Professional SQL Server® 2008 Administration with Windows PowerShell™

WITHDRAWN

Professional
SQL Server® 2008 Administration with Windows PowerShell™

Professional

SQL Server® 2008 Administration with Windows PowerShell™

Muthusamy Anantha Kumar
Yan Pan

WILEY

Wiley Publishing, Inc.

Professional SQL Server® 2008 Administration with Windows PowerShell™

Published by
Wiley Publishing, Inc.
10475 Crosspoint Boulevard
Indianapolis, IN 46256
www.wiley.com

Published by Wiley Publishing, Inc., Indianapolis, Indiana

Published simultaneously in Canada

ISBN: 978-0-470-47728-1

Manufactured in the United States of America

10 9 0 7 6 5 1 3 2 1

Library of Congress Cataloging-in-Publication Data

Kumar, Muthusamy Anantha, 1974-
    Microsoft SQL server 2008 administration with Windows Powershell / Muthusamy Anantha Kumar, Yan Pan.
        p. cm.
    Includes index.
    ISBN 978-0-470-47728-1 (paper/website)
    1. SQL server. 2. Windows PowerShell (Computer program language) I. Pan, Yan, 1976- II. Title.
    QA76.73.W56K96 2009
    005.2'82--dc22

                                                        2009013304

About the Authors

Muthusamy Anantha Kumar, aka MAK (MCTS, MCITP: Database Administrator 2008), is currently the Senior SQL Server Database Engineer for a leading global financial services firm on Wall Street. He has published many online articles as a contributing columnist for `DatabaseJournal.com`. He also published online articles for `SQL-Server-Performance.com` and `SQLServercentral.com`. His articles can be found at `www.mssqlengineering.com`. He also teaches SQL Server Database Administration online at the University of West Florida.

MAK has been working in information technology for more than 10 years. He has worked in the technology side of the finance, dot com, B2B, and software industries. His past clients include Fort James, Boston Financial, PCConnection, PurchaseSoft, Merrill Lynch, and Jefferies. MAK holds an M.B.A. degree and various certifications in the computer field.

He also teaches Microsoft SQL Server and has taught many SQL Server developers and DBAs. He has master's degree in Business Administration.

MAK lives in New Jersey. He can be reached at `mak_999@yahoo.com`.

Yan Pan (MCITP, MCDBA, OCA) is a Senior DBA for a leading global financial services firm, where her daily duties include administering hundreds of SQL Server and Oracle servers of every possible version, working with business units, and troubleshooting database performance problems. She is also a contributing columnist for `DatabaseJournal.com`. Her articles can be found at `www.yanpansql.com`.

Previously, Yan worked as a SQL Server DBA and a .NET developer at Data Based Ads, Inc., and developed two .NET Web applications. Before that, she worked at AT&T Research Labs. She designed OLAP cubes with SQL Server Analysis Services and developed PivotTable reports for regional managers. She has master's degrees in Computer Science and Physics.

Yan lives in Chicago, IL. She can be reached at `yanpansql@yahoo.com`.

Credits

Executive Editor
Robert Elliott

Development Editor
Rosanne Koneval

Technical Editor
Haidong Ji

Production Editor
Daniel Scribner

Copy Editor
Luann Rouff

Editorial Manager
Mary Beth Wakefield

Production Manager
Tim Tate

Vice President and Executive Group Publisher
Richard Swadley

Vice President and Executive Publisher
Barry Pruett

Associate Publisher
Jim Minatel

Project Coordinator, Cover
Lynsey Stanford

Proofreader
Jen Larsen, Word One

Indexer
Robert Swanson

Acknowledgments

First of all, I would like to thank my fiancée, Claire Hsu. Without her moral support, this book would not have been possible. I would like to thank my mom, Jayalakshmi Muthusamy, for bringing me into this world. I still admire her for not losing her patience and always keeping her sense of humor. I would like to thank my dad, Muthusamy Srinivasan, for being a friend and a teacher. I want to take this opportunity to thank both my parents for all the compromises they made to raise both my sister and me. I would also like to thank my sister, Anuradha, for supporting me and taking care of me.

I would like to thank my co-author, Yan Pan, especially for being both very patient when needed and pushing me when necessary. She is a very good friend and colleague. She could always get me back on track when I was distracted with other projects.

I would also like to thank all my friends, current and past colleagues, and relatives for their constant inspiration.

I am very grateful to all the readers and fans of my online articles from various parts of the world. Without their support, comments, motivation, and critiques, this book wouldn't have shaped up so well.

Yan and I are both grateful to Haidong Ji, aka Alex, for introducing us to Wrox-Wiley and being our knowledgeable technical editor. We also want to thank Bob Elliot for bringing our book proposal to the executive team and making it happen.

Last but not least, we would like to thank Rosanne Koneval and Daniel Scribner. Your questioning at the right place, proper decision-making, and quick turnaround made this book much neater and clearer.

It is hoped that I haven't forgotten anyone, but if I have, it was an oversight. Honest.

— *MAK*

First and foremost, I would like to thank my beloved husband, Yue Guo. You have always supported and encouraged me in everything I have ever done. Thank you for your incredible patience throughout the writing of this book. I would also like to thank my parents for all they have done for me to give me the best life they could possibly give.

I would like to express my sincere appreciation to MAK for introducing me to technical writing and sharing the book idea with me. Your optimism, enthusiasm, and humor have made the book-writing journey a wonderful experience.

I am also deeply indebted to Haidong (Alex) Ji. Haidong, thank you for introducing us to Wrox. Thank you for your suggestions, guidance, and encouragement throughout the course of this book. Your technical input and attention to detail helped us improve the quality of this book greatly.

I would also like to thank Bob Elliot, Rosanne Koneval and Daniel Scribner at Wrox. Bob, thank you for believing in us. We started this project with plenty of enthusiasm and passion for new technology, but not a book contract. Thank you for making our dream come true and allowing our vision of a Windows

Acknowledgments

PowerShell–powered SQL Server enterprise infrastructure to reach thousands of readers, and hopefully making their lives easier. Rosanne, thank you for your incredible patience in cleaning up the words and polishing everything up to get this book ready for the printer. Daniel, thank you for giving a final touch to this book.

Finally, I'd like to thank you, my readers, for reading what I have written! Without your support and feedback, I could not have accomplished so much.

— *Yan*

Contents

Contents

Contents

Contents

Contents

Introduction

Welcome to *SQL Server 2008 Administration with Windows PowerShell*. This book is a nuts-and-bolts guide to creating Windows PowerShell scripts that can be used to administer every aspect of the SQL Server 2008 Database Engine. Using a very hands-on approach, this book guides you through the basics of Windows PowerShell, the available Windows PowerShell components that have been integrated into SQL Server 2008, and the actual administration tasks. By providing clear, well-structured examples, *SQL Server 2008 Administration with Windows PowerShell* shows you how to construct effective and practical solutions that can improve SQL Server administration and monitoring at your company.

SQL Server 2008 delivers a dynamic, smart, and productive data platform for all your data-related needs. SQL Server 2008 offers secure, reliable, and consistent performance. It is also very scalable and flexible, handling any form of data. It is well known in the technology world that SQL Server 2008 is not only a RDBMS, but also has built-in features such as Integration Services for ETL, Analysis Services for Business Intelligence, Reporting Services for report management, and more. This is why Microsoft SQL Server is a cut above all other database products.

Windows PowerShell 2.0 is the new extensible command-line interface shell and scripting language that provides an environment for interactive scripting and non-interactive scripted administration of local and remote computers. Because Windows PowerShell integrates with the Microsoft .NET Framework, we can take advantage of all the features of .NET as well. Windows PowerShell 2.0 helps system administrators to automate and manage various aspects of the Windows environment. PowerShell 2.0 also has many new and useful features such as remoting, eventing, and many more. For these reasons, Windows PowerShell 2.0 stands above all the system administration products on the market.

This book brings together the best of both worlds — namely, the database world and the administration world — to help you manage, automate, and control your environment. This book combines three technologies — SQL Server 2008, the .NET Framework, and Windows PowerShell 2.0 — and guides SQL Server database administrators in managing a server plant using Windows PowerShell 2.0.

We've provided a wide range of material in a tutorial-based book to get you over the learning curve of Windows PowerShell 2.0 and SQL Server 2008 database administration.

Who This Book Is For

Whether you are a SQL Server database administrator, a developer, or a systems administrator, at some point you probably have had to develop or administer the system or the database in your organization. It is also common for the people in these roles to wear each other's hats in order to get things done.

If you are a Microsoft SQL Server database administrator, you know that you cannot manage and access all the system resources from SQL Server. Because SQL Server runs on top of the Windows operating system and relies on the health of the system, you need information from the system side as well. This book will teach you to manage both SQL Server and system resources using Windows PowerShell 2.0.

If you are a systems administrator and would like to know more about SQL Server database administration, this book introduces you to the features in SQL Server 2008 and provides plenty of examples demonstrating how to manage SQL Server 2008 using Windows PowerShell 2.0.

This book is also appropriate for those who have some exposure to systems administration and SQL Server administration, or for those who want to expand their skill set to include administration.

What This Book Covers

This book covers the fundamentals of Windows PowerShell 2.0 cmdlets. It includes programming, scripting, debugging, and error handling in PowerShell. It covers all Windows administration related to SQL Server 2008 using Windows PowerShell 2.0.

It also introduces Windows Management Instrumentation (WMI) and explains how to write WMI scripts in Windows PowerShell to perform system and SQL Server 2008 administrative tasks.

This book also covers the WMI providers for SQL Server. These useful providers enable you to manage SQL Server services and network connectivity, and proactively monitor SQL Server events. You will also discover the new Eventing feature in Windows PowerShell 2.0.

Additionally, the new SQL Server 2008 support for Windows PowerShell is presented. It illustrates the SQL Server PowerShell provider and SQLSERVER: drive. You will also learn how to manage SQL Server objects, including the new policy objects.

One more important topic this book covers is using SQL Server Management Objects (SMO) to create databases and tables and perform backups and restores. The SMO scripts shown in this book are all written in Windows PowerShell 2.0.

This book also explains the need for SQL Server standards; and you will learn how to build a SQL Server inventory over an existing or new environment.

Finally, you will learn how to perform the various SQL Server administrative tasks on servers in the inventory, such as installation, monitoring, performance data collection, policy definition, backups, restores, database scripting, and more, using Windows PowerShell 2.0.

How This Book Is Structured

Windows PowerShell 2.0 is introduced in the first eight chapters. If you do not have any background in Windows PowerShell 2.0, these chapters are critical. They help you understand the basics of writing Windows PowerShell 2.0 scripts, and you will learn how to use the scripts to administer the overall operating system.

Chapter 1 covers installation of prerequisites, and installation and configuration of Windows PowerShell 2.0.

Chapters 2, 3, and 4 cover the various cmdlets available in Windows PowerShell, and the various programming features such as inputs, outputs, debugging, error handling, functions, profiles, and so on.

Chapters 5, 6, 7, and 8 cover the various systems administration features, including accessing file systems, registry information, variables, and Event logs. It also explains the Windows Management Instrumentation (WMI) model and shows you how to use WMI to manage system resources.

Chapters 9 and 10 show you how to access the WMI providers for SQL Server. You will learn how to use the WMI Provider for Configuration Management to manage SQL Server services and network connectivity, and the WMI Provider for Server Events to manage SQL Server events. You will also discover the new Eventing feature in Windows PowerShell 2.0.

Chapters 11 and 12 take on the Windows PowerShell support that has been integrated into SQL Server 2008, namely, the SQLSERVER: drive. These two chapters will focus on the SQL and SQLPolicy folders separately.

Chapter 13 shows you how to write SQL Server Management Objects (SMO) programs in Windows PowerShell 2.0. This chapter covers various tasks such as creating a database and database objects, and backing up and restoring a database.

Chapters 14 and 15 provide you with ample examples of building a SQL Server tasks inventory over an existing or new environment, and how to define various standards. Standards include both SQL Server standards and Windows PowerShell standards.

The remaining chapters explain installation, data collection, monitoring, and how to create Windows PowerShell scripts to handle a wide range of SQL Server administrative tasks for servers in the inventory.

Chapter 16 illustrates the installation of SQL Server 2008. Chapter 17 covers tasks related to collecting SQL Server host and server performance data. Chapters 18 and 19 cover monitoring aspects of SQL Server 2008 administration. Chapter 20 defines policies to enforce SQL Server standards, and Chapter 21 generates various scripts at both the database level and the database object level.

What You Need to Use This Book

This book covers SQL Server 2008 administration with Windows PowerShell 2.0. In order to use this book, you need both a server-side component and client-side components:

❑   For the server-side component, you need SQL Server 2008 Developer or Enterprise or Standard edition.

❑   For client-side components, you need Windows PowerShell 2.0 CTP3. To install Windows PowerShell 2.0 CTP3, the operating system of your computer needs to be either Windows XP Service Pack 3, Windows 2003 Service Pack 2, Windows Vista Service Pack 1, or Windows Server 2008. You also need to pre-install the following components on your computer:

   ❑   Microsoft .NET Framework 2.0 or greater

   ❑   Windows Remote Management 2.0 CTP3 for Windows PowerShell remoting and background jobs

We discuss the prerequisites of Windows PowerShell 2.0 in Chapter 1 in detail.

All the scripts and codes in the book have been tested on SQL Server 2008 with .NET Framework 3.5 and Windows PowerShell 2.0 CTP3. We tested all the scripts on Windows XP, Windows Server 2008, and Windows Vista. Most of the scripts and code illustrated here work under Windows PowerShell 1.0 as well, although you may notice that the output of such scripts and codes differs slightly, and that remoting under Windows PowerShell 1.0 is not possible unless you use WMI objects.

In order to install Windows PowerShell 2.0 and Windows Remote Management, and to store all the scripts provided in the book, you need a minimum of 100MB of hard disk space.

Conventions

To help you get the most from the text and keep track of what's happening, we've used a number of conventions throughout the book.

> *Notes, tips, hints, tricks, and asides to the current discussion are offset and placed in italics like this.*

As for styles in the text:

❑ We *highlight* new terms and important words when we introduce them.

❑ We show filenames, URLs, and code within the text like so: `persistence.properties`.

❑ We present code like this:

```
We use a monofont type with no highlighting for most code examples.
```

Source Code

As you work through the examples in this book, you may choose either to type in all the code manually or to use the source code files that accompany the book. All of the source code used in this book is available for download at `www.wrox.com`. Once at the site, simply locate the book's title (either by using the Search box or by using one of the title lists) and click the Download Code link on the book's detail page to obtain all the source code for the book.

> *Because many books have similar titles, you may find it easiest to search by ISBN; this book's ISBN is 978-0-470-47728-1.*

Once you download the code, just decompress it with your favorite compression tool. Alternately, you can go to the main Wrox code download page at `www.wrox.com/dynamic/books/download.aspx` to see the code available for this book and all other Wrox books.

Errata

We make every effort to ensure that there are no errors in the text or in the code. However, no one is perfect, and mistakes do occur. If you find an error in one of our books, such as a spelling mistake or a faulty piece of code, we would be very grateful for your feedback. By sending in errata, you may save another reader hours of frustration, and at the same time you will be helping us provide even higher quality information.

To find the errata page for this book, go to www.wrox.com and locate the title using the Search box or one of the title lists. Then, on the book details page, click the Book Errata link. On this page you can view all errata submitted for this book and posted by Wrox editors. A complete book list, including links to each book's errata, is also available at www.wrox.com/misc-pages/booklist.shtml.

If you don't spot "your" error on the Book Errata page, go to www.wrox.com/contact/techsupport.shtml and complete the form there to send us the error you have found. We'll check the information and, if appropriate, post a message to the book's errata page and fix the problem in subsequent editions of the book.

p2p.wrox.com

For author and peer discussion, join the P2P forums at p2p.wrox.com. The forums are a Web-based system for you to post messages relating to Wrox books and related technologies and interact with other readers and technology users. The forums offer a subscription feature to e-mail you topics of interest of your choosing when new posts are made to the forums. Wrox authors, editors, other industry experts, and your fellow readers are present on these forums.

At http://p2p.wrox.com you will find a number of different forums that will help you not only as you read this book, but also as you develop your own applications. To join the forums, just follow these steps:

1. Go to p2p.wrox.com and click the Register link.

2. Read the terms of use and click Agree.

3. Enter the required information to join as well as any optional information you wish to provide and click Submit.

4. You will receive an e-mail with information describing how to verify your account and complete the joining process.

You can read messages in the forums without joining P2P but in order to post your own messages, you must join.

Once you join, you can post new messages and respond to messages other users post. You can read messages at any time on the Web. If you would like to have new messages from a particular forum e-mailed to you, click the Subscribe to this Forum icon by the forum name in the forum listing.

For more information about how to use the Wrox P2P, be sure to read the P2P FAQs for answers to questions about how the forum software works, as well as many common questions specific to P2P and Wrox books. To read the FAQs, click the FAQ link on any P2P page.

What Is Windows PowerShell?

Windows PowerShell is the extensible command-line interface shell and scripting language that provides a command-line environment for interactive exploration and administration of computers. In addition, it provides developers with an opportunity to script these commands, enabling them to be automated, scheduled, and run multiple times.

This chapter covers the following topics:

❑   A brief overview of command-line interfaces

❑   Prerequisites for installing PowerShell

❑   Installing PowerShell 2.0 CTP3.

Command-Line Interfaces versus Graphical User Interfaces

Before UNIX, Linux, and Windows surfaced in the information technology market, input media such as punched card and punched tape were used. All the input and instructions to the computer used command lines.

When UNIX and Linux were released, administrators started managing the operating system using command-line interfaces, which were also used by the day-to-day users and programmers to interact with the operating system.

UNIX and Linux are built on command-line interfaces, so there has always been administrative scripting and different shells, such as the Korn shell, the C shell, and the Bourne shell. Programming languages such as TCL and PERL were immediately available.

Originally, when Microsoft released MS-DOS, it was not used as a shell. It was entirely a standalone operating system. The initial and original Microsoft Windows release was a graphical shell that sat on top of the MS-DOS operating system. Once Windows NT was introduced, this situation was reversed. MS-DOS became the shell in the graphical Windows operating system.

Graphical user interfaces (GUIs) were basically developed for users with less technical background who were looking for a friendly interface. Because graphical interfaces are limited to fewer functions, once you hit their limitations you will start relying on the command-line interface. For example, with a GUI, if you want to rename all the extensions of a group of files and suffix each file with the current day's timestamp, it will take a while because you have to select and rename each file individually.

Therefore, command-line interfaces and their commands are very commonly used for administrative tasks and automation. They also help to consolidate functionality in batches, through MS-DOS batch files.

command.com was used as the command-line user interface in early versions of Microsoft Windows. cmd.exe was introduced in Windows NT.

When administrators reached the limit of command-line batch files, they started looking for a language that could do both command shell functions and programming. Microsoft introduced the Visual Basic scripting language, which helped administrators initially. However, there were limitations in VBScript as well. Administrators started relying on Windows Management Instrumentation (WMI) and COM objects introduced later by Microsoft for many other administrative functions.

The administrative command-line interface started becoming more complicated with internal DOS commands, external DOS commands, batch files, executables, VBScripts, WMI, and so forth.

It was with all of this in mind that Microsoft developed and introduced Windows PowerShell.

Prerequisites for Installing Windows PowerShell 2.0

Windows PowerShell can be installed and run on Windows XP, Windows Vista, Windows Server 2003, and Windows Server 2008. Although Windows PowerShell is included as part of Windows Server 2008, it is not installed by default on Windows XP, Windows 2003, or Windows Vista. At the time of writing, Windows PowerShell 1.0 is visible as a feature in Windows Server 2008 that can be turned on.

Windows PowerShell 1.0 is also installed with Exchange Server 2007, System Center Operations Manager 2007, System Center Data Protection Manager V2, and System Center Virtual Machine Manager because they leverage Windows PowerShell to improve administrator control, efficiency, and productivity.

This book uses Windows PowerShell 2.0 CTP3. Before installing Windows PowerShell 2.0 CTP3, you should ensure that your system has the following software programs it requires:

❑ Windows XP Service Pack 3, Windows 2003 Service Pack 2, Windows Vista Service Pack 1, or Windows Server 2008

❑ Microsoft .NET Framework 2.0 or greater

❑ Windows Remote Management 2.0 CTP3 for Windows PowerShell remoting and background jobs

❑ Microsoft .NET Framework 3.5 Service Pack 1 for Windows PowerShell Integrated Scripting Environment (ISE) and the Out-GridView cmdlet

If .NET Framework 2.0 is not installed on your computer, the error message shown in Figure 1-1 will pop up when you try to install Windows PowerShell 2.0 CTP3.

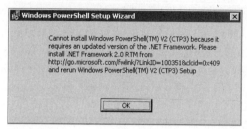

Figure 1-1

After installing the .NET Framework, if you continue to install on a non-standard operating system such as Windows Server 2000, Windows NT, and so on, you may get the error shown in Figure 1-2.

Figure 1-2

Although Figure 1-2 shows v1.0 in the title bar and file path, it is actually PowerShell 2.0 CTP3. Community Technology Preview, also known as CTP3, is basically the bug fix that Microsoft relies on, adding new features based on feedback from the technology community. The folder may be changed to v2.0 once the release to manufacturing (RTM) version is released.

In order to check the prerequisites for the PowerShell installation, we created a batch file to run all the necessary checks. Listing 1-1 shows the MS-DOS batch script, CheckPowershellPreqs.bat, which uses Windows Management Instrumentation Command-line (WMIC) to check the requirements before you install Windows PowerShell. WMIC enables you to access WMI information via the command line. In some respects, you can think of WMIC as an early prototype of PowerShell. However, WMIC can only output its results as text. It doesn't return programming objects that can be further processed, as Window PowerShell does, and as you will see later.

Listing 1-1: CheckPowershellPreqs.bat

```
@ECHO Off

REM *************************************************************
REM *Objective: TO check if the current windows version is        *
REM *           Compatible for PowerShell 2.0 and its pre-requisites*
REM *Created by: Yan and MAK                                        *
REM *Created Date: 2008/09/01                                       *
```

Continued

Listing 1-1: CheckPowershellPreqs.bat *(continued)*

```
REM *                                                                      *
REM ************************************************************************


SET OS_VERSION=
SET Service_Pack=

REM Find OS version
FOR /F "delims== tokens=2" %%i IN ('wmic os get Version /value')
   DO SET OS_VERSION=%%i

IF NOT DEFINED OS_VERSION (
    ECHO WMIC is not installed on this system.
    GOTO :END_SCRIPT
)

REM Find service pack value
FOR /F "delims== tokens=2" %%i IN ('wmic os get ServicePackMajorVersion /value')
   DO SET Service_Pack=%%i

REM Windows XP
IF "%OS_VERSION%"=="5.1.2600" (
    @IF "%Service_Pack%" LSS "3" (
        ECHO %OS_NAME% Service Pack 3 is required
        GOTO :END_SCRIPT
    )
    GOTO :DOTNETFRAMEWORK_CHECK
)

REM Windows Server 2003
IF "%OS_VERSION%"=="5.2.3790" (
    @IF "%Service_Pack%" LSS "2" (
        ECHO %OS_NAME% Service Pack 2 is required
        GOTO :END_SCRIPT
    )
    GOTO :DOTNETFRAMEWORK_CHECK
)


REM Windows Vista
IF "%OS_VERSION%"=="6.0.6001" (
    @IF "%Service_Pack%" LSS "1" (
        ECHO %OS_NAME% Service Pack 1 is required
        GOTO :END_SCRIPT
    )
    GOTO :DOTNETFRAMEWORK_CHECK
)

IF "%OS_VERSION%" GTR "5.2.3790" (
    GOTO :DOTNETFRAMEWORK_CHECK
)
ELSE (
    GOTO :END_SCRIPT
)
```

Listing 1-1: CheckPowershellPreqs.bat *(continued)*

```
REM Check .NET framework
:DOTNETFRAMEWORK_CHECK
wmic product where (caption like "Microsoft .NET Framework%%") get Version /value |
    findstr "=[2-9]\.*" > nul
IF "%ERRORLEVEL%"=="1" (
    ECHO .NET Framework 2.0 or greater is required
    GOTO :END_SCRIPT
)

REM Check Windows remote management
:WINRMCHECK
wmic path Win32_service where caption="Windows Remote Management (WS-Management)" |
    findstr /i "(WS-Management)" > nul
IF "%ERRORLEVEL%"==1 (
    ECHO Windows Remote Management is required
    GOTO :END_SCRIPT
)

ECHO Your system meets the requirements

:END_SCRIPT
```

From a Windows command console, run `CheckPowershellPreqs.bat` from the script directory `C:\DBAScripts`. You should get a message similar to the one shown in Figure 1-3 if your system meets the requirements for a PowerShell installation.

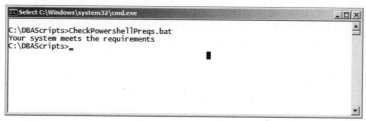

Figure 1-3

You may run into an error as follows on Windows Server 2003:

```
ERROR:
Code = 0x80041010
Description = Invalid class
Facility = WMI
```

This means that you need to install the WMI Windows Installer Provider in order for WMIC to work. To do so, open Control Panel ➢ Add/Remove Programs. Select Add/Remove Windows Components. Double-click Management and Monitoring Tools. Select WMI Windows Installer Provider, and then click OK to install.

If your operating system is Windows XP Service Pack 2 and you install Windows PowerShell 2.0 CTP3, it may or may not work. The officially supported service pack for Windows XP when installing Windows

PowerShell 2.0 CPT3 is Service Pack 3, so when executing `C:\DBAScripts\CheckPowershellPreqs.bat` it will complain that Service Pack 3 is required.

Installing the Microsoft .NET Framework

Windows PowerShell integrates with the .NET Framework and provides a shell environment to perform administrative tasks. PowerShell exposes the .NET classes as built-in commands, and when these commands are executed they produce one or more structured objects as output.

Download the .NET Framework from `http://download.microsoft.com` and install .NET Framework 2 or later. It is recommended that you use .NET 3.5, although all the code in this book works on .NET Framework 2 and later. In Chapter 11, you will see that an SQL Server 2008 installation installs .NET 3.5 by default.

Installing Windows Remote Management

Another prerequisite is to install Windows Remote Management (WinRM). WinRM is required for Windows PowerShell remoting and background jobs. You can download WinRM 2.0 CTP3 (also known as Ws-Management) from `https://connect.microsoft.com/WSMAN/Downloads` for Windows Vista and Windows Server 2008. The installation procedures of the executable `Windows6.0-KB950099-x86.msu` for 32-bit and `Windows6.0-KB950099-x64.msu` for 64-bit are shown in Figure 1-4 and Figure 1-5.

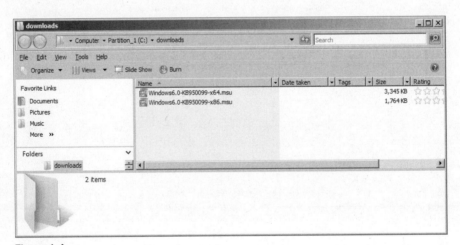

Figure 1-4

Figure 1-5

Double-click on `Windows6.0-KB950099-x86.msu` if you are installing WinRM on a 32-bit Windows operating system. Double-click on `Windows6.0-KB950099-x64.msu` if you are installing it on a 64-bit Windows operating system.

If you already have Windows PowerShell 1.0 installed on your machine, then you have to uninstall PowerShell 1.0 first and then install PowerShell 2.0 CTP3.

To uninstall Windows PowerShell 1.0, follow these steps:

1. Click Start ➪ Run, type **appwiz.cpl**, and then click OK.

2. Select the Show Updates check box (on the top in the middle).

3. In the list of currently installed programs, click Windows PowerShell(TM) 1.0, and then click Remove. If you don't see Windows PowerShell(TM) 1.0, please look for Windows Hotfix 926139, 926140, or 926141.

4. Follow the instructions to remove Windows PowerShell(TM) 1.0.

If you already have Windows PowerShell 2.0 CTP1 or CTP2, you have to uninstall them also. They appear as "Windows PowerShell V2 (TM)" in the program list.

In Windows 2008, Windows PowerShell 1.0 is made visible as a Windows feature. You can disable and uninstall the `PowerShell` feature as described here:

1. Click Start at the Windows taskbar.

2. Click Server Manager ➢ Features ➢ Add Feature, and uncheck the Windows PowerShell check box.

3. Click Next to uninstall.

Now that you have the acceptable operating system, the .NET Framework, and Windows Remote Management, the next section provides the steps needed to actually install Windows PowerShell 2.0 CTP3.

Installing Windows PowerShell

To install Windows PowerShell on Windows XP or Windows 2003 systems, do the following:

1. Download the Windows PowerShell 2.0 CTP3 installation file from `www.Microsoft.com/downloads`. The name of the installation file varies according to platform, operating system, and language pack. Choose the appropriate version for your operating system. If you have a 64-bit Windows operating system, then please download `PowerShell_Setup_amd64.msi`, as shown in Figure 1-6. If you have a 32-bit Windows operating system, then please download `PowerShell_Setup_x86.msi`, as shown in Figure 1-7.

2. After downloading the appropriate version for your operating system, you will see the initial screen of the installation wizard, similar to the one shown in Figure 1-8. Click Next.

3. Accept the license agreement, as shown in Figure 1-9, and click Next.

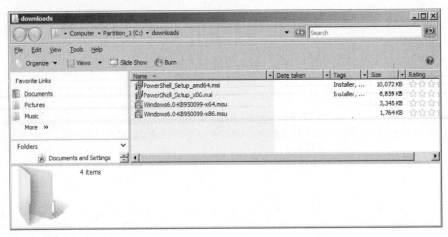

Figure 1-6

Figure 1-7

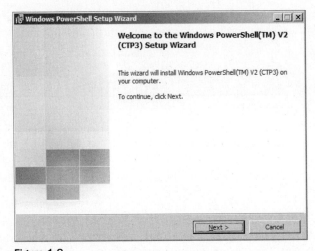

Figure 1-8

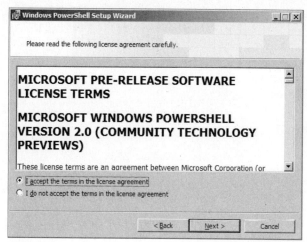

Figure 1-9

4. It takes a few minutes to complete the install. As shown in Figure 1-10, click Install to begin the installation process. You will see the progress of the installation, as shown in Figure 1-11.

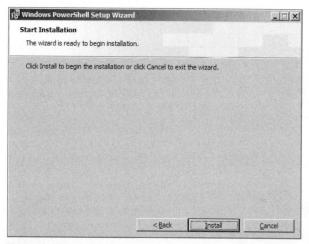

Figure 1-10

5. When installation is completed successfully, you will see a screen similar to the one shown in Figure 1-12. Click Finish.

On 32-bit versions of Windows, Windows PowerShell is installed by default in the `%SystemRoot%\System32\WindowsPowerShell\v1.0` directory.

On 64-bit versions of Windows, a 32-bit version of Windows PowerShell is installed in the `%SystemRoot%\SystemWow64\WindowsPowerShell\v1.0` directory and a 64-bit version of Windows PowerShell is installed in the `%SystemRoot%\System32\WindowsPowerShell\v1.0` directory.

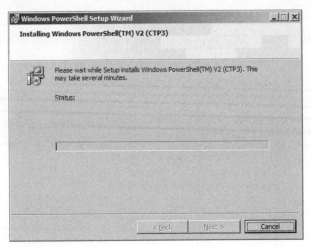

Figure 1-11

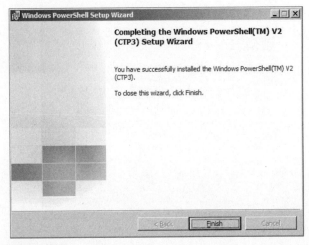

Figure 1-12

This book covers Windows PowerShell 2.0 CTP3. The installation file replaces the executables in the v1.0 folder. The actual folders for Windows PowerShell may change to v2.0 when PowerShell 2.0 RTM is released.

Launching Windows PowerShell

Windows PowerShell can be launched in several ways. This section describes the different methods. No method is superior to the others. It is just a matter of preference.

Using the Command console

To launch Windows PowerShell using the command console, open the command console and then type **powershell**, as shown in Figure 1-13.

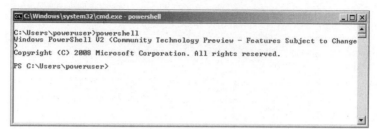

Figure 1-13

Using All Programs

You can also click Start ➢ All Programs ➢ Windows PowerShell V2 (CTP3), and then select and click Windows PowerShell V2 (CTP3), as shown in Figure 1-14.

Figure 1-14

You may also see Windows PowerShell ISE (CTP3) in the Windows Program menu. The Windows Power-Shell Integrated Scripting Environment (ISE) is a host application for Windows PowerShell. In Windows PowerShell ISE, you can run commands and write, test, and debug scripts in a single Windows graphical user interface. This book illustrates all Windows PowerShell-related cmdlets and scripts using a command-line interface. It does not illustrate PowerShell scripts using the ISE.

Once PowerShell is launched, you can see the command prompt. The prompt in the PowerShell command window varies according to the operating system used.

To be consistent with the PowerShell window title, you could update the shortcut, as illustrated in Figure 1-15. Right-click on the Windows PowerShell V2 (CTP3) shortcut, click Properties, and under the General tab, update the title to "Windows PowerShell" and click OK.

Using Start Run

You can also launch PowerShell by clicking Start ➢ Run and typing the following: **%systemroot% \system32\windowsPowerShell\v1.0\PowerShell.exe.** Then click OK, as shown in Figure 1-16.

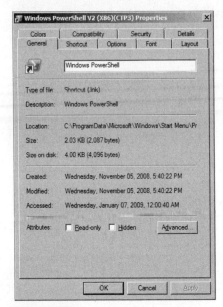

Figure 1-15

Figure 1-16

Alternatively, you can also launch PowerShell by clicking Start ➤ Run and typing **PowerShell**.

Windows finds the PowerShell.exe executable from the environment PATH variable and then launches it.

This opens the PowerShell command console, shown in Figure 1-17.

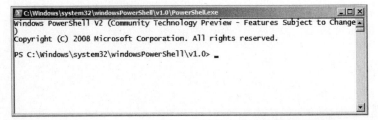

Figure 1-17

If you are using 64-bit PowerShell, then you can launch PowerShell by clicking Start ➤ Run and typing the following: **%systemroot%\SysWOW64\WindowsPowerShell\v1.0\PowerShell.exe.** Then click OK, as shown in Figure 1-18.

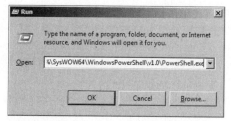

Figure 1-18

This opens the PowerShell command console, as shown in Figure 1-19.

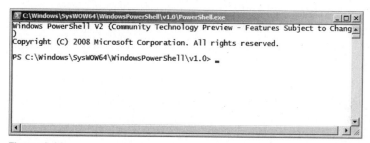

Figure 1-19

Summary

This chapter discussed the prerequisites for Windows PowerShell, described how to install Windows PowerShell 2.0 CTP3, and showed various methods to launch PowerShell.

The next chapter covers the various command types and commonly used *cmdlets* that appear throughout the book. A Windows PowerShell cmdlet is a simple command used for interaction with any managed application, including the Windows operating system and applications such as SQL Server, Microsoft Exchange, and so on.

2

Windows PowerShell Command Types, Snap-ins, and cmdlets

Now that you've installed Windows PowerShell on your computer, I bet you can't wait to start running your own commands to unravel the power of Microsoft's new command shell. This chapter introduces you to the new PowerShell commands, or cmdlets. It also introduces you to the collections of cmdlets called snap-ins. By following all of the examples in this book, you will become comfortable working with the cmdlets, and you will even be able to tweak the output to your liking. First, however, this chapter gives you a quick-start on how to run PowerShell commands interactively.

This chapter covers the following topics:

❑   PowerShell command types

❑   PowerShell snap-ins

❑   Syntax of cmdlets

❑   Command chaining

❑   Getting help

❑   Filtering

❑   Sorting

❑   Formatting

PowerShell Command Types

When you launch a new PowerShell window, you are basically executing a small `PowerShell.exe` executable, which provides a command-line interface and issues instructions on how to make the functionality in the PowerShell Engine available.

Those instructions are written in .NET language and are available in the form of commands called *cmdlets* (pronounced "command lets"). All the cmdlets, when executed, process the instructions and return an object, not just text.

The following four different command types are available in the PowerShell environment. Don't panic. PowerShell understands and performs the different types of functions based on the type of commands that you execute.

- ❑ Native commands
- ❑ PowerShell cmdlets
- ❑ Shell functions
- ❑ Script commands

The following sections take a closer look at the differences between the different command types in PowerShell and how each can be used.

Native Commands

Native commands are external executables that the Windows operating system can run. For example, `notepad.exe`, `calc.exe`, or even a batch file can be run from the PowerShell command-line interface.

The following example executes a Windows command shell `cmd.exe` with the `system.ini` file as a parameter, as shown in Figure 2-1:

```
cmd /c c:\windows\system.ini
```

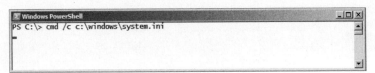

Figure 2-1

Once this command is executed, PowerShell recognizes the executable file and passes the command to the operating system directly. The operating system basically opens the file using the default editor `Notepad.exe`, as shown in the Figure 2-2.

If the default editor on your machine is not `Notepad.exe`, *then the operating system opens this executable file with your default editor, rather than* `Notepad.exe`.

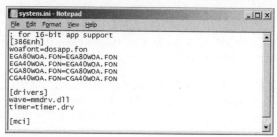

Figure 2-2

The next example will launch the Windows calculator. Enter the following command into PowerShell, as shown in Figure 2-3:

```
calc
```

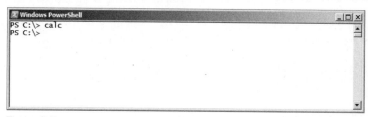

Figure 2-3

Once this command is executed, PowerShell recognizes the executable file and passes the command to the operating system directly. The operating system launches the calculator, as shown in Figure 2-4.

Figure 2-4

You can also execute a batch file within the Windows PowerShell environment. Create a small batch file, C:\Batch-Test.bat, that displays the current date and time, as shown here:

```
@Echo off
Echo The current date is : %date%
Echo The current time is : %time%
```

You can execute the batch file in the Windows PowerShell environment using `.\` or `./`, as shown in Figure 2-5:

```
.\Batch-Test.bat
```

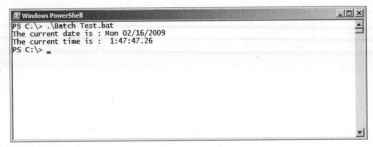

Figure 2-5

PowerShell cmdlets

PowerShell cmdlets are compiled DLL files that are loaded into PowerShell at runtime. Anybody can write custom cmdlets using the PowerShell Software Development Kit (SDK). You can get more information on the PowerShell SDK from `http://msdn.microsoft.com/en-us/library/ms714469 (VS.85).aspx`.

The cmdlets are constructed in *verb-noun* format. The verb specifies the action that it is going to perform and the noun specifies the object being operated on. The noun is always singular (not plural), even if it retrieves or acts on multiple objects.

The following example is a cmdlet that gets all the processes running on the current host machine, as shown in Figure 2-6:

```
Get-Process
```

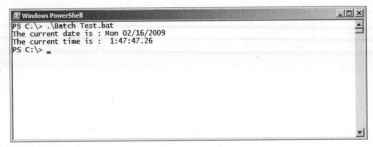

Figure 2-6

The term `get` in this command is the verb, and the term `process` is the noun, so the cmdlet "gets" all the "processes" running on the current host.

Amazing, isn't it? You don't have to use VBScript to query the WMI win32_process class and get the process information and format the result. Just a simple `Get-Process` command will do that for you.

We know this makes you wonder what other amazing cmdlets are available that you could use in your environment. If you would like to know the basic definitions of cmdlets and other elements of all the PowerShell commands in the current PowerShell environment, you can run the following cmdlet, as shown in Figure 2-7:

```
Get-Command
```

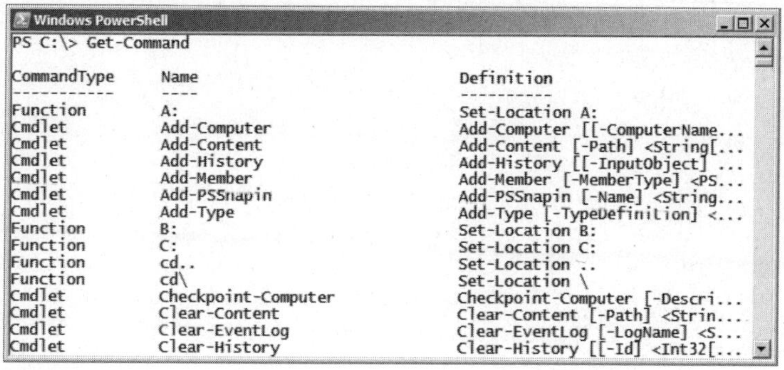

Figure 2-7

Figure 2-7 shows the names of the cmdlets and their definitions.

Windows PowerShell 2.0 CTP3 also has a feature called Tab Completion. With this feature, you don't have to type the entire cmdlet every time it is used. You can just type the beginning of the cmdlet — for example, Get-PS, and press the Tab key. PowerShell will automatically complete your cmdlet with the cmdlet starting with Get-PS. If more than one cmdlet starts with Get-PS, then press the Tab key again and PowerShell will show you the next available cmdlet that starts with Get-PS. Continue pressing the Tab key until you see the cmdlet that you want to use.

For example, if you type **Get-PS** and press the Tab key several times, all of the following cmdlets will appear, in ascending order:

❑ Get-PSBreakpoint

❑ Get-PSCallStack

❑ Get-PSDrive

❑ Get-PSProvider

❑ Get-PSSession

❑ Get-PSSessionConfiguration

❑ Get-PSSnapin

Shell Function Commands

Shell function commands are subroutines that you can create and have available throughout the current PowerShell session. If a block of code is often re-used in the main code, then you can create a function and call the function wherever necessary within the main code.

Here is an example of how to create a simple function. This function lists all the files with the extension .ini under the C:\Windows folder. Shell functions are discussed in more detail in Chapter 4.

```
function list-ini {Get-ChildItem c:\windows\*.ini}
```

Once the preceding command is executed (see Figure 2-8), the function list-ini is created.

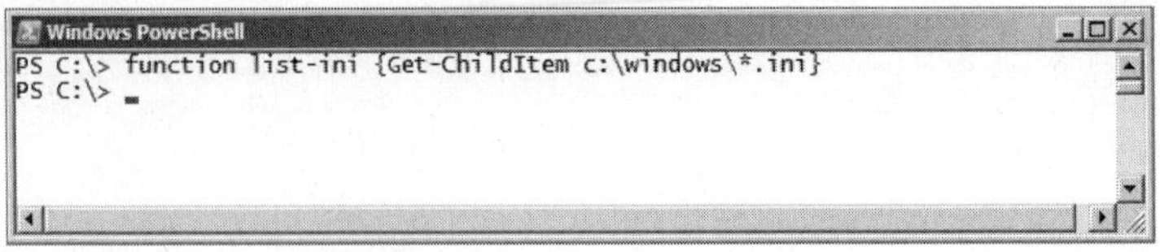

Figure 2-8

This list-ini function can be called anywhere in the current session. Execute the function as shown in Figure 2-9. Once the function name is called, PowerShell recognizes it as a function code block and executes the code block defined in the actual function list-ini. The following command requests all the files with the extension .ini under C:\Windows folder:

```
list-ini
```

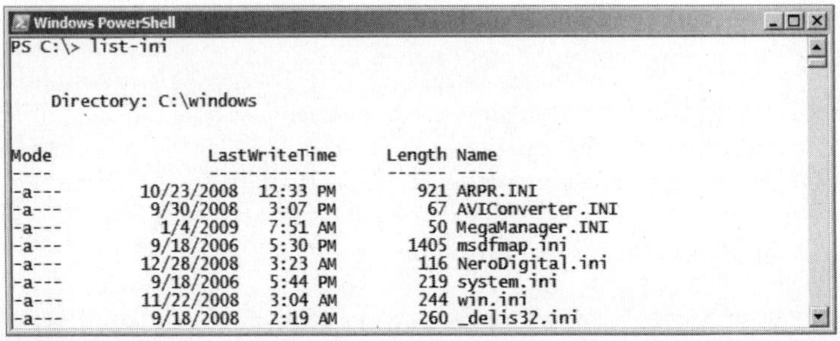

Figure 2-9

Functions can be made persistently available in all the Windows PowerShell sessions by adding them to the PowerShell profile. You will see examples of the Windows PowerShell profile and its uses in detail in Chapter 5.

Script Commands

Script commands are a set of executable PowerShell cmdlets stored in a file with the .ps1 extension.

You can create a simple Add-Num.ps1 script using Notepad under the directory C:\DBAScripts, as shown in the following example. This script file, shown in Figure 2-10, accepts two variables, $variable1 and $variable2, as parameters and stores the sum to a third variable, $variable3. It then displays the value of $variable3.

```
# ===========================================================
#
# NAME: Add-Num.ps1
```

```
#
# AUTHOR: Yan and MAK
# DATE   : 4/26/2008
#
# COMMENT: This script accepts two numbers, sums the
# two numbers and display the result
#
# ======================================================

param (
[int] $variable1,
[int] $variable2
)

$variable3=$variable1+$variable2;
$variable3
```

You can use any text editor to write a PowerShell Script file, not just Notepad.

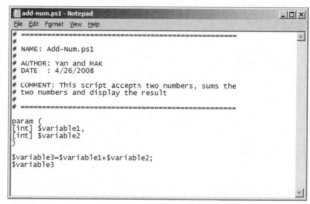

Figure 2-10

Here, all the information that appears after the pound symbol (#) will be ignored by Windows PowerShell because that tells PowerShell that those are comments. Beginning with PowerShell 2.0 CTP3, you can use multi-line comments using <# and #>.

Because you created the PowerShell script Add-Num.ps1 under C:\DBAScripts, you have to navigate to the folder DBAScripts. The cmdlet Set-Location can be used to move the location from the current folder to the DBAScripts folder, as shown in Figure 2-11.

Then the PowerShell script Add-Num.ps1 can be executed using .\ or ./, as shown in Figure 2-11.

```
Set-Location C:\DBAScripts
.\add-num.ps1 100 200
./add-num.ps1 10 200
```

When executing the script, if PowerShell returns the warning message "Script cannot be loaded because execution of script is disabled," then execute the following command, followed by the script shown in

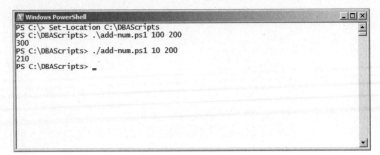

Figure 2-11

Figure 2-12. By default, execution of any PowerShell script is restricted for security reasons, but you can use the cmdlet set-executionpolicy to make it unrestricted.

```
Set-ExecutionPolicy Unrestricted
```

```
Windows PowerShell
PS C:\DBAScripts> .\add-num.ps1 100 200
File C:\DBAScripts\add-num.ps1 cannot be loaded because the execution of script
s is disabled on this system. Please see "get-help about_signing" for more deta
ils.
At line:1 char:14
+ .\add-num.ps1 <<<< 100 200
    + CategoryInfo          : NotSpecified: (:) [], PSSecurityException
    + FullyQualifiedErrorId : RuntimeException

PS C:\DBAScripts> Set-ExecutionPolicy Unrestricted
PS C:\DBAScripts> .\add-num.ps1 100 200
300
PS C:\DBAScripts>
```

Figure 2-12

More PowerShell scripts and securities are shown in detail in later chapters.

Calling PowerShell cmdlets or Scripts from the Command Shell

PowerShell functionality can be used from other shells such as command shell. The PowerShell.exe executable accepts numerous parameters, such as a console file or a command.

You can execute .ps1 files by passing them as parameters to the PowerShell executable, as shown in Figures 2-13 and 2-14. Launch the command shell by running the following command from Start ➢ Run, as shown in Figure 2-13:

```
cmd.exe
```

At the command prompt, execute the following command as shown in Figure 2-14. This PowerShell.exe executable accepts the parameter name -command and the parameter value Add-Num.ps1 with parameters 100 and 400:

```
PowerShell -command C:\DBAScripts\add-num.ps1 100 400
```

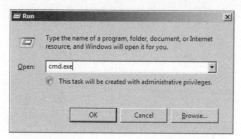

Run
Type the name of a program, folder, document, or Internet resource, and Windows will open it for you.
Open: cmd.exe
This task will be created with administrative privileges.
OK
Cancel
Browse...

Figure 2-13

Administrator: C:\Windows\system32\cmd.exe
C:\Users\poweruser>PowerShell -command c:\DBAScripts\add-num.ps1 100 400
500
C:\Users\poweruser>_

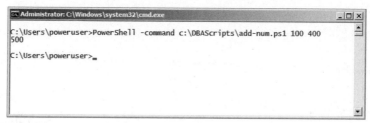

Figure 2-14

You can execute a PowerShell cmdlet directly from the command shell as shown here and in Figure 2-15:

```
PowerShell -command Get-Process
```

Windows PowerShell
PS C:\DBAScripts> PowerShell -command Get-Process
Handles NPM(K) PM(K) WS(K) VM(M) CPU(s) Id ProcessName
124 9 21668 24996 65 460 audiodg
186 15 36292 36448 188 153.46 3688 ButtonMonitor
195 13 35668 1780 107 0.31 1908 ccSvcHst
830 13 3216 7756 168 60.90 520 csrss
631 29 15504 22240 144 99.03 580 csrss
52 5 3196 4776 72 0.02 3600 dpupdchk
119 8 3712 9656 85 0.30 2780 dwm
1595 102 81588 99156 371 293.03 3176 explorer
151 10 30208 6392 70 0.08 4932 fdhost
46 4 1648 3988 28 0.03 4156 fdlauncher
580 86 170512 185320 437 356.99 5068 firefox
0 0 0 24 0 0 Idle
354 23 13280 24616 129 3.07 764 iexplore
683 51 75436 67852 278 3.01 4008 iexplore

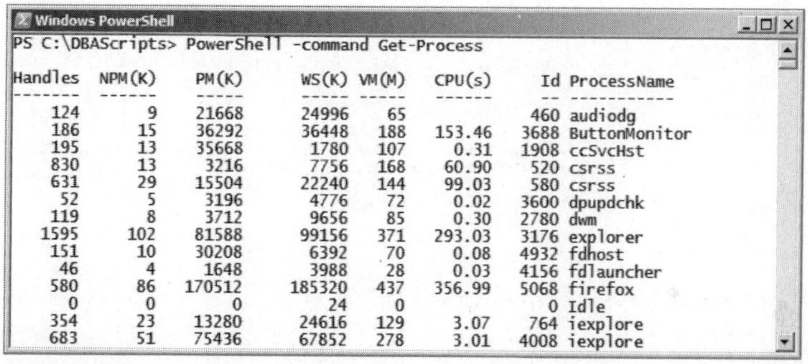

Figure 2-15

PowerShell Snap-ins

PowerShell cmdlets are contained in PowerShell snap-ins. PowerShell *snap-ins* are a group of PowerShell cmdlets or providers that extend the functionality of the shell. When a snap-in is loaded into the PowerShell environment, the cmdlets and providers contained in it are registered with the shell.

By default, seven core snap-ins are loaded, and their corresponding cmdlets are available when PowerShell is launched. Each core snap-ins has its own namespace:

- Core
- Host

- ❑ Management
- ❑ Security
- ❑ Utility
- ❑ Diagnostics
- ❑ WSMAN.Management

Execute the following PowerShell cmdlet to see all the snap-ins that are loaded into the current Power-Shell environment, as shown in Figure 2-16.

```
Get-PSSnapin
```

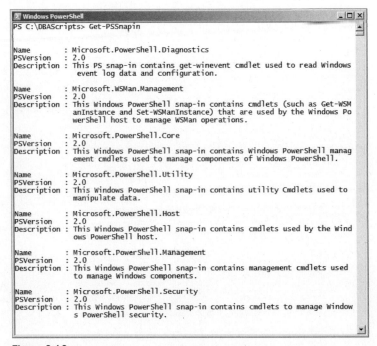

Figure 2-16

The following sections describe each of the snap-ins and their cmdlets. Most of the cmdlets listed here are described and demonstrated throughout the remaining chapters. The following section provides basic information about how to get all the cmdlets available in each snap-in.

You can also check Appendix A for more details about each cmdlet in each snap-in.

Core

The namespace of the Core snap-in is Microsoft.PowerShell.core. This snap-in contains cmdlets related to the PowerShell engine, such as aliases, environments, variables, and functions.

You can find all the cmdlets available in the namespace Microsoft.PowerShell.core using the simple cmdlet shown in Figure 2-17.

Here, two cmdlets are used. One is Get-Command, which provides the commands available in Power-Shell. The other is Where-Object, which is used for filtering the result. The pipe (|) is used for command chaining. More about command chaining is explained later in this chapter.

```
Get-Command -commandtype cmdlet | Where-Object {$_.PSSnapin -match "core"}
```

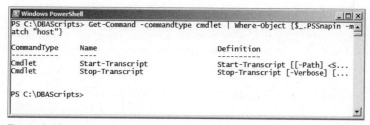

Figure 2-17

Host

The namespace of the Host snap-in is Microsoft.PowerShell.Host. This snap-in contains cmdlets related to hosting, such as start-transcript and stop-transcript.

You can find all the cmdlets available in the namespace Microsoft.PowerShell.host using the following cmdlet, shown in Figure 2-18:

```
Get-Command -commandtype cmdlet | Where-Object {$_.PSSnapin -match "host"}
```

```
Windows PowerShell                                                    _|□|×|
PS C:\DBAScripts> Get-Command -commandtype cmdlet | Where-Object {$_.PSSnapin -m
atch "host"}

CommandType      Name                              Definition
-----------      ----                              ----------
Cmdlet           Start-Transcript                  Start-Transcript [[-Path] <S...
Cmdlet           Stop-Transcript                   Stop-Transcript [-Verbose] [...

PS C:\DBAScripts>
```

Figure 2-18

PowerShell.Management

The namespace of the Management snap-in is Microsoft.PowerShell.Management. This snap-in contains cmdlets related to windows management, such as managing services and processes, and so on.

You can find all the cmdlets available in the namespace Microsoft.PowerShell.Management using the following cmdlet, shown in Figure 2-19:

```
Get-Command -commandtype cmdlet | Where-Object {$_.PSSnapin -match
    "PowerShell.Management"}
```

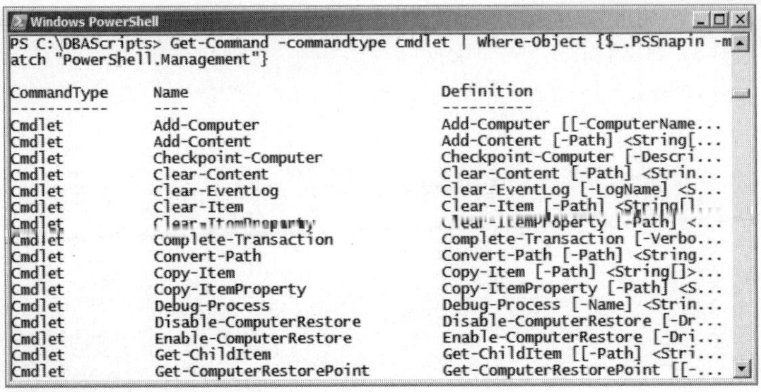

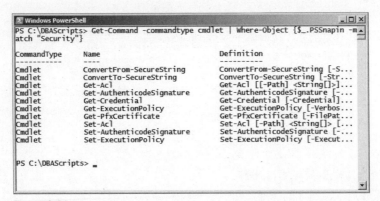

Figure 2-19

Security

The namespace of the Security snap-in is Microsoft.PowerShell.Security. This snap-in contains cmdlets related to PowerShell security, such as Get-Acl and Set-ExecutionPolicy.

You can find all the cmdlets available in the namespace Microsoft.PowerShell.Security using the following cmdlet:

```
Get-Command -commandtype cmdlet | Where-Object {$_.PSSnapin -match "Security"}
```

Figure 2-20 shows some of the commonly used cmdlets, including their descriptions, related to the Security snap-in.

Figure 2-20

Utility

The namespace of the Utility snap-in is Microsoft.PowerShell.Utility. This snap-in contains cmdlets that can retrieve and manipulate data, such as `write-host`, `Format-List`, and so on.

You can find all the cmdlets available in the namespace Microsoft.PowerShell.Utility using the following cmdlet:

```
Get-Command -commandtype cmdlet | Where-Object {$_.PSSnapin -match "Utility"}
```

Figure 2-21 shows some of the commonly used cmdlets, including their descriptions, related to the Utility snap-in.

```
Windows PowerShell
PS C:\DBAScripts> Get-Command -commandtype cmdlet | Where-Object {$_.PSSnapin -m
atch "Utility"}

CommandType     Name                            Definition
-----------     ----                            ----------
Cmdlet          Add-Member                      Add-Member [-MemberType] <PS...
Cmdlet          Add-Type                        Add-Type [-TypeDefinition] <...
Cmdlet          Clear-Variable                  Clear-Variable [-Name] <Stri...
Cmdlet          Compare-Object                  Compare-Object [-ReferenceOb...
Cmdlet          ConvertFrom-Csv                 ConvertFrom-Csv [-InputObjec...
Cmdlet          ConvertFrom-StringData          ConvertFrom-StringData [-Str...
Cmdlet          ConvertTo-Csv                   ConvertTo-Csv [-InputObject]...
Cmdlet          ConvertTo-Html                  ConvertTo-Html [[-Property] ...
Cmdlet          ConvertTo-Xml                   ConvertTo-Xml [-InputObject]...
Cmdlet          Disable-PSBreakpoint            Disable-PSBreakpoint [-Break...
Cmdlet          Enable-PSBreakpoint             Enable-PSBreakpoint [-Id] <I...
Cmdlet          Export-Alias                    Export-Alias [-Path] <String...
Cmdlet          Export-Clixml                   Export-Clixml [-Path] <Strin...
Cmdlet          Export-Csv                      Export-Csv [-Path] <String> ...
Cmdlet          Export-FormatData               Export-FormatData [-InputObj...
Cmdlet          Export-PSSession                Export-PSSession [-Session] ...
```

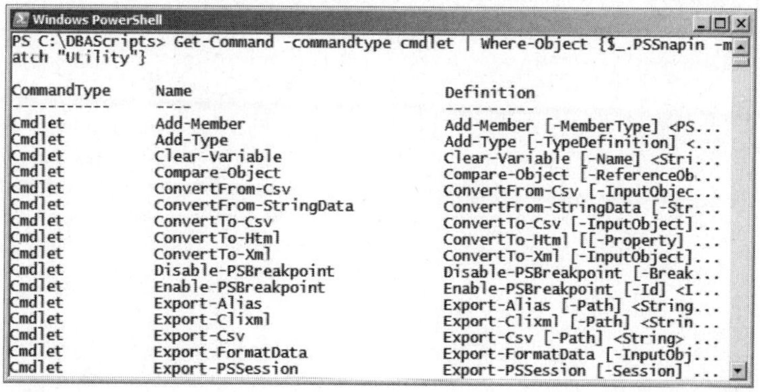

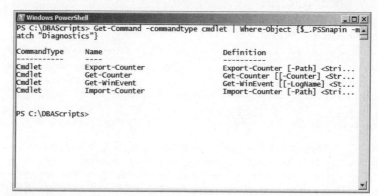

Figure 2-21

Diagnostics

The namespace of the Diagnostic snap-in is Microsoft.PowerShell.Diagnostics. This snap-in contains cmdlets related to performance counters and event logs.

You can find all the cmdlets available in the namespace Microsoft.PowerShell.Diagnostics using the following cmdlet, shown in Figure 2-22:

```
Get-Command -commandtype cmdlet | Where-Object {$_.PSSnapin -match "Diagnostics"}
```

```
Windows PowerShell
PS C:\DBAScripts> Get-Command -commandtype cmdlet | Where-Object {$_.PSSnapin -m
atch "Diagnostics"}

CommandType     Name                            Definition
-----------     ----                            ----------
Cmdlet          Export-Counter                  Export-Counter [-Path] <Stri...
Cmdlet          Get-Counter                     Get-Counter [[-Counter] <Str...
Cmdlet          Get-WinEvent                    Get-WinEvent [[-LogName] <St...
Cmdlet          Import-Counter                  Import-Counter [-Path] <Stri...


PS C:\DBAScripts>
```

Figure 2-22

WsMan.Management

The namespace of the WsMAN.Management snap-in is Microsoft.WsMan.Management. This snap-in contains cmdlets related to WsMan.

You can find all the cmdlets available in the namespace Microsoft.WsMan.Management using the following cmdlet, shown in Figure 2-23:

```
Get-Command -commandtype cmdlet | Where-Object {$_.PSSnapin -match
    "WsMan.Management"}
```

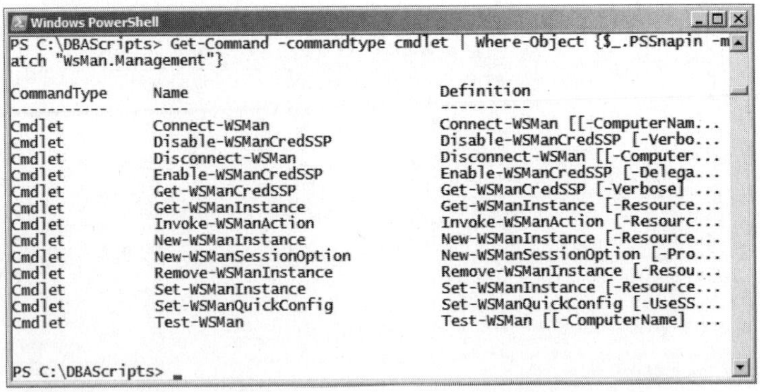

Figure 2-23

cmdlets related to WsManagement are very new and currently there is little documentation for Power-Shell 2.0 CTP3. This should change, however, after its official release. Such documentation, when it becomes available, will help you understand more about each of the cmdlets and enable you to explore their functionality and usage.

PowerShell cmdlet Syntax

As stated earlier in this chapter, cmdlets are constructed in *verb-noun* format. The verb specifies the action to be performed and the noun specifies the object being operated on. Recall that the noun is always singular, even if it retrieves or acts on multiple objects or data.

Two examples are the cmdlet `Get-process` and `Write-host`.

Most cmdlets accept parameters. All parameters names are prefixed with a hyphen, and all the parameter values are prefixed with a blank space after the parameter name. There are two types of parameters: *named parameters* and *positional parameters*.

Named Parameter

This is the easiest and most common way to use parameters. Basically, you specify the name of the parameter followed by its value — for example, `Get-Process -Name smss`:

```
Get-Process -Name smss
```

`Get-process` is the cmdlet, `Name` is the parameter name, and `smss` is the parameter value.

Parameter values can be substituted with wildcards as well, as shown here and in Figure 2-24:

```
Get-Process -Name s*
```

```
Windows PowerShell                                                    _ □ ×
PS C:\DBAScripts> Get-Process -Name s*

Handles  NPM(K)      PM(K)      WS(K) VM(M)    CPU(s)     Id ProcessName
-------  ------      -----      ----- -----    ------     -- -----------
   1804      29    276316      96976   772    533.94   2208 SearchIndexer
    235      14      5552      11692    87      0.45   3068 SearchSettings
    219      13      4140      12464    96      0.14   3592 SearchSettings
    257      23      4000       8888    48      5.85    628 services
    461      30     24984      42828   178     37.58   5908 sidebar
     97       6      7884      12748    62      2.12    536 SLsvc
     31       2       568       1064     6      0.08    452 smss
     89       7      3224       6540    72      0.20   7068 splwow64
    320      18      7768      13300   114      6.96   1532 spoolsv
    797      42    193188     199808   369  1,072.19    208 svchost
   1366    1968     88768     105336   510     84.85    284 svchost
    163       8      4756       8712    44      0.31    512 svchost
    646      49     13676      21404   114     15.96    572 svchost
    327       9      4740       8988    54    101.24    800 svchost
    408      66      7620      11916    63     17.19    908 svchost
    505      43     21396      20096    94     32.65   1012 svchost
    676      44     37704      42672   462     49.41   1092 svchost
```

Figure 2-24

Positional Parameter

PowerShell allows us to omit the parameter name completely for certain parameters. In the previous example, `name` is a positional parameter in the first position; therefore, it can be called without the parameter name (see Figure 2-25), as shown here:

```
Get-Process s*
```

```
Windows PowerShell                                                    _ □ ×
PS C:\DBAScripts> Get-Process s*

Handles  NPM(K)      PM(K)      WS(K) VM(M)    CPU(s)     Id ProcessName
-------  ------      -----      ----- -----    ------     -- -----------
   1808      29    276316      96984   772    533.94   2208 SearchIndexer
    235      14      5552      11692    87      0.45   3068 SearchSettings
    219      13      4140      12464    96      0.14   3592 SearchSettings
    257      23      4000       8888    48      5.85    628 services
    461      30     24984      42828   178     38.42   5908 sidebar
     97       6      7884      12748    62      2.12    536 SLsvc
     31       2       568       1064     6      0.08    452 smss
     89       7      3224       6540    72      0.20   7068 splwow64
    320      18      7768      13300   114      6.96   1532 spoolsv
    790      42    193084     199780   368  1,072.24    208 svchost
   1364    1968     88712     105312   509     84.88    284 svchost
    163       8      4756       8712    44      0.31    512 svchost
    646      49     13676      21404   114     15.96    572 svchost
    327       9      4740       8988    54    101.24    800 svchost
    412      67      7728      11964    64     17.19    908 svchost
    503      43     21312      20080    93     32.65   1012 svchost
    674      44     37656      42660   462     49.41   1092 svchost
```

Figure 2-25

You can easily find all the positional parameter of a PowerShell cmdlet by executing the following cmdlet (see Figure 2-26):

```
(Get-Help Get-Process).parameters.parameter
```

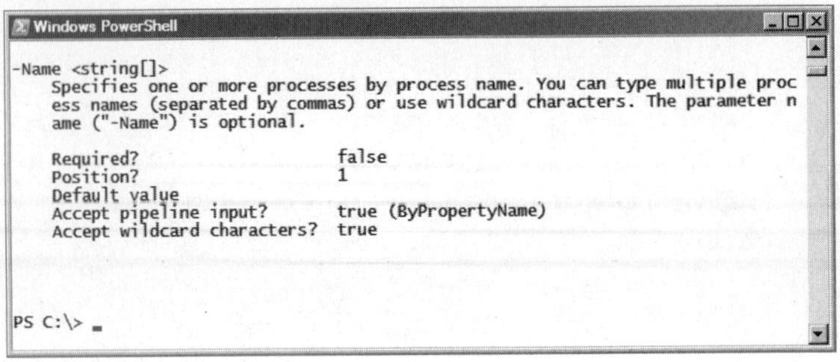

```
Windows PowerShell                                                    _ □ ×

-Name <string[]>
     Specifies one or more processes by process name. You can type multiple proc
     ess names (separated by commas) or use wildcard characters. The parameter n
     ame ("-Name") is optional.

     Required?                    false
     Position?                    1
     Default value
     Accept pipeline input?       true (ByPropertyName)
     Accept wildcard characters?  true


PS C:\> _
```

Figure 2-26

Figure 2-26 shows the end of the output. As you can see, the value of the Position? property of the Name parameter is 1, so Name is a positional parameter at position 1.

Windows PowerShell supports the following six common parameters on all the cmdlets:

❑   Debug

❑   ErrorAction

❑   ErrorVariable

❑   OutputBuffer

❑   OutputVariable

❑   Verbose

Two other commonly used parameters available in certain cmdlets provide options for "what if" scenarios and choosing confirmation (Yes/No):

❑   WhatIf

❑   Confirm

For more information regarding the common parameters, run the following command:

```
Get-Help about_CommonParameters
```

Command Chaining

As in UNIX and Linux, PowerShell cmdlets can be chained together using a pipeline. *Command chaining* is having the output of one command feed into, or act as the input to, another command. This was shown earlier in Figure 2-23.

In the following command example, the output of Get-Process is fed to the cmdlet Where-Object. The output of the cmdlet Where-Object is fed to the cmdlet Sort-Object.

As you already know, the cmdlet Get-Process shows all the processes on the current local machine. When the output of the Get-Process is fed to Where-Object using command chaining, the Where-Object processes each item from the output of Get-Process and looks for the processname equal to the value "rundll32". Then the filtered output of Where-Object is passed to Sort-Object, which sorts the database based on the Object ID value in descending order (see Figure 2-27).

```
Get-Process | Where-Object {$_.Processname -eq "rundll32"} | Sort-Object ID -desc
```

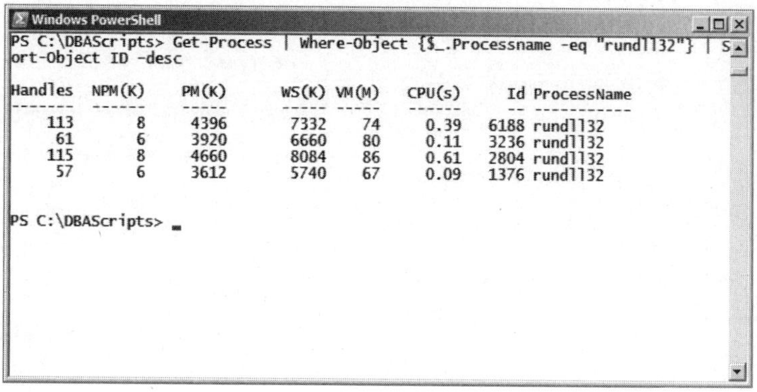

Figure 2-27

Hence, the output shown in Figure 2-27 is the result of command chaining. You will be using command chaining throughout this book.

Getting Help

Microsoft documented all the cmdlets and that documentation can be retrieved using the cmdlet Get-Help. This documentation is similar to using the man command in the UNIX and Linux environment. In addition, certain parameters can be used with Get-Help to get detailed information and examples.

The cmdlet Get-Help can be used in three different ways:

❑   Get-Help with no parameter:

```
Get-Help Get-Process
```

This provides the minimal information needed to understand and use the cmdlet. The following information is returned when executed (see Figure 2-28):

❑   Name

❑   Synopsis

❑   Detailed Description

❑   Related Links

❑   Remarks

❑   Get-Help with the -detailed parameter:

```
Get-Help Get-Process -detailed
```

```
Windows PowerShell                                                    _ |□| x|
PS C:\DBAScripts> Get-Help Get-Process

NAME
    Get-Process

SYNOPSIS
    Gets the processes that are running on the local computer or a remote compu
    ter.


SYNTAX
    Get-Process [-ComputerName <string[]>] [-FileVersionInfo] [-Module] -Id <In
    t32[]> [<CommonParameters>]

    Get-Process [-ComputerName <string[]>] [-FileVersionInfo] [-Module] -InputO
    bject <Process[]> [<CommonParameters>]

    Get-Process [-ComputerName <string[]>] [-FileVersionInfo] [-Module] [[-Name
    ] <string[]>] [<CommonParameters>]
```

Figure 2-28

This returns the following information when executed (see Figure 2-29):

❑   Name

❑   Synopsis

❑   Syntax

❑   Detailed Description

❑   Parameters

❑   Examples

❑   Remarks

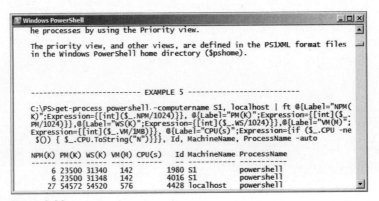

```
Windows PowerShell                                                    _ |□| x|
he processes by using the Priority view.

The priority view, and other views, are defined in the PS1XML format files
in the Windows PowerShell home directory ($pshome).



---------------------------- EXAMPLE 5 ----------------------------

C:\PS>get-process powershell -computername S1, localhost | ft @{Label="NPM(
K)";Expression={[int]($_.NPM/1024)}}, @{Label="PM(K)";Expression={[int]($_.
PM/1024)}},@{Label="WS(K)";Expression={[int]($_.WS/1024)}},@{Label="VM(M)";
Expression={[int]($_.VM/1MB)}}, @{Label="CPU(s)";Expression={if ($_.CPU -ne
$()) { $_.CPU.ToString("N")}}}, Id, MachineName, ProcessName -auto

NPM(K) PM(K) WS(K) VM(M) CPU(s)    Id MachineName ProcessName
------ ----- ----- ----- ------    -- ----------- -----------
     6 23500 31340   142         1980 S1          powershell
     6 23500 31348   142         4016 S1          powershell
    27 54572 54520   576         4428 localhost    powershell
```

Figure 2-29

❑   Get-Help with the -full parameter:

    Get-Help Get-Process -full

This provides all of the following (see Figure 2-30):

❑   Name

❑   Synopsis

- ❏ Syntax
- ❏ Detailed Description
- ❏ Parameters
- ❏ Input Types
- ❏ Return Type
- ❏ Notes
- ❏ Examples
- ❏ Related Links

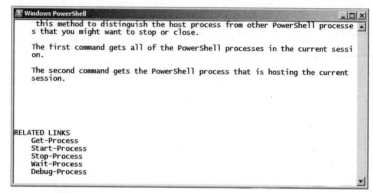

Figure 2-30

When using the `-full` and `-detailed` parameters, the documentation expands to several pages and flashes through screen and it is very difficult to read all of them if you do not have enough screen buffer. You can use command chaining with the MS-DOS executable `more` to page the documentation, as shown here:

```
Get-Help Get-Process -Full | more
```

This causes the output to be displayed one screen at a time. You can scroll the pages from one screen to another by pressing the spacebar or Enter key. You can abort the display of paging using Ctrl + C. Figure 2-31 shows the same `Get-Help Get-Process` cmdlet using `more`.

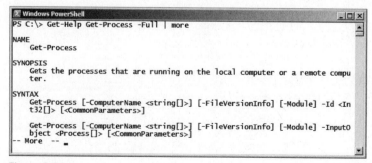

Figure 2-31

Alternatively, you can just use the built-in Help function. The Help function actually pipes the result from the `Get-Help` cmdlet to `more` to support paging, as shown in the following example:

```
Help Get-Process -Full
```

Filtering

The cmdlets can produce humongous results. Not all of the columns and rows that are displayed as output are useful all the time. You may need to filter the results. PowerShell provides two cmdlets for filtering: `Where-Object` and `Select-Object`.

As shown earlier when you ran the `Get-Process` cmdlet, it returns all the processes running on the current host (see Figure 2-32):

```
Get-Process
```

```
Windows PowerShell
PS C:\DBAScripts> Get-Process

Handles  NPM(K)    PM(K)      WS(K) VM(M)   CPU(s)     Id ProcessName
-------  ------    -----      ----- -----   ------     -- -----------
    133      10    23328      26448    76             488 audiodg
    189      15    36196      36760   189    55.21    936 ButtonMonitor
    187      15    19284      19172   160     3.68   5044 ButtonMonitor
    198      13    54220       1828   122     0.28   2700 ccSvcHst
     45       5     4176       6908    53     0.33   2404 cmd
    598      11     3108       7516   164     4.96    532 csrss
    278      10     6540      13224   167     3.12   3604 csrss
    524      32    14828      20520   176    14.38   5436 csrss
     54       5     3848       4556    71     0.00   2172 dpupdchk
    220      13     6324      10696   106     0.22   3308 dpupdchk
     92       7     6800       3192    69    10.02   3376 dwm
     83       6     2736       5244    57     0.05   4092 dwm
    686      49    35708      58136   253    42.81    164 explorer
    833      66    49748      67736   280    26.46   2316 explorer
    378      50   103144     113024   295    47.61   5956 firefox
    223      15     4872       2928    76     0.19   5880 GoogleUpdate
    104       8     2512       5540    75     0.02   1256 ICQ Service
```

Figure 2-32

If, for example, you're only interested in the processes that start with "s", then you can use the `Where-Object` cmdlet as shown here and in Figure 2-33:

```
Get-Process | Where-Object {$_.Processname -like "s*"}
```

```
Windows PowerShell
PS C:\DBAScripts> Get-Process | Where-Object {$_.Processname -like "s*"}

Handles  NPM(K)    PM(K)      WS(K) VM(M)   CPU(s)     Id ProcessName
-------  ------    -----      ----- -----   ------     -- -----------
   1804      29   276316      96980   772   533.94   2208 SearchIndexer
    235      14     5552      11692    87     0.45   3068 SearchSettings
    219      13     4140      12464    96     0.14   3592 SearchSettings
    257      23     4000       8884    48     6.04    628 services
    461      30    25032      42876   178    40.19   5908 sidebar
     97       6     7884      12748    62     2.12    536 SLsvc
     31       2      568       1064     6     0.08    452 smss
     89       7     3224       6540    72     0.20   7068 splwow64
    320      18     7768      13300   114     6.96   1532 spoolsv
    799      42   193084     199788   368 1,074.35    208 svchost
   1366    1968    88720     105324   509    85.11    284 svchost
    163       8     4756       8712    44     0.31    512 svchost
    645      49    13676      21400   114    15.97    572 svchost
    327       9     4736       8972    54   101.26    800 svchost
    410      66     7676      11952    64    17.19    908 svchost
    512      44    21448      20140    94    32.79   1012 svchost
    676      44    37652      42652   462    49.51   1092 svchost
```

Figure 2-33

Basically, $_ is substituted with the actual output of Get-Process row by row and evaluated against the -like operator with the value s*.

If you want to list all the processes that start with "s" excluding the process name svchost, then you can use the and and ne operators in the Where-Object, as shown here (see Figure 2-34):

```
Get-Process | Where-Object {$_.Processname -like "s*" -and $_.Processname -ne
    "svchost" }
```

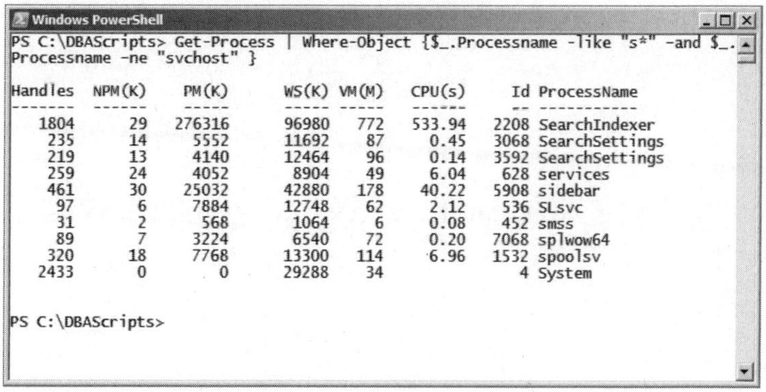

Figure 2-34

The following table shows the comparison operators available in PowerShell.

Comparison Operator	Meaning	Example (returns true)
-eq	Is equal to	1 -eq 1
-ne	Is not equal to	1 -ne 2
-lt	Is less than	1 -lt 2
-le	Is less than or equal to	1 -le 2
-gt	Is greater than	2 -gt 1
-ge	Is greater than or equal to	2 -ge 1
-like	Is like (wildcard comparison for text)	"file.doc" -like "f*.do?"
-notlike	Is not like (wildcard comparison for text)	"file.doc" -notlike "p*.doc"
-contains	Contains	1,2,3 -contains 1
-notcontains	Does not contain	1,2,3 -notcontains 4
-ceq	Case sensitive equal to	a -ceq a
-cne	Is not equal to	a -cne A

The next table shows the logical operators available.

Logical Operator	Meaning	Example (returns true)
-and	Logical and; true if both sides are true	(1 -eq 1) -and (2 -eq 2)
-or	Logical or; true if either side is true	(1 -eq 1) -or (1 -eq 2)
-not	Logical not; reverses true and false	-not (1 -eq 2)
!	Logical not; reverses true and false	! (1 -eq 2)

You can also filter items up front in the Get-Process itself, as shown here and in Figure 2-35:

```
Get-Process s* | Where-Object {$_.Processname -ne "svchost"}
```

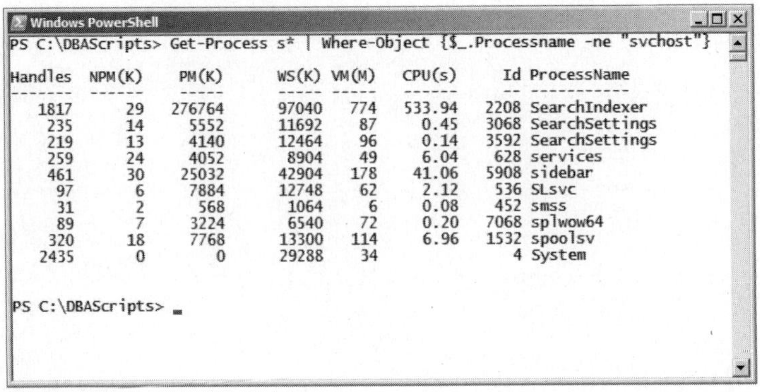

Figure 2-35

If the operator needs to use numerical values, then you can use numerical operators, as shown here and in Figure 2-36:

```
Get-Process | Where-Object {$_.Handles -gt 1100 -and $_.CPU -gt 5}
```

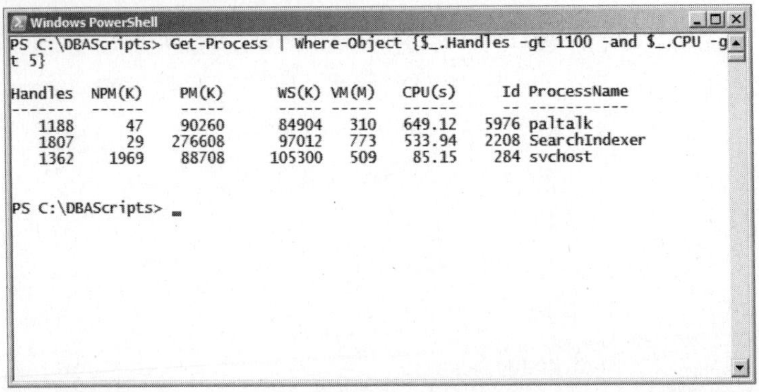

Figure 2-36

When you execute the `Get-Process` cmdlet, the default display of a process is a table that includes the following columns:

- ❏ Handles
- ❏ NPM(K)
- ❏ PM(K)
- ❏ WS(K)
- ❏ VM(M)
- ❏ CPU(s)
- ❏ ID
- ❏ ProcessName

However, if you only want to view some of the columns in the output, use the cmdlet `Select-Object`, as shown here (see Figure 2-37):

```
Get-Process | Select-Object ID, Processname
```

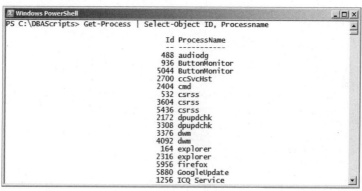

Figure 2-37

With `Select-Object`, you can select unique values, as shown here (see Figure 2-38):

```
Get-Process | Select-Object Processname -unique
```

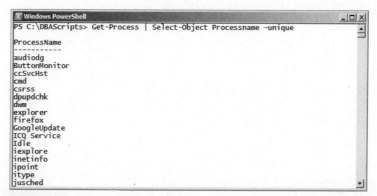

Figure 2-38

As shown in Figure 2-38, duplicate `csrss`, `fdhost` and `fdlauncher` processes have been filtered out.

Sorting

When executed, cmdlets produce output based on the default sort order of the cmdlet. You can change this output behavior using `Sort-Object`.

You can sort the output in ascending, descending, or alphabetical order using `Sort-Object` as shown in Figures 2-39, Figure 2-40, and Figure 2-41, respectively.

This cmdlet sorts the output in ascending order:

```
Get-Process s* | Sort-Object CPU
```

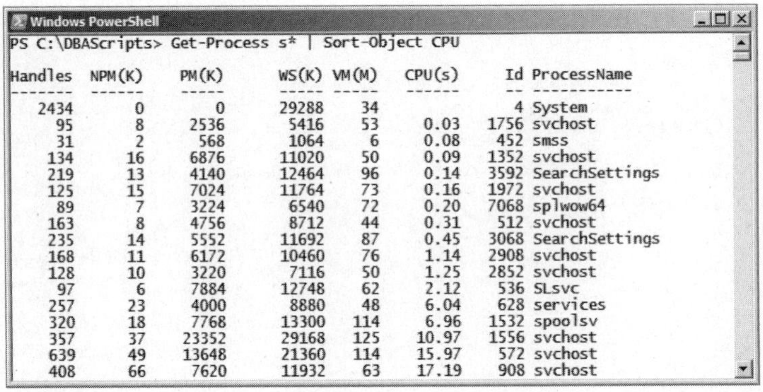

```
PS C:\DBAScripts> Get-Process s* | Sort-Object CPU

Handles  NPM(K)    PM(K)      WS(K) VM(M)   CPU(s)     Id ProcessName
-------  ------    -----      ----- -----   ------     -- -----------
   2434       0        0      29288    34               4 System
     95       8     2536       5416    53     0.03   1756 svchost
     31       2      568       1064     6     0.08    452 smss
    134      16     6876      11020    50     0.09   1352 svchost
    219      13     4140      12464    96     0.14   3592 SearchSettings
    125      15     7024      11764    73     0.16   1972 svchost
     89       7     3224       6540    72     0.20   7068 splwow64
    163       8     4756       8712    44     0.31    512 svchost
    235      14     5552      11692    87     0.45   3068 SearchSettings
    168      11     6172      10460    76     1.14   2908 svchost
    128      10     3220       7116    50     1.25   2852 svchost
     97       6     7884      12748    62     2.12    536 SLsvc
    257      23     4000       8880    48     6.04    628 services
    320      18     7768      13300   114     6.96   1532 spoolsv
    357      37    23352      29168   125    10.97   1556 svchost
    639      49    13648      21360   114    15.97    572 svchost
    408      66     7620      11932    63    17.19    908 svchost
```

Figure 2-39

This cmdlet sorts the output in descending order because the `-desc` parameter is used:

```
Get-Process s* | Sort-Object CPU -desc
```

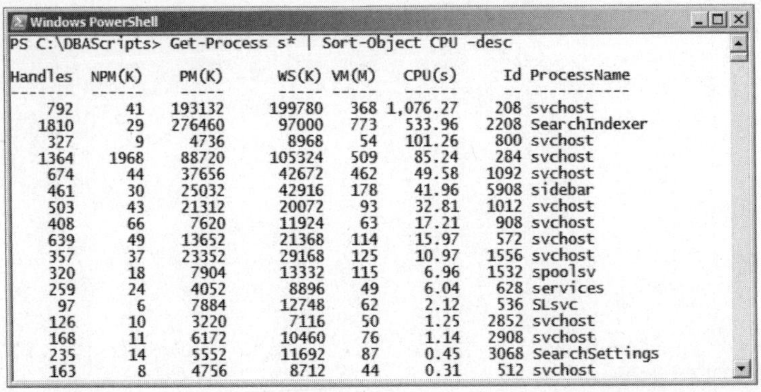

```
PS C:\DBAScripts> Get-Process s* | Sort-Object CPU -desc

Handles  NPM(K)    PM(K)      WS(K) VM(M)   CPU(s)     Id ProcessName
-------  ------    -----      ----- -----   ------     -- -----------
    792      41   193132     199780   368 1,076.27    208 svchost
   1810      29   276460      97000   773   533.96   2208 SearchIndexer
    327       9     4736       8968    54   101.26    800 svchost
   1364    1968    88720     105324   509    85.24    284 svchost
    674      44    37656      42672   462    49.58   1092 svchost
    461      30    25032      42916   178    41.96   5908 sidebar
    503      43    21312      20072    93    32.81   1012 svchost
    408      66     7620      11924    63    17.21    908 svchost
    639      49    13652      21368   114    15.97    572 svchost
    357      37    23352      29168   125    10.97   1556 svchost
    320      18     7904      13332   115     6.96   1532 spoolsv
    259      24     4052       8896    49     6.04    628 services
     97       6     7884      12748    62     2.12    536 SLsvc
    126      10     3220       7116    50     1.25   2852 svchost
    168      11     6172      10460    76     1.14   2908 svchost
    235      14     5552      11692    87     0.45   3068 SearchSettings
    163       8     4756       8712    44     0.31    512 svchost
```

Figure 2-40

This command sorts the output of the `Get-Service` cmdlet alphabetically based on the column `DisplayName`. The default sort order for `Get-Service` is based on the column `Name`:

```
Get-Service | Sort-Object DisplayName
```

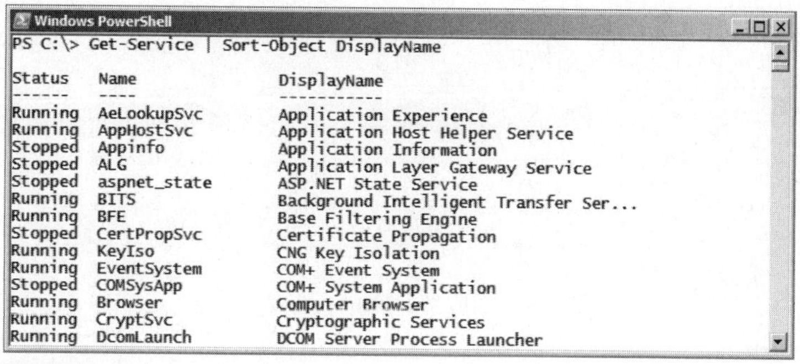

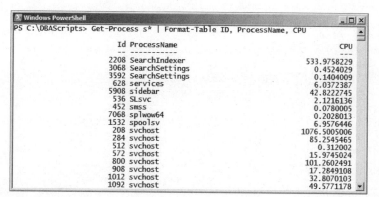

Figure 2-41

Formatting

Any cmdlet you execute is piped to a default cmdlet, `Out-Default`. The `Out-Default` cmdlet, in turn, pipes the output to the default formatter. The default formatter then displays the output.

The `PowerShellcore.format.ps1xml` file under the PowerShell installation directory contains extensive information explaining how different types of objects are displayed.

The default formatter can be overridden by the `Format-Table`, `Format-List`, `Format-Wide`, and `Format-Custom` cmdlets, as shown in Figure 2-42. Here is an example:

```
Get-Process s* | Format-Table ID, ProcessName, CPU
```

Figure 2-42

Formatting with autosize will show the results in more readable output (see Figure 2-43):

```
Get-Process s* | Format-Table ID, ProcessName, ID, CPU -autosize
```

```
Windows PowerShell                                                        _ □ ×
PS C:\DBAScripts> Get-Process s* | Format-Table ID, ProcessName, ID, CPU -autos
ize

  Id ProcessName       Id        CPU
  -- -----------       --        ---
2208 SearchIndexer   2208   533.991423
3068 SearchSettings  3068     0.4524029
3592 SearchSettings  3592     0.1404009
 628 services         628     6.0372387
5908 sidebar         5908    42.8222745
 536 SLsvc            536     2.1216136
 452 smss             452     0.0780005
7068 splwow64        7068     0.2028013
1532 spoolsv         1532     6.9576446
 208 svchost          208  1076.5473009
 284 svchost          284    85.2545465
 512 svchost          512     0.312002
 572 svchost          572    15.9745024
 800 svchost          800   101.2602491
 908 svchost          908    17.2849108
1012 svchost         1012    32.8070103
```

Figure 2-43

You can format the output by grouping it based on a property (see Figure 2-44):

```
Get-Process s* | Group-Object ProcessName
```

```
Windows PowerShell                                                        _ □ ×
PS C:\DBAScripts> Get-Process s* | Group-Object ProcessName

Count Name                  Group
----- ----                  -----
    1 SearchIndexer         {System.Diagnostics.Process (SearchIndexer)}
    2 SearchSettings        {System.Diagnostics.Process (SearchSettings)...
    1 services              {System.Diagnostics.Process (services)}
    1 sidebar               {System.Diagnostics.Process (sidebar)}
    1 SLsvc                 {System.Diagnostics.Process (SLsvc)}
    1 smss                  {System.Diagnostics.Process (smss)}
    1 splwow64              {System.Diagnostics.Process (splwow64)}
    1 spoolsv               {System.Diagnostics.Process (spoolsv)}
   14 svchost               {System.Diagnostics.Process (svchost), Syste...
    1 System                {System.Diagnostics.Process (System)}

PS C:\DBAScripts> _
```

Figure 2-44

You can also group using `Format-Table`. The result is different because you are not using `Group-Object` (see Figure 2-45):

```
Get-Process s* | Format-Table -group ProcessName
```

As shown in Figure 2-46, you can format the output column names using expressions:

```
Get-Process s* | Format-Table @{expression="Processname"; width=25; label="Process
    Name"},   @{expression = "CPU"; width=15; label = "CPU Used"}
```

You can also output the result in the form of a list by using the `Format-List` cmdlet, as shown in Figure 2-47:

```
Get-Process s* | Format-List
```

```
Windows PowerShell                                                          _ □ ×
PS C:\DBAScripts> Get-Process s* | Format-Table -group ProcessName

    ProcessName: SearchIndexer

Handles  NPM(K)    PM(K)      WS(K) VM(M)   CPU(s)      Id ProcessName
-------  ------    -----      ----- -----   ------      -- -----------
   1805      29   276312      96968   772   533.99    2208 SearchIndexer

    ProcessName: SearchSettings

Handles  NPM(K)    PM(K)      WS(K) VM(M)   CPU(s)      Id ProcessName
-------  ------    -----      ----- -----   ------      -- -----------
    235      14     5552      11692    87     0.45    3068 SearchSettings
    219      13     4140      12464    96     0.14    3592 SearchSettings

    ProcessName: services

Handles  NPM(K)    PM(K)      WS(K) VM(M)   CPU(s)      Id ProcessName
```

Figure 2-45

```
Windows PowerShell                                                          _ □ ×
PS C:\DBAScripts> Get-Process s* | Format-Table @{expression="Processname"; widt
h=25; label="Process Name"},   @{expression = "CPU"; width=15; label = "CPU Used
"}

Process Name                    CPU Used
------------                    --------
SearchIndexer                 533.991423
SearchSettings                  0.468003
SearchSettings                 0.1404009
services                       6.0372387
sidebar                       42.8378746
SLsvc                          2.1216136
smss                           0.0780005
splwow64                       0.2028013
spoolsv                        6.9576446
svchost                     1077.9513099
svchost                       85.3013468
svchost                        0.312002
svchost                       16.0057026
svchost                      101.2602491
svchost                       17.3005109
```

Figure 2-46

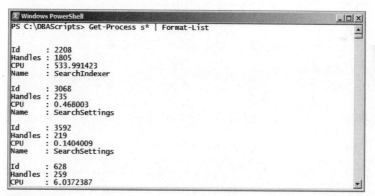

```
Windows PowerShell                                                          _ □ ×
PS C:\DBAScripts> Get-Process s* | Format-List


Id      : 2208
Handles : 1805
CPU     : 533.991423
Name    : SearchIndexer

Id      : 3068
Handles : 235
CPU     : 0.468003
Name    : SearchSettings

Id      : 3592
Handles : 219
CPU     : 0.1404009
Name    : SearchSettings

Id      : 628
Handles : 259
CPU     : 6.0372387
```

Figure 2-47

Another use of `Format-List` is to list all the properties of the cmdlet (see Figure 2-48):

```
Get-Process s* | Format-List -property *
```

```
Windows PowerShell                                                        _ □ x
PS C:\DBAScripts> Get-Process s* | Format-List -property *

__NounName            : Process
Name                  : SearchIndexer
Handles               : 1809
VM                    : 809590784
WS                    : 99299328
PM                    : 282943488
NPM                   : 28464
Path                  : C:\Windows\system32\SearchIndexer.exe
Company               : Microsoft Corporation
CPU                   : 533.991423
FileVersion           : 7.0.6001.16503 (longhorn(wmbla).080526-2159)
ProductVersion        : 7.0.6001.16503
Description           : Microsoft Windows Search Indexer
Product               : Microsoft® Windows® Operating System
Id                    : 2208
PriorityClass         : Normal
HandleCount           : 1809
WorkingSet            : 99299328
```

Figure 2-48

After you get the list of all the properties, you can override the default column display with your own list, as shown in Figure 2-49:

```
Get-Process s* | Format-Table -property Name, Company, Product
```

```
Windows PowerShell                                                        _ □ x
PS C:\DBAScripts> Get-Process s* | Format-Table -property Name, Company, Product

Name                  Company                    Product
----                  -------                    -------
SearchIndexer         Microsoft Corporation      Microsoft® Windows® Op...
SearchSettings        Vendio Services, Inc.      Search Settings
SearchSettings        Vendio Services, Inc.      Search Settings
services              Microsoft Corporation      Microsoft® Windows® Op...
sidebar               Microsoft Corporation      Microsoft® Windows® Op...
SLsvc                 Microsoft Corporation      Microsoft® Windows® Op...
smss                  Microsoft Corporation      Microsoft® Windows® Op...
splwow64              Microsoft Corporation      Microsoft® Windows® Op...
spoolsv               Microsoft Corporation      Microsoft® Windows® Op...
svchost               Microsoft Corporation      Microsoft® Windows® Op...
svchost               Microsoft Corporation      Microsoft® Windows® Op...
svchost               Microsoft Corporation      Microsoft® Windows® Op...
svchost               Microsoft Corporation      Microsoft® Windows® Op...
svchost               Microsoft Corporation      Microsoft® Windows® Op...
svchost               Microsoft Corporation      Microsoft® Windows® Op...
svchost               Microsoft Corporation      Microsoft® Windows® Op...
```

Figure 2-49

Summary

This chapter illustrated the various command types — namely, native commands, shell function commands, script commands, and cmdlets. In the rest of the chapters, you will use these four command types in various situations. This chapter also demonstrated different types of snap-ins and their corresponding cmdlets. When it comes to handling the output of the cmdlets, this chapter illustrated cmdlets related to command chaining, formatting, grouping and sorting, and more. All the formatting procedures and command chaining described in this chapter are used throughout the book. You will revisit functionality such as creating functions in future chapters. The next two chapters show you how to re-use a set of commands by encapsulating them in scripts and functions.

3

Windows PowerShell Programming, Scripting, Error Handling, and Debugging

In Chapter 2, you learned how to use PowerShell cmdlets, command chaining, and command snap-ins. You also learned about formatting, grouping, and sorting. This chapter discusses and illustrates all the PowerShell programming constructs, including using variables, arrays, looping, inputs and outputs, and more. Though all the programming constructs discussed in this chapter can be used in the Windows PowerShell interactive mode, they are primarily used inside the Windows PowerShell scripts. Scripts are a group of PowerShell cmdlets that, for the most part, accept input as parameters and output in the form of files, and all programming logic is encapsulated in the script. These scripts are used for automation.

This chapter covers the following topics:

- ❑ PowerShell variables
- ❑ Arrays
- ❑ Expressions
- ❑ Conditional expressions
- ❑ Loop construct
- ❑ Inputs
- ❑ PowerShell scripting
- ❑ Text file as input

- ❏ Writing to a file

- ❏ Error handling

- ❏ Debugging

PowerShell Scripts

PowerShell scripts are cmdlets put together in a .ps1 file. This is similar to any programming language. The basic requirement of any programming language is input commands, processing commands, and output commands. Other commands, such as error handling and debugging, are also required.

PowerShell provides all the basic requirements for programming PowerShell scripts, and all these commands available in the form of cmdlets are object oriented.

The following list contains the basic requirements of any programming language:

- ❏ Input
    - ❏ User input from the console
    - ❏ User input as parameters
    - ❏ File input
- ❏ Processing
    - ❏ Operators
    - ❏ Expressions
    - ❏ Loop constructs
    - ❏ Variables
- ❏ Output
    - ❏ Output to users on the console
    - ❏ File output
- ❏ Error Handling
- ❏ Debugging

Before jumping into input and output, it's useful to take a look at where the input data and intermediate processing results are stored, namely, the *variables*. All types of variables and how they store information are discussed in the following section.

PowerShell Variables

PowerShell variables are not the same as variables in other languages where only scalar values are stored. Rather, PowerShell variables hold the entire object. They are not just a placeholder for scalar values.

PowerShell variables are prefixed with the dollar symbol ($). You can assign the variable as you would in any other language using the equals operator (=).

Before exploring the variables, navigate to the root folder of the current drive in PowerShell by executing the following cmdlet. This will give you more screen room to work with all the illustrations in this chapter.

```
Set-location C:\
```

Now assign the cmdlet string to a variable as shown in the following example. Here you are using a variable $myvar and assigning the resulting object of the get-process cmdlet to it using the = assignment operator.

```
$myvar=get-process s*
```

Execute the variable as shown in Figure 3-1.

```
$myvar
```

```
Windows PowerShell                                                          _ □ ×
PS C:\users\poweruser> Set-location C:\
PS C:\> $myvar=get-process s*
PS C:\> $myvar

Handles  NPM(K)    PM(K)     WS(K) VM(M)   CPU(s)      Id ProcessName
-------  ------    -----     ----- -----   ------      -- -----------
   1035      24   107472     59072   515    56.97    2944 SearchIndexer
    154      10     3736      8904    90     0.12    1716 SearchSettings
    256      23     3744      7216    34    21.12     616 services
    481      29    24904     43824   166    62.37    1768 sidebar
     98       6     7888     12648    56     1.92      12 SLsvc
     28       2      564      1060     6     0.06     448 smss
     89       7     3608      7052    74     1.62    3772 splwow64
    324      18     8452     12880   101     0.73    1520 spoolsv
    675      37   154172    159988   297   157.34     196 svchost
```

Figure 3-1

You can use various operators in Windows PowerShell, many of which are used throughout the rest of this book. For a complete list of Windows PowerShell operators, jump to the "Operators" section located at the end of this chapter.

Now assign a numerical value to a variable $mynumvar and a string value to another variable $mystrvar, as shown here:

```
$mynumvar=100
$mystrvar="This is test"
```

As discussed earlier, all the variables are basically an object. In the preceding example, two kinds of variables were used. One is a numeric variable and the other is a string variable. In order to find out the properties and methods of those defined variables, use the Get-Member cmdlet, as shown here (see Figure 3-2 and Figure 3-3):

```
$mynumvar | get-member
$mystrvar | get-member
```

```
Windows PowerShell                                                    _|□|x|
PS C:\> $mynumvar=100
PS C:\> $mystrvar="This is test"
PS C:\> $mynumvar | get-member


   TypeName: System.Int32

Name          MemberType Definition
----          ---------- ----------
CompareTo     Method     System.Int32 CompareTo(Object value), System.Int32 Co...
Equals        Method     System.Boolean Equals(Object obj), System.Boolean Equ...
GetHashCode   Method     System.Int32 GetHashCode()
GetType       Method     System.Type GetType()
GetTypeCode   Method     System.TypeCode GetTypeCode()
ToString      Method     System.String ToString(), System.String ToString(Stri...
```

Figure 3-2

```
Windows PowerShell                                                    _|□|x|
PS C:\> $mystrvar | get-member


   TypeName: System.String

Name          MemberType      Definition
----          ----------      ----------
Clone         Method          System.Object Clone()
CompareTo     Method          System.Int32 CompareTo(Object value),...
Contains      Method          System.Boolean Contains(String value)
CopyTo        Method          System.Void CopyTo(Int32 sourceIndex,...
EndsWith      Method          System.Boolean EndsWith(String value)...
Equals        Method          System.Boolean Equals(Object obj), Sy...
GetEnumerator Method          System.CharEnumerator GetEnumerator()
GetHashCode   Method          System.Int32 GetHashCode()
GetType       Method          System.Type GetType()
```

Figure 3-3

You can see that all the methods and properties of both variables are listed. You can use any of the methods and properties for that object. The following example calls the ToUpper method and converts the string to uppercase:

```
$mystrvar.ToUpper()
```

The following example gets the value of the property Length and displays the value (see Figure 3-4):

```
$mystrvar.Length
```

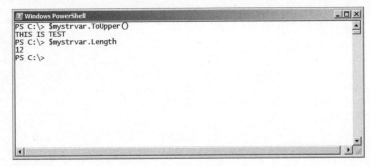

```
Windows PowerShell                                                    _|□|x|
PS C:\> $mystrvar.ToUpper()
THIS IS TEST
PS C:\> $mystrvar.Length
12
PS C:\>
```

Figure 3-4

The following expressions assign, concatenate, replace, and repeat (see Figure 3-5). Here, the operator = is for assignment and the operator + is for concatenation. The operator -replace replaces "World" with "universe".

```
$var1="hello"
$var2="world"
$var1.toupper()+$var2.toupper()

$var1.toupper()*2+$var2.toupper()

$var1.toupper()*2+$var2.toupper() -replace "World","universe"
```

```
Windows PowerShell
PS C:\> $var1="hello"
PS C:\> $var2="world"
PS C:\> $var1.toupper()+$var2.toupper()
HELLOWORLD
PS C:\>
PS C:\> $var1.toupper()*2+$var2.toupper()
HELLOHELLOWORLD
PS C:\>
PS C:\> $var1.toupper()*2+$var2.toupper() -replace "World","universe"
HELLOHELLOuniverse
PS C:\>
```

Figure 3-5

You can assign date values to a variable as shown and manipulate the output by using simple expressions.

In the next example, the expression $mydate=get-date assigns the object get-date, which has the current date and time value, to a variable $mydate. $mydate.year will display the value of the object property year. The expression $mydate.month displays the value of the object property month. $mydate.day +1 adds 1 to the object property day and displays the resulting value (see Figure 3-6):

```
$mydate=get-date
$mydate.year
$mydate.month
$mydate.day
$mydate.day+1
```

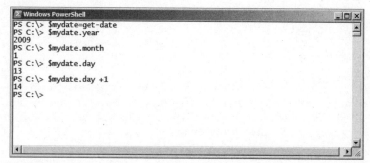

```
Windows PowerShell
PS C:\> $mydate=get-date
PS C:\> $mydate.year
2009
PS C:\> $mydate.month
1
PS C:\> $mydate.day
13
PS C:\> $mydate.day +1
14
PS C:\>
```

Figure 3-6

Arrays

Arrays are used to implement mathematical vectors and matrices, as well as other kinds of rectangular tables. PowerShell variables can also store array values. The following example creates a numerical array with five elements, 10, 20, 30, 40, and 50, as shown in Figure 3-7:

```
$mynumarray =10,20,30,40,50
```

This example displays the fourth element from the array:

```
$mynumarray[3]
```

Array elements are accessed using an *index*, also known as an *origin*. There are different kinds of index implementations: zero-based, one-based, n-based, and so on. Windows PowerShell arrays follow a zero-based index. Hence, in the preceding example, `$mynumarray[3]` is basically pointing to the fourth element in the array.

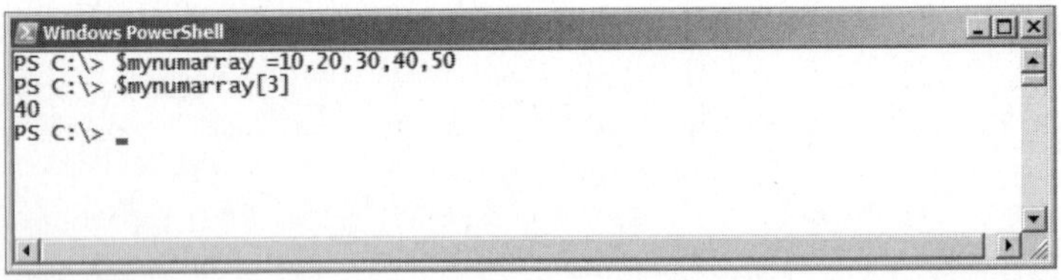

Figure 3-7

Next, create a string array with three elements using the following code. Assigning a string to an array is similar to assigning numerical values to an array. The following example assigns three string values to an array and displays the second position. After that, it displays all the elements available in the array. When you call the array without any address, it displays all the elements, as shown in Figure 3-8.

```
$mystrarray="Alan","Charlie","Jake"
$mystrarray[1]
$mystrarray
```

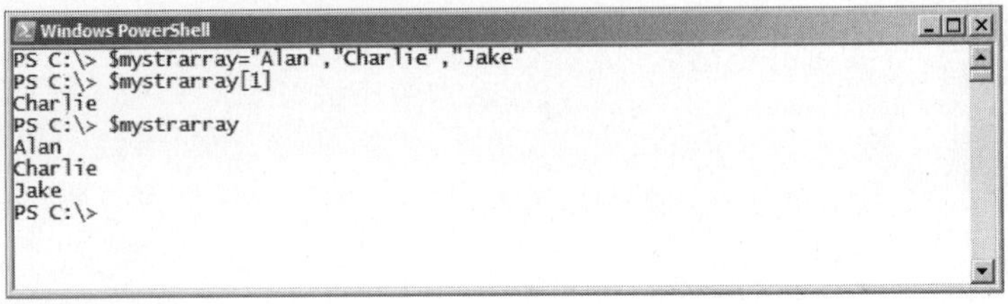

Figure 3-8

PowerShell can also store associative arrays. An associative array stores data in the form of paired keys and values. The following example stores the three keys FirstName, LastName, and Salary with the values "Alan", "Harper", and 1000.00, respectively. You can retrieve the value of the array by calling the address, which in this case is the key (see Figure 3-9).

```
$myhash=@{FirstName="Alan";Lastname="Harper";Salary=1000.000}
$myhash["FirstName"]
$myhash.FirstName
```

```
PS C:\> $myhash=@{FirstName="Alan";Lastname="Harper";Salary=1000.000}
PS C:\> $myhash["FirstName"]
Alan
PS C:\> $myhash.FirstName
Alan
PS C:\>
```

Figure 3-9

Expressions

In any programming language, expressions are a combination of values, operators, variables, and functions that are evaluated by the program and produce results.

Expressions in PowerShell are very straightforward. The following example demonstrates how arithmetic expressions work. In this example, you assign the value 100 to $myvar1 and the value 75 to $myvar2. Then you basically multiply, divide, and get the modulus between the two variables (see Figure 3-10).

```
$myvar1=100
$myvar2=75
$myvar1*$myvar2
$myvar1/$myvar2
$myvar1%$myvar2
```

```
PS C:\> $myvar1=100
PS C:\> $myvar2=75
PS C:\> $myvar1*$myvar2
7500
PS C:\> $myvar1/$myvar2
1.33333333333333
PS C:\> $myvar1%$myvar2
25
PS C:\>
```

Figure 3-10

The following example demonstrates how to assign string values to two variables and then concatenate both string values by using the plus (+) operator (see Figure 3-11):

```
$mystr1="Hello"
$mystr2="World"
$mystr1+$mystr2
```

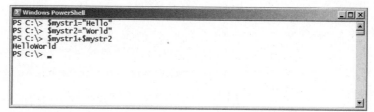

```
PS C:\> $mystr1="Hello"
PS C:\> $mystr2="World"
PS C:\> $mystr1+$mystr2
HelloWorld
PS C:\>
```

Figure 3-11

Expressions cannot exist without operators, described in the next section.

Chapter 3: Programming, Scripting, Error Handling, and Debugging

Operators

Any programming language generally supports numeric operators similar to mathematical operators. In addition to the numeric operators, PowerShell also supports other operators. The following tables describe the operators available in PowerShell.

Numeric Assignment Operator	Description
=	Assigns a value to a variable
+=	Adds the value of the right side of the assignment to the existing value of the left side and assigns the result to the variable on the left side
-=	Subtracts the value of the right side of the assignment from the existing value of the left side and assigns the result to the variable on the left side
*=	Multiplies the value of the right side of the assignment and the existing value of the left side and assigns the result to the variable on the left side
/=	Divides the value of the left side of the assignment into the existing value of the right side and assigns the result to the variable on the left side
%=	Divides the value of the left side of the assignment into the existing value of the right side and assigns the remainder to the variable on the left side

Logical Operator	Description
-and	Is true if both comparisons are true and only then
-or	Is true if one or both comparisons is true
-not	Negation
!	Negation. Synonym for -not.

Unary Operator	Description
+	Signifies explicitly that a number is a positive number
-	Signifies that a number is a negative number
++	Increments a value or variable
-	Decrements a value or variable

Comparison Operator	Description
-eq	Tests for equality
-ne	Tests for inequality
-gt	Tests whether the value on the left is greater than the value on the right
-ge	Tests whether the value on the left is greater than or equal to the value on the right
-lt	Tests whether the value on the left is less than the value on the right
-le	Tests whether the value on the left is less than or equal to the value on the right
-like	Tests, using wildcards, whether two values match. The wildcard(s) go on the right side.
-notlike	Tests, using wildcards, whether two values fail to match. The wildcard(s) go on the right side.
-match	Tests, using regular expressions, whether two values match. The regular expression goes on the right side.
-notmatch	Tests, using regular expressions, whether two values fail to match. The regular expression goes on the right side.
-ceq	Tests for case-sensitive equality
-cne	Tests for case-sensitive inequality
-cgt	Tests whether the value on the left is greater than the value on the right. Case-sensitive comparison.
-cge	Tests whether the value on the left is greater than or equal to the value on the right. Case-sensitive comparison.
-clt	Tests whether the value on the left is less than the value on the right. Case-sensitive comparison.
-cle	Tests whether the value on the left is less than or equal to the value on the right. Case-sensitive comparison.
-clike	Tests, using wildcards, whether two values match. The wildcard(s) go on the right side. Case-sensitive comparison.
-cnotlike	Tests, using wildcards, whether two values fail to match. The wildcard(s) go on the right side. Case-sensitive comparison.
-cmatch	Tests, using regular expressions, whether two values match. The regular expression goes on the right side. Case-sensitive matching.
-cnotmatch	Tests, using regular expressions, whether two values fail to match. The regular expression goes on the right side. Case-sensitive matching.
-ieq	Tests for case-insensitive equality

Continued

Comparison Operator	Description
-ine	Tests for case-insensitive inequality
-igt	Tests whether the value on the left is greater than the value on the right. Case-insensitive comparison.
-ige	Tests whether the value on the left is greater than or equal to the value on the right. Case-insensitive comparison.
-ilt	Tests whether the value on the left is less than the value on the right. Case-insensitive comparison.
-ile	Tests whether the value on the left is less than or equal to the value on the right. Case-insensitive comparison.
-ilike	Tests, using wildcards, whether two values match. The wildcard(s) go on the right side. Case-insensitive comparison.
-inotlike	Tests, using wildcards, whether two values fail to match. The wildcard(s) go on the right side. Case-insensitive comparison.
-imatch	Tests, using regular expressions, whether two values match. The regular expression goes on the right side. Case-insensitive matching.
-inotmatch	Tests, using regular expressions, whether two values fail to match. The regular expression goes on the right side. Case-insensitive matching.

String Operator	Description
+	Concatenates two strings
*	Repeats a string some number of times
-f	Formats a string
-replace	Replaces the string with another string
-match	Regular expression match
-like	Wildcard matching

Now that you are familiar with the various operators, the next section describes how the comparison operators are used.

Conditional Expressions

As you likely already know, conditional statements, conditional expressions, or conditional constructs are features of a programming language that perform various computations or actions depending on whether a programmer-specified condition evaluates to true or false. Windows PowerShell also has such a feature, called the *IF statement*.

IF Statement

An IF statement is one of the basic decision-making statements based on the evaluation of a particular condition.

The following example illustrates whether (if) one of the assigned variable values is greater than the other. It uses the IF statement to compare two variables and displays the results (see Figure 3-12):

```
$myvar1=100
$myvar2=200
if ($myvar1 -gt $myvar2)
{write-host $myvar1" is Greater than" $myvar2}
else
{write-host $myvar2" is Greater than" $myvar1}
```

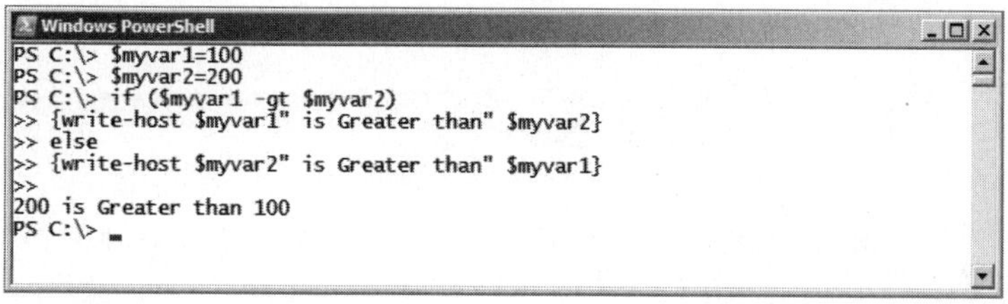

Figure 3-12

IF statements can also be used with multiple ELSEIF conditions. The following example demonstrates different grades based on actual scores using multiple IF conditions (see Figure 3-13):

```
$myscore=75
if ($myscore -gt 50 -and $myscore -lt 60)
{write-host "Grade C"}
elseif ($myscore -gt 60 -and$myscore -lt 70)
{write-host "Grade B"}
elseif ($myscore -gt 70 -and $myscore -lt 80)
{write-host "Grade B+"}
elseif ($myscore -gt 80 -and$myscore -lt 90)
{write-host "Grade A"}
elseif ($myscore -gt 90)
{write-host "Grade A+"}
else
{write-host "Grade C-"
```

Multiple ELSEIF statements can be rewritten using a switch statement, as shown here (see Figure 3-14):

```
$Disk = get-WmiObject win32_logicaldisk
foreach ($Drive in $Disk)
{switch ($Drive.DriveType) {
1{ $Drive.DeviceID + " Unknown" }
2{ $Drive.DeviceID + " Floppy" }
3{ $Drive.DeviceID + " Hard Drive" }
4{ $Drive.DeviceID + " Network Drive" }
```

```
5{ $Drive.DeviceID + " CD" }
6{ $Drive.DeviceID + " RAM Disk" }
}}
```

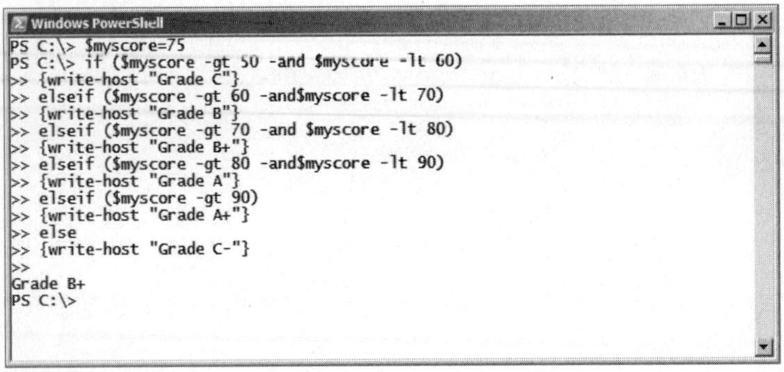

```
Windows PowerShell
PS C:\> $myscore=75
PS C:\> if ($myscore -gt 50 -and $myscore -lt 60)
>> {write-host "Grade C"}
>> elseif ($myscore -gt 60 -and$myscore -lt 70)
>> {write-host "Grade B"}
>> elseif ($myscore -gt 70 -and $myscore -lt 80)
>> {write-host "Grade B+"}
>> elseif ($myscore -gt 80 -and$myscore -lt 90)
>> {write-host "Grade A"}
>> elseif ($myscore -gt 90)
>> {write-host "Grade A+"}
>> else
>> {write-host "Grade C-"}
>>
Grade B+
PS C:\>
```

Figure 3-13

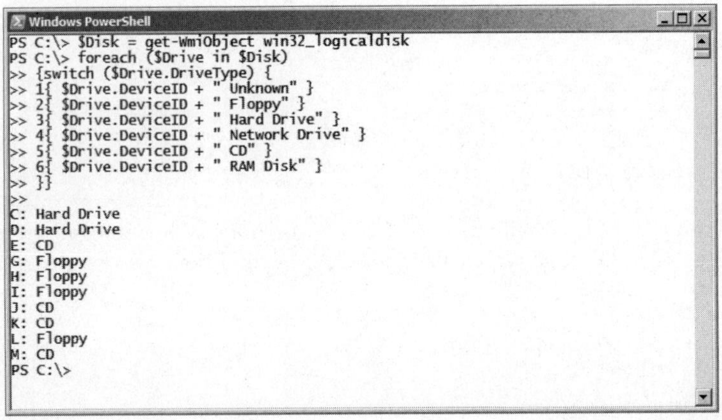

```
Windows PowerShell
PS C:\> $Disk = get-WmiObject win32_logicaldisk
PS C:\> foreach ($Drive in $Disk)
>> {switch ($Drive.DriveType) {
>> 1{ $Drive.DeviceID + " Unknown" }
>> 2{ $Drive.DeviceID + " Floppy" }
>> 3{ $Drive.DeviceID + " Hard Drive" }
>> 4{ $Drive.DeviceID + " Network Drive" }
>> 5{ $Drive.DeviceID + " CD" }
>> 6{ $Drive.DeviceID + " RAM Disk" }
>> }}
>>
C: Hard Drive
D: Hard Drive
E: CD
G: Floppy
H: Floppy
I: Floppy
J: CD
K: CD
L: Floppy
M: CD
PS C:\>
```

Figure 3-14

Note that the preceding example also includes a `foreach` loop. We discuss that in detail in the next section.

Loop Construct

In any programming language, loops are statements that enable a piece of code to be executed repeatedly. Windows PowerShell provides a few looping constructs.

Loops are very important and significant when you have to iterate through all the items in an object. This section covers the following loop constructs:

- ❑ `For` loop
- ❑ `While` loop
- ❑ `Do-While` loop

❑   `Do-Until` loop

❑   `foreach` statement

For Loop

`For` loop is one of the most commonly used loops in programming languages. This `for` loop construct is similar to C language and has three parts:

1.   `init-expr`, if it exists, is executed. Typically this initializes one or more counters, and may also declare them as well.

2.   `eval-expr` evaluates the current condition. If it is true, then it continues the loop.

3.   `increment-expr` is executed if it exists. Typically this increases or increments by one or more counters.

The next example, shown in Figure 3-15, illustrates the multiplication table for 5. Basically, it starts the loop with value 0, evaluates the value, and determines whether it is less than 11. The loop continues until the condition is true and increases the value by 1 each time it loops:

```
$myvar=5
for ($i = 0; $i -lt 11; $i++)
{write-host $i "X" $myvar "=" ($myvar*$i)}
```

```
Windows PowerShell                                                 _ □ x
PS C:\> $myvar=5
PS C:\> for ($i = 0; $i -lt 11; $i++)
>> {write-host $i "X" $myvar "=" ($myvar*$i)}
>>
0 X 5 = 0
1 X 5 = 5
2 X 5 = 10
3 X 5 = 15
4 X 5 = 20
5 X 5 = 25
6 X 5 = 30
7 X 5 = 35
8 X 5 = 40
9 X 5 = 45
10 X 5 = 50
PS C:\>
```

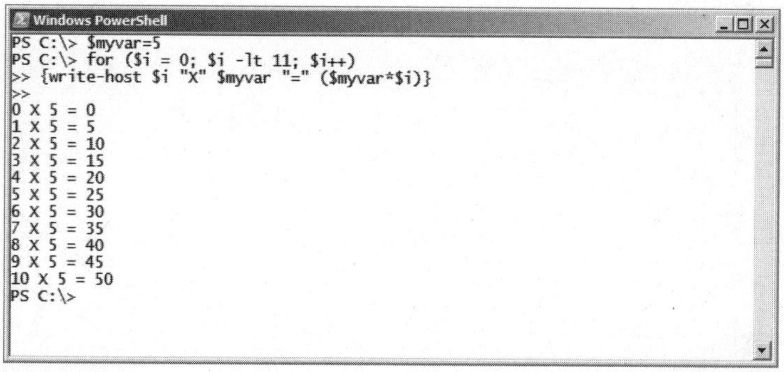

Figure 3-15

While Loop

The same multiplication table can be written using a `while` loop statement. The difference between a `for` loop and a `while` loop is that the value is initialized before the `while` loop. With the `while` loop construct, the evaluation and the incremental portion of the loop is written inside the loop as an expression. Here the looping continues until the condition is true (see Figure 3-16):

```
$myvar=5
$i = 0
while ($i -le 10)
{ write-host $i "X" $myvar "=" ($myvar*$i) ;$i++}
```

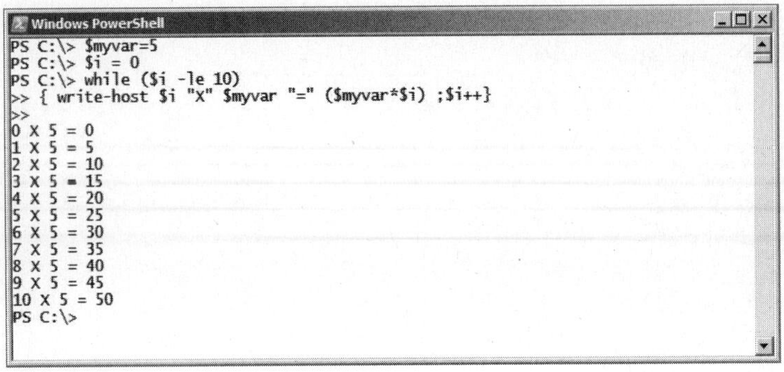

```
Windows PowerShell                                              _ □ ×
PS C:\> $myvar=5
PS C:\> $i = 0
PS C:\> while ($i -le 10)
>> { write-host $i "X" $myvar "=" ($myvar*$i) ;$i++}
>>
0 X 5 = 0
1 X 5 = 5
2 X 5 = 10
3 X 5 = 15
4 X 5 = 20
5 X 5 = 25
6 X 5 = 30
7 X 5 = 35
8 X 5 = 40
9 X 5 = 45
10 X 5 = 50
PS C:\>
```

Figure 3-16

Do-While Loop

Additionally, the same multiplication table can be written using the Do while loop statement. The Do while construct consists of a block of code and a condition. First the code within the block is executed, and then the condition is evaluated. If the condition is true, then the code within the block is executed again. Here, the looping continues until the condition becomes false (see Figure 3-17):

```
$myvar=5
$i = 0
do { write-host $i "X" $myvar "=" ($myvar*$i) ;$i++}
while ($i -le 10)
```

```
Windows PowerShell                                              _ □ ×
PS C:\> $myvar=5
PS C:\> $i = 0
PS C:\> do { write-host $i "X" $myvar "=" ($myvar*$i) ;$i++}
>> while ($i -le 10)
>>
0 X 5 = 0
1 X 5 = 5
2 X 5 = 10
3 X 5 = 15
4 X 5 = 20
5 X 5 = 25
6 X 5 = 30
7 X 5 = 35
8 X 5 = 40
9 X 5 = 45
10 X 5 = 50
PS C:\>
```

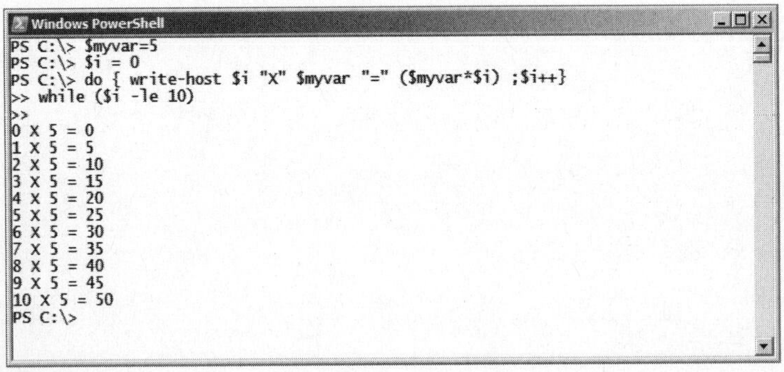

Figure 3-17

Do-Until Loop

In the next example, shown in Figure 3-18, the same multiplication table is written using the Do until loop statement. The Do until construct consists of a block of code and a condition. First the code within the block is executed, and then the condition is evaluated. If the condition is false, then the code within the block is executed again. The looping continues until the condition becomes true.

```
$myvar=5
$i = 0
do { write-host $i "X" $myvar "=" ($myvar*$i) ;$i++}
until ($i -eq 11)
```

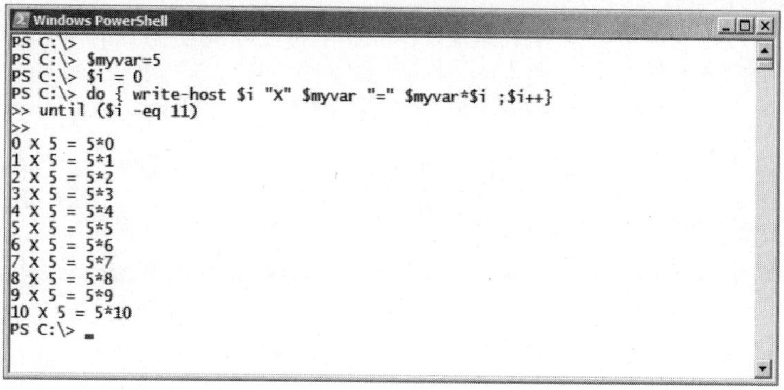

Figure 3-18

Foreach Statement

A `foreach` statement is widely used when you want to iterate through an array or through all the items in an object.

The following example, shown in Figure 3-19, assigns the resulting object of the `Get-process` cmdlet to a variable, and then iterates through all the items in the object and displays them with incremental numbers on the fly:

```
$Processes=get-process | select-object ProcessName
$i=1
foreach ($process in $Processes)
{write-host $i "Process Name is " $process.Processname;$i++; }
```

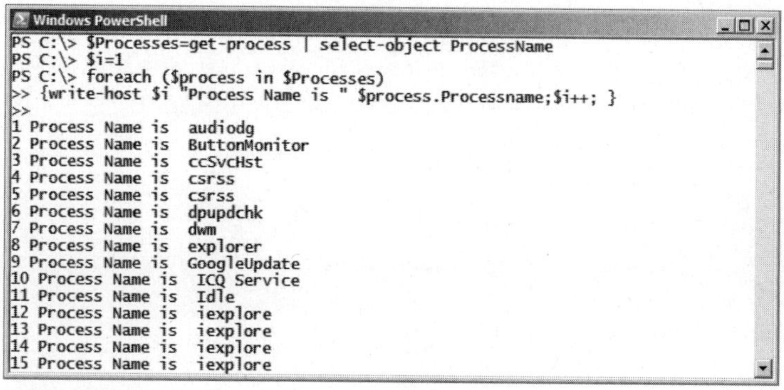

Figure 3-19

The same `foreach` statement can be used to iterate through an array. The following example, shown in Figure 3-20, lists all the elements in an array, does a cumulative addition, and computes the total:

```
$myarray=10,50,60,22,44,55,667,88
$i=0
$j=0
foreach ($element in $myarray)
{ $j=$j+$element;
```

```
Write-host "Array Element Position =" $i "Element value =" $element "Cumulative
    Sum =" $j ;
$i++ }
Write-host "Total of all the elements in the array is " $j
```

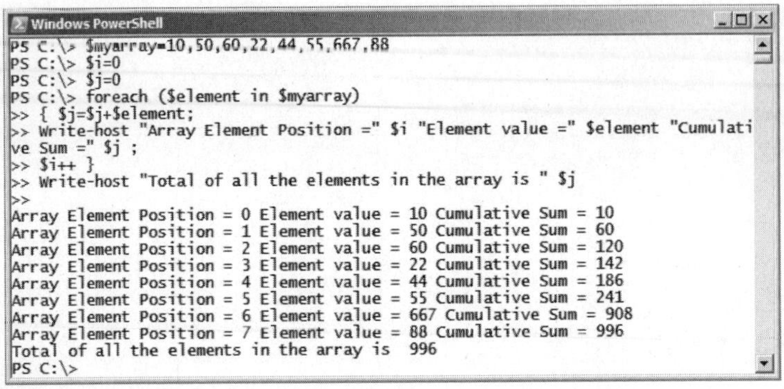

Figure 3-20

Now that you have an understanding of the processing elements of a basic programming language, including variables, operators, expressions, and programming constructs, it's time to move on to the various inputs and outputs of the programming.

Input

This section illustrates the various input cmdlets that can be used in the PowerShell environment. The Read-Host cmdlet is used when you want PowerShell to be very interactive with the user. This is the basic input command.

The following example requests that the user input two numbers, displaying their sum. Read-Host cmdlet displays a message to ask the user to provide a value. The message is specified by the Prompt parameter. Read-Host then assigns the value provided by the user to the variable:

```
$a = read-host -prompt "Enter a number please"
10
$b = read-host -prompt "Enter a another number please"
25
$a+$b
```

The result would be as follows (see Figure 3-21):

```
1025
```

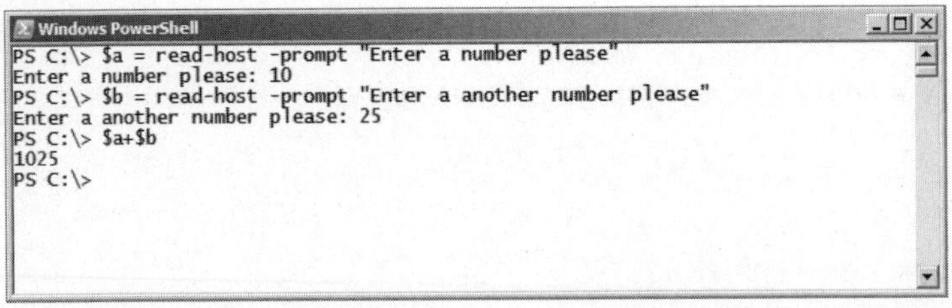

Figure 3-21

As you can see, PowerShell did a string concatenation of the two values entered, instead of adding the two values. If you want PowerShell to treat those variables as integers, you can explicitly define them as such.

The following example explicitly defines two variables as integers and reads the values from the host using the `Read-host` cmdlet (see Figure 3-22):

```
[int]$a = read-host -prompt "Enter a number please"
10
[int]$b = read-host -prompt "Enter a another number please"
25
$a+$b
```

The result would be as follows:

```
35
```

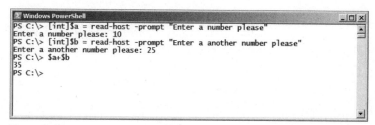

Figure 3-22

There is one other way to provide input to Windows PowerShell: using parameters. Parameters are discussed briefly in the following section, and in detail in Chapter 4.

PowerShell Scripting

A PowerShell script contains a set of cmdlets that will perform certain tasks. You can create your first PowerShell script using `read-host` as input and `write-host` cmdlets for output display.

First, you need to change your current location from the C:\ folder to the DBAScripts directory using the following cmdlet. You need to change location to `C:\DBAScripts` because all the PowerShell scripts that you are going to write will reside in this folder. It is easier to execute the script in the current folder than by typing **C:\DBAScripts\<scriptname>** all the time.

```
Set-location C:\DBAScripts
```

Create the following `calculate-arith.ps1` PowerShell script as shown here. (You can create it using Notepad or any other text editor).

```
# =========================================================
#
# NAME: Calculate-arith.ps1
#
# AUTHOR: Yan and MAK
```

```
# DATE   : 4/26/2008
#
# COMMENT: Simple Calculator
#
# =====================================================
 [int]$a = read-host -prompt "Enter a number please"
[int]$b = read-host -prompt "Enter a number please"
$c = read-host -prompt "Please select any one of the following operator - + / *

"
Switch ($c){
+ {$a+$b}
- {$a-$b}
* {$a*$b}
/ {$a/$b}
default {write-host "Wrong arithmetic operation" $a $c $b}
}
```

Execute the PowerShell script `calculate-arith.ps1` as shown here. When executing the script, it prompts for three inputs: Two prompts are for integer values and the third prompt is for the operator. Provide the values and select the operators several times when prompted (see Figure 3-23).

```
.\calculate-arith.ps1
```

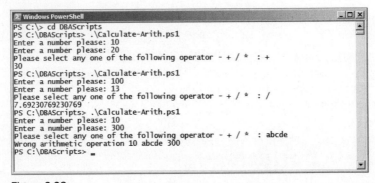

Figure 3-23

When a line starts with #, it comments the entire line. PowerShell totally ignores that line. Comments are very useful for documentation and describing the script.

You can also write a non-interactive PowerShell script by accepting the input values as parameters, as shown in the following example.

Create the `calculate-arith2.ps1` PowerShell script as follows:

```
# =====================================================
#
# NAME: Calculate-arith2.ps1
#
# AUTHOR: Yan and MAK
# DATE   : 4/26/2008
#
```

```
# COMMENT: Simple Calculator using parameters
#
# =======================================================
param (
  [int] $a,
  [string] $c,
  [int] $b
)

Switch ($c){
+ {$a+$b}
- {$a-$b}
* {$a*$b}
/ {$a/$b}
% {$a%$b}
default {write-host "Invalid arithmetic operator" $a $c $b}
}
```

Execute the PowerShell script `calculate-arith2.ps1` (see Figure 3-24).

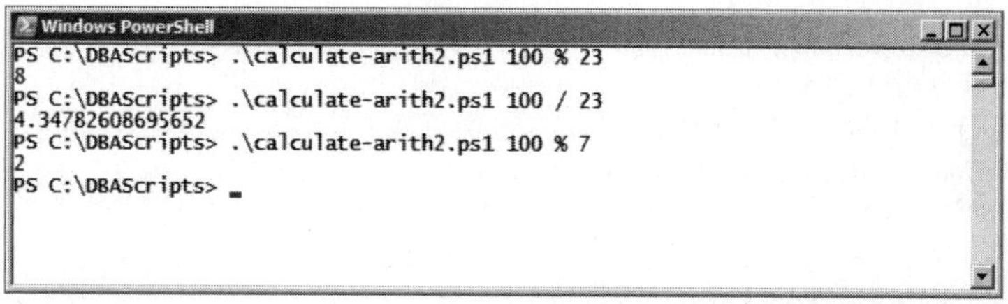

Figure 3-24

Now create a small PowerShell script that accepts three parameters and displays the multiplication table for the given number and range. The first parameter accepts the multiplication table number. The second and third parameters specify the starting and ending range of the multiplication table.

Create the following `multi-table.ps1` PowerShell script:

```
# =======================================================
#
# NAME: multiple-table.ps1
#
# AUTHOR: Yan and MAK
# DATE   : 4/26/2008
#
# COMMENT: Multiplication table generator
#
# =======================================================
param (
  [double] $MultiplyNumber,
  [double] $Startingrange,
  [double] $Endingrange
)
```

```
$calcnum=0
Write-host "Multiplication table of "$MultiplyNumber
for($i=$Startingrange;$i -le $Endingrange;$i++)
{$calcnum=$MultiplyNumber*$i; write-output "$MultiplyNumber x $i = $calcnum"  }
```

Execute the PowerShell script, as shown in Figure 3-25.

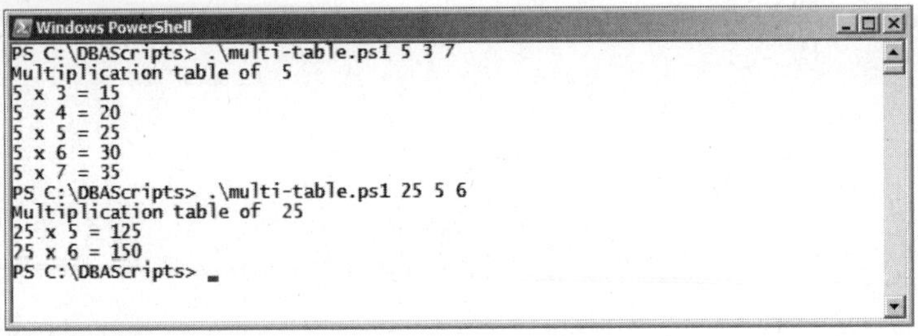

Figure 3-25

Text File As Input

Reading a text file and manipulating the output is very common in the scripting world. You can create a PowerShell script that will read any file passed as a parameter and display its content with line numbers. In this next example you will use the cmdlet `get-content` to read the entire table and assign that to a variable. Then you use the `foreach` loop to loop through line by line and display the entire text file.

Create the following `read-file.ps1` PowerShell script:

```
# =====================================================
#
# NAME: Read-File.ps1
#
# AUTHOR: Yan and MAK
# DATE  : 4/26/2008
#
# COMMENT: Read file and display with line numbers
#
# =====================================================

param (
  [string] $filename
)

$readbuffer=get-content -path $filename
$i=0;
foreach($line in $readbuffer)
{$i++;write-output "$i : $line"}
```

Execute the PowerShell script `read-file.ps1` as shown here (see Figure 3-26):

```
.\read-file.ps1 c:\windows\system.ini
```

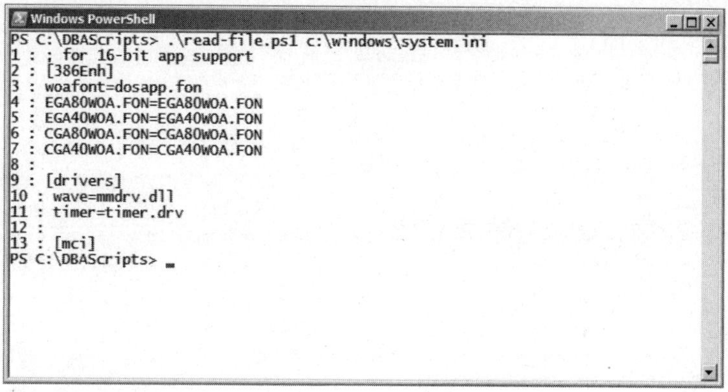

Figure 3-26

Next, read the SQL Server error log with a new script, `read-errorlog.ps1`. This script accepts three parameters. The first parameter is the filename, which is basically the SQL Server error log location. The second parameter is the date. The script reads the entire error log and displays only the information after this date value. The third parameter is the number, which represents the number of lines you want the output to display.

The following script looks for the keyword "Error:" in the error log file and displays only those messages. It also filters the results based on the date and time. The filtering basically ignores all the lines with the keyword "Error:" before the date and time passed as a parameter. Filtering also helps in showing only the number of lines that are passed as a parameter.

You can also see that we use the `-encoding unicode` parameter name and parameter value when using the `get-content` cmdlet. This is because SQL Server 2005 and later creates the error log in Unicode format.

Create the following `read-errorlog.ps1` PowerShell script using Notepad:

```
# ========================================================
#
# NAME: read-errorlog.ps1
#
# AUTHOR: Yan and MAK
# DATE   : 4/26/2008
#
# COMMENT: Read SQL Server error log for errors
#
# ========================================================

param (
  [string] $filename,
  [datetime] $date,
  [int] $last
)

$readbuffer=get-content -path $filename -encoding unicode |select-object -last $last
$i=0
[datetime] $mydate
```

```
foreach($line in $readbuffer)
{
        $i++;
        $mydate=$line.substring(0,22)

        if($line -ne "")
        {

                if($mydate -ge $date)
                {

                        if ($line -like "*Error:*")
                        {
                                write-output "$i: $line"
                        }

                }
        }

}
```

Execute the script as shown here (see Figure 3-27):

```
.\read-errorlog.ps1 "C:\Program Files\Microsoft SQL Server\MSSQL10.
    MSSQLSERVER\MSSQL\Log\ERRORLOG" "2008-11-11 12:53:16.49" 10
```

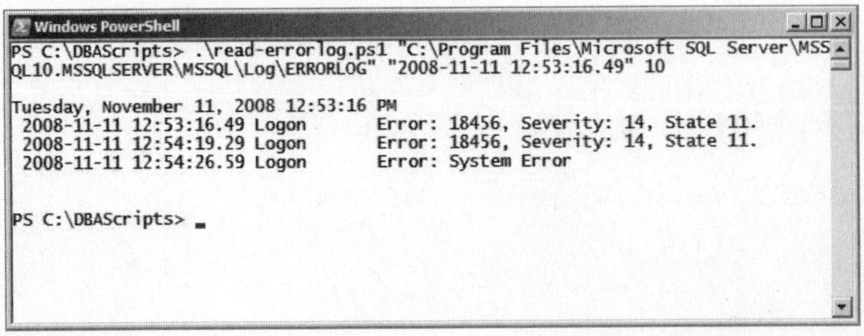

Figure 3-27

Output

As mentioned earlier in this chapter, output is also one of the basic requirements in any programming language. PowerShell has various output-related cmdlets. This section illustrates how to write the output to a file.

Writing to the Console

Writing to the console is a common way of treating output in any programming language. The commonly used output-related PowerShell cmdlets for the console are Write-Output and Write-Host.

The `Write-Output` cmdlet sends the specified object down the pipeline to the next command. If the command is the last in the pipeline, the object is displayed on the console.

If you just need to display the objects at the end of a pipeline on the console, it is generally not necessary to use the cmdlet. For example, `Get-Process | Write-Output` is equivalent to `Get-Process`.

`Write-Host` is another commonly used cmdlet in PowerShell scripting and in interactive mode. You have already seen various uses of the `Write-Host` cmdlet in this chapter and previous chapters.

The `Write-Host` cmdlet customizes output. For example, you can specify the color of text. However, the blue background color of course doesn't show up in the black-and-white Figure 3-28.

```
Write-Host "SQL Server 2008 Administration with Windows PowerShell" -Foregroundcolor
    White -Backgroundcolor blue
```

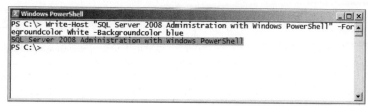

Figure 3-28

The `Write-Host` cmdlet is used throughout the rest of the book.

Writing to a File

You can write the output to a local file by using the cmdlet `Set-Content`. This example creates a script that will read the SQL Server error log to find lines with the keyword "Error" and write them to a log file. The `read-errorlog2.ps1` file is mostly similar to `read-errorlog.ps1` but the cmdlet `Set-Content` redirects the output to a filename that is passed as a parameter.

Create the following `read-errorlog2.ps1` PowerShell script:

```
# ========================================================
#
# NAME: read-errorlog2.ps1
#
# AUTHOR: Yan and MAK
# DATE  : 4/26/2008
#
# COMMENT: Read SQL Server error log for errors
# and save it a text file.
# ========================================================

param (
  [string] $infile,
```

```
    [datetime] $date,
    [int] $last,
    [string] $Outfile
)

$readbuffer=get-content -path $infile -encoding unicode |select-object -last $last
$i=0

[datetime] $date
[string] $outbuffer
$outbuffer=""

foreach($line in $readbuffer)
{
$i++;
$mydate=$line.substring(0,22)

if($line -ne "")
{
if($mydate -ge $date)
{
if ($line -like "*Error:*")
{
write-output "$i: $line"
$outbuffer=$outbuffer + $line

}

}
}

}

set-content -path $outfile -value $outbuffer
```

Execute the `read-errorlog2.ps1` script with the same parameters as before, and with the addition of an output filename (see Figure 3-29):

```
.\read-errorlog2.ps1 "C:\Program Files\Microsoft SQL Server\MSSQL10.
    MSSQLSERVER\MSSQL\Log\ERRORLOG" "2008-11-11 12:53:16.49" 10 c:\test.log
```

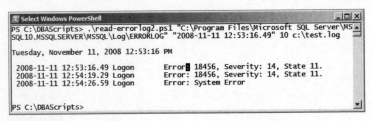

Figure 3-29

When the script is executed, it both displays the results on the screen and writes to the log file `C:\test.log`, as shown in Figure 3-30.

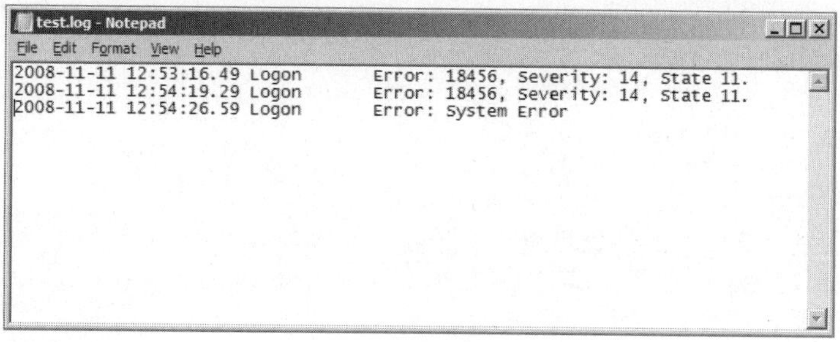

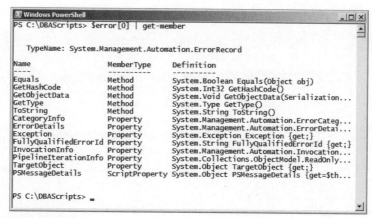

Figure 3-30

Error Handling

The last basic requirement in any programming language is handling exceptions and errors. Windows PowerShell provides different methods for handling errors.

There are two types of PowerShell errors: *terminating* and *nonterminating*. Terminating errors stop further execution soon after the error occurs. Conversely, nonterminating errors generally report the error and continue running.

Both types of errors are logged in the variable $Error. $Error contains all the errors that occurred in the current session. The collection of errors contains the most recent error in Error[0] until $MaximumErrorCount, which is 256 by default.

$Error is handled by System.Management.Automation.ErrorRecord.

```
$error[0] | get-member
```

The get-member cmdlet, when used in conjunction with $error, will provide all the properties and methods of this object, as shown in Figure 3-31.

Figure 3-31

The following example attempts to retrieve the content of a file that doesn't exist in order to simulate an error, as shown in Figure 3-32, and then tries to get the error information (see Figure 3-36 and Figure 3-37):

```
get-content testerror.txt
$error[0].InvocationInfo
```

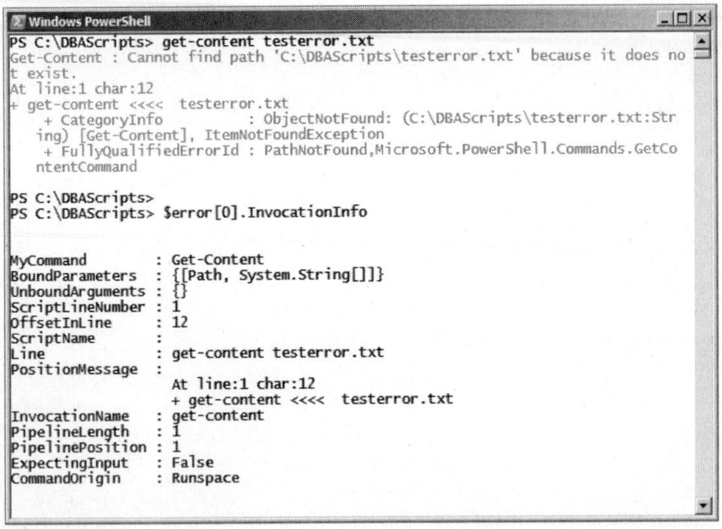

Figure 3-32

You can display all the errors on the screen just by calling the error variable, $error, as shown here (see Figure 3-33):

```
$error
```

Figure 3-33

There are three ways to handle errors. The first method is by using the parameters `ErrorAction` and `ErrorVariable` (see Figure 3-34).

In the following example, both parameters are used. The parameter `ErrorVariable` stores the error details to the error variable `MyError`. The parameter `ErrorAction`, with the value `SilentlyContinue`, causes PowerShell to continue operation silently:

```
get-content testerror.txt -ErrorVariable MyError -ErrorAction Silentlycontinue
```

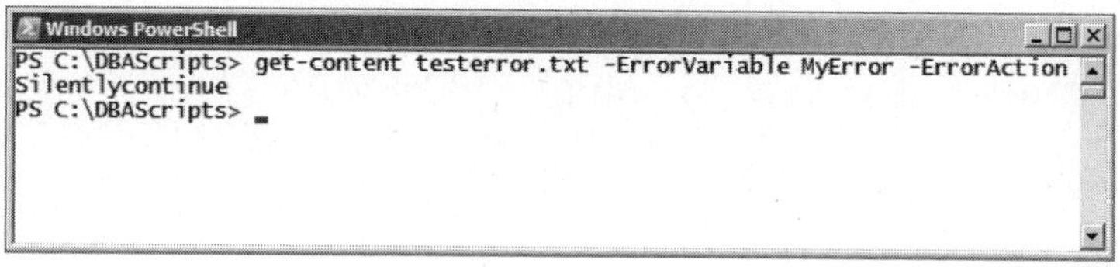

Figure 3-34

Because the error is stored in the error variable `MyError`, now the error can be accessed easily (see Figure 3-35):

```
if ($MyError) {write-host "File Not Found"}
```

Figure 3-35

The second method for handling errors is to use the "throw" keyword. Use the Throw keyword when you want to throw your own terminating errors.

The following example uses the throw keyword if a parameter is not passed to the script. Create the PowerShell script `calculate-arith3.ps1` as shown here:

```
# ======================================================
#
# NAME: calculate-arith3.ps1
#
# AUTHOR: Yan and MAK
# DATE   : 4/26/2008
#
# COMMENT: Simple calculator with "Throw"
#
# ======================================================

param (
  [int] $a = $(Throw "Please provide Number as first parameter"),
  [string] $c,
```

```
    [int] $b
)

Switch ($c){
+ {$a+$b}
- {$a-$b}
* {$a*$b}
/ {$a/$b}
% {$a%$b}
default {write-host "Invalid arithmetic operator" $a $c $b}
}
```

Now execute the PowerShell script `calculate-arith3` with no parameters:

```
.\calculate-arith3.ps1
```

The script will stop by throwing the error defined, as shown in Figure 3-36.

Figure 3-36

The third method for handling exceptions is to use TRAP. When encountering an error, PowerShell's default behavior is to halt and display the error. However, if you just want to trap the error and continue the rest of the script, then TRAP is very useful.

Create `test-trap.ps1`, shown here, which checks the Z: drive (which doesn't exist) and uses the TRAP command to trap that error and continue the operation:

```
# =====================================================
#
# NAME: test-trap.ps1
#
# AUTHOR: Yan and MAK
# DATE  : 4/26/2008
#
# COMMENT: Simple demo of  "TRAP"
#
# =====================================================
function checkdrive ($drive)
{

trap {
write-host "Drive error"
write-host $_.Errorid
```

```
write-host $_.Exception.message
}

get-location $drive -Erroraction stop
}

write-host "Starting..."
write-host "Going to check drive"
checkdrive("Z:")
write-host "Completed checking drive"
write-host "Ending"
```

Now you can execute the PowerShell script `testtrap.ps1` as shown here (see Figure 3-37):

```
.\test-trap.ps1
```

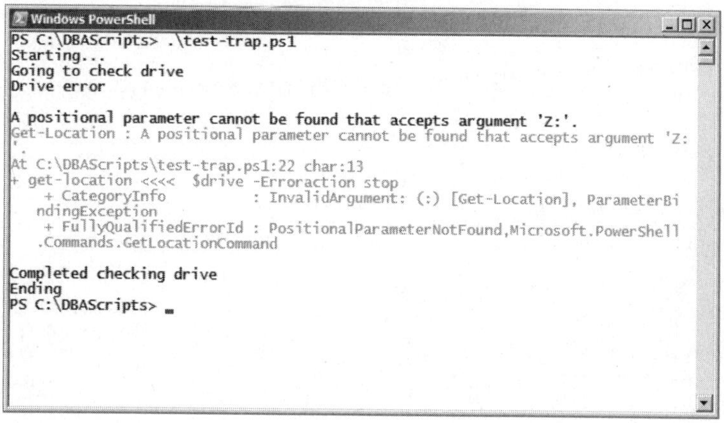

Figure 3-37

From the output shown, you can see that despite getting the error upon checking the drive, it continued executing the remaining commands in the script file.

Debugging

PowerShell provides the cmdlet Set-PSDebug to turn debugging on and off.

This section runs some cmdlets with debugging on. The cmdlet Set-PSDebug can be run with two different parameters: Step and Trace. The Step parameter basically makes the script of cmdlets into a very interactive mode.

Execute the following Set-PSDebug cmdlet with Step as a parameter, as shown here (see Figure 3-38):

```
Set-PSDebug -Step
$myvar=100
$myvar+20
```

Now, any cmdlet executed after this will be prompted by the PSDebug cmdlet with Yes/No/Suspend, as shown in Figure 3-38.

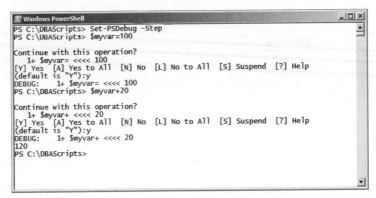

Figure 3-38

PSDebug can be turned off by using Set-PSDebug with -Off as a parameter:

```
Set-PSDebug -Off
```

Now execute the calculate-arith2.ps1 script with PSDebug turned on:

```
Set-PSDebug -Step
.\calculate-arith2.ps1 4 + 5
```

As shown in Figure 3-39, PSDebug prompts for confirmation at every line in the script. You use "A" to pass "Yes" for all the prompts.

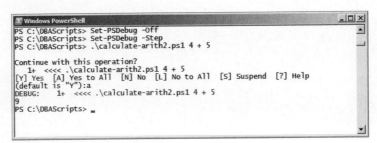

Figure 3-39

You can also debug the scripts and cmdlets using set-PSDebug with trace as a parameter.

When PSDebug is executed with trace as a parameter, instead of stepping through line by line, it executes the whole script and generates the trace.

Execute calculate-arith2.ps1 with Set-PSDebug and the parameter Trace.

```
Set-PSDebug -Off
```

```
Set-PSDebug -Trace 2
.\calculate-arith2.ps1 4 + 5
```

As shown in Figure 3-40, PowerShell displays the debug information line by line.

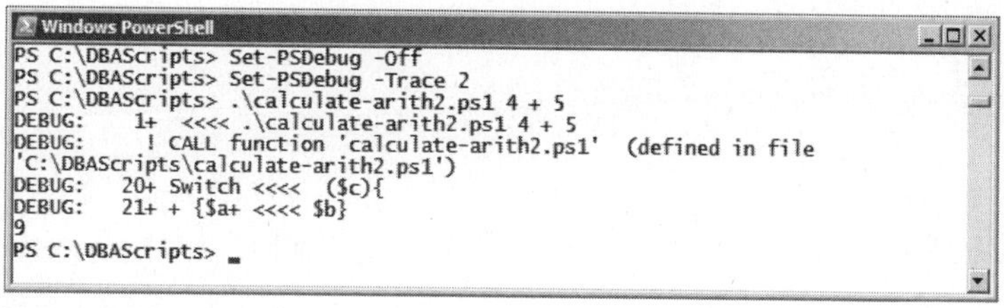

Figure 3-40

Trace accepts three different parameter values:

Trace Parameter Value	Meaning
0	No debugging
1	Trace script lines
2	Trace script lines, variable assignments, function calls, and scripts

You can also use the `Write-Debug` cmdlet in the code, which will be executed only in debug mode.

For example, create the following script, `calculate-arith4.ps1`:

```
# ========================================================
#
# NAME: calculate-arith4.ps1
#
# AUTHOR: Yan and MAK
# DATE   : 4/26/2008
#
# COMMENT: Demo for "Write-Debug"
#
# ========================================================
param (
   [int] $a,
   [string] $c,
   [int] $b
)
write-debug "Getting parameters"
write-debug "Parameter 1 is $a"
write-debug "Parameter 2 is $c"
write-debug "Parameter 3 is $b"

write-debug "Checking parameter 2"
Switch ($c){
```

```
+ {$a+$b}
- {$a-$b}
* {$a*$b}
/ {$a/$b}
% {$a%$b}
default {write-host "Invalid arithmetic operator" $a $c $b}
}
```

With Set-PSDebug –Off, execute the following calculate-arith4.ps1 script as shown here (see Figure 3-41):

```
Set-PSDebug -Off
.\calculate-arith4.ps1 4 + 5
```

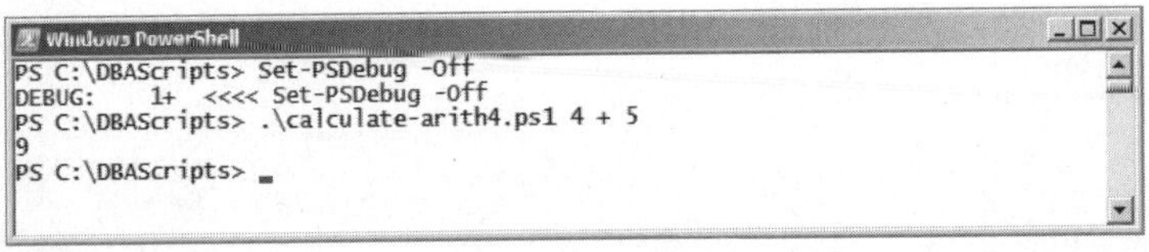

Figure 3-41

From the output, it is clear that Write-Debug did nothing when the script is executed.

Now execute the same script with Set-PSDebug –step. You can see all the statements that you wrote with the Write-Debug cmdlet in Figure 3-42.

```
Set-PSDebug -Off

Set-PSDebug -Step
.\calculate-arith4.ps1 4 + 5
```

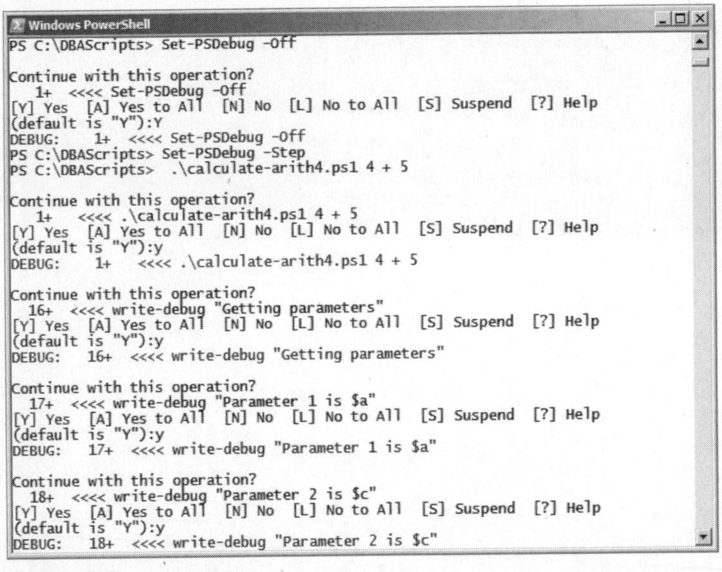

Figure 3-42

74

The behavior of the `Write-Debug` cmdlet can also be controlled by the preference variable `$DebugPreference`. The default value of this variable is `SilentlyContinue`, i.e., debug messages are not displayed. However, you can change its value to `"Continue"`, which displays debug messages and continues with execution. Run the following commands (see Figure 3-43):

```
Set-PSDebug -Off
$DebugPreference
$DebugPreference="Continue"
.\calculate-arith4.ps1 4 + 5
```

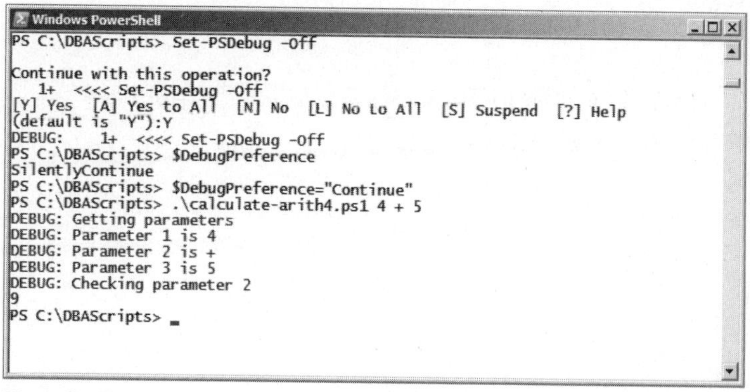

Figure 3-43

As shown in Figure 3-43, after the value of `$DebugPreference` changes from `SilentlyContinue` to `Continue`, the debug messages from the `calculate-arith4.ps1` script are printed out along with the result.

Summary

This chapter illustrated various input and output methods, along with various programming elements such as variables, expressions, operators, and loop constructs, in Windows PowerShell. It also illustrated the various error-handling and debugging methods both inside PowerShell's interactive mode and inside the scripts.

The next chapter continues to explore the programming side of subroutines, user profiles, and the sourcing of scripts and functions.

4

Windows PowerShell Functions, Parameters, Sourcing, Scopes, and User Profiles

In any programming language, code reusability is both common and important. It increases productivity and decreases the need to write redundant code blocks. Another important basic functionality in any programming language is the scope of variables and functions.

This chapter focuses on the reusability of PowerShell scripting. You will learn how to reuse code blocks through functions, sourcing files, and user profiles. You will also be introduced to variable scopes and function scopes. Finally, this chapter also covers transcripts.

Functions

Functions are modules or blocks of code that can be reused repeatedly in programming by just calling the block of code by name. Creating functions reduces the writing of redundant code and increases productivity. Functions can be written inside the main script or can be sourced in from a file.

The following code creates a simple function that displays a welcome message to the user:

```
function Hello
{
write-host "Welcome to PowerSQL"
}
```

You can call the function by just typing "Hello," as shown in Figure 4-1. This function has no return value or parameters.

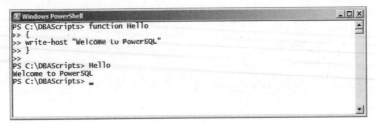

Figure 4-1

Arguments in Functions

Functions accept arguments or parameters if you define them in the function. There are two ways to define arguments. One is using the argument variable args. This is the array variable in which each element represents one argument.

Arguments and parameters refer to the same thing.

The following example creates a function that accepts two arguments using the args variable. Here the parameters are not predefined. The function basically accepts all arguments passed and makes use of only the first two. The arguments are stored in an array and $args[0] represents argument 1, $args[1] represents argument 2, and so on.

```
Function ConcatName
{
[string] $args[0] + [string] $args[1]
}
```

This function can be executed as shown here:

```
ConcatName "Sam" "Rooban" "Test"
```

This passes three string arguments. The function accepts all the arguments "Sam", "Rooban", and "Test", and concatenates only the first two, displaying them as shown in Figure 4-2.

```
Windows PowerShell
PS C:\DBAScripts> Function ConcatName
>> {
>> [string] $args[0] + [string] $args[1]
>> }
>>
PS C:\DBAScripts> ConcatName "Sam" "Rooban" "Test"
SamRooban
PS C:\DBAScripts>
```

Figure 4-2

The arguments of the same function ConcatName can be defined in a different way, as shown next. In the following example, the arguments are predefined and assigned to the string variables $Firstname and $Lastname, respectively:

```
Function ConcatName ([string] $Firstname ,[string] $Lastname )
{
$Firstname + $LastName
}
```

This function can also be called like this (see Figure 4-3):

```
ConcatName "Sam" "Rooban"
```

Here we are passing two string arguments. The function accepts the two arguments "Sam" and "Rooban" and assigns that to the variables $FirstName and $LastName and then concatenates the two variables, displaying them as shown in Figure 4-3.

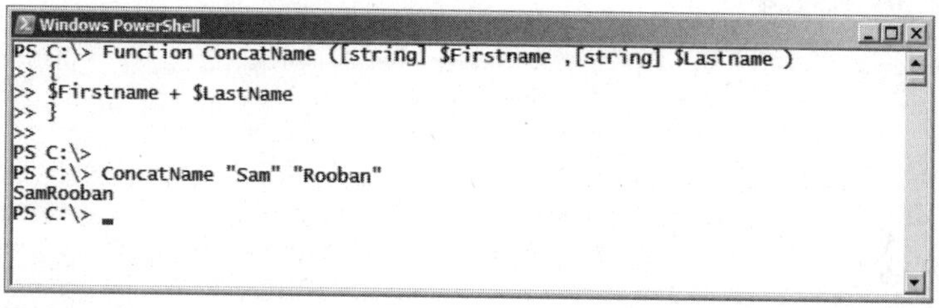

Figure 4-3

An arguments can be created as a *switch*. The difference between a parameter and a switch is that a switch does not take a value, whereas a parameter can. A switch is typically used like a flag or an ON/OFF switch.

Now create the following ConcatName function with three parameters, with one as a switch. Whenever the switch is used when calling the function, it will display the usage information:

```
Function ConcatName ([string] $x ,[string] $y, [switch] $help)
{
if ($help)
{
write-host "Usage: Concatename 'Firstname' 'Lastname'"
}
else
{
Write-host $x$y
}
}
```

As shown in Figure 4-4, when executing the function with the -help parameter, it just displays the usage information of the function. If you don't use the -help parameter, it will display the concatenation of the two string values that are passed as parameters.

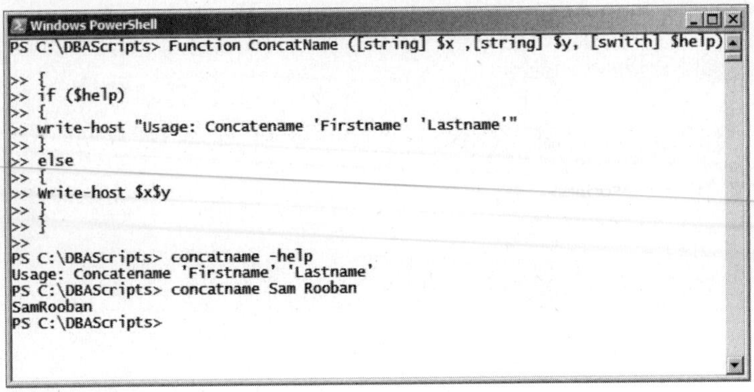

Figure 4-4

Returning Values

Typically, a function should return values so that the calling program can manipulate or make use of the returned values.

The following example creates a compute function that can add, delete, multiply, or divide based on the parameter. Then it returns the computed value to the calling script. Create this in a PowerShell script `calculate-arith1.ps1`, and save the script file under the directory `C:\DBAScripts`. The script passes 1, +, and 20 to the function, The function adds 1 to 20 and passes the result 21 back to the script, and then the script prints out 21:

```
# ======================================================
#
# NAME: calculate-arith1.ps1
#
# AUTHOR: Yan and MAK
# DATE   : 4/26/2008
#
# COMMENT: Demo for "Return value"
#
# ======================================================
Function compute([int] $x ,[string] $y, [int] $z)
{
switch ($y)
{
"+" { $computed=$x+$z }
"-" { $computed=$x-$z }
"/" { $computed=$x/$z }
"*" { $computed=$x*$z }
"%" { $computed=$x%$z }
}
return $computed
}

$a=compute 1 "+" 20

write-host $a
```

Now execute the `calculate-arith1.ps1` script as shown here (see Figure 4-5):

```
.\calculate-arith1.ps1
```

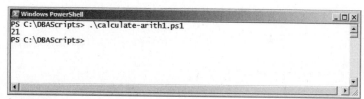

Figure 4-5

Script Parameters

Arguments or parameters can also be used in scripts. Scripts accept arguments or parameters if you define them inside the script. There are two ways to define arguments. One is using the argument variable `args`. This is the array variable in which each element represents one argument.

You can create a script that accepts two arguments using the `args` variable. Here the parameters are not predefined. It basically accepts all arguments passed and makes use of only the first two. The arguments are stored in an array; `$args[0]` represents argument 1, `$args[1]` represents argument 2, and so on:

```
# =======================================================
#
# NAME: Test-Args1.ps1
#
# AUTHOR: Yan and MAK
# DATE   : 4/26/2008
#
# COMMENT: Demo for arguments in script that are not
# pre-defined.
# =======================================================

write-host $args[0]
write-host $args[1]
```

Try to execute the script with no parameters and then with the two parameters shown here:

```
.\Test-Args1.ps1
.\Test-Args1.ps1 MyPparam1 MyParam2
```

You can see that when the script `Test-Args1` is executed without parameters, the `$ARGS[0]` and `$ARGS[0]` are empty and do not display any values. However, when executed with the parameters `MyParam1` and `MyParam2`, it displays the parameter values, as shown in Figure 4-6.

The next example creates a script that accepts two arguments. Here the parameters are predefined, and the values are stored in the variables `$firstname` and `$lastname`:

```
# =======================================================
#
# NAME: Test-Args2.ps1
#
```

```
# AUTHOR: Yan and MAK
# DATE  : 4/26/2008
#
# COMMENT: Demo for arguments in script that are
# pre-defined.
# =========================================================
param
(
[String] $firstname,
[String] $Lastname

)
write-host "First Name is " $firstname
write-host "Last Name is " $lastname
```

Now try to execute the script with no parameters and then with two parameters:

```
.\Test-Args2.ps1 Adam Smith
.\Test-Args2.ps1 Adam
.\Test-Args2.ps1 Smith
```

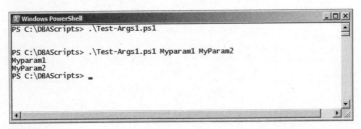

Figure 4-6

In Figure 4-7, you can see that when the script Test-Args2 is executed with the parameter values Adam or Smith or Adam and Smith, it accepts the argument values and stores that to $firstname and $lastname and displays them. However, when passed only one parameter value, it always passes to the first parameter variable $firstname.

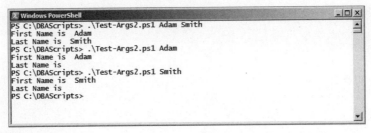

Figure 4-7

In order to ensure that the first parameter value is passed to the first parameter variable $firstname and the second parameter value is passed to the second parameter variable $lastname, you can use the parameter name and parameter value.

The same script `Test-args2.ps1` can be used for this. The following code executes the script with parameter name and parameter value:

```
.\Test-Args2.ps1 -FirstName Adam -LastName Smith
.\Test-Args2.ps1 -FirstName Adam
.\Test-Args2.ps1 -LastName Smith
```

As shown in Figure 4-8, when the parameter name is used, the parameter value is passed on to the right parameter variable.

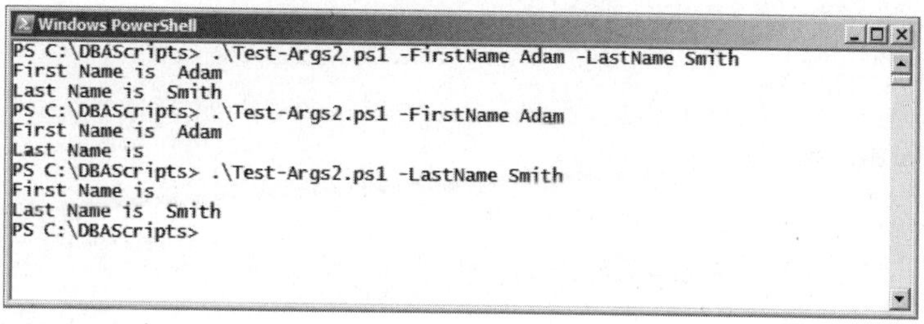

```
Windows PowerShell                                                    _ □ ×
PS C:\DBAScripts> .\Test-Args2.ps1 -FirstName Adam -LastName Smith
First Name is  Adam
Last Name is  Smith
PS C:\DBAScripts> .\Test-Args2.ps1 -FirstName Adam
First Name is  Adam
Last Name is
PS C:\DBAScripts> .\Test-Args2.ps1 -LastName Smith
First Name is
Last Name is  Smith
PS C:\DBAScripts>
```

Figure 4-8

Just as you can with functions, you can also create a parameter variable with a switch as an option. The behavior of the switch parameter is exactly the same as in a function.

Next, create a script `Test-args3.ps1` with a couple of switch parameters, as shown here:

```
# =======================================================
#
# NAME: Test-Args3.ps1
#
# AUTHOR: Yan and MAK
# DATE   : 4/26/2008
#
# COMMENT: Demo for arguments in script that are
# pre-defined switch.
# =======================================================
param
(
[String] $firstname,
[String] $lastname,
[switch] $help,
[switch] $version

)

$versionval=1.0
if ($help)
{
write-host "Usage: .\Test-Args3.ps1 Firstname LastName"
}
```

```
if ($version)
{
write-host "Version number of Test-Args3.ps1 is $versionval"
}

write-host "First Name is " $firstname
write-host "Last Name is " $lastname
```

Now execute the script with the parameter name and parameter value and switches as shown here:

```
.\Test-Args3.ps1 -FirstName Adam -LastName Smith
.\Test-Args3.ps1 -FirstName Adam -Help
.\Test-Args3.ps1 -LastName Smith -Help -Version
```

As shown in Figure 4-9, when a switch is used while executing the script, it displays the information provided inside the if block.

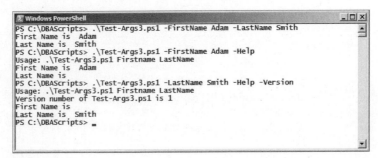

Figure 4-9

Sourcing

When all the related functions are put together in a file, the file can be sourced into the current Windows PowerShell environment or any script so that they will all be available.

Create a script file Mymodule.ps1 under the C:\DBAScripts directory with the following three functions in it:

```
# =====================================================
#
# NAME: MyModule.ps1
#
# AUTHOR: Yan and MAK
# DATE   : 4/26/2008
#
# COMMENT: Demo for Sourcing all the functions
# defined in this file
# =====================================================
function Hello
```

```
{
write-host "Welcome to PowerSQL"
}

Function ConcatName
{
[string] $args[0] + [string] $args[1]
}

Function compute([int] $x ,[string] $y, [int] $z)
{
switch ($y)
{
"+" { $computed=$x+$z }
"-" { $computed=$x-$z }
"/" { $computed=$x/$z }
"*" { $computed=$x^$z }
"%" { $computed=$x%$z }
}
return $computed
}
```

Now source the module so that it will be available for the session and then try to call all the functions.

Sourcing can be done by using . *script's file path* as shown here (see Figure 4-10):

```
. .\mymodule.ps1
Concatname "Sam" "Rooban"
Hello
Compute 5 * 20
```

Once `Mymodule.ps1` is sourced, all the functions that define the `Mymodule.ps1` become available in the current session. All the functions can be used.

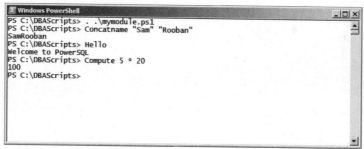

Figure 4-10

Variable Scope

PowerShell offers scope when defining variables. There are three variable scopes. *Global scope* is the scope of the current Windows PowerShell instance. Variables defined in this scope are visible to all the cmdlets, scripts, and functions executed in the Windows PowerShell instance. *Local scope* is the current scope. A new local scope is created whenever you run a function, script, or start a new instance of the Windows PowerShell. *Script scope* is created when the script is started, and removed when the script is completed. Variables in script scope are visible only when the script is running.

By default, a variable is created in the local scope. When a variable is accessed, it is also searched from the local scope. If it is there, you can use it; if it is not there, look at the parent's scope (and upward until you find the variable or reach to the global scope).

You can create a small script `Myscope.ps1` under `C:\DBAScripts` as shown here:

```
# ====================================================
#
# NAME: MyScope.ps1
#
# AUTHOR: Yan and MAK
# DATE   : 4/26/2008
#
# COMMENT: Demo for variable scope
#
# ====================================================
$myvar=1 # This variable is created in the scope of myscope.ps1.
write-host "Myvar defined as $myvar"

function myfunction
{
write-host "Myvar inside the myfunction is $myvar"
write-host "Updating myvar inside the myfunction... "
$myvar=2 # This variable is created in the scope of myfunction, a child scope of the
myscope.ps1 script scope.
write-host "Value of myvar after being updating inside myfunction is $myvar "
}
write-host "Calling myfunction"
myfunction

write-host "Value of myvar after calling the function is $myvar"
```

Define a global variable $myvar in Windows PowerShell:

```
$myvar=100
```

Now execute the `myscope.ps1` script as shown here:

```
.\myscope.ps1
$myvar
```

As shown in Figure 4-11, the `Myscope.ps1` script first calls the `myvar` variable, and its value is 1 in that scope. Then the variable is overridden with a value of 2 in the `myfunction` function inside the script. After exiting the function, the value of the variable changes back to 1 because the current scope changed back to the script scope. After exiting the function, you are in the global scope. PowerShell maintained a value of 100 for the variable in the global scope.

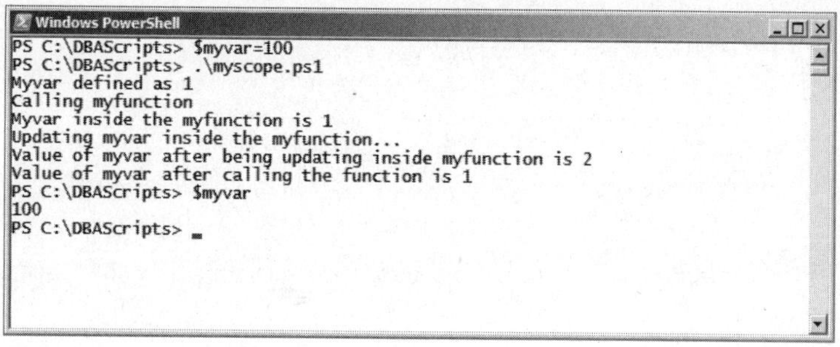

Figure 4-11

A variable can be read by the scope where it was created, and the child scopes of that scope. It can be changed in its scope, or the child scopes, by explicitly referring to it using a script label. Windows PowerShell provides three labels for identifying the scope of a variable: local, global, and script. To refer to a variable in another scope, place the scope label before the variable name, separating them by a colon (:) — for example, $global:myvar, $local:myvar, $myscript:myvar, and $myfunction:myvar.

Note that a variable cannot be read or changed in the parent scope of the scope where it was created.

Function Scope

Similar to the variable scope described in the previous section, scope is available for functions as well. If you declare a function, it is available only within the scope in which you declared it and any child scopes. The scope of the function can be illustrated by the following example.

Create Functionscope.ps1 as shown in the following example. In the script, the function innerfunction is defined in the scope of the outerfunction.

```
# ========================================================
#
# NAME: FunctionScope.ps1
#
# AUTHOR: Yan and MAK
# DATE   : 4/26/2008
#
# COMMENT: Demo for Function scope
#
# ========================================================

function outerfunction
{
        function innerfunction
        {
                write-host "Inside the innerfunction..."
        }

Write-Host "Calling innerfunction inside outerfunction..."
innerfunction
}
```

```
outerfunction
Write-Host "Trying to call innerfunction outside outerfunction..."
innerfunction
```

Execute the `functionscope.ps1` as shown here:

```
.\FunctionScope.ps1
```

From the output shown in Figure 4-12, you can see that `innerfunction` is out of scope and not recognized when called outside the `outerfunction` function.

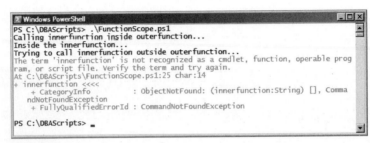

Figure 4-12

Note also that the global variable can be accessed and updated anywhere in the script. The local variable with the same name as its parent scope, however, is always overridden in the local scope.

More information on variables and scopes is provided in Chapter 5 when we discuss the variable drive.

User Profiles

To reuse a function, you can source in the script file that contains the function, as shown earlier. However, you can also put the function in your profile. A *profile* is a script that runs automatically when Windows PowerShell starts up. It can contain functions, variables, and aliases so that every time Windows Power-Shell starts, the functions, variables, and aliases are loaded into the new session automatically.

Four different profiles are available in Windows PowerShell, as listed in the following load order. If there is any conflict between these files, the commands in the more specific profile, which is loaded later, take precedence.

❑ **%windir%\system32\WindowsPowerShell\v2.0\profile.ps1**

This profile applies to all users and all shells.

❑ **%windir%\system32\WindowsPowerShell\v2.0\Microsoft.PowerShell_profile.ps1**

This profile applies to all users, but only to the Microsoft.PowerShell shell. For example, the Microsoft SQL Server PowerShell shell that the `SQLPS` utility starts is not a default Microsoft. PowerShell shell (we discuss it in Chapter 11). Therefore, this profile doesn't apply to it.

❑ **%UserProfile%\My Documents\WindowsPowerShell\profile.ps1** or **%UserProfile% \Documents\WindowsPowerShell\profile.ps1** on Windows Vista and Windows Server 2008.

This profile applies only to the current user but affects all shells.

❏ **%UserProfile%\My Documents\WindowsPowerShell\Microsoft.PowerShell_profile.ps1** or
   %UserProfile%\Documents\WindowsPowerShell\Microsoft.PowerShell_profile.ps1 on
   Windows Vista and Windows Server 2008.

This profile applies only to the current user and the Microsoft.PowerShell shell.

An administrator can set up profiles that are run for all users by using the first two profile files in the
folder `%windir%\System32\WindowsPowerShell\v2.0`. Aliases, functions, and variables defined in the
two files, if present, are used for all users of that machine.

For the current user, to ensure that no conflicts between profile files would overwrite a function you want
to use, it makes sense to put the function in the user-specific and shell-specific profile file. The path of this
file is actually stored in the built-in variable `$profile`. To determine if this profile already exists, enter
the following:

```
test-path $profile
```

If the profile exists, the command returns `True`. Otherwise, you need to create the profile file using the
following command (see Figure 4-13):

```
new-item -path $profile -type file -force
```

```
Windows PowerShell
PS C:\DBAScripts> test-path $profile
False
PS C:\DBAScripts> new-item -path $profile -type file -force


        Directory: C:\Users\MAK\Documents\WindowsPowerShell


Mode                LastWriteTime        Length Name
----                -------------        ------ ----
-a---         1/19/2009   6:36 AM             0 Microsoft.PowerShell_profile.ps1


PS C:\DBAScripts> _
```

Figure 4-13

After the profile specified in the `$profile` variable has been created, you can enter aliases, functions, and
scripts in the profile to customize your shell. For example, if you want to reuse all the functions defined
earlier in the `Mymodule.ps1` script, you can copy the content of the script to the profile by running the
following command (see Figure 4-14). The `Get-Content` and `Set-Content` cmdlets are covered in detail
in Chapter 5.

```
Get-Content C:\DBAScripts\mymodule.ps1 | Set-Content $profile
Get-Content $profile
```

After you set up the profile file, open a new shell and try to call the functions defined in the profile (see
Figure 4-15):

```
Concatname "Sam" "Rooban"
Hello
Compute 5 * 20
```

As you can see, the preceding three functions are loaded to the shell automatically.

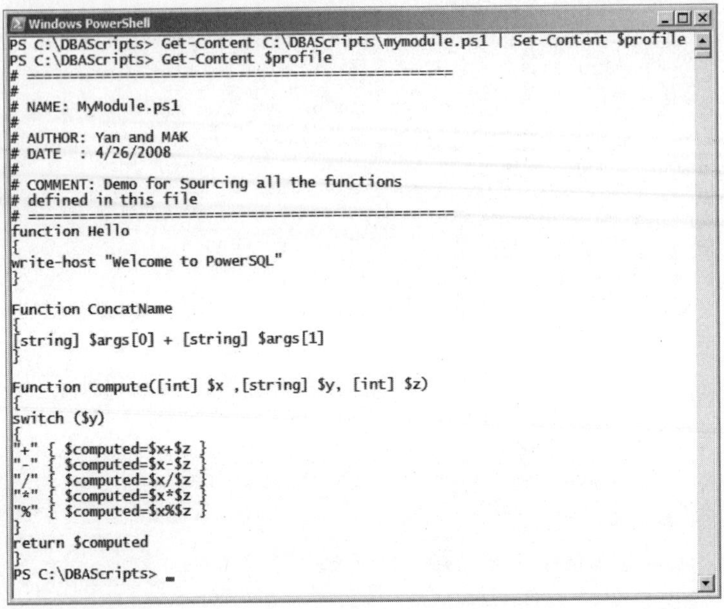

```
PS C:\DBAScripts> Get-Content C:\DBAScripts\mymodule.ps1 | Set-Content $profile
PS C:\DBAScripts> Get-Content $profile
# ===================================================
#
# NAME: MyModule.ps1
#
# AUTHOR: Yan and MAK
# DATE   : 4/26/2008
#
# COMMENT: Demo for Sourcing all the functions
# defined in this file
# ===================================================
function Hello
{
write-host "Welcome to PowerSQL"
}

Function ConcatName
{
[string] $args[0] + [string] $args[1]
}

Function compute([int] $x ,[string] $y, [int] $z)
{
switch ($y)
{
"+" { $computed=$x+$z }
"-" { $computed=$x-$z }
"/" { $computed=$x/$z }
"*" { $computed=$x*$z }
"%" { $computed=$x%$z }
}
return $computed
}
PS C:\DBAScripts> _
```

Figure 4-14

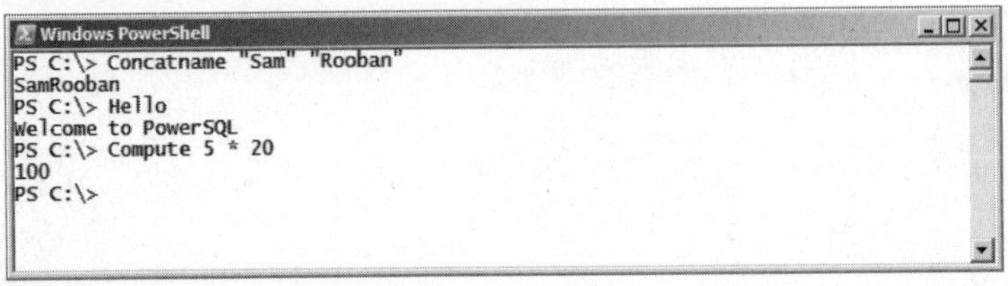

```
PS C:\> Concatname "Sam" "Rooban"
SamRooban
PS C:\> Hello
Welcome to PowerSQL
PS C:\> Compute 5 * 20
100
PS C:\>
```

Figure 4-15

Transcripts

PowerShell also provides a feature that records everything that happens during the PowerShell session. This can be turned on and off by using the following Start-Transcript and Stop-transcript cmdlets.

Start the transcript with the execute few cmdlets, functions, and scripts shown here:

```
Start-transcript -path C:\MyPsTranscripts.txt
Hello
Concatname "Sam" "Rooban"
./test-args3.ps1 -Firstname Sam -LastName Rooban
```

Figure 4-16 shows that the transcript started and began, recording all the cmdlets, functions, and scripts in the PowerShell session.

You can open the C:\MyPsTranscripts.txt file using Notepad and see all the recordings (see Figure 4-17).

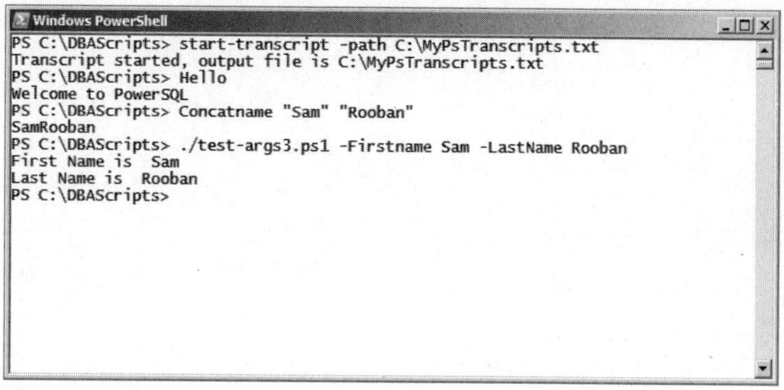

Figure 4-16

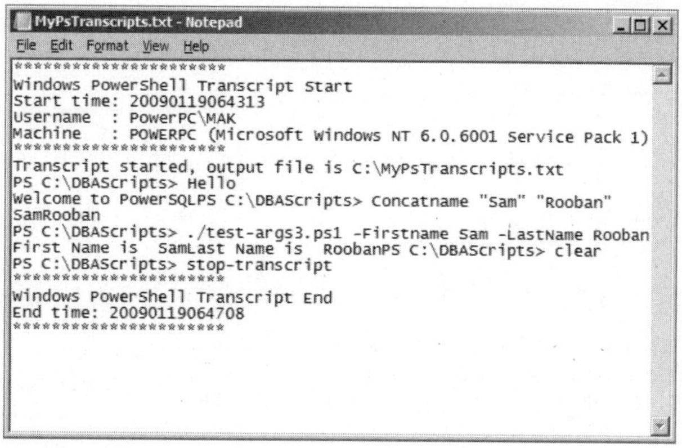

Figure 4-17

Use the following `Stop-Transcript` cmdlet to stop the transcript:

```
Stop-Transcript
```

You can enable and disable transcripts in every script you create, recording each and every cmdlet, expression, and different construct used in the script to a file, and stopping the recording at the end of the script.

Summary

This chapter covered how to create functions and function arguments, defining parameters in scripts, and sourcing a script file. It also demonstrated the various scopes related to variables and functions and explained the use of profiles and transcripts.

This chapter and the previous chapter illustrated the various programming functionalities in Windows PowerShell. The next chapter describes how to work with the system registry, file system, environment variables, and more.

5

Working with the File System, Registry, and Variables

One of the most powerful features of Windows PowerShell is the ability to navigate through many different data stores in a consistent manner. In addition to the familiar file system drives, such as C: and D:, Windows PowerShell includes drives that represent the registry hives, variables, aliases, environment variables, functions, certificates, and more. This chapter demonstrates how to work with four drives: the File System drive, the Registry drive, the Variable drive, and the Environment drive.

More specifically, this chapter covers the following topics:

❑   Using `Get-PSDrive` and `Get-PSProvider` to retrieve Windows PowerShell drives and providers

❑   Working with the file system

❑   Working with the registry

❑   Working with variables

❑   Working with environment variables

Using Get-PSDrive and Get-PSProvider

You can use the cmdlet `Get-PSDrive` to obtain a list of all Windows PowerShell drives. Run the following command at the Windows PowerShell prompt:

```
Get-PSDrive | Format-Table -auto
```

Figure 5-1 shows the list of drives on a default installation of Windows PowerShell. In this example, all of the following are on the local machine: one alias drive, which contains aliases for commands; one certificate drive, cert:, which contains digital signature certificates; three file system drives, C:, D: and E:; one environment drive, Env:, which contains environmental variables; one function drive, Function:, which contains functions declared in PowerShell; two registry drives, HKCU: and HKLM:; one variable drive, Variable:, which contains variables declared in Windows PowerShell; and one WSMan: drive that contains Windows Remote Management configurations.

The Windows PowerShell providers, shown in the second column of Figure 5-1, provide the Windows PowerShell drives to the Windows PowerShell console. These providers are .NET assemblies that make the data in a specialized data store available in Windows PowerShell in a format that resembles file system drives.

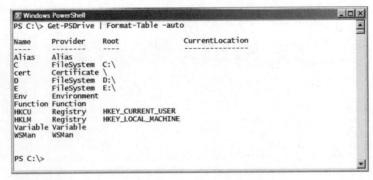

Figure 5-1

You can use the Get-PSProvider cmdlet to obtain a list of all the providers:

```
Get-PSProvider
```

Figure 5-2 shows how the cmdlet prints out a list of providers. Again, these are the providers listed in the second column of Figure 5-1.

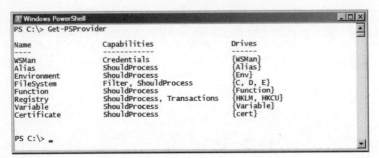

Figure 5-2

The associated drives that each of the providers expose are shown in the third column of the output. These providers are installed in Windows PowerShell by default. You can write your own provider in .NET to surface data stores specific to your own product or database, and add the drives by using the New-PSDrive command.

Working with File System

As shown in the preceding section, file system drives are Windows PowerShell drives that are made available through the FileSystem provider. In order to get a list of file system drives, you can execute the following command:

```
Get-PSDrive -pSProvider FileSystem | Format-Table -auto
```

The output is shown in Figure 5-3. However, the information you can get from Get-PSDrive is limited. You can only see the drive name and your current location — that's about it.

```
Windows PowerShell
PS C:\> Get-PSDrive -pSProvider FileSystem | Format-Table -auto

Name Provider    Root CurrentLocation
---- --------    ---- ---------------
C    FileSystem C:\
D    FileSystem D:\
E    FileSystem E:\


PS C:\>
```

Figure 5-3

Let's say you want to view the amount of free space on each logical drive. Unfortunately, the drive objects returned by Get-PSDrive won't get it for you. This is where *Windows Management Instrumentation (WMI)* comes into play. WMI is the infrastructure for managing data and operations on Windows-based operating systems. WMI is available on all Windows operating systems since Windows NT 4.0 (long before Windows PowerShell was introduced). WMI is described in more detail in Chapter 8.

The Get-WmiObject cmdlet is used to make a connection into the WMI. It creates instances of WMI classes. The Win32_LogicalDisk WMI class represents all local storage devices on a computer system. The DriveType property of this class represents the type of disk drive. A value of 3 corresponds to a local disk. You will first create an instance of the Win32_LogicalDisk WMI class. Then you'll use the Select-Object cmdlet to get the name and free space of each local drive. The complete command is shown here:

```
Get-WmiObject -class Win32_LogicalDisk -filter "DriveType=3" | Select-Object
    DeviceID, FreeSpace | Format-Table -auto
```

The output is shown in Figure 5-4. The FreeSpace shown is in bytes. As you can see, the C: drive has 22334136320 bytes free. Because this is such a large value it is a little hard to read. You can convert the bytes to GB for easy viewing by running the following command:

```
Get-WmiObject -class Win32_LogicalDisk -filter "DriveType=3" | ForEach-Object
    -Process {Write-Host $_.DeviceID "has" ($_.FreeSpace/1GB) "GB free"}
```

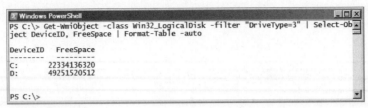

Figure 5-4

As shown in Figure 5-5, drive C: has 20GB free, and drive D: has 45GB free.

```
Windows PowerShell
PS C:\> Get-WmiObject -class Win32_LogicalDisk -filter "DriveType=3" | ForEach-O
bject -Process {Write-Host $_.DeviceID "has" ($_.FreeSpace/1GB) "GB free"}
C: has 20.8000640869141 GB free
D: has 45.8690528869629 GB free
PS C:\> _
```

Figure 5-5

Navigating the File System

After you have the list of file system drives, you can navigate through them for files and directories. In Windows PowerShell, the working directory, or the current directory you are in, is called *location*. As in command-line interfaces such as Cmd.exe, you can refer to all the objects under the current location using a relative path. Alternately, you can refer to them using an absolute path from the root of the file system drive.

The core cmdlets you can use to change the current location are listed in Table 5-1.

Table 5-1: cmdlets to Change Location

cmdlet Name	Alias	Description
Set-Location	sl, cd, chdir	Sets the current working location to a specified location
Get-Location	gl, pwd	Gets information about the current working location
Push-Location	Pushd	Pushes the current location onto the stack that contains the ordered history of locations where you have been
Pop-Location	Popd	Changes the current location to the location most recently pushed onto the stack

The Set-Location command enables you to specify the current location. Suppose you are in the root of the C: drive. The following command changes the current location to C:\Windows:

```
Set-Location -Path C:\Windows
```

After you enter the command, you will notice the PowerShell prompt changes to C:\Windows, as shown in Figure 5-6.

Figure 5-6

However, if you want direct feedback from the command, you can include the –passThru parameter in the command. The –Path parameter immediately following Set-Location can be omitted because it is a positional parameter in position 1. You can simply provide the path value in position 1.

```
Set-Location C:\Windows -passThru
```

The new directory C:\Windows is returned, as shown in Figure 5-7.

Figure 5-7

You can specify paths relative to the current location in the same way as you would in Windows command shells. A period (.) represents the current directory, and a double period (..) represents the parent directory of the current location. For example, you can change from the current location C:\Windows to its parent, the root of the C: drive, as shown here and in Figure 5-8:

```
Set-Location ..
```

Figure 5-8

You can verify the current location from the command prompt or by entering the Get-Location cmdlet, as shown in Figure 5-9. The Get-Location cmdlet retrieves the current working location:

```
Get-Location
```

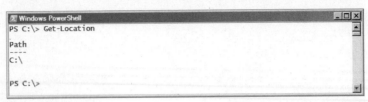

Figure 5-9

It is helpful to be able to keep track of where you have been and return to previous locations. The Push-Location cmdlet in Windows PowerShell pushes the current location onto a stack that contains an ordered history of locations you have been, and enables you to return using the Pop-Location cmdlet.

To push the current location onto the stack and then move to the Program Files\Microsoft SQL Server directory, run the following command:

```
Push-Location -Path "C:\Program Files\Microsoft SQL Server"
```

Notice that the current location changes to C:\Program Files\Microsoft SQL Server in Figure 5-10.

Figure 5-10

You can then return to the root directory of the C: drive by entering the Pop-Location command:

```
Pop-Location
```

Notice that the current location changes back to C:\ in Figure 5-11.

Figure 5-11

Managing Files and Directories

After you navigate the file system, you may want to manage the files and directories, such as creating a new file, writing to a file, deleting an existing directory, and so on. The core cmdlets you can use to manage files and directories are listed in Table 5-2.

Table 5-2: cmdlets to Manage Files and Directories

cmdlet Name	Alias	Description
Get-ChildItem	gci	Gets the items and child items in one or more specified locations
New-Item	ni	Creates a new file or directory
Copy-Item	cpi, copy	Copies files
Remove-Item	ri, del, rd	Removes files or directories
Move-Item	mi, move	Moves a file
Rename-Item	rni, rn	Renames a file

To obtain a directory listing of the C:\ drive, use the Get-ChildItem cmdlet:

```
Get-ChildItem C:\
```

This cmdlet returns all the files and directories under C:\, as shown in Figure 5-12.

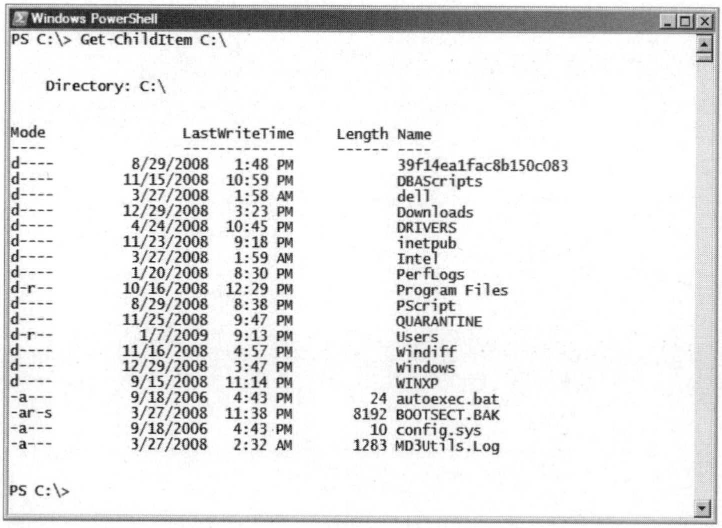

Figure 5-12

To get the methods and properties associated with the objects, use the Get-Member cmdlet:

```
Get-ChildItem | Get-Member
```

As shown in Figure 5-13, the available methods for directory and file objects are listed separately.

Figure 5-13

If you want to get a list of only the directories, you can use the `Where-Object` cmdlet to filter the objects whose `PSIsContainer NoteProperty` returns true because only directory objects are containers (the output is shown in Figure 5-14):

```
Get-ChildItem | Where-Object {$_.PSIsContainer}
```

If you want to view only the directory names, you can use the `Select-Object` cmdlet to select only the `Name` property of the directory objects (the output is shown in Figure 5-15):

```
Get-ChildItem | Where-Object {$_.psIsContainer} | Select-Object Name
```

The `Get-ChildItem` command also accepts wildcards in the path of the items to list. The Windows Power-Shell wildcard notation includes the following:

❑ **Asterisk (*)**: Matches zero or more occurrences of any character

```
Windows PowerShell                                                    _ |□| X
PS C:\> Get-ChildItem | Where-Object {$_.PSIsContainer}

    Directory: C:\

Mode                LastWriteTime     Length Name
----                -------------     ------ ----
d----        8/29/2008     1:48 PM           39f14ea1fac8b150c083
d----       11/15/2008    10:59 PM           DBAScripts
d----        3/27/2008     1:58 AM           dell
d----       12/29/2008     3:23 PM           Downloads
d----        4/24/2008    10:45 PM           DRIVERS
d----       11/23/2008     9:18 PM           inetpub
d----        3/27/2008     1:59 AM           Intel
d----        1/20/2008     8:30 PM           PerfLogs
d-r--       10/16/2008    12:29 PM           Program Files
d----        8/29/2008     8:38 PM           PScript
d----       11/25/2008     9:47 PM           QUARANTINE
d-r--         1/7/2009     9:13 PM           Users
d----       11/16/2008     4:57 PM           Windiff
d----       12/29/2008     3:47 PM           Windows
d----        9/15/2008    11:14 PM           WINXP

PS C:\> _
```

Figure 5-14

```
Windows PowerShell                                                    _ |□| X
PS C:\> Get-ChildItem | Where-Object {$_.psIsContainer} | Select-Object Name

Name
----
39f14ea1fac8b150c083
DBAScripts
dell
Downloads
DRIVERS
inetpub
Intel
PerfLogs
Program Files
PScript
QUARANTINE
Users
Windiff
Windows
WINXP

PS C:\> _
```

Figure 5-15

- ❑ **Question mark (?)**: Matches exactly one character
- ❑ **Left bracket ([) and right bracket (])**: Surround a set of characters to be matched

For example, if you want to view a list of available assemblies only under the .NET Framework v3.5 directory, run the following command:

```
Get-ChildItem C:\Windows\Microsoft.NET\Framework\v3.5\*.dll
```

Figure 5-16 shows the assemblies under the directory.

The New-Item cmdlet enables you to create a file or directory. Use the -Type parameter to tell Windows PowerShell that the new item will be a file or directory. For example, the following command creates a new directory called psDir under the root directory of the C: drive, and then creates a new file, psFile.txt, under the new directory, C:\psDir. The output is shown in Figure 5-17.

```
New-Item -Path C:\ -Name psDir -Type directory
```

```
Windows PowerShell                                                          _□×
PS C:\> Get-ChildItem C:\Windows\Microsoft.NET\Framework\v3.5\*.dll


    Directory: C:\Windows\Microsoft.NET\Framework\v3.5


Mode            LastWriteTime     Length Name
----            -------------     ------ ----
-a---       7/29/2008   11:40 PM  802816 Microsoft.Build.Tasks.v3.5.dll
-a---       7/29/2008   11:40 PM   40960 Microsoft.Data.Entity.Build.Tasks.
                                          dll
-a---       7/29/2008   11:40 PM   41984 Microsoft.VisualC.STLCLR.dll
-a---       7/29/2008   11:40 PM    5632 Sentinel.v3.5Client.dll


PS C:\>
```

Figure 5-16

```
Windows PowerShell                                                          _□×
PS C:\> New-Item -Path C:\ -Name psDir -Type directory


    Directory: C:\


Mode            LastWriteTime     Length Name
----            -------------     ------ ----
d----       1/7/2009    9:40 PM          psDir


PS C:\>
```

Figure 5-17

You can omit the optional -Path parameter when creating the new file psFile.txt because it is a positional parameter in position 1. Simply provide the path value in position 1. The output is shown in Figure 5-18.

```
New-Item C:\psDir -Name psFile.txt -Type file
```

```
Windows PowerShell                                                          _□×
PS C:\> New-Item C:\psDir -Name psFile.txt -Type file


    Directory: C:\psDir


Mode            LastWriteTime     Length Name
----            -------------     ------ ----
-a---       1/7/2009    9:40 PM        0 psFile.txt


PS C:\> _
```

Figure 5-18

The Copy-Item cmdlet enables you to copy a file or directory from one location to another. However, unlike Windows command shells, Copy-Item does not copy the files and subfolders contained in a directory by default.

For example, if you try to copy the psDir directory you just created from the root of the C: drive to the C:\Windows\Temp directory, the command will succeed, but the psFile.txt file you created under C:\psDir directory will not be copied:

```
Set-Location C:\psdir
Copy-Item C:\psDir C:\Windows\Temp
```

```
Get-ChildItem C:\Windows\Temp
Get-ChildItem C:\Windows\Temp\psDir
```

Notice that only the psDir directory is copied in Figure 5-19.

```
Windows PowerShell                                                      _ □ ×
PS C:\> Set-location C:\psdir
PS C:\psDir> Copy-Item C:\psDir C:\Windows\Temp
PS C:\psDir> Get-ChildItem C:\Windows\Temp


    Directory: C:\Windows\Temp


Mode                LastWriteTime     Length Name
----                -------------     ------ ----
d----        1/6/2009     5:01 PM            54bd
d----       12/15/2008    9:02 AM            MPTelemetrySubmit
d----        1/7/2009     9:42 PM            psDir
-a---       12/29/2008   10:54 AM      13786 coinlog.log
-a---       12/28/2008   11:24 PM        632 fwtsqmfile01.sqm
-a---        1/7/2009     8:01 PM      63028 MpCmdRun.log
-a---        1/5/2009     6:52 PM     208450 MpSigStub.log
-a---        1/7/2009     7:41 PM   50806784 WFVDD34.tmp


PS C:\psDir> Get-ChildItem C:\Windows\Temp\psDir
PS C:\psDir>
```

Figure 5-19

To copy the contents of a folder, include the recurse parameter of the Copy-Item cmdlet in the command. If you have already copied the directory without its contents, add the force parameter, which enables you to overwrite the empty folder, as shown in Figure 5-20.

```
Copy-Item C:\psDir C:\Windows\Temp -recurse -force
Get-ChildItem C:\Windows\Temp
Get-ChildItem C:\Windows\Temp\psDir
```

```
Windows PowerShell                                                      _ □ ×
PS C:\psDir> Copy-Item C:\psDir C:\Windows\Temp -recurse -force
PS C:\psDir> Get-ChildItem C:\Windows\Temp


    Directory: C:\Windows\Temp


Mode                LastWriteTime     Length Name
----                -------------     ------ ----
d----        1/6/2009     5:01 PM            54bd
d----       12/15/2008    9:02 AM            MPTelemetrySubmit
d----        1/7/2009     9:43 PM            psDir
-a---       12/29/2008   10:54 AM      13786 coinlog.log
-a---       12/28/2008   11:24 PM        632 fwtsqmfile01.sqm
-a---        1/7/2009     8:01 PM      63028 MpCmdRun.log
-a---        1/5/2009     6:52 PM     208450 MpSigStub.log
-a---        1/7/2009     7:41 PM   50806784 WFVDD34.tmp


PS C:\psDir> Get-ChildItem C:\Windows\Temp\psDir


    Directory: C:\Windows\Temp\psDir


Mode                LastWriteTime     Length Name
----                -------------     ------ ----
-a---        1/7/2009     9:40 PM          0 psFile.txt


PS C:\psDir>
```

Figure 5-20

To remove files or directories, use the `Remove-Item` cmdlet. Unlike the `New-Item` cmdlet, Windows PowerShell does not provide different type parameters for removing directories and files.

In the next example, run the following commands to remove the `psFile.txt` file under `C:\psDir`, and then the empty `psDir` directory.

```
Set-Location C:\
Remove-Item C:\psDir\psFile.txt
Remove-Item C:\psDir
Get-ChildItem C:\
```

Figure 5-21 shows that the `psFile.txt` was removed first, followed by the `C:\psDir` directory.

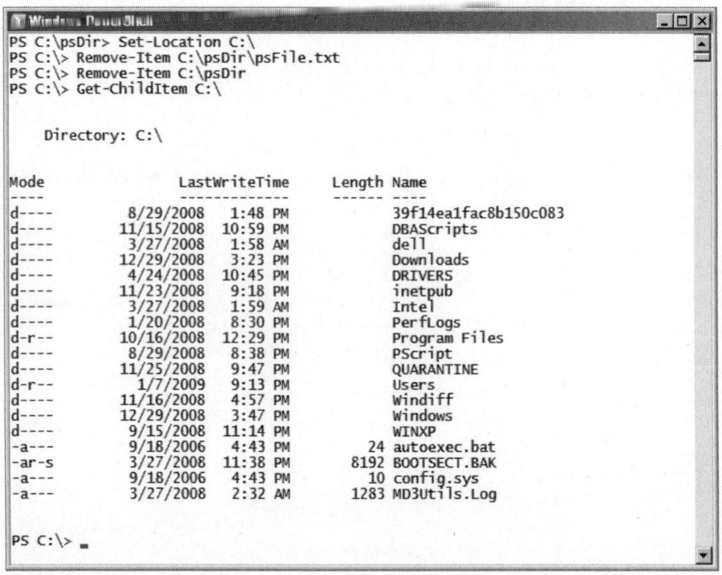

Figure 5-21

If you want to delete the `C:\Windows\Temp\psDir` directory that you copied earlier from `C:\psDir`, with everything it contains in one shot, simply specify the `-recurse` parameter:

```
Remove-Item C:\Windows\Temp\psDir -recurse
```

If you try to delete the `C:\Windows\Temp\psDir` directory without the `-recurse` parameter, Windows PowerShell prompts you to confirm the deletion because the directory is non-empty. The output is shown in Figure 5-22.

```
Remove-Item C:\Windows\Temp\psDir
```

You need to select Y (Yes) or A (Yes to All) to delete the directory and everything in it.

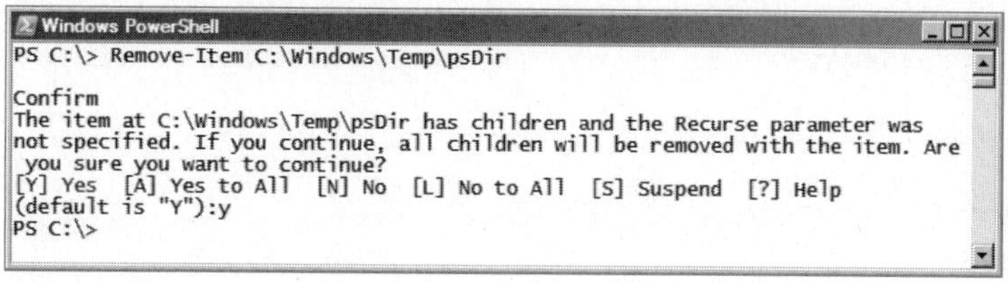

Figure 5-22

To move a file or folder, use the Move-Item cmdlet. The following commands create a directory C:\psDir (this directory was removed in previous examples), and then move the psDir directory from the C:\ directory to the root of the C:\Windows\Temp directory. The output is shown in Figure 5-23.

```
New-Item -Path C:\ -Name psDir -Type directory
Move-Item -Path C:\psDir -Destination C:\Windows\Temp
Get-ChildItem C:\Windows\Temp
```

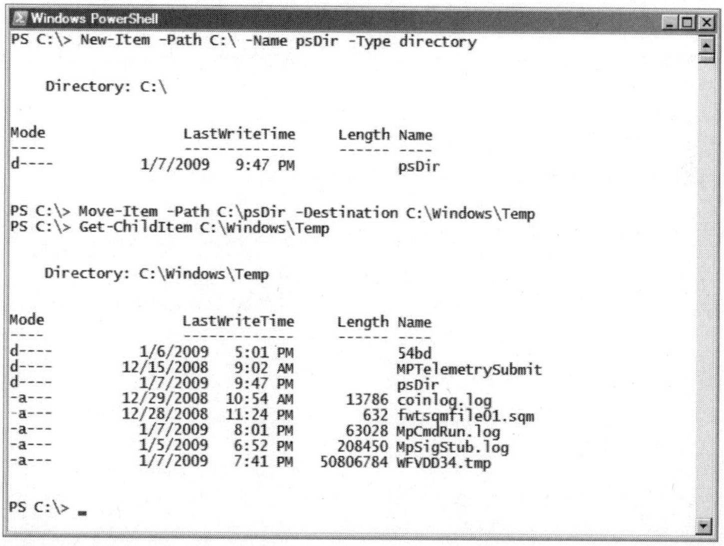

Figure 5-23

To change the name of a file or folder, use the Rename-Item cmdlet. The following command creates a new file, psFile.txt, in the C:\psDir directory and then changes the name of the file from psFile.txt to rnFile.txt. The output is shown in Figure 5-24.

```
New-Item C:\Windows\Temp\psDir -Name psFile.txt -Type file
Rename-Item -Path C:\Windows\Temp\psDir\psFile.txt rnFile.txt
Get-ChildItem C:\Windows\Temp\psDir
```

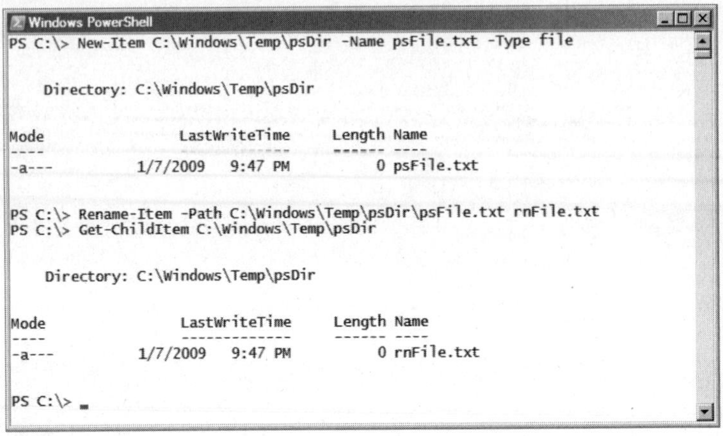

```
Windows PowerShell                                                      _ □ ×
PS C:\> New-Item C:\Windows\Temp\psDir -Name psFile.txt -Type file

    Directory: C:\Windows\Temp\psDir

Mode            LastWriteTime       Length Name
----            -------------       ------ ----
-a---           1/7/2009   9:47 PM       0 psFile.txt

PS C:\> Rename-Item -Path C:\Windows\Temp\psDir\psFile.txt rnFile.txt
PS C:\> Get-ChildItem C:\Windows\Temp\psDir

    Directory: C:\Windows\Temp\psDir

Mode            LastWriteTime       Length Name
----            -------------       ------ ----
-a---           1/7/2009   9:47 PM       0 rnFile.txt

PS C:\> _
```

Figure 5-24

Managing File Contents

The previous sections explained how to manage the objects in the file system. This section examines how to read and write a file. The core cmdlets you can use to manage file contents are listed in Table 5-3.

Table 5-3: cmdlets to Manage File Contents

cmdlet Name	Alias	Description
Set-Content	Si	Sets the contents of a file
Add-Content	Sc	Appends to the contents of a file
Get-Content	gc, type	Sends the contents of a file to the output stream
Clear-Content	Cli	Clears the contents of a file

To overwrite the contents of a file, use the Set-Content cmdlet. The following command overwrites the contents of the rnFile.txt file you created earlier. The new content is specified by the -value argument.

```
Set-Content C:\Windows\Temp\psDir\rnFile.txt -Value "This is new content."
```

If you just want to append to the end of the rnFile.txt file but not overwrite the entire contents, use the Add-Content cmdlet. The following command appends to the end of the rnFile.txt file:

```
Add-Content C:\Windows\Temp\psDir\rnFile.txt -Value "More content"
```

To read the contents of a file, use the Get-Content cmdlet:

```
Get-Content C:\Windows\Temp\psDir\rnfile.txt
```

Notice that the contents of the rnFile.txt file includes what was written by Set-Content and Add-Content in Figure 5-25.

```
Windows PowerShell                                                    _ □ ×
PS C:\> Set-Content C:\Windows\Temp\psDir\rnFile.txt -Value "This is new content
."
PS C:\> Add-Content C:\Windows\Temp\psDir\rnFile.txt -Value "More content"
PS C:\> Get-Content C:\Windows\Temp\psDir\rnfile.txt
This is new content.
More content
PS C:\>
```

Figure 5-25

Get-Content and Set-Content can also be used to merge files. Write a simple string to a new file called file1.txt with the Set-Content cmdlet. Then write a simple string to another new file called file2.txt. You can use the Get-Content cmdlet to retrieve the contents of the two files as a string object, and pipe the object to the Set-Content cmdlet to write to a new file, file3.txt. The complete commands are as follows:

```
Set-Location C:\Windows\Temp\psDir
Set-Content file1.txt -Value "File 1."
Set-Content  file2.txt -Value "File 2."
Get-Content file1.txt,file2.txt | Set-Content file3.txt
Get-Content file3.txt
```

As shown in Figure 5-26, the Set-Content cmdlet actually created file1.txt, file2.txt, and file3.txt. The file3.txt file contains the contents of both file1.txt and file2.txt.

```
Windows PowerShell                                                    _ □ ×
PS C:\> Set-Location C:\Windows\Temp\psDir
PS C:\Windows\Temp\psDir> Set-Content file1.txt -Value "File 1."
PS C:\Windows\Temp\psDir> Set-Content  file2.txt -Value "File 2."
PS C:\Windows\Temp\psDir> Get-Content file1.txt,file2.txt | Set-Content file3.tx
t
PS C:\Windows\Temp\psDir> Get-Content file3.txt
File 1.
File 2.
PS C:\Windows\Temp\psDir>
```

Figure 5-26

To delete the contents of a file, such as its text, but not delete the item, use the Clear-Content cmdlet:

```
Clear-Content file3.txt
Get-Content file3.txt
```

Notice that the file3.txt file has been emptied in Figure 5-27.

```
Windows PowerShell                                                    _ □ ×
PS C:\Windows\Temp\psDir> Clear-Content file3.txt
PS C:\Windows\Temp\psDir> Get-Content file3.txt
PS C:\Windows\Temp\psDir>
```

Figure 5-27

Working with the Registry

This section looks at the registry drives. There are two built-in registry drives in Windows PowerShell: HKCU and HKLM. They are made available through the Registry provider. You can execute the following command to retrieve them:

```
Get-PSDrive -pSProvider Registry
```

Figure 5-28 shows the registry drives.

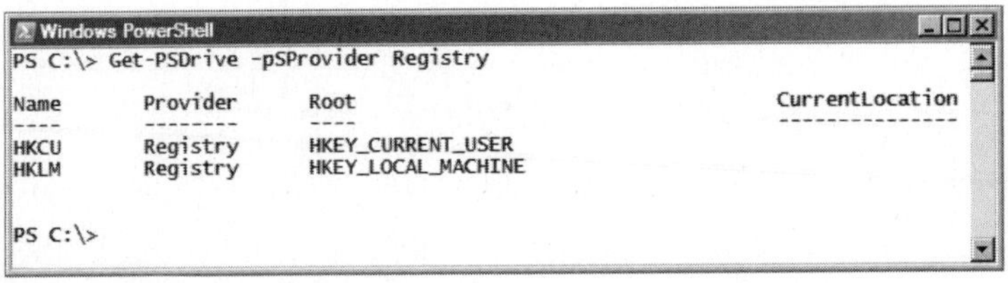

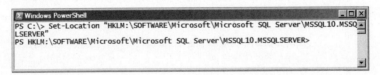

Figure 5-28

You can change the current location to a path under a registry drive using the `Set-Location` cmdlet, and then get the keys under the registry path with the `Get-ChildItem` cmdlet. For example, the following command sets the current location to the registry root of the default SQL Server 2008 instance on the local computer, as shown in Figure 5-29.

```
Set-Location "HKLM:\SOFTWARE\Microsoft\Microsoft SQL Server\MSSQL10.MSSQLSERVER"
```

```
Windows PowerShell
PS C:\> Set-Location "HKLM:\SOFTWARE\Microsoft\Microsoft SQL Server\MSSQL10.MSSQ
LSERVER"
PS HKLM:\SOFTWARE\Microsoft\Microsoft SQL Server\MSSQL10.MSSQLSERVER>
```

Figure 5-29

Once you are at the registry root of the default SQL Server 2008 instance, you can view all the subkeys related to the default instance using the `Get-ChildItem` cmdlet:

```
Get-ChildItem
```

The subkeys are shown in Figure 5-30. The MSSQLServer subkey contains the configuration information about the data engine, including registry values related to audit level, authentication mode, and so on.

Because Windows PowerShell considers a registry value a property of a key, you need to use the `Get-ItemProperty` cmdlet to retrieve the registry values under MSSQL:

```
Get-ItemProperty MSSQLServer
```

As shown in Figure 5-31, the command returns only the registry values.

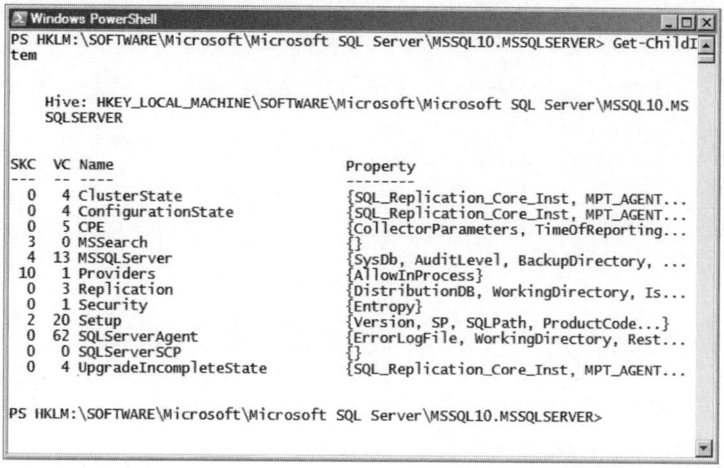

```
PS HKLM:\SOFTWARE\Microsoft\Microsoft SQL Server\MSSQL10.MSSQLSERVER> Get-ChildI
tem


    Hive: HKEY_LOCAL_MACHINE\SOFTWARE\Microsoft\Microsoft SQL Server\MSSQL10.MS
    SQLSERVER


SKC  VC Name                           Property
---  -- ----                           --------
  0   4 ClusterState                   {SQL_Replication_Core_Inst, MPT_AGENT...
  0   4 ConfigurationState             {SQL_Replication_Core_Inst, MPT_AGENT...
  0   5 CPE                            {CollectorParameters, TimeOfReporting...
  3   0 MSSearch                       {}
  4  13 MSSQLServer                    {SysDb, AuditLevel, BackupDirectory, ...
 10   1 Providers                      {AllowInProcess}
  0   3 Replication                    {DistributionDB, WorkingDirectory, Is...
  0   1 Security                       {Entropy}
  2  20 Setup                          {Version, SP, SQLPath, ProductCode...}
  0  62 SQLServerAgent                 {ErrorLogFile, WorkingDirectory, Rest...
  0   0 SQLServerSCP                   {}
  0   4 UpgradeIncompleteState         {SQL_Replication_Core_Inst, MPT_AGENT...


PS HKLM:\SOFTWARE\Microsoft\Microsoft SQL Server\MSSQL10.MSSQLSERVER>
```

Figure 5-30

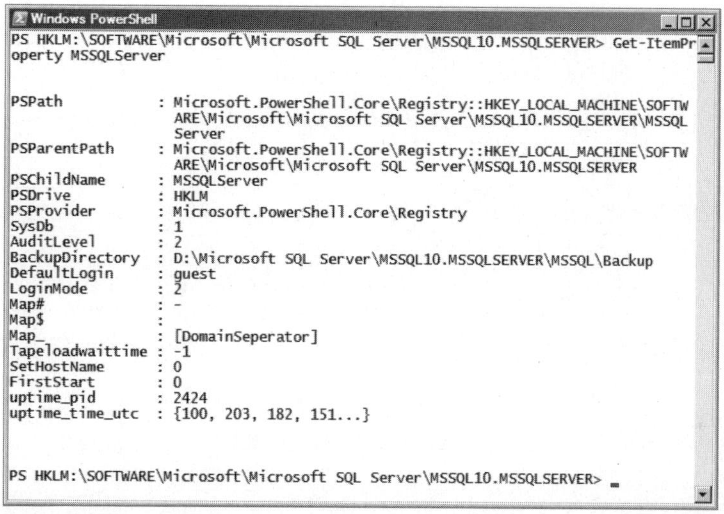

```
PS HKLM:\SOFTWARE\Microsoft\Microsoft SQL Server\MSSQL10.MSSQLSERVER> Get-ItemPr
operty MSSQLServer


PSPath            : Microsoft.PowerShell.Core\Registry::HKEY_LOCAL_MACHINE\SOFTW
                    ARE\Microsoft\Microsoft SQL Server\MSSQL10.MSSQLSERVER\MSSQL
                    Server
PSParentPath      : Microsoft.PowerShell.Core\Registry::HKEY_LOCAL_MACHINE\SOFTW
                    ARE\Microsoft\Microsoft SQL Server\MSSQL10.MSSQLSERVER
PSChildName       : MSSQLServer
PSDrive           : HKLM
PSProvider        : Microsoft.PowerShell.Core\Registry
SysDb             : 1
AuditLevel        : 2
BackupDirectory   : D:\Microsoft SQL Server\MSSQL10.MSSQLSERVER\MSSQL\Backup
DefaultLogin      : guest
LoginMode         : 2
Map#              : -
Map$              :
Map_              : [DomainSeperator]
Tapeloadwaittime  : -1
SetHostName       : 0
FirstStart        : 0
uptime_pid        : 2424
uptime_time_utc   : {100, 203, 182, 151...}


PS HKLM:\SOFTWARE\Microsoft\Microsoft SQL Server\MSSQL10.MSSQLSERVER> _
```

Figure 5-31

The registry value `AuditLevel` controls the audit levels on SQL Server. The value `2` shown in the figure means that only failed logins are audited on the default instance. If you want to audit all the logins, including the successful ones, you need to change the value to `3` and bounce the instance. The `Set-ItemProperty` cmdlet sets the registry value:

```
Set-ItemProperty -path MSSQLServer -name AuditLevel -value 3
```

To verify that the registry value has been changed, run the following command:

```
(Get-ItemProperty MSSQLServer).AuditLevel
```

As shown in Figure 5-32, the registry value `AuditLevel` is now changed to 3.

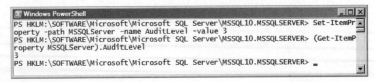

Figure 5-32

Besides the registry values, the `MSSQLServer` registry key also has its own subkeys. To get the subkeys, use the `Get-ChildItem` cmdlet:

```
Get-ChildItem -path MSSQLServer
```

As shown in Figure 5-33, the subkeys contain information related to the version of the SQL Server, the FILESTREAM availability on the instance, the startup parameters, and server network configuration settings.

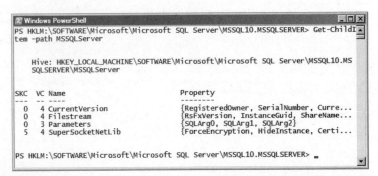

Figure 5-33

To list all the registry values under these subkeys, run the following command:

```
Get-ChildItem MSSQLServer | ForEach-Object {Get-ItemProperty $_.PSPath | Select * }
```

The output is shown in Figure 5-34.

You can ignore the properties prefixed with "PS." These are Windows PowerShell-related properties. For example, the `CurrentVersion` subkey has four values — `RegisteredOwner`, `SerialNumber`, `CurrentVersion`, and `Language` — which provide useful information about the SQL Server instance.

The registry path can be very long, such as `HKEY_LOCAL_MACHINE\SOFTWARE\Microsoft \Microsoft SQL Server\MSSQL10.MSSQLSERVER\MSSQLServer`. As it is cumbersome to type such long paths, you can create a custom Windows PowerShell drive that is rooted in that key by executing the following command:

```
New-PSDrive -Name mssqlkey -PSProvider Registry -Root "HKLM\SOFTWARE\Microsoft
    \Microsoft SQL Server\MSSQL10.MSSQLSERVER\MSSQLServer"
Get-ChildItem mssqlkey:
```

```
 Windows PowerShell                                               _ B X
PS HKLM:\SOFTWARE\Microsoft\Microsoft SQL Server\MSSQL10.MSSQLSERVER> Get-ChildI
tem MSSQLServer | ForEach-Object {Get-ItemProperty $_.PSPath | Select * }


PSPath             : Microsoft.PowerShell.Core\Registry::HKEY_LOCAL_MACHINE\SOFTWA
                     RE\Microsoft\Microsoft SQL Server\MSSQL10.MSSQLSERVER\MSSQLSe
                     rver\CurrentVersion
PSParentPath       : Microsoft.PowerShell.Core\Registry::HKEY_LOCAL_MACHINE\SOFTWA
                     RE\Microsoft\Microsoft SQL Server\MSSQL10.MSSQLSERVER\MSSQLSe
                     rver
PSChildName        : CurrentVersion
PSProvider         : Microsoft.PowerShell.Core\Registry
RegisteredOwner    :
SerialNumber       :
CurrentVersion     : 10.0.1600.22
Language           : 1033

PSPath             : Microsoft.PowerShell.Core\Registry::HKEY_LOCAL_MACHINE\SOFTWARE\
                     Microsoft\Microsoft SQL Server\MSSQL10.MSSQLSERVER\MSSQLServer\F
                     ilestream
PSParentPath       : Microsoft.PowerShell.Core\Registry::HKEY_LOCAL_MACHINE\SOFTWARE\
                     Microsoft\Microsoft SQL Server\MSSQL10.MSSQLSERVER\MSSQLServer
PSChildName        : Filestream
PSProvider         : Microsoft.PowerShell.Core\Registry
RSFxVersion        : 0102
InstanceGuid       : {24603d9b-0a54-4bfb-9814-8836f60b0c51}
ShareName          : MSSQLSERVER
EnableLevel        : 2

PSPath             : Microsoft.PowerShell.Core\Registry::HKEY_LOCAL_MACHINE\SOFTWARE\
                     Microsoft\Microsoft SQL Server\MSSQL10.MSSQLSERVER\MSSQLServer\P
                     arameters
PSParentPath       : Microsoft.PowerShell.Core\Registry::HKEY_LOCAL_MACHINE\SOFTWARE\
                     Microsoft\Microsoft SQL Server\MSSQL10.MSSQLSERVER\MSSQLServer
PSChildName        : Parameters
PSProvider         : Microsoft.PowerShell.Core\Registry
SQLArg0            : -dD:\Microsoft SQL Server\MSSQL10.MSSQLSERVER\MSSQL\DATA\master.
                     mdf
SQLArg1            : -eD:\Microsoft SQL Server\MSSQL10.MSSQLSERVER\MSSQL\Log\ERRORLOG
SQLArg2            : -lD:\Microsoft SQL Server\MSSQL10.MSSQLSERVER\MSSQL\DATA\mastlog
                     .ldf

PSPath             : Microsoft.PowerShell.Core\Registry::HKEY_LOCAL_MACHINE\SOFTWA
                     RE\Microsoft\Microsoft SQL Server\MSSQL10.MSSQLSERVER\MSSQLSe
                     rver\SuperSocketNetLib
PSParentPath       : Microsoft.PowerShell.Core\Registry::HKEY_LOCAL_MACHINE\SOFTWA
                     RE\Microsoft\Microsoft SQL Server\MSSQL10.MSSQLSERVER\MSSQLSe
                     rver
PSChildName        : SuperSocketNetLib
PSProvider         : Microsoft.PowerShell.Core\Registry
ForceEncryption    : 0
HideInstance       : 0
Certificate        :
DisplayName        : SQL Server Network Configuration
```

Figure 5-34

As shown in Figure 5-35, you can then use the mssqlkey: drive to access the default instance registry key.

Working with Variables

The Variable: drive provides access to the variables created in Windows PowerShell. Windows PowerShell includes a set of cmdlets designed specifically to view and change variables. They are listed in Table 5-4.

When you use these particular cmdlets, you do not need to specify the Variable: drive. Windows PowerShell assumes that you are working with the Variable: drive.

You can also set the location or specify the path parameter to the Variable: drive, and work with the variables in the same manner as you would with file system objects using the `Item` cmdlets: `Get-Item`, `New-Item`, `Set-Item`, `Remove-Item`, and `Clear-Item`.

For example, you can get a list of variables available in the current shell by using one of three commands, as shown in Figure 5-36. The first command is as follows:

```
Get-Variable
```

111

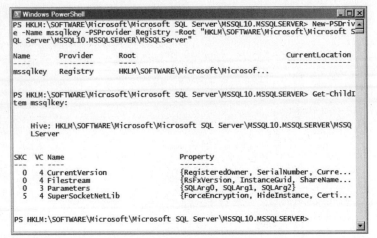

```
Windows PowerShell                                                    _ □ X
PS HKLM:\SOFTWARE\Microsoft\Microsoft SQL Server\MSSQL10.MSSQLSERVER> New-PSDriv
e -Name mssqlkey -PSProvider Registry -Root "HKLM\SOFTWARE\Microsoft\Microsoft S
QL Server\MSSQL10.MSSQLSERVER\MSSQLServer"

Name        Provider        Root                                    CurrentLocation
----        --------        ----                                    ---------------
mssqlkey    Registry        HKLM\SOFTWARE\Microsoft\Microsof...


PS HKLM:\SOFTWARE\Microsoft\Microsoft SQL Server\MSSQL10.MSSQLSERVER> Get-ChildI
tem mssqlkey:


    Hive: HKLM\SOFTWARE\Microsoft\Microsoft SQL Server\MSSQL10.MSSQLSERVER\MSSQ
    LServer


SKC  VC Name                         Property
---  -- ----                         --------
  0   4 CurrentVersion               {RegisteredOwner, SerialNumber, Curre...
  0   4 Filestream                   {RsFxVersion, InstanceGuid, ShareName...
  0   3 Parameters                   {SQLArg0, SQLArg1, SQLArg2}
  5   4 SuperSocketNetLib            {ForceEncryption, HideInstance, Certi...


PS HKLM:\SOFTWARE\Microsoft\Microsoft SQL Server\MSSQL10.MSSQLSERVER>
```

Figure 5-35

Table 5-4: cmdlets to Manage Variables

cmdlet Name	Alias	Description
Get-Variable	Gv	Gets the variables in the current console
New-Variable	Nv	Creates a new variable
Set-Variable	sv, set	Sets the value of a variable. Creates the variable if one with the requested name does not exist.
Remove-Variable	Rv	Deletes a variable and its value
Clear-Variable	Clv	Deletes the value of a variable

This is the second command you could use:

```
Set-Location Variable:
Get-ChildItem
```

Finally, the third command is as follows:

```
Get-ChildItem -Path Variable:
```

Obviously, the variable cmdlets are the easiest to use when working with variables. You will see more examples of the cmdlets later in this section.

Three types of variables are available in Windows PowerShell: automatic, preference, and user-created.

```
Windows PowerShell                                                    _ □ X
PS C:\> Get-Variable

Name                              Value
----                              -----
$                                 cls
?                                 True
^                                 cls

args                              {}
ConfirmPreference                 High
ConsoleFileName
DebugPreference                   SilentlyContinue
Error                             {Cannot find drive. A drive with name 'mssqlk...
ErrorActionPreference             Continue
ErrorView                         NormalView
ExecutionContext                  System.Management.Automation.EngineIntrinsics
false                             False
FormatEnumerationLimit            4
HOME                              C:\Users\poweruser
Host                              System.Management.Automation.Internal.Host.In...
input                             System.Collections.ArrayList+ArrayListEnumera...
MaximumAliasCount                 4096
MaximumDriveCount                 4096
MaximumErrorCount                 256
MaximumFunctionCount              4096
MaximumHistoryCount               64
MaximumVariableCount              4096
MyInvocation                      System.Management.Automation.InvocationInfo
NestedPromptLevel                 0
null
OutputEncoding                    System.Text.ASCIIEncoding
PID                               6068
PROFILE                           C:\Users\poweruser\Documents\WindowsPowerShel...
ProgressPreference                Continue
PSBoundParameters                 {}
PSCmdlet
PSCulture                         en-US
PSEmailServer
PSHOME                            C:\Windows\system32\WindowsPowerShell\v1.0\
PSMaximumReceivedDataSizePe...     2047
PSMaximumReceivedObjectSizeMB     2047
PSSessionApplicationName          wsman
PSSessionConfigurationName        http://schemas.microsoft.com/powershell/Micro...
PSTypePath
```

Figure 5-36

Automatic Variables

Automatic variables store the state information for Windows PowerShell. These variables are created and populated automatically by Windows PowerShell to return information about the execution environment. Users cannot change the value of these variables. If you try to overwrite an automatic variable — for example, $PsHome, the variable containing the installation directory for Windows PowerShell — you will get an error, as shown in Figure 5-37.

```
Set-Variable -name PsHome -value "C:\"
```

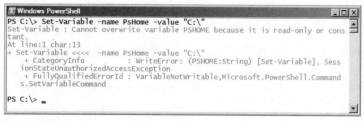

```
Windows PowerShell                                                    _ □ X
PS C:\> Set-Variable -name PsHome -value "C:\"
Set-Variable : Cannot overwrite variable PSHOME because it is read-only or cons
tant.
At line:1 char:13
+ Set-Variable <<<<  -name PsHome -value "C:\"
    + CategoryInfo          : WriteError: (PSHOME:String) [Set-Variable], Sess
  ionStateUnauthorizedAccessException
    + FullyQualifiedErrorId : VariableNotWritable,Microsoft.PowerShell.Command
  s.SetVariableCommand

PS C:\> _
```

Figure 5-37

The following list describes some of the automatic variables:

❑ $?: Contains the execution status of the last individual command or Windows PowerShell script. It contains TRUE if last command or script succeeded, and FALSE if it failed.

❑ $_: Contains the current object in a pipelined script block. You can use this variable in commands that perform an action on every object or on selected objects in a pipeline.

❑ $Error: Contains an array of error objects that represent the recent errors. The most recent error is the first in the array ($error[0]).

❑ $False: Represents FALSE in commands and scripts.

❑ $ForEach: Contains the enumerator of a foreach-object loop. You can use the properties and methods of enumerators on the value of $foreach. For example, the Current property returns the current object in the loop, and the MoveNext() method moves to the next object.

The following examples show how the MoveNext() method moves the enumerator forward inside the loop. When the loop starts, the $foreach enumerator points the first number 1. Inside the loop, the MoveNext() method moves the enumerator to the second number 2, and 2 is returned by the Current property. In the second iteration, 4 is printed. Then 6, 8, 10 are printed. Therefore, only even numbers are printed out.

```
foreach ($i in 1..10)
{

        [Void] $foreach.MoveNext()

        $foreach.Current
}
```

Figure 5-38 shows the output.

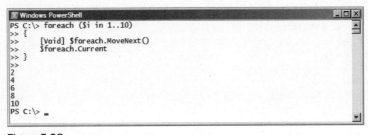

Figure 5-38

❑ $Home: Contains the full path to the user's home directory.

❑ $LastExitCode: Contains the exit code of the last native Windows program or Windows Power-Shell script that was executed. This variable does not store the result of individual commands.

❑ $PID: Contains the process identifier of the Windows PowerShell process associated with the current console or the current execution of a script. You can use $PID to distinguish among executions of a script. For example, each time the script runs, you can create a unique log file whose name ends with the $PID.

❑ $Profile: Contains the full path to the user-specific profile for the default shell. It is equivalent to %UserProfile%\My Documents\WindowsPowerShell\Microsoft.PowerShell_profile.ps1 on Windows Server 2003 and XP, or %UserProfile%\Documents\WindowsPowerShell\ Microsoft.PowerShell_profile.ps1 on Windows Vista. You can use this variable to represent the profile in commands, as described in Chapter 4.

❑ $PsHome: Contains the full path to the installation directory for Windows PowerShell.

❑ $pwd: Contains a path object that represents the current location.

❑ $True: Represents TRUE in commands and scripts.

Preference Variables

Preference variables store user preferences that control the behavior of debugging, verbosity, and errors. These variables are created by Windows PowerShell and are populated with default values. Users can change the value of a preference variable using the Set-Variable cmdlet or an assignment statement. For example, you could use either:

```
Set-Variable -name MaximumHistoryCount -value (100)
```

Or the following:

```
$MaximumHistoryCount = 100
```

Here are some of the preference variables:

❑ $DebugPreference: Determines how the current shell responds to debugging messages generated by a script, cmdlet, or provider, such as the debug messages generated by the Write-Debug cmdlet. The default value is SilentlyContinue, which suppresses the debug messages and continues with execution. Other possible values include Continue, Inquire, and Stop. They all display the debug message, but Continue allows the shell to continue with execution, Inquire asks the user whether execution should continue, and Stop stops execution.

❑ $ErrorActionPreference: This variable determines how the current shell responds to nonterminating errors generated by a script, cmdlet, or provider, such as the errors generated by the Write-Error cmdlet. It has the same four possible values as $DebugPreference. The default value is Continue, which displays the error message and continues with execution. SlientlyContinue suppresses the error message and continues with execution. Inquire displays the error message and asks the user whether execution should continue. Stop displays the error message and stops execution.

❑ $MaximumHistoryCount: Determines how many commands are saved in the command history of the current session. Only the saved commands can be retrieved. By default, 64 commands are saved. As mentioned earlier, you can change the number of commands saved using the Set-Variable cmdlet or an assignment statement.

You can use the Get-History cmdlet to display the command history and then run a command from the history list with the Invoke-History cmdlet (Figure 5-39 shows how to run the command of ID number 8):

```
Get-History
Invoke-History -id 8
```

```
Windows PowerShell                                                    _ □ x
PS C:\> Get-History

  Id CommandLine
  -- -----------
   1 (Get-Host).UI.RawUI.WindowTitle = "Windows PowerShell"
   2 Set-Location C:\
   3 Get-Variable
   4 Get-History
   5 Get-Location
   6 Get-History
   7 Get-Variable
   8 Set-Location C:\Windows\Temp
   9 Set-Location C:\
  10 cls


PS C:\> Invoke-History 8
Set-Location C:\Windows\Temp
PS C:\Windows\Temp> _
```

Figure 5-39

You can also use the up arrow key to retrieve the previous command, the down arrow key to display the next command, F7 to display the command history, F8 to find the most recent command that begins with specific characters, and F9 to find a command by history ID.

❑ $WarningPreference: Determines how the current shell responds to warning messages generated by a script, cmdlet or provider, such as the messages generated by the Write-Warning cmdlet. It has the same four possible values as $DebugPreference. The default value is Continue, which displays the error message and continues with execution. Other possible values include SilentlyContinue, Inquire and Stop. SilentlyContinue suppresses the warning message and continues with execution. Inquire displays the warning message and asks the users if execution should continue. Stop displays the warning message and stop execution.

❑ $WhatIfPreference: Determines whether WhatIf is automatically enabled for every cmdlet that supports it. When the value of $WhatIfPreference is 1, WhatIf is enabled. When the cmdlet runs, it only explains what will happen if it executes, instead of actually executing it. When the value of $WhatIfPreference is 0, Whatif is disabled and the cmdlet executes. However, the -WhatIf common parameter overrides this preference variable. You can use the -Whatif parameter of the cmdlet to enable/disable WhatIf regardless of how the $WhatIfPreference is set.

User-Created Variables

As the name suggests, users create *user-created variables*. By default, the variables that you create in the Windows PowerShell command line exist only while the Windows PowerShell window is open and are lost when you close the window. To save a variable, add it to the Windows PowerShell profile.

For example, to create a new System.DateTime variable that has the current date and time, you can use a simple assignment statement:

```
$myVar = Get-Date
$myVar = Get-Date
```

You can also use the following New-Variable cmdlet:

```
New-Variable -name myVar -value (Get-Date)
```

Alternately, you use the New-Item cmdlet:

```
New-Item -Path Variable: -name myVar -value (Get-Date)
```

What are the advantages of the New-Variable cmdlet versus the assignment and the New-Item cmdlet? Let's look at the syntax for the New-Variable cmdlet.

New-Variable: Creates a new variable

```
New-Variable [-name] <string> [[-value] <Object>] [-scope <string>] [-description
    <string>] [-option {<None> | <ReadOnly> | <Constant> | <Private> | <AllScope>}]
    [-force] [-passThru] [-whatIf] [-confirm] [<CommonParameters>]
```

As shown here, other than the name parameter that specifies the names of the variables to be changed, some parameters are not available in the assignment or the New-Item cmdlet. The following list describes them:

- -scope <string>: Determines the scope of the variable's visibility. There are three variable scopes: *global*, *local*, or *script*. Local is the default. Global scope is the scope of the current Windows PowerShell instance. Variables defined in this scope are visible to all the cmdlets, scripts, and functions executed in the Windows PowerShell instance. Local scope is the current scope. A new local scope is created whenever you run a function or a script, or start a new instance of Windows PowerShell. Script scope is created when the script is started, and removed when the script is finished. Variables in the script scope are visible only when the script is running. By default, a variable is created with local scope.

  The value can be a number relative to the current scope (0 through the number of scopes, where 0 is the current scope, and increasing the number by 1 moves to the parent scope of the current scope).

  A variable can be read by the scope where it was created, and the child scopes of the scope where it was created. It can only be changed in its scope, unless the child scopes explicitly refers to it using a script label. It cannot be read or changed in the parent scopes of its scope.

- -description <string>: Describes the purpose of the variable.

- -option <ScopedItemOptions>: Provides optional properties of the variable. Possible values include None, ReadOnly, Constant, Private and AllScope. ReadOnly defines a read-only variable that cannot be deleted or changed without using the Force parameter in Remove-Variable, Set-Variable or Clear-Variable. Constant defines a variable that cannot be deleted or changed, even with the Force parameter. It can only be removed when the Windows PowerShell instance exits. Constant is valid only when creating a new variable. Private makes the variable visible only in the scope in which it was created, not even in the child scopes. AllScope copies the variable to all scopes that are created. You don't need to refer to the variable with a script label.

- -passThru <SwitchParameter>: Passes the variable created by this cmdlet through the pipeline and allows it to be further used.

The parameters of the New-Variable cmdlet provide you with more options to manage variables than the simple assignment statement and the Item cmdlets. They enable you to define a variable in a scope that is different from the local scope. They also enable you to define a read-only variable or a constant. For example, you can define a read-only variable called rovar with a value of 1, and try to change its value by running the following commands:

```
New-Variable rovar -value 1 -option ReadOnly
$rovar=10
```

Figure 5-40 shows the read-only variable rovar is defined. The attempt to change its value fails.

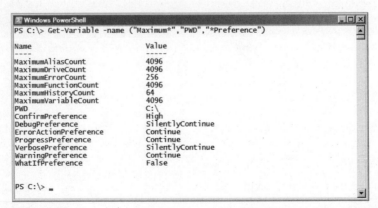

```
Windows PowerShell                                                    _□×
PS C:\> New-Variable rovar -value 1 -option ReadOnly
PS C:\> $rovar=10
Cannot overwrite variable rovar because it is read-only or constant.
At line:1 char:7
+ $rovar <<<< =10
    + CategoryInfo          : WriteError: (rovar:String) [], SessionStateUnaut
      horizedAccessException
    + FullyQualifiedErrorId : VariableNotWritable

PS C:\>
```

Figure 5-40

Other variable cmdlets are also tailored for variables and provide more options. Let's look at other variable cmdlets and their parameters.

Get-Variable: Gets the variables

```
Get-Variable [[-name] <string[]>] [-include <string[]>] [-exclude <string[]>]
    [-valueOnly] [-scope <string>] [<CommonParameters>]
```

Here we only list the parameters that are different from those in the New-Variable cmdlet:

```
-name <string[]>
```

Unlike the name parameter in the New-Variable cmdlet, this parameter accepts a string array containing variable names. Wildcards are also permitted. For example, the following command retrieves the variables beginning with "Maximum", matching "PWD", and ending with "Preference":

```
Get-Variable -name ("Maximum*","PWD","*Preference")
```

The variables are shown in Figure 5-41.

```
Windows PowerShell                                                    _□×
PS C:\> Get-Variable -name ("Maximum*","PWD","*Preference")

Name                      Value
----                      -----
MaximumAliasCount         4096
MaximumDriveCount         4096
MaximumErrorCount         256
MaximumFunctionCount      4096
MaximumHistoryCount       64
MaximumVariableCount      4096
PWD                       C:\
ConfirmPreference         High
DebugPreference           SilentlyContinue
ErrorActionPreference     Continue
ProgressPreference        Continue
VerbosePreference         SilentlyContinue
WarningPreference         Continue
WhatIfPreference          False

PS C:\> _
```

Figure 5-41

❑ `-include <string[]>`: Specifies only the items upon which the cmdlet will act, excluding all others. A string array containing names is passed, and wildcards are permitted. If the same string array is passed to this parameter and the –name parameter, the same set of variables will be returned. The only difference is the order in which the variables are returned.

❑ `-exclude <string[]>`: Excludes the specified items. A string array containing names is passed, and wildcards are permitted.

❑ `-valueOnly <SwitchParameter>`: Returns only the values of the variables.

You can filter the variables based on their optional properties. The following command uses the `Where-Object` cmdlet to filter out read-only variables whose options are equal to `ReadOnly`:

```
Get-Variable | Where-Object {$_.options -eq 'ReadOnly'}
```

As shown in Figure 5-42, the read-only variable `rovar` defined earlier was returned.

Figure 5-42

Set-Variable: Sets the value of variables or changes the properties of the variables

```
Set-Variable [-name] <string[]> [[-value] <Object>] [-include <string[]>]
    [-exclude <string[]>] [-scope <string>] [-description <string>] [-option {<None> |
    <ReadOnly> | <Constant> | <Private> | <AllScope>}] [-force] [-passThru]
    [-whatIf] [-confirm] [<CommonParameters>]
```

You have seen all the parameters in the `New-Variable` and `Get-Variable` cmdlets except the `force` parameter. This parameter forces the cmdlet to make the best attempt at setting the variable. This parameter is needed to change the value of a read-only variable. However, it has no effect on a constant. For example, to change the value of the read-only variable `rovar` that was defined earlier, run the following command:

```
 Set-Variable rovar -value 5 –force
$rovar
```

Figure 5-43 shows that the value of the read-only variable `rovar` is changed to 5.

Remove-Variable: Removes variables

```
Remove-Variable [-name] <string[]> [-include <string[]>] [-exclude <string[]>]
    [-scope <string>] [-force] [-whatIf] [-confirm] [<CommonParameters>]
```

119

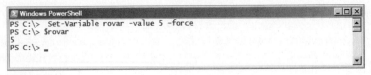

Figure 5-43

You have seen all the parameters in other cmdlets. To remove the read-only variable defined earlier, you need to use the -force parameter (see Figure 5-44):

```
Remove-Variable rovar -force
```

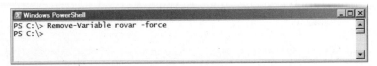

Figure 5-44

Clear-Variable: Deletes the value of variables and makes the variables null

```
Clear-Variable [-name] <string[]> [-include <string[]>] [-exclude <string[]>]
    [-scope <string>] [-force] [-passThru] [-whatIf] [-confirm] [<CommonParameters>]
```

These parameters are also available in other cmdlets. You can define a variable myVar and set its value to "hello", then use the Clear-Variable cmdlet to delete its value and make it NULL:

```
New-Variable myVar -value "hello"
$myVar
Clear-Variable myVar
$myVar
$myVar -eq $NULL # Confirm that the myVar variable has been nulled.
Remove-Variable myVar     #Tidy up
```

As shown in Figure 5-45, after the myVar variable is cleared by the Clear-Variable cmdlet, it is equal to NULL.

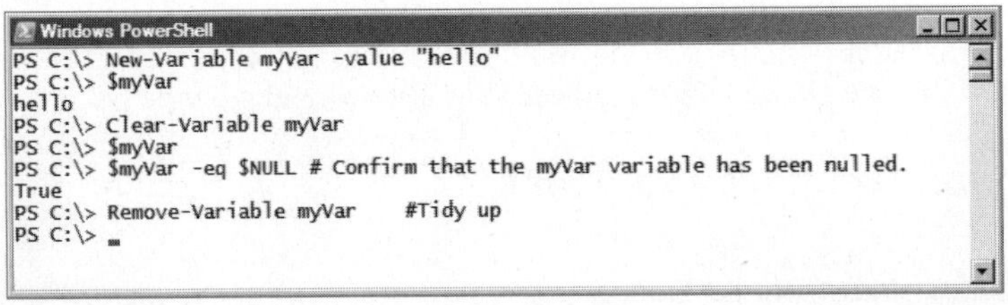

Figure 5-45

Working with Environment Variables

Besides the variables available through the Variable: drive, Windows environmental variables are also available in Windows PowerShell through the Env: drive. To get a list of the environmental variables, you can either change the current location to Env: and run `Get-ChildItem`, or you can specify the `-Path` parameter to Env: in the `Get-ChildItem` cmdlet. The following example shows the former option:

```
Set-Location Env:
Get-ChildItem
```

Here is the latter option, as shown in Figure 5-46:

```
Get-ChildItem -Path Env:
```

Figure 5-46

You can use the `Set-Item` cmdlet to change the value of an environment variable. For example, you can pre-append "C:\" to the `Path` environment variable. The following command gets the value of the `-Path` variable, uses the `Set-Item` cmdlet to append "C:\" to the beginning of the value, and then confirms the changed value:

```
(Get-Item Env:\Path).Value
Set-Item Env:\Path -Value ("C:\;" + (Get-Item Env:\Path).Value)
(Get-Item Env:\Path).Value
```

The output is shown in Figure 5-47. Note that this change is effective only in the current PowerShell window. If you need to change an environmental variable permanently, you need to use the `SetX.exe` executable.

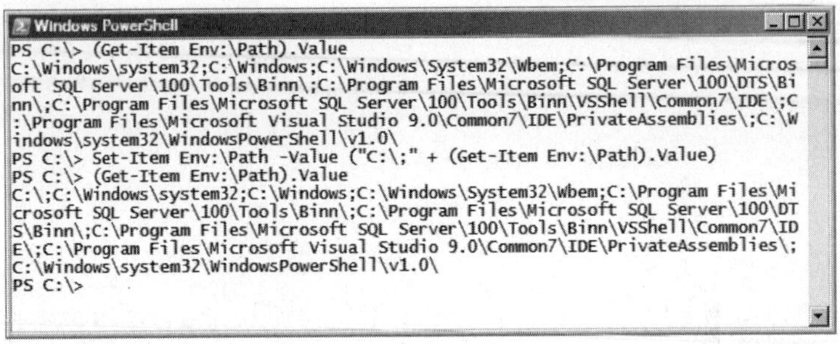

```
Windows PowerShell                                                    _ □ ×
PS C:\> (Get-Item Env:\Path).Value
C:\Windows\system32;C:\Windows;C:\Windows\System32\Wbem;C:\Program Files\Micros
oft SQL Server\100\Tools\Binn\;C:\Program Files\Microsoft SQL Server\100\DTS\Bi
nn\;C:\Program Files\Microsoft SQL Server\100\Tools\Binn\VSShell\Common7\IDE\;C
:\Program Files\Microsoft Visual Studio 9.0\Common7\IDE\PrivateAssemblies\;C:\W
indows\system32\WindowsPowerShell\v1.0\
PS C:\> Set-Item Env:\Path -Value ("C:\;" + (Get-Item Env:\Path).Value)
PS C:\> (Get-Item Env:\Path).Value
C:\;C:\Windows\system32;C:\Windows;C:\Windows\System32\Wbem;C:\Program Files\Mi
crosoft SQL Server\100\Tools\Binn\;C:\Program Files\Microsoft SQL Server\100\DT
S\Binn\;C:\Program Files\Microsoft SQL Server\100\Tools\Binn\VSShell\Common7\ID
E\;C:\Program Files\Microsoft Visual Studio 9.0\Common7\IDE\PrivateAssemblies\;
C:\Windows\system32\WindowsPowerShell\v1.0\
PS C:\>
```

Figure 5-47

Summary

This chapter demonstrated how to use Windows PowerShell cmdlets to manage system resources, including the file system, the registry, and environment variables. It also looked at the three types of variables declared in Windows PowerShell: automatic, preference, and user-created, and their different purposes. The next chapter discusses how to access event logs in PowerShell, and the various cmdlets related to event log access and handling.

6

Working with Event Logs

Chapter 5 discussed features related to navigating through the many different data stores in a consistent way. PowerShell also provides the functionality to access the event logs. This chapter discusses the various cmdlets related to accessing and handling event logs. As you know, the behaviors of hardware, software, and users on your system are recorded as events in the Windows event logs. Therefore, the event logs provide very helpful insight into what is happening on your system. For example, if your SQL Server doesn't start automatically as expected, then the Application event log would be the first place you want to look to troubleshoot the problem. However, the large volume of information contained in the event logs can sometimes make it difficult to find the particular events you are interested in.

This chapter introduces you to the available event logs and the different types of information they contain. It also shows you how to sift through the information more effectively with Windows PowerShell.

This chapter covers the following topics:

- ❑ Event Log Service

- ❑ Event Viewer

- ❑ Event logs

- ❑ Log entry types

- ❑ Exporting the event logs

- ❑ PowerShell cmdlets related to event logs

Event Log Service

The Windows Event Log service enables an application to publish, access, and process events. Events are stored in event logs, which can be routinely checked by an administrator or monitoring tool to detect certain occurrences or problems on a computer.

In Windows 2003 and Windows XP, the Event Log service uses `services.exe` (see Figure 6-1).

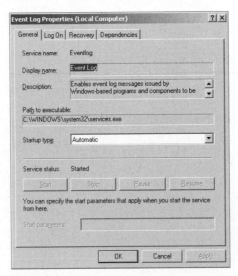

Figure 6-1

In Windows 2008 and Windows Vista, the Windows event log has been rewritten around a well-defined, structured XML log format and designated log types in order to enable applications to more precisely log events and make it easier for support technicians and developers to interpret the events. The XML representation of the event can be viewed on the Details tab in an event's properties. It is also possible to view all potential events, their structure, registered event publishers, and their configurations using the *wevtutil* utility, even before the events are fired.

Numerous types of event logs are available, including *administrative*, *operational*, *analytic*, and *debug* event log types. Analytic and debug events of high frequency are directly saved into a trace file, while administrative and operational events are infrequent enough to allow additional processing without affecting system performance, so they are delivered to the Event Log service. Events are published asynchronously to reduce the performance impact on the event publishing application. Event attributes are also much more detailed, and include `EventID`, `Level`, `Task`, `Opcode`, and `Keywords` properties.

Two main event subscribers include the Event Collector service and Task Scheduler 2.0. The Event Collector service can automatically forward event logs to other remote systems running Windows Vista, Windows Server 2008, or Windows Server 2003 R2 on a configurable schedule. Event logs can also be remotely viewed from other computers, and multiple event logs can be centrally logged and monitored without any agent and managed from a single computer. Events can also be directly associated with tasks, which run in the redesigned Task Scheduler and trigger automated actions when particular events take place.

In Windows 2008 and Vista operating systems, the Event Log service runs using `svchost.exe`, as shown in Figure 6-2.

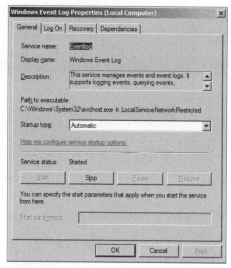

Figure 6-2

Event Viewer

Event logs on a host machine can be viewed with Microsoft's *Event Viewer*. Event Viewer is available as a Microsoft Management console snap-in, `EventVwr`.

There are two ways to launch `EventVwr`.

From the Control Panel, select Administrative Tools ➢ Event Viewer, as shown in Figure 6-3.

Alternately, you could simply click Start ➢ Run, type **eventvwr**, and click OK on Windows XP and Windows Server 2003, as shown in Figure 6-4; or you can click Start and type **eventvwr** in the Search box on Windows Vista and Windows Server 2008.

Event Logs

There are three main event logs:

- ❑ Application Log
- ❑ Security Log
- ❑ System Log

There are also other event logs dedicated for Windows PowerShell, Office Diagnostics, Office Sessions, and more in Windows XP and Windows 2003, as shown in Figure 6-5.

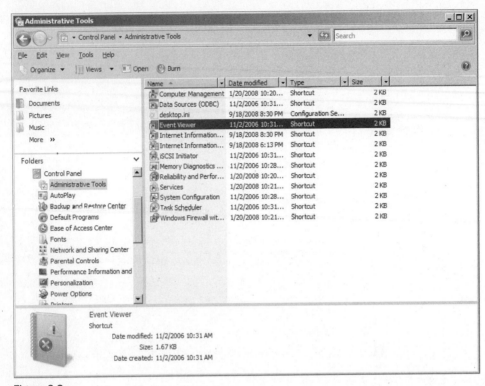

Figure 6-3

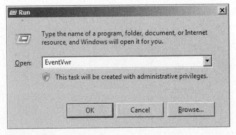

Figure 6-4

In Windows 2008 and Windows Vista operating systems, Event Viewer looks much different than in Windows XP or Windows 2003 (see Figure 6-6). Windows logs, including the Application Log, the Security Log, and the System Log, are separated from logs for other applications and services.

This chapter concentrates only on the major event logs such as Application, Security, and System:

❑ **Application log:** The Application log contains events logged by programs. For example, a database program may record a file error in the Application log. Events written to the Application log are determined by the developer(s) of the software program.

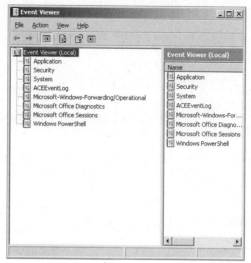

Figure 6-5

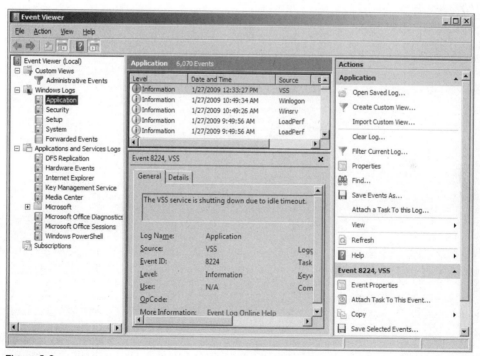

Figure 6-6

❑ **Security log**: The Security log records events such as valid and invalid logon attempts, as well as events related to resource use, such as creating, opening, or deleting files. For example, when logon auditing is enabled, an event is recorded in the Security log each time a user attempts to log on to the computer. You must be logged on either as Administrator or as a member of the Administrators group in order to turn on, use, and specify which events are recorded in the Security log.

❑ **System log**: The System log contains events logged by Windows system components. For example, if a driver fails to load during startup, an event is recorded in the System log. Windows predetermines the events that are logged by system components.

Event Viewer settings for each log can be updated, and the events it contains can be filtered using the Properties and Filter dialogs, respectively, as shown in Figure 6-7 and Figure 6-8.

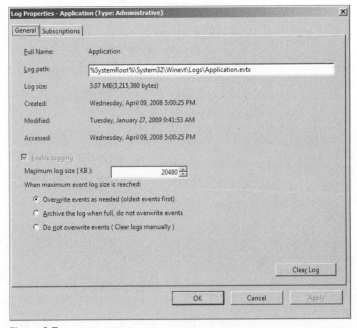

Figure 6-7

Log Entry Types

Each event log contains different types of information. The information is categorized into five entry types:

❑ **Information**: Indicates the successful operation of, for example, an application or service

❑ **Warning**: Indicates an event that may not necessarily be significant but which could indicate a current or future problem

❑ **Error**: Indicates a significant problem, such as the failure of a service to start

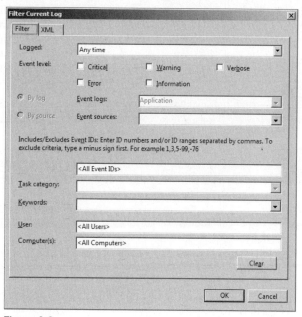

Figure 6-8

❑ **Success Audit**: An audited security access attempt that succeeds

❑ **Failure Audit**: An audited security access attempt that fails

PowerShell provides the following dedicated cmdlet for accessing the Windows event log:

```
Get-EventLog
```

To find all the log types available on the local computer, execute the following command (see Figure 6-9):

```
Get-EventLog -list
```

```
Windows PowerShell                                                      _|□|x|
PS C:\> Get-EventLog -list

Max(K) Retain OverflowAction      Entries Name
------ ------ --------------      ------- ----
20,480      0 OverwriteAsNeeded     6,070 Application
15,168      0 OverwriteAsNeeded         0 DFS Replication
20,480      0 OverwriteAsNeeded         0 HardwareEvents
   512      7 OverwriteOlder            0 Internet Explorer
20,480      0 OverwriteAsNeeded         0 Key Management Service
 8,192      0 OverwriteAsNeeded         0 Media Center
16,384      0 OverwriteAsNeeded         0 ODiag
16,384      0 OverwriteAsNeeded     1,010 OSession
20,480      0 OverwriteAsNeeded    17,529 Security
20,480      0 OverwriteAsNeeded    45,895 System
15,360      0 OverwriteAsNeeded       678 Windows PowerShell

PS C:\> _
```

Figure 6-9

To find the log types available on a remote computer, you just need to pass the remote computer name to the `ComputerName` parameter.

The following example uses the remote hostname `PowerServer3` (see Figure 6-10):

```
Get-EventLog -computerName PowerServer3 -list
```

```
Windows PowerShell                                                      _ □ x
PS C:\> Get-EventLog -computerName PowerServer3 -list

    Max(K) Retain OverflowAction          Entries Name
    ------ ------ --------------          ------- ----
       512      7 OverwriteOlder              120 ACEEventLog
    16,384      0 OverwriteAsNeeded         2,272 Application
    20,480      0 OverwriteAsNeeded             0 Microsoft-Windows-Forwarding/O...
    16,384      0 OverwriteAsNeeded             0 ODiag
    16,384      0 OverwriteAsNeeded           143 OSession
    16,384      0 OverwriteAsNeeded        12,777 Security
    16,384      0 OverwriteAsNeeded         2,552 System
    15,360      0 OverwriteAsNeeded           199 Windows PowerShell


PS C:\> _
```

Figure 6-10

In other examples of `Get-EventLog` shown later in this chapter, you can simply add "-computerName PowerServer3" to see the results on the remote computer PowerServer3.

If you would like to query all the entries in the Application event log or the Windows PowerShell log, all you have to do is pass the log name as a parameter. Execute the following commands, as shown in Figure 6-11 and Figure 6-12:

```
Get-EventLog -LogName "Application"
Get-EventLog -LogName "Windows PowerShell"
```

```
Windows PowerShell                                                      _ □ x
PS C:\> Get-EventLog -LogName "Application"

    Index Time             EntryType    Source               InstanceID Message
    ----- ----             ---------    ------               ---------- -------
     6727 Jan 27 12:33     Information  VSS                        8224 The VSS...
     6726 Jan 27 10:49     Information  Winlogon             3221229476 The Win...
     6725 Jan 27 10:49     Information  Microsoft-Windows...      10002 The des...
     6724 Jan 27 09:49     Information  LoadPerf             1073742824 The des...
     6723 Jan 27 09:49     Information  LoadPerf             1073742825 The des...
     6722 Jan 27 09:46     Information  SecurityCenter                1 The Win...
     6721 Jan 27 09:44     Information  Windows Search Se... 1073742827 The Win...
     6720 Jan 27 09:44     Information  ESENT                       302 Windows...
     6719 Jan 27 09:44     Information  ESENT                       301 Windows...
     6718 Jan 27 09:44     Information  ESENT                       300 Windows...
     6717 Jan 27 09:44     Information  ESENT                       102 Windows...
     6716 Jan 27 09:44     Information  VMware Server              1103 Virtual...
     6715 Jan 27 09:43     Error        WinMgmt              3221225482 The des...
     6714 Jan 27 09:43     Information  Microsoft-Windows...          1 The des...
     6713 Jan 27 09:43     Information  Microsoft-Windows...          1 The des...
     6712 Jan 27 09:42     Information  Windows Search Se... 1073742827 The Win...
```

Figure 6-11

As you know now, the `Get-Member` cmdlet provides all the methods and properties of any cmdlet. Therefore, you could find information about `Get-Eventlog` by executing the following command (see Figure 6-13):

```
Get-Eventlog -LogName "Application" -newest 1 | Get-Member | sort MemberType
```

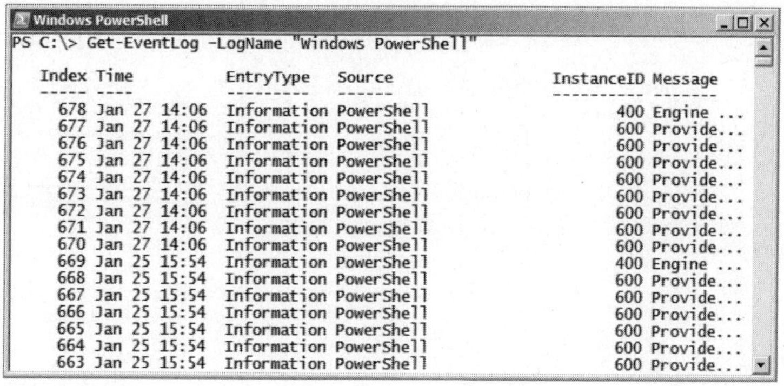

```
PS C:\> Get-EventLog -LogName "Windows PowerShell"

  Index Time          EntryType   Source                 InstanceID Message
  ----- ----          ---------   ------                 ---------- -------
    678 Jan 27 14:06  Information PowerShell                    400 Engine ...
    677 Jan 27 14:06  Information PowerShell                    600 Provide...
    676 Jan 27 14:06  Information PowerShell                    600 Provide...
    675 Jan 27 14:06  Information PowerShell                    600 Provide...
    674 Jan 27 14:06  Information PowerShell                    600 Provide...
    673 Jan 27 14:06  Information PowerShell                    600 Provide...
    672 Jan 27 14:06  Information PowerShell                    600 Provide...
    671 Jan 27 14:06  Information PowerShell                    600 Provide...
    670 Jan 27 14:06  Information PowerShell                    600 Provide...
    669 Jan 25 15:54  Information PowerShell                    400 Engine ...
    668 Jan 25 15:54  Information PowerShell                    600 Provide...
    667 Jan 25 15:54  Information PowerShell                    600 Provide...
    666 Jan 25 15:54  Information PowerShell                    600 Provide...
    665 Jan 25 15:54  Information PowerShell                    600 Provide...
    664 Jan 25 15:54  Information PowerShell                    600 Provide...
    663 Jan 25 15:54  Information PowerShell                    600 Provide...
```

Figure 6-12

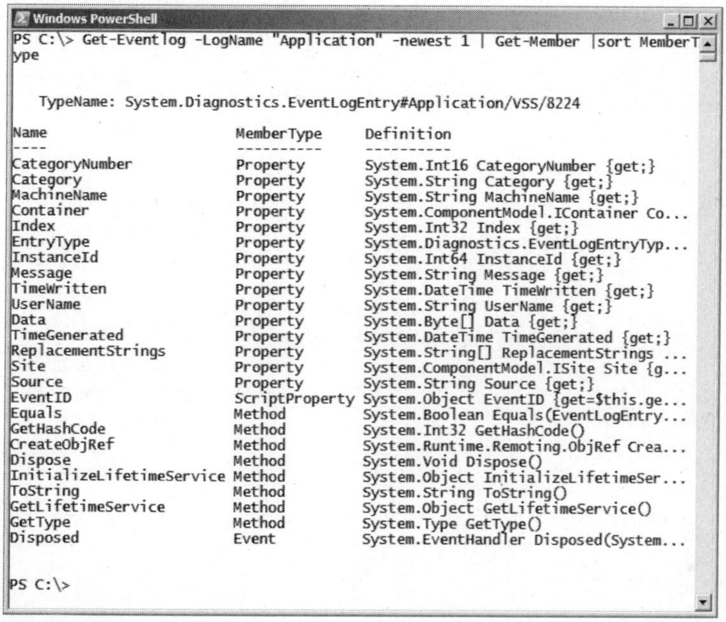

```
PS C:\> Get-Eventlog -LogName "Application" -newest 1 | Get-Member |sort MemberT
ype


   TypeName: System.Diagnostics.EventLogEntry#Application/VSS/8224

Name                      MemberType     Definition
----                      ----------     ----------
CategoryNumber            Property       System.Int16 CategoryNumber {get;}
Category                  Property       System.String Category {get;}
MachineName               Property       System.String MachineName {get;}
Container                 Property       System.ComponentModel.IContainer Co...
Index                     Property       System.Int32 Index {get;}
EntryType                 Property       System.Diagnostics.EventLogEntryTyp...
InstanceId                Property       System.Int64 InstanceId {get;}
Message                   Property       System.String Message {get;}
TimeWritten               Property       System.DateTime TimeWritten {get;}
UserName                  Property       System.String UserName {get;}
Data                      Property       System.Byte[] Data {get;}
TimeGenerated             Property       System.DateTime TimeGenerated {get;}
ReplacementStrings        Property       System.String[] ReplacementStrings ...
Site                      Property       System.ComponentModel.ISite Site {g...
Source                    Property       System.String Source {get;}
EventID                   ScriptProperty System.Object EventID {get=$this.ge...
Equals                    Method         System.Boolean Equals(EventLogEntry...
GetHashCode               Method         System.Int32 GetHashCode()
CreateObjRef              Method         System.Runtime.Remoting.ObjRef Crea...
Dispose                   Method         System.Void Dispose()
InitializeLifetimeService Method         System.Object InitializeLifetimeSer...
ToString                  Method         System.String ToString()
GetLifetimeService        Method         System.Object GetLifetimeService()
GetType                   Method         System.Type GetType()
Disposed                  Event          System.EventHandler Disposed(System...


PS C:\>
```

Figure 6-13

You can find all the types of information available by querying the `EntryType` as follows (see Figure 6-14, Figure 6-15, and Figure 6-16).

```
Get-EventLog -LogName "Application" | Select-Object EntryType -unique | Format-
Table -auto
```

Entry type 0 means the type information was not available.

```
Get-EventLog -LogName "System" -computername PowerServer3 | Select-Object
EntryType -unique | Format-Table -auto
```

```
Get-EventLog -LogName "Windows PowerShell" | Select-Object EntryType -unique |
Format-Table -auto
```

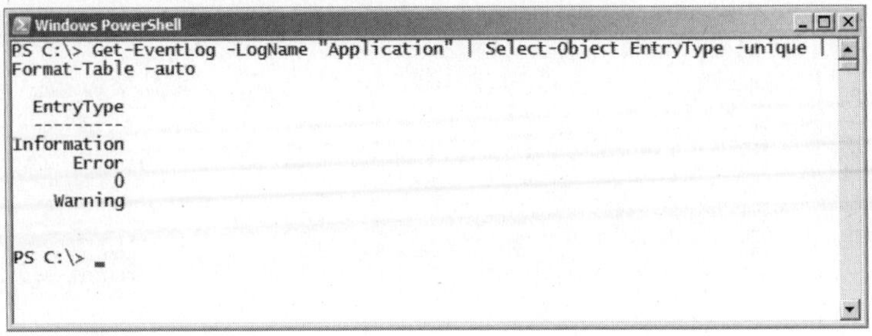

```
Windows PowerShell                                           _ □ x
PS C:\> Get-EventLog -LogName "Application" | Select-Object EntryType -unique |
Format-Table -auto

    EntryType
    ---------
Information
      Error
          0
    Warning


PS C:\> _
```

Figure 6-14

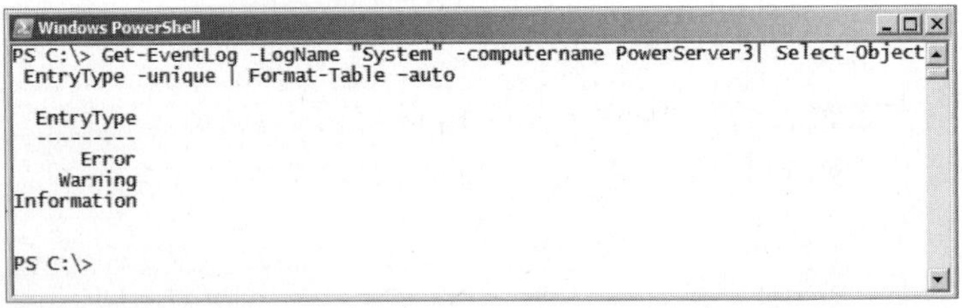

```
Windows PowerShell                                           _ □ x
PS C:\> Get-EventLog -LogName "System" -computername PowerServer3| Select-Object
  EntryType -unique | Format-Table -auto

    EntryType
    ---------
        Error
      Warning
Information


PS C:\>
```

Figure 6-15

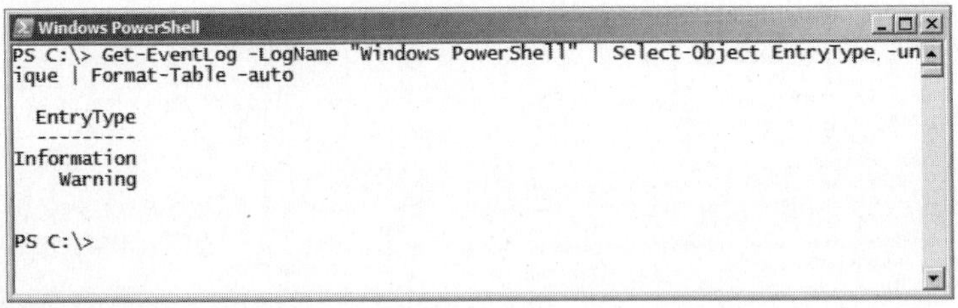

```
Windows PowerShell                                           _ □ x
PS C:\> Get-EventLog -LogName "Windows PowerShell" | Select-Object EntryType. -un
ique | Format-Table -auto

    EntryType
    ---------
Information
    Warning


PS C:\>
```

Figure 6-16

Browsing through a lot of lines in an event log is tedious. With the Get-EventLog cmdlet, you can filter the entries that you would like to see. One of the parameters in the Get-EventLog cmdlet is newest.

As its name suggests, the newest parameter shows the newest entries in the event log. Execute the following command to show the newest ten entries from the event log (see Figure 6-17):

```
Get-EventLog -LogName "application" -newest 10
```

You could apply all the formatting techniques that you learned in Chapter 2 on this cmdlet, such as the Where-Object cmdlet. For example, assume that you want to see all SQL Server–related errors in the Application event log. You could achieve that by using the Where-Object cmdlet, as shown here (see Figure 6-18):

```
Get-EventLog -LogName "Application" -computername PowerServer3 | Where-Object
{$_.Source -like "*SQL*"} | Where-Object {$_.EntryType -eq "Error"}
```

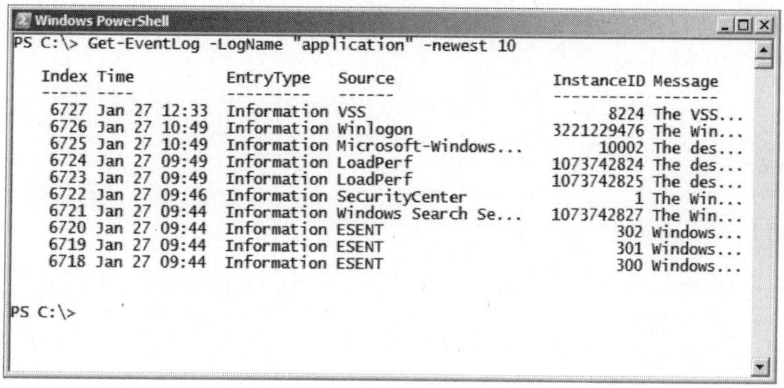

```
Windows PowerShell
PS C:\> Get-EventLog -LogName "application" -newest 10

   Index Time          EntryType   Source                 InstanceID Message
   ----- ----          ---------   ------                 ---------- -------
    6727 Jan 27 12:33  Information VSS                          8224 The VSS...
    6726 Jan 27 10:49  Information Winlogon               3221229476 The Win...
    6725 Jan 27 10:49  Information Microsoft-Windows...        10002 The des...
    6724 Jan 27 09:49  Information LoadPerf               1073742824 The des...
    6723 Jan 27 09:49  Information LoadPerf               1073742825 The des...
    6722 Jan 27 09:46  Information SecurityCenter                  1 The Win...
    6721 Jan 27 09:44  Information Windows Search Se...   1073742827 The Win...
    6720 Jan 27 09:44  Information ESENT                         302 Windows...
    6719 Jan 27 09:44  Information ESENT                         301 Windows...
    6718 Jan 27 09:44  Information ESENT                         300 Windows...

PS C:\>
```

Figure 6-17

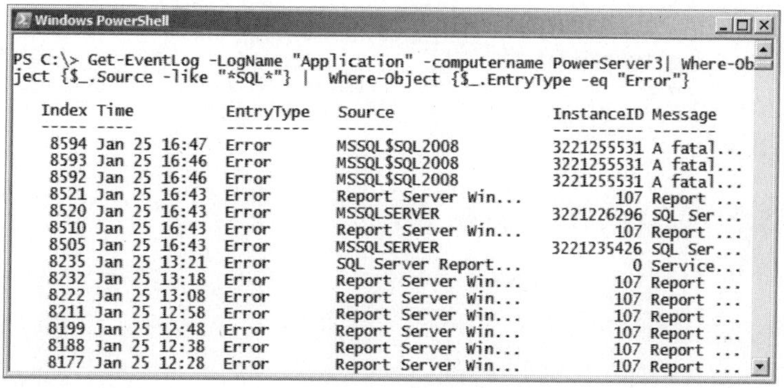

```
Windows PowerShell

PS C:\> Get-EventLog -LogName "Application" -computername PowerServer3| Where-Ob
ject {$_.Source -like "*SQL*"} |  Where-Object {$_.EntryType -eq "Error"}

   Index Time          EntryType   Source                 InstanceID Message
   ----- ----          ---------   ------                 ---------- -------
    8594 Jan 25 16:47  Error       MSSQL$SQL2008          3221255531 A fatal...
    8593 Jan 25 16:46  Error       MSSQL$SQL2008          3221255531 A fatal...
    8592 Jan 25 16:46  Error       MSSQL$SQL2008          3221255531 A fatal...
    8521 Jan 25 16:43  Error       Report Server Win...          107 Report ...
    8520 Jan 25 16:43  Error       MSSQLSERVER            3221226296 SQL Ser...
    8510 Jan 25 16:43  Error       Report Server Win...          107 Report ...
    8505 Jan 25 16:43  Error       MSSQLSERVER            3221235426 SQL Ser...
    8235 Jan 25 13:21  Error       SQL Server Report...            0 Service...
    8232 Jan 25 13:18  Error       Report Server Win...          107 Report ...
    8222 Jan 25 13:08  Error       Report Server Win...          107 Report ...
    8211 Jan 25 12:58  Error       Report Server Win...          107 Report ...
    8199 Jan 25 12:48  Error       Report Server Win...          107 Report ...
    8188 Jan 25 12:38  Error       Report Server Win...          107 Report ...
    8177 Jan 25 12:28  Error       Report Server Win...          107 Report ...
```

Figure 6-18

You could also use date ranges and sort the results. For example, the following will find all the error messages generated on January 27, 2009 (see Figure 6-19):

```
Get-EventLog -LogName "Application" | Where-Object {$_.EntryType -eq "Error"} |
Where-Object {($_.TimeGenerated -gt "2009/01/27") -and ($_.TimeGenerated -lt
"2009/01/28")} | Sort-Object TimeGenerated -descending | Format-Table -auto
```

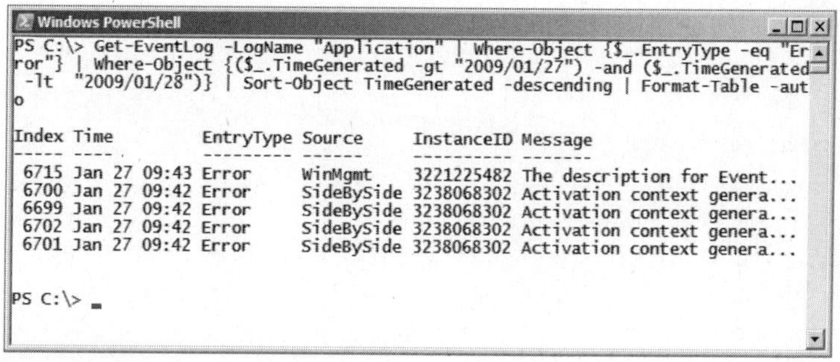

```
Windows PowerShell
PS C:\> Get-EventLog -LogName "Application" | Where-Object {$_.EntryType -eq "Er
ror"} | Where-Object {($_.TimeGenerated -gt "2009/01/27") -and ($_.TimeGenerated
 -lt  "2009/01/28")} | Sort-Object TimeGenerated -descending | Format-Table -aut
o

Index Time         EntryType Source     InstanceID Message
----- ----         --------- ------     ---------- -------
 6715 Jan 27 09:43 Error     WinMgmt    3221225482 The description for Event...
 6700 Jan 27 09:42 Error     SideBySide 3238068302 Activation context genera...
 6699 Jan 27 09:42 Error     SideBySide 3238068302 Activation context genera...
 6702 Jan 27 09:42 Error     SideBySide 3238068302 Activation context genera...
 6701 Jan 27 09:42 Error     SideBySide 3238068302 Activation context genera...

PS C:\> _
```

Figure 6-19

If you want to see the error messages that occurred on the remote computer PowerServer3 in the month of January, you can run this command (see Figure 6-20):

```
Get-EventLog -ComputerName PowerServer3 -LogName "Application" | Where-Object
{$_.EntryType -eq "Error"} | Where-Object {($_.TimeGenerated -gt "2009/01/01") -and
($_.TimeGenerated -lt "2009/01/31")} | Sort-Object TimeGenerated -descending |
Format-Table -auto
```

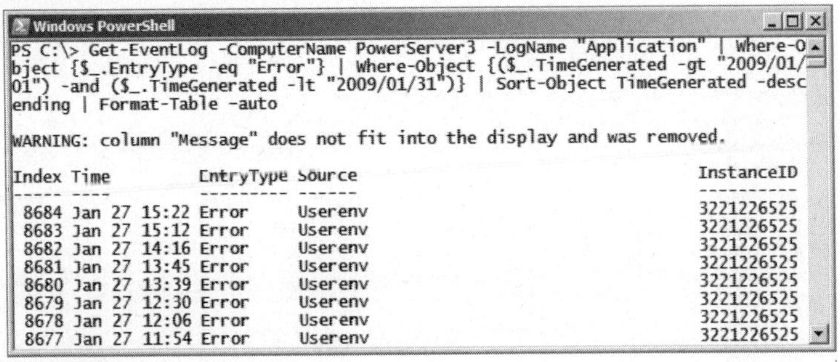

Figure 6-20

Exporting the event logs

You can export event log entries to an XML or CSV file or a simple text file for archiving or forwarding purposes.

Let's assume that you want to see all the application errors related to SQL Server and export them to a .csv file. The following command would do that for you (see Figure 6-21). The cmdlet that you are going to use is Get-EventLog. Get-EventLog cmdlet hands the collection to the next cmdlet, Where-Object. In turn, Where-Object filters out any item namely "*SQL*." After it finishes filtering, Where-Object hands the remaining item to another Where-Object. The second Where-Object filters the collection further and hands the remaining items to the Export-Csv object.

```
Get-EventLog -LogName "Application" -computername PowerServer3 | Where-Object
{$_.Source -like "*SQL*"} | Where-Object {$_.EntryType -eq "Error"} | Export-Csv
C:\PowerServer3_sqlevents.csv
```

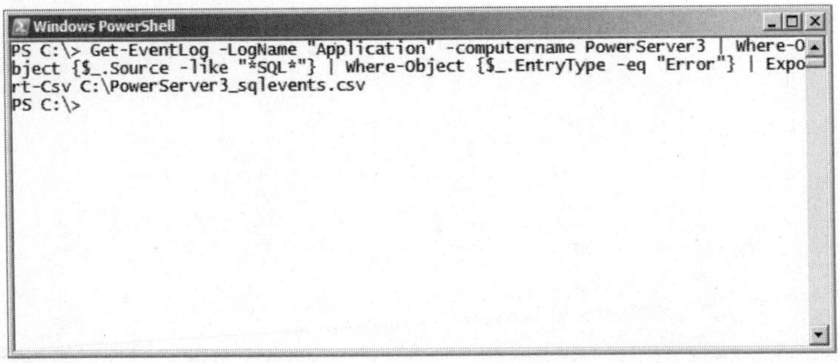

Figure 6-21

The `C:\PowerServer3_sqlevents.csv` file can be opened in Excel, as shown in Figure 6-22.

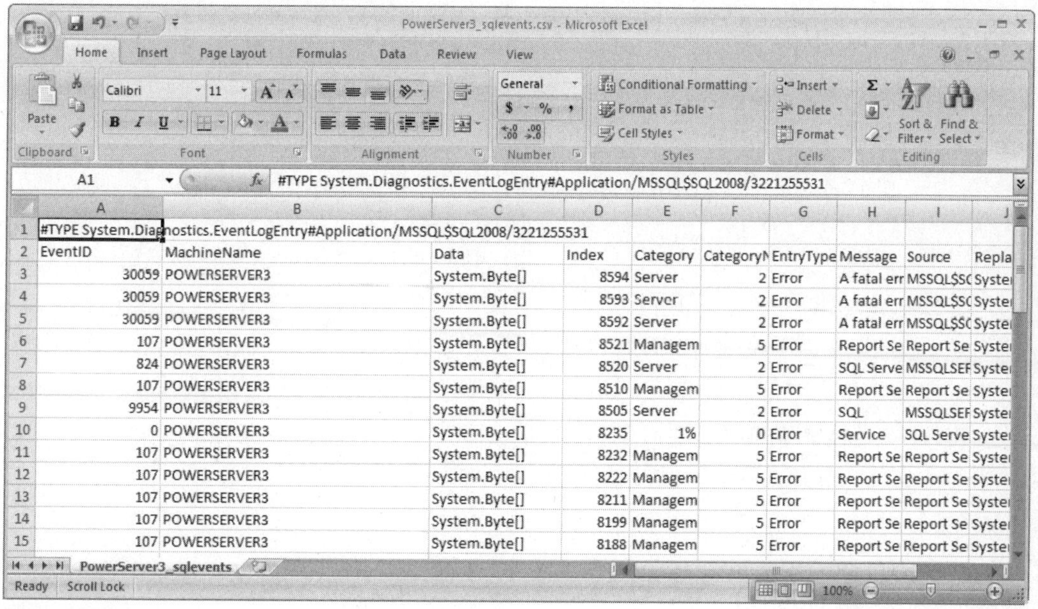

Figure 6-22

You could export the same SQL Server events to an XML file, as shown in Figure 6-23. Here, you use the cmdlet `Export-Clixml` to export the output of all the cmdlets before the pipeline:

```
Get-EventLog -LogName "Application" -computername PowerServer3 | Where-Object
{$_.Source -like "*SQL*"} | Where-Object {$_.EntryType -eq "Error"} | Export-Clixml
C:\PowerServer3_sqlevents.xml
```

```
Windows PowerShell
PS C:\> Get-EventLog -LogName "Application" -computername PowerServer3 | Where-O
bject {$_.Source -like "*SQL*"} | Where-Object {$_.EntryType -eq "Error"} | Expo
rt-Clixml C:\PowerServer3_sqlevents.xml
PS C:\>
```

Figure 6-23

The `PowerServer3_sqlevents.xml` file can be opened with any browser that is compatible with XML browsing (see Figure 6-24).

Figure 6-24

You could also export the file to a simple text file, as shown in Figure 6-25. Here you are using the cmdlet `Out-File` to export the output of all the cmdlets before the pipeline:

```
Get-EventLog -LogName "Application" -computername PowerServer3 | Where-Object
{$_.Source -like "*SQL*"} | Where-Object {$_.EntryType -eq "Error"} | Out-File
C:\PowerServer3_sqlevents.txt
```

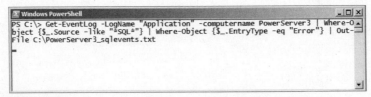

Figure 6-25

You can open the `sqlevents.txt` file using Notepad, as shown in Figure 6-26.

PowerShell cmdlets Related to event log

The most commonly used cmdlets related to event logging are as follows:

- ❑ `Get-EventLog`
- ❑ `Clear-EventLog`
- ❑ `Show-EventLog`
- ❑ `Limit-EventLog`
- ❑ `Write-EventLog`

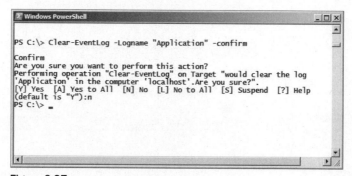

```
PowerServer3_sqlevents.txt - Notepad

File  Edit  Format  View  Help

Index  Time         EntryType    Source              InstanceID Message
-----  ----         ---------    ------              ---------- -------
 8594  Jan 25 16:47 Error        MSSQL$SQL2008       3221255531 A fatal...
 8593  Jan 25 16:46 Error        MSSQL$SQL2008       3221255531 A fatal...
 8592  Jan 25 16:46 Error        MSSQL$SQL2008       3221255531 A fatal...
 8521  Jan 25 16:43 Error        Report Server Win...        107 Report ...
 8520  Jan 25 16:43 Error        MSSQLSERVER         3221226296 SQL Ser...
 8510  Jan 25 16:43 Error        Report Server Win...        107 Report ...
 8505  Jan 25 16:43 Error        MSSQLSERVER         3221235426 SQL Ser...
 8235  Jan 25 13:21 Error        SQL Server Report...          0 Service...
 8232  Jan 25 13:18 Error        Report Server Win...        107 Report ...
 8222  Jan 25 13:08 Error        Report Server Win...        107 Report ...
 8211  Jan 25 12:58 Error        Report Server Win...        107 Report ...
 8199  Jan 25 12:48 Error        Report Server Win...        107 Report ...
 8188  Jan 25 12:38 Error        Report Server Win...        107 Report ...
 8177  Jan 25 12:28 Error        Report Server Win...        107 Report ...
 8166  Jan 25 12:18 Error        Report Server Win...        107 Report ...
 8155  Jan 25 12:08 Error        Report Server Win...        107 Report ...
 8143  Jan 25 11:58 Error        Report Server Win...        107 Report ...
 8123  Jan 25 11:48 Error        Report Server Win...        107 Report ...
 8093  Jan 25 11:38 Error        Report Server Win...        107 Report ...
```

Figure 6-26

Windows PowerShell also provides two other cmdlets, New-EventLog and Remove-EventLog, which are widely used for creating custom event logs. These cmdlets are not discussed here because they are not useful for SQL Server administration.

The Clear-EventLog cmdlet deletes all of the entries from the specified event logs on either the local computer or remote computers.

The next example attempts to clear the events from the Application event log using the -confirm switch. Execute the following command, as shown in Figure 6-27. Select "No" when asked for confirmation.

```
Clear-EventLog -Logname "Application" -confirm
```

```
Windows PowerShell

PS C:\> Clear-EventLog -Logname "Application" -confirm

Confirm
Are you sure you want to perform this action?
Performing operation "Clear-EventLog" on Target "would clear the log
'Application' in the computer 'localhost'.Are you sure?".
[Y] Yes  [A] Yes to All  [N] No  [L] No to All  [S] Suspend  [?] Help
(default is "Y"):n
PS C:\>
```

Figure 6-27

Now clear the event log related to Windows PowerShell using the -confirm switch. This time, select "Yes" when it prompts for confirmation, as shown in Figure 6-28.

Now use Event Viewer to see whether all the information in the Windows PowerShell event log has been cleared. Launch EventVwr using one of the methods illustrated in the beginning of this chapter (see Figure 6-29).

Another useful cmdlet is Show-EventLog, which when executed opens the EventVwr on the local machine. If you want to see the event logs of a remote computer using EventVwr, you could execute the

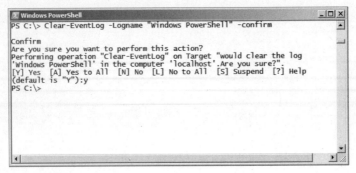

Figure 6-28

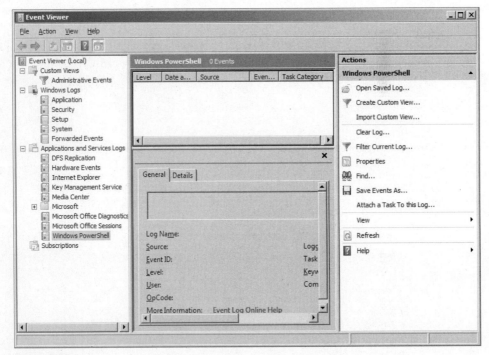

Figure 6-29

Show-EventLog cmdlet as shown in the following example. Here, you are going to see the event logs of the server PowerServer3 opened by the cmdlet (see Figure 6-30):

```
Show-EventLog -computername PowerServer3
```

The Write-EventLog cmdlet writes an event to an event log. In order to write the event to an event log, you need to know the event source and the log type.

The -Source option specifies the event source, which is typically the name of the application that is writing the event to the log. You could use the existing source available and write the log to that event or create a new source using the New-EventLog cmdlet.

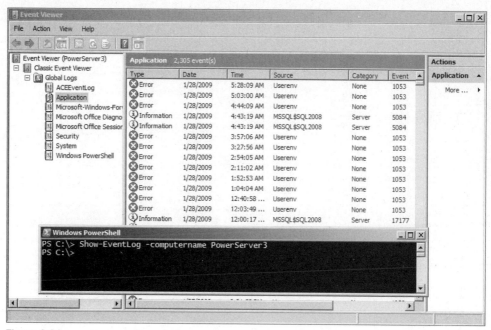

Figure 6-30

The following example shows all the sources available on the current host machine (see Figure 6-31):

```
Get-EventLog -logname "Application" | Select-Object Source -unique
```

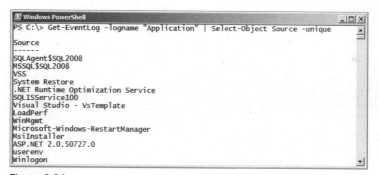

Figure 6-31

In the next example, you write the message "SQL Server 2008 administration with Windows PowerShell" under the Application event log using the event source Userenv. This message is going to be inserted in the log as an Information entry type (see Figure 6-32).

```
Write-EventLog -logname "Application" -source userenv -eventID 3001 -entrytype
Information -message "SQL Server 2008 administration with Windows PowerShell"
-category 1 -rawdata 10,20
```

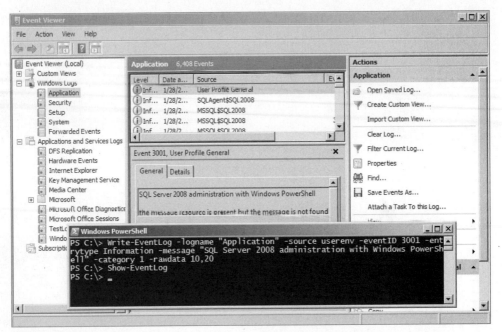

Figure 6-32

You can limit the size of the event log retention period using the `Limit-EventLog` cmdlet. The following command keeps the log entries for seven days and overwrites the log when it is overflowing:

```
Limit-EventLog -logname "Windows PowerShell" -overflowaction OverwriteOlder -
retention 7
```

Summary

This chapter discussed event logs and types of event entries. It showed you how to query different event logs and get the information you need based on log names, entry types, and dates. It also demonstrated how to export event logs into files. Finally, you learned how to clear an event log, write to an event log, and launch Event Viewer using the `Show-EventLog` cmdlet.

Chapter 8 discusses the WMI method of accessing the event logs in detail.

## 7

Working with Windows Services and Processes

This chapter looks at the cmdlets related to Windows services and processes in detail. It covers the following topics:

❏ Windows services

❏ Windows PowerShell and Windows services

❏ Windows processes

❏ Windows PowerShell and Windows processes

What Is a Windows Service?

A Windows service is a long-running executable that performs specific functions and is designed not to require user intervention. By definition, it's a program that runs invisibly in the background. These services load and start running whether or not anyone logs into the computer, unlike a program that is launched from the Startup folder under All Programs.

Many of the Windows services start when the Microsoft Windows operating system is booted, and run in the background as long as Windows is running. They are similar in concept to a UNIX daemon. They appear in the Processes list in Windows Task Manager, most often with a username of SYSTEM, LOCAL SERVICE, or NETWORK SERVICE, though not all processes with the SYSTEM username are services.

Once a service is installed, it can be managed by launching Services from the Windows Control Panel ➤ Administrative Tools, or by selecting Start ➤ Run and typing **Services.msc**. The Services window shown in Figure 7-1 will open.

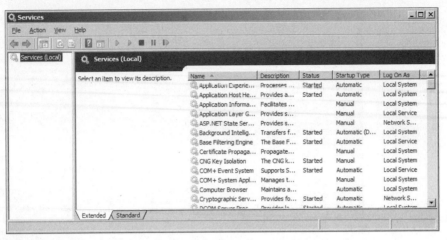

Figure 7-1

As shown in Figure 7-1, the Services management console provides a brief description of each service function and displays the path to the service executable, its current status, its startup type, dependencies, and the account under which the service is running. It enables users to do the following:

❑ Start, stop, pause, or restart services

❑ Specify service parameters

❑ Change the startup type, which includes Automatic, Manual, Disabled, and Automatic (Delayed):

    ❑ **Automatic**: Starts the services at system logon

    ❑ **Manual**: Starts a service as required or when called from an application (according to definition, but only some of the time in practice, depending on the service)

    ❑ **Disabled**: Completely disables the service and prevents it and its dependencies from running

    ❑ **Automatic (Delayed)**: A new startup type introduced in Windows Vista that waits for the system to complete the booting process and finish the initial busy operations

❑ Change the account under which the service logs on

❑ Configure recovery options upon service failure

❑ Export the list of services as a text file or a CSV file

If you want a quick visual of which items are running or stopped, you can also use the MS Configuration Utility by selecting Start ➤ Run and typing **msconfig.exe**. However, the information provided is limited, as shown in Figure 7-2.

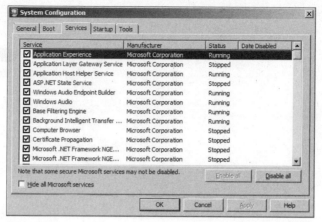

Figure 7-2

Windows PowerShell and Windows Services

Windows PowerShell provides a list of cmdlets that can be used to create, manage, and delete Windows services.

To find all the cmdlets that are related to Windows services, execute the following command (see Figure 7-3):

```
Get-Command -CommandType cmdlet *service*
```

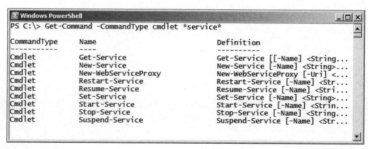

Figure 7-3

The following Windows PowerShell cmdlets are related to accessing Windows services:

❑ Get-Service

❑ New-Service

❑ New-WebServiceProxy

- ❑ Restart-Service
- ❑ Resume-Service
- ❑ Set-Service
- ❑ Start-Service
- ❑ Stop-Service
- ❑ Suspend-Service

The following sections describe some of the commonly used and useful cmdlets related to Windows services.

Get-Service

The Get-Service cmdlet lists all the services on a local or remote computer. For example, you can find all the running services that start with SQL by executing the following command (see Figure 7-4).

```
Get-Service -DisplayName "SQL*" -Computername PowerServer3 | Where-Object
{$_.status -eq "Running"}
```

As shown by the results in Figure 7-4, you can see that all the services whose display name starts with SQL are listed from the remote computer PowerServer3.

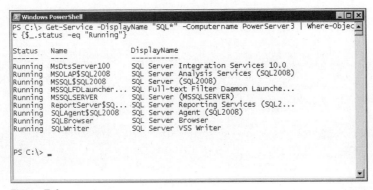

Figure 7-4

If you want to see all the services whose name begins with "SQL" but exclude any service name that has the word "Writer" from the output, you can use the -Exclude parameter as shown here (see Figure 7-5):

```
Get-Service  -Include "SQL*" -Exclude "*Writer*" -ComputerName PowerServer3 |
Where-Object {$_.status -eq "Running"}
```

Now let's list all the properties associated with the Get-Service cmdlet. Execute the following Get-Service cmdlet with the Get-Member cmdlet (see Figure 7-6):

```
Get-Service | Get-Member -MemberType properties
```

```
Windows PowerShell                                                      _ □ ×
PS C:\> Get-Service  -Include "SQL*" -Exclude "*Writer*" -ComputerName PowerServ
er3 | Where-Object {$_.status -eq "Running"}

Status    Name              DisplayName
------    ----              -----------
Running   SQLAgent$SQL2008  SQL Server Agent (SQL2008)
Running   SQLBrowser        SQL Server Browser


PS C:\>
```

Figure 7-5

```
Windows PowerShell                                                      _ □ ×
PS C:\> Get-Service | Get-Member -MemberType properties


   TypeName: System.ServiceProcess.ServiceController

Name                   MemberType     Definition
----                   ----------     ----------
Name                   AliasProperty  Name = ServiceName
CanPauseAndContinue    Property       System.Boolean CanPauseAndContinue {get;}
CanShutdown            Property       System.Boolean CanShutdown {get;}
CanStop                Property       System.Boolean CanStop {get;}
Container              Property       System.ComponentModel.IContainer Container...
DependentServices      Property       System.ServiceProcess.ServiceController[] ...
DisplayName            Property       System.String DisplayName {get;set;}
MachineName            Property       System.String MachineName {get;set;}
ServiceHandle          Property       System.Runtime.InteropServices.SafeHandle ...
ServiceName            Property       System.String ServiceName {get;set;}
ServicesDependedOn     Property       System.ServiceProcess.ServiceController[] ...
ServiceType            Property       System.ServiceProcess.ServiceType ServiceT...
Site                   Property       System.ComponentModel.ISite Site {get;set;}
Status                 Property       System.ServiceProcess.ServiceControllerSta...

PS C:\> _
```

Figure 7-6

Now list all the methods associated with the Get-Service cmdlet. Execute the following Get-Service cmdlet with the Get-Member cmdlet (see Figure 7-7):

```
Get-Service | Get-Member -MemberType methods
```

```
Windows PowerShell                                                      _ □ ×
PS C:\> Get-Service | Get-Member -MemberType methods


   TypeName: System.ServiceProcess.ServiceController

Name                       MemberType Definition
----                       ---------- ----------
Close                      Method     System.Void Close()
Continue                   Method     System.Void Continue()
CreateObjRef               Method     System.Runtime.Remoting.ObjRef CreateOb...
Dispose                    Method     System.Void Dispose()
Equals                     Method     System.Boolean Equals(Object obj)
ExecuteCommand             Method     System.Void ExecuteCommand(Int32 command)
GetHashCode                Method     System.Int32 GetHashCode()
GetLifetimeService         Method     System.Object GetLifetimeService()
GetType                    Method     System.Type GetType()
InitializeLifetimeService  Method     System.Object InitializeLifetimeService()
Pause                      Method     System.Void Pause()
Refresh                    Method     System.Void Refresh()
Start                      Method     System.Void Start(), System.Void Start(...
Stop                       Method     System.Void Stop()
ToString                   Method     System.String ToString()
WaitForStatus              Method     System.Void WaitForStatus(ServiceContro...
```

Figure 7-7

You can start and stop a Windows service using the methods available for `Get-Service`. The following example displays the status of the Windows service `"aspnet_state"` and then tries to start and then stop the service (see Figure 7-8):

```
(Get-Service -Name "aspnet_state").status
(Get-Service -Name "aspnet_state").start()
(Get-Service -Name "aspnet_state").status
Start-Sleep 5
(Get-Service -Name "aspnet_state").status
(Get-Service -Name "aspnet_state").stop()
(Get-Service -Name "aspnet_state").status
Start-Sleep 5
(Get-Service -Name "aspnet_state").status
```

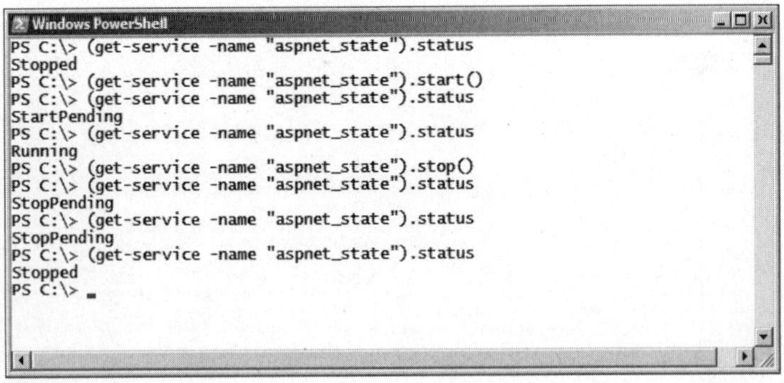

Figure 7-8

From the preceding snapshot, you can see that we got the status of the service using properties, and started and stopped the service using the `start()` and `stop()` methods, respectively. You can also see the status changing from "StartPending" and "StopPending" to "Running" and "Stopped", respectively.

Stop-Service

Instead of using the methods from `Get-Service` to stop a service, you could use the cmdlet `Stop-Service`.

Assume that you want to stop the aspnet_state service using the `stop-service` cmdlet. The following example shows the status of the service, stops the service, and then shows the status of the service again (see Figure 7-9).

```
Get-Service -Name aspnet_state
Stop-Service -Name aspnet_state
Get-Service -Name aspnet_state
```

Now assume that you want to stop all the SQL Server–related services on the local machine. You can use the `Get-Service` and `Stop-Service` cmdlets together. The following steps lead to stopping all running SQL-related services. It would be a disaster if you ran the `Stop-Service` cmdlet on a production machine, so you can use the `-WhatIf` switch parameter with the `Stop-Service` cmdlet and preview the results (see Figure 7-10):

```
Get-Service -DisplayName *sql* | Where-Object {$_.Status -eq "Running"} | Stop-
Service -WhatIf
```

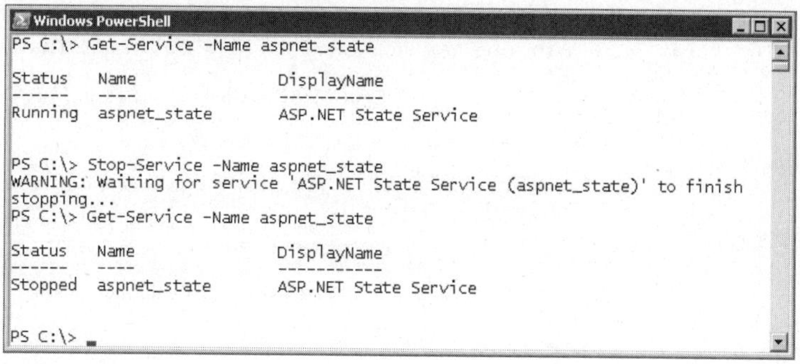

Figure 7-9

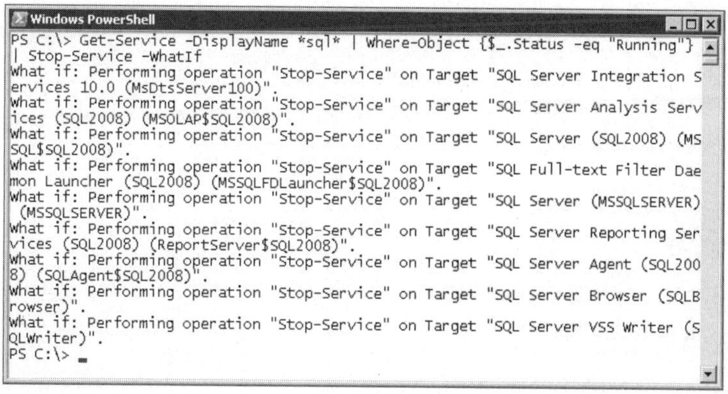

Figure 7-10

All these services can be stopped one by one with confirmation using the -confirm parameter, as shown in the following example. This enables users to choose which service to stop (see Figure 7-11).

```
Get-Service -Displayname *sql* | Where-Object {$_.Status -eq "Running"}| Stop-
Service -confirm
```

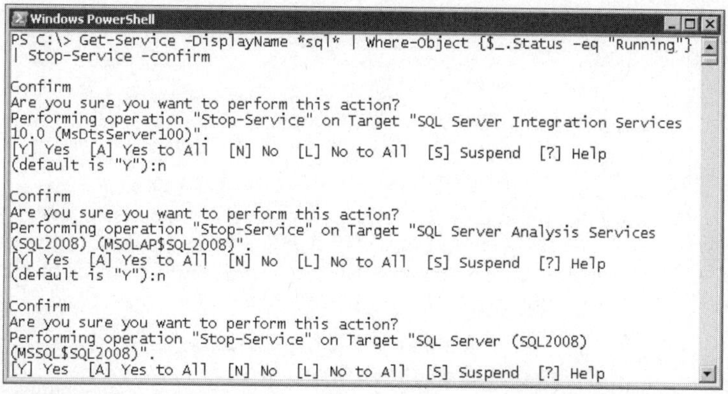

Figure 7-11

You could also use the `Stop-Service` cmdlet with the `-confirm` parameter directly, as shown here (see Figure 7-12):

```
Stop-Service -Displayname *sql* -Confirm
```

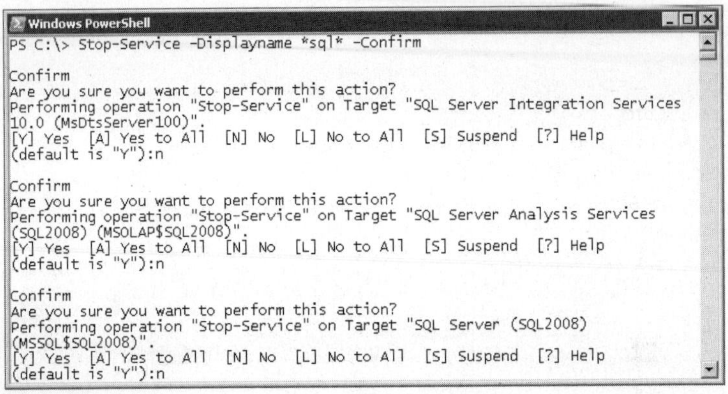

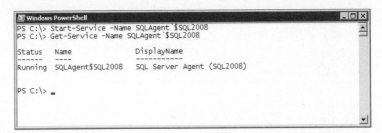

Figure 7-12

Start-Service

Instead of using the methods from `Get-Service` to start a service, you could use the cmdlet `Start-Service`.

Now try to start a stopped SQL Server Agent service. The following example will try to start the SQLAgent$SQL2008 service (see Figure 7-13):

```
Start-Service -Name SQLAgent`$SQL2008
Get-Service -Name SQLAgent`$SQL2008
```

PowerShell assumes that anything prefixed with the dollar sign ($) is a variable. The backtick sign (`) is used to escape the $ sign.

Figure 7-13

Now use the following to find all the SQL server–related services that are not started (see Figure 7-14):

```
Get-Service -DisplayName *sql* | Where-Object {$_.Status -eq "Stopped"}
```

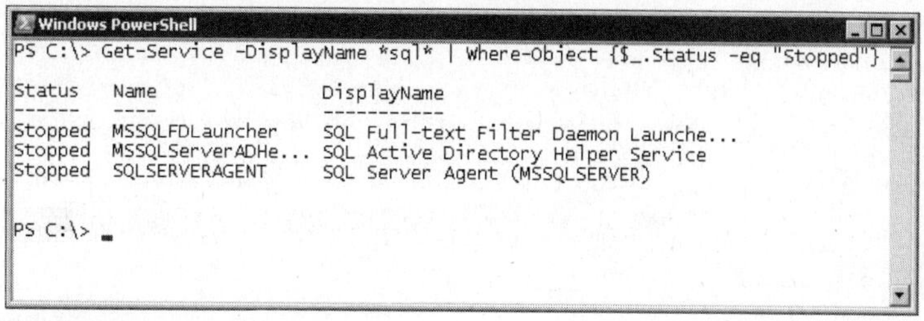

Figure 7-14

As you did in `Stop-Service`, you can try to start all the SQL Server–related services that are stopped with a `WhatIf` scenario, as shown in the following example (see Figure 7-15):

```
Get-Service -DisplayName *sql* | Where-Object {$_.Status -eq "Stopped"} |
Start-Service -WhatIf
```

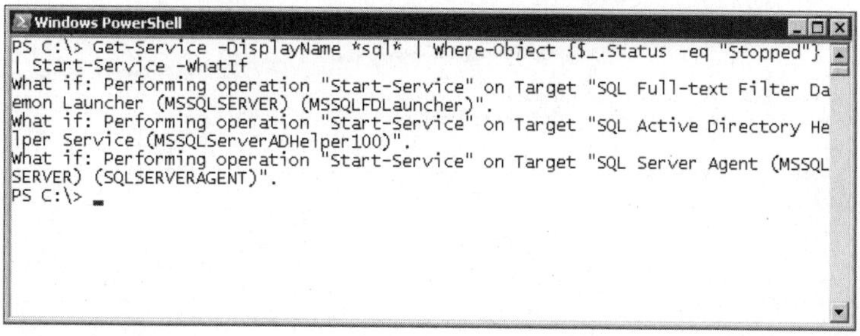

Figure 7-15

Similarly, just as you did with `Stop-Service`, you can try to start all the SQL Server–related services that are stopped with the `-confirm` parameter (see Figure 7-16):

```
Get-Service -DisplayName *sql* | Where-Object {$_.Status -eq "Stopped"} |
Start-Service -confirm
```

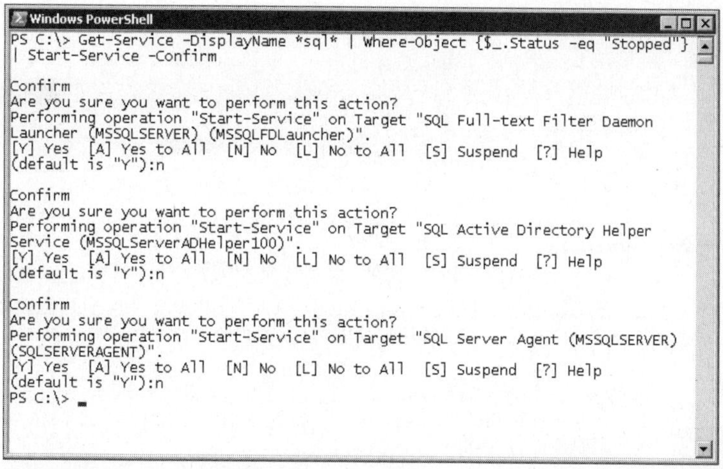

Figure 7-16

Set-Service

The next useful cmdlet related to Windows services is `Set-Service`. `Set-Service` is very useful for changing configurations on the Windows service. One of the commonly used configurations in any Windows service is the startup type.

Let's see the startup option of SQL Server Agent by launching `Services.msc` and double-clicking the SQLAgent$SQL2008 service.

As shown in Figure 7-17, the service startup type is set to Manual, meaning when windows starts, it won't automatically start the SQLAgent$SQL2008 service.

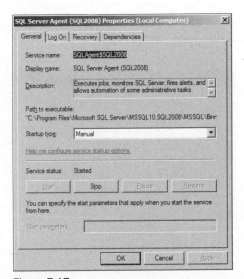

Figure 7-17

Now you can use `Set-Service` to change the startup type from Manual to Automatic, as shown in Figure 7-18:

```
Set-Service -Name "SQLAGENT`$SQL2008" -StartupType "Automatic"
```

Figure 7-18

When you launch `Services.msc` and open SQLAgent$SQL2008, you can see that the startup type changed from Manual to Automatic (see Figure 7-19).

The WMI method of accessing the Windows services on a local and remote machine are discussed in Chapter 8 in detail.

Note that you cannot stop and start a service on a remote machine using Stop-Service and Start-Service yet. The -computername option may become available in the official Windows PowerShell 2.0 RTM release.

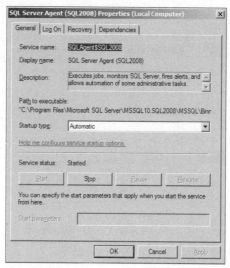

Figure 7-19

Working with Windows Processes

Windows processes are executables that are currently running on the host. All the Windows processes can be viewed and managed using Task Manager.

Task Manager can be launched by executing TaskMgr. It can also be launched by selecting Start ➤ Run and entering **taskmgr**, as shown in Figure 7-20.

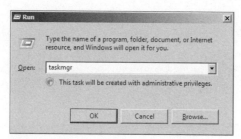

Figure 7-20

When TaskMgr is launched, you can manage Window processes, such as killing the process, setting process priority, and so on, under the Processes tag (refer to Figure 7-21 and Figure 7-22).

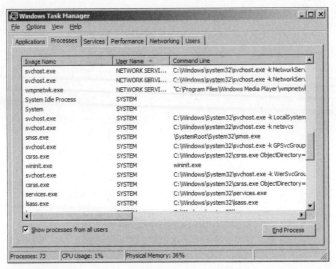

Figure 7-21

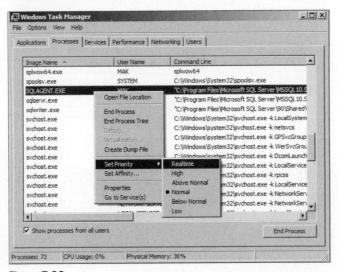

Figure 7-22

There are three commonly used cmdlets that you can use to access the processes on a host machine:

- ❏ `Get-Process`
- ❏ `Start-Process`
- ❏ `Stop-Process`

Two other cmdlets available are as follows:

- ❏ `Wait-Process`
- ❏ `Debug-Process`

All the available cmdlets related to processes can be found by executing the following cmdlet (see Figure 7-23):

```
Get-Command *process* -CommandType "cmdlet"
```

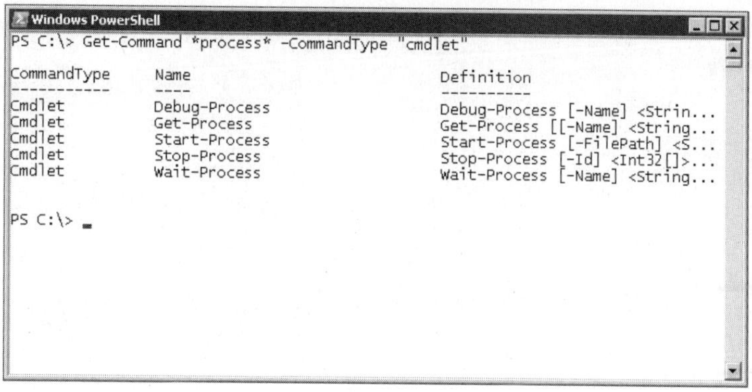

Figure 7-23

Get-Process

Windows PowerShell provides the cmdlet `Get-Process`, which enables you to get information on Windows processes and manage them. To get a list of processes running on the local computer, execute the following command (see Figure 7-24):

```
Get-Process
```

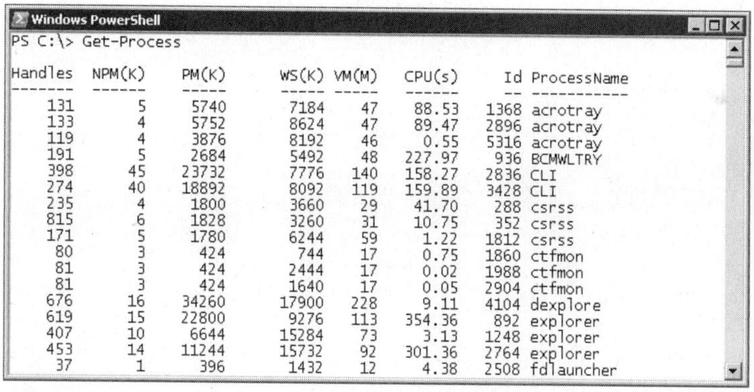

Figure 7-24

The default output of the `Get-Process` cmdlet is the process ID, process name, and six performance counters on memory and CPU usage. Each counter corresponds to a property of the process object.

Besides these six properties, there are many others. The mostly commonly used properties get information such as priority, location, CPU and memory usage of the executable, and more.

Now query all the properties available in the Get-Process cmdlet. Execute the following Get-Process cmdlet with the Get-Member cmdlet as shown here (see Figure 7-25):

```
Get-Process |Get-Member -MemberType properties
```

```
Windows PowerShell                                                    _ □ ×
PS C:\> Get-Process |Get-Member -MemberType properties


   TypeName: System.Diagnostics.Process

Name                    MemberType      Definition
----                    ----------      ----------
Handles                 AliasProperty   Handles = Handlecount
Name                    AliasProperty   Name = ProcessName
NPM                     AliasProperty   NPM = NonpagedSystemMemorySize
PM                      AliasProperty   PM = PagedMemorySize
VM                      AliasProperty   VM = VirtualMemorySize
WS                      AliasProperty   WS = WorkingSet
__NounName              NoteProperty    System.String __NounName=Process
BasePriority            Property        System.Int32 BasePriority {get;}
Container               Property        System.ComponentModel.IContainer C...
EnableRaisingEvents     Property        System.Boolean EnableRaisingEvents...
ExitCode                Property        System.Int32 ExitCode {get;}
ExitTime                Property        System.DateTime ExitTime {get;}
Handle                  Property        System.IntPtr Handle {get;}
HandleCount             Property        System.Int32 HandleCount {get;}
```

Figure 7-25

To query all the methods available in the Get-Process cmdlet, execute the following with the Get-Member cmdlet as shown here (see Figure 7-26):

```
Get-Process |Get-Member -MemberType methods
```

```
Windows PowerShell                                                    _ □ ×
PS C:\> Get-Process |Get-Member -MemberType methods


   TypeName: System.Diagnostics.Process

Name                        MemberType Definition
----                        ---------- ----------
BeginErrorReadLine          Method     System.Void BeginErrorReadLine()
BeginOutputReadLine         Method     System.Void BeginOutputReadLine()
CancelErrorRead             Method     System.Void CancelErrorRead()
CancelOutputRead            Method     System.Void CancelOutputRead()
Close                       Method     System.Void Close()
CloseMainWindow             Method     System.Boolean CloseMainWindow()
CreateObjRef                Method     System.Runtime.Remoting.ObjRef CreateOb...
Dispose                     Method     System.Void Dispose()
Equals                      Method     System.Boolean Equals(Object obj)
GetHashCode                 Method     System.Int32 GetHashCode()
GetLifetimeService          Method     System.Object GetLifetimeService()
GetType                     Method     System.Type GetType()
InitializeLifetimeService   Method     System.Object InitializeLifetimeService()
Kill                        Method     System.Void Kill()
```

Figure 7-26

As shown in the list of properties in Figure 7-25, you can see there are many properties related to memory, the CPU, and so on. You can call some of the useful properties according to your requirements.

Let's look at the resources used by SQL Server–related services. The following command gets information about priority, location of the executable, the CPU, and memory usage. Here, we use the -Name parameter to filter out the processes (see Figure 7-27):

```
Get-Process -Name "sql*" | Format-List ProcessName, Id, BasePriority,
PriorityClass, PriorityBoostEnabled, MachineName, Path, UserProcessorTime,
```

PrivilegedProcessorTime, Threads, WorkingSetSize, PagedSystemMemorySize, PrivateMemorySize, VirtualMemorySize

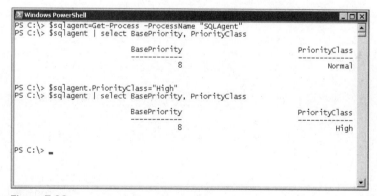

```
PS C:\> Get-Process -Name "sql*" | Format-List ProcessName, Id, BasePriority, Pr
iorityClass, PriorityBoostEnabled, MachineName, Path, UserProcessorTime, Privile
gedProcessorTime, Threads, WorkingSetSize, PagedSystemMemorySize, PrivateMemoryS
ize, VirtualMemorySize


ProcessName             : SQLAGENT
Id                      : 2736
BasePriority            : 8
PriorityClass           : Normal
PriorityBoostEnabled    : True
MachineName             : .
Path                    : C:\Program Files\Microsoft SQL Server\MSSQL10.SQL2008
                          \MSSQL\Binn\SQLAGENT.EXE
UserProcessorTime       : 00:00:00.1875000
PrivilegedProcessorTime : 00:00:00.1562500
Threads                 : {1324, 5336, 5792, 4700...}
PagedSystemMemorySize   : 114540
PrivateMemorySize       : 8806400
VirtualMemorySize       : 103317504
```

Figure 7-27

Changing the priority of a process is a common task. For example, if you want to change the priority of the SQLAGENT.exe process just shown from Normal to High, you can accomplish that by executing the following cmdlet:

```
$sqlagent=Get-Process -ProcessName "SQLAgent"
$sqlagent | select BasePriority, PriorityClass
$sqlagent.PriorityClass="High"
$sqlagent | select BasePriority, PriorityClass
```

The preceding example verified the Priority class initially, and then updated the Priority class and again verified the change. As shown in Figure 7-28, the priority of the SQLAGENT.exe process changed from Normal to High.

```
PS C:\> $sqlagent=Get-Process -ProcessName "SQLAgent"
PS C:\> $sqlagent | select BasePriority, PriorityClass

             BasePriority                    PriorityClass
             ------------                    -------------
                        8                           Normal

PS C:\> $sqlagent.PriorityClass="High"
PS C:\> $sqlagent | select BasePriority, PriorityClass

             BasePriority                    PriorityClass
             ------------                    -------------
                        8                             High

PS C:\> _
```

Figure 7-28

Stop-Process

You can stop a process using the kill method. However, Windows PowerShell already provides a separate cmdlet for that: Stop-Process. The Stop-Process cmdlet stops one or more running processes. You can specify a process by process name or process ID (PID), or pass a process object to `Stop-Process`. For `Get-Process`, the default is by process name. For `Stop-Process`, the default is by process ID. If you want to stop a process by name, you need to use the `-Processname` parameter.

In the example from the last section, you saw a few SQL Server–related processes such as `SQLAGENT.exe` and `SQLservr.exe` running on the local machine. You could stop those processes using `Stop-Process` by executing the following command (see Figure 7-29):

```
Get-Process "SQL*"
Stop-Process -ProcessName "SQL*" -Confirm
```

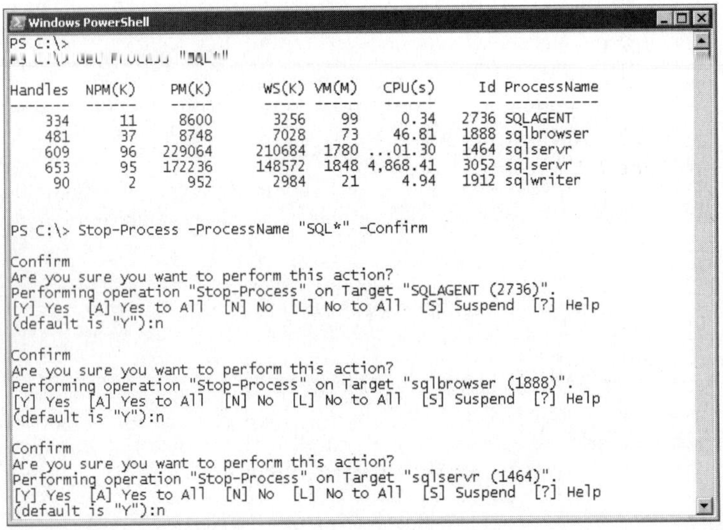

Figure 7-29

However, if you have two `SQLServer.exe` processes running and you want to kill only the `SQLServr.exe` process, then you need to find the unique process ID for `SQLServr.exe`. Once the unique process ID is found, you can kill the process. This is illustrated in the following example:.

```
Get-Process -ProcessName sqlservr | Select-Object ID, ProcessName
```

To terminate the correct process, you can execute `Stop-Process` by passing the correct process ID, as shown here:

```
Stop-Process 2308
```

If you want to access the processes from a remote computer, you can use the parameter `-computername` (see Figure 7-30):

```
Get-Process -ComputerName "PowerServer3"
```

Note that PowerServer3 is the remote host name.

```
Windows PowerShell                                                    _ □ ×
PS C:\> Get-Process -ComputerName "PowerServer3"

Handles  NPM(K)   PM(K)    WS(K)  VM(M)   CPU(s)     Id ProcessName
-------  ------   -----    -----  -----   ------     -- -----------
    131       5    5740     7184     47    88.53   1368 acrotray
    133       4    5752     8624     47    89.47   2896 acrotray
    119       4    3876     8192     46     0.55   5316 acrotray
    191       5    2684     5492     48   228.59    936 BCMWLTRY
    398      45   23732     7776    140   158.30   2836 CLI
    274      40   18892     8092    119   159.91   3428 CLI
    236       4    1800     3660     29    41.70    288 csrss
    814       6    1828     3260     31    10.75    352 csrss
    169       5    1792     6260     59     1.58   1812 csrss
     80       3     424      744     17     0.75   1860 ctfmon
     81       3     424     2444     17     0.02   1988 ctfmon
     81       3     424     1640     17     0.05   2904 ctfmon
    676      16   34260    17900    228     9.11   4104 dexplore
    617      15   22736     9268    112   354.48    892 explorer
    407      10    6644    15288     73     3.42   1248 explorer
    451      14   11180    15724     91   301.47   2764 explorer
     37       1     396     1432     12     4.38   2508 fdlauncher
    348      20   88276    52732    206   231.27   5220 firefox
     63       2   17652    16732     49    29.56   3604 FNPLicensingService
    112       4    1548     1840     43     1.09   1348 GrooveMonitor
    112       4    1548     3732     43     0.89   2844 GrooveMonitor
    112       4    1568     5324     43     0.13   3212 GrooveMonitor
    255       6    5036     8716     67     0.52   1268 helpctr
    181       5    1760     3868     45     0.02   3140 helphost
```

Figure 7-30

Summary

This chapter has discussed Windows services and Windows processes. In particular, you learned how to query services and processes using PowerShell cmdlets.

The chapter also illustrated how to start and stop Windows services and Windows processes with the WhatIf and confirm switch parameters.

8

Working with WMI

Chapters 5, 6, and 7 showed how to manage event logs, services, processes, environment variables, and the registry with Windows PowerShell cmdlets. In this chapter, you will learn how to manage the same resources through Windows Management Instrumentation (WMI) classes. WMI is Microsoft's primary technology for managing Windows systems. WMI is so essential to Windows management that it has been included in every operating system released by Microsoft since Windows NT 4.0. WMI includes a large collection of classes that represent various system components, which enables Windows-based operating systems to be monitored and controlled, both locally and remotely. Since SQL Server 2005, new WMI classes were introduced to manage SQL Server configuration settings and events. This chapter focuses on the operating system components; the WMI classes specific to SQL Server administration are explained in Chapters 9 and 10.

This chapter covers the following topics:

- ❑   Permission issues regarding WMI

- ❑   The WMI model

- ❑   Working with Event Log

- ❑   Working with services

- ❑   Working with processes

- ❑   Working with environment variables

- ❑   Working with the registry

Permission Issues and WMI

In order for WMI to work, the Windows Management Instrumentation service must be running. The service cannot be disabled and it must run under the local system account. If this account is changed, WMI will not have the permissions needed to operate properly.

If you connect with WMI remotely with a user account that is not a member of the Administrators group on the server computer, then you will probably encounter problems. In this case, you need to examine the DCOM security and Windows Firewall settings. To do this, perform the following steps:

❏ On the client computer, enable Windows Management Instrumentation (WMI) for remote administration.

   1. Click Start ➢ Run, type **gpedit.msc**, and then click OK.

   2. In the Group Policy Object Editor, expand Computer Configuration, expand Administrative Templates, and then expand Network.

   3. Expand Network Connections, expand Windows Firewall, and then click Domain Profile.

   4. In Windows XP or Windows Server 2003, right-click Windows Firewall: Allow remote administration exception ➢ Properties. In Windows Vista or Windows Server 2008, right-click Windows Firewall: Allow inbound remote administration exception.

   5. In the dialog, click Enabled ➢ OK.

❏ On the server and on the client computer, specify that DCOM is available for all Microsoft COM applications.

   1. Click Start ➢ Run, type **dcomcnfg**, and then click OK.

   2. In the Component Services dialog, expand Component Services, expand Computers, and right-click My Computer ➢ Properties.

   3. In the My Computer Properties dialog, click the Default Properties tab.

   4. On the Default Properties tab, select the Enable Distributed COM on this computer check box, and then click OK.

❏ On the server computer, add the user account you are connecting with to the Distributed COM Users group.

   1. Click Start ➢ Run, type **lusrmgr.msc**, and then click OK.

   2. In the Local Users and Groups dialog, click Groups, and then double-click Distributed COM Users.

   3. In the Distributed COM Users Properties dialog, click Add.

   4. In the Select Users dialog, type the user name under "Enter the object names to select," and then click OK twice.

If your server computer is a Windows XP machine, you won't see the Distributed COM Users group. If you still have problems connecting with WMI remotely, perform the following steps.

On the server computer, make sure the user account you are connecting with has the rights to launch and activate COM applications remotely.

   1. Click Start ➢ Run, type **dcomcnfg**, and then click OK.

   2. In the Component Services dialog, expand Component Services, expand Computers, and right-click My Computer ➢ Properties.

   3. In the My Computer Properties dialog, click the Default Properties tab.

4. On the COM Security tab, click Edit Limits under Launch and Activation Permissions.

5. On the Launch and Activation Permission window, make sure the user account is allowed for Local Launch, Remote Launch, Local Activation, and Remote Activation, and then click OK.

The WMI Model

Before you start writing scripts to access SQL Server WMI objects, it is helpful to first look at the WMI model and examine some basic concepts.

The WMI model has three layers, as shown in Figure 8-1.

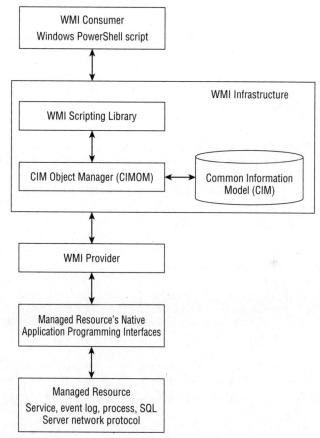

Figure 8-1

The lowest layer in the WMI model is *managed resource*. Windows resources that can be managed using WMI include event logs, services, processes, environment variables, registry settings, networking components and many more.

The middle layer is the *WMI infrastructure*. It consists of four components. WMI providers act as an intermediary between managed resources and WMI. WMI providers can access managed resources through the resources' native Win32 APIs, then forward the resource information to the Common Information Model Object Manager (CIMOM) for integration and interpretation. The CIMOM handles consumer requests for managed resources, and uses the information obtained from the CIM repository to direct the consumer's requests to the appropriate provider. The CIM repository stores the class definitions that model the managed resources and provides provider and class information to CIMOM. Last but not least, the WMI scripting library provides a set of automation objects through which scripting languages, such as Windows PowerShell script, VBScript, and JScript, access the WMI infrastructure.

The top layer in the WMI model is *WMI consumer*. A consumer can be a Windows PowerShell script, a VB script, or a managed application. The consumer accesses the management information available through the WMI infrastructure.

The classes stored in the CIM repository are grouped into namespaces. Each namespace can contain one or more of the following groups of classes: system classes, core and common classes, and/or extension classes. System classes are classes that support internal WMI configuration and operations. They can be identified by the two underscores prefacing their names, such as `_Provider` and `_NAMESPACE`. The core and common classes are derived from the system classes. They define resources common to particular management areas, such as systems and networks, but independent of platform. They can be identified by the `CIM_` prefix. Extension classes are technology-specific classes created by system and application software developers; an example of the `Win32_LogicalDisk` class was shown in Chapter 5. Because extension classes provide platform-specific information, they are the primary group of classes you will use in your scripts.

The CIM is based on object-oriented design principles, so CIM classes can also be divided into three primary class types in the object hierarchy: abstract, static, and dynamic. An abstract class is a template used to derive new abstract and non-abstract classes, and cannot be used to retrieve instances of managed resources. A static class defines data physically stored in the CIM repository, the most common of which is WMI configuration and operational data. A dynamic class models a WMI managed resource that is dynamically retrieved from a provider. The most common use of the dynamic class type is in the definition of extension classes. Therefore, the classes you will use in WMI scripts are most likely to be dynamic and extension.

If you are not familiar with the WMI class hierarchy, you can go to `www.microsoft.com/downloads/details.aspx?FamilyID=6430f853-1120-48db-8cc5-f2abdc3ed314&DisplayLang=en` and download WMI Administrative Tools. The tools include WMI CIM Studio, WMI Object Browser, WMI Event Registration Tool, and WMI Event Viewer. WMI CIM Studio and WMI Object Browser are nice tools to view classes and their properties, methods, associations, and instances in a CIM repository.

WMI organizes classes into a hierarchy of namespaces. You can use the `Get-WmiObject` cmdlet shown in Chapter 5 to query the available namespaces under the root level. The namespaces are the class type of `_Namespace`. The following command queries the namespaces at the root level:

```
Get-WmiObject -class __Namespace -namespace root | Select-Object Name
```

Figure 8-2 shows the output.

The `root\CIMV2` namespace is the default namespace for the `Get-WmiObject` cmdlet, meaning you do not have to specify the namespace in `Get-WmiObject` if you are referring to this namespace. Although you can change the default namespace for VB scripting by changing the Default Namespace value under the registry key HKEY_LOCAL_MACHINE\SOFTWARE\Microsoft\WBEM\Scripting, this registry key has no effect on the Get-WmiObject cmdlet.

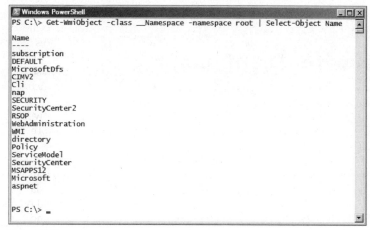

Figure 8-2

The root\CIMV2 namespace contains the core Windows OS classes. You can retrieve a list of classes under root\CIMV2 using this command:

```
Get-WmiObject –list
```

However, the list is quite long. The following abbreviated list contains only the classes for the event logs, services, and processes used in this chapter:

- ❏ Win32_NTEventlogFile
- ❏ Win32_NTLogEvent
- ❏ Win32_Service
- ❏ Win32_Process

In Chapters 5, 6, and 7 you learned how to work with the registry, environment variables, event logs, services, and processes on the local and remote computer with the built-in cmdlets in Windows PowerShell. Here you will see how to access the same resources through WMI classes both locally and remotely.

To connect to a remote computer, simply specify the computer name as the value for the –computerName parameter of the Get-WmiObject cmdlet. You may be wondering why we are showing you an alternative method to manage the same resources. The reason is because WMI classes enable you to access more Windows resources or get more information about the same resources than the built-in cmdlets provide you with. For example, the Win32_LogicalDisk class shown in Chapter 5 provides much more information about logical drives than the Get-PSDrive cmdlet, such as free space. Other examples are the Start-Service and Stop-Service cmdlets. As mentioned in Chapter 7, even with Windows Power-Shell CTP3, you cannot start or stop a remote service using the cmdlets yet, whereas you can with the Win32_Service WMI class.

This chapter is intended to give you an overview of how to work with WMI classes in Windows Power-Shell. There are a lot more WMI classes that won't be covered in this chapter that you are encouraged to explore on your own.

Note that we are using a local computer, PowerPC, and a remote computer, PowerServer3. We ran all the commands in our examples on the local computer PowerPC. Before you run the commands in your environment, you will need to change the value of the `-computerName` parameter from PowerServer3 to your remote computer name.

Working with Event Log

The `Win32_NTEventlogFile` class represents event log files of the operating system. To get a list of log files available on your local computer, execute the following command:

```
Get-WmiObject -class Win32_NTEventlogFile | Format-Table -wrap
```

As shown in Figure 8-3, the `LogfileName` column contains the names of the log files. The `Name` column contains the log file locations. The `NumberOfRecords` column shows the number of entries in each log file. Seven event logs are non-empty and contain entries on the local computer.

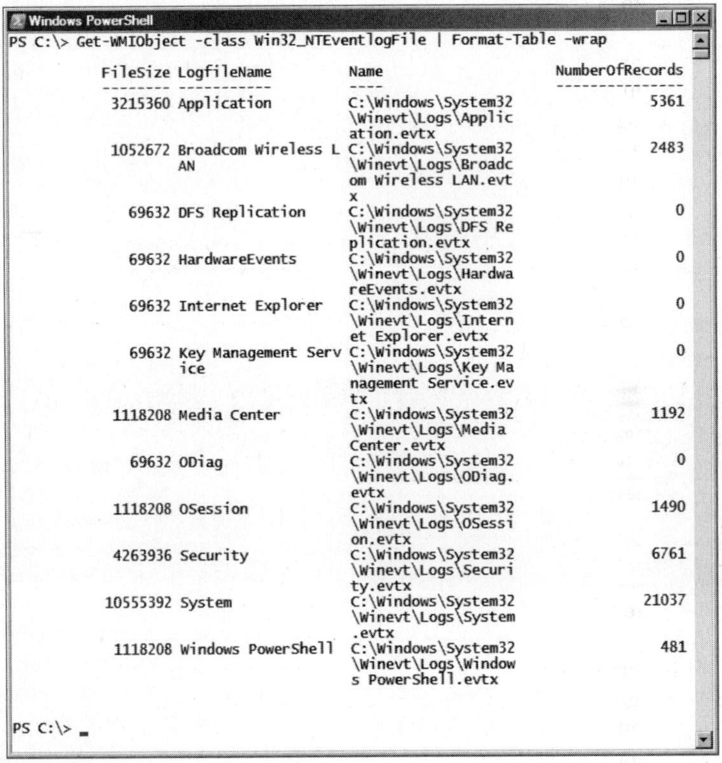

```
Windows PowerShell
PS C:\> Get-WMIObject -class Win32_NTEventlogFile | Format-Table -wrap

         FileSize LogfileName          Name                          NumberOfRecords
         -------- -----------          ----                          ---------------
          3215360 Application          C:\Windows\System32                      5361
                                       \Winevt\Logs\Applic
                                       ation.evtx
          1052672 Broadcom Wireless L  C:\Windows\System32                      2483
                  AN                   \Winevt\Logs\Broadc
                                       om Wireless LAN.evt
                                       x
            69632 DFS Replication      C:\Windows\System32                         0
                                       \Winevt\Logs\DFS Re
                                       plication.evtx
            69632 HardwareEvents       C:\Windows\System32                         0
                                       \Winevt\Logs\Hardwa
                                       reEvents.evtx
            69632 Internet Explorer    C:\Windows\System32                         0
                                       \Winevt\Logs\Intern
                                       et Explorer.evtx
            69632 Key Management Serv  C:\Windows\System32                         0
                  ice                  \Winevt\Logs\Key Ma
                                       nagement Service.ev
                                       tx
          1118208 Media Center         C:\Windows\System32                      1192
                                       \Winevt\Logs\Media
                                       Center.evtx
            69632 ODiag                C:\Windows\System32                         0
                                       \Winevt\Logs\ODiag.
                                       evtx
          1118208 OSession             C:\Windows\System32                      1490
                                       \Winevt\Logs\OSessi
                                       on.evtx
          4263936 Security             C:\Windows\System32                      6761
                                       \Winevt\Logs\Securi
                                       ty.evtx
         10555392 System               C:\Windows\System32                     21037
                                       \Winevt\Logs\System
                                       .evtx
          1118208 Windows PowerShell   C:\Windows\System32                       481
                                       \Winevt\Logs\Window
                                       s PowerShell.evtx

PS C:\> _
```

Figure 8-3

To access the log files on a remote computer, use the `-computerName` parameter and pass the remote computer name. For example, to connect to the remote computer PowerServer3, run the following command:

```
Get-WmiObject -computerName PowerServer3 -class Win32_NTEventlogFile | select
FileSize, LogfileName, Name, NumberOfRecords, CSName | Format-Table -wrap
```

Figure 8-4 shows a list of event log files, including Application, Security, System, and Windows Power-Shell event log files on the remote computer PowerServer3.

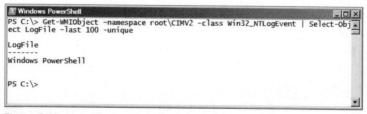

```
Windows PowerShell                                                   _ □ ×
PS C:\> Get-WMIObject -computerName PowerServer3 -class Win32_NTEventlogFile | s
elect FileSize, LogfileName, Name, NumberOfRecords, CSName | Format-Table -wrap

       FileSize LogfileName      Name             NumberOfRecords CSName
       -------- -----------      ----             --------------- ------
         327680 Application      C:\WINDOWS\syst             1002 POWERSERVER3
                                 em32\config\App
                                 Event.Evt
         983040 Security         C:\WINDOWS\Syst             2560 POWERSERVER3
                                 em32\config\Sec
                                 Event.Evt
         262144 System           C:\WINDOWS\syst              716 POWERSERVER3
                                 em32\config\Sys
                                 Event.Evt
          65536 Windows PowerSh  C:\WINDOWS\Syst                8 POWERSERVER3
                ell              em32\config\Win
                                 dowsPowerShell.
                                 evt

PS C:\> _
```

Figure 8-4

The `Win32_NTLogEvent` class represents instances from the Windows NT event logs. Every entry in the event log makes up an instance of this class. The `LogFile` property of this class has the name of the Windows NT event log file. To get a list of the log files that contain the last 100 entries on the local computer, execute the following command. The `-unique` switch parameter in the `Select-Object` cmdlet is used to eliminate duplicates in the result set and retrieve only unique log file names.

```
Get-WmiObject -namespace root\CIMV2 -class Win32_NTLogEvent | Select-Object
LogFile -last 100 -unique
```

As shown in Figure 8-5, the last 100 entries all come from the Windows PowerShell event log.

```
Windows PowerShell                                                   _ □ ×
PS C:\> Get-WMIObject -namespace root\CIMV2 -class Win32_NTLogEvent | Select-Obj
ect LogFile -last 100 -unique

LogFile
-------
Windows PowerShell

PS C:\>
```

Figure 8-5

If you encounter the error "Quota violation" when running this command, you can increase the `MemoryPerHost` setting of the `_ProviderHostQuotaConfiguration` class to fix it. However, be careful when changing this setting, as it increases the amount of private memory that can be held by every host provider process. To increase the value, perform the following steps:

1. Select Start ➤ Run and type **wbemtest.exe**.

2. Click Connect on the Windows Management Instrumentation Tester.

3. In the Namespace text box, just enter **root**. Click Connect.

4. Select Enum Instances.

5. In the Class Info dialog, enter the superclass name as **__ProviderHostQuotaConfiguration** and click OK.

6. In the Query Result window, double-click _ProviderHostQuotaConfiguration=@.

7. In the Object Editor window, under Properties, find the property MemoryPerHost and double-click it.

8. Increase the value and select Save Property. Close the windows and restart the machine.

An excellent blog about the setting is available at http://blogs.technet.com/askperf/archive/2008/09/16/memory-and-handle-quotas-in-the-wmi-provider-service.aspx.

To get a list of log files that contain the last 100 entries on the remote computer PowerServer3, run the following command:

```
Get-WmiObject -computerName PowerServer3 -namespace root\CIMV2 -class
Win32_NTLogEvent | Select-Object LogFile -last 100 -unique
```

Figure 8-6 shows the list.

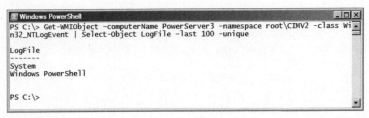

Figure 8-6

If you want to query all of the entries in the Application event log, all you have to do is pass LogFile as a filter to the Get-WmiObject cmdlet:

```
Get-WmiObject -namespace root\CIMV2 -class Win32_NTLogEvent -filter
"LogFile='Application'"
```

Alternately, you can issue a WQL query that uses a where condition on the LogFile property:

```
Get-WmiObject -namespace root\CIMV2 -query "Select * from Win32_NTLogEvent where
LogFile='Application'"
```

In most cases, you will want to view only some of the thousands of entries in the Application event log. For example, you might want to view only the last entry. You can use the Select-Object cmdlet and its -last parameter to filter the last entry:

```
Get-WmiObject -namespace root\CIMV2 -class Win32_NTLogEvent -filter
"LogFile='Application'" | Select-Object -last 1
```

Figure 8-7 shows the last Application event log entry on the local computer.

Figure 8-7

To see all the properties of instances of the `Win32_NTLogEvent` class, you just need to pipe the last event log object to the `Get-Member` cmdlet:

```
Get-WmiObject -namespace root\CIMV2 -class Win32_NTLogEvent | Select-Object -last 1 |
Get-Member -MemberType Property
```

Figure 8-8 shows all the properties of the event class. The `Category` property is a number specific to the event source. The `EventType` property describes the type of event.

Possible values for the event types are listed in the following table.

Value	Meaning
1	Error
2	Warning
3	Information
4	Security Audit Success
5	Security Audit Failure

```
PS C:\> Get-WMIObject -namespace root\CIMV2 -class Win32_NTLogEvent | Select-Obj
ect -last 1 | Get-Member -MemberType Property


   TypeName: System.Management.ManagementObject#root\CIMV2\Win32_NTLogEvent

Name                   MemberType Definition
----                   ---------- ----------
Category               Property   System.UInt16 Category {get;set;}
CategoryString         Property   System.String CategoryString {get;set;}
ComputerName           Property   System.String ComputerName {get;set;}
Data                   Property   System.Byte[] Data {get;set;}
EventCode              Property   System.UInt16 EventCode {get;set;}
EventIdentifier        Property   System.UInt32 EventIdentifier {get;set;}
EventType              Property   System.Byte EventType {get;set;}
InsertionStrings       Property   System.String[] InsertionStrings {get;set;}
Logfile                Property   System.String Logfile {get;set;}
Message                Property   System.String Message {get;set;}
RecordNumber           Property   System.UInt32 RecordNumber {get;set;}
SourceName             Property   System.String SourceName {get;set;}
TimeGenerated          Property   System.String TimeGenerated {get;set;}
TimeWritten            Property   System.String TimeWritten {get;set;}
Type                   Property   System.String Type {get;set;}
User                   Property   System.String User {get;set;}
__CLASS                Property   System.String __CLASS {get;set;}
__DERIVATION           Property   System.String[] __DERIVATION {get;set;}
__DYNASTY              Property   System.String __DYNASTY {get;set;}
__GENUS                Property   System.Int32 __GENUS {get;set;}
__NAMESPACE            Property   System.String __NAMESPACE {get;set;}
__PATH                 Property   System.String __PATH {get;set;}
__PROPERTY_COUNT       Property   System.Int32 __PROPERTY_COUNT {get;set;}
__RELPATH              Property   System.String __RELPATH {get;set;}
__SERVER               Property   System.String __SERVER {get;set;}
__SUPERCLASS           Property   System.String __SUPERCLASS {get;set;}


PS C:\> _
```

Figure 8-8

The Message property contains the event message as it appears in the Windows NT event log. The SourceName property contains the name of the source that generated the entry. For SQL Server–related events, the source name can be an instance name, such as MSSQLServer or MSSQL$INST2008, or a service name, such as SQLBrowser. The TimeGenerated property contains the date and time the event was generated. The TimeWritten property contains the date and time the event was written to the log file. The Type property also contains the type of event, and is an enumerated string. The User property contains the user name of the logged-on user when the event occurred. If the user name cannot be determined, then this will be NULL.

You can find all the types of events available in the Application event log on the local computer by querying EventType and type. Use the Select-Object cmdlet to select the two properties and use the -unique parameter to discard duplicates. Then you can use the Sort-Object cmdlet to sort the event types:

```
Get-WmiObject -namespace root\CIMV2 -class Win32_NTLogEvent -Filter
"LogFile='Application'" | Select-Object EventType, Type -unique | Sort-Object
EventType
```

Figure 8-9 shows the output.

You can also filter events based on the event source. For example, if you want to look at the error events generated by the default SQL Server instance in the Application log, instead of using the -filter parameter as in the previous command, you can use the Where-Object cmdlet to do the filtering based on the LogFile name, SourceName, and EventType:

```
Get-WmiObject -namespace root\CIMV2 -class Win32_NTLogEvent  | Where-Object {
($_.LogFile -eq 'Application') -and ($_.SourceName -eq "MSSQLSERVER") -and
($_.EventType -eq 1) }  | Format-List SourceName, Message, TimeGenerated
```

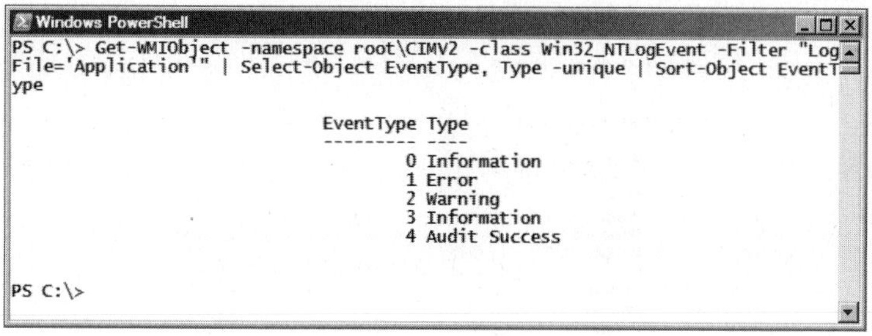

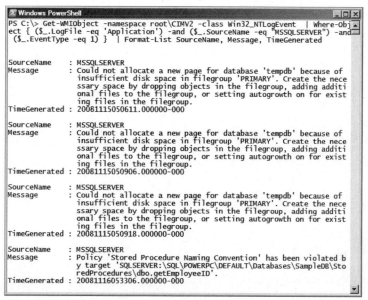

Figure 8-9

The SQL Server–specific error messages are shown in Figure 8-10.

Figure 8-10

You can also filter events based on date ranges. The following example uses the `Where-Object` cmdlet to filter the events whose `TimeGenerated` property is greater than `20081130` (Nov 30, 2008) and less than `20081201` (Dec 1, 2008), thus getting the error events that occurred on Nov 30, 2008. Then the events are sorted in descending order by time, and displayed in a list:

```
Get-WmiObject -namespace root\CIMV2 -class Win32_NTLogEvent  -Filter
"LogFile='Application'" | Where-Object { ($_.EventType -eq 1) -and ($_.TimeGenerated
-gt "20081130") -and ($_.TimeGenerated -lt "20081201") } | Sort-Object
TimeGenerated -descending | Format-List
```

Figure 8-11 shows the events generated on Nov 30, 2008.

```
Windows PowerShell                                                    _ □ ×
PS C:\> Get-WMIObject -namespace root\CIMV2 -class Win32_NTLogEvent  | Where-Obj
ect { ($_.EventType -eq 1) -and ($_.TimeGenerated -gt "20081130") -and ($_.TimeG
enerated -lt "20081201") } | Sort-Object TimeGenerated -descending | Format-List


__GENUS          : 2
__CLASS          : Win32_NTLogEvent
__SUPERCLASS     :
__DYNASTY        : Win32_NTLogEvent
__RELPATH        : Win32_NTLogEvent.Logfile="System",RecordNumber=100001
__PROPERTY_COUNT : 16
__DERIVATION     : {}
__SERVER         : POWERPC
__NAMESPACE      : root\CIMV2
__PATH           : \\POWERPC\root\CIMV2:Win32_NTLogEvent.Logfile="System",Recor
                   dNumber=100001
Category         : 0
CategoryString   :
ComputerName     : PowerPC.powerdomain.com
Data             :
EventCode        : 7000
EventIdentifier  : 3221232472
EventType        : 1
InsertionStrings : {BCM42RLY, %%2}
Logfile          : System
Message          : The BCM42RLY service failed to start due to the following er
                   ror:
                   The system cannot find the file specified.
RecordNumber     : 100001
SourceName       : Service Control Manager
TimeGenerated    : 20081130230520.000000-000
TimeWritten      : 20081130230520.000000-000
Type             : Error
User             :

__GENUS          : 2
__CLASS          : Win32_NTLogEvent
__SUPERCLASS     :
__DYNASTY        : Win32_NTLogEvent
__RELPATH        : Win32_NTLogEvent.Logfile="System",RecordNumber=100000
__PROPERTY_COUNT : 16
__DERIVATION     : {}
__SERVER         : POWERPC
__NAMESPACE      : root\CIMV2
__PATH           : \\POWERPC\root\CIMV2:Win32_NTLogEvent.Logfile="System",Recor
                   dNumber=100000
Category         : 0
CategoryString   :
ComputerName     : PowerPC.powerdomain.com
Data             :
```

Figure 8-11

Working with Services

The `Win32_Service` class represents the services on a computer. To get a list of services on the local computer, run the following command. Notice that the root\CIMV2 namespace is omitted in the command because it is the default namespace:

```
Get-WmiObject -class Win32_Service
```

Figure 8-12 shows the output.

To get a list of services on the remote computer PowerServer3, execute the following command:

```
Get-WmiObject -computerName PowerServer3 -class Win32_Service
```

Six properties are listed for each service, as shown in Figure 8-13. The `ExitCode` property represents the Windows error code that defines errors encountered when starting or stopping the service. In our example, 0 means the operation to start or stop the service was completed successfully, and 1077 means no attempts to start the service were made since the last reboot. The `Name` property provides a name that uniquely identifies the service. The `ProcessId` contains the process identifier under which the service is running. The `StartMode` property determines how the service is started. In our example, `Auto` means the service is started automatically by the service control manager (SCM) during system startup. `Manual` means the service is started by the SCM only when a process calls the `StartService` method. The `State` property contains the current state of the service. The `Status` property indicates the current status of the object. This can be an operational status, such as OK, Degraded, or Pred Fail, or a non-operational status, such as Error, Starting, Stopping, or Service.

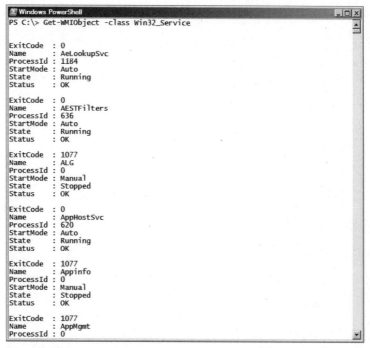

```
Windows PowerShell                                                   _ □ X
PS C:\> Get-WMIObject -class Win32_Service

ExitCode  : 0
Name      : AeLookupSvc
ProcessId : 1184
StartMode : Auto
State     : Running
Status    : OK

ExitCode  : 0
Name      : AESTFilters
ProcessId : 636
StartMode : Auto
State     : Running
Status    : OK

ExitCode  : 1077
Name      : ALG
ProcessId : 0
StartMode : Manual
State     : Stopped
Status    : OK

ExitCode  : 0
Name      : AppHostSvc
ProcessId : 620
StartMode : Auto
State     : Running
Status    : OK

ExitCode  : 1077
Name      : Appinfo
ProcessId : 0
StartMode : Manual
State     : Stopped
Status    : OK

ExitCode  : 1077
Name      : AppMgmt
ProcessId : 0
```

Figure 8-12

Besides the six properties just described for each service, other commonly used properties and methods for the `Win32_Service` class are as follows:

- ❑ **Description**: Contains the detailed description of the service.

- ❑ **DisplayName**: Contains the display name of the service. For SQL Server services, it can be SQL Server (MSSQLSERVER), SQL Server Agent (INSTANCE1), and SQL Server Browser.

- ❑ **ErrorControl**: Indicates the severity of the error if this service fails to start during startup. The value defines the action taken by the startup program if failure occurs. Most of the services are installed using the Normal error control code; and if they fail before the user logs on, the user receives the notification "At least one service or device failed during startup."

- ❑ **PathName**: Contains the full path to the service binary file that implements the service.

- ❑ **Started**: A Boolean variable indicating whether the service has been started.

❑ **StartName**: Account name under which a service runs. The account name can be a local account, such as LocalSystem or NT AUTHORITY\NetworkService, or a domain account in the format of *DomainName\Username*.

❑ **SystemName**: Name of the computer that hosts this service.

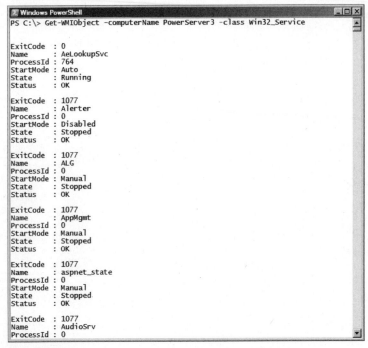

```
Windows PowerShell
PS C:\> Get-WMIObject -computerName PowerServer3 -class Win32_Service

ExitCode  : 0
Name      : AeLookupSvc
ProcessId : 764
StartMode : Auto
State     : Running
Status    : OK

ExitCode  : 1077
Name      : Alerter
ProcessId : 0
StartMode : Disabled
State     : Stopped
Status    : OK

ExitCode  : 1077
Name      : ALG
ProcessId : 0
StartMode : Manual
State     : Stopped
Status    : OK

ExitCode  : 1077
Name      : AppMgmt
ProcessId : 0
StartMode : Manual
State     : Stopped
Status    : OK

ExitCode  : 1077
Name      : aspnet_state
ProcessId : 0
StartMode : Manual
State     : Stopped
Status    : OK

ExitCode  : 1077
Name      : AudioSrv
ProcessId : 0
```

Figure 8-13

Consider the SQL Server service of the default instance on the local computer and its properties. The following command uses the `Where-Object` cmdlet to filter the service, and uses the `Select-Object` cmdlet to retrieve its properties:

```
Get-WmiObject -class Win32_Service | Where-Object {$_.Name -eq 'MSSQLSERVER'} |
    Select-Object Name, ExitCode, ProcessId, StartMode, State, Status, Description,
    DisplayName, ErrorControl, PathName, Started, StartName, SystemName
```

As shown in Figure 8-14, the SQL Server service of the default instance started successfully with an exit code 0, and has been running under a process ID of 5548 on the local computer, PowerPC.

The Auto StartMode indicates that this service starts automatically at system startup. This service is displayed as SQL Server (MSSQLSERVER) in the Service Management Console. The service binary file `sqlservr.exe` is located under `C:\Program Files\Microsoft SQL Server\MSSQL10.MSSQLSERVER\MSSQL\`
`Binn`. The service account of this service is the domain account SqlService in the PowerDomain domain.

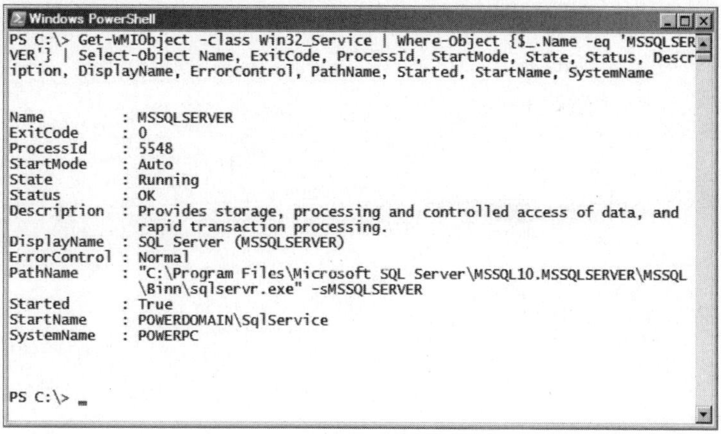

Figure 8-14

The `Win32_Service` class also provides methods for working with the services. Some of them are listed in the following table.

Method	Description
StartService	Attempts to place a service into the startup state.
StopService	Places a service in the stopped state.
ChangeStartMode	Modifies the start mode of a service.
Change	Modifies a service.
GetSecurityDescriptor	Returns the security descriptor that controls access to the service. This method is available starting with Windows Vista.
SetSecurityDescriptor	Writes an updated version of the security descriptor that controls access to the service. This method is available starting with Windows Vista.

The `StartService` method starts a service. Let's start a stopped SQL Server–related service. To filter the stopped SQL Server–related services with the `Where-Object` cmdlet, execute this command:

```
Get-WmiObject -class Win32_Service | Where-Object { ($_.Name -like '*SQL*') -and
($_.State -eq 'Stopped') }
```

As shown in Figure 8-15, the last service, the SQL Server Agent service for the default instance, is stopped.

To start it, invoke the `StartService` method on the object associated with the SQLSERVERAGENT service:

```
(Get-WmiObject -class Win32_Service | Where-Object {$_.Name -eq
'SQLSERVERAGENT'}).StartService()
```

Figure 8-15

As shown in Figure 8-16, the 0 return code from the StartService method indicates the agent started successfully.

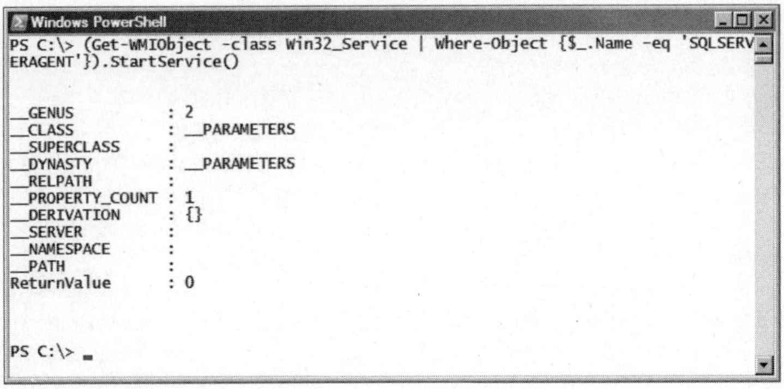

```
Windows PowerShell                                                    _ □ ×
PS C:\> (Get-WMIObject -class Win32_Service | Where-Object {$_.Name -eq 'SQLSERV
ERAGENT'}).StartService()


__GENUS            : 2
__CLASS            : __PARAMETERS
__SUPERCLASS       :
__DYNASTY          : __PARAMETERS
__RELPATH          :
__PROPERTY_COUNT   : 1
__DERIVATION       : {}
__SERVER           :
__NAMESPACE        :
__PATH             :
ReturnValue        : 0


PS C:\> _
```

Figure 8-16

To verify that the SQLSERVERAGENT service started, run the following command:

```
Get-WmiObject -class Win32_Service | Where-Object { ($_.Name -like 'SQLSERVERAGENT') }
```

As shown in Figure 8-17, the state of the service has changed from Stopped to Running, and the service is running under process ID 1548.

```
Windows PowerShell                                                    _ □ ×
PS C:\> Get-WMIObject -class Win32_Service | Where-Object { ($_.Name -like 'SQLS
ERVERAGENT') }


ExitCode  : 0
Name      : SQLSERVERAGENT
ProcessId : 1548
StartMode : Manual
State     : Running
Status    : OK


PS C:\> _
```

Figure 8-17

To start a service on a remote computer, you just need to add the -computerName parameter. For example, the following command starts the SQLSERVERAGENT service on the remote computer PowerServer3:

```
(Get-WmiObject -class Win32_Service -computerName PowerServer3 | Where-Object {
($_.Name -eq 'SQLSERVERAGENT') }).StartService()
```

```
Windows PowerShell                                                    _ □ ×
PS C:\> (Get-WMIObject -class Win32_Service -computerName PowerServer3 | Where-O
bject { ($_.Name -eq 'SQLSERVERAGENT') }).StartService()


__GENUS         : 2
__CLASS         : __PARAMETERS
__SUPERCLASS    :
__DYNASTY       : __PARAMETERS
__RELPATH       :
__PROPERTY_COUNT : 1
__DERIVATION    : {}
__SERVER        :
__NAMESPACE     :
__PATH          :
ReturnValue     : 0


PS C:\>
```

Figure 8-18

As shown in Figure 8-18, the 0 return code from the StartService method indicates that the agent started successfully on the remote computer, PowerServer3. The built-in cmdlet Start-Service in Windows PowerShell 2.0 CTP3 cannot be used to start or stop remote services, so you have more flexibility using the WMI class Win32_Service.

The StopService method places a service in the stopped state. Let's stop all the running SQL Server–related services on the local computer. To filter these services with the Where-Object cmdlet, execute the following command:

```
Get-WmiObject -class Win32_Service | Where-Object { ($_.Name -like '*SQL*') -and
($_.State -eq 'Running') }
```

Figure 8-19 shows all the running services.

Figure 8-19

Similar to the StartService method, the StopService method is applied to only one service object; you cannot just pipeline multiple service objects and invoke the method on them. You need to use the ForEach-Object cmdlet, and apply the method against each service object. Furthermore, note that the SQL Server Agent service for the default instance (SQLSERVERAGENT) is below the SQL Server service (MSSQLSERVER). Because the agent service depends on the SQL Server service, you need to stop the agent service first, followed by the SQL Server service. You can use the Sort-Object cmdlet to reverse the order of the services. You also need to add a 15-second delay between each stop attempt to ensure that each operation is given enough time to process:

```
Get-WmiObject -class Win32_Service | Where-Object{ ($_.Name -like '*SQL*') -and
($_.State -eq 'Running') } | Sort-Object Name -desc | ForEach-Object -process {
$_.StopService(); Start-Sleep -s 15 }
```

The 0 return values (ReturnValue) shown in Figure 8-20 indicate that the services stopped successfully.

To verify that all the SQL Server–related services have stopped, execute the previous command again:

```
Get-WmiObject -class Win32_Service | Where-Object{ ($_.Name -like '*SQL*') -and
($_.State -eq 'Running')}
```

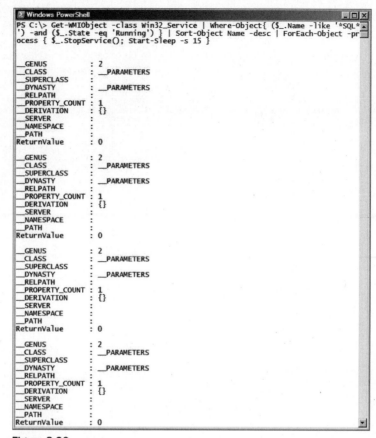

Figure 8-20

As shown in Figure 8-21, none of the SQL Server–related services are running.

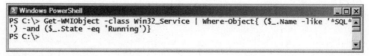

Figure 8-21

The `ChangeStartMode` method modifies the start mode of a service. This method takes one parameter: `StartMode`. Possible values for the parameter include `Boot`, `System`, `Automatic`, `Manual`, and `Disabled`. For example, if you would like to change the start mode of the SQL Server Agent service of the default instance from Manual to Auto (so the agent starts automatically at system startup), run the following command:

```
(Get-WmiObject -class Win32_Service | Where-Object{ ($_.Name -like
'SQLSERVERAGENT') }).ChangeStartMode('Automatic')
```

```
#To confirm that the StartMode has been changed.
Get-WmiObject -class Win32_Service | Where-Object{ ($_.Name -like 'SQLSERVERAGENT') }
```

As shown in Figure 8-22, after the command is executed, the start mode of the agent service changes from Manual to Auto.

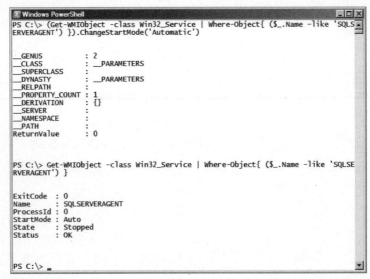

Figure 8-22

Another method, `Change`, can be used to modify the start mode of a service as well. This method can also modify other properties of a service, including display name, binary file path, error control, service account, loading order, and service dependencies. Here is the definition of the method:

```
System.Management.ManagementBaseObject  Change(System.String DisplayName,
System.String PathName, System.Byte ServiceType, System.Byte ErrorControl,
System.String StartMode, System.Boolean DesktopInteract, System.String StartName,
System.String StartPassword, System.String LoadOrderGroup, System.String[]
LoadOrderGroupDependencies, System.String[] ServiceDependencies)
```

You can use this method to change the service account of the SQL Server. Currently, the SQL Server service for the default instance is running under the PowerUser account PowerDomain\SqlService, but you can change it to the local system account temporarily. If you want to populate the parameters, you need to get the parameter collection for the `Change` method. The raw view, `psbase`, of the service object provides a way to get the native methods for WMI, including the `GetMethodParameters` method to get the parameter collection, and another method, `InvokeMethod`, to invoke the `Change` method on the service object:

```
# Gets the SQL Server service object
$service = Get-WmiObject -class Win32_Service | Where-Object{ ($_.Name -eq
'MSSQLSERVER') }
# Gets the parameter collection of the Change method for the service object
$params = $service.psbase.GetMethodParameters('Change')
# Set the new service account
```

```
$params["StartName"] = [String] "LocalSystem"
# Apply the Change method to the SQL Server service object
$result= $service.psbase.InvokeMethod('Change', $params, $Null)
"The return code of the Change method is " + $result["ReturnValue"]
```

To verify that the service account has been changed, run the following command:

```
Get-WmiObject -class Win32_Service | Where-Object{ ($_.Name -like 'MSSQLSERVER') } |
select StartName
```

Figure 8-23 shows that the SQL Server service account has been changed to LocalSystem.

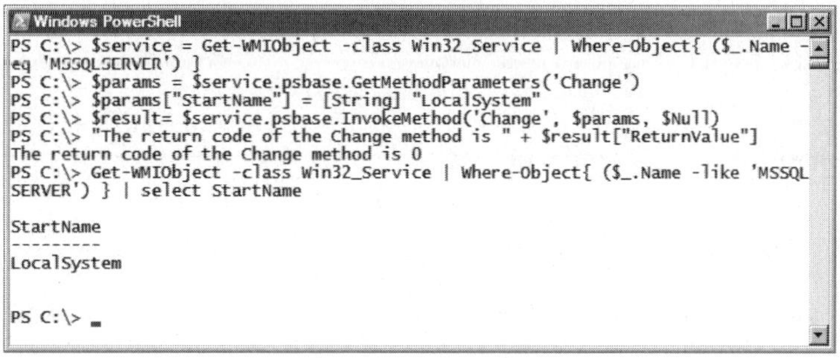

Figure 8-23

Working with Processes

The `Win32_Process` class represents processes on an operating system. To get a list of processes on your local computer, run the following command:

```
Get-WmiObject -class Win32_Process
```

There are many properties associated with each process. Some of the properties are static and don't change after the process starts, such as those that provide the process identifier, the underlying binary file, and the operating system of the process. Following is a list of static properties:

- ❑ **Caption**: Contains a short description of the process

- ❑ **CommandLine**: Contains the command line used to start a specific process. For example, for the SQL Server service for the default instance installed in the default directory, it is `C:\Program Files\Microsoft SQL Server\MSSQL10.MSSQLSERVER\MSSQL\Binn\sqlservr.exe. -sMSSQLSERVER`.

- ❑ **CreationDate**: Contains the date the process begins executing.

- ❑ **CSName**: Contains the name of the computer system on which the process is running.

- ❑ **Description**: Contains a detailed description of the process, if available.

- ❑ **ExecutablePath**: Contains the path to the executable file of the process. It doesn't include the parameters used to start the process.

❑ **Name**: Contains the name for the process.

❑ **OSName**: Contains the name of the operating system on which the process is running — for example, Microsoft Windows Vista Ultimate.

❑ **ParentProcessId**: Contains the unique identifier of the process that invokes the process. The parent process for SQL Server–related services is always the Service Control Manager process, `services.exe`.

❑ **Priority**: Contains the scheduling priority of a process within an operating system. The higher the value, the higher priority a process receives. Priority values can range from 0 (zero), the lowest priority, to 31, the highest priority. The default priority for SQL Server–related services is 8.

❑ **ProcessId**: Contains the process identifier.

❑ **WindowsVersion**: Contains the version of Windows in which the process is running   for example, 6.0.6001 for Windows Vista Service Pack 1 Build 6001.

Let's first look at the values of these properties for the process `sqlservr.exe`, the SQL Server service. The following command filters the service with the `Where-Object` cmdlet, and then uses the `Select-Object` to select its properties:

```
Get-WmiObject -class Win32_Process | Where-Object{ ($_.Name -eq 'sqlservr.exe') } |
Select-Object Caption, CommandLine, CreationDate, CSName, Desciption, ExecutablePath,
Name, OSName, ParentProcessId, Priority, ProcessId, WindowsVersion
```

The `CommandLine` contains the command to start the default instance (see Figure 8-24).

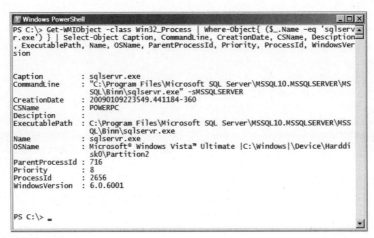

Figure 8-24

In this case, the instance was started at 22:35 on January 9. It is running under the process ID 2656 on the Windows Vista machine PowerPC. The parent process, `services.exe`, is running under the process ID 716. The priority base for the SQL Server process is 8, which is normal.

Some properties of the `Win32_Process` class are dynamic. They provide detailed usage information about the system resources for the process. This information can be very useful for troubleshooting performance problems.

Following are the CPU-related properties of the `Win32_Process` class:

❏ **KernelModeTime**: CPU time in kernel mode, in 100 nanosecond units. If this information is not available, then the value is 0.

❏ **UserModeTime**: CPU time in user mode, in 100 nanosecond units. If this information is not available, then the value is 0.

❏ **ThreadCount**: Number of active threads in a process. Each running process has at least one thread.

❏ **HandleCount**: Total number of handles currently opened by all the threads in this process. A handle is used to examine or modify the system resources. Each handle has an entry in a table that is maintained internally. Entries contain the addresses of the resources, and data to identify the resource type.

Before looking at the memory-related properties of the `Win32_Process` class, let's look at how the memory for a process works. The set of memory pages visible to the process in physical RAM is the working set of a process. These pages are resident, and available for an application to use without triggering a page fault. However, the operating system uses paging files as virtual memory, and makes the virtual memory available to all processes as if it were real RAM.

The operating system, in coordination with the CPU, saves portions of RAM to the paging file and loads portions of the paging file back into RAM as the running applications need them. Pages are swapped between memory and paging files, which result in page faults. A page fault can be soft or hard. If the faulted page is found elsewhere in physical memory, then it is a soft page fault. A hard page fault occurs when a process requires code or data that is not in its working set or elsewhere in physical memory and must be retrieved from disk. A soft page fault has much less effect on performance compared to a hard page fault. When the system does not have enough memory for the working set size the process needs, thrashing and extensive paging occur.

The virtual address space for a process is the set of virtual memory addresses that it can use. Using virtual address space does not necessarily imply corresponding use of either disk or main memory pages. However, virtual space is finite; if a process uses too much, it might not be able to load libraries.

Following are the memory-related properties:

❏ **MaximumWorkingSetSize**: Maximum working set size of the process, in kilobytes.

❏ **MinimumWorkingSetSize**: Minimum working set size of the process, in kilobytes.

❏ **PeakWorkingSetSize**: Peak working set size of a process.

❏ **WorkingSetSize**: Amount of memory, in bytes, that a process needs to execute efficiently (for an operating system that uses page-based memory management).

❏ **PageFaults**: Number of page faults that a process generates. This includes both soft and hard page faults.

❏ **PageFileUsage**: Amount of page file space that a process is using currently, in kilobytes.

❏ **PeakPageFileUsage**: Maximum amount of page file space used during the life of a process, in kilobytes.

❏ **PeakVirtualSize**: Maximum virtual address space a process uses at any one time.

❏ **PrivatePageCount**: Current number of pages allocated that are only accessible to the process represented by this `Win32_Process` instance.

❑ **QuotaNonPagedPoolUsage**: Quota amount of nonpaged pool usage for a process.

❑ **QuotaPagedPoolUsage**: Quota amount of paged pool usage for a process.

❑ **QuotaPeakNonPagedPoolUsage**: Peak quota amount of nonpaged pool usage for a process.

❑ **QuotaPeakPagedPoolUsage**: Peak quota amount of paged pool usage for a process.

❑ **VirtualSize**: Current size of the virtual address space that a process is using, not the physical or virtual memory actually used by the process.

Following are the I/O–related properties of the `Win32_Process` class:

❑ **OtherOperationCount**: Number of I/O operations performed that are not read or write operations.

❑ **OtherTransferCount**: Amount of data transferred during operations that are not read or write operations.

❑ **ReadOperationCount**: Number of read operations performed.

❑ **ReadTransferCount**: Amount of data read, in bytes.

❑ **WriteOperationCount**: Number of write operations performed.

❑ **WriteTransferCount**: Amount of data written, in bytes.

In Chapter 7, you saw the output from the `Get-Process` cmdlet. Actually, each performance counter in the output can be mapped to one or two properties from the `Win32_Process` class. The following table shows the mappings.

Get-Process	W32_Process
Handles	HandleCount
NPM(K)	QuotaNonPagedPoolUsage
PM(K)	PageFileUsage
WS(K)	WorkingSetSize
VM(M)	VirtualSize
CPU(s)	KernelModeTime + UserModeTime

The following command shows the output from the `Get-Process` cmdlet and the properties from the `Win32_Process` for the `sqlservr.exe` process.

```
Get-Process | Where-Object{$_.Name -eq 'sqlservr' }
Get-WmiObject -class Win32_Process | Where-Object{$_.Name -eq 'sqlservr.exe'} |
foreach -process ("Handles: " + $_.HandleCount; "NPM(K): " + $_.QuotaNonPagedPool
Usage; "PM(K): " + $_.PageFileUsage; "WS(K): " + $_.WorkingSetSize/1024; "VM(M): " +
$_.VirtualSize/1024/1024; "CPU(s): " +
($_.KernelModeTime/10e6+$_.UserModeTime/10e6).ToString(); "Id: " + $_.ProcessId;
"ProcessName: " + $_.Name}
```

As shown in Figure 8-25, you can get the same resource usage information from both the `Get-Process` cmdlet and the `Win32_Process` class.

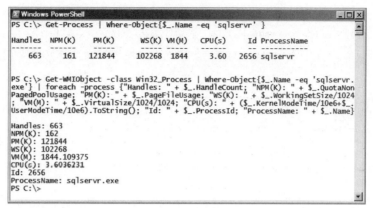

```
Windows PowerShell
PS C:\> Get-Process | Where-Object{$_.Name -eq 'sqlservr' }

Handles  NPM(K)    PM(K)      WS(K) VM(M)   CPU(s)      Id ProcessName
-------  ------    -----      ----- -----   ------      -- -----------
    663     161   121844     102268  1844     3.60    2656 sqlservr

PS C:\> Get-WMIObject -class Win32_Process | Where-Object{$_.Name -eq 'sqlservr.
exe'} | foreach -process {"Handles: " + $_.HandleCount; "NPM(K): " + $_.QuotaNon
PagedPoolUsage; "PM(K): " + $_.PageFileUsage; "WS(K): " + $_.WorkingSetSize/1024
; "VM(M): " + $_.VirtualSize/1024/1024; "CPU(s): " + ($_.KernelModeTime/10e6+$_.
UserModeTime/10e6).ToString(); "Id: " + $_.ProcessId; "ProcessName: " + $_.Name}

Handles: 663
NPM(K): 162
PM(K): 121844
WS(K): 102268
VM(M): 1844.109375
CPU(s): 3.6036231
Id: 2656
ProcessName: sqlservr.exe
PS C:\>
```

Figure 8-25

To get a list of processes running on a remote computer named PowerServer3, run the following command:

```
Get-WmiObject -computerName PowerServer3 -class Win32_Process
```

Figure 8-26 shows part of the output.

The `Win32_Process` class also provides methods to manage processes. Two of them are listed here.

Method	Description
SetPriority	Changes the execution priority of a process
Terminate	Terminates a process and all of its threads

The `SetPriority` method changes the execution priority of a process. This method takes only one parameter, `priority`. Possible values for the parameter are listed in the following table.

Priority	Description
Idle	Specified for a process with threads that run only when the system is idle.
Normal	Specified for a process with no special scheduling needs.
High Priority	Specified for a process that performs time-critical tasks that must be executed immediately.
Real Time	Specified for a process with the highest priority possible. The threads of this process preempt the threads of any other processes, including other OS processes that perform important tasks.

Figure 8-26

The default priority for the SQL Server service is 8. However, you can use this method to promote the priority of the SQL Server service to High, a Windows scheduling priority higher than other processes on the same computer. The following commands promote the priority of the SQL Server service of the default instance on the local computer:

```
$sqlprocess = Get-WmiObject -class Win32_Process | Where-Object{$_.Name -eq
'sqlservr.exe' -and $_.CommandLine -like '*-sMSSQLSERVER'}
"Priority of the process of the default SQL Server instance is " +
$sqlprocess.Priority $sqlprocess.SetPriority(128)
$sqlprocess = Get-WmiObject -class Win32_Process | Where-Object{$_.Name -eq
'sqlservr.exe' -and $_.CommandLine -like '*-sMSSQLSERVER'}
"Priority of the process of the default SQL Server instance is " +
$sqlprocess.Priority
```

Note that if you do not have a default instance, but only a named instance, on your computer, then you should update MSSQLSERVER with the name of the named instance before running the commands. For example, for the named instance INSTANCE1, the first command line should be as follows:

```
$sqlprocess = Get-WmiObject -class Win32_Process | Where-Object{$_.Name -eq
'sqlservr.exe' -and $_.CommandLine -like '*-sINSTANCE1'}
```

As shown in Figure 8-27, you first get the process object for the SQL Server service of the default instance.

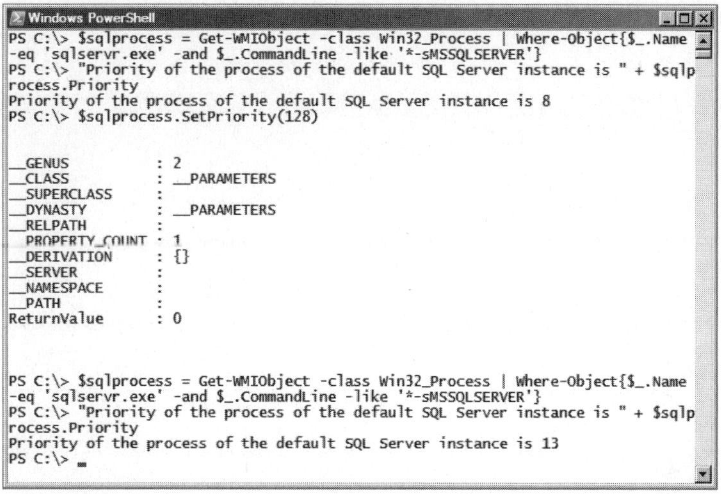

Figure 8-27

Then you raise the priority of the process from Normal to High using the SetPriority method. The priority number increases from 8 to 13 after the change. Actually, the commands have the same effect as enabling the "priority boost" option on the SQL Server. However, the SetPriority method changes only the process the SQL Server service is currently running on, whereas the option affects any process the SQL Server service is associated with after it is enabled.

```
exec sp_configure 'priority boost', 1
reconfigure
```

The Terminate method terminates a process and all of its threads. For example, to terminate a running Notepad process, you first need to determine its process ID. Then pass the ID as a parameter to the method.

Open a Notepad window and run the following command to terminate the Notepad process:

```
$proc=Get-WmiObject -class Win32_Process | Where-Object{$_.name -eq 'notepad.exe'}
$proc.Terminate($proc.ProcessID)
```

As shown in Figure 8-28, the Terminate method executed with a success code of 0. You should have noticed that the Notepad window closed.

Configuration Manager should be used to stop SQL Server–related services. However, in rare cases, a SQL Server instance becomes unresponsive. For example, suppose a User Mode Scheduler inside SQL Server hangs and you are unable to stop the service with Configuration Manager. In this case, you need to terminate the SQL Server process directly. The following commands filter out the SQL Server service for the default instance based on the `Name` and `CommandLine` properties, and then invoke the `Terminate` method on the service:

```
$proc=Get-WmiObject -class Win32_Process | Where-Object{$_.Name -eq 'sqlservr.exe'
-and $_.CommandLine -like '*-sMSSQLSERVER'}
$proc.Terminate($proc.ProcessID)
```

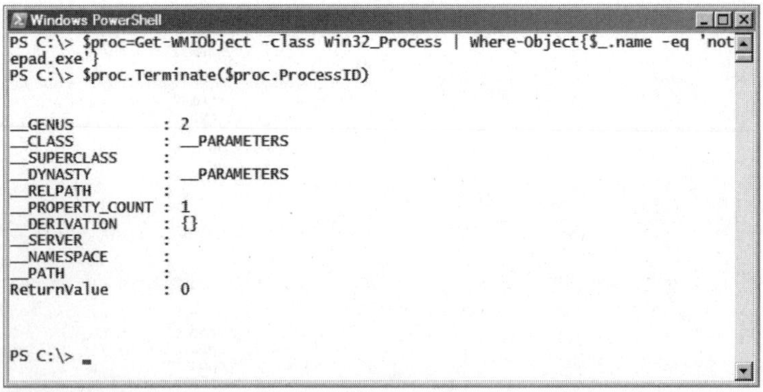

Figure 8-28

If there are multiple instances on the same computer, then you certainly don't want to stop the healthy instances by accident. You need to specify the name of the instance you are trying to stop in the `CommandLine` property as shown in the preceding example.

Working with Environment Variables

The `Win32_Environment` WMI class represents system environment settings on a Windows computer system. Querying this class returns environment variables found under the registry key `HKLM\System\CurrentControlSet\Control\Sessionmanager\Environment`.

The properties of the class are as follows:

- ❏ **Caption**: Short description (one-line string) of the environment variable.
- ❏ **Description**: Description of the environment variable.
- ❏ **InstallDate**: When the environment variable was installed.
- ❏ **Name**: Name of a Windows-based environment variable.
- ❏ **SystemVariable**: Indicates whether the variable is a system variable. A system variable is set by the operating system, and is independent from user environment settings.
- ❏ **UserName**: Name of the owner of the environment setting. It is set to <SYSTEM> for settings that are specific to the system, and <DEFAULT> for default user settings.
- ❏ **VariableValue**: Value of the variable.

You can access all the variables and their values by executing the following command:

```
Get-WmiObject -class Win32_Environment | Select-Object Name, VariableValue
```

The output is shown in Figure 8-29.

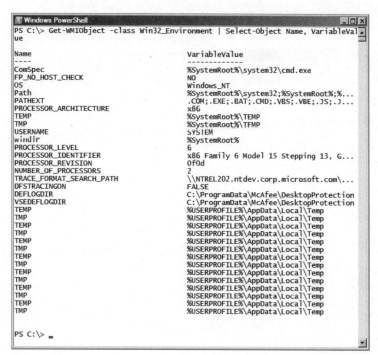

Figure 8-29

You can get all the properties and methods of the `Win32_Environment` class by passing the environment variable objects in a pipeline to the `Get-Member` cmdlet:

```
Get-WmiObject -class Win32_Environment | Get-Member
```

As shown in Figure 8-30, there are other properties you can access.

You can use the `Select-Object` cmdlet to get the owner of the variables from the `Win32_Environment` class:

```
Get-WmiObject -class Win32_Environment | Select-Object Name, UserName, SystemVariable
```

As shown in Figure 8-31, all the system variables are owned by `SYSTEM`.

You can first filter the variable objects returned by `Get-WmiObject` with the `Where-Object` cmdlet to get the TMP setting for the user PowerDomain\PowerUser:

```
Get-WmiObject -class Win32_Environment | Where-Object {$_.Name -eq "TMP" -and
$_.Username -eq "PowerDomain\PowerUser"}
```

```
Windows PowerShell                                                    _ □ X
PS C:\> Get-WMIObject -class Win32_Environment | Get-Member


   TypeName: System.Management.ManagementObject#root\cimv2\Win32_Environment

Name                   MemberType    Definition
----                   ----------    ----------
Caption                Property      System.String Caption {get;set;}
Description            Property      System.String Description {get;set;}
InstallDate           Property      System.String InstallDate {get;set;}
Name                   Property      System.String Name {get;set;}
Status                 Property      System.String Status {get;set;}
SystemVariable        Property      System.Boolean SystemVariable {get;set;}
UserName               Property      System.String UserName {get;set;}
VariableValue         Property      System.String VariableValue {get;set;}
__CLASS                Property      System.String __CLASS {get;set;}
__DERIVATION          Property      System.String[] __DERIVATION {get;set;}
__DYNASTY             Property      System.String __DYNASTY {get;set;}
__GENUS                Property      System.Int32 __GENUS {get;set;}
__NAMESPACE           Property      System.String __NAMESPACE {get;set;}
__PATH                 Property      System.String __PATH {get;set;}
__PROPERTY_COUNT      Property      System.Int32 __PROPERTY_COUNT {get;set;}
__RELPATH             Property      System.String __RELPATH {get;set;}
__SERVER               Property      System.String __SERVER {get;set;}
__SUPERCLASS          Property      System.String __SUPERCLASS {get;set;}
PSStatus               PropertySet   PSStatus {Status, Name, SystemVariable}
ConvertFromDateTime    ScriptMethod  System.Object ConvertFromDateTime();
ConvertToDateTime      ScriptMethod  System.Object ConvertToDateTime();


PS C:\> _
```

Figure 8-30

```
Windows PowerShell                                                    _ □ X
PS C:\> Get-WMIObject -class Win32_Environment | Select-Object Name, UserName, S
ystemVariable

Name                         UserName                    SystemVariable
----                         --------                    --------------
ComSpec                      <SYSTEM>                              True
FP_NO_HOST_CHECK             <SYSTEM>                              True
OS                           <SYSTEM>                              True
Path                         <SYSTEM>                              True
PATHEXT                      <SYSTEM>                              True
PROCESSOR_ARCHITECTURE       <SYSTEM>                              True
TEMP                         <SYSTEM>                              True
TMP                          <SYSTEM>                              True
USERNAME                     <SYSTEM>                              True
windir                       <SYSTEM>                              True
PROCESSOR_LEVEL              <SYSTEM>                              True
PROCESSOR_IDENTIFIER         <SYSTEM>                              True
PROCESSOR_REVISION           <SYSTEM>                              True
NUMBER_OF_PROCESSORS         <SYSTEM>                              True
TRACE_FORMAT_SEARCH_PATH     <SYSTEM>                              True
DFSTRACINGON                 <SYSTEM>                              True
DEFLOGDIR                    <SYSTEM>                              True
VSEDEFLOGDIR                 <SYSTEM>                              True
TEMP                         NT AUTHORITY\SYSTEM                   False
TMP                          NT AUTHORITY\SYSTEM                   False
TEMP                         NT AUTHORITY\LOCAL SERVICE            False
TMP                          NT AUTHORITY\LOCAL SERVICE            False
TEMP                         NT AUTHORITY\NETWORK SE...            False
TMP                          NT AUTHORITY\NETWORK SE...            False
TEMP                         POWERDOMAIN\PowerUser                 False
TMP                          POWERDOMAIN\PowerUser                 False
TEMP                         POWERDOMAIN\SqlService                False
TMP                          POWERDOMAIN\SqlService                False
TEMP                         POWERPC\Yan                           False
TMP                          POWERPC\Yan                           False
TEMP                         POWERPC\Administrator                 False
TMP                          POWERPC\Administrator                 False


PS C:\> _
```

Figure 8-31

The output is shown in Figure 8-32.

```
Windows PowerShell                                                    _ □ ×
PS C:\> Get-WMIObject -class Win32_Environment | Where-Object {$_.Name -eq "TMP"
-and $_.Username -eq "PowerDomain\PowerUser"}

VariableValue                    Name                    UserName
-------------                    ----                    --------
%USERPROFILE%\AppData\L... TMP                           POWERDOMAIN\PowerUser


PS C:\> _
```

Figure 8-32

The `Delete` method deletes a variable from the system environment. For example, to delete the variable TMP, you can filter the variable object as shown in the previous command, and then invoke the `Delete` object on the object. However, before deleting a variable, ensure that the OS and applications are not using it. Otherwise, some applications might not work correctly.

```
$a= Get-WmiObject -class Win32_Environment| Where-Object {$_.Name -eq "TMP"
-and $_.Username -eq "PowerDomain\PowerUser"}
$a.Delete()
```

In order to access system variables on a remote machine, you can add an additional parameter: `-computerName`:

```
Get-WmiObject -class Win32_Environment -computerName PowerServer3 | Select-Object
Name, UserName, SystemVariable
```

The environment variables on the remote computer PowerServer3 are shown in Figure 8-33.

```
Windows PowerShell                                                    _ □ ×
PS C:\> Get-WMIObject -class Win32_Environment -computerName PowerServer3 | Sele
ct-Object Name, UserName, SystemVariable

Name                     UserName                        SystemVariable
----                     --------                        --------------
ComSpec                  <SYSTEM>                         True
Path                     <SYSTEM>                         True
windir                   <SYSTEM>                         True
OS                       <SYSTEM>                         True
PROCESSOR_ARCHITECTURE   <SYSTEM>                         True
PROCESSOR_LEVEL          <SYSTEM>                         True
PROCESSOR_IDENTIFIER     <SYSTEM>                         True
PROCESSOR_REVISION       <SYSTEM>                         True
NUMBER_OF_PROCESSORS     <SYSTEM>                         True
ClusterLog               <SYSTEM>                         True
PATHEXT                  <SYSTEM>                         True
TEMP                     <SYSTEM>                         True
TMP                      <SYSTEM>                         True
FP_NO_HOST_CHECK         <SYSTEM>                         True
TEMP                     NT AUTHORITY\SYSTEM              False
TMP                      NT AUTHORITY\SYSTEM              False
TEMP                     NT AUTHORITY\LOCAL SERVICE       False
TMP                      NT AUTHORITY\LOCAL SERVICE       False
TEMP                     NT AUTHORITY\NETWORK SE...       False
TMP                      NT AUTHORITY\NETWORK SE...       False
TEMP                     POWERDOMAIN\PowerUser            False
TMP                      POWERDOMAIN\PowerUser            False
TEMP                     POWERDOMAIN\sqlservice           False
TMP                      POWERDOMAIN\sqlservice           False
TEMP                     POWERDOMAIN\Administrator        False
TMP                      POWERDOMAIN\Administrator        False
TEMP                     POWERSERVER3\Administrator       False
TMP                      POWERSERVER3\Administrator       False


PS C:\>
```

Figure 8-33

Working with the Registry

The StdRegProv class contains methods that manipulate system registry keys and values. On Windows Server 2003, Windows XP, Windows 2000, Windows NT 4.0, and Windows Me/98/95, StdRegProv is available only in the root\default namespace. On Windows Vista and Windows Server 2008, StdRegProv is preinstalled in the WMI namespaces root\default and root\cimv2.

Now check all the methods that are available from the class StdRegProv:

```
$Reg = [WMIClass]"root\default:stdRegProv"
$Reg | Get-Member
```

Figure 8-34 shows the results.

Figure 8-34

Registry keys are classified into six different categories (hives) identified by the following unique registry hive constants. You need these unique numbers to access the right keys and their values.

Hive	Decimal Value	Hexidecimal Value
HKEY_CLASSES_ROOT	2147483648	0x80000000
HKEY_CURRENT_USER	2147483649	0x80000001
HKEY_LOCAL_MACHINE	2147483650	0x80000002
HKEY_USERS	2147483651	0x80000003
HKEY_CURRENT_CONFIG	2147483653	0x80000005
HKEY_DYN_DATA	2147483654	0x80000006

To get a list of service names listed as subkeys under the SYSTEM\CurrentControlSet\Services key in the HKEY_LOCAL_MACHINE registry hive, you can use the Enumkey method. This method accepts a hive constant and a registry path. In this case, you pass the value of the HKEY_LOCAL_MACHINE hive and the path SYSTEM\CurrentControlSet\Services, as shown in the following command:

```
$Reg = [WMIClass]"root\default:stdRegProv"
$HKEY_LOCAL_MACHINE = 2147483650 $strKeyPath = "SYSTEM\CurrentControlSet\Services"
$services=$Reg.EnumKey($HKEY_LOCAL_MACHINE,$strKeyPath)
$services.sNames
```

Figure 8-35 shows part of the services.

Figure 8-35

You may want to query certain information about SQL Server, such as what network libraries are installed and whether they are enabled. The server network protocols for the default instance are listed as subkeys under SOFTWARE\Microsoft\Microsoft SQL Server\MSSQL10.MSSQLSERVER\ MSSQLServer\SuperSocketNetLib in the HKEY_LOCAL_MACHINE registry hive. You can use the EnumKey method to retrieve all the protocol subkeys. For each protocol, the Enabled registry value of each protocol indicates whether the protocol is enabled (1) or disabled (0). The value is of type REG_DWORD, so you need to use the GetDWORDValue method to get it:

```
$Reg = [WMIClass]"root\default:stdRegProv"
$HKEY_LOCAL_MACHINE = 2147483650
$strKeyPath = "SOFTWARE\Microsoft\Microsoft SQL
Server\MSSQL10.MSSQLSERVER\MSSQLServer\SuperSocketNetLib"
$netlib=$Reg.EnumKey($HKEY_LOCAL_MACHINE,$strKeyPath)
$netlib.sNames | Foreach-Object { $_ + "=" +
$Reg.GetDWORDValue($HKEY_LOCAL_MACHINE,$strKeyPath+'\'+ $_,"Enabled").uValue}
```

As shown in Figure 8-36, both the Named Pipes and TCP/IP protocols are enabled.

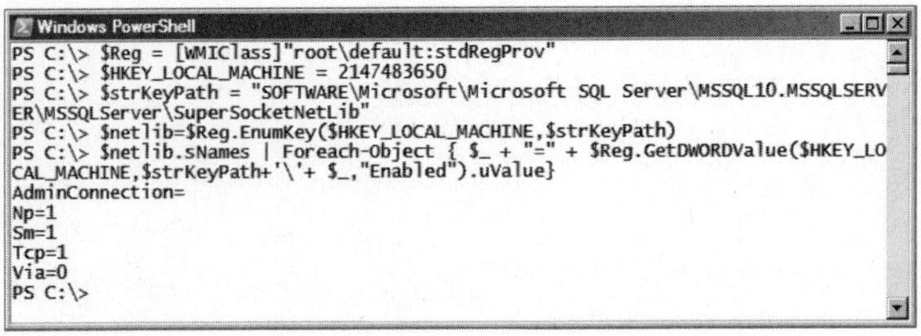

Figure 8-36

To get the registry values under a key, you can use the EnumValues method. For example, to obtain all the values under the Named Pipes registry key, use the following commands (the sNames property contains an array of named registry values):

```
$Reg = [WMIClass]"root\default:stdRegProv"
$HKEY_LOCAL_MACHINE = 2147483650
$strKeyPath = "SOFTWARE\Microsoft\Microsoft SQL
Server\MSSQL10.MSSQLSERVER\MSSQLServer\SuperSocketNetLib\Np"
$namedpipe=$Reg.EnumValues($HKEY_LOCAL_MACHINE,$strKeyPath)
$namedpipe.sNames
```

Figure 8-37 shows three named nondefault values under the Named Pipes key, which includes the Enabled key shown in the previous example.

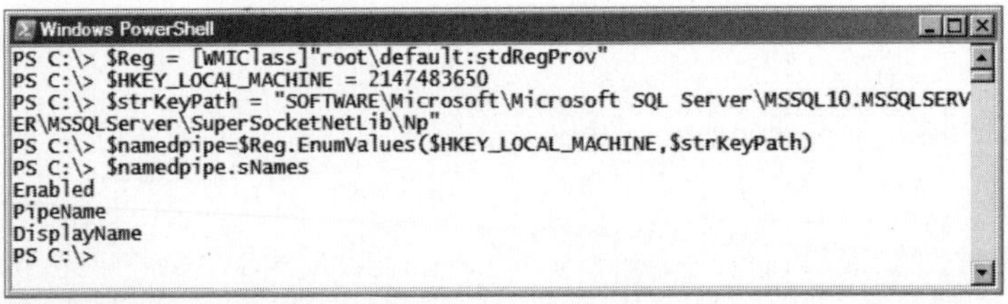

Figure 8-37

Figure 8-38 shows the same values in the Registry Editor.

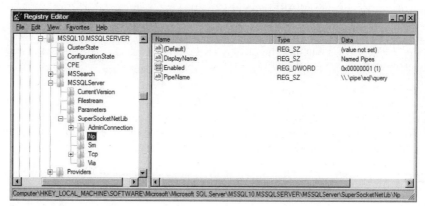

Figure 8-38

The name of the named pipe and the TCP/IP port number are of type REG_SZ, which is a string. You can obtain them with the GetStringValue method using the following commands:

```
$Reg = [WMIClass]"root\default:stdRegProv"
$HKEY_LOCAL_MACHINE = 2147483650

$strKeyPath = "SOFTWARE\Microsoft\Microsoft SQL
Server\MSSQL10.MSSQLSERVER\MSSQLServer\SuperSocketNetLib\Np"
$pipeName=$reg.GetStringValue($HKEY_LOCAL_MACHINE,$strKeyPath,"Pipename").svalue
$pipeName

$strKeyPath = "SOFTWARE\Microsoft\Microsoft SQL
Server\MSSQL10.MSSQLSERVER\MSSQLServer\SuperSocketNetLib\Tcp\IPAll"
$TcpPort=$reg.GetStringValue($HKEY_LOCAL_MACHINE,$strKeyPath,"TcpPort").svalue
$TcpPort
```

The pipe name is \\.\pipe\sql\query, and the TCP/IP port number is 1433 (see Figure 8-39).

```
PS C:\> $Reg = [WMIClass]"root\default:stdRegProv"
PS C:\> $HKEY_LOCAL_MACHINE = 2147483650
PS C:\>
PS C:\> $strKeyPath = "SOFTWARE\Microsoft\Microsoft SQL Server\MSSQL10.MSSQLSERV
ER\MSSQLServer\SuperSocketNetLib\Np"
PS C:\> $pipeName=$reg.GetStringValue($HKEY_LOCAL_MACHINE,$strKeyPath,"Pipename"
).svalue
PS C:\> $pipeName
\\.\pipe\sql\query
PS C:\>
PS C:\> $strKeyPath = "SOFTWARE\Microsoft\Microsoft SQL Server\MSSQL10.MSSQLSERV
ER\MSSQLServer\SuperSocketNetLib\Tcp\IPAll"
PS C:\> $TcpPort=$reg.GetStringValue($HKEY_LOCAL_MACHINE,$strKeyPath,"TcpPort").
svalue
PS C:\> $TcpPort
1433
PS C:\>
```

Figure 8-39

Now try to create a new value name and value data under SOFTWARE\Microsoft\MSSQLServer\ MSSQLServer\SuperSocketNetLib\Np in the registry. The CreateKey method creates the subkey and the `SetStringValue` method adds a registry value of type `REG_SZ`. The new registry value is called `TestValueName`, and its value is `TestValue`. You can verify the creation of the new registry value by querying it with the `GetStringValue` method:

```
$HKEY_LOCAL_MACHINE = 2147483650
$Reg = [WMIClass]"root\default:stdRegProv"
$strKeyPath = "SOFTWARE\Microsoft\Microsoft SQL
Server\MSSQL10.MSSQLSERVER\MSSQLServer\SuperSocketNetLib\Np"
$strValueName = "TestValueName"
$strValue = "TestValue"
$Reg.CreateKey($HKEY_LOCAL_MACHINE,$strKeyPath)
$Reg.SetStringValue($HKEY_LOCAL_MACHINE,$strKeyPath,$strValueName,$strValue)
$Reg.GetStringValue($HKEY_LOCAL_MACHINE,$strKeyPath,"TestValueName").svalue
```

As shown in Figure 8-40, a new registry key value, `TestValueName`, has been created.

Figure 8-40

If you want to delete this key, use the `DeleteValue` method:

```
$Reg.DeleteValue($HKEY_LOCAL_MACHINE, $strKeyPath, "TestValueName")
```

Figure 8-41 shows the 0 return code, which indicates that the value was deleted successfully.

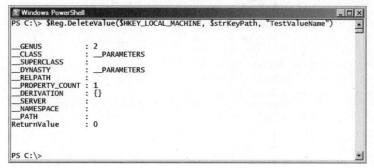

Figure 8-41

Summary

This chapter discussed the WMI model, and worked with different WMI classes to manage Windows event logs, services, processes, environment variables, and the registry. In the next two chapters, we will use the WMI classes to manage SQL Server configurations and server events.

9

WMI Provider for Configuration Management

Since the release of Microsoft SQL Server 2005, Microsoft has included two WMI providers for SQL Server: the WMI Provider for Configuration Management to manage SQL Server services and network connectivity, and the WMI Provider for Server Events, to manage SQL Server events. This chapter illustrates how to access the SQL Server 2008 WMI providers using Windows PowerShell, and how to perform administrative tasks using the WMI Provider for Configuration Management. The WMI Provider for Server Events is explained in detail in Chapter 10.

The WMI Provider for Configuration Management is a published layer that is used with the SQL Server Configuration Manager snap-in for the Microsoft Management Console (MMC) and the Microsoft SQL Server Configuration Manager. By writing a Windows PowerShell script, you can connect to the Configuration Manager and take advantage of all the services it provides.

In this chapter, you will learn how to manage SQL Server services, client and server protocols, and server aliases, both locally and remotely, using Windows PowerShell and the WMI Provider for Configuration Management. As you know, the Configuration Manager can be used to manage only local SQL Server instances. Therefore, the approach introduced in this chapter is far more flexible.

This chapter covers the following topics:

- ❏ Managing SQL Server services

- ❏ Managing client network protocols

- ❏ Managing SQL Server client aliases

- ❏ Managing server network protocols

- ❏ Changing FILESTREAM settings

- ❏ Changing SQL Server advanced properties

Managing SQL Server Services

The WMI Provider for Configuration Management provides access to WMI objects in the root\Microsoft\SqlServer\ComputerManagement namespace for SQL Server 2005, and the root\Microsoft\SqlServer\ComputerManagement10 namespace for SQL Server 2008. Because objects are instances of classes, we'll look at the classes available under the namespace for SQL Server 2008. As stated in Chapter 8, the extension classes (the classes without a prefix of two underscores) are technology-specific classes. This chapter covers only the extension classes that are specific to SQL Server. As shown in previous chapters, you can use the Get-WmiObject cmdlet to connect with WMI. The following command uses the -list parameter to list all the classes under the namespace, and the Where-Object cmdlet to filter the extension classes:

```
Get-WmiObject -namespace root\Microsoft\SqlServer\ComputerManagement10 -list | Where-
Object {-not ($_.Name -like '__*')}
```

Figure 9-1 shows the extension classes. As suggested by their names, they can be used to instantiate objects for client network protocols, server network protocols, SQL Server services, and server aliases.

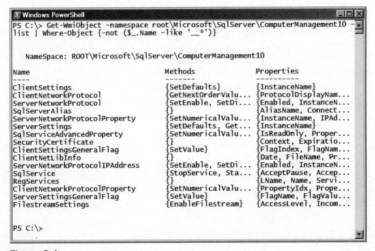

Figure 9-1

The SqlService class represents the objects for SQL services. To view a list of available services on your local computer, you can pass the class name SqlService to the -class parameter, and then use the Select-Object cmdlet to get the name, type, state, and process ID of each service. By default, the services are returned in a list. For easy viewing, you can use the Format-Table cmdlet to format the output as a table:

```
Get-WmiObject -namespace root\Microsoft\SqlServer\ComputerManagement10 -class
SqlService | Select-Object ServiceName, DisplayName, SQLServiceType, State,
ProcessId | Format-Table -wrap
```

Figure 9-2 shows that the local computer has a default instance MSSQLSERVER and a named instance INSTANCE1 installed. The command returns 10 service instances representing SQL Server Integration Services, SQL Server Analysis Service, SQL Server Service, SQL Server Full-Text Filter Daemon Launcher Service, SQL Server Reporting Services, SQL Server Agent Service, and SQL Server Browser Service.

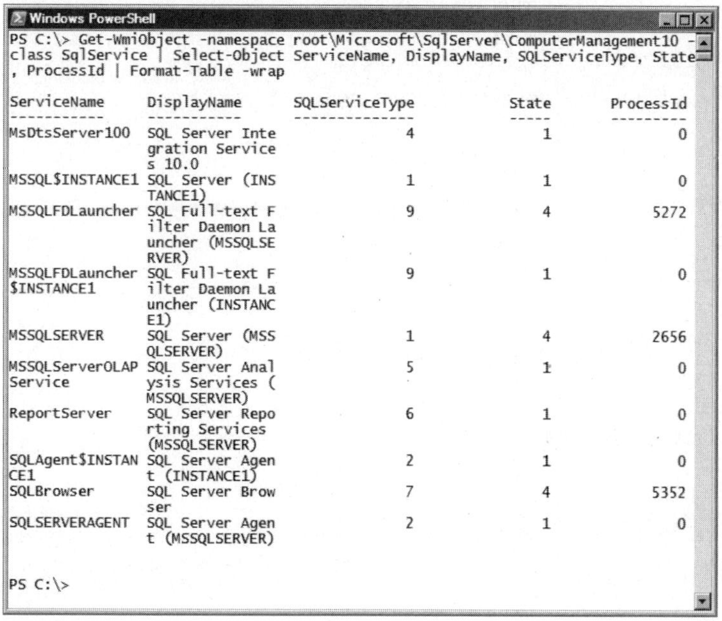

Figure 9-2

As you can see, each service has a SQLServiceType. The service types are defined in Table 9-1.

The running state of each service is also represented by a value, as defined in Table 9-2.

Figure 9-2 shows that the SQL Server Service for the default instance MSSQLSERVER, the SQL Full-Text Filter Daemon Launcher service MSSQLFDLauncher, and the SQL Server Browser service SQLBrowser, are running.

To see all the methods that you can apply to the service instances, run the following command.

```
Get-WmiObject -namespace root\Microsoft\SqlServer\ComputerManagement10 -class
SqlService | Get-Member -MemberType method
```

You can use the methods shown in Figure 9-3 to manage the state of the services and change the service accounts.

Table 9-1: SQL Server Service Types

Type	Description
1	SQL Server service
2	SQL Server Agent service
4	SQL Server Integration Services
5	SQL Server Analysis Services
6	SQL Server Reporting Services
7	SQL Server Browser service
8	NsService is the SQL Server Notification Services service. However, this service is not available in SQL Server 2008.
9	SQL Server Full-Text Filter Daemon

Table 9-2: Service States

State	Description
1	Stopped. The service is stopped.
2	Start Pending. The service is waiting to start.
3	Stop Pending. The service is waiting to stop.
4	Running. The service is running.
5	Continue Pending. The service is waiting to continue.
6	Pause Pending. The service is waiting to pause.
7	Paused. The service is paused.

You can change the SQL Server service account from the local system account to a domain account, PowerDomain\SqlService, and then restart the service for the change to take effect. A sample of such a script is shown in the following example. The script first uses Get-WmiObject to instantiate an object associated with the default SQL Server service, MSSQLSERVER. Then it invokes the SetServiceAccount method of the object to change the service account to the domain account PowerDomain\SqlService. After the service account has been changed, it invokes the StopService and StartService methods to stop and restart the SQL Server service:

```
$strUserName = "PowerDomain\SqlService"
# Password for the PowerDomain\SqlService account
```

```
$strPassword= "P@ssw0rd"
$sqlservice = Get-WmiObject -namespace
root\Microsoft\SqlServer\ComputerManagement10
-class SqlService -filter "ServiceName='MSSQLSERVER'"

$sqlservice.SetServiceAccount($strUserName, $strPassword)

$sqlservice.StopService()

$sqlservice.StartService()
```

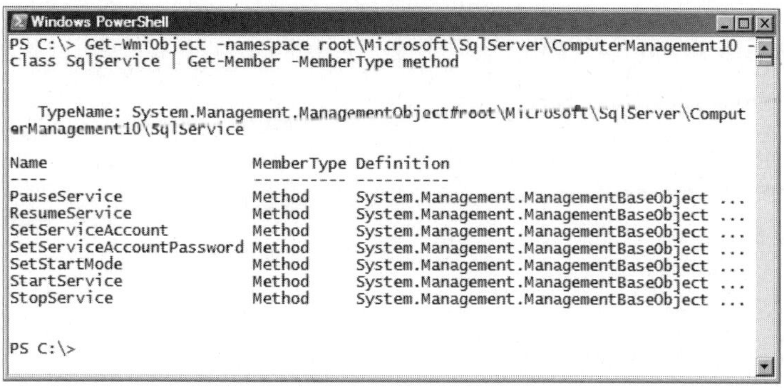

Figure 9-3

The output is shown in Figure 9-4. A return value of 0 means that the operation was successful.

If you have only named instances on your computer, you will need to change the -filter parameter in the Get-WmiObject cmdlet before running the script. For example, for a named instance INSTANCE1, you should change the filter to "ServiceName='MSSQL`$INSTANCE1'". The backtick character (`) is used to escape the dollar sign ($) character in the service name.

As demonstrated in the previous chapters, WMI enables system components to be controlled remotely. The -computerName flag is used to specify the name of the remote computer to connect with. The following example shows how to change a named instance called CH0DE1 on a remote computer DEMOPC. You can change the first line of the preceding script as follows:

```
$sqlservice = Get-WmiObject -computerName DEMOPC -namespace
root\Microsoft\SqlServer\ComputerManagement10 -class SqlService -filter
"ServiceName='MSSQL`$CH0DE1'"
```

For a local computer, you can omit the -computerName parameter and use "." or "localhost" as its value.

A complete sample script can be found in ManageSQLServerService.ps1 under the C:\DBAScripts directory. This directory is going to hold all of your administrative scripts, and will be the default location from which your scripts run. This script uses Out-Null to suppress the informational messages returned by the SetServiceAccount, StopService, and StartService methods. As shown in Figure 9-5, this script was executed to change the SQL Server service account. Notice that no informational messages were printed out.

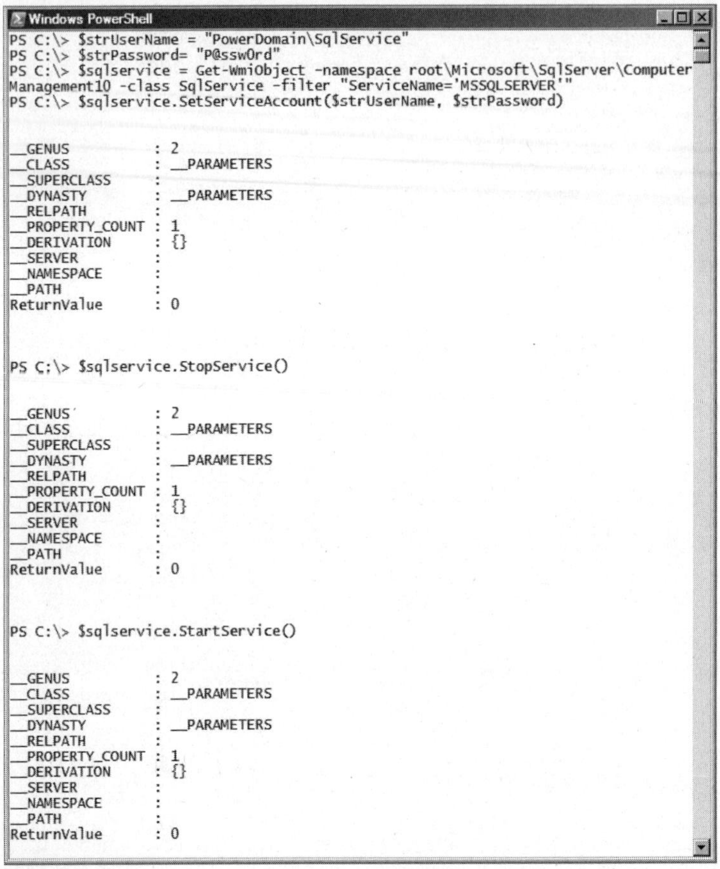

```
Windows PowerShell                                                    _ □ ×
PS C:\> $strUserName = "PowerDomain\SqlService"
PS C:\> $strPassword= "P@ssw0rd"
PS C:\> $sqlservice = Get-WmiObject -namespace root\Microsoft\SqlServer\Computer
Management10 -class SqlService -filter "ServiceName='MSSQLSERVER'"
PS C:\> $sqlservice.SetServiceAccount($strUserName, $strPassword)


__GENUS         : 2
__CLASS         : __PARAMETERS
__SUPERCLASS    :
__DYNASTY       : __PARAMETERS
__RELPATH       :
__PROPERTY_COUNT : 1
__DERIVATION    : {}
__SERVER        :
__NAMESPACE     :
__PATH          :
ReturnValue     : 0



PS C:\> $sqlservice.StopService()


__GENUS         : 2
__CLASS         : __PARAMETERS
__SUPERCLASS    :
__DYNASTY       : __PARAMETERS
__RELPATH       :
__PROPERTY_COUNT : 1
__DERIVATION    : {}
__SERVER        :
__NAMESPACE     :
__PATH          :
ReturnValue     : 0



PS C:\> $sqlservice.StartService()


__GENUS         : 2
__CLASS         : __PARAMETERS
__SUPERCLASS    :
__DYNASTY       : __PARAMETERS
__RELPATH       :
__PROPERTY_COUNT : 1
__DERIVATION    : {}
__SERVER        :
__NAMESPACE     :
__PATH          :
ReturnValue     : 0
```

Figure 9-4

```
Windows PowerShell                                                    _ □ ×
PS C:\DBAScripts> .\ManageSQLServerService.ps1
PS C:\DBAScripts> _
```

Figure 9-5

You can also change the start mode of a SQL Server service with the SetStartMode method. If the SQL Server Agent service is currently set to start manually but you want it to start automatically to support jobs and alerts, you can run the AutostartSQLServerAgent.ps1 script shown here:

```
$strComputer = "."

$sqlservice = Get-WmiObject -computerName $strComputer -namespace
root\Microsoft\SqlServer\ComputerManagement10 `
-class SqlService -filter "ServiceName='SQLSERVERAGENT'"
$sqlservice.SetStartMode(2)
```

The script first uses Get-WmiObject to instantiate an object associated with the default SQL Server Agent service, SQLSERVERAGENT. It then invokes the SetStartMode method of the object to change the start mode to 2. The parameter 2 corresponds to the Auto start mode. All the start modes are defined in Table 9-3.

Table 9-3: Service Start Modes

Start Mode	Description
2	Service is started automatically
3	Service is started manually
4	Service is disabled

Note that if you only have named instances on your computer, you need to change the -filter parameter in the Get-WmiObject cmdlet before running the script. For example, for a named instance INSTANCE1, you should change the filter to "ServiceName=' SQLAgent`$INSTANCE1'". The backtick character (`) is used to escape the dollar sign ($) character in the service name.

As shown in Figure 9-6, the script was executed to change the start mode of the SQL Server Agent for the default instance. The 0 value was returned from successfully executing the SetStartMode method.

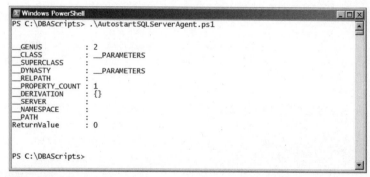

Figure 9-6

Managing Client Network Protocols

The ClientNetworkProtocol class represents the objects for client network protocols. To see the list of protocols, you can use the Get-WmiObject cmdlet and pass the class name ClientNetworkProtocol to the -class parameter. Then use the Select-Object cmdlet to get the protocol names and their order:

```
Get-WmiObject -namespace root\Microsoft\SqlServer\ComputerManagement10 -class
ClientNetworkProtocol  | Select-Object ProtocolName, ProtocolDisplayName,
ProtocolOrder
```

The `ProtocolOrder` column, as shown in Figure 9-7, specifies the order of the client network protocol that is currently referenced. In this case, when connecting with a SQL Server instance, the Microsoft SQL Server client first uses the Shared Memory protocol.

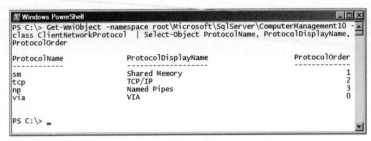

Figure 9-7

If the first protocol doesn't work (i.e., the connection is remote), the client tries the `TCP/IP` protocol next, and then the `Named Pipes` protocol. The `0` value of the `ProtocolOrder` property of the `VIA` protocol means it is disabled.

To see all the methods you can apply to the client network protocol instances, use the `Get-Member` cmdlet to get the members of type `Method`. Then use the `Select-Object` cmdlet to get only the names of the methods:

```
Get-WmiObject -namespace root\Microsoft\SqlServer\ComputerManagement10 -class
ClientNetworkProtocol | Get-Member -memberType Method | Select-Object Name
```

Figure 9-8 shows the list of methods available. These methods can be used to select the protocol that is in the next position in the list of protocols, to disable or enable a protocol, and to change the protocol order.

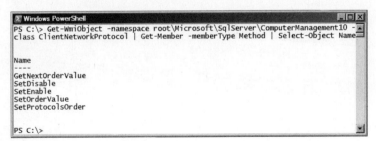

Figure 9-8

For example, if you want to disable the `Named Pipes` protocol, you can use the `Get-WmiObject` method to instantiate the objects for the client network protocols, and filter the `Named Pipes` protocol object with the `ProtocolName` property. Then invoke the `SetDisable` method on the object:

```
$clientprotocol=Get-WmiObject -namespace
root\Microsoft\SqlServer\ComputerManagement10 -class ClientNetworkProtocol -filter
```

```
"ProtocolName='np'"
$clientprotocol.SetDisable()
```

The 0 return value shown in Figure 9-9 indicates that the Named Pipes protocol was disabled successfully.

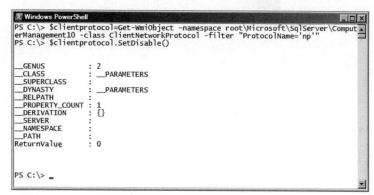

Figure 9-9

You can run the following command again for verification:

```
Get-WmiObject -namespace root\Microsoft\SqlServer\ComputerManagement10 -class
ClientNetworkProtocol | Select-Object ProtocolName, ProtocolDisplayName,
ProtocolOrder
```

As shown in Figure 9-10, the order of the Named Pipes protocol changed to 0 (i.e., it is disabled).

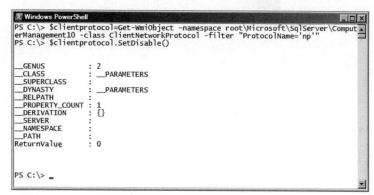

Figure 9-10

If you'd like to re-enable the Named Pipes protocol and place it above the TCP/IP protocol, which has an order of 2 in the list, you can simply use the SetOrderValue method to set the order of the Named Pipes protocol to 2, to take the place of the TCP/IP protocol:

```
$clientprotocol=Get-WmiObject -namespace root\Microsoft\SqlServer
\ComputerManagement10 -class ClientNetworkProtocol -filter "ProtocolName='np'"
$clientprotocol.SetOrderValue(2)
```

To verify the result, sort all the client network protocols by their order:

```
Get-WmiObject -namespace root\Microsoft\SqlServer\ComputerManagement10 -class
ClientNetworkProtocol | Select-Object ProtocolName, ProtocolDisplayName,
ProtocolOrder | Sort-Object ProtocolOrder
```

Figure 9-11 shows that the Named Pipes protocol is now above the TCP/IP protocol.

Figure 9-11

Some settings are specific to each protocol. For example, the TCP/IP protocol must define a default listening port. The properties specific to each protocol can be accessed through the ClientNetworkProtocolProperty class. The following command instantiates all the objects of this class with the Get-WmiObject cmdlet, and then uses the Select-Object cmdlet to get the property names and their associated protocol names:

```
Get-WmiObject -namespace root\Microsoft\SqlServer\ComputerManagement10 -class
ClientNetworkProtocolProperty | Select-Object PropertyName, ProtocolName
```

As shown in Figure 9-12, the TCP/IP protocol owns the first three properties.

If you want to change the default port of the TCP/IP protocol from 1433 to 7001, you can use the SetNumericalValue method of the ClientNetworkProtocolProperty class. A sample script is shown here:

```
$strComputer = "."

$protocolproperty=Get-WmiObject -computerName $strComputer -namespace
root\Microsoft\SqlServer\ComputerManagement10 -class ClientNetworkProtocolProperty
-filter "PropertyName='Default Port'"

$protocolproperty.SetNumericalValue(7001)
```

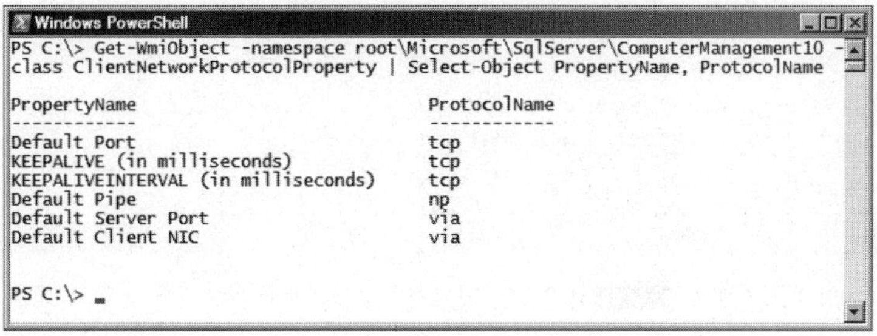

Figure 9-12

Figure 9-13 shows the output from running the above commands.

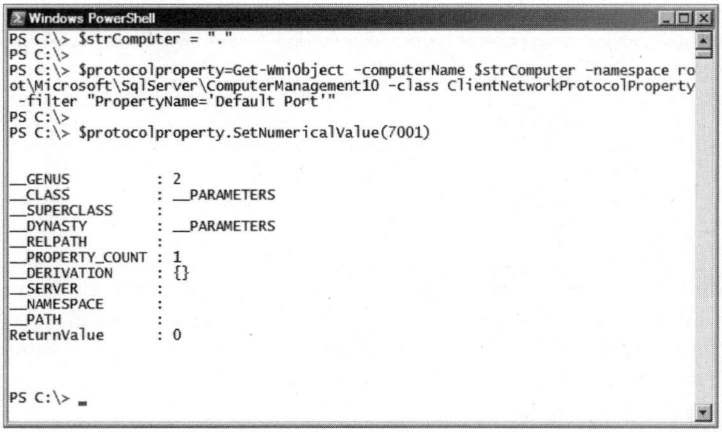

Figure 9-13

To verify that the default port has been changed, you can run this command:

```
Get-WmiObject -namespace root\Microsoft\SqlServer\ComputerManagement10 -class
ClientNetworkProtocolProperty -filter "PropertyName='Default Port'"
```

Figure 9-14 shows that the default TCP/IP port has been changed to 7001. The complete script is in
ChangeTCPIPDefaultPort.ps1.

Managing SQL Server Client Aliases

SQL Server client aliases make user connections easier, faster, and more convenient. Each alias saves all
the information you need to connect to a SQL Server, such as the server name and the client protocol
used to connect to a server. By using an alias, you do not need to enter the information each time you
connect. You can also use an easy-to-remember nickname for your application that is different from the
actual server name.

```
Windows PowerShell                                                    _ □ ×
PS C:\> Get-WmiObject -namespace root\Microsoft\SqlServer\ComputerManagement10 -
class ClientNetworkProtocolProperty -filter "PropertyName='Default Port'"


__GENUS          : 2
__CLASS          : ClientNetworkProtocolProperty
__SUPERCLASS     :
__DYNASTY        : ClientNetworkProtocolProperty
__RELPATH        : ClientNetworkProtocolProperty.PropertyIdx=1,PropertyType=1,P
                   rotocolName="tcp"
__PROPERTY_COUNT : 7
__DERIVATION     : {}
__SERVER         : POWERPC
__NAMESPACE      : root\Microsoft\SqlServer\ComputerManagement10
__PATH           : \\POWERPC\root\Microsoft\SqlServer\ComputerManagement10:Clie
                   ntNetworkProtocolProperty.PropertyIdx=1,PropertyType=1,Proto
                   colName="tcp"
PropertyIdx      : 1
PropertyName     : Default Port
PropertyNumVal   : 7001
PropertyStrVal   :
PropertyType     : 1
PropertyValType  : 4
ProtocolName     : tcp


PS C:\>
```

Figure 9-14

The SqlServerAlias class represents the objects for SQL Server client aliases. To view a list of aliases defined on the local computer, you again use the Get-WmiObject cmdlet, but then pass the class name SqlServerAlias to the class parameter:

```
Get-WmiObject -namespace root\Microsoft\SqlServer\ComputerManagement10 -class
SqlServerAlias
```

As shown in Figure 9-15, only a SQL Server client alias CH0DE1 is defined on the local computer, which points to a named instance CH0DE1 on a remote computer DEMOPC that listens on TCP/IP port 7001. To manage an alias on a remote computer, use the -computerName parameter to specify the remote computer name.

```
Windows PowerShell                                                    _ □ ×
PS C:\> Get-WmiObject -namespace root\Microsoft\SqlServer\ComputerManagement10 -
class SqlServerAlias


__GENUS          : 2
__CLASS          : SqlServerAlias
__SUPERCLASS     :
__DYNASTY        : SqlServerAlias
__RELPATH        : SqlServerAlias.AliasName="CH0DE1"
__PROPERTY_COUNT : 4
__DERIVATION     : {}
__SERVER         : POWERPC
__NAMESPACE      : root\Microsoft\SqlServer\ComputerManagement10
__PATH           : \\POWERPC\root\Microsoft\SqlServer\ComputerManagement10:SqlS
                   erverAlias.AliasName="CH0DE1"
AliasName        : CH0DE1
ConnectionString : 7001
ProtocolName     : tcp
ServerName       : DEMOPC\CH0DE1


PS C:\> _
```

Figure 9-15

The `SqlServerAlias` class does not define any methods. It inherits the methods from its parent class, `ManagementObject`. The `Delete` method of the `ManagementObject` class can be used to delete an existing alias. For example, if you want to delete the alias `CH0DE1` above, you can use the `Delete` method. The backtick character (`` ` ``) in the following script is used to concatenate the script lines:

```
$strComputer = "."
# Name of the alias
$strAliasName = "CH0DE1"

$oldalias=Get-WmiObject -computerName $strComputer -namespace
root\Microsoft\SqlServer\ComputerManagement10 `
-class SqlServerAlias -filter "AliasName='$strAliasName'"

$oldalias.Delete()
```

The complete script `DeleteClientAlias.ps1` is saved in the script directory `C:\DBAScripts`. In Figure 9-16, the script is run to delete the alias. Then the previous command is run to verify the deletion of the alias. Notice that no aliases are returned.

```
C:DBAScripts\DeleteClientAlias.ps1
Get-WmiObject -namespace root\Microsoft\SqlServer\ComputerManagement10 -class
SqlServerAlias
```

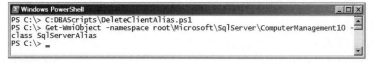

```
Windows PowerShell
PS C:\> C:\DBAScripts\DeleteClientAlias.ps1
PS C:\> Get-WmiObject -namespace root\Microsoft\SqlServer\ComputerManagement10 -
class SqlServerAlias
PS C:\> _
```

Figure 9-16

`Get-WmiObject` can only be used to manage the existing SQL Server client aliases. To create a new alias, you need to use the `New-Object` cmdlet to create an alias object from the corresponding .NET class, `Microsoft.SqlServer.Management.Smo.Wmi.ServerAlias`. The `Microsoft.SqlServer.Management.Smo` namespace contains classes that represent the core SQL Server Management Objects (SMOs). You will find more examples on SMO in Chapter 13. The `Microsoft.SqlServer.Management.Smo.Wmi.ServerAlias` class is contained in the assembly `Microsoft.SqlServer.SqlWmiManagement.dll` for SQL Server 2008, and in the assembly `Microsoft.SqlServer.Smo.dll` for SQL Server 2005.

Before PowerShell can call a .NET class, the assembly containing the .NET class must be loaded first. By default, PowerShell loads a small list of assemblies. To get a list of loaded assemblies, you can use the `GetAssemblies` method of the current Windows PowerShell application domain. For each assembly, use the `Split-Path` cmdlet to get only the filename. Thereafter, sort the assembly filenames alphabetically with the `Sort-Object` cmdlet:

```
[System.AppDomain]::CurrentDomain.GetAssemblies() | ForEach-Object { split-path
$_.Location -leaf } | Sort-Object
```

As shown in Figure 9-17, neither the `Microsoft.SqlServer.SqlWmiManagement.dll` assembly nor the `Microsoft.SqlServer.Smo.dll` assembly have been loaded by default.

```
Windows PowerShell                                                    _ □ ×
PS C:\> [System.AppDomain]::CurrentDomain.GetAssemblies() | ForEach-Object { spl
it-path $_.Location -leaf } | Sort-Object
Microsoft.PowerShell.Commands.Diagnostics.dll
Microsoft.PowerShell.Commands.Management.dll
Microsoft.PowerShell.Commands.Utility.dll
Microsoft.PowerShell.ConsoleHost.dll
Microsoft.PowerShell.Security.dll
Microsoft.WSMan.Management.dll
Microsoft.WSMan.Runtime.dll
mscorlib.dll
System.Configuration.Install.dll
System.Data.dll
System.DirectoryServices.dll
System.dll
System.Management.Automation.dll
System.Management.dll
System.ServiceProcess.dll
System.Transactions.dll
System.Xml.dll
PS C:\>
```

Figure 9-17

To load the `Microsoft.SqlServer.SqlWmiManagement.dll` assembly for SQL Server 2008, use the `LoadWithPartialName` method of the `System.Reflection.Assembly` class. The `Out-Null` cmdlet is used to suppress the informational message:

```
[reflection.assembly]::LoadWithPartialName("Microsoft.SqlServer.SqlWmiManagement")
| Out-Null
```

For SQL Server 2005, the command should be as follows:

```
[reflection.assembly]::LoadWithPartialName("Microsoft.SqlServer.Smo") | Out-Null
```

After the assembly is loaded, you need to first create an SMO object that represents the WMI installation for SQL Server on the local computer. This object will be the parent of the alias you create. The following commands instantiate an object for the SQL Server WMI installation on the local computer:

```
$strComputer='.'  # '.' or 'localhost' for local computer.
$objComputer=New-Object Microsoft.SqlServer.Management.Smo.Wmi.ManagedComputer
$strComputer
```

Now create an alias object from the `Microsoft.SqlServer.Management.Smo.Wmi.ServerAlias` class and set the parent of this alias to the `ManagedComptuer` object you created:

```
$newalias=New-Object ("Microsoft.SqlServer.Management.Smo.Wmi.ServerAlias")
$newalias.Parent=$objComputer
```

Each alias has a few properties, such as the name of the server to connect to and the client protocol, that need to be populated before it can be created. In this example, you recreate the CH0DE1 alias you deleted earlier. This alias connects to the named instance DEMOPC\CH0DE1 at port 7001 using the TCP/IP protocol:

```
$newalias.Name='CH0DE1' # name of the new alias
# DEMOPC\CH0DE1 is the SQL Server instance the alias points to
$newalias.ServerName='DEMOPC\CH0DE1'
# 7001 is the port the SQL Server instance DEMOPC\CH0DE1 is listening on
$newalias.ConnectionString=7001
$newalias.ProtocolName='tcp'
$newalias.Create()
```

The complete script, `CreateServerAlias2008.ps1`, is saved in our script directory, `C:\DBAScripts`. Run the script from the directory and then verify the creation of the alias by selecting all the objects of the `SqlServerAlias` class with the `Get-WmiObject` cmdlet:

```
C:\DBAScripts\CreateServerAlias2008.ps1
Get-WmiObject -namespace root\Microsoft\SqlServer\ComputerManagement10 -class
SqlServerAlias
```

The output is shown in Figure 9-18. As you can see, the new alias has been created.

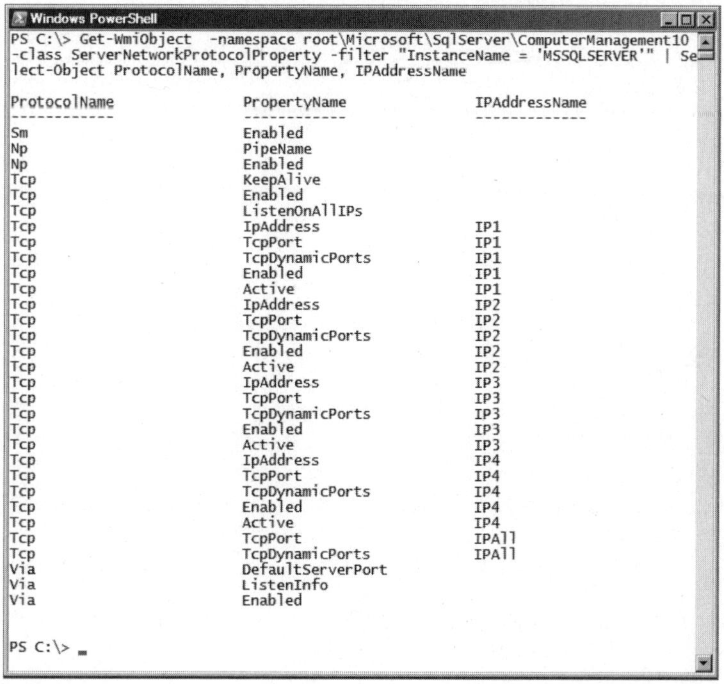

Figure 9-18

Managing Server Network Protocols

The `ServerNetworkProtocolProperty` class represents the properties of server network protocols. To view the list of properties associated with each network protocol for the default instance on the local computer, use the `Get-WmiObject` cmdlet and pass the class name `ServerNetworkProtocolProperty` to the `-class` parameter:

```
Get-WmiObject  -namespace root\Microsoft\SqlServer\ComputerManagement10 -class
ServerNetworkProtocolProperty -filter "InstanceName = 'MSSQLSERVER'" | Select-Object
ProtocolName, PropertyName, IPAddressName
```

As shown in Figure 9-19, besides the common property `Enabled`, each protocol has its own properties. The `Named Pipe` protocol has a property called `PipeName` that specifies the named pipe on which the default SQL Server instance listens. The TCP/IP protocol is associated with IP addresses on the computer, including the loopback address, 127.0.0.1. The names of the IP addresses are in the format IP1, IP2, and so on, up to IPAll, which denotes all the IP addresses.

```
Windows PowerShell
PS C:\> Get-WmiObject  -namespace root\Microsoft\SqlServer\ComputerManagement10
-class ServerNetworkProtocolProperty -filter "InstanceName = 'MSSQLSERVER'" | Se
lect-Object ProtocolName, PropertyName, IPAddressName

ProtocolName            PropertyName            IPAddressName
------------            ------------            -------------
Sm                      Enabled
Np                      PipeName
Np                      Enabled
Tcp                     KeepAlive
Tcp                     Enabled
Tcp                     ListenOnAllIPs
Tcp                     IpAddress               IP1
Tcp                     TcpPort                 IP1
Tcp                     TcpDynamicPorts         IP1
Tcp                     Enabled                 IP1
Tcp                     Active                  IP1
Tcp                     IpAddress               IP2
Tcp                     TcpPort                 IP2
Tcp                     TcpDynamicPorts         IP2
Tcp                     Enabled                 IP2
Tcp                     Active                  IP2
Tcp                     IpAddress               IP3
Tcp                     TcpPort                 IP3
Tcp                     TcpDynamicPorts         IP3
Tcp                     Enabled                 IP3
Tcp                     Active                  IP3
Tcp                     IpAddress               IP4
Tcp                     TcpPort                 IP4
Tcp                     TcpDynamicPorts         IP4
Tcp                     Enabled                 IP4
Tcp                     Active                  IP4
Tcp                     TcpPort                 IPAll
Tcp                     TcpDynamicPorts         IPAll
Via                     DefaultServerPort
Via                     ListenInfo
Via                     Enabled

PS C:\> _
```

Figure 9-19

By default, the ListenOnAllIPs property is enabled and SQL Server listens on all the IP addresses. The settings of the IPAll address apply to all the IP addresses.

To prevent hackers from using the default port 1433 to "slam" the default instance, you might want to change the port number for IPAll from 1433 to another port — for example, 3660. You can use the Get-WmiObject cmdlet to instantiate a network protocol property object that represents the TCPPort property of the IPAll address for the default instance. Then invoke the SetStringValue method of the object to change the port number to 3660. You also need to stop and restart the default instance with the SqlService class as illustrated in the first part of this chapter in order for the new port number to take effect. The complete script, ChangeDefaultPortNumber.ps1, is shown here:

```
$wmi=Get-WmiObject -namespace root\Microsoft\SqlServer\ComputerManagement10
-class ServerNetworkProtocolProperty `
-filter "PropertyName='TcpPort' and IPAddressName='IPAll' and
InstanceName='MSSQLSERVER'"

$wmi.SetStringValue(3660) | Out-Null

$sqlservice = Get-WmiObject -namespace
root\Microsoft\SqlServer\ComputerManagement10 -class SqlService `
```

```
-filter "ServiceName='MSSQLSERVER'"

$sqlservice.StopService() | Out-Null

$sqlservice.StartService() | Out-Null

# Confirm the default port number has been changed
Get-WmiObject -namespace root\Microsoft\SqlServer\ComputerManagement10 -class
ServerNetworkProtocolProperty `
-filter "PropertyName='TcpPort' and IPAddressName='IPAll' and
InstanceName='MSSQLSERVER'" | Select-Object PropertyStrVal
```

The `ChangeDefaultPortNumber.ps1` script is saved in the script directory, `C:\DBAScripts`:

```
C:\DBAScripts\ChangeDefaultPortNumber.ps1
```

Figure 9-20 shows the output from running the script. As you can see, the new port number is changed to 3660.

Figure 9-20

Note that if you only have named instances on your computer, you need to change the `-filter` parameter in the `Get-WmiObject` cmdlet before running the script. For example, for a named instance `INSTANCE1`, you should change the filter to `ServiceName='MSSQL`$INSTANCE1'`. The backtick character (`` ` ``) is used to escape the dollar sign ($) character in the service name.

If you want to assign different port numbers to different IP addresses — for example, to associate different TCP/IP ports with different non-uniform memory access (NUMA) nodes — then you can disable the `ListenOnAllIPs` property and configure the settings of each IP address. You can use the `Get-WmiObject` cmdlet to instantiate a network protocol property object that is associated with the `ListenOnAllIPs` property for the default instance. Because the value of the property is of type `Boolean`, you need to invoke the `SetFlag` method to set the Boolean value to 0, and thus disable the property. You also need to stop and restart the default instance in order for the new setting to take effect. The complete script, `DisableListenOnAllIPs.ps1`, is shown here:

```
# . for the local computer
# If you want to connect to a remote machine, specify the machine name here.
$strComputer = "."
# Name of the targeted SQL Server instance. Here the default instance is targeted.
# For a named instance INSTANCE1, use "INSTANCE1".
$strInstanceName = "MSSQLSERVER"

$wmi=Get-WmiObject -computerName $strComputer -namespace
root\Microsoft\SqlServer\ComputerManagement10 `
```

213

```
        -class ServerNetworkProtocolProperty -filter "PropertyName='ListenOnAllIPs'
and InstanceName='$strInstanceName'"

$wmi.SetFlag(0) | Out-Null

$sqlservice = Get-WmiObject -computerName $strComputer -namespace
root\Microsoft\SqlServer\ComputerManagement10 `
 -class SqlService -filter "ServiceName='MSSQL`$$strInstanceName'"

$sqlservice.StopService() | Out-Null

$sqlservice.StartService() | Out-Null

$wmi=Get-WmiObject -computerName $strComputer -namespace
root\Microsoft\SqlServer\ComputerManagement10 `
 -class ServerNetworkProtocolProperty -filter "PropertyName='ListenOnAllIPs'
and InstanceName='$strInstanceName'"

# Confirm the ListenOnAllIPs property has been disabled.
Write-Host "The value of the ListenOnAllIPs property is set to " $wmi.PropertyNumVal
```

The `DisableListenOnAllIPs.ps1`script is also saved in our script directory, `C:\DBAScripts`:

```
C:\DBAScripts\DisableListenOnAllIPs.ps1
```

Figure 9-21 shows the output from running the script. As you can see, the value of the `ListenOnAllIPs` property is now 0, which means that it is disabled.

Figure 9-21

Changing FILESTREAM Settings

SQL server 2008 introduced a new feature called FILESTREAM. FILESTREAM integrates the SQL Server Database Engine with an NTFS file system by storing varbinary(max) binary large object (BLOB) data as files on the file system. This separates the storage of unstructured data, such as bitmap images, text files, videos, audio files, and so on from structured data into data files. At the same time, this still allows unstructured data to be queried, inserted, updated, deleted, and backed up like structured data using Transact-SQL statements.

By default, FILESTREAM is disabled. Before starting to use it on a SQL Server instance, FILESTREAM needs to be enabled on the instance. The `FILESTREAMSettings` class provides an `EnableFILESTREAM` method that accepts two parameters:

```
EnableFILESTREAM(System.UInt32 AccessLevel, System.String ShareName)
```

The `AccessLevel` parameter specifies the access level of FILESTREAM storage, and it can have one of the values shown in Table 9-4.

Table 9-4: FILESTREAM Access Level Values

Value	Description
0	Disables FILESTREAM support for this instance
1	Enables FILESTREAM for Transact-SQL access
2	Enables FILESTREAM for Transact-SQL and local file system access
3	Enables FILESTREAM for Transact-SQL, local file system access, and remote file system access

The ShareName parameter specifies the file share name that is used to enable local and remote clients to obtain streaming access to FILESTREAM data through the file system. This value can be changed only when the enabled state changes from 0 (disabled) or 1 (Transact-SQL only) to file system access (2 or 3).

In our example, FILESTREAM is disabled on the default instance. The following EnableFileStream.ps1 script enables FILESTREAM for Transact-SQL and local file system access. It uses the Get-WmiObject cmdlet to instantiate a FILESTREAMSettings object associated with the default instance. Next, it invokes the EnableFILESTREAM method of the object to enable FILESTREAM for Transact-SQL and local file system access and set the share name to MSSQLSERVER. Then it confirms the changes by printing out the access level and share name:

```
# . for the local computer
# If you want to connect to a remote machine, specify the machine name here.
$strComputer = "."
# Name of the targeted SQL Server instance. Here the default instance is targeted.
# For a named instance INSTANCE1, use "INSTANCE1".
$strInstanceName = "MSSQLSERVER"

$wmi=Get-WmiObject -computerName $strComputer -namespace
root\Microsoft\SqlServer\ComputerManagement10 `
 -class FILESTREAMSettings -filter "InstanceName='$strInstanceName'"

# Prints out the AccessLevel property before changing it.
Write-Host "The access level of FILESTREAM before the change is set to"
$wmi.AccessLevel ", and the file share name is " $wmi.ShareName

$wmi.EnableFILESTREAM(2, 'MSSQLSERVER') | Out-Null

$wmi=Get-WmiObject -computerName $strComputer -namespace
root\Microsoft\SqlServer\ComputerManagement10 `
 -class FILESTREAMSettings -filter "InstanceName='$strInstanceName'"

# Confirm the AccessLevel property has been set.
Write-Host "The access level of FILESTREAM after the change is set to"
$wmi.AccessLevel ", and the file share name is " $wmi.ShareName
```

Save the script in your script directory, C:\DBAScripts:

```
C:\DBAScripts\EnableFILESTREAM.ps1
```

215

Figure 9-22 shows the output from running the script. As shown, the access level of the FILESTREAM property is changed from 0 to 2 for Transact-SQL and local file system. The share name is set to MSSQLSERVER.

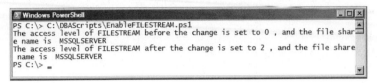

Figure 9-22

However, please note that you still need to restart the SQL Server instance and reconfigure the server option in SSMS to fully enable FILESTREAM. For example, run the following statement in SSMS to enable FILESTREAM for Transact-SQL and Win32 streaming access:

```
EXEC sp_configure filestream_access_level, 2
RECONFIGURE
```

Changing SQL Server Advanced Properties

In addition to the common properties that are available for the SQLService class, each SQL service has its own unique properties, which are represented in the SqlServiceAdvancedProperty class. For example, a SQL Server service has startup parameters, a dump directory for memory dumps in case of an error, and read-only properties such as version, INSTALLPATH, and DATAPATH. A SQL Browser service has a BROWSER property that indicates whether the Browser service is listening.

Let's focus on the properties of the SQL Server services. Suppose the file system is corrupted, in which case you need to restore every database, including the master database. To restore the master database, you need to start the SQL Server in single-user mode. Insert the -m option into the existing startup options, and then restart the database. The ChangeStartupParameters.ps1 script is shown in the following example. The script first uses the Get-WmiObject cmdlet to instantiate a SqlServiceAdvancedProperty object that corresponds to the STARTUPPARAMETERS property of the default instance. Next, it invokes the SetStringValue method to pre-append the -m option to the string of startup parameters. The "`n" in the script is used to print out the new line character.

```
# . for the local computer
# If you want to connect to a remote machine, specify the machine name here.
$strComputer='.'
# Name of the targeted service. Here the default SQL Server service is targeted.
# For a named instance INSTANCE1, use "MSSQL`$INSTANCE1"
$strServiceName = "MSSQLSERVER"

$ap=Get-WmiObject -computerName $strComputer -namespace
root\Microsoft\SqlServer\ComputerManagement10  -class SqlServiceAdvancedProperty `
-filter "ServiceName='$strServiceName' and PropertyName='STARTUPPARAMETERS'"
```

```
$ap.SetStringValue("-m " + $ap.PropertyStrValue) | Out-Null

# Confirm the "-m" option has been added.
$ap=Get-WmiObject -computerName $strComputer -namespace
root\Microsoft\SqlServer\ComputerManagement10  -class SqlServiceAdvancedProperty `
-filter "ServiceName='$strServiceName' and PropertyName='STARTUPPARAMETERS'"

Write-Host "The startup parameters have been changed to `n" $ap.PropertyStrValue
```

The ChangeStartupParameters.ps1script is saved in our script directory, `C:\DBAScripts`:

```
C:\DBAScripts\ChangeStartupParameters.ps1
```

Figure 9-23 shows the output from running the script. As you can see, the `-m` option is added as a startup parameter. The new startup option will take effect the next time SQL Server starts.

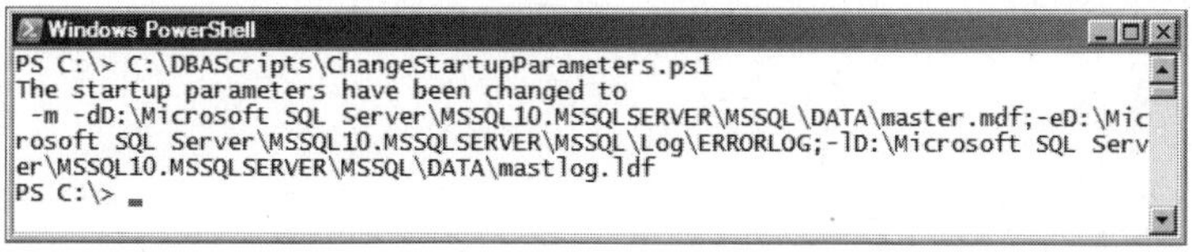

Figure 9-23

The following example looks at the read-only properties of the SQL Server service. You can use the `Get-WmiObject` cmdlet to instantiate all the objects of the `SqlServiceAdvancedProperty` class that are associated with the default instance. Next, the `Where-Object` cmdlet is used to filter the read-only properties based on the Boolean property `IsReadOnly`. Then the `Format-Table` cmdlet is used to select only the property names, and their values in string or numerical format.

```
$strComputer='.'
$strServiceName = "MSSQLSERVER"

$properties=Get-WmiObject -computerName $strComputer -namespace
root\Microsoft\SqlServer\ComputerManagement10  -class SqlServiceAdvancedProperty
-filter "ServiceName='$strServiceName'"

$properties | Where-Object {$_.IsReadOnly} | Format-table -wrap PropertyName,
PropertyStrValue, PropertyNumValue
```

As shown in Figure 9-24, the version number of our SQL Server instance is 10.0.1600.22, which corresponds to SQL Server 2008 RTM.

The binaries of the instance are under the directory `C:\Program Files\Microsoft SQL Server\MSSQL10.MSSQLSERVER\MSSQL`. The default path for the data folder points to the directory `D:\Microsoft SQL Server\MSSQL10.MSSQLSERVER\MSSQL`. The default language is 1033, English (United States). The registry root for the default instance is Software\Microsoft\Microsoft SQL Server\MSSQL10.MSSQLSERVER. The product edition of the instance is Developer Edition, and the instance name is MSSQLSERVER.

```
Windows PowerShell                                              _ □ X
PS C:\> $strComputer='.'
PS C:\> $strServiceName = "MSSQLSERVER"
PS C:\>
PS C:\> $properties=Get-WmiObject -computerName $strComputer -namespace root\Mic
rosoft\SqlServer\ComputerManagement10  -class SqlServiceAdvancedProperty -filter
 "ServiceName='$strServiceName'"
PS C:\>
PS C:\> $properties | Where-Object {$_.IsReadOnly} | Format-table -wrap Property
Name, PropertyStrValue, PropertyNumValue

PropertyName            PropertyStrValue                 PropertyNumValue
------------            ----------------                 ----------------
SQLSTATES                                                       2099205
VERSION                 10.0.1600.22
SPLEVEL                                                              0
CLUSTERED                                                            0
INSTALLPATH             C:\Program Files\Microsoft
                          SQL Server\MSSQL10.MSSQLS
                        ERVER\MSSQL
DATAPATH                D:\Microsoft SQL Server\MS
                        SQL10.MSSQLSERVER\MSSQL
LANGUAGE                                                          1033
FILEVERSION             2007.100.1600.22
VSNAME
REGROOT                 Software\Microsoft\Microso
                        ft SQL Server\MSSQL10.MSSQ
                        LSERVER
SKU                                                          2176971986
SKUNAME                 Developer Edition
INSTANCEID              MSSQL10.MSSQLSERVER
ISWOW64                                                             0


PS C:\> _
```

Figure 9-24

Summary

This chapter covered some of the classes available through the WMI Provider for Configuration Management. You can use these classes to manage SQL Server services, client network protocols, client aliases, server network protocols, FILESTREAM settings, and startup parameters. Although all these configuration settings can be controlled in SQL Server Configuration Manager, the scripts shown in this chapter are more flexible and powerful because they can be used to manage SQL Server instances remotely.

The next chapter discusses the SQL Server 2008 WMI Provider.

10

WMI Provider for Server Events

In addition to the WMI Provider for Configuration Management discussed in Chapter 9, SQL Server 2008 includes one other WMI provider: the WMI Provider for Server Events. This provider transforms SQL Server event data into WMI class instances, and enables you to use WMI to monitor events in SQL Server. This chapter shows you how to monitor Data Definition Language (DDL) and trace events in a SQL Server instance by leveraging this provider in Windows PowerShell. This chapter covers the following:

❑ WMI Provider for Server Events

❑ WMI Query Language (WQL)

❑ Event handling with Windows PowerShell 2.0

❑ Monitoring errors from the SQL Server error log

❑ Monitoring deadlocks

❑ Monitoring blockings

❑ Monitoring login changes and failed login attempts

❑ Monitoring databases and database objects

WMI Provider for Server Events

The WMI Provider for Server Events turns SQL Server into a managed WMI object and enables you to use WMI to monitor server events. This provider manages a WMI namespace for each instance of SQL Server 2008. The name of the namespace is in the format root\Microsoft\SqlServer\ServerEvents\instance_name.

For a default instance, the namespace is root\Microsoft\SqlServer\ServerEvents\MSSQLSERVER.

For a named instance INSTANCE1, the namespace is root\Microsoft\SqlServer\ServerEvents\INSTANCE1.

To monitor a default instance on a remote computer — for example, DEMOPC — you can use a named space, \\DEMOPC\root\Microsoft\SqlServer\ServerEvents\MSSQLSERVER.

The WMI Provider for Server Events leverages event notification in SQL Server. When WMI events in the namespace of a SQL Server instance are monitored for the first time, the provider creates a target service in the msdb database called SQL/Notifications/ProcessWMIEventProviderNotification/v1.0, and a queue for the target service WMIEventProviderNotificationQueue. When a WMI management application issues a WMI Query Language (WQL) query to access SQL Server events, the WMI Provider for Server Events translates the query into an event notification. If events on the server level are queried, the provider creates a server event notification. If events in a database or on a particular database object are queried, the provider creates an event notification in the target database.

After the required event notification is created, it sends event data to the target service SQL/Notifications/ProcessWMIEventProviderNotification/v1.0 in the msdb database. The target service puts the event into the WMIEventProviderNotificationQueue queue in the msdb database. You can query the catalog views, sys.services, and sys.service_queues, to confirm the creation of the service and queue. The provider reads the XML event data from this queue and transforms it into managed object format before returning it to the client application.

Because Service Broker services are used by the event notification to send messages about server events, Service Broker must be enabled in the msdb database and the target database wherever the events are generated. To check whether the Service Brokers are enabled on a SQL Server instance, and to get the Service Broker instance GUID in each database, run the following query on the instance:

```
SELECT name, is_broker_enabled, service_broker_guid FROM sys.databases;
```

If the is_broker_enable column for a database has a value of 0, it means that Service Broker is not enabled for the database. The broker instance in the msdb database is the most useful because msdb hosts the target service and the service queue. To enable Service Broker for a database — for example, the msdb database — use the ALTER DATABASE statement:

```
ALTER DATABASE msdb SET ENABLE_BROKER
```

A complete list of server events classes for SQL Server 2008 can be found at http://msdn.microsoft.com/en-us/library/ms186449(SQL.100).aspx.

WMI Query Language (WQL)

The WMI Query Language (WQL) is designed to perform queries against the CIM repository to retrieve WMI information. WQL is a subset of ANSI SQL with minor semantic changes to support WMI. Therefore, it is very straightforward to write WQL queries.

WQL queries can be divided into three types: data, event, and schema.

Data queries are used to retrieve class instances and data associations. For example, every Get-WmiObject command with a -filter parameter in Chapter 9 can be mapped to a data query — a Select statement with the -filter parameter being mapped to a Where clause. For example, the following command is equivalent to the command listed after it:

```
Get-WmiObject -namespace root\Microsoft\SqlServer\ComputerManagement10 -class
ClientNetworkProtocol -filter "ProtocolName='np'"
```

The preceding command is equivalent to this:

```
Get-WmiObject -namespace root\Microsoft\SqlServer\ComputerManagement10 -query
"Select * From ClientNetworkProtocol Where ProtocolName='np'"
```

Event queries are used to subscribe to WMI events. Event providers use event queries to register one or more events. Event queries are completely supported in Windows PowerShell 2.0. They are used in this chapter.

Schema queries are used to retrieve class definitions and schema associations. They are the least used of all WQL queries. Because they are not used in this book, schema queries are not covered here.

Event Handling with Windows PowerShell 2.0

Unlike Windows PowerShell 1.0, for which you need to use .NET classes, such as the System. Management.ManagementEventWatcher class to subscribe and monitor events, Windows PowerShell 2.0 CTP3 provides a full-blown eventing infrastructure for event queries. The following list describes some eventing cmdlets:

❑   Register-WmiEvent: Create an event subscription of WMI events on the local or a remote computer

❑   Get-Event: Receive subscribed WMI events in the event queue in the current Windows Power-Shell session.

❑   Remove-Event: Remove subscribed WMI events in the event queue in the current Windows PowerShell session.

❑   Unregister-Event: Cancel an event subscription.

❑   Get-EventSubscriber: Get the event subscribers in the current Windows PowerShell session.

Before you create an event subscription, you need to write a WQL query that specifies the kinds of events you would like to subscribe to and monitor. For example, to subscribe to any DDL activity in the AdventureWorks2008 database on the default SQL Server instance on the local computer PowerPC, query the DDL_DATABASE_LEVEL_EVENTS event class and use the DatabaseName property to filter the events in AdventureWorks2008. The WQL query is shown here:

```
$eventQuery = "SELECT * FROM DDL_DATABASE_LEVEL_EVENTS WHERE DatabaseName=
'AdventureWorks2008'"
```

If you want new events to be checked every 10 seconds, you can add WITHIN 10 to the WQL query:

```
$eventQuery = "SELECT * FROM DDL_DATABASE_LEVEL_EVENTS WITHIN 10 WHERE DatabaseName=
'AdventureWorks2008'"
```

The events on the default instance on the local computer are available under the namespace root\Microsoft\SqlServer\ServerEvents\MSSQLSERVER:

```
$namespace = "root\Microsoft\SqlServer\ServerEvents\MSSQLSERVER"
```

To monitor the events on a named instance CH0DE1 on a remote computer — say, DEMOPC — you only need to change the namespace to \\DEMOPC\root\Microsoft\SqlServer\ServerEvents\ MSSQLSERVER\CH0DE1. For simplicity and clarity, the examples in this chapter focus on a local computer. You can just change the namespace in the examples to monitor remote instances.

Use the Register-WmiEvent cmdlet to register an event subscription associated with the WQL query and the namespace. A WMI event specified by the WQL query will be added to the event queue in the current Windows PowerShell session:

```
Register-WmiEvent -Namespace $namespace -Query $eventQuery -SourceIdentifier
    "sqlevents"
```

To check whether new events have arrived in the event queue, use the Get-Event cmdlet to get the events identified by the name of the event subscription. Next, you can use a for loop to iterate through the events. Usually you won't be interested in WMI system properties such as __GENUS, __DYNASTY, and __PATH. You can use a string array variable, $properties, to explicitly select the event properties by their names. After you get the information of an event, the event is still in the event queue. To avoid duplicate information, you need to remove the event with the Remove-Event cmdlet after you get its information:

```
while ($true) {
        # Get new events
        $objEvents=Get-Event -SourceIdentifier "sqlevents" -ErrorAction
SilentlyContinue

        # If new events arrive, then retrieve the event information.
        if ($objEvents) {
            # Loop through the collection of new events
            for ($i=0; $i -lt $objEvents.Count; $i++) {
                    $objEvents[$i].SourceEventArgs.NewEvent | Select-Object
$properties

                    # Remove the event after its information has been processed.
                    Remove-Event -EventIdentifier $objEvents[$i].EventIdentifier -
ErrorAction SilentlyContinue


    }
        }
}
```

In the preceding code, the events are monitored in an infinite loop. Some kind of stop mechanism should be introduced to break out of the loop without aborting brutally by using Ctrl+C. The following code enables the loop to be broken by pressing the Esc key:

```
$ESCkey = 27 # 27 is the key number for the Esc button.

# Check if the Esc key is pressed
```

```
if ($host.ui.RawUi.KeyAvailable) {
        $key = $host.ui.RawUI.ReadKey("NoEcho,IncludeKeyUp")

        # If the Esc key is pressed, unregister the event subscription, break the loop,
and exit this function.
        if ($key.VirtualKeyCode -eq $ESCkey) {
                Unregister-Event "sqlevents"
                break
        }
}
```

To retrieve different events, you only need to change the particular WQL query, the namespace, and the selected properties of the events. Therefore, it makes sense to encapsulate the preceding steps in a function, and reuse the function to monitor different events throughout this chapter. The complete function Get-WMIEvent.ps1 is shown here:

```
function Get-WMIEvent([string] $eventQuery, [string] $namespace, [string[]]
$properties)
{
$ESCkey = 27 # 27 is the key number for the Esc button.

# If an event subscription called "sqlevents" already exists, unregister it first.
if (Get-EventSubscriber 'sqlevents' -ErrorAction SilentlyContinue) {
        Unregister-Event "sqlevents"
}

# Create an event subscription called "sqlevents" that registers to the events
specified by the $eventQuery under the $namespace.
Register-WmiEvent -Namespace $namespace -Query $eventQuery -SourceIdentifier
"sqlevents"

while ($true) {
        # Get new events
        $objEvents=Get-Event -SourceIdentifier "sqlevents" -ErrorAction
SilentlyContinue

        # If new events arrive, then retrieve the event information.
        if ($objEvents) {
                # Loop through the collection of new events
                for ($i=0; $i -lt $objEvents.Count; $i++) {
                        $objEvents[$i].SourceEventArgs.NewEvent | Select-Object
$properties

                        # Remove the event after its information has been processed.
                        Remove-Event -EventIdentifier $objEvents[$i].EventIdentifier -
ErrorAction SilentlyContinue


        }
        }

        # Check if the Esc key is pressed
        if ($host.ui.RawUi.KeyAvailable) {
                $key = $host.ui.RawUI.ReadKey("NoEcho,IncludeKeyUp")
```

```
                        # If the Esc key is pressed, unregister the event subscription, break the
        loop, and exit this function.
                        if ($key.VirtualKeyCode -eq $ESCkey) {
                                Unregister-Event "sqlevents"
                                break
                        }
                }
        }
}
```

As discussed in Chapter 4, to reuse a function, you can put it in the user-specific, shell-specific profile: `%UserProfile%\My Documents\WindowsPowerShell\Microsoft.PowerShell_profile.ps1` or `%UserProfile%\Documents\WindowsPowerShell\Microsoft.PowerShell_profile.ps1` on Windows Vista. Alternately, you can put the function in a library file and source in the file each time prior to executing a script. In this case, the library file is called `dbaLib.ps1` under the `C:\DBAScripts` directory. The examples in this chapter use the `Get-WMIEvent` function to print out event information in the console for demonstration purposes.

In real practice, it is more common to save the output into a log file, or notify support personnel through e-mail or page based on the event received, or send an alert to an event management system such as Netcool. The following function is a more flexible version of the `Get-WMIEvent` function that accepts a script block:

```
function Get-WMIEvent([string] $eventQuery, [string] $namespace, [ScriptBlock]
$sblock)
{
$ESCkey = 27 # 27 is the key number for the Esc button.

# If an event subscription called "sqlevents" already exists, unregister it first.
if (Get-EventSubscriber 'sqlevents' -ErrorAction SilentlyContinue) {
        Unregister-Event "sqlevents"
}

# Create an event subscription called "sqlevents" that registers to the events
specified by the $eventQuery under the $namespace.
Register-WmiEvent -Namespace $namespace -Query $eventQuery -SourceIdentifier
"sqlevents"

while ($true) {
        # Get new events
        $objEvents=Get-Event -SourceIdentifier "sqlevents" -ErrorAction
SilentlyContinue

        # If new events arrive, then retrieve the event information.
        if ($objEvents) {
                # Loop through the collection of new events
                for ($i=0; $i -lt $objEvents.Count; $i++) {
                        $objEvents[$i].SourceEventArgs.NewEvent | &$sblock

                        # Remove the event after its information has been processed.
                        Remove-Event -EventIdentifier $objEvents[$i].EventIdentifier -
ErrorAction SilentlyContinue
```

```
        }
            }

            # Check if the Esc key is pressed
            if ($host.ui.RawUi.KeyAvailable) {
                    $key = $host.ui.RawUI.ReadKey("NoEcho,IncludeKeyUp")

                # If the Esc key is pressed, unregister the event subscription, break the
        loop, and exit this function.
                    if ($key.VirtualKeyCode -eq $ESCkey) {
                            Unregister-Event "sqlevents"
                            break
                    }
            }
        }
    }
```

The differences between the Get-WmiEvent functions have been highlighted. You can utilize the script block to save the event information into a log file C:\sqlevents.log. The script block is as follows:

```
$sblock = { $input | Select-Object ObjectType, SPID, SQLInstance, TSQLCommand
| Out-File "c:\sqlevents.log" }
```

The $input variable enumerates the event objects in the incoming pipeline.

Monitoring Errors from the SQL Server Error Log

The errors identified in the SQL Server error log help to detect any current or potential problems, including data file growth problems, backup device problems, failed logins, insufficient lock resources, and so on. The trace event class for the SQL Server error log is ERRORLOG. In the real world, DBAs are usually more interested in errors with a severity level of 17 and higher, which indicate software or hardware errors, rather than informational messages or user errors. In SQL Server 2008, error messages with severity 16, from policy violations, are also worth monitoring.

In the script that follows, MonitorErrorLog.ps1, the event query to subscribe to errors from the SQL Server error log, the namespace of the default instance, and the properties of the events are defined. Then the script calls the Get-WMIEvent function to capture and print out the error events. The backtick characters (`) are used to concatenate the script lines:

```
$query = "SELECT * FROM ERRORLOG WHERE Severity >= 16"
$sqlnamespace = "root\Microsoft\SqlServer\ServerEvents\MSSQLSERVER"
$selections= "LoginSid","PostTime","SQLInstance","IsSystem","DatabaseID", `
"ComputerName","SessionLoginName","SPID","TransactionID","EventSequence", `
"HostName","ClientProcessID","NTUserName","RequestID","DatabaseName", `
"Error","Severity","TextData","NTDomainName","LoginName","StartTime",
"ApplicationName"

Get-WMIEvent $query $sqlnamespace $selections
```

Run the script in a Windows PowerShell console:

```
. C:\DBAScripts\dbaLib.ps1
C:\DBAScripts\MonitorErrorLog.ps1
```

While the script is running, open a SQL Server Management Studio (SSMS) query window and run the following SQL query on the default instance to generate an error message with severity 16:

```
Use AdventureWorks2008
Raiserror ('This is a test message', 16, 1) with log
```

Figure 10-1 shows the output after the script captures the error.

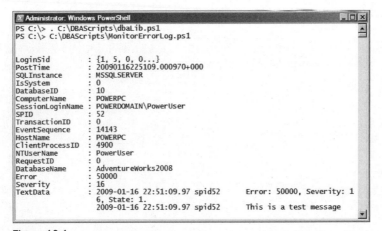

Figure 10-1

As shown in the output, the login PowerDomain\PowerUser connects with the default instance MSSQLSERVER on POWERPC in a session with SPID 52. The login causes an error with error number 50000 and severity 16 in the AdventureWorks2008 database. The TextData column provides the complete error information. After you are notified of the errors from the SQL Server error log, you can take appropriate action.

Monitoring Deadlocks

A deadlock occurs when two or more sessions permanently block each other because each session has a lock on a resource which the other sessions are trying to acquire. The SQL Server Database Engine has a lock monitor thread that periodically initiates a search through all of the tasks to detect deadlocks. After a deadlock is detected, the Database Engine ends a deadlock by choosing one of the threads as a deadlock victim, and a 1205 error is thrown by SQL Server. To collect information about the threads and the resources involved in the deadlock, you can monitor the DEADLOCK_GRAPH trace event class. The MonitorDeadlocks.ps1 script defines the event query, the namespace for the default instance, and the properties of deadlock events:

```
$query = "SELECT * FROM DEADLOCK_GRAPH"
$sqlnamespace = "root\Microsoft\SqlServer\ServerEvents\MSSQLSERVER"
$selections= "LoginSid", "LoginName", "SQLInstance", "IsSystem", "PostTime", `
"ComputerName", "SessionLoginName", "SPID", "StartTime", "TransactionID", `
"EventSequence", "TextData"

Get-WMIEvent $query $sqlnamespace $selections
```

Run the script in a Windows PowerShell console:

```
. C:\DBAScripts\dbaLib.ps1
C:\DBAScripts\MonitorDeadlocks.ps1
```

In order to test this script, run the following query in a SSMS query window:

```
CREATE TABLE Test (i int)

INSERT Test SELECT 1
GO
BEGIN TRAN
UPDATE Test SET i = 1
WAITFOR DELAY '00:00:30'
UPDATE Test2 SET i = 1
WAITFOR DELAY '00:02:00'
COMMIT

DROP TABLE Test
```

This session holds exclusive locks on the Test table, and tries to update the Test2 table.

Within 30 seconds, in another SSMS query window, run this query:

```
CREATE TABLE Test2 (i int)

INSERT Test2 SELECT 1
GO
BEGIN TRAN
UPDATE Test2 SET i = 1
WAITFOR DELAY '00:00:30'
UPDATE Test SET i = 1
WAITFOR DELAY '00:02:00'
COMMIT

DROP TABLE Test2
```

This session holds exclusive locks on the Test2 table, and tries to update the Test table. You have a deadlock situation here because these two sessions are blocking each other, trying to update the table the other process is holding. Our script, MonitorDeadlocks.ps1, detects the deadlock and prints out the deadlock graph.

Figure 10-2 shows the output. The last property, TextData, cannot be shown in full.

Figure 10-2

The complete TextData is shown here:

```
<TextData><deadlock-list>&#x0A; <deadlock victim="processc6b558">&#x0A; <process-
list>&#x0A; <process id="processc6b558" taskpriority="0" logused="248"
waitresource="RID: 1:1:304:0" waittime="2234" ownerId="291807"
transactionname="user_transaction" lasttranstarted="2009-01-16T22:38:55.550"
XDES="0x58b8280" lockMode="U" schedulerid="1" kpid="4272" status="suspended"
spid="55" sbid="0" ecid="0" priority="0" trancount="2" lastbatchstarted="2009-01-
16T22:38:55.550" lastbatchcompleted="2009-01-16T22:38:55.550" lastattention="2009-
01-16T22:38:26.867" clientapp="Microsoft SQL Server Management Studio - Query"
hostname="POWERPC" hostpid="4900" loginname="POWERDOMAIN\PowerUser"
isolationlevel="read committed (2)" xactid="291807" currentdb="1"
lockTimeout="4294967295" clientoption1="671088672" clientoption2="128056">
&#x0A; <executionStack>&#x0A; <frame procname="adhoc" line="4" stmtstart="16"
sqlhandle="0x02000000c1081407296ca08140bec8aa7e80cbe6b1ce3619">&#x0A;UPDATE [Test]
set [i] = @1 </frame>&#x0A; <frame procname="adhoc" line="4" stmtstart="130"
stmtend="176"sqlhandle="0x020000003c79c7207829ee6fa84ad47a7c28afb36a2e72eb">
&#x0A;UPDATE Test SET i = 1 </frame>&#x0A; </executionStack>&#x0A;
<inputbuf>&#x0A;BEGIN TRAN &#x0A;UPDATE Test2 SET i = 1 &#x0A;WAITFOR
DELAY &apos;00:00:30&apos; &#x0A;UPDATE Test SET i = 1 &#x0A;WAITFOR
DELAY &apos;00:02:00&apos; &#x0A;COMMIT &#x0A;&#x0A;DROP TABLE Test2&#x0A;
&#x0A; </inputbuf>&#x0A; </process>&#x0A; <process id="process6350aa8"
taskpriority="0" logused="248" waitresource="RID:1:1:309:0" waittime="9332"
ownerId="291761" transactionname="user_transaction" lasttranstarted="2009-01-16T22:
38:48.447" XDES="0x52cdb30" lockMode="U" schedulerid="1" kpid="4580"
status="suspended" spid="52" sbid="0" ecid="0" priority="0" trancount="2"
lastbatchstarted="2009-01-16T22:38:48.447" lastbatchcompleted="2009-01-16T22:
```

```
38:48.447" lastattention="2009-01-16T22:38:05.337" clientapp="Microsoft SQL
Server Management Studio - Query" hostname="POWERPC" hostpid="4900"
loginname="POWERDOMAIN\PowerUser" isolationlevel="read committed (2)"
xactid="291761" currentdb="1" lockTimeout="4294967295" clientoption1="671090784"
clientoption2="390200">&#x0A;   <executionStack>&#x0A;      <frame procname="adhoc"
line="4" stmtstart="16" sqlhandle="0x02000000d754ba259586cc023c12b6e68ced80a
43710ab21">&#x0A;UPDATE [Test2] set [i] = @1     </frame>&#x0A;
<frame procname="adhoc" line="4" stmtstart="128" stmtend="176"
sqlhandle="0x02000000952d5a0eee199c15bbafd5addc0f91981b230c11">&#x0A;UPDATE
Test2 SET i = 1 </frame>&#x0A;      </executionStack>&#x0A;   <inputbuf>&#x0A;
BEGIN TRAN &#x0A;UPDATE Test SET i = 1 &#x0A;WAITFOR DELAY
&apos;00:00:30&apos; &#x0A;UPDATE Test2 SET i = 1 &#x0A;WAITFOR DELAY
&apos;00:02:00&apos; &#x0A;COMMIT &#x0A;&#x0A;DROP TABLE Test&#x0A;&#x0A;
</inputbuf>&#x0A;   </process>&#x0A;  </process-list>&#x0A;  <resource-list>&#x0A;
<ridlock fileid="1" pageid="304" dbid="1" objectname="master.dbo.Test"
id="lock511fec0" mode="X" associatedObjectId="72057594039697408">&#x0A;
<owner-list>&#x0A;      <owner id="process6350aa8" mode="X"></owner>&#x0A;
</owner-list>&#x0A;     <waiter-list>&#x0A;       <waiter id="processc6b558" mode="U"
requestType="wait"></waiter>&#x0A;    </waiter-list>&#x0A; </ridlock>&#x0A;
<ridlock fileid="1" pageid="309" dbid="1" objectname="master.dbo.Test2"
id="lock8015180" mode="X" associatedObjectId="72057594039762944">&#x0A;
<owner-list>&#x0A;      <owner id="processc6b558" mode="X"></owner>&#x0A;
</owner-list>&#x0A;     <waiter-list>&#x0A;       <waiter id="process6350aa8"
mode="U" requestType="wait"></waiter>&#x0A;    </waiter-list>&#x0A;   </ridlock>
&#x0A;   </resource-list>&#x0A;  </deadlock>&#x0A;</deadlock-list>&#x0A;</TextData>
```

Spid 10, shown in the SPID property, was the lock detection thread initiated by SQL Server, run under the sa login. The XML text in the TextData property might look cryptic, but if you examine it carefully the victim in this deadlock situation had a process ID processc6b558, which matched the process ID in the first <process> tag. The content in this <process> tag indicates that the SPID of the victim is 55, and the login POWERDOMAIN\PowerUser owned this SPID.

The <frame> tag inside the process tag indicates that the statement SPID 55 was executing at the time of the deadlock. If you are interested in the entire input buffer of this SPID, you can look at the <inputbuf> tag. The second <process> tag shows that the winner in this deadlock situation is spid 52, and that the login POWERDOMAIN\PowerUser also owns this SPID. Again, the <frame> tag shows the statement spid 52 was executing at the time of the deadlock, and the <inputbuf> tag shows its entire input buffer.

The <resource-list> tag shows the resource each process is holding exclusively and the resource it was waiting for. Although only process IDs processc6b558 and process6350aa8 were included in the <resource-list> tag, you can match them with SPID 55 and 52 individually in the <process> tags. The objectname attribute shows you the resource names.

Monitoring Blockings

Blocking occurs when a process is waiting for a resource that another process is holding. Excessive blocking can increase process wait time and slow down overall SQL Server performance. The trace event class BLOCKED_PROCESS_REPORT can be used to monitor blocked processes that are waiting for resources. However, by default, this event class is disabled. You need to run sp_configure to reconfigure the *blocked process threshold* option. This option specifies the threshold, in seconds, at which blocked process reports are generated. For example, if you want a blocked process report to be generated for each session that is blocked for 30 seconds, run the following query on the SQL Server:

```
Exec sp_configure 'show advanced options', 1
RECONFIGURE
GO
Exec sp_configure 'blocked process threshold', 30
RECONFIGURE
GO
```

The setting change becomes effective immediately without a server stop and restart. Please note that each report contains only two connections of a blocking. Unlike the DEADLOCK_GRAPH event, which shows a deadlock chain, this event class does not show the complete chain. You have to work through all the reports gathered at the same time to figure out which process is at the head of the chain.

The MonitorBlockings.ps1 script defines the event query, the namespace for the default instance, and the properties of blocked process reports:

```
$query = "SELECT * FROM BLOCKED_PROCESS_REPORT"
$sqlnamespace = "root\Microsoft\SqlServer\ServerEvents\MSSQLSERVER"
$selections= "LoginSid","PostTime","SQLInstance","IsSystem",`
"DatabaseID","ComputerName","SessionLoginName","SPID", `
"TransactionID","EventSequence","IndexID","ObjectID", "TextData", `
"EndTime","Duration","Mode"

Get-WMIEvent $query $sqlnamespace $selections
```

Run the script in a Windows PowerShell session:

```
. C:\DBAScripts\dbaLib.ps1
C:\DBAScripts\MonitorBlockings.ps1
```

While the scripts are running, open a query window in SSMS and run this query:

```
USE AdventureWorks2008

IF  EXISTS (SELECT * FROM sys.objects WHERE object_id = OBJECT_ID(N'[dbo].[Test]')
AND
type in (N'U'))
DROP TABLE [dbo].[Test]
GO

CREATE TABLE Test (i int)

INSERT Test SELECT 1
GO
BEGIN TRAN
UPDATE Test SET i = 1
WAITFOR DELAY '00:01:00'
COMMIT
```

This session holds exclusive locks for one minute on the Test table.

In another query window in SSMS, run the following query:

```
USE AdventureWorks2008
UPDATE Test SET i = 1
```

Because this session is trying to update the `Test` table, it is blocked by the first session. The `Monitor-Blockings.ps1` script detects the blocking and picks up the process report.

Figure 10-3 shows the output. Similar to the deadlock graph shown in the last section, `spid 7`, shown in the `SPID` property, is the blocking detection thread initiated by SQL Server.

Figure 10-3

The XML text in the `TextData` property shows the blocked process in the `<blocked-process>` tag. The blocked process is running under SPID 54, owned by the login `POWERDOMAIN\PowerUser`. The entire input buffer of this SPID is in the `<inputbuf>` tag. The blocking process is included in the `<blocking-process>` tag. It is running under SPID 52, owned by the login `POWERDOMAIN\PowerUser`. Its entire input buffer can be found in the `<inputbuf>` tag. The `waitresource` attribute (`waitresource="RID: 10:1:23082:0"`) inside the `<process>` tag of the `<blocked-process>` tag identifies the ID of the page that the waiter waits for, `RID: 10:1:23082` (note that a lock on a data row is actually on the data page that contains the row). The first number, 10, is the ID of the database to which the resource belongs, which you could also get from the `currentdb` attributes inside the `<process>` tag. In this case, database ID 10 corresponds to the `AdventureWorks2008` database. To determine the resource, you can run the undocumented `dbcc page` command in the `AdventureWorks2008` database (see Figure 10-4):

```
dbcc traceon(3604)
dbcc page (10,1,23082,0)
```

Figure 10-4

The `Metadata:ObjectId 711673583` under the `PAGE HEADER` in the result is the ID of the `Test` table that owns the locked page. You can confirm this by running the following command:

```
select OBJECT_NAME(711673583)
```

This command should return the table name, `Test`. Therefore, the output indicates that SPID 54 is waiting for a data page of the `Test` table to be released by SPID 52.

Monitoring Login Changes and Failed Login Attempts

As a DBA working at a financial company, I often face questions from business units on security auditing. They're usually concerned with unauthorized server access or malicious security exploitation. To help them meet auditing requirements, I can create SQL Server traces using extended procedures, such as `sp_trace_setevent` and `sp_trace_setstatus`, to monitor login events in the background. However, it is not an easy task. It involves creating a trace with the right events, creating a startup procedure to kick off the trace when SQL Server starts, and outputting the trace to a readable file. The following example shows an approach to monitoring login changes and failed login attempts with the WMI Provider for Server Events, which is much easier and cleaner.

`DDL_LOGIN_EVENTS` is the DDL event class for login events. It has three child classes:

- ❏   `ALTER_LOGIN`: Captures changes to properties of SQL Server logins and Windows logins
- ❏   `CREATE_LOGIN`: Captures new account creations
- ❏   `DROP_LOGIN`: Captures account deletions

In the script that follows, called `MonitorLogins.ps1`, the event query is defined to subscribe to events from the `DDL_LOGIN_EVENTS` class. The namespace of the default instance and the properties of the events are also defined. Then the script calls the `Get-WMIEvent` function to capture and print out the login DDL events:

```
$query = "SELECT * FROM DDL_LOGIN_EVENTS"
$sqlnamespace = "root\Microsoft\SqlServer\ServerEvents\MSSQLSERVER"
$selections= "__CLASS", "SID", "ObjectName", "ObjectType", `
"PostTime", "ComputerName", "DefaultLanguage", "DefaultDatabase", `
"SPID", "LoginName", "SQLInstance", "LoginType"

Get-WMIEvent $query $sqlnamespace $selections
```

In this script, we add a general property `_CLASS` to specify whether a login is altered, created, or dropped. This is necessary because the three child classes don't return any class-specified properties to identify the type of action, although `DROP_LOGIN` returns the `TSQLCommand` executed to drop the login.

Run the script in a Windows PowerShell session:

```
. C:\DBAScripts\dbaLib.ps1
C:\DBAScripts\MonitorLogins.ps1
```

Open a query window in SSMS and run the following query on the default instance:

```
CREATE LOGIN sqluser WITH PASSWORD='Welcome123'
ALTER LOGIN sqluser WITH PASSWORD='Er34jkOio'
DROP LOGIN sqluser
```

As you can see, the query creates a SQL Server login, `sqluser`, changes its password, and then drops the login. Our script, `MonitorLogins.ps1`, captures all three login events.

Figure 10-5 shows the output. The script prints out the type of events that happened (__CLASS), the login that was changed (ObjectName), and the login that issued the change (LoginName). From the information, you can track down unplanned or malicious changes.

Figure 10-5

In addition to login changes, failed login attempts also need to be monitored to prevent malicious security exploitation. The trace event class AUDIT_LOGIN_FAILED is used for this purpose. The MonitorFailed-LoginAttempts.ps1 script shown here captures failed login attempts:

```
$query = "SELECT * FROM AUDIT_LOGIN_FAILED"
$sqlnamespace = "root\Microsoft\SqlServer\ServerEvents\MSSQLSERVER"
$selections= "HostName","NTUserName","SQLInstance","Success","IsSystem",`
"RequestID","DatabaseID","DatabaseName","ComputerName","SessionLoginName",`
"SPID","NTDomainName","LoginName","StartTime","ApplicationName",`
"EventSequence","PostTime","ClientProcessID","Error","TextData"

Get-WMIEvent $query $sqlnamespace $selections
```

Run the script in a Windows PowerShell session:

```
. C:\DBAScripts\dbaLib.ps1
C:\DBAScripts\MonitorFailedLoginAttempts.ps1
```

Open SQL Server Management Studio. Try to log in as sa with an invalid password. You should get a pop-up message like the one shown in Figure 10-6.

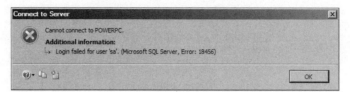

Figure 10-6

The login attempt failed, of course, because the password was incorrect. The output from the script is shown in Figure 10-7.

Figure 10-7

The TextData property shows the same message shown in the pop-up window. The ComputerName property indicates from which workstation the login was attempted. By capturing all the failed login attempts, you can track down malicious security exploitation.

Monitoring Databases

On the server level, you need to audit database events to guard against accidental database deletions. In a shared database environment, you also need to monitor the addition of new databases in order to manage backups and disk space effectively.

Database events are included in the DDL_SERVER_LEVEL_EVENTS class. Three child classes of this class are associated with database changes:

❑   ALTER_DATABASE: Captures changes to properties of databases

❑   CREATE_DATABASE: Captures new database creations

❑   DROP_DATABASE: Captures database deletions

There are other child classes under the DDL_SERVER_LEVEL_EVENTS class. To retrieve only events from the preceding three child classes, you need to use the identifier __CLASS to filter the events from the DDL_SERVER_LEVEL_EVENTS class in the event query. The sample script, MonitorDatabases.ps1, is shown here:

```
$query = "SELECT * FROM DDL_SERVER_LEVEL_EVENTS `
WHERE __CLASS = 'CREATE_DATABASE' or __CLASS = 'ALTER_DATABASE' `
or __CLASS = 'DROP_DATABASE'"
$sqlnamespace = "root\Microsoft\SqlServer\ServerEvents\MSSQLSERVER"
$selections= "SQLInstance","PostTime","ComputerName","SPID",`
"LoginName","TSQLCommand","DatabaseName"

Get-WMIEvent $query $sqlnamespace $selections
```

Run this script in a Windows PowerShell session:

```
. C:\DBAScripts\dbaLib.ps1
C:\DBAScripts\MonitorDatabases.ps1
```

Open a query window in SSMS and run the following query on the default instance:

```
CREATE DATABASE testDB
ALTER DATABASE testDB modify file (name=testDB, size=10MB)
DROP DATABASE testDB
```

As shown here, this SQL query creates a testDB database, changes the size of the database's data file, and then drops the database.

The MonitorDatabases.ps1 script captures all three events.

Figure 10-8 shows the output. The DatabaseName property shows the database that is being changed.

The TSQLCommand property shows the actual T-SQL statement that is run against the server. You can also see details about the sessions that make the changes, such as SPID, login name, and computer name.

Monitoring Database Objects

In a development team where each developer can make his or her own changes to the database schema, a developer might make unplanned changes, and overwrite the work done by another developer. To ensure that the change process is transparent and manageable, you should track down planned and unplanned changes to minimize the risk of improper changes causing a database outage.

Let's take the stored procedure as an example. The DDL_PROCEDURE_EVENTS class is the event class for stored procedure events. It has three child classes:

❑   ALTER_PROCEDURE: Captures changes to properties of stored procedures

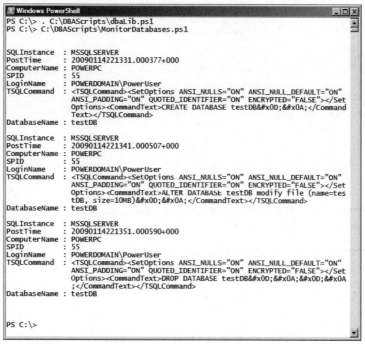

Figure 10-8

❑ `CREATE_PROCEDURE`: Captures the creation of new stored procedures

❑ `DROP_PROCEDURE`: Captures deletions of existing stored procedures

The `MonitorStoredProcs.ps1` script shown here monitors stored procedure changes in the `AdventureWorks2008` database:

```
$query = "SELECT * FROM DDL_PROCEDURE_EVENTS WHERE DatabaseName like
'AdventureWorks2008%' "
$sqlnamespace = "root\Microsoft\SqlServer\ServerEvents\MSSQLSERVER"
$selections = "SchemaName","TSQLCommand","PostTime","SQLInstance",`
"ObjectName","ObjectType","DatabaseName","ComputerName","SPID",`
"LoginName","UserName"

Get-WMIEvent $query $sqlnamespace $selections
```

Run the script in a Windows PowerShell console:

```
. C:\DBAScripts\dbaLib.ps1
C:\DBAScripts\MonitorStoredProcs.ps1
```

Open a query window in SSMS and run the following query in the `AdventureWorks2008` database on the default instance:

```
USE AdventureWorks2008
GO
```

```
CREATE PROCEDURE getBlockedProcessesDetails
AS
SELECT session_id, blocking_session_id
FROM sys.dm_exec_requests
WHERE blocking_session_id > 0
GO
ALTER PROCEDURE getBlockedProcessesDetails
AS
SELECT session_id, command, blocking_session_id
FROM sys.dm_exec_requests
WHERE blocking_session_id > 0
GO
DROP PROCEDURE getBlockedProcessesDetails
```

The query first creates a stored procedure called getBlockedProcessesDetails. This stored procedure gets a list of blocked and blocking sessions. Then the stored procedure is modified to include the T-SQL command from the blocked session. Finally, the stored procedure is dropped.

As shown in Figure 10-9, the MonitorStoredProcs.ps1 script captures all three events.

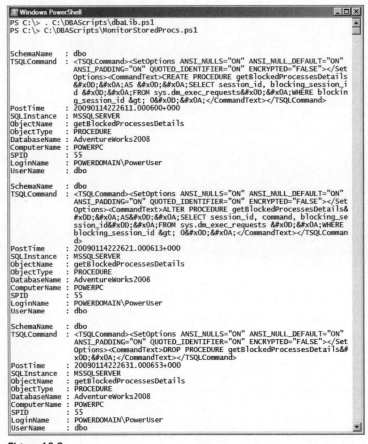

Figure 10-9

The `ObjectName` property shows which stored procedure is being changed. The `TSQLCommand` property shows the actual T-SQL statement that is run against the database to change the stored procedure. The `LoginName` property shows the login that makes the changes.

Summary

This chapter demonstrated the uses of the WMI Provider for Server Events in event monitoring. You learned how to leverage the eventing infrastructure in Windows PowerShell 2.0 to create a function, `Get-WMIEvent`, to monitor DDL and trace events. The examples include errors from SQL Server error log, deadlocks, blockings, login changes, failed login attempts, database changes, and database object changes. You can mimic the scripts in this chapter, and easily extend the monitoring function, to other events in SQL Server instances. For more information on this provider and available event classes, you can refer to BOL or visit the MSDN website, http://msdn.microsoft.com/en-us/library/ms180560.aspx.

In the next two chapters, you will discover a new feature in SQL Server 2008, Windows PowerShell support for SQL Server. This new feature highlights Microsoft's determination to use Windows PowerShell to automate server administration.

11

Windows PowerShell in SQL Server 2008 Environment, SQL Server PowerShell Provider

When installing SQL Server 2008, SQL Server installs Windows PowerShell and two SQL Server PowerShell snap-ins that expose SQL Server functionality in PowerShell. You may remember from Chapter 2 that PowerShell Snap-ins are .NET assemblies that contain Windows PowerShell providers and/or Windows PowerShell cmdlets that extend the functionality of the shell. When a snap-in is loaded into the PowerShell environment, the cmdlets and providers contained in it are registered with the shell. SQL Server 2008 installs its own snap-ins, which are covered in detail in the latter part of this chapter.

This chapter discusses the new features in SQL Server 2008 that integrate SQL Server and Power-Shell:

❏ `sqlps` utility

❏ SQLSERVER: `Drive` and `Invoke-Sqlcmd` cmdlets

❏ Encoding and decoding the Uniform Resource Name (URN)

sqlps Utility

The `sqlps` utility is included with SQL Server 2008; you don't have to install it separately. When the `sqlps` utility is launched, it starts a PowerShell session with the SQL Server PowerShell provider. This means that SQL Server PowerShell snap-ins and all SQL Server–related cmdlets are loaded, registered, and ready to be executed. The SQL Server PowerShell provider exposes SQL Server objects in a hierarchy similar to the file system.

In addition to `sqlps`, the following components are also already installed at the time of SQL Server 2008 installation:

❑ **.NET Framework 3.5:** The SQL Server 2008 installation process installs .NET Framework 3.5 and then requires a reboot.

❑ **Windows PowerShell 1.0:** If Windows PowerShell is not already installed, SQL Server installs it.

❑ **SQL Server PowerShell Snap-ins:**

    ❑ Includes a set of SQL Server cmdlets

    ❑ A SQL Server PowerShell provider enables you to navigate SQL Server objects using paths similar to file system paths.

❑ **`sqlps` utility:** `sqlps` starts the PowerShell environment and then loads and registers the SQL Server PowerShell Snap-ins. With `sqlps`, you can run PowerShell commands and scripts, and run SQL Server cmdlets with `sqlps`.

You can invoke and use PowerShell on a SQL Server 2008 server in four different ways. The first way is through the `sqlps` utility. `sqlps.exe` is copied to the `\Program Files\Microsoft SQL Server\100\Tools\Binn` folder at the time of installation. Because the Binn folder is added to the System PATH variable, you can launch the `sqlps` utility by selecting Start ➢ Run and entering `sqlps`, as shown in Figure 11-1.

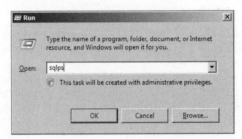

Figure 11-1

Once you click OK, you can see that SQL Server PowerShell [`sqlps`] is launched (see Figure 11-2).

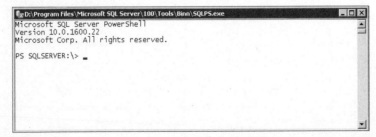

Figure 11-2

PowerShell can also be launched from SQL Server Management Studio by right-clicking on an object in Object Explorer, as shown in Figure 11-3. SQL Server Management Studio launches the sqlps and sets the location to the object to which you were pointing. In this case, it is the AWBuildVersion table in the database AdventureWorks2008 (see Figure 11-4).

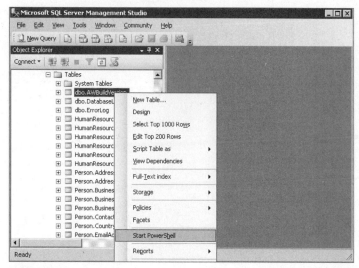

Figure 11-3

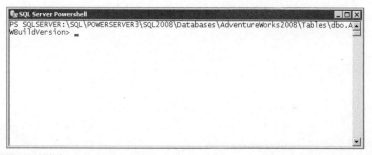

Figure 11-4

PowerShell scripts and cmdlets can also be launched inside a SQL Server Agent job. Figure 11-5 shows that by setting the type of SQL Server Agent job step to PowerShell, you can insert PowerShell cmdlets and scripts.

You can also launch Windows PowerShell and add the SQL Server PowerShell provider functionality using the Add-PSSnapin cmdlet, as shown in Figure 11-6. In order to launch PowerShell in this way, follow these steps:

1. Launch Windows PowerShell from Start ➤ Program ➤ Windows PowerShell.
2. Add the SQL Server PowerShell snap-ins as shown. In the following example, the cmdlet Get-PSSnapin —registered shows all the available registered snap-ins in the system.

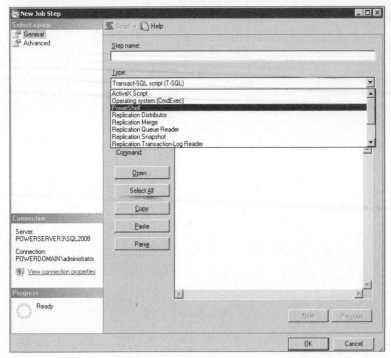

Figure 11-5

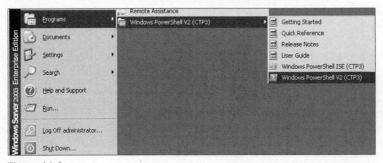

Figure 11-6

3.　The two cmdlets `Add-PSSnapin SqlServerProviderSnapin100` and `Add-PSSnapin SqlServerCmdletSnapin100` add the SQL Server 2008 PowerShell snap-ins and the SQL Server PowerShell provider functionality to the current PowerShell Session (see Figure 11-7):

```
Get-PSSnapin -registered
Add-PSSnapin SqlServerProviderSnapin100
Add-PSSnapin SqlServerCmdletSnapin100
```

You can also load the Type Data and Format Data files used by `sqlps`. The files are located in the directory `C:\Program Files\Microsoft SQL Server\100\Tools\Binn` by default. If your installation changes the default location, then you will need to change the path in the following script:

```
Update-TypeData "C:\Program Files\Microsoft SQL
Server\100\Tools\Binn\SQLProvider.Types.ps1xml"
Update-FormatData "C:\Program Files\Microsoft SQL
Server\100\Tools\Binn\SQLProvider.Format.ps1xml"
```

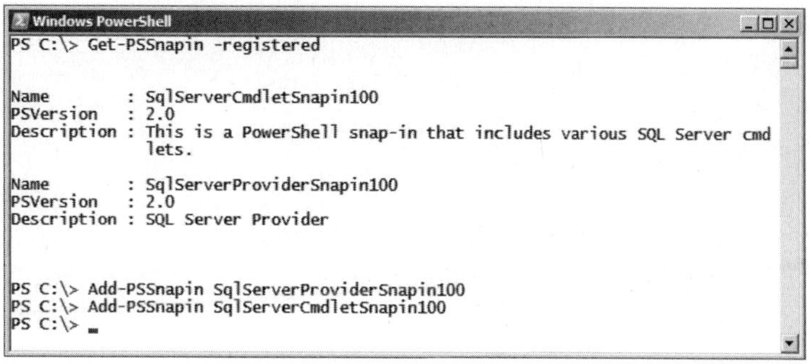

Figure 11-7

The four methods just described can be used in different scenarios. If SQL Server Management Studio is already launched and you want to open a PowerShell session with the SQL Server PowerShell provider, then methods 2 and 3 are very useful. The last method is very useful when you are already in a powerful session and want to load the SQL Server PowerShell provider onto the current session. If SQL Server Management Studio is not launched and you don't have an existing PowerShell session, then you could use the first method.

SQLSERVER: Drive and Invoke-Sqlcmd cmdlet

To confirm that SQL Server PowerShell snap-ins are added to your Windows PowerShell session, you can query the SQL Server–related snap-ins in the current PowerShell environments by executing the cmdlet Get-PSSnapin:

```
Get-PSSnapin Sql*
```

Figure 11-8 shows that the following snap-ins are loaded and available:

❑ SqlServerCmdletSnapin100

❑ SqlServerProviderSnapin100

SQL Snap-ins

At this point, you must be curious to find all the available cmdlets related to SQL Server 2008. To do so, you can use the Get-Command cmdlet (see Figure 11-9):

```
Get-Command -commandtype cmdlet | where-object {$_.PSSnapin -match
"SqlServerCmdletSnapin100"}
Get-Command -commandtype cmdlet | where-object {$_.PSSnapin -match
"SqlServerProviderSnapin100"}
```

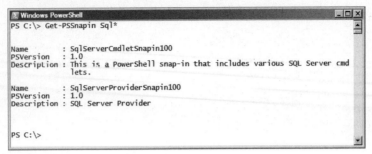

Figure 11-8

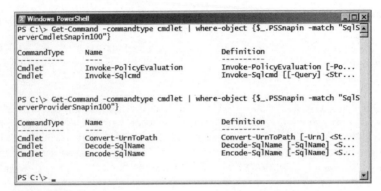

Figure 11-9

As shown in the results, the following cmdlets are available:

❑   Invoke-PolicyEvaluation

❑   Invoke-Sqlcmd

❑   Convert-UrnToPath

❑   Decode-SqlName

❑   Encode-SqlName

Except for Invoke-PolicyEvaluation, all of these cmdlets are covered in detail later in the chapter. The Invoke-PolicyEvaluation cmdlet is related to SQL Server policy evaluation and is discussed in the next chapter.

Because the SqlServerProviderSnapin100 snap-in is available in the current session, it contains the SQL Server PowerShell provider that exposes SQL Server objects in a hierarchy similar to file system paths, under a drive named SQLSERVER. It is very easy to navigate to a particular object type and execute all Data Definition Language (DDL) statements in the form of file system commands. You can see the SQLSERVER: drive, along with other PowerShell drives available in the current environment, by executing the cmdlet Get-PSDrive, as shown here (see Figure 11-10):

```
Get-PSDrive
```

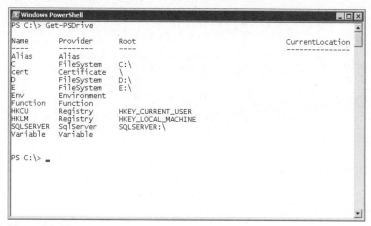

Figure 11-10

The output shows that a new drive is available, `SQLSERVER:\`. This is the root drive. Now navigate to SQLSERVER: and query the child items as shown here:

```
Set-Location SQLSERVER:
Get-ChildItem | Select-Object Name
```

As shown in Figure 11-11, the following child items are listed:

- ❑ SQL
- ❑ SQLPolicy
- ❑ SQLRegistration
- ❑ DataCollection

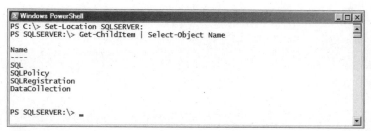

Figure 11-11

SQLSERVER: is the root folder, which contains a child item named "SQL." You can navigate to this subfolder using the cmdlet `Set-Location`, as shown here:

```
Set-Location SQL
Get-ChildItem
```

From the output, shown in Figure 11-12, you can see that the default instance is listed as DEFAULT, and the named instance is listed as SQL2008 under the property Servers.

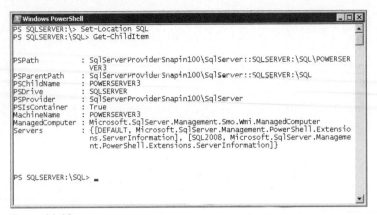

Figure 11-12

You can query all the available SQL Server instances by navigating to the machine name subfolder PowerServer3 (see Figure 11-13):

```
Set-Location PowerServer3
Get-Childitem | Select-Object Name
```

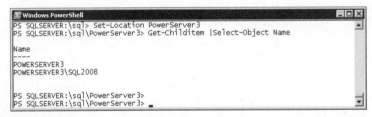

Figure 11-13

You can also query all the registered servers by navigating to the SQLRegistration folder under SQLServer:\SQL\SQLRegistration, as shown here (see Figure 11-14):

```
Set-Location SQLServer:\SQLRegistration
Get-ChildItem | select RegisteredServers
```

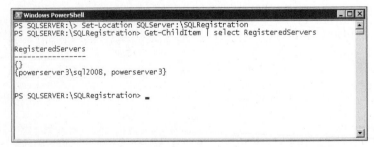

Figure 11-14

If you wanted to list all the available folders under the DEFAULT instance, you could navigate to the DEFAULT folder using the Get-Location cmdlet and then list all the folders using the Get-ChildItem cmdlet (see Figure 11-15):

```
Set-Location \
Set-Location SQL
Set-Location PowerServer3
Set-Location DEFAULT
Get-ChildItem
```

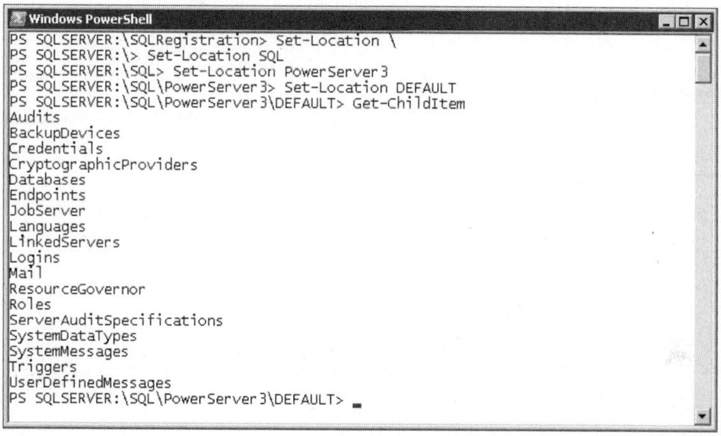

Figure 11-15

You can keep navigating the hierarchy until the last node available, as shown in Figure 11-16. The following example navigates all the way to the ExtendedProperties of the City column in the Person.Address table in the AdventureWorks2008 database:

```
Set-Location Databases
Set-Location 'AdventureWorks2008'
Set-Location Tables
Set-Location Person.Address
Set-Location Columns
Set-Location City
Set-Location ExtendedProperties
```

Every folder contains different methods that can be invoked and different properties you can access and set values to. In order to find all the methods and properties available under a hierarchal folder, you can use the Get-item and Get-member cmdlets, as shown in Figure 11-17.

In order to find all the methods available under the folder Databases, use the following code:

```
Set-Location SQLSERVER:\SQL
Set-Location PowerServer3\DEFAULT\Databases
Get-Item . | Get-Member -Type Methods
```

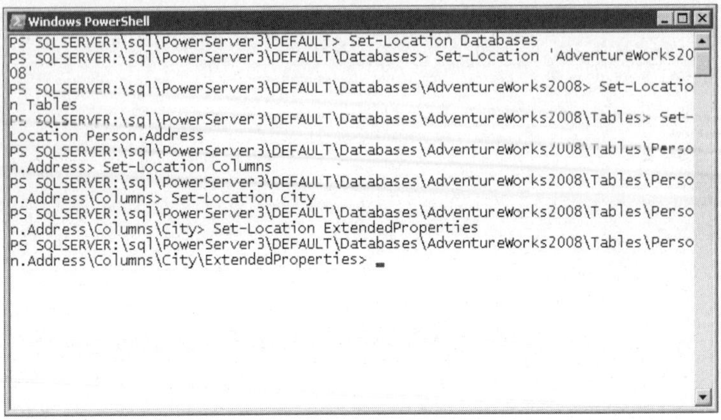

Figure 11-16

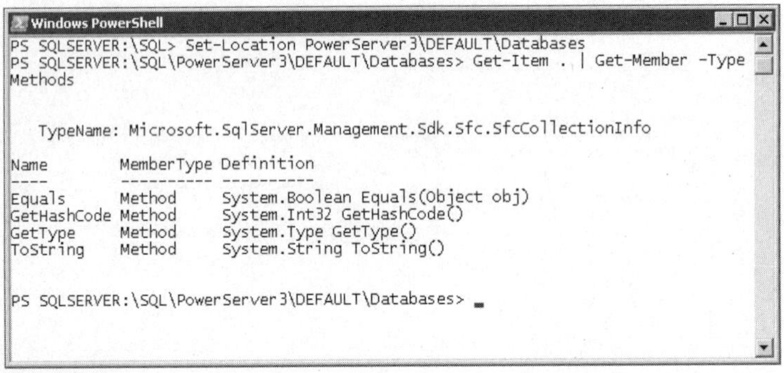

Figure 11-17

You can also get server information about the default instance by using the `Get-Item` cmdlet and its properties, as shown here (see Figure 11-18):

```
Set-Location SQLSERVER:\SQL\PowerServer3\
$server = Get-Item Default
$server.get_VersionString()
$Server.Settings.Properties | Select-Object Name, Value | Format-Table -auto
```

In addition, you can list the databases and their recovery model on the default instance using the cmdlet `Get-item` (see Figure 11-19):

```
Set-Location SQLSERVER:\SQL\PowerServer3\
$server = Get-Item Default
$server.Databases | Select-Object Name,RecoveryModel | Format-Table -auto
```

One of the restrictions of the SQL Server PowerShell provider is that you cannot create objects using the normal provider methods.

```
Windows PowerShell                                                      _ □ ✕
PS C:\> Set-Location SQLSERVER:\SQL\PowerServer3\
PS SQLSERVER:\SQL\PowerServer3> $server = Get-Item Default
PS SQLSERVER:\SQL\PowerServer3> $server.get_VersionString()
10.0.1600.22
PS SQLSERVER:\SQL\PowerServer3> $Server.Settings.Properties | Select-Object Name
, Value | Format-Table -auto

Name                                                                   Value
----                                                                   -----
AuditLevel                                                             Failure
BackupDirectory   ...Files\Microsoft SQL Server\MSSQL10.MSSQLSERVER\MSSQL\Backup
DefaultFile
DefaultLog
LoginMode                                                              Mixed
MailProfile
NumberOfLogFiles                                                          -1
PerfMonMode                                                             None
TapeLoadWaitTime                                                          -1
```

Figure 11-18

```
Windows PowerShell                                                      _ □ ✕
PS SQLSERVER:\SQL\PowerServer3> Set-Location SQLSERVER:\SQL\PowerServer3\
PS SQLSERVER:\SQL\PowerServer3> $server = Get-Item default
PS SQLSERVER:\SQL\PowerServer3> $server.Databases | Select-Object Name,RecoveryM
odel | Format-Table -auto

Name                  RecoveryModel
----                  -------------
admin                     Full
Admin2                    Full
AdventureWorks2008        Simple
master                    Simple
model                     Full
msdb                      Simple
SQL_Inventory             Full
tempdb                    Simple
TestDatabase              Full


PS SQLSERVER:\SQL\PowerServer3> _
```

Figure 11-19

You have to rely on SQL Server SMO to create objects such as a new database. The following example creates the database "TestDatabase" on the SQL Server default instance using SQL Server Management Object (SMO), as shown in Figure 11-20. Chapter 13 illustrates the use of SMO objects in detail.

```
$Server = New-Object Microsoft.SqlServer.Management.Smo.Server("PowerServer3")
$database = New-Object Microsoft.SqlServer.Management.Smo.Database($server,
"TestDatabase")
$database.create()
```

```
Windows PowerShell                                                      _ □ ✕
PS SQLSERVER:\SQL\PowerServer3> $Server = New-Object Microsoft.SqlServer.Managem
ent.Smo.Server("PowerServer3")
PS SQLSERVER:\SQL\PowerServer3> $database = New-Object Microsoft.SqlServer.Manag
ement.Smo.Database($server, "TestDatabase")
PS SQLSERVER:\SQL\PowerServer3> $database.create()
PS SQLSERVER:\SQL\PowerServer3> _
```

Figure 11-20

You can navigate to the `Databases` folder and see all the database names by using a simple cmdlet `Get-ChildItem`:

```
Set-Location SQLSERVER:\SQL\PowerServer3\DEFAULT\Databases
Get-ChildItem | Select-Object Name
```

As shown in Figure 11-21, notice that only user databases were returned.

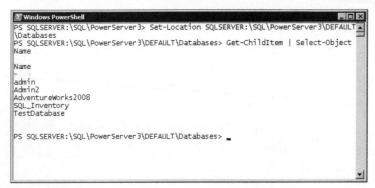

Figure 11-21

To view the system databases such as `master` and `msdb`, include the `-force` parameter (see Figure 11-22):

```
Set-Location SQLSERVER:\SQL\PowerServer3\DEFAULT\Databases
Get-ChildItem -force | Select-Object Name
```

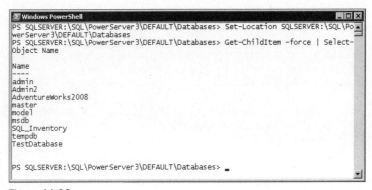

Figure 11-22

You can query the same information about database names from the named instance `SQL2008` using the instance name instead of the instance name `DEFAULT` (see Figure 11-23):

```
Get-ChildItem SQLSERVER:\SQL\PowerServer3\SQL2008\Databases -force |
Select-Object Name
```

```
Windows PowerShell                                                    _ □ ×
PS SQLSERVER:\SQL\PowerServer3\DEFAULT\Databases> Get-ChildItem SQLSERVER:\SQL\P
owerServer3\SQL2008\Databases -force | Select-Object Name

Name
----
Admin
AdventureWorksDW2008
AdventureWorksLT2008
AdventureWorksTest
edw
master
model
msdb
MyDB2
MyDBTest
pdw
PerfMon_DB
ReportServer$SQL2008
ReportServer$SQL2008TempDB
tempdb
test

PS SQLSERVER:\SQL\PowerServer3\DEFAULT\Databases>  _
```

Figure 11-23

The SQL Server PowerShell provider also includes the cmdlet `Invoke-Sqlcmd`, which is very useful in querying and executing ad hoc queries and stored procedures.

The following example will query all the data from a table Address in the database AdventureWorks2008 by executing the `Invoke-Sqlcmd` cmdlet (see Figure 11-24):

```
Set-Location SQLSERVER:\SQL\PowerServer3\DEFAULT\Databases\AdventureWorks2008

Invoke-Sqlcmd -Query "select top 10 * from Person.Address" | format-table -Auto
```

```
Windows PowerShell                                                    _ □ ×
PS SQLSERVER:\SQL\PowerServer3\DEFAULT\Databases>
PS SQLSERVER:\SQL\PowerServer3\DEFAULT\Databases> Set-Location SQLSERVER:\SQL\Po
werServer3\DEFAULT\Databases\AdventureWorks2008
PS SQLSERVER:\SQL\PowerServer3\DEFAULT\Databases\AdventureWorks2008>
PS SQLSERVER:\SQL\PowerServer3\DEFAULT\Databases\AdventureWorks2008> Invoke-Sqlc
md -Query "select top 10 * from Person.Address" | format-table -Auto
WARNING: Using provider context. Server = PowerServer3, Database =
AdventureWorks2008.

WARNING: 3 columns do not fit into the display and were removed.

AddressID AddressLine1          AddressLine2 City    StateProvinceID PostalCode
--------- ------------          ------------ ----    --------------- ----------
        1 1970 Napa Ct.                      Bothell              79 98011
        2 9833 Mt. Dias Blv.                 Bothell              79 98011
        3 7484 Roundtree Drive               Bothell              79 98011
        4 9539 Glenside Dr                   Bothell              79 98011
        5 1226 Shoe St.                      Bothell              79 98011
        6 1399 Firestone Drive               Bothell              79 98011
        7 5672 Hale Dr.                      Bothell              79 98011
        8 6387 Scenic Avenue                 Bothell              79 98011
        9 8713 Yosemite Ct.                  Bothell              79 98011
       10 250 Race Court                     Bothell              79 98011

PS SQLSERVER:\SQL\PowerServer3\DEFAULT\Databases\AdventureWorks2008>
```

Figure 11-24

You can find all the methods and properties available for the object returned from `Invoke-Sqlcmd` by using the `Get-Member` cmdlet. This example uses the parameter `-ServerInstance` with the cmdlet `Get-Item`. The `(Get-Item .)` gets the current server instance name (see Figure 11-25).

```
Set-Location SQLSERVER:\SQL\PowerServer3\DEFAULT\

$myTable =Invoke-Sqlcmd -Query "SELECT * from master.dbo.sysobjects " -ServerInstance
(Get-Item .)

$mMyTtable | get-member
```

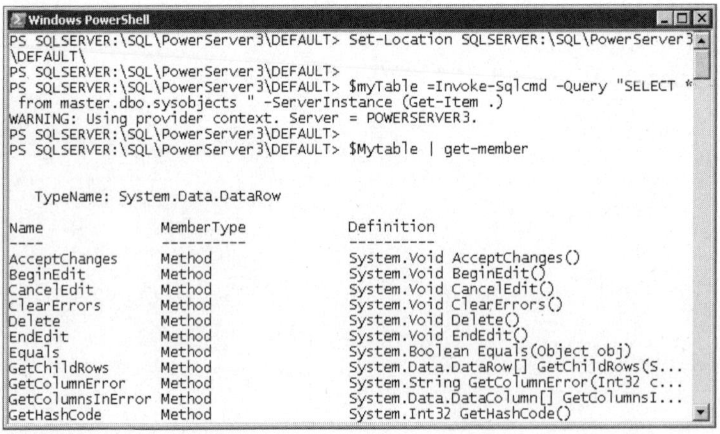

Figure 11-25

The output object from the `Invoke-Sqlcmd` cmdlet is basically a `System.Data.DataRow` object. You can access the row information using the `Foreach-Object` cmdlet (see Figure 11-26):

```
$myTable =Invoke-Sqlcmd -Query "SELECT * from master.dbo.sysdatabases "
-ServerInstance (Get-Item .)
$Mytable| Foreach-Object {$_.db_id;$_.name;$_.crdate;} | Format-Table -Auto
```

In the event that you want to access information from a particular server, you can use the `-Servername` parameter with the actual server name (see Figure 11-27):

```
Invoke-Sqlcmd -Query "SELECT @@servername" -ServerInstance "PowerServer3"
```

The next example shows how to use SQL Server authentication to access the remote server by executing the `Invoke-Sqlcmd` cmdlet using the `-User` and `-Password` parameters (see Figure 11-28):

```
Invoke-Sqlcmd -Query "SELECT @@servername+': '+@@version" -ServerInstance
"PowerServer3" -User "sa" -Password "P@ssw0rd"
```

From the preceding two examples, you can see that you don't have to be under a certain folder to execute the `Invoke-Sqlcmd` cmdlet if you are passing the actual instance name.

```
Windows PowerShell                                                    _□×
PS SQLSERVER:\SQL\PowerServer3\DEFAULT> $myTable =Invoke-Sqlcmd -Query "SELECT *
 from master.dbo.sysdatabases " -ServerInstance (Get-Item .)
WARNING: Using provider context. Server = POWERSERVER3.
PS SQLSERVER:\SQL\PowerServer3\DEFAULT> $Mytable| Foreach-Object {$_.db_id;$_.na
me;$_.crdate;} | Format-Table -Auto
master

WARNING: 2 columns do not fit into the display and were removed.

Date                 Day DayOfWeek DayOfYear Hour      Kind Millisecond Min
                                                                        ute
----                 --- --------- --------- ----      ---- ----------- ---
4/8/2003 12:00:00 AM   8 Tuesday          98    9 Unspecified       390  13
tempdb
2/6/2009 12:00:00 AM   6 Friday           37   21 Unspecified        13   3
model
4/8/2003 12:00:00 AM   8 Tuesday          98    9 Unspecified       390  13
msdb
7/9/2008 12:00:00 AM   9 Wednesday       191   16 Unspecified       767  46
admin
9/20/2008 12:00:00 AM 20 Saturday        264    3 Unspecified       357  34
Admin2
9/20/2008 12:00:00 AM 20 Saturday        264    4 Unspecified       437   2
SQL_Inventory
10/18/2008 12:00:00 AM 18 Saturday       292    0 Unspecified        33  22
AdventureWorks2008
2/6/2009 12:00:00 AM   6 Friday           37   21 Unspecified       640   8
TestDatabase
2/6/2009 12:00:00 AM   6 Friday           37   21 Unspecified       280  20
```

Figure 11-26

```
Windows PowerShell                                                    _□×
PS SQLSERVER:\> Invoke-Sqlcmd -Query "SELECT @@servername" -ServerInstance "Powe
rServer3"

Column1
-------
POWERSERVER3


PS SQLSERVER:\> _
```

Figure 11-27

```
Windows PowerShell                                                    _□×
PS SQLSERVER:\> Invoke-Sqlcmd -Query "SELECT @@servername+': '+@@version" -Serve
rInstance "PowerServer3" -User "sa" -Password "P@ssw0rd"

Column1
-------
POWERSERVER3: Microsoft SQL Server 2008 (RTM) - 10.0.1600.22 (Intel X86) ...


PS SQLSERVER:\> _
```

Figure 11-28

In order to use SQL Server authentication to access the remote named instance, execute the
Invoke-Sqlcmd cmdlet using the -ServerInstance, -User, and -Password parameters, as shown here
(see Figure 11-29):

```
Invoke-Sqlcmd -Query "SELECT @@servername+': '+@@version" -ServerInstance
"PowerServer3\SQL2008" -User "sa" -Password "P@ssw0rd"
```

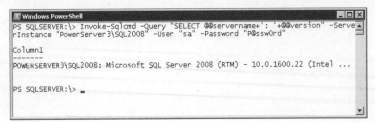

Figure 11-29

Encoding and Decoding Uniform Resource Name (URN)

In some cases you have to use special characters when using SQL providers. In those cases, the `Encode-SqlName` and `Decode-SqlName` cmdlets come in handy. The following example shows a table named `[my\table:s]` in the `admin` database:

```
use admin
go
create table [my\table:s] (id int, name varchar(100))
go
```

Try to access the table using the `Set-Location` cmdlets shown here:

```
Set-Location SQLSERVER:\SQL\powerserver3\default\databases\admin\tables
Set-Location dbo.my\table:s
Set-Location "dbo.my\table:s"
Set-Location "dbo.[my\table:s]"
```

If you use the `SQLSERVER:` drive and navigate to the tables as shown in Figure 11-30, you will have difficulty because the backslash (\) and colon (:) are special characters.

This problem can be easily solved using the `Encode-SqlName` cmdlet (see Figure 11-31).

```
$tbname=(Encode-SqlName "my\table:s")
Set-Location dbo.$tbname
```

If you already have an encoded SQL name and you want to decode it, you could use the `Decode-SqlName` cmdlet (see Figure 11-32):

```
Decode-SqlName "my%5Ctable%3As"
```

The SQL Server Management Object (SMO) model builds Uniform Resource Names (URNs) for every object. You can access the URN information of table objects as shown here (see Figure 11-33):

```
Set-Location SQLSERVER:\SQL\powerserver3\default\databases\admin\tables
Get-ChildItem | Select-Object Urn
```

```
Windows PowerShell                                                      _ □ ×
PS SQLSERVER:\> Set-Location SQLSERVER:\SQL\powerserver3\default\databases\admin
\tables
PS SQLSERVER:\SQL\powerserver3\default\databases\admin\tables> Set-Location dbo.
my\table:s
Set-Location : Cannot find drive. A drive with name 'dbo.my\table' does not exi
st.
At line:1 char:13
+ Set-Location <<<<  dbo.my\table:s
    + CategoryInfo          : ObjectNotFound: (dbo.my\table:String) [Set-Locat
   ion], DriveNotFoundException
    + FullyQualifiedErrorId : DriveNotFound,Microsoft.PowerShell.Commands.SetL
   ocationCommand

PS SQLSERVER:\SQL\powerserver3\default\databases\admin\tables> Set-Location "dbo
.my\table:s"
Set-Location : Cannot find drive. A drive with name 'dbo.my\table' does not exi
st.
At line:1 char:13
+ Set-Location <<<<   "dbo.my\table:s"
    + CategoryInfo          : ObjectNotFound: (dbo.my\table:String) [Set-Locat
   ion], DriveNotFoundException
    + FullyQualifiedErrorId : DriveNotFound,Microsoft.PowerShell.Commands.SetL
   ocationCommand

PS SQLSERVER:\SQL\powerserver3\default\databases\admin\tables> Set-Location "dbo
.[my\table:s]"
Set-Location : Cannot find drive. A drive with name 'dbo.[my\table' does not ex
ist.
At line:1 char:13
+ Set-Location <<<<   "dbo.[my\table:s]"
    + CategoryInfo          : ObjectNotFound: (dbo.[my\table:String) [Set-Loca
   tion], DriveNotFoundException
    + FullyQualifiedErrorId : DriveNotFound,Microsoft.PowerShell.Commands.SetL
   ocationCommand

PS SQLSERVER:\SQL\powerserver3\default\databases\admin\tables> _
```

Figure 11-30

```
Windows PowerShell                                                      _ □ ×
PS SQLSERVER:\SQL\powerserver3\default\databases\admin\tables> $tbname=(Encode-S
qlName "my\table:s")
PS SQLSERVER:\SQL\powerserver3\default\databases\admin\tables> Set-Location dbo.
$tbname
PS SQLSERVER:\SQL\powerserver3\default\databases\admin\tables\dbo.my%5Ctable%3As
> _
```

Figure 11-31

```
Windows PowerShell                                                      _ □ ×
PS SQLSERVER:\SQL\powerserver3\default\databases\admin\tables\dbo.my%5Ctable%3As
> Decode-SqlName "my%5Ctable%3As"
my\table:s
PS SQLSERVER:\SQL\powerserver3\default\databases\admin\tables\dbo.my%5Ctable%3As
> _
```

Figure 11-32

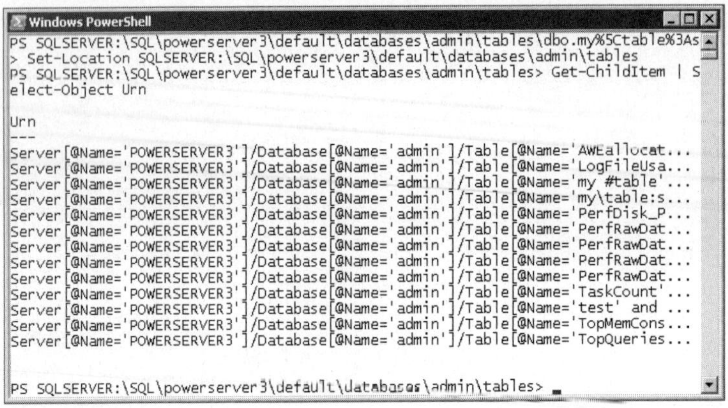

Figure 11-33

If you want to convert these URNs to an actual PowerShell provider path, then the `Convert-UrnToPath` cmdlet comes in handy. The next example converts one of the URNs listed to the actual PowerShell provider path (see Figure 11-34):

```
Convert-UrnToPath "Server[@Name='POWERSERVER3']/Database[
@Name='admin']/Table[@Name='my #table' and @Schema='dbo']"
```

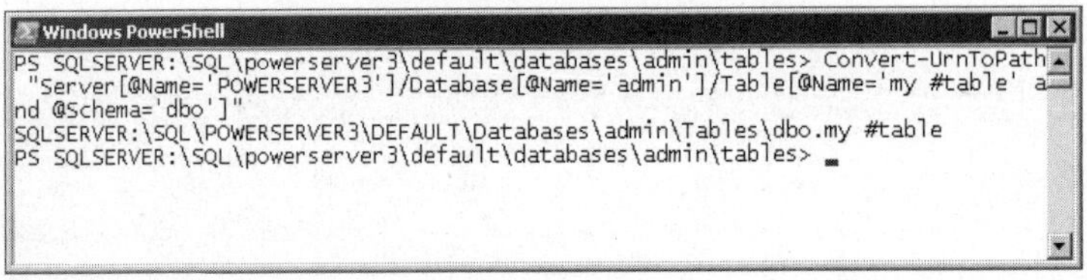

Figure 11-34

Summary

This chapter explained how the `sqlps` utility and the SQL Server PowerShell provider are used in a Windows PowerShell environment. It also covered different ways to access PowerShell in a SQL Server 2008 environment. You now know how to access different objects through the SQLSERVER: drive and are more familiar with the various cmdlets related to SQL Server, such as `Invoke-Sqlcmd`, `Convert-UrnToPath`, `Encode-SqlName`, and `Decode-SqlName`.

You have also seen that you can use SQL Server provider to navigate SQL Server objects in any level of the hierarchy. Additionally, this chapter showed you how to invoke different methods and access different properties at any level. The next chapter discusses the `SQLSERVER:\SQLPolicy` folder in detail.

12

Managing Policies through SQLSERVER:\SQLPolicy

Policy-Based Management (PBM) is a new feature in SQL Server 2008 that helps SQL Server administration. It enables database administrators to manage SQL Server instances by intent through clearly defined policies, thus reducing the potential for administrative errors. In Chapter 11, managing databases and database objects through the SQL folder under the SQLSERVER: drive was discussed. In this chapter, you will learn how to access Policy-Based Management objects, such as policies and conditions, through the other folder, SQLSERVER:\SQLPolicy.

This chapter covers the following topics:

- ❏ SQLSERVER:\SQLPolicy folder
- ❏ Conditions
- ❏ Policies

SQLSERVER:\SQLPolicy Folder

If you are not familiar with the Policy-Based Management (PBM) feature in SQL Server 2008, here is a brief introduction. As mentioned in the introduction to this chapter, Policy-Based Management helps database administrators manage SQL Server instances by applying clearly defined policies that reduce the potential for errors. The Policy-Based Framework implements the policies behind the scenes with a policy engine, SQL Server Agent jobs, SQLCLR, DDL triggers, and Service Broker. Policies can be applied or evaluated against a single server or a group of servers, improving the scalability of monitoring and administration. The operative terms used in Policy-Based Management include target, facet, condition, policy, and category.

Before creating a policy, you need to identify the entities in SQL Server to which you want to apply the policy. The entities are the *targets* of the policy. A target could be a SQL Server instance, a database, a table, a login, and so on. You can also apply conditions to filter the targets in a server instance in order to get a *target set*, such as all the user databases on an instance.

You can define multiple target sets for a policy, and they will all be contained in an object set. Targets have their own logical properties. For example, a login has a name, a login type (SQL Server or Windows login), a default database, and the enforcement of password policy.

A set of logical properties that model the behavior or characteristics of a certain type of target is called a *facet*. A target can have one or more facets. For example, a server target can have a configuration facet that includes the options configured by sp_configure, and an audit facet that includes the security login auditing settings on the server. You can define a Boolean expression that specifies the allowed states of the properties in a facet. For example, you can specify that the only allowed authentication mode of an SQL Server instance is Windows Authentication.

This Boolean expression is called a *condition*. Once you have targets and a condition, you can define a policy to check the condition against the targets. You can also assign the policy to a user-defined *category*. Policy categories help manage the policies and facilitate database subscriptions to all the policies in a category instead of as individual policies. For more information on Policy-Based Management, you can refer to SQL Server 2008 Books Online.

All of these PBM objects are available under the SQLSERVER:\SQLPolicy folder. Chapter 11 discussed the SQLSERVER: drive that is implemented by the SQL Server PowerShell provider. It also demonstrated how to register the provider and SQL Server cmdlets in your session by adding SQL Server Power-Shell snap-ins. To make it easier for you to add the snap-ins to your Windows PowerShell session, the following script can be added to the dbaLib.ps1 file:

```
############################################################################
# Add SQL Server Powershell snap-ins if they are not added yet
############################################################################
# Check if SQL Server Powershell snap-ins have not been added to the current
Windows PowerShell session
if (-not (Get-PSSnapin "SqlServer*" -ea SilentlyContinue)) {

        # If SQL Server Powershell snap-ins have not been added, then check if they
are registered on the system.
        $PSSnapIn=Get-PSSnapin SqlServer* -Registered
        if ($PSSnapIn) {
                #Add SQL Server 2008 PowerShell snap-ins
                $PSSnapIn | foreach { Add-PSSnapin $_.Name }

                # Load Type Data and Format Data used by SQLPS

                if(Test-Path -Path "C:\Program Files\Microsoft SQL Server\100\
Tools\Binn\SQLProvider.Types.ps1xml" ) {
                        Update-TypeData "C:\Program Files\Microsoft SQL Server\100\
Tools\Binn\SQLProvider.Types.ps1xml"
                }
                else {
                        Write-Host "SQLProvider.Types.ps1xml not found in
C:\Program Files\Microsoft SQL Server\100\Tools\Binn."
                        Write-Host "Please find the file on your machine and
update the path in dbaLib.ps1."
                }

                if(Test-Path -Path "C:\Program Files\Microsoft SQL Server\100\
Tools\Binn\SQLProvider.Format.ps1xml" ) {
                        Update-FormatData "C:\Program Files\Microsoft
```

```
SQL Server\100\Tools\Binn\SQLProvider.Format.ps1xml"
                }
        else {
                Write-Host "SQLProvider.Format.ps1xml not found in
C:\Program Files\Microsoft SQL Server\100\Tools\Binn."
                Write-Host "Please find the file on your machine and update
the path in dbaLib.ps1."
                }

        }
        else {
                Write-Output "No SQL Server Powershell snap-ins are registered!"
        }
}
```

If the snap-ins have not been added to the current Windows PowerShell session, then the script
checks whether the snap-ins are registered. If they are registered, then the script adds them with the
Add-PSSnapin cmdlet. The script also adds type data and format data used by SQLPS. By default,
the type data and format data files, SQLProvider.Types.ps1xml and SQLProvider.Format.ps1xml,
reside in the C:\Program Files\Microsoft SQL Server\100\Tools\Binn directory. If you changed the
default location of the SQL Server binaries to a different folder during your SQL Server installation,
please change the Binn path in the dbaLib.ps1 file before running the scripts.

As in Chapter 10, you can just source in the dbaLib.ps1 file to work with the SQLSERVER: drive and the
SQL Server cmdlets that are contained in the snap-ins:

```
. C:\DBAScripts\dbaLib.ps1
```

To access the SQLSERVER:\SQLPolicy folder and set the working location to the folder, you can use the
Set-Location cmdlet:

```
Set-Location SQLSERVER:\SQLPolicy
```

Following the folder is the computer name. You can connect to the local computer or a remote computer. The commands in the following example connect to the local computer, PowerPC, and a remote
computer, PowerServer3:

```
Set-Location SQLSERVER:\SQLPolicy\PowerPC
Set-Location SQLSERVER:\SQLPolicy\PowerServer3
```

The instance name is entered after the computer name. You can connect to any of the instances on the
specific computer. Let's say you have a default instance and a named instance, INSTANCE1, on the local
computer, PowerPC. You can connect to them individually using the following commands:

```
Set-Location SQLSERVER:\SQLPolicy\PowerPC\default
Set-Location SQLSERVER:\SQLPolicy\PowerPC\INSTANCE1
```

You can navigate the Policy-Based Management objects under each instance using the same cmdlets for
the file system:

```
Get-ChildItem
Get-Item
Move-Item
```

```
Rename-Item
Remove-Item
```

The following `Get-ChildItem` cmdlet shows the five types of Policy-Based Management objects available under the default instance on PowerPC in Figure 12-1:

```
. C:\DBAScripts\dbaLib.ps1
Set-Location SQLSERVER:\SQLPolicy\PowerPC\default
Get-ChildItem
```

Figure 12-1

We'll focus on conditions and policies because they contain the most useful information about the Policy-Based Management Framework. In order to have sample conditions and policies to work with, import the policies that are shipped with SQL Server 2008. Right-click Policies under Policy Management, and select Import Policy. This brings up an Import dialog box. Click the ellipses (. . .) button in the Files to Import box. Another Select Policy box pops up. Navigate to the directory `C:\Program Files\Microsoft SQL Server\100\Tools\Policies\DatabaseEngine\1033`, and select all the files under this folder. Click Open and the Select Policy box will be closed. Click OK to close the Import dialog box. SQL Server will import all the policies under that directory (see Figure 12-2).

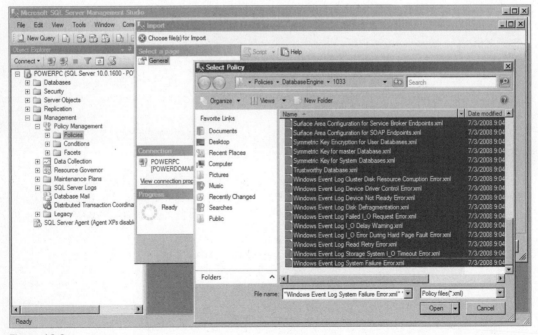

Figure 12-2

Conditions

Each policy has one and only one condition that defines the allowed states of the properties in the facet shared by the targets of the policy. Before defining a policy, its condition needs to be created first. To view all the conditions under the default instance on the computer PowerPC, run either one of the following commands:

```
. C:\DBAScripts\dbaLib.ps1
Set-Location SQLSERVER:\SQLPolicy\PowerPC\default\Conditions
Get-ChildItem | Sort-Object Name
```

Alternately, you can run the next command:

```
. C:\DBAScripts\dbaLib.ps1
Get-ChildItem -path SQLSERVER:\SQLPolicy\PowerPC\default\Conditions |
Sort-Object Name
```

Part of the output is shown in Figure 12-3. You can use the `Select-Object` cmdlet to select the `ExpressionNode` property, which contains the Boolean expression set in the condition, and the facet property to which the expression applies.

```
Windows PowerShell                                                           _|□|x|
PS C:\> . C:\DBAScripts\dbaLib.ps1
PS C:\> Set-Location SQLSERVER:\SQLPolicy\PowerPC\default\Conditions
PS SQLSERVER:\SQLPolicy\PowerPC\default\Conditions> Get-ChildItem | Sort-Object
Name

Name                          Facet                      Created
----                          -----                      -------
32-bit Affinity Mask Overla... IServerPerformanceFacet   9/19/2008 10:53 PM
32-bit Configuration          Server                     9/19/2008 10:53 PM
32-bit Configuration of SQL... Server                    9/19/2008 10:53 PM
64-bit Affinity Mask Overla... IServerPerformanceFacet   9/19/2008 10:53 PM
64-bit Configuration          Server                     9/19/2008 10:53 PM
64-bit Configuration of SQL... Server                    9/19/2008 10:53 PM
Affinity Mask Default         IServerPerformanceFacet    9/19/2008 10:53 PM
Auto Close Disabled           IDatabasePerformanceFacet  9/19/2008 10:53 PM
Auto Shrink Disabled          IDatabasePerformanceFacet  9/19/2008 10:53 PM
Auto-configured Dynamic Locks IServerPerformanceFacet    9/19/2008 10:53 PM
Auto-configured Maximum Wor... IServerPerformanceFacet   9/19/2008 10:53 PM
Auto-configured Open Objects  IServerPerformanceFacet    9/19/2008 10:53 PM
Blocked Process Threshold O... IServerPerformanceFacet   9/19/2008 10:53 PM
Cluster Disk Resource Corru... Server                    9/19/2008 10:53 PM
CmdExec Rights for sysadmin... IServerSecurityFacet      9/19/2008 10:53 PM
Collation Matches master or... IDatabasePerformanceFacet 9/19/2008 10:53 PM
Data and Backup on Separate... IDatabaseMaintenanceFacet 9/19/2008 10:53 PM
Data and Log Files on Separ... IDatabasePerformanceFacet 9/19/2008 10:53 PM
Database Owner Not sysadmin   IDatabaseSecurityFacet     9/19/2008 10:53 PM
Default Trace Enabled         IServerAuditFacet          9/19/2008 10:53 PM
Device Driver Control Error... Server                    9/19/2008 10:53 PM
Device Not Ready Error Check  Server                     9/19/2008 10:53 PM
Disk Defragmentation Result... Server                    9/19/2008 10:53 PM
Domain Guest Login            Login                      10/28/2008 5:49 PM
Endpoint Disabled             Endpoint                   9/19/2008 10:53 PM
Endpoint Stopped              Endpoint                   9/19/2008 10:53 PM
Enterprise or Standard Edition Server                    9/19/2008 10:53 PM
Fail For Any Symmetric Key    SymmetricKey               9/19/2008 10:53 PM
Failed I/O Request Check      Server                     9/19/2008 10:53 PM
File is 1GB or Larger         DataFile                   9/19/2008 10:53 PM
Growth Type Not Percent       DataFile                   9/19/2008 10:53 PM
Guest                         User                       9/19/2008 10:53 PM
```

Figure 12-3

Take the `Auto Close Disabled` condition as an example:

```
Get-ChildItem | Where-Object {$_.Name -eq 'Auto Close Disabled' } |
Select-Object Name, ExpressionNode, Facet | Format-List
```

As shown in Figure 12-4, this condition tests the `@AutoClose` property of the `IDatabasePerformanceFacet` facet.

```
Windows PowerShell                                                    _□×
PS SQLSERVER:\SQLPolicy\PowerPC\default\Conditions> Get-ChildItem | Where-Object
 {$_.Name -eq 'Auto Close Disabled' } | Select-Object Name, ExpressionNode, Face
t | Format-List


Name            : Auto Close Disabled
ExpressionNode  : @AutoClose = False()
Facet           : IDatabasePerformanceFacet



PS SQLSERVER:\SQLPolicy\PowerPC\default\Conditions>
```

Figure 12-4

If the `AutoClose` property is set to `False`, i.e., the database is not closed automatically, then the condition is not violated.

Some conditions contain complex expressions using functions such as `ExecuteSql()` or `ExecuteWql()`. To list these conditions, check whether the `HasScript` property is not `NULL` with the `Where-Object` cmdlet (see Figure 12-5):

```
Get-ChildItem | Where-Object {$_.HasScript} | Select-Object Name, ExpressionNode
```

```
Windows PowerShell                                                    _□×
PS SQLSERVER:\SQLPolicy\PowerPC\default\Conditions> Get-ChildItem | Where-Object
 {$_.HasScript} | Select-Object Name, ExpressionNode

Name                                    ExpressionNode
----                                    --------------
Cluster Disk Resource Corruption Err... IsNull(ExecuteWql('Numeric', 'root\C...
Device Driver Control Error Check       IsNull(ExecuteWql('Numeric', 'root\C...
Device Not Ready Error Check            IsNull(ExecuteWql('Numeric', 'root\C...
Disk Defragmentation Resulting Data ... IsNull(ExecuteWql('Numeric', 'root\C...
Failed I/O Request Check                IsNull(ExecuteWql('Numeric', 'root\C...
I/O Delay Warning Check                 IsNull(ExecuteWql('Numeric', 'root\C...
I/O Error During Hard Page Fault Err... IsNull(ExecuteWql('Numeric', 'root\C...
No Suspect Database Pages               ExecuteSql('Numeric', 'SELECT COUNT(...
Read Retry Error Check                  IsNull(ExecuteWql('Numeric', 'root\C...
Storage System I/O Timeout Error Check  IsNull(ExecuteWql('Numeric', 'root\C...
System Failure Error Check              IsNull(ExecuteWql('Numeric', 'root\C...


PS SQLSERVER:\SQLPolicy\PowerPC\default\Conditions>
```

Figure 12-5

You may also want to know the history of a condition, such as the creator, the creation date, the last time it was modified, and who modified it. To do that, you can just select the `CreatedBy`, `CreateDate`, `ModifiedBy` and `DataModified` properties and format the results with the `Format-List` cmdlet:

```
Get-ChildItem | Format-List CreatedBy, CreateDate, ModifiedBy, DateModified
```

The output is shown in Figure 12-6. As you can see, the policies were created on September 19, 2008, and none of them have been modified.

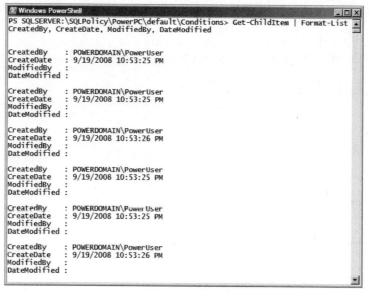

Figure 12-6

You can also create, alter, or drop a condition using the methods of the Condition class.

For example, you can create a condition called No server access using the Create method. This condition can be applied to certain logins to prevent them from accessing the SQL Server instance. You need to first create a policy store instance of the Microsoft.SqlServer.Management.Dmf.PolicyStore .NET class that represents the SQL Server instance. In case you are curious about the name DMF, Policy-Based Management (PBM) used to be called Declarative Management Framework (DMF) during SQL Server 2008 development. This policy store instance will contain the condition. Next, you assign to the condition a facet and an expression containing the properties from the facet; and then you create the new condition by invoking the Create method. Finally, you verify success of the creation with the Get-ChildItem cmdlet (the output is shown in Figure 12-7):

```
# Create a policy store instance to represent the default instance on PowerPC
$sqlConnection=New-Object System.Data.SqlClient.SqlConnection
$sqlConnection.ConnectionString="Server=PowerPC;Database=master;Integrated
Security=True"
$storeConnection=New-Object  Microsoft.SqlServer.Management.Sdk.Sfc
.SqlStoreConnection($sqlConnection)
$store=New-Object Microsoft.SqlServer.Management.Dmf.PolicyStore ($storeConnection)

# Create the new condition "No server access"
$condition=New-Object Microsoft.SqlServer.Management.Dmf.Condition
($store, 'No server access')
$condition.ExpressionNode='@HasAccess = False()'
$condition.Facet='Login'
$condition.Create()
Get-ChildItem -path SQLSERVER:\SQLPolicy\PowerPC\default\Conditions | Where-Object
{$_.Name -eq 'No server access' } | Format-List *
```

Figure 12-7

You can also use the Drop method to drop the newly created condition, and confirm the drop with Get-ChildItem, as shown in Figure 12-8:

```
$condition=Get-ChildItem -path SQLSERVER:\SQLPolicy\PowerPC\default\Conditions |
Where-Object {$_.Name -eq 'No server access'}
$condition.Drop()
#To confirm the condition has been dropped.
Get-ChildItem -path SQLSERVER:\SQLPolicy\PowerPC\default\Conditions | Where-Object
{$_.Name -eq 'No server access'}
```

Figure 12-8

If for some reason the `Drop` method does not work, try to open another Windows PowerShell console and run the commands again.

You can also use the `ScriptCreate`, `ScriptAlter`, and `ScriptDrop` methods to generate the SQL scripts that can be used to create, alter, and drop a condition, respectively. The following recreates the `No server access` condition and generates the scripts for it:

```
# Create the new condition "No server access"
$sqlConnection=New-Object System.Data.SqlClient.SqlConnection
$sqlConnection.ConnectionString="Server=PowerPC;Database=master;Integrated
Security=True"
$storeConnection=New-Object  Microsoft.SqlServer.Management.Sdk.Sfc.
SqlStoreConnection($sqlConnection)
$store=New-Object Microsoft.SqlServer.Management.Dmf.PolicyStore ($storeConnection)
$condition=New-Object Microsoft.SqlServer.Management.Dmf.Condition ($store,
'No server access')
$condition.ExpressionNode='@HasAccess = False()'
$condition.Facet='Login'
$condition.Create()

# Generate SQL scripts that can be used to create, alter and drop the condition
$condition.ScriptCreate().ToString()
$condition.ScriptAlter().ToString()
$condition.ScriptDrop().ToString()
```

However, notice that in Figure 12-9 the create and alter scripts are not complete.

Figure 12-9

They do not include the facet parameter and the expression parameter that should be specified in XML format.

Policies

A condition is just a Boolean expression. The expected behavior it specifies can only be enforced until it is used in a policy. To view all the policies under the default instance on the computer PowerPC, set the current location to the Policies node, and get the policies under the location with the `Get-ChildItem` cmdlet. Alternatively, just pass the path to the Policies node to the `-path` parameter in the `Get-ChildItem` cmdlet. Then sort the policy names alphabetically with the `Sort-Object` cmdlet:

```
Set-Location SQLSERVER:\SQLPolicy\PowerPC\default\Policies
Get-ChildItem | Sort-Object Name
```

Another alternative is to use the `-path` parameter:

```
Get-ChildItem -path SQLSERVER:\SQLPolicy\PowerPC\default\Policies |
Sort-Object Name
```

As shown in Figure 12-10, all the policies that are shipped with SQL Server 2008 have been imported into the default instance.

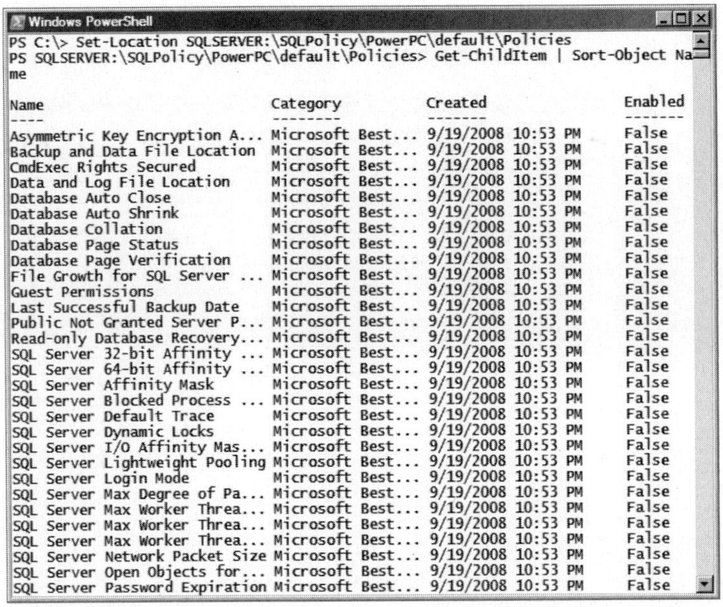

Figure 12-10

Let's look at the properties of the Policy class. Take the `Last Successful Backup Date` policy as an example. You can use the `Where-Object` cmdlet to filter the particular policy based on its `Name` property. Then format the properties with the `Format-List` cmdlet:

```
$pbk=Get-ChildItem -path SQLSERVER:\SQLPolicy\PowerPC\default\Policies |
Where-Object {$_.Name -eq 'Last Successful Backup Date'}
$pbk | Format-List AutomatedPolicyEvaluationMode, CategoryId, Condition,
Description, Enabled, HasScript, HelpLink, HelpText, ID, IdentityKey, ModifiedBy,
Name, ObjectSet, Parent, RootCondition, ScheduleUid
```

As shown in Figure 12-11, the policy has a value of None for the AutomatedPolicyEvaluationMode property, which means it is evaluated only on demand.

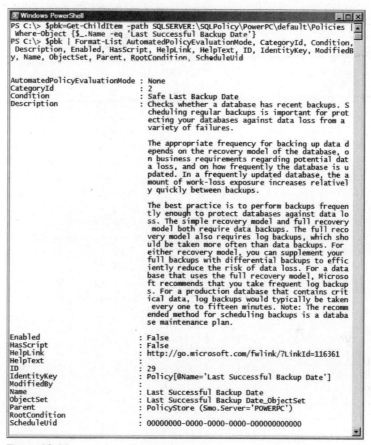

Figure 12-11

The possible values of the property are listed in Table 12-1.

The policy category ID is 2, as shown in the CategoryId property. To get more information on the policy category, you need to look at the associated object with an ID of 2 under the SQLSERVER:\SQLPolicy\PowerPC\default\PolicyCategories path:

```
Get-ChildItem -path SQLSERVER:\SQLPolicy\PowerPC\default\PolicyCategories |
Where-Object {$_.ID -eq 2}  | Select-Object Name, MandateDatabaseSubscriptions
```

Table 12-1: AutomatedPolicyEvaluationMode Values

Value	Execution Mode
CheckOnChanges	Uses event notification to evaluate the policy when changes are made.
CheckOnSchedule	Uses a SQL Server Agent job to schedule the evaluations of the policy.
Enforce	Uses DDL triggers to evaluate and prevent policy violations.
None	The policy is evaluated only on demand.

As shown in Figure 12-12, the category of this policy is called Microsoft Best Practices: Maintenance.

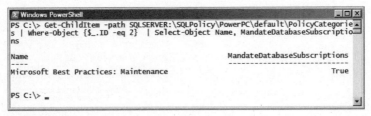

Figure 12-12

Every database is mandated to subscribe to the policies in this category, as MandateDatabaseSubscriptions is set to True.

Referring back to Figure 12-11, look at the rest of the properties. The policy is using the Safe Last Backup Date condition, and is disabled for automation, as the Enabled property is set to False. It does not have scripts. The ID of this policy is 29.

The name of the associated object set is Last Successful Backup Date_ObjectSet. The object set can be found under the SQLSERVER:\SQLPolicy\PowerPC\default\ObjectSets path using the following command:

```
Get-ChildItem -path SQLSERVER:\SQLPolicy\PowerPC\default\ObjectSets |
Where-Object {$_.Name -eq 'Last Successful Backup Date_ObjectSet'}
```

However, as shown in Figure 12-13, the preceding command gives you the facet for the object set only. It doesn't provide much information about the target sets contained in the object set because the TargetSets property is a collection.

You can use the Serialize method to get the XML presentation of the target sets. The Serialize method populates an XmlWriter object, so you first define an XmlTextWriter object:

```
$stringWriter = New-Object System.IO.StringWriter
$xmlWriter = New-Object System.Xml.XmlTextWriter($stringWriter)
$xmlWriter.Formatting = "indented"
$xmlWriter.Indentation = 2
```

270

```
$os= Get-ChildItem -path SQLSERVER:\SQLPolicy\PowerPC\default\ObjectSets |
Where-Object {$_.Name -eq 'Last Successful Backup Date_ObjectSet'}
$os.Serialize($xmlWriter)
$xmlWriter.Flush()
$stringWriter.Flush()
Write-Output $stringWriter.ToString()
$stringWriter.Close()
$xmlWriter.Close()
```

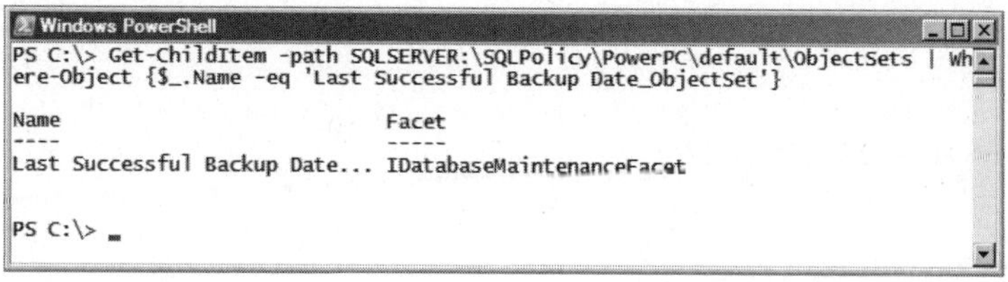

Figure 12-13

The entire XML string shown in Figure 12-14 is saved in the objectSet.xml file.

Figure 12-14

Alternately, you can print out the XML data for each target set in the object set separately. The following script uses foreach to loop through the collection of target sets, and uses the Serialize method of each target set to flush out the XML presentation to the XMLTextWriter:

```
$stringWriter = New-Object System.IO.StringWriter
$xmlWriter = New-Object System.Xml.XmlTextWriter($stringWriter)
$xmlWriter.Formatting = "indented"
$xmlWriter.Indentation = 2
$os= Get-ChildItem -path SQLSERVER:\SQLPolicy\PowerPC\default\ObjectSets |
Where-Object {$_.Name -eq 'Last Successful Backup Date_ObjectSet'}
foreach ($t in $os.TargetSets)
{
        $stringWriter = New-Object System.IO.StringWriter
        $xmlWriter = New-Object System.Xml.XmlTextWriter($stringWriter)
        $xmlWriter.Formatting = "indented"
        $xmlWriter.Indentation = 2
        $t.Serialize($xmlWriter)
        $xmlWriter.Flush()
        $stringWriter.Flush()
        Write-Output $stringWriter.ToString()
        $stringWriter.Close()
        $xmlWriter.Close()
}
```

Figure 12-15 shows only part of the output.

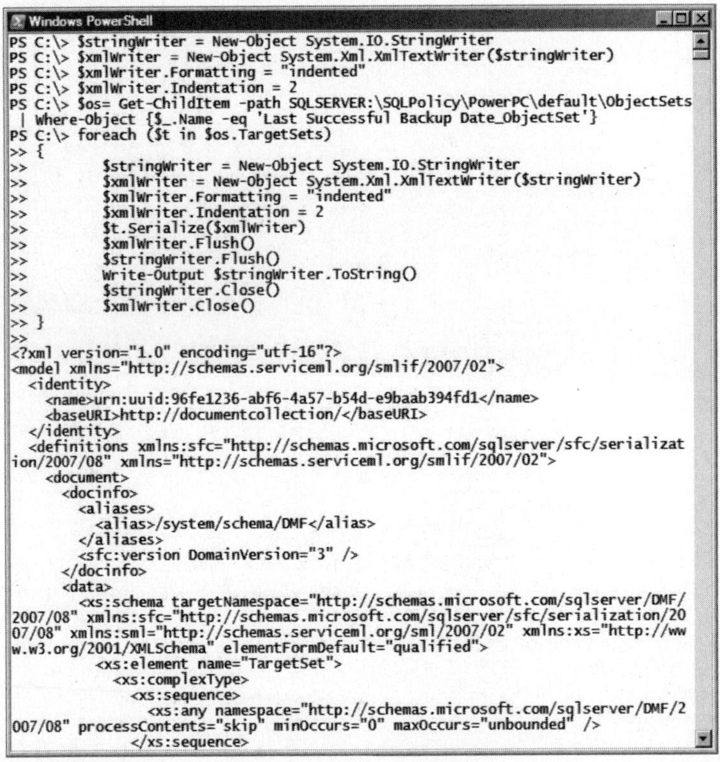

Figure 12-15

For the `Last Successful Backup Date` policy, there is only a target set. The entire XML string for the target set shown in Figure 12-15 is saved in the `targetSet.xml` file.

Now look at the `DMF:TargetSet` node in Microsoft Word (see Figure 12-16). The target set includes targets of type Server/Database. Because no condition is applied to the Server/Database level, all the databases are included.

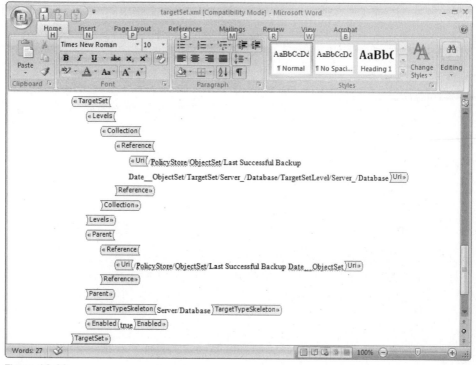

Figure 12-16

You can also create, alter, or drop a policy using the methods of the `Policy` class. For example, suppose you want to create a policy called `Domain guest cannot access server`. This policy uses the `No server access` condition you created earlier, and applies it to a login called `POWERDOMAIN\Guest` to capture violations that allow domain guests to connect to the SQL Server. To filter the login, you need to create a condition that uses the Login facet and includes only the `POWERDOMAIN\Guest` login. The script, `CreatePolicy.ps1`, is shown here:

```
$domainName="POWERDOMAIN"
$hostName="PowerPC"
$instanceName="default" # "default"
for default instance

# Create a policy store instance to represent the default instance on PowerPC
$sqlConnection=New-Object System.Data.SqlClient.SqlConnection
$sqlConnection.ConnectionString="Server=$serverName;Database=master;Integrated
Security=True"
$storeConnection=New-Object  Microsoft.SqlServer.Management.Sdk.
Sfc.SqlStoreConnection($sqlConnection)
```

```
$store=New-Object Microsoft.SqlServer.Management.Dmf.PolicyStore ($storeConnection)

# Create a condition called "No server access" that prevents logins
from accessing the SQL Server instance.
if (-not (Get-ChildItem -path SQLSERVER:\SQLPolicy\$hostName\
$instanceName\Conditions | Where-Object {$_.Name -eq 'No server access'}))
{
        $condition=New-Object Microsoft.SqlServer.Management.Dmf.Condition ($store,
'No server access')
        $condition.ExpressionNode='@HasAccess = False()'
        $condition.Facet='Login'
        $condition.Create()
}

# Create a condition called "Domain Guest Login" to filter only the
POWERDOMAIN\Guest login.
if (-not (Get-ChildItem -path SQLSERVER:\SQLPolicy\$hostName\$instanceName\
Conditions | Where-Object {$_.Name -eq 'Domain Guest Login'}))
{
        $condition=New-Object Microsoft.SqlServer.Management.Dmf.Condition
($store, 'Domain Guest Login')
        $condition.ExpressionNode="@Name = '$domainName\Guest'"
        $condition.Facet="Login"
        $condition.Create()
}

# Create an object set that uses the "Domain Guest Login" condition
to filter only the POWERDOMAIN\Guest login.
if (-not (Get-ChildItem -path SQLSERVER:\SQLPolicy\$hostName\$instanceName\
ObjectSets | Where-Object {$_.Name -eq 'Domain
guest cannot access server_ObjectSet'}))
{
        $objectSet=New-Object Microsoft.SqlServer.Management.Dmf.ObjectSet($store,
'Domain guest cannot access server_ObjectSet')
        $objectSet.Facet="Login"
        $targetSet=$objectSet.TargetSets["Server/Login"]
        $targetSet.Enabled=1
        $targetSet.SetLevelCondition($targetSet.GetLevel("Server/Login"),
"Domain Guest Login")
        $objectSet.Create()
}

# Create a policy called "Domain guest cannot access server"
# that applies the condition "No server access" to the object set containing
only the POWERDOMAIN\Guest login.
#The execution mode of this policy is set to None - On Demand.
if (-not (Get-ChildItem -path SQLSERVER:\SQLPolicy\$hostName\
$instanceName\Policies | Where-Object {$_.Name -eq
'Domain guest cannot access server'}))
{
        $policy=New-Object Microsoft.SqlServer.Management.Dmf.Policy ($store,
'Domain guest cannot access server')
        $policy.Condition="No server access"
        $policy.AutomatedPolicyEvaluationMode="None"
        $policy.ObjectSet="Domain guest cannot access server_ObjectSet"
```

```
        $policy.Create()
}

# Confirm the policy and its target sets have been created correctly.
(Get-ChildItem -path SQLSERVER:\SQLPolicy\$hostName\$instanceName\ObjectSets `
| Where-Object {$_.Name -eq 'Domain guest cannot access
server_ObjectSet'}).TargetSets `
| foreach -process { $_.GetLevelsSorted() }

Get-ChildItem -path SQLSERVER:\SQLPolicy\$hostName\$instanceName\Policies `
| Where-Object {$_.Name -eq 'Domain guest cannot access server'} `
| Select-Object AutomatedPolicyEvaluationMode, Condition, Enabled, ID,
IdentityKey, Name, ObjectSet, Parent, CreateDate, CreatedBy
```

Now run the script:

```
. C:\DBAScripts\dbaLib.ps1
C:\DBAScripts\CreatePolicy.ps1
```

As shown in Figure 12-17, the policy Domain guest cannot access server has been created.

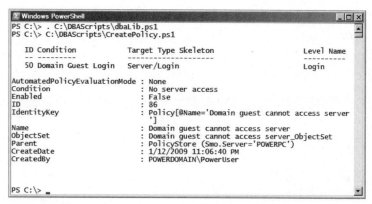

Figure 12-17

Its target set filters logins based on the Domain Guest Login condition at the Server/Login level. The policy tests the No server access condition against its target set. The policy is evaluated on demand, as its AutomatedPolicyEvaluationMode is set to None. You can change the mode and schedule its evaluation based on auditing requirements.

To drop this policy and its associated object set, use the Get-ChildItem cmdlet to get all the policies, and filter the Domain guest cannot access server policy object with the Where-Object cmdlet, based on the Name property. Next, invoke the Drop method on the policy to drop it. Then confirm the success of the drop:

```
$policy=Get-ChildItem -path SQLSERVER:\SQLPolicy\PowerPC\default\Policies |
Where-Object {$_.Name -eq 'Domain guest cannot access server'}
$policy.Drop()
Get-ChildItem -path SQLSERVER:\SQLPolicy\PowerPC\default\Policies | Where-Object
{$_.Name -eq 'Domain guest cannot access server'}
```

As shown in Figure 12-18, the Get-ChildItem cmdlet returns nothing. The policy has been dropped.

Figure 12-18

You can use the EvaluationHistories, EnumPolicyExecutionHistoryDetail, and EnumPolicyExecutionHistoryDetailResults methods to view the execution history of a policy. For example, to view the history of the Last Successful Backup Date policy, query the EvaluationHistories property. This property contains a collection. Use a for loop to loop through the collection and get the StartDate, EndDate, ID, and Result of each evaluation:

```
$pbk=Get-ChildItem -path SQLSERVER:\SQLPolicy\PowerPC\default\Policies |
Where-Object {$_.Name -eq 'Last Successful Backup Date'}
$histories=$pbk.EvaluationHistories
for ($i=1; $i -le $histories.Count; $i++) {
$histories.Item($i) | Format-List PolicyName, StartDate, EndDate, ID, Result
}
```

As shown in Figure 12-19, three evaluations of the policy are stored in the history. The start date, end date, ID, and result of each evaluation are listed. The ID property is actually the position of the evaluation in the EvaluationHistories collection.

Figure 12-19

As you can see, the evaluation with an ID of 2 has a `False` result. You can also get the result by querying the `Result` property of the second item in the `EvaluationHistories` collection:

```
$histories.Item(2).Result
```

As shown in Figure 12-20, the evaluation with an ID of 2 failed.

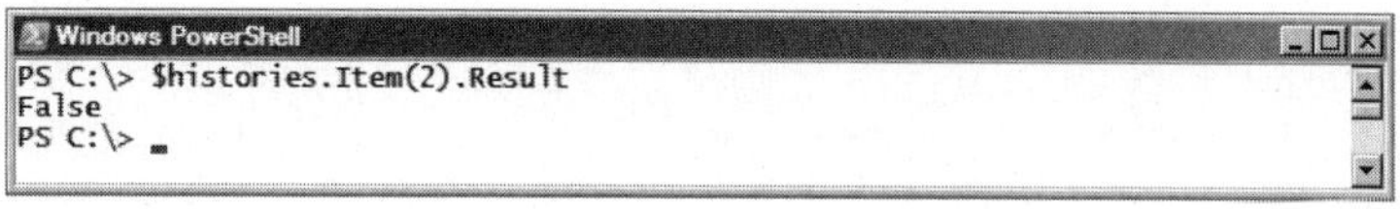

Figure 12-20

To find out why the evaluation fails, you can look at the `ConnectionEvaluationHistories` property. Because a policy can be evaluated against a single server or a group of servers, each member of the property has the information for a specific server. Each `ConnectionEvaluationHistories` member has an `EvaluationDetails` property that has the evaluation information for all the targets of the policy. Each member of the `EvaluationDetails` property has the evaluation details for a target in the `ResultDetail` property, and the target information in the `TargetQueryExpression` property. To loop through the `ConnectionEvaluationHistories` and `EvaluationDetails` collections, you need to use the `GetEnumerator` method to get two enumerators, and then use the `MoveNext` method and the `Current` property of the enumerators to iterate through the collections:

```
$evalHist=$histories.Item(2).ConnectionEvaluationHistories
$enum1=$evalHist.GetEnumerator()
if ($enum1.MoveNext()) {
        $details=$evalHist.Item($enum1.Current.ID).EvaluationDetails
        $enum2=$details.GetEnumerator()
        if ($enum2.MoveNext()) {
                $details.Item($enum2.Current.ID) | Format-List ResultDetail,
TargetQueryExpression, Result
        }
}
```

Figure 12-21 shows the part of the output for the `admin` database.

Here, the policy is evaluated against all the databases, including the `admin` database listed in the `TargetQueryExpression` property. The `admin` database violates the policy, thus the result is `False`. The details of the evaluation are shown in the `ResultDetail` property. The Boolean expression of the evaluation uses the operator `GE` (greater than) to compare the database attribute `LastBackupDate` with `DateAdd('day', -1, GetDate())`.

The `ScriptCreate`, `ScriptAlter`, and `ScriptDrop` methods of the `Policy` class generate the SQL scripts that can be used to create, alter, and drop a policy, respectively. Because the associated object set needs to be created before the policy can be created, you also generate the object set creation script here. This example uses the `Guest Permissions` policy:

```
# Get an object associated with the Guest Permissions policy
$policy=Get-ChildItem -path SQLSERVER:\SQLPolicy\PowerPC\default\Policies |
Where-Object {$_.Name -eq 'Guest Permissions'}
```

```
$policy.ScriptCreate().ToString()
$policy.ScriptAlter().ToString()
$policy.ScriptDrop().ToString()

# Get the object set for the Guest Permissions policy
$objectSet=Get-ChildItem -path SQLSERVER:\SQLPolicy\PowerPC\default\ObjectSets |
Where-Object {$_.Name -eq $policy.ObjectSet.ToString()}
$objectSet.ScriptCreate().ToString()
```

```
Windows PowerShell                                                                    _ □ X
PS C:\> $evalHist=$histories.Item(2).ConnectionEvaluationHistories
PS C:\> $enum1=$evalHist.GetEnumerator()
PS C:\> if ($enum1.MoveNext()) {
>>          $details=$evalHist.Item($enum1.Current.ID).EvaluationDetails
>>          $enum2=$details.GetEnumerator()
>>          if ($enum2.MoveNext()) {
>>                  $details.Item($enum2.Current.ID) | Format-List ResultDetail,
TargetQueryExpression, Result }}
>>


ResultDetail            : <Operator>
                            <TypeClass>Bool</TypeClass>
                            <OpType>GE</OpType>
                            <ResultObjType>System.Boolean</ResultObjType>
                            <ResultValue>False</ResultValue>
                            <Count>2</Count>
                            <Attribute>
                              <TypeClass>Unsupported</TypeClass>
                              <Name>LastBackupDate</Name>
                              <ResultObjType>System.DateTime</ResultObjType>
                              <ResultValue>0</ResultValue>
                            </Attribute>
                            <Function>
                              <TypeClass>DateTime</TypeClass>
                              <FunctionType>DateAdd</FunctionType>
                              <ReturnType>DateTime</ReturnType>
                              <ResultObjType>System.DateTime</ResultObjType>
                              <ResultValue>-8589798097196628080</ResultValue>
                              <Count>3</Count>
                              <Constant>
                                <TypeClass>String</TypeClass>
                                <ObjType>System.String</ObjType>
                                <Value>day</Value>
                              </Constant>
                              <Constant>
                                <TypeClass>Numeric</TypeClass>
                                <ObjType>System.Int32</ObjType>
                                <Value>-1</Value>
                              </Constant>
                              <Function>
                                <TypeClass>DateTime</TypeClass>
                                <FunctionType>GetDate</FunctionType>
                                <ReturnType>DateTime</ReturnType>
                                <ResultObjType>System.DateTime</ResultObjType>
                                <ResultValue>-8589797233196628080</ResultValue>
                                <Count>0</Count>
                              </Function>
                            </Function>
                          </Operator>
TargetQueryExpression : SQLSERVER:\SQL\POWERPC\DEFAULT\Databases\admin
Result                : False
```

Figure 12-21

Part of the output is shown in Figure 12-22.

How do you evaluate a policy manually? The Evaluate method of the Policy class did not work at the
time this chapter was written. However, you can use the Invoke-PolicyEvaluation cmdlet provided by
the SqlServerCmdletSnapin100 snap-in. The policy to be evaluated is specified in the -Policy parameter
of this cmdlet. The -Policy parameter can take policies stored in an SQL Server instance or in XML files.
It can even take a string that specifies the names of one or more XML policy files, or a set of policy
objects, or a set of FileInfo objects that represent XML policy files. The policy objects can be passed
from a pipeline as well.

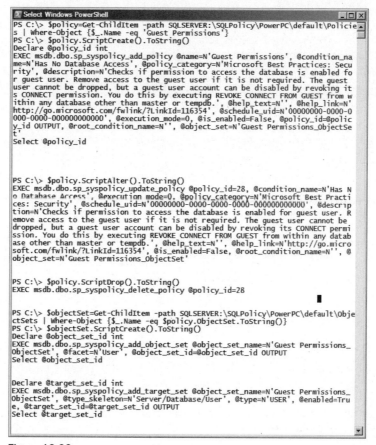

Figure 12-22

The cmdlet also has a `-AdHocPolicyEvaluationMode` parameter to specify the evaluation modes. The possible values are as follows:

❑ `Check`: Reports the compliance status of the target objects using the credentials of the current login. Does not reconfigure any objects. This is the default setting.

❑ `CheckSqlScriptAsProxy`: Reports the compliance status of the target objects using the credentials of the `##MS_PolicyTSQLExecutionLogin##` proxy login. Does not reconfigure any objects.

❑ `Configure`: Reports the compliance status of the target objects using the credentials of the current login. Reconfigures any settable and deterministic options that are not in compliance with the policies.

The target sets of the policy evaluation can be specified in two ways. You can evaluate the policy against all the qualified objects on a server instance specified in the `-TargetServerName` parameter. To fine-tune the target set further, use the `-TargetExpression` parameter.

You can use the `-TargetObjects` parameter to specify a `PSObject` or an array of `PSObjects` that define the set of SQL Server objects.

The next example shows how to evaluate the Database Page Status policy against the admin database on the default instance to ensure that it has no suspect database pages. First, you get a policy object that represents the Database Page Status policy, and pass it to the Invoke- PolicyEvaluation cmdlet. In the TargetServer parameter, specify the default instance PowerPC, and in the TargetExpression parameter, specify the filter Server[@Name='PowerPC']/Database[@Name='admin'] to narrow down the targets on the instance to only the admin database. Then you query the Result property from the evaluation.

```
Get-ChildItem -path SQLSERVER:\SQLPolicy\PowerPC\default\Policies |
Where-Object {$_.Name -eq 'Database Page Status'} | Invoke-PolicyEvaluation
-TargetServer "PowerPC" -TargetExpression "Server[@Name='PowerPC']/Database
[@Name='admin']" | Format-Table Result -AutoSize
```

Figure 12-23 shows that the result of the evaluation is True, which means that the admin database does not have any suspect database pages.

```
Windows PowerShell

PS C:\> Get-ChildItem -path SQLSERVER:\SQLPolicy\PowerPC\default\Policies | Wher
e-Object {$_.Name -eq 'Database Page Status'} | Invoke-PolicyEvaluation -TargetS
erver "PowerPC" -TargetExpression "Server[@Name='PowerPC']/Database[@Name='admin
']" | Format-Table Result -AutoSize

Result
------
  True


PS C:\>
```

Figure 12-23

You can also pass a PSObject to the TargetObjects property to represent the admin database to the Invoke-PolicyEvaluation cmdlet. The first line of the following script uses the Get-Item cmdlet to get an object that represents the admin database (see Figure 12-24):

```
$db=Get-Item SQLSERVER:\SQL\PowerPC\default\Databases\admin
Get-ChildItem -path SQLSERVER:\SQLPolicy\PowerPC\default\Policies |
Where-Object {$_.Name -eq 'Database Page Status'} |
Invoke-PolicyEvaluation -TargetObjects $db | Format-Table Result -AutoSize
```

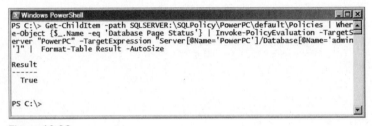

```
Windows PowerShell

PS C:\> $db=Get-Item SQLSERVER:\SQL\PowerPC\default\Databases\admin
PS C:\> Get-ChildItem -path SQLSERVER:\SQLPolicy\PowerPC\default\Policies | Wher
e-Object {$_.Name -eq 'Database Page Status'} | Invoke-PolicyEvaluation -TargetO
bjects $db | Format-Table Result -AutoSize

Result
------
  True


PS C:\> _
```

Figure 12-24

There is another database called admin2 on the same SQL Server instance. This database was intentionally corrupted. Suppose that you want to evaluate the Database Page Status policy against the database. You can run the following command:

```
$db=Get-Item SQLSERVER:\SQL\PowerPC\default\Databases\admin2
Get-ChildItem -path SQLSERVER:\SQLPolicy\PowerPC\default\Policies | Where-Object
{$_.Name -eq 'Database Page Status'} | Invoke-PolicyEvaluation -TargetObjects
$db | Format-Table Result -AutoSize
```

Figure 12-25 shows the evaluation result is False, which means that the admin2 database does have suspect database pages.

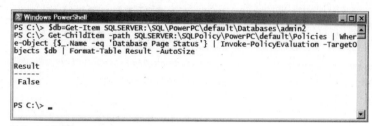

Figure 12-25

Summary

This chapter explored the Policy-Based Management objects stored under the SQLSERVER:\SQLPolicy folder. It demonstrated how to query, create, and drop policies and conditions, and the associated object sets and target sets with Windows PowerShell. In addition, it demonstrated how to generate scripts for existing objects, and how to evaluate policies manually with the Invoke-PolicyEvaluation cmdlet. Chapter 20 follows the same approach and uses Windows PowerShell scripts to define policies on multiple servers, thus enforcing SQL Server standards with minimum effort.

13

Windows PowerShell and SMO

In the previous chapters, you learned how to connect and query SQL Server 2008 instances using the new features SQLPS and the SQL and SQLPolicy folder under the SQLSERVER: drive. In this chapter, you will use Windows PowerShell in conjunction with .NET class libraries to connect to SQL Server. You will also use SQL Server Management Objects (SMO) to connect to SQL Server and access the SQL Server–related objects, features, and functionalities. This chapter covers the alternative ways to connect to SQL Server.

The PowerShell and SMO portions of this chapter cover the following:

- ❑ PowerShell and the SQLConnection .NET class

- ❑ Working with SQL Server using SMO

- ❑ Working with databases using SMO

- ❑ Working with tables using SMO

- ❑ Backup and Restore with SMO

PowerShell and the SQLConnection .NET Class

The .NET class System.Data.SqlClient.SqlConnection represents an open connection to a SQL Server database. You can leverage this class via PowerShell to connect to SQL Server, retrieve data, and execute procedures.

The following example retrieves the SQL Server version number from the default instance:

```
#Let's set the location to the script folder C:\DBAScripts

Set-Location C:\DBAScripts
$SqlConnection = New-Object System.Data.SqlClient.SqlConnection
$SqlConnection.ConnectionString = "Server=PowerServer3;Database=master;Integrated
Security=True"
$SqlCmd = New-Object System.Data.SqlClient.SqlCommand
$SqlCmd.CommandText = "Select @@version as SQLServerVersion"
$SqlCmd.Connection = $SqlConnection
$SqlAdapter = New-Object System.Data.SqlClient.SqlDataAdapter
$SqlAdapter.SelectCommand = $SqlCmd
$DataSet = New-Object System.Data.DataSet
$SqlAdapter.Fill($DataSet)
$SqlConnection.Close()
$DataSet.Tables[0]
```

The results are similar to the screenshot shown in Figure 13-1, which shows the version number.

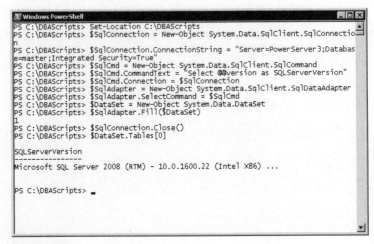

Figure 13-1

The preceding example used four classes:

❑   System.Data.SqlClient.SqlConnection

❑   System.Data.SqlClient.SqlCommand

❑   System.Data.SqlClient.SqlDataAdapter

❑   System.Data.DataSet

The SQLConnection class represents an open connection to a SQL Server database. The SQLCommand class represents a Transact-SQL statement or stored procedure to execute against a SQL Server database. The SQLDataAdapter class represents a set of data commands and a database connection that are used to fill the dataset class. The data set represents in-memory cache data. Basically, the script first opens a connection to the default instance PowerServer3. Next, it creates a command object and sets the T-SQL statement to `"select @@version"`. Then the script creates a data adapter to fill a data set with the results from the SqlCommand. Finally, the data set is displayed. You will use these four classes throughout this chapter.

You can also connect to a named instance of the SQL Server using the same .NET Framework class library System.Data.SqlClient.SqlConnection via PowerShell, as shown here:

```
$SqlConnection = New-Object System.Data.SqlClient.SqlConnection
$SqlConnection.ConnectionString = "Server=PowerServer3\SQL2008;Database=master;
Integrated Security=True"
$SqlCmd = New-Object System.Data.SqlClient.SqlCommand
$SqlCmd.CommandText = "select @@version as SQLServerVersion"
$SqlCmd.Connection = $SqlConnection
$SqlAdapter = New-Object System.Data.SqlClient.SqlDataAdapter
$SqlAdapter.SelectCommand = $SqlCmd
$DataSet = New-Object System.Data.DataSet
$SqlAdapter.Fill($DataSet)
$SqlConnection.Close()
$DataSet.Tables[0]
```

Note that PowerServer3 is the host name and SQL2008 is the instance name in this example.

The results of the T-SQL command `"select @@version as SQLServerVersion"` are shown in Figure 13-2.

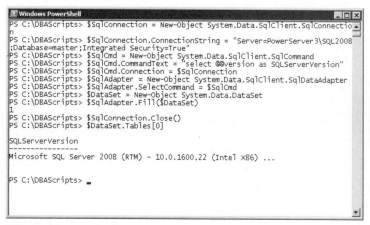

Figure 13-2

You can also execute a stored procedure and retrieve the results from a named instance of the SQL Server using the same .NET Framework class library System.Data.SqlClient.SqlConnection via PowerShell, as shown here:

```
$SqlConnection = New-Object System.Data.SqlClient.SqlConnection
$SqlConnection.ConnectionString = "Server=PowerServer3\SQL2008;Database=master;
```

```
Integrated Security=True"
$SqlCmd = New-Object System.Data.SqlClient.SqlCommand
$SqlCmd.CommandText = "sp_who"
$SqlCmd.Connection = $SqlConnection
$SqlAdapter = New-Object System.Data.SqlClient.SqlDataAdapter
$SqlAdapter.SelectCommand = $SqlCmd
$DataSet = New-Object System.Data.DataSet
$SqlAdapter.Fill($DataSet)
$SqlConnection.Close()
$DataSet.Tables[0]
```

You can see the results of the stored procedure `"sp_who"` in Figure 13-3.

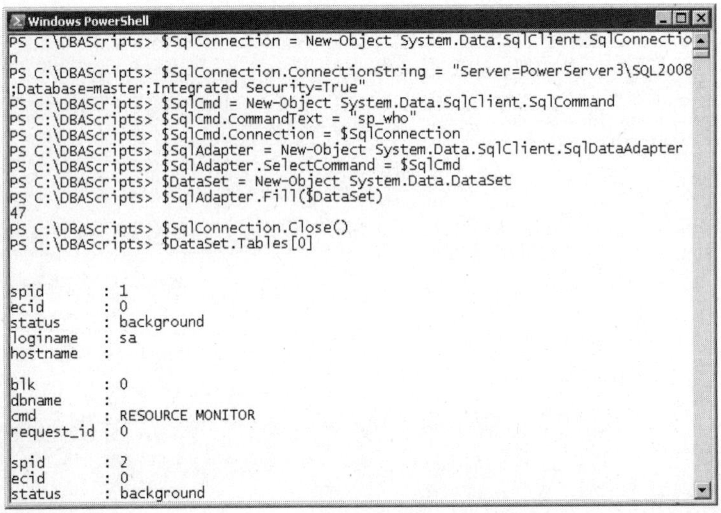

Figure 13-3

Because you often want to know the version of SQL Server that is installed, the next example creates a generic PowerShell script Get-SQLVersion.ps1, which can be used to retrieve the version number of any SQL Server instance. This example basically guides you through executing a T-SQL command:

```
Param (
  [string] $SQLSERVER
)
$SqlConnection = New-Object System.Data.SqlClient.SqlConnection
$SqlConnection.ConnectionString = "Server=$SQLSERVER;Database=master;Integrated
Security=True"
$SqlCmd = New-Object System.Data.SqlClient.SqlCommand
$SqlCmd.CommandText = "Select @@version as SQLServerVersion"
$SqlCmd.Connection = $SqlConnection
$SqlAdapter = New-Object System.Data.SqlClient.SqlDataAdapter
$SqlAdapter.SelectCommand = $SqlCmd
$DataSet = New-Object System.Data.DataSet
$SqlAdapter.Fill($DataSet)
```

```
$SqlConnection.Close()
$DataSet.Tables[0]
```

You can execute the `Get-SQLVersion.ps1` PowerShell script by passing the SQL Server instance name:

```
.\Get-SQLVersion.ps1 "PowerServer3"
.\Get-SQLVersion.ps1 "PowerServer3\SQL2008"
```

Figure 13-4 reveals the results of the `"select @@version"`:

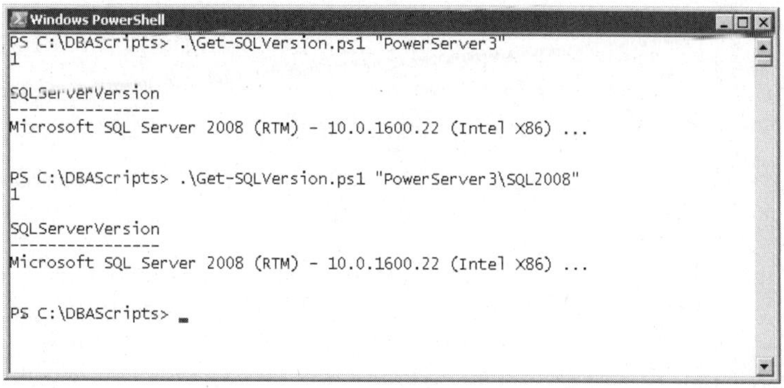

Figure 13-4

It is common practice to navigate all the database objects in a given database. The next example creates the PowerShell script to retrieve all the table names from a SQL Server database. The script takes two parameters, server name and database name, and uses them to construct the connection string:

```
Param (
  [string] $SQLSERVER,
  [string] $DATABASE
)
$SqlConnection = New-Object System.Data.SqlClient.SqlConnection
$SqlConnection.ConnectionString =  "Server=$SQLSERVER;Database=$DATABASE;Integrated
Security=True"
$SqlCmd = New-Object System.Data.SqlClient.SqlCommand
$SqlCmd.CommandText = "Select name from sysobjects where type = N'U'"
$SqlCmd.Connection = $SqlConnection
$SqlAdapter = New-Object System.Data.SqlClient.SqlDataAdapter
$SqlAdapter.SelectCommand = $SqlCmd
$DataSet = New-Object System.Data.DataSet
$SqlAdapter.Fill($DataSet)
$SqlConnection.Close()
$DataSet.Tables[0]
```

Next, retrieve the table names from the named instance `SQL2008`, as shown here:

```
.\Get-Tables.ps1 "PowerServer3\SQL2008" "msdb"
```

Figure 13-5 shows the results of the Get-Tables PowerShell script:

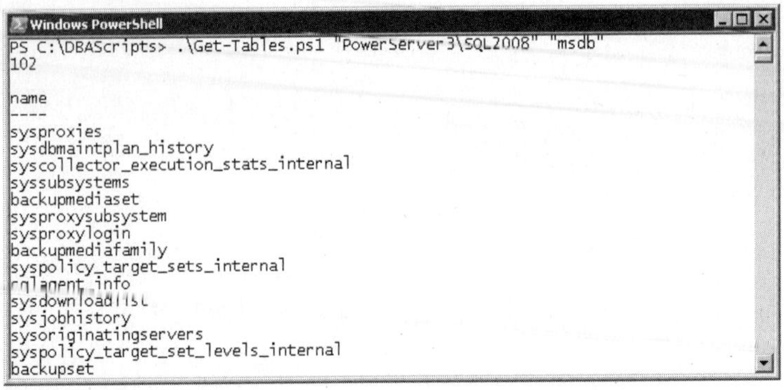

Figure 13-5

When it comes to SQL Server stored procedures that accept parameters, you also need to set the CommandType property to StoredProcedure, and define the parameters in the Parameters property.

As a DBA, it is your task to create backups on all the databases. The following example creates a small stored procedure uspBackupDB in the master database of the default SQL Server instance that would take backups of any database in a given location. This stored procedure accepts three parameters: a database name, a backup folder path, and a backup type. The backup type has three possible values — Full, Tran, or Diff — that correspond to full database backup, transaction log backup, and differential database backup, respectively:

```
set quoted_identifier off
go
USE [master]
GO
/****** Object:  StoredProcedure [dbo].[uspBackupDB]    Script Date: 08/31/2008
21:43:41 ******/
IF  EXISTS (SELECT * FROM sys.objects WHERE object_id =
OBJECT_ID(N'[dbo].[uspBackupDB]') AND type in (N'P', N'PC'))
DROP PROCEDURE [dbo].[uspBackupDB]
GO
USE [master]
GO
/****** Object:  StoredProcedure [dbo].[uspBackupDB]    Script Date: 08/31/2008
21:34:59 ******/
SET ANSI_NULLS ON
GO
SET QUOTED_IDENTIFIER OFF
GO
Create  proc [dbo].[uspBackupDB] @databasename varchar(128), @FolderPath
varchar(1000), @BackupType varchar(4)
as
set quoted_identifier off
declare @query varchar(2000)
If @Backuptype="Full"
begin
set @query ="backup database "+@databasename+" to disk =
```

```
'"+@Folderpath+@databasename+"_"+convert(varchar(8),getdate(),112)+".bak'"
end
If @Backuptype="Tran"
begin
set @query ="backup database "+@databasename+" to disk =
'"+@Folderpath+@databasename+"_"+convert(varchar(8),getdate(),112)+".trn'"
end
If @Backuptype="Diff"
begin
set @query ="backup database "+@databasename+" to disk =
'"+@Folderpath+@databasename+"_"+convert(varchar(8),getdate(),112)+".Dif'"
end
print @query
exec (@query)
GO
```

Next, create a PowerShell script `Backup-DataBase.ps1`. This script connects to a SQL Server instance and executes the `uspBackupDB` stored procedure. You can copy the code from the uspBackupDB.sql file:

```
Param (
    [string] $SQLSERVER,
    [string] $DATABASE,
    [string] $LOCATION,
    [string] $BACKTUPTYPE
)

$SQL="master.dbo.uspBackupDB"
#write-host $SQL
$conn = New-Object System.Data.SqlClient.SqlConnection("Data
Source=$SQLSERVER;Initial Catalog=master;Integrated Security=SSPI")
$cmd = New-Object System.Data.SqlClient.SqlCommand("$SQL", $conn)
$cmd.CommandType = [System.Data.CommandType]'StoredProcedure'
$cmd.Parameters.Add("@databasename",[System.Data.SqlDbType]"VarChar",128) | Out-Null
$cmd.Parameters.Add("@Folderpath",[System.Data.SqlDbType]"VarChar",1000) | Out-Null
$cmd.Parameters.Add("@BackupType",[System.Data.SqlDbType]"VarChar",4) | Out-Null
$cmd.Parameters["@databasename"].Value = $DATABASE
$cmd.Parameters["@Folderpath"].Value = $LOCATION
$cmd.Parameters["@BackupType"].Value = $BACKTUPTYPE
$conn.Open()
$cmd.ExecuteNonQuery() | Out-Null
$conn.Close()
```

Now you can create a folder "Backup" on the C: drive to store all the backup files. Here you are going to use the cmdlet `New-Item` to create the folder:

```
New-Item -Path C:\ -Name Backup -Type directory
```

Now execute the PowerShell script `backup-database.ps1` and take a backup of the `master` database as shown here:

```
.\Backup-DataBase.ps1 PowerServer3 AdventureWorks2008 c:\Backup\ Full
.\Backup-DataBase.ps1 PowerServer3 AdventureWorks2008 c:\Backup\ Tran
.\Backup-DataBase.ps1 PowerServer3 AdventureWorks2008 c:\Backup\ Diff
```

This script takes full backup, transactional log backup, and differential backup, as shown in Figure 13-6 and Figure 13-7.

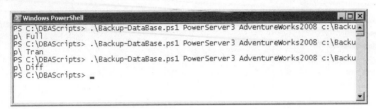

Figure 13-6

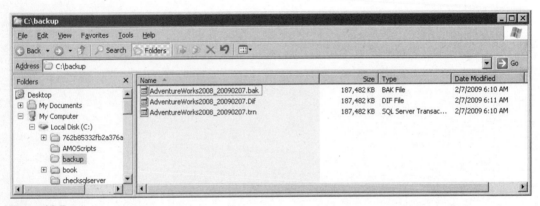

Figure 13-7

This section has covered the connection to SQL Server and various methods of accessing SQL Server databases and objects using the `SqlConnection` .NET class, but there is another method of connecting to SQL Server and accessing information: SQL SMO. The next section covers SMO in detail.

Working with SQL Server using SMO

You can leverage the class library SQL Server SMO via PowerShell to connect to SQL server and manipulate and retrieve data. This section examines some of the useful properties and methods of SMO, which in turn retrieves information from SQL Server.

Before you use the SMO objects, you need to load the SMO class library, the `Microsoft.SqlServer.Smo.dll` assembly, as you did in Chapter 9. The `LoadWithPartialName` method loads an assembly from the application directory or from the global assembly cache using a partial name. You can connect to a SQL Server instance using SQL Server SMO as shown here:

```
[System.Reflection.Assembly]::LoadWithPartialName('Microsoft.SqlServer.SMO')  |
Out-Null
$smovar = New-Object ('Microsoft.SqlServer.Management.Smo.Server')
'PowerServer3\SQL2008'
```

Note that `PowerServer3` is the host name of the computer and `SQL2008` is the named instance. The results look like Figure 13-8.

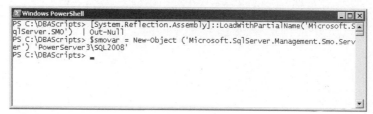

Figure 13-8

Methods and Properties

You can use the `Get-Member` cmdlet to retrieve all of the properties and methods of the SMO object:

```
$smovar | Get-Member
```

The results are shown in Figure 13-9.

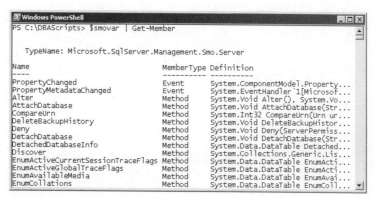

Figure 13-9

Getting Version Information

The next example uses the `Version`, `VersionMajor`, `VersionMinor`, and `VersionString` properties to get the SQL Server version number, as shown in Figure 13-10:

```
$smovar.Version
$smovar.VersionMajor
$smovar.VersionMinor
$smovar.VersionString
```

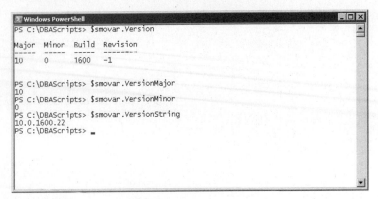

Figure 13-10

SQL Server SPID Information

You can also retrieve all the SPID information connected to SQL Server using the `EnumProcess()` method, as shown in the following example. The equivalent SQL command would be `sp_who`.

```
$smovar.EnumProcesses() | Select-Object Spid, Command, Program | Format-Table -auto
```

The results appear in Figure 13-11.

Figure 13-11

SQL Server Server-Related Information

The following example shows how you can get SQL Server–related properties such as error log path, data file path, edition, and more:

```
$smovar.Name
$smovar.InstanceName
$smovar.OSVersion
$smovar.Product
$smovar.ProductLevel
$smovar.SqlCharSetName
$smovar.CollationName
$smovar.MasterDBPath
$smovar.MasterDBLogPath
$smovar.LoginMode
$smovar.ErrorLogPath
```

Figure 13-12 shows the results.

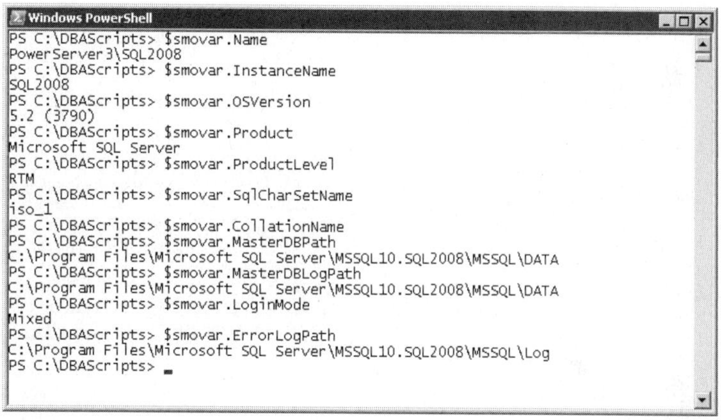

Figure 13-12

You already know that it is easy to access information from one array, rather than storing the information in multiple variables. The following example puts all the properties into a hash table:

```
$SQLServerProperty=@{Poperties_of_SQLServer=""}
$SQLServerProperty =$SQLServerProperty+@{SQLServerName=$smovar.Name}
$SQLServerProperty =$SQLServerProperty+@{OSVersion=$smovar.OSVersion}
$SQLServerProperty =$SQLServerProperty+@{LoginMode=$smovar.LoginMode}
$SQLServerProperty =$SQLServerProperty+@{Product=$smovar.Product}
$SQLServerProperty =$SQLServerProperty+@{ProductLevel=$smovar.ProductLevel}
$SQLServerProperty =$SQLServerProperty+@{SqlCharSetName=$smovar.SqlCharSetName}
$SQLServerProperty =$SQLServerProperty+@{Collation=$smovar.Collation}
$SQLServerProperty =$SQLServerProperty+@{MasterDBPath=$smovar.MasterDBPath}
$SQLServerProperty=$SQLServerProperty+@{MasterDBLogPath=$smovar.MasterDBLogPath}
$SQLServerProperty =$SQLServerProperty+@{ErrorLogPath=$smovar.ErrorLogPath}
$SQLServerProperty
```

The results are shown in Figure 13-13.

Figure 13-13

You can get the entire server configuration information by calling the `Configuration` method and its properties, as shown here. The equivalent T-SQL command would be `sp_configure`.

```
$smovar.Configuration.Properties | Select-Object DisplayName, Number, Minimum,
Maximum
```

The results would look like Figure 13-14.

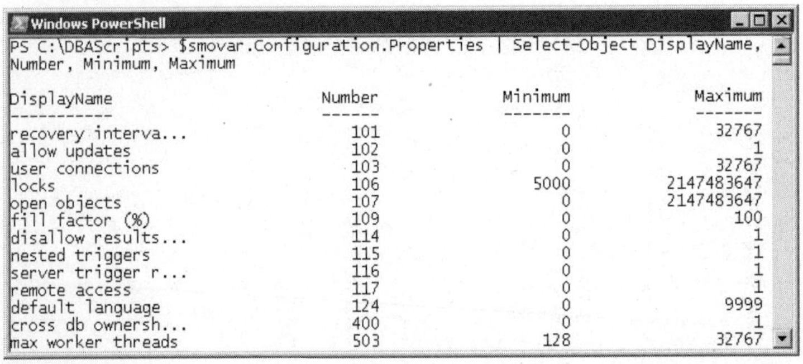

Figure 13-14

SQL Server Database-Related Information

You can query all the database-related information available on the SQL Server instance via SMO. The following cmdlet shows the database name, the date created, and collation:

```
$smovar.Databases | Select-Object Name, CreateDate, Collation
```

Figure 13-15 shows the results.

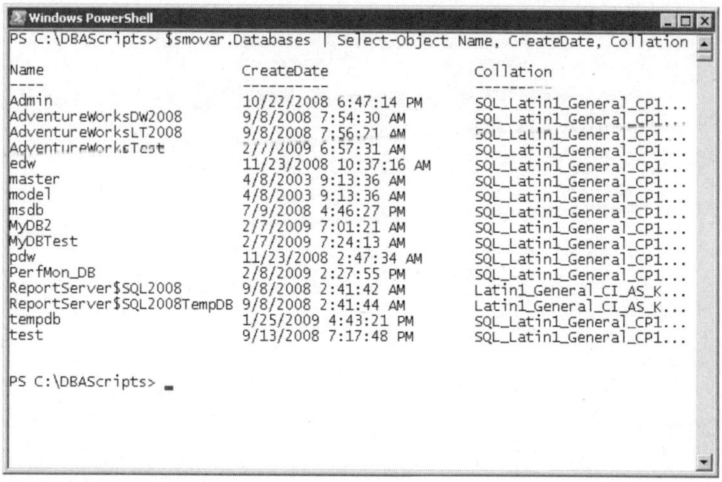

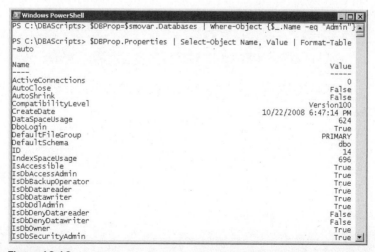

Figure 13-15

In order to get all the database properties on a particular database, in this case `Admin`, execute the following cmdlet (see Figure 13-16):

```
$DBProp=$smovar.Databases | Where-Object {$_.Name -eq "Admin"}
$DBProp.Properties | Select-Object Name, Value | Format-Table -auto
```

Figure 13-16

Changing the Login Mode

SQL Server enables you to change the server login mode from Mixed to Windows authentication by executing the following cmdlet:

```
$smovar.Loginmode
$smovar.set_LoginMode("Integrated")
$smovar.Loginmode
```

Figure 13-17 shows the results.

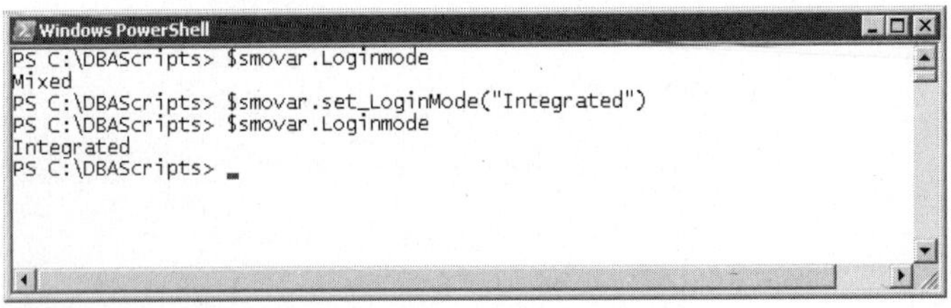

Figure 13-17

Host Information

You can also get some hardware and host-related information from SMO — for example, NetBIOS, platform, number of processors, and size of physical memory — by executing the following cmdlets:

```
$smovar.Get_ComputerNamePhysicalNetBIOS()
$smovar.Get_ServerType()
$smovar.Get_Platform()
$smovar.Get_Processors()
$smovar.Get_Physicalmemory()
```

Figure 13-18 shows the results.

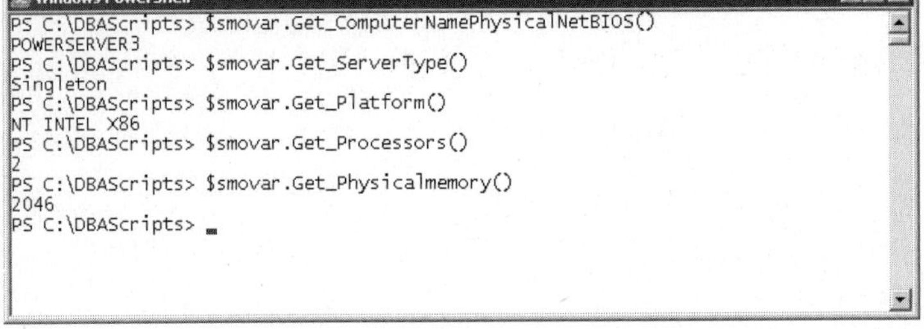

Figure 13-18

Performance Counters

You can enumerate all the performance counters available for a particular SQL Server instance by executing the following cmdlet (see Figure 13-19):

```
$perfcount=$smovar.EnumPerformanceCounters()
$perfcount
```

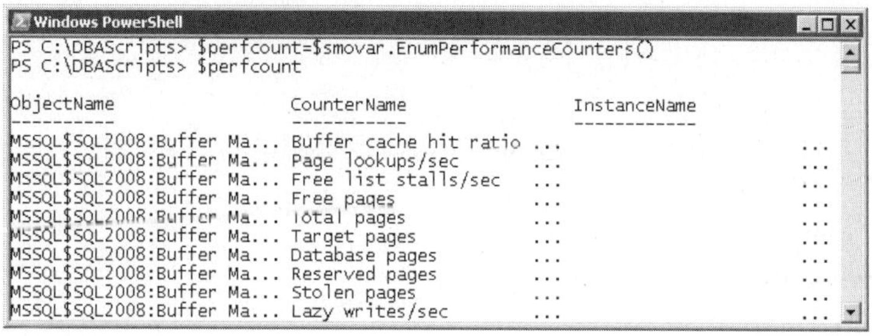

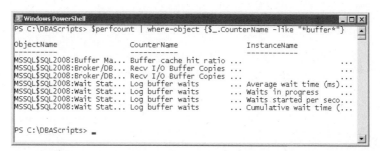

Figure 13-19

You can also use a filtering cmdlet. This example displays all the performance counters that are related to "Buffer" (see Figure 13-20):

```
$perfcount | where-object {$_.CounterName -like "*buffer*"}
```

Figure 13-20

Working with Databases using SMO

SMO can be used to create a database using the class `Microsoft.SqlServer.Management.Smo.Database`.

The next example creates a database called `AdventureWorksTest` using PowerShell and SMO. This example uses the `Create` method of the `smo.database` object (see Figure 13-21):

```
[System.Reflection.Assembly]::LoadWithPartialName('Microsoft.SqlServer.SMO') |
Out-Null
```

```
$Server = New-Object ('Microsoft.SqlServer.Management.Smo.Server')
'PowerServer3\SQL2008'
$DataBase = New-Object ('Microsoft.SqlServer.Management.Smo.Database')
($Server, "AdventureWorksTest")
$Database.Create()
$Server.databases | Select-Object name
```

Figure 13-21

In this case the database was created with all the default options. The next example shows how to create a database with proper data file, log file, log location, data location, and file size.

Create another database called `"MyDB2"` using PowerShell and SMO (see Figure 13-22). This time you need to specify the data filename and file location, data file size, log file name and log file location, and log file size. Create a primary file group using the SMO.Filegroup class, and a data file and a log file using the SMO.DataFile class. You can then set the file size, location, and growth size using various properties of the DataFile class:

```
[System.Reflection.Assembly]::LoadWithPartialName("Microsoft.SqlServer.SMO") |
Out-Null
$Server = New-Object ('Microsoft.SqlServer.Management.Smo.Server')
'PowerServer3\SQL2008'
$DataBase = New-Object ('Microsoft.SqlServer.Management.Smo.Database')
($Server, "MyDB2")
$FileGroup = New-Object ('Microsoft.SqlServer.Management.Smo.FileGroup')
($DataBase, "PRIMARY")
$DataBase.FileGroups.Add($FileGroup)
$DataBaseDataFile = New-Object ('Microsoft.SqlServer.Management.Smo.DataFile')
($FileGroup, "MyDB2_Data")
$FileGroup.Files.Add($DataBaseDataFile)
$DataBaseDataFile.FileName = "C:\MyDb2_Data.mdf"
$DataBaseDataFile.Size = [double](25.0 * 1024.0)
```

```
$DataBaseDataFile.GrowthType = "Percent"
$DataBaseDataFile.Growth = 25.0
$DataBaseDataFile.MaxSize = [double](100.0 * 1024.0)
$DataBaseLogFile = new-object ('Microsoft.SqlServer.Management.Smo.LogFile')
($DataBase, "MyDb2_Log")
$DataBaseLogFile.FileName = "C:\MyDb2_Log.ldf"
$DataBase.Create()
```

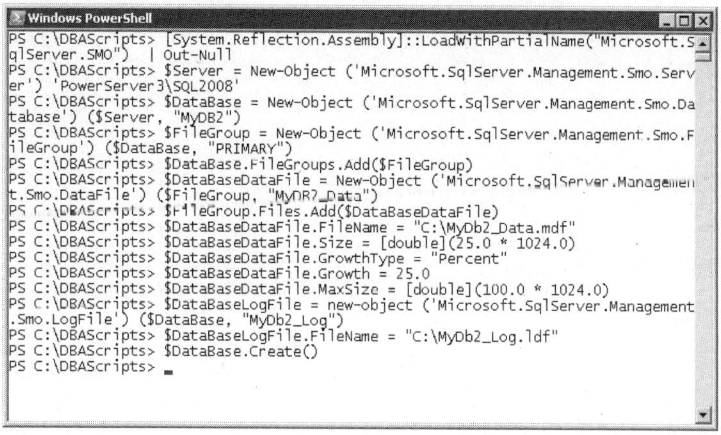

Figure 13-22

The database files created in the C: drive are shown in Figure 13-23.

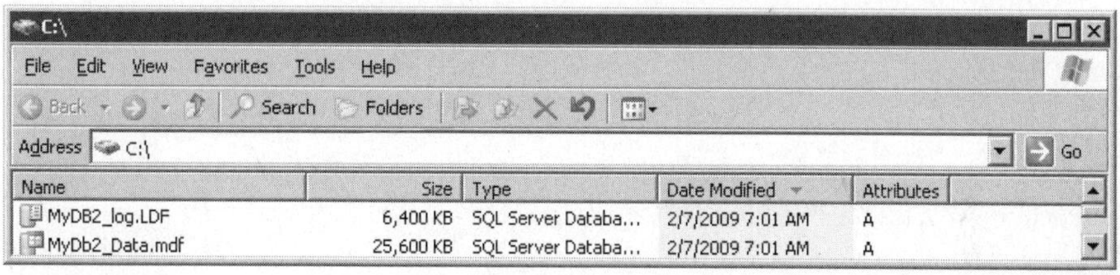

Figure 13-23

The next example creates a database with a primary group and a user-defined filegroup. This code creates the database "MyDBTest"(see Figure 13-24). This time you need to specify the data file name, data file location, data file size, log file name, log file location, and log file size on both the primary filegroup and a user-defined filegroup "SalesFileGrp". You will create a data file on each filegroup, and a log file.

```
[System.Reflection.Assembly]::LoadWithPartialName("Microsoft.SqlServer.SMO")

$Server = New-Object ('Microsoft.SqlServer.Management.Smo.Server')
'PowerServer3\SQL2008'

$DataBase = New-Object ('Microsoft.SqlServer.Management.Smo.Database')
($Server, "MyDBTest")

# Create primary and user-defined filegroups.
```

```
$PrimaryFileGroup = New-Object ('Microsoft.SqlServer.Management.Smo.FileGroup')
($DataBase, "PRIMARY")
$DataBase.FileGroups.Add($PrimaryFileGroup)
$SalesFileGroup  = New-Object ('Microsoft.SqlServer.Management.Smo.FileGroup')
($DataBase, "SalesFileGrp")
$DataBase.FileGroups.Add($SalesFileGroup)

# Create the data files.
$DataBaseDataFile = New-Object ('Microsoft.SqlServer.Management.Smo.DataFile')
($PrimaryFileGroup, "MyDBTest_Primary_Data")
$DataBaseDataFile2 = New-Object ('Microsoft.SqlServer.Management.Smo.DataFile')
($SalesFileGroup, "MyDBTest_SalesFileGrp_Data")

# Add the data files to their respective filegroups.
$PrimaryFileGroup.Files.Add($DataBaseDataFile)
$SalesFileGroup.Files.Add($DataBaseDataFile2)

# Define the data file location, size and growth
$DataBaseDataFile.FileName = "E:\Data\MyDBTest_Data_primary.mdf"
$DataBaseDataFile2.FileName = "E:\Data\MyDBTest_Data_SalesFileGrp.ndf"

$DataBaseDataFile.Size = [double](25.0 * 1024.0)
$DataBaseDataFile.GrowthType = "Percent"
$DataBaseDataFile.Growth = 25.0
$DataBaseDataFile.MaxSize = [double](100.0 * 1024.0)
$DataBaseDataFile.IsPrimaryFile = 'True'

$DataBaseDataFile2.Size = [double](25.0 * 1024.0)
$DataBaseDataFile2.GrowthType = "Percent"
$DataBaseDataFile2.Growth = 25.0
$DataBaseDataFile2.MaxSize = [double](100.0 * 1024.0)

# Create the log file.
$DataBaseLogFile = new-object ('Microsoft.SqlServer.Management.Smo.LogFile')
($DataBase, "MyDBTest_Log")
$DataBase.Logfiles.add($DataBaseLogFile)
$DataBaseLogFile.FileName = "E:\Data\MyDBTest_Log.ldf"

$DataBase.Create()
```

Figure 13-25 shows the database files created in the E: drive.

You can change the recovery model by using the set_RecoveryModel method (see Figure 13-26). In this example, you change the FULL recovery of the database "MyDBTest" to simple recovery:

```
$server = New-Object ('Microsoft.SqlServer.Management.Smo.Server')
'PowerServer3\SQL2008'
$database = New-Object ('Microsoft.SqlServer.Management.Smo.Database')
($server, "MyDBTest")
$database.RecoveryModel
#Recovery model values 1 is FULL, 2 is BulkLogged, 3 is Simple
$rmodel=3
$database.Set_RecoveryModel($rmodel)
$database.RecoveryModel
```

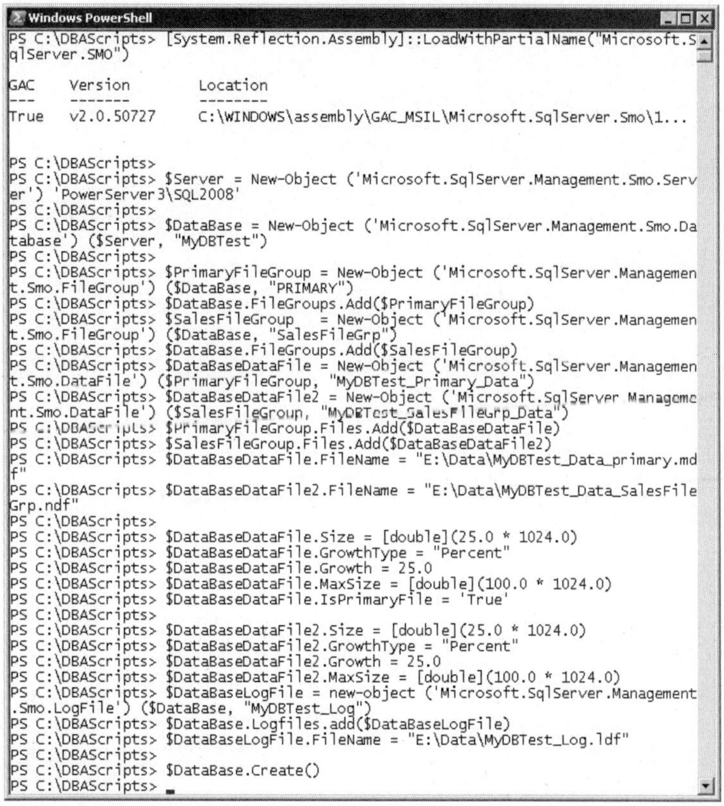

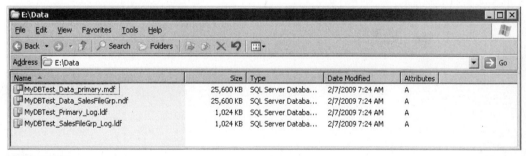

Figure 13-24

Figure 13-25

You can execute a stored procedure or a query in the database using the following code (see Figure 13-27):

```
$server = New-Object ('Microsoft.SqlServer.Management.Smo.Server')
'PowerServer3\SQL2008'
$database = New-Object ('Microsoft.SqlServer.Management.Smo.Database')
($server, "MyDBTest")
$result=$dataBase.ExecuteWithResults("sp_who")
$result.Tables | Format-Table -auto
```

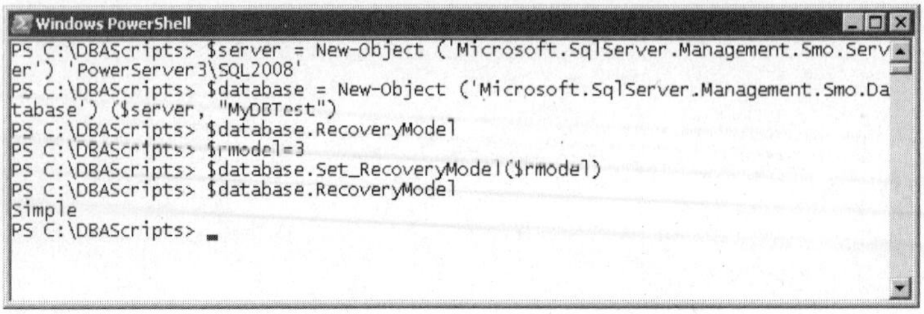

Figure 13-26

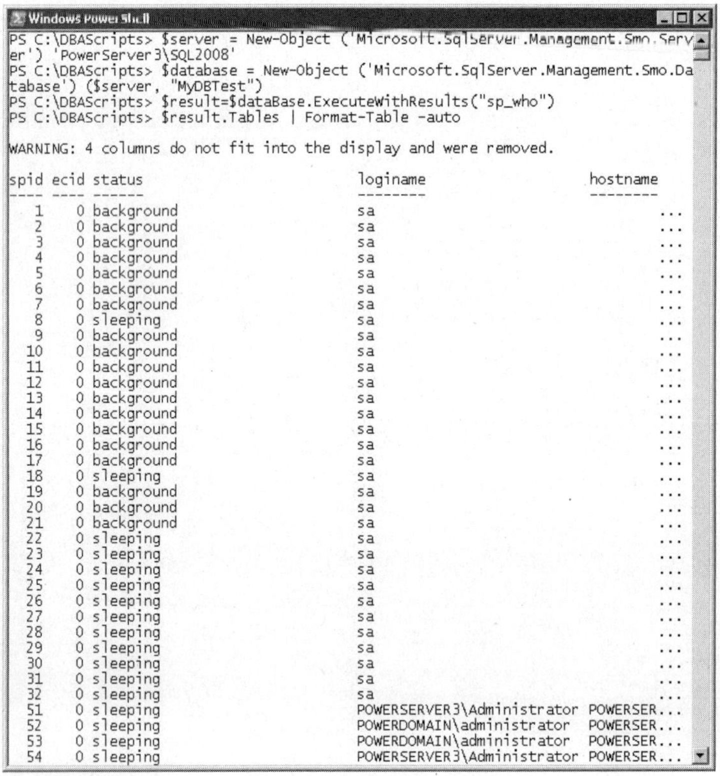

Figure 13-27

In order to change the compatibility level of the database from SQL Server 2008 to SQL Server 2000, you need to execute the following code (see Figure 13-28):

```
$server = New-Object ('Microsoft.SqlServer.Management.Smo.Server')
'PowerServer3\SQL2008'
$database = New-Object ('Microsoft.SqlServer.Management.Smo.Database')
($server, "MyDBTest")
$dataBase.CompatibilityLevel
$dataBase.Set_CompatibilityLevel(80)
$dataBase.CompatibilityLevel
```

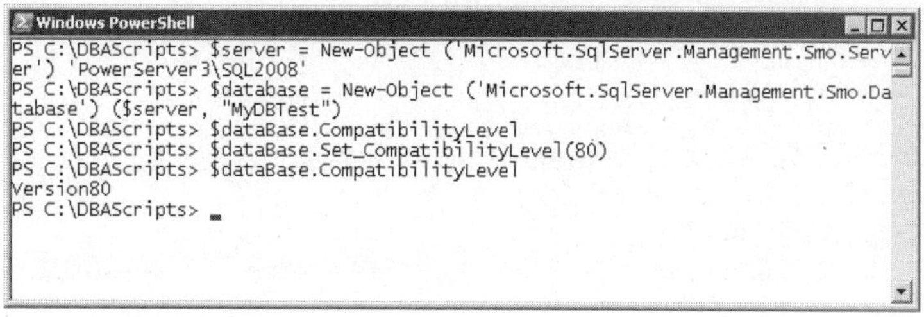

Figure 13-28

You could use the `Microsoft.SqlServer.Management.Smo.Scripter` class to script the database. The next example shows you how. The database in this example is called `"MyDBTEST"` (see Figure 13-29). Chapter 21 discusses scripting of the database, the schema, and database objects in detail.

```
[System.Reflection.Assembly]::LoadWithPartialName('Microsoft.SqlServer.SMO')  |
Out-Null
$MyScripter=New-Object
("Microsoft.SqlServer.Management.Smo.Scripter")
$server = New-Object ('Microsoft.SqlServer.Management.Smo.Server')
'PowerServer3\SQL2008'
$MyScripter.Server=$server
$MyScripter.Script($server.databases["MyDBTEST"])
```

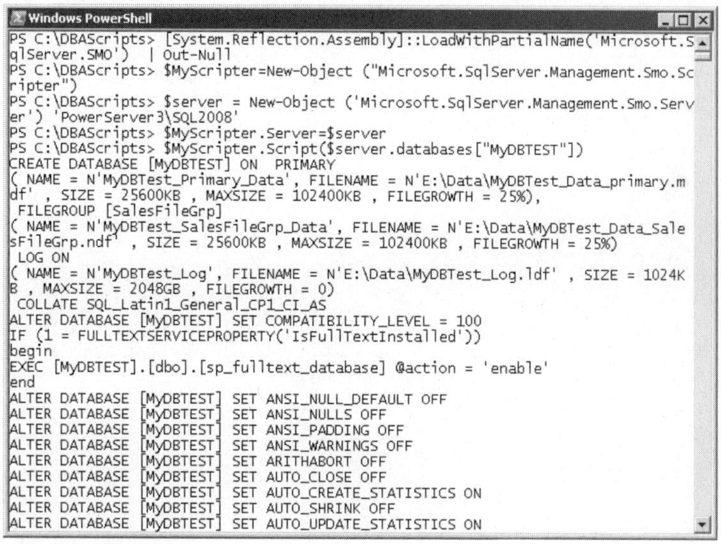

Figure 13-29

You can list database objects such as tables, views, and stored procedures using the `Database` property of the class `Microsoft.SqlServer.Management.Smo.Server`, as shown here (see Figure 13-30 and Figure 13-31):

```
$server = New-Object ('Microsoft.SqlServer.Management.Smo.Server')
"PowerServer3\SQL2008"
$database = $server.Databases["msdb"]
$database.Views | Select-Object Name
$database.StoredProcedures | Select-Object Name
```

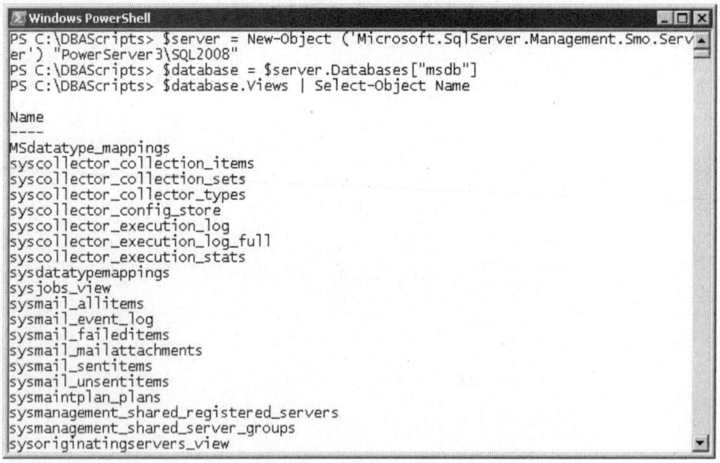

```
PS C:\DBAScripts> $server = New-Object ('Microsoft.SqlServer.Management.Smo.Serv
er') "PowerServer3\SQL2008"
PS C:\DBAScripts> $database = $server.Databases["msdb"]
PS C:\DBAScripts> $database.Views | Select-Object Name

Name
----
MSdatatype_mappings
syscollector_collection_items
syscollector_collection_sets
syscollector_collector_types
syscollector_config_store
syscollector_execution_log
syscollector_execution_log_full
syscollector_execution_stats
sysdatatypemappings
sysjobs_view
sysmail_allitems
sysmail_event_log
sysmail_faileditems
sysmail_mailattachments
sysmail_sentitems
sysmail_unsentitems
sysmaintplan_plans
sysmanagement_shared_registered_servers
sysmanagement_shared_server_groups
sysoriginatingservers_view
```

Figure 13-30

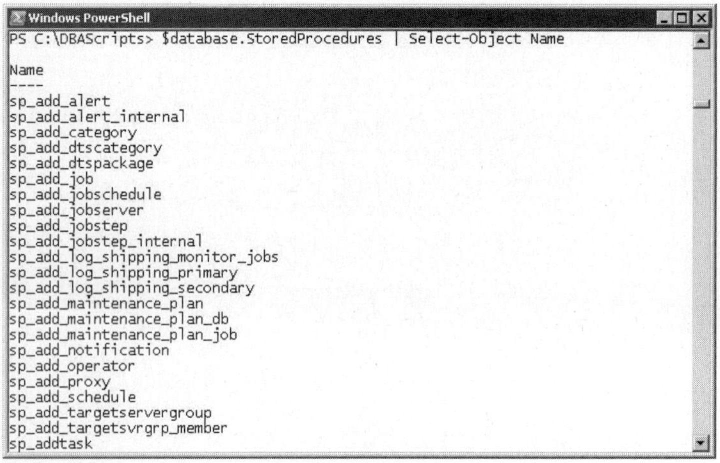

```
PS C:\DBAScripts> $database.StoredProcedures | Select-Object Name

Name
----
sp_add_alert
sp_add_alert_internal
sp_add_category
sp_add_dtscategory
sp_add_dtspackage
sp_add_job
sp_add_jobschedule
sp_add_jobserver
sp_add_jobstep
sp_add_jobstep_internal
sp_add_log_shipping_monitor_jobs
sp_add_log_shipping_primary
sp_add_log_shipping_secondary
sp_add_maintenance_plan
sp_add_maintenance_plan_db
sp_add_maintenance_plan_job
sp_add_notification
sp_add_operator
sp_add_proxy
sp_add_schedule
sp_add_targetservergroup
sp_add_targetsvrgrp_member
sp_addtask
```

Figure 13-31

Working with Tables using SMO

So far, you have seen the various uses of SMO. SMO can also be used to create and manipulate database objects such as tables, stored procedures, functions, and more. This section illustrates the use of SMO in accessing and manipulating the database object tables.

Creating Tables

Creating tables in SMO is a pretty straightforward process. For the next example, create a table "MyTable" in the database "MyDBTest" with two columns named ID and Name, as shown below. Here we use the Microsoft.SqlServer.Management.SMO.Table and Microsoft.SqlServer.Management.SMO.Column class to create the table. Using the SMO.column class, set the property Collation to a specific collation value. We use the method columns.Add() in the Table object (see Figure 13-32).

```
[System.Reflection.Assembly]::LoadWithPartialName('Microsoft.SqlServer.SMO')
| Out-Null

$server = New-Object ('Microsoft.SqlServer.Management.Smo.Server')
'PowerServer3\SQL2008'

$database = $server.Databases["MyDBTest"]

$table = New-Object Microsoft.SqlServer.Management.Smo.Table($database, "MyTable")

$datatype1 = [Microsoft.SqlServer.Management.Smo.Datatype]::int
$datatype2 = [Microsoft.SqlServer.Management.Smo.Datatype]::Nchar(50)
$col1 = New-Object Microsoft.SqlServer.Management.Smo.Column($table,
"ID",$datatype1)
$col1.Collation = "Latin1_General_CI_AS"
$col1.Nullable = $false

$col2 = New-Object Microsoft.SqlServer.Management.Smo.Column($table,
"Name",$datatype2)
$col2.Collation = "Latin1_General_CI_AS"
$col2.Nullable = $false

$table.Columns.Add($col1)
$table.Columns.Add($col2)

$table.Create()
```

Listing Columns

You can use SMO to display all the columns available in a table. In the following example, we iterate through all the tables in the database until we find the table "Mytable" using a foreach loop. Once we find the table, we iterate through all the columns in the table and display the column name (see Figure 13-33):

```
[System.Reflection.Assembly]::LoadWithPartialName("Microsoft.SqlServer.Smo")  |
Out-Null
$server=New-Object "Microsoft.SqlServer.Management.Smo.Server"
'PowerServer3\SQL2008'
$database = $server.Databases["MyDBTest"]
foreach ($table in $database.tables)
{
        if($table.name -eq "MyTable")
        { Write-Host "Table Name="$table.Name;
                foreach ($col in $table.columns) { Write-Host "ColumnName="$col.Name}
        }
```

```
Windows PowerShell                                                          _ □ X
PS C:\DBAScripts> [System.Reflection.Assembly]::LoadWithPartialName("Microsoft.S
qlServer.ConnectionInfo") | Out-Null
PS C:\DBAScripts> [System.Reflection.Assembly]::LoadWithPartialName("Microsoft.S
qlServer.SmoEnum") | Out-Null
PS C:\DBAScripts> [System.Reflection.Assembly]::LoadWithPartialName('Microsoft.S
qlServer.SMO') | Out-Null
PS C:\DBAScripts>
PS C:\DBAScripts> $server = New-Object ('Microsoft.SqlServer.Management.Smo.Serv
er') 'PowerServer3\SQL2008'
PS C:\DBAScripts>
PS C:\DBAScripts> $database = $server.Databases["MyDBTest"]
PS C:\DBAScripts>
PS C:\DBAScripts> $table = New-Object Microsoft.SqlServer.Management.Smo.Table($
database, "MyTable")
PS C:\DBAScripts>
PS C:\DBAScripts>
PS C:\DBAScripts> $datatype1 = [Microsoft.SqlServer.Management.Smo.Datatype]::in
t
PS C:\DBAScripts> $datatype2 = [Microsoft.SqlServer.Management.Smo.Datatype]::Nc
har(50)
PS C:\DBAScripts> $col1 = New-Object Microsoft.SqlServer.Management.Smo.Column($
table, "ID",$datatype1)
PS C:\DBAScripts> $col1.Collation = "Latin1_General_CI_AS"
PS C:\DBAScripts> $col1.Nullable = $false
PS C:\DBAScripts>
PS C:\DBAScripts> $col2 = New-Object Microsoft.SqlServer.Management.Smo.Column($
table, "Name",$datatype2)
PS C:\DBAScripts> $col2.Collation = "Latin1_General_CI_AS"
PS C:\DBAScripts> $col2.Nullable = $false
PS C:\DBAScripts>
PS C:\DBAScripts> $table.Columns.Add($col1)
PS C:\DBAScripts> $table.Columns.Add($col2)
PS C:\DBAScripts>
PS C:\DBAScripts> $table.Create()
PS C:\DBAScripts> _
```

Figure 13-32

```
Windows PowerShell                                                          _ □ X
PS C:\DBAScripts> [System.Reflection.Assembly]::LoadWithPartialName("Microsoft.S
qlServer.Smo") | Out-Null
PS C:\DBAScripts> $server=New-Object "Microsoft.SqlServer.Management.Smo.Server"
 'PowerServer3\SQL2008'
PS C:\DBAScripts> $database = $server.Databases["MyDBTest"]
PS C:\DBAScripts> foreach ($table in $database.tables)
>> {
>> if($table.name -eq "MyTable")
>> { Write-Host "Table Name="$table.Name;
>> foreach ($col in $table.columns) { Write-Host "ColumnName="$col.Name}
>> }
>> }
>>
Table Name= MyTable
ColumnName= ID
ColumnName= Name
PS C:\DBAScripts> _
```

Figure 13-33

Removing Columns

You can use SMO to drop a column from a table. In the next example, shown in Figure 13-34, we iterate through all the tables in the database until we find the table "Mytable" using a foreach loop. Once we find the table, we iterate through all the columns until we find the column "ID". Once found, we drop the column using the drop() method:

```
[System.Reflection.Assembly]::LoadWithPartialName("Microsoft.SqlServer.Smo")  |
Out-Null
$srv=New-Object "Microsoft.SqlServer.Management.Smo.Server" 'PowerServer3\SQL2008'
$db = $srv.Databases["MyDBTest"]
```

```
foreach ($table in $db.Tables)
{
        if ($table.name -eq "MyTable")
        {
                foreach ($col in $table.columns)
                {
                        if($col.name -eq "ID")
                        {
                                $dropcolumn=$col
                        }


                }
        }
}

$dropcolumn.Drop();
$table.Alter();
```

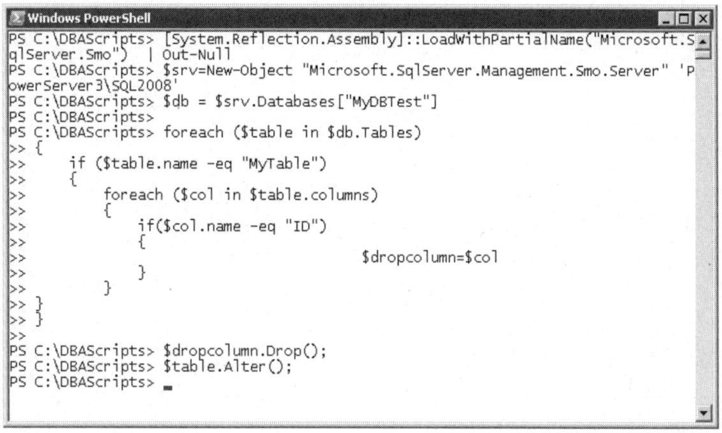

Figure 13-34

Adding Columns

SMO can also be used for adding new columns to existing tables. Execute the cmdlets as shown in the following example. Here, we use the class 'Microsoft.SqlServer.Management.Smo.Column' to add new columns. We also use the properties Name, columns, Nullable and datatype and the Add() method to add the column to the table "MyTable" (see Figure 13-35):

```
[System.Reflection.Assembly]::LoadWithPartialName("Microsoft.SqlServer.Smo")  |
Out-Null

$srv = New-Object ('Microsoft.SqlServer.Management.Smo.Server')
'PowerServer3\SQL2008'

$db = $srv.Databases["MyDBTest"]
$table = $db.Tables["MyTable"]
```

```
$datatype0 =[Microsoft.SqlServer.Management.Smo.Datatype]::datetime
$datatype1 =[Microsoft.SqlServer.Management.Smo.Datatype]::int
$datatype2 =[Microsoft.SqlServer.Management.Smo.Datatype]::Money
$datatype3 =[Microsoft.SqlServer.Management.Smo.Datatype]::Nchar(50)

$col0 = New-Object 'Microsoft.SqlServer.Management.Smo.Column'
$col0.Name="DOB"
$table.Columns.Add($col0)
$col0.Nullable = $false
$col0.Datatype=$datatype0

$col1 = New-Object 'Microsoft.SqlServer.Management.Smo.Column'
$col1.Name="ID"
$table.Columns.Add($col1)
$col1.Nullable = $false
$col1.Datatype=$datatype1

$col2 = New-Object 'Microsoft.SqlServer.Management.Smo.Column'
$col2.Name="Salary"
$table.Columns.Add($col2)
$col2.Nullable = $false
$col2.Datatype=$datatype2

$col3 = New-Object 'Microsoft.SqlServer.Management.Smo.Column'
$col3.Name="Address"
$table.Columns.Add($col3)
$col3.Nullable = $false
$col3.Datatype=$datatype3

$table.alter()
```

Dropping a Table

SMO can also be used to drop existing tables. Execute the cmdlets as shown here (see Figure 13-36):

```
[System.Reflection.Assembly]::LoadWithPartialName("Microsoft.SqlServer.Smo") |
Out-Null
$srv = New-Object ('Microsoft.SqlServer.Management.Smo.Server')
'PowerServer3\SQL2008'
$db = $srv.Databases["MyDBTest"]

$table = $db.Tables["MyTable"]
$table.drop()
```

Backup and Restore with SMO

SMO can also be used to back up and restore a database.

Database Backup

As you already know, there are three different backups — namely, full backup, differential, and transactional log backup. SMO can be used to take backups of all databases as well. Earlier in this chapter, you saw an example of taking backups of databases using the `SqlConnection` class and a stored procedure. This section illustrates how to take backups using SMO classes without using any stored procedures. The next example takes a full backup of the database `"MyDBTest"`, as shown in Figure 13-37 and Figure 13-38. Here we use the `SMO.Backup` and `SMO.BackupDeviceitem` classes for restoring a database. In SQL Server 2008, Microsoft moved all of the classes related to backup and restore to `SMOExtended.dll`.

```
Windows PowerShell                                                    _ □ x
PS C:\DBAScripts>  [System.Reflection.Assembly]::LoadWithPartialName("Microsoft.
SqlServer.Smo")  | Out-Null
PS C:\DBAScripts>
PS C:\DBAScripts> $srv = New-Object ('Microsoft.SqlServer.Management.Smo.Server'
) 'PowerServer3\SQL2008'
PS C:\DBAScripts>
PS C:\DBAScripts> $db = $srv.Databases["MyDBTest"]
PS C:\DBAScripts> $table = $db.Tables["MyTable"]
PS C:\DBAScripts>
PS C:\DBAScripts> $datatype0 -[Microsoft.SqlServer.Management.Smo.Datatype]::dat
etime
PS C:\DBAScripts> $datatype1 =[Microsoft.SqlServer.Management.Smo.Datatype]::int

PS C:\DBAScripts> $datatype2 =[Microsoft.SqlServer.Management.Smo.Datatype]::Mon
ey
PS C:\DBAScripts> $datatype3 =[Microsoft.SqlServer.Management.Smo.Datatype]::Nch
ar(50)
PS C:\DBAScripts>
PS C:\DBAScripts> $col0 = New-Object 'Microsoft.SqlServer.Management.Smo.Column'

PS C:\DBAScripts> $col0.Name="DOB"
PS C:\DBAScripts> $table.Columns.Add($col0)
PS C:\DBAScripts> $col0.Nullable = $false
PS C:\DBAScripts> $col0.Datatype=$datatype0
PS C:\DBAScripts>
PS C:\DBAScripts> $col1 = New-Object 'Microsoft.SqlServer.Management.Smo.Column'

PS C:\DBAScripts> $col1.Name="ID"
PS C:\DBAScripts> $table.Columns.Add($col1)
PS C:\DBAScripts> $col1.Nullable = $false
PS C:\DBAScripts> $col1.Datatype=$datatype1
PS C:\DBAScripts>
PS C:\DBAScripts> $col2 = New-Object 'Microsoft.SqlServer.Management.Smo.Column'

PS C:\DBAScripts> $col2.Name="Salary"
PS C:\DBAScripts> $table.Columns.Add($col2)
PS C:\DBAScripts> $col2.Nullable = $false
PS C:\DBAScripts> $col2.Datatype=$datatype2
PS C:\DBAScripts>
PS C:\DBAScripts> $col3 = New-Object 'Microsoft.SqlServer.Management.Smo.Column'

PS C:\DBAScripts> $col3.Name="Address"
PS C:\DBAScripts> $table.Columns.Add($col3)
PS C:\DBAScripts> $col3.Nullable = $false
PS C:\DBAScripts> $col3.Datatype=$datatype3
PS C:\DBAScripts>
PS C:\DBAScripts> $table.alter()
PS C:\DBAScripts> _
```

Figure 13-35

```
Windows PowerShell                                                    _ □ x
PS C:\DBAScripts>  [System.Reflection.Assembly]::LoadWithPartialName("Microsoft.
SqlServer.Smo")  | Out-Null
PS C:\DBAScripts>
PS C:\DBAScripts> $srv = New-Object ('Microsoft.SqlServer.Management.Smo.Server'
) 'PowerServer3\SQL2008'
PS C:\DBAScripts>
PS C:\DBAScripts> $db = $srv.Databases["MyDBTest"]
PS C:\DBAScripts>
PS C:\DBAScripts> $table = $db.Tables["MyTable"]
PS C:\DBAScripts> $table.drop()
PS C:\DBAScripts> _
```

Figure 13-36

You can see that we load that assembly in the beginning:

```
[System.Reflection.Assembly]::LoadWithPartialName("Microsoft.SqlServer.Smo") |
Out-Null
[System.Reflection.Assembly]::LoadWithPartialName("Microsoft.SqlServer.SmoExtended")
| Out-Null

[System.IO.Directory]::CreateDirectory("C:\Backup")
| Out-Null
$srv=New-Object "Microsoft.SqlServer.Management.Smo.Server" "PowerServer3\SQL2008"
$bck=New-Object "Microsoft.SqlServer.Management.Smo.backup"
$bck.Action = 'Database'
$fil=New-Object "Microsoft.SqlServer.Management.Smo.BackupDeviceItem"
$fil.DeviceType='File'
$timestamp=((get-date).toString('yyyy_MM_dd_hh_mm'))
$fil.Name=[System.IO.Path]::Combine("C:\Backup", "MyDBtest" +"_"+$timestamp+".bak")
$bck.Devices.Add($fil)
$bck.Database="MyDBTest"
$bck.SqlBackup($srv)
```

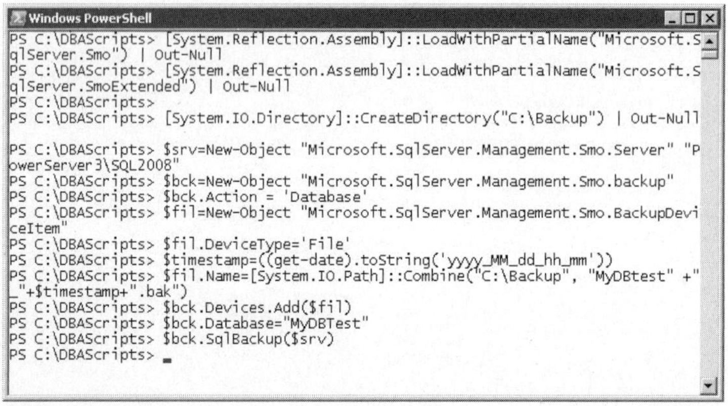

Figure 13-37

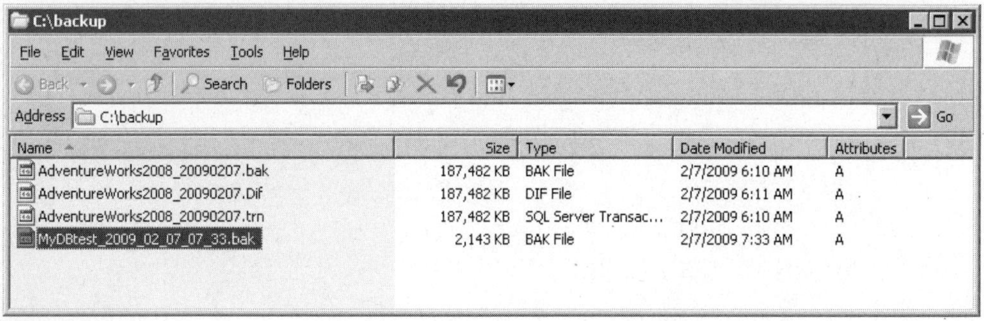

Figure 13-38

Transaction Log Backup

SMO can also be used to take transactional backups of a database. The next example takes a transaction log backup of the database "MyDBTest", as shown here (see Figure 13-39 and Figure 13-40):

```
[System.Reflection.Assembly]::LoadWithPartialName("Microsoft.SqlServer.Smo") |
Out-Null
[System.Reflection.Assembly]::LoadWithPartialName("Microsoft.SqlServer.SmoExtended")
| Out-Null
$srv=New-Object "Microsoft.SqlServer.Management.Smo.Server" "PowerServer3\SQL2008"
$bck=New-Object "Microsoft.SqlServer.Management.Smo.Backup"
$bck.Action = 'Log'
$fil=New-Object "Microsoft.SqlServer.Management.Smo.BackupDeviceItem"
$fil.DeviceType='File'
$timestamp=((get-date).toString('yyyy_MM_dd_hh_mm'))
$fil.Name=[System.IO.Path]::Combine("C:\Backup", "MyDBTest" +"_"+$timestamp+".log")
$bck.Devices.Add($fil)
$bck.Database="MyDBTest"
$bck.SqlBackup($srv)
```

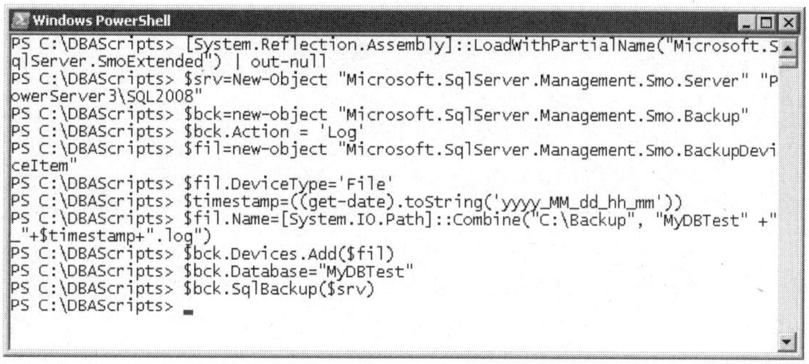

Figure 13-39

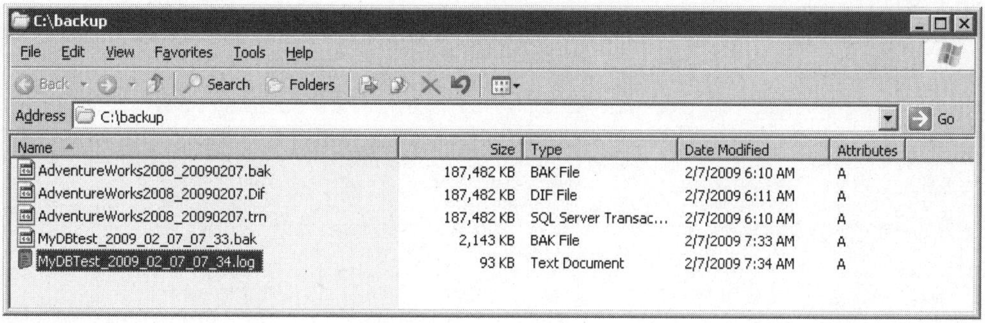

Figure 13-40

Differential Backup

SMO can also be used to take Differential backups of a database. In order to take the Differential backup of the database "MyDBTest", use the following code (see Figure 13-41 and Figure 13-42):

```
[System.Reflection.Assembly]::LoadWithPartialName("Microsoft.SqlServer.Smo") |
Out-Null

[System.Reflection.Assembly]::LoadWithPartialName("Microsoft.SqlServer.SmoExtended")
| Out-Null
$srv=New-Object "Microsoft.SqlServer.Management.Smo.Server" "PowerServer3\SQL2008"
$bck=New-Object "Microsoft.SqlServer.Management.Smo.Backup"
$bck.Incremental = 1
$fil=New-Object "Microsoft.SqlServer.Management.Smo.BackupDeviceItem"
$fil.DeviceType='File'
$timestamp=((get-date).toString('yyyy_MM_dd_hh_mm'))
$fil.Name=[System.IO.Path]::Combine("C:\Backup", "MyDBTest"
+"_"+$timestamp+".diff")
$bck.Devices.Add($fil)
$bck.Database="MyDBTest"
$bck.SqlBackup($srv)
```

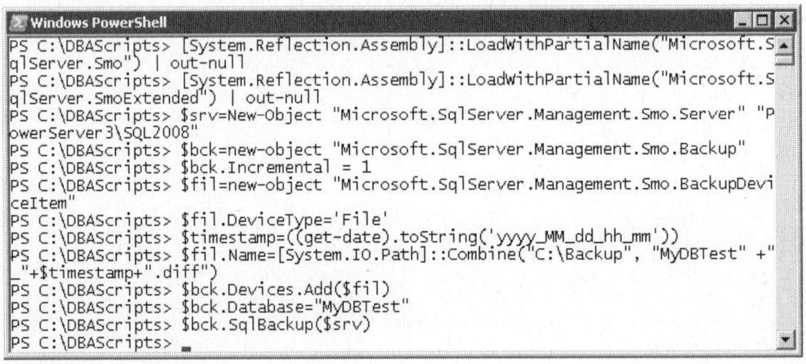

Figure 13-41

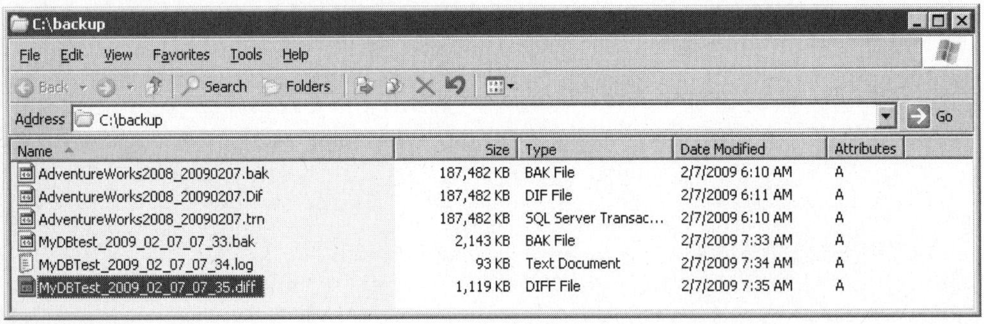

Figure 13-42

Restoring Full Backup

SMO can also be used to restore a full backup. In this example, the `SQLRestore()` method is used to restore the backup file. We also use the class `Microsoft.SqlServer.Management.Smo.relocatefile` to move the data files and log files to a different location. In addition, the `ReplaceDatabase` property is used to restore the backup file to a new database, `"MyDBTest2"` (see Figure 13-43):

```
[System.Reflection.Assembly]::LoadWithPartialName("Microsoft.SqlServer.Smo") |
Out-Null
[System.Reflection.Assembly]::LoadWithPartialName("Microsoft.SqlServer.SmoExtended")
| Out-Null
$srv=New-Object "Microsoft.SqlServer.Management.Smo.Server" "PowerServer3\SQL2008"
$srv.ConnectionContext.SqlExecutionModes =
[Microsoft.SqlServer.Management.Common.SqlExecutionModes]::executesql
$res=New-Object "Microsoft.SqlServer.Management.Smo.restore"
$fil=New-Object "Microsoft.SqlServer.Management.Smo.BackupDeviceItem"
$relofil=New-Object "Microsoft.SqlServer.Management.Smo.relocatefile"
$relofil2=New-Object "Microsoft.SqlServer.Management.Smo.relocatefile"
$relofil3=New-Object "Microsoft.SqlServer.Management.Smo.relocatefile"
$relofil4=New-Object "Microsoft.SqlServer.Management.Smo.relocatefile"
$fil.DeviceType='File'
$fil.Name="c:\backup\MyDBtest_2009_02_07_07_33.bak"
$res.Action = "Database"
$res.Database="MyDBTest2"
$res.Devices.add($fil)
$res.ReplaceDatabase=1
$relofil.LogicalFilename="MyDBTest_Primary_Data"
$relofil.PhysicalFilename="E:\Data\MyDBTest_Data_primary2.mdf"
$res.RelocateFiles.add($relofil)
$relofil2.LogicalFilename="MyDBTest_SalesFileGrp_Data"
$relofil2.PhysicalFilename="E:\Data\MyDBTest_Data_SalesFileGrp2.ndf"
$res.RelocateFiles.add($relofil2)
$relofil3.LogicalFilename="MyDBTest_Primary_Log"
$relofil3.PhysicalFilename="E:\Data\MyDBTest_Primary_Log2.ldf"
$res.RelocateFiles.add($relofil3)
$relofil4.LogicalFilename="MyDBTest_SalesFileGrp_Log"
$relofil4.PhysicalFilename="E:\Data\MyDBTest_SalesFileGrp_Log2.ldf"
$res.RelocateFiles.add($relofil4)
$res.SqlRestore($srv)
Write-Host "Restored the database backup."
```

Restoring a Full Backup and Transaction Log Backup

In this example, we use the `SQLRestore()` method to restore the backup file. We also use the class `Microsoft.SqlServer.Management.Smo.relocatefile` to move the data files and log files to a different location. The `ReplaceDatabase` property restores the backup file onto a new database, `"MyDBTest2"`.

You can see that we repeat the same restore step we used in restoring a full backup to restore the transaction log backup. Because we are restoring multiple files, we use the property `set_NoRecovery(1)` to keep the database in `Norecovery` mode. As shown in Figure 13-44, the following code restores both `Full` backup and `transactionlog` backup:

```
[System.Reflection.Assembly]::LoadWithPartialName("Microsoft.SqlServer.Smo") |
Out-Null
[System.Reflection.Assembly]::LoadWithPartialName("Microsoft.SqlServer.SmoExtended")
| Out-Null
$srv=New-Object "Microsoft.SqlServer.Management.Smo.Server" "PowerServer3\SQL2008"
$srv.ConnectionContext.SqlExecutionModes =
[Microsoft.SqlServer.Management.Common.SqlExecutionModes]::executesql
$res=New-Object "Microsoft.SqlServer.Management.Smo.restore"
$fil=New-Object "Microsoft.SqlServer.Management.Smo.BackupDeviceItem"
$relofil=New-Object "Microsoft.SqlServer.Management.Smo.relocatefile"
$relofil2=New-Object "Microsoft.SqlServer.Management.Smo.relocatefile"
$relofil3=New-Object "Microsoft.SqlServer.Management.Smo.relocatefile"
$relofil4=New-Object "Microsoft.SqlServer.Management.Smo.relocatefile"

$fil.DeviceType='File'
$fil.Name="c:\backup\MyDBtest_2009_02_07_07_33.bak "
$res.Action = "Database"
$res.Database="MyDBTest2"
$res.Devices.add($fil)
$res.ReplaceDatabase=1

$relofil.LogicalFilename="MyDBTest_Primary_Data"
$relofil.PhysicalFilename="E:\Data\MyDBTest_Data_primary2.mdf"
$res.RelocateFiles.add($relofil)

$relofil2.LogicalFilename="MyDBTest_SalesFileGrp_Data"
$relofil2.PhysicalFilename=" E:\Data\MyDBTest_Data_SalesFileGrp2.ndf"
$res.RelocateFiles.add($relofil2)

$relofil3.LogicalFilename="MyDBTest_Primary_Log"
$relofil3.PhysicalFilename=" E:\Data\MyDBTest_Primary_Log2.ldf"
$res.RelocateFiles.add($relofil3)

$relofil4.LogicalFilename="MyDBTest_SalesFileGrp_Log"
$relofil4.PhysicalFilename="E:\Data\MyDBTest_SalesFileGrp_Log2.ldf"
$res.RelocateFiles.add($relofil4)

$res.set_NoRecovery(1)

$res.SqlRestore($srv)
Write-Host "Restored the database backup."

$res=New-Object "Microsoft.SqlServer.Management.Smo.restore"
$fil=New-Object "Microsoft.SqlServer.Management.Smo.BackupDeviceItem"
$relofil=New-Object "Microsoft.SqlServer.Management.Smo.relocatefile"
$relofil2=New-Object "Microsoft.SqlServer.Management.Smo.relocatefile"
$relofil3=New-Object "Microsoft.SqlServer.Management.Smo.relocatefile"
$relofil4=New-Object "Microsoft.SqlServer.Management.Smo.relocatefile"

$fil.DeviceType='File'
$fil.Name="c:\backup\MyDBTest_2009_02_07_07_34.log"
$res.Action = "Log"
$res.Database="MyDBTest2"
$res.Devices.add($fil)
$res.ReplaceDatabase=1
```

```
$relofil.LogicalFilename="MyDBTest_Primary_Data"
$relofil.PhysicalFilename=" E:\Data\MyDBTest_Data_primary2.mdf"
$res.RelocateFiles.add($relofil)

$relofil2.LogicalFilename="MyDBTest_SalesFileGrp_Data"
$relofil2.PhysicalFilename=" E:\Data\MyDBTest_Data_SalesFileGrp2.ndf"
$res.RelocateFiles.add($relofil2)

$relofil3.LogicalFilename="MyDBTest_Primary_Log"
$relofil3.PhysicalFilename=" E:\Data\MyDBTest_Primary_Log2.ldf"
$res.RelocateFiles.add($relofil3)

$relofil4.LogicalFilename="MyDBTest_SalesFileGrp_Log"
$relofil4.PhysicalFilename=" E:\Data\MyDBTest_SalesFileGrp_Log2.ldf"
$res.RelocateFiles.add($relofil4)

$res.set_NoRecovery(0)

$res.SqlRestore($srv)
Write-Host "Restored the transaction log backup."
```

Figure 13-43

```
Windows PowerShell                                                    _ □ ×
PS C:\DBAScripts> $relofil4.LogicalFilename="MyDBTest_SalesFileGrp_Log"
PS C:\DBAScripts> $relofil4.PhysicalFilename="E:\Data\MyDBTest_SalesFileGrp_Log2
.ldf"
PS C:\DBAScripts> $res.RelocateFiles.add($relofil4)
3
PS C:\DBAScripts> $res.set_NoRecovery(1)
PS C:\DBAScripts> $res.SqlRestore($srv)
PS C:\DBAScripts> Write-Host "Restored the database backup."
Restored the database backup.
PS C:\DBAScripts> $res=New-Object "Microsoft.SqlServer.Management.Smo.restore"
PS C:\DBAScripts> $fil=New-Object "Microsoft.SqlServer.Management.Smo.BackupDevi
ceItem"
PS C:\DBAScripts> $relofil=New-Object "Microsoft.SqlServer.Management.Smo.reloca
tefile"
PS C:\DBAScripts> $relofil2=New-Object "Microsoft.SqlServer.Management.Smo.reloc
atefile"
PS C:\DBAScripts> $relofil3=New-Object "Microsoft.SqlServer.Management.Smo.reloc
atefile"
PS C:\DBAScripts> $relofil4=New-Object "Microsoft.SqlServer.Management.Smo.reloc
atefile"
PS C:\DBAScripts> $fil.DeviceType='File'
PS C:\DBAScripts> $fil.Name="c:\backup\MyDBTest_2009_02_07_07_34.log"
PS C:\DBAScripts> $res.Action = "Log"
PS C:\DBAScripts> $res.Database="MyDBTest2"
PS C:\DBAScripts> $res.Devices.add($fil)
PS C:\DBAScripts> $res.ReplaceDatabase=1
PS C:\DBAScripts> $relofil.LogicalFilename="MyDBTest_Primary_Data"
PS C:\DBAScripts> $relofil.PhysicalFilename="E:\Data\MyDBTest_Data_primary2.mdf"

PS C:\DBAScripts> $res.RelocateFiles.add($relofil)
0
PS C:\DBAScripts> $relofil2.LogicalFilename="MyDBTest_SalesFileGrp_Data"
PS C:\DBAScripts> $relofil2.PhysicalFilename="E:\Data\MyDBTest_Data_SalesFileGrp
2.ndf"
PS C:\DBAScripts> $res.RelocateFiles.add($relofil2)
1
PS C:\DBAScripts> $relofil3.LogicalFilename="MyDBTest_Primary_Log"
PS C:\DBAScripts> $relofil3.PhysicalFilename="E:\Data\MyDBTest_Primary_Log2.ldf"

PS C:\DBAScripts> $res.RelocateFiles.add($relofil3)
2
PS C:\DBAScripts> $relofil4.LogicalFilename="MyDBTest_SalesFileGrp_Log"
PS C:\DBAScripts> $relofil4.PhysicalFilename="E:\Data\MyDBTest_SalesFileGrp_Log2
.ldf"
PS C:\DBAScripts> $res.RelocateFiles.add($relofil4)
3
PS C:\DBAScripts> $res.set_NoRecovery(0)
PS C:\DBAScripts> $res.SqlRestore($srv)
PS C:\DBAScripts> Write-Host "Restored the transaction log backup."
Restored the transaction log backup.
PS C:\DBAScripts>
```

Figure 13-44

Summary

This chapter illustrated connection methods using the SqlConnection class and SQL Server Management Objects (SMO). It also illustrated the various administrative functions such as creating a database, creating objects, getting server information and database information, object creation, and backup and restore using Windows PowerShell and SQL Server Management Objects. Although you can always use plain T-SQL for doing all the tasks mentioned in this chapter, when it comes to automation, SMO and the SQLConnection class always come in handy. The next chapter discusses various SQL Server and PowerShell standards used in the industry.

14

Building SQL Server Standards and PowerShell Coding Standards

Defining and documenting SQL Server's standards is very important for any organization. Standards are important because they improve database manageability, platform scalability, Transact-SQL readability, and database performance, in addition to making troubleshooting easier. This chapter deals with SQL Server standards in a shop. SQL Server is not just a RDBMS; it contains many features. Based on the environment and resource availability, the features that are supported in an organization should be defined. Although it is easy and useful to adopt Microsoft's recommended standards and best practices, depending on your environment and the features that your department is going to support, you also need to define your own standards.

The standards illustrated in this chapter are a compilation of different scenarios drawn from our personal experiences in various companies. If you are already following SQL Server standards in your company, you may not need to review this chapter. However, we recommend you to go through the Windows PowerShell standards and at least glance through this entire chapter. It will definitely give you more insight and help you improve your current standards.

This chapter covers the following topics:

- ❏ SQL Server standards
- ❏ SQL Server development standards
- ❏ SQL Server database design standards and best practices
- ❏ Data protection standards
- ❏ SQL Server production standards
- ❏ Windows PowerShell coding standards

SQL Server Standards

The scope of the SQL Server standards defined in this chapter cover SQL Server 2000, 2005, and 2008 databases and related systems. Although not all of the standards discussed in this chapter may apply to your organization completely, you can still use this chapter as a general guideline. Once your standards are defined, you can enforce them by regular auditing, or policies, as you will see in Chapter 20.

SQL Server Development Standards

SQL Server development standards establish the programming standards for SQL Server development. Various components are involved when developing or programming in the SQL Server environment. These development standards help to improve T-SQL readability, troubleshooting, and performance.

Naming Conventions

A clear and consistent naming convention related to naming any element of the database is a vital part of any development standards. Just by reading the name of a database or an object, you should be able to tell its character and function.

Databases

Databases should be named to identify the application. Database names should not include versions or environment information or any other variables that may change over time and become meaningless. For example, do not name a database `VisualReporting_PROD`, `VisualReporting_test`. The naming convention should reflect the application name — for example, `RiskReporting`.

Tables

Tables should be named to identify the entities they represent, and be placed in the appropriate schema. Don't include spaces within object names, as square brackets or quotation marks will be needed when referring to the object. Similar to databases, you should use a descriptive application name such as `HumanResources.Employee`, `Production.Product`.

Views

View names should be descriptive and prefixed with a "v." A view cannot be named identically to a table, as they reside in the same namespace. A view should be placed in the appropriate schema.

Views do not always represent a single entity. A view can be a combination of two or more tables based on a join condition. When possible, combine the names of the base tables. For example, if you have a view combining two tables `Employee` and `Department` in the `HumanResources` schema, name the view `vEmployeeDepartment` and placed it in the `HumanResources` schema.

Views can summarize data from existing base tables in the form of reports. For example, you might use `vProductsSales` or `vOrderSummary`.

Stored Procedures

Stored procedure names should describe the work they do and be prefixed with `usp`. Use a verb abbreviation to describe the action name or tasks. Action names could be `Insert`, `Delete`, `Update`, `Select`, `Upsert`, or `Get`.

Never prefix your stored procedures with `sp_` unless you are storing the procedure in the `master` database. If you call a stored procedure prefixed with `sp_`, SQL Server always looks for this procedure in the `master` database. Only after checking in the master database (if not found) does it search the current database.

For example, you could name a stored procedure `uspInsertCustomer`, `uspUpsertEmployeeDetails`.

In Chapter 20, you will see an exemplary policy "Stored Procedure Naming Convention" that enforces the stored procedure naming convention.

User-Defined Functions

In Microsoft SQL Server, user-defined functions (UDFs) are similar to stored procedures, except that UDFs can be used in `SELECT` statements. Therefore, the naming conventions discussed in the preceding section for stored procedures apply to UDFs as well. UDFs should be prefixed with `ufn`. The only actions that apply here are `Select` and `Get`. For example, a user-defined function can be named something like `ufnGetCustomerAddress`.

Triggers

Use the `dml` or `ddl` prefix to specify the trigger type.

For DML triggers, use actions to specify the type of T-SQL events that cause the DML trigger to fire. Incorporate the table or view name in the trigger name to indicate the table or view on which the DML trigger is executed. Combine the actions as necessary to reflect the activity against the table.

For DDL triggers, append the server or database event that causes the trigger to fire. Microsoft SQL Server allows more than one trigger per action per table, but this is not recommended because it becomes too hard to manage and is very difficult to debug.

Examples of acceptable trigger names might be `dmlInsertEmployeeDetails` and `ddlCreateTable`.

Indexes

Indexes are dependent on the underlying base tables or views, so it makes sense to include the name of the table and the column(s) on which it is built in the index name. The prefix of `IX_` is used for nonprimary indexes. If the index is a unique index, then prefix it with `UIX_`. For a clustered index, use the prefix `CIX_`; and for a unique clustered index, use the prefix `UCIX_`.

For example, an index name might be defined as `IX_Address_AddressLine1_AddressLine2_City _StateProvinceID_PostalCode`.

Columns

Columns are attributes of an entity — that is, columns describe the properties of an entity. Therefore, column names should be meaningful and natural. For example, useful column names could be defined as `ProductID`, `ProductName`, `FirstName`, and `LastName`.

User-Defined Data Types

Using CamelCase (also known as Hungarian Notation) and the prefix `udt`, name user-defined data types to describe the attribute of the column. User-defined data types are used to maintain consistency of data types across different tables for the same attribute. For example, a user-defined data types could be defined as udtCustomerID.

Primary Keys

A primary key should be prefixed by PK_ and followed by the table name and the primary column names, such as PK_Customer_CustomerID.

Foreign Keys

Foreign keys should be prefixed by FK_ and followed with the table name and the parent table name (referenced table name), and the referenced column name.

For performance reasons, an index must be created on the columns(s) that match the foreign key. Follow the index-naming standards during the creation of this index. An example might be FK_Product_ProductSubcategory_ProductSubcategoryID.

Default and Check Constraints

Use the DF_ and CK_ prefixes, respectively, for Default and Check constraints, followed by the table name and the column name on which the constraint is enforced (e.g., DF_Order_OrderDate, CK_Product_ProductNumber).

Variables

A variable name should describe what it represents. For variables that store the contents of columns, you should use the same naming convention that you use for column names (e.g., @LastName, @databaseID).

Roles

A role name should be made up of the application name it is used for and the function it performs. Standard role names would include the following: dev, online, batch, report. Use PascalCase. For example, assume "Pluto" is the application name. "Dev" stands for developers, so the role for the developers that work on the Pluto application is PlutoDev.

General Rules

When creating a naming convention, keep the following general rules in mind:

- ❏ Keep it as simple as possible.
- ❏ Use mixed case names to be clear. When you use mixed case names, be consistent with case throughout the code on case-sensitive SQL Servers.
- ❏ Do not use spaces within the name of database objects, as spaces confuse front-end data access tools and applications. Use underscores instead.
- ❏ Be sure not to use any reserved words when naming your database objects, as that can lead to some unpredictable results. To get a list of reserved words for Microsoft SQL Server, search Books Online for "Reserved keywords."

Stored Procedure Standards

When developers are ready to create their stored procedures, the DBA should take the time to review their code and ensure that it follows documented standards, including proper formatting, good usage, and good design. If problems are identified, the DBA must notify the developers, explaining the need for the change. This provides an opportunity to review and optimize the code before it causes a production problem. The following sections offer some guidelines on creating stored procedures.

Keep Them Small

Keep stored procedures as small as possible. If necessary, create several small procedures that are called from one "driver" procedure.

When calling a stored procedure from your application, it is important that you call it using its fully qualified name, such as `exec database_name.dbo.myProcedure` instead of `exec myProcedure`.

Using fully qualified names helps to eliminate any potential confusion about which stored procedure you want to run, which prevents bugs and other potential problems. More important, doing so enables SQL Server to access the stored procedure's execution plan more directly, which in turn speeds up the performance of the stored procedure.

"DBO" As Object Owner

In SQL Server 2000, the schema was synonymous with the owner. Unless unavoidable, all objects within a database should be owned by dbo; if they are not, SQL Server must perform name resolution on the objects if the object names are the same but the owners are different. When this happens, SQL Server cannot use a stored procedure using the existing execution plan. Instead, it has to recompile and execute the procedure.

Beginning with SQL Server 2005, the behavior of schemas changed. Schemas are no longer equivalent to database users. Each user has a default schema, which can be set and changed. Therefore, defining all objects in the dbo schema is not always appropriate. Because any given database user might belong to a different default schema, it's a good idea to always refer to tables, views, stored procedures, and so on by schema name.

Use Comments Generously

Using comments helps others understand the code clearly, and it won't affect performance. Changes to database objects made by the developer should be logged with comments. The following listing shows an example:

```
-------------------------------------------------------------------------------
--Object Name:     uspGetPatientRate
--Author:          MAK & Yan
--Created Dt:
--Function:        Provide information for Rate info Screen
--*************************************************************
--        Modification Log
--*************************************************************
```

```
--Modified by:  Modified Date:   Modification:
--MAK           Dec-27-2008      4. Add DefaultCharge indicator in charge information
--                               3. Update obsolete information in charge
                                     information, default to 100
--Yan           Nov-20-2008      2. Add PatientStatusFlag indicator in rate
                                     information to
--                               differentiate physical and virtual rate info
--MAK           Mar-03-2007      1. Change virtual_flag to VirtualFlag
--*********************************************************************
```

Using comments to provide a history of changes over time can help any developers who work with your code later to understand what was changed and why.

Select *

Do not use SELECT * in your queries. Always write the required column names after the SELECT, INSERT, and UPDATE statements, such as SELECT CustomerID, CustomerName, and City. This technique results in less disk I/O and hence better performance.

Cursors

Avoid cursors as much as possible. Cursors can be avoided by using SELECT statements in many cases. Try to use a WHILE loop instead. Testing has shown that a WHILE loop is always faster than a cursor. For a WHILE loop to replace a cursor, you need a column (primary key or unique key) to identify each row uniquely. Generally, cursors use a lot of resources and reduce performance. If you have to use a cursor, then make sure you close it and DEALLOCATE it when you are finished with it. Deallocation is required to free up the SQL Server resources used by the cursor.

Each time you fetch a row from a cursor, it results in a network round-trip, whereas a normal SELECT query makes only one round-trip regardless of the size of the resultset. Cursors require more resources and temporary storage (more I/O operations). Alternatives include using SET-based operations or WHILE loops.

Temporary Tables

Avoid the use of temporary tables while processing data. Creating a temporary table means more disk I/O. Moreover, when SQL Server is shut down, any data in tempdb is deleted permanently. For this reason, don't store any application-specific data in the tempdb database. Leave it exclusively for use by SQL Server. Tempdb should only be thought of as transitional storage space. Because tempdb has a limited size, care must be taken that when you do use it, it doesn't become filled with records in tables from rogue procedures that indefinitely create tables with too many records. If this were to happen, not only would your process stop working, but the entire server could stop functioning, affecting everyone on that server.

Things to Avoid

Avoid wildcard characters at the beginning of a word when using the LIKE keyword. This results in an index scan, which defeats the purpose of an index.

Avoid searching with not equal operators (<> and NOT). This results in an index scan, which could potentially cause performance problems.

Prefix table names with owner names. This improves readability and avoids confusion. BOL even states that qualifying table names with owner names helps in reuse of execution plans.

Things to Use

Use SET NOCOUNT ON. This improves the performance of stored procedures by reducing network traffic by suppressing messages like "(1 row(s) affected)." Use this at the beginning of SQL batches, stored procedures, and triggers in production environments.

Use foreign key and check constraints. Perform all your referential integrity checks and data validations using constraints (either foreign key or check constraints). These constraints are faster than triggers. Use triggers only for auditing, custom tasks and validations that cannot be performed using these constraints.

Front-end applications should be deadlock-intelligent. They should be able to resubmit the transaction in case the previous transaction fails with error 1205, but not infinitely or the application could loop.

Check @@ERROR

Always check the global variable @@ERROR immediately after executing a data manipulation statement such as INSERT, UPDATE, or DELETE. Alternately, try to use TRY . . . CATCH wherever possible. This way, you can roll back the transaction in case of an error (@@ERROR will be greater than 0 in the case of an error). By default, SQL Server will not roll back all the previous changes within a transaction if a particular statement fails. If you SET XACT_ABORT ON at execute or run time, this behavior is changed. If you are on SQL Server 2005 or later, try to use TRY . . . CATCH.

- ❑ TRY block: The TRY block contains the instructions that might cause an exception.

- ❑ CATCH block: If an exception occurs from one of the statements in the TRY block, then control is branched to the CATCH block, where the exception can be handled, logged, and so on.

Use SQL Server Date Data Types

Always use SQL Server date and datetime data types for storing dates. This ensures that years are stored in a four-digit format.

DML Statements

Do not use DML statements within applications. Front-end apps should not query/manipulate data directly using DML statements. Create stored procedures, and the apps should access these stored procedures. This helps execute plan caching and keeps the data access clean and consistent across all the modules of your application. It also avoids SQL injection.

ANSI-Standard Join Clauses

The more readable ANSI-standard join clauses should be used instead of the old-style joins. With the ANSI joins, the WHERE clause is used only for filtering data. In the older-style joins, the WHERE clause handles both the join condition and filtering data. The preferred ANSI-standard join is as follows:

```
select Orders.OrderID,
Employees.LastName,
Customers.CompanyName,
Orders.ShipCity
from    Orders inner join Employees
on      Orders.employeeID = Employees.EmployeeID
inner   join Customers
on      Orders.customerID = Customers.CustomerID
where   Orders.ShipCity > 'T';
```

This is the old-style join:

```
select Orders.OrderID,
Employees.LastName,
Customers.CompanyName,
Orders.ShipCity
from    Orders, Employees, Customers
where   Orders.ShipCity > 'T'
and     Orders.EmployeeID  = Employees.EmployeeID
and     Orders.CustomerID = Customers.CustomerID;
```

Deprecated Features

Try to avoid any features or objects that will be deprecated in the future. When a new SQL Server version is released, make sure you do not continue using any deprecated features.

Database Design Standards and Best Practices

In a table that conforms to the third normal form, no column can depend on a non-key column. However, denormalize your database as needed for specific performance reasons. For reporting purposes, a denormalized database design is more preferable than a normalized database design. In the OLAP environment, denormalization works better.

User-Defined Tables

System databases should not contain user-defined tables. There are exceptional cases for which you have to create a stored procedure and table in master databases — for example, using a startup procedure.

Logs

If you have physically separate disk systems, place the logs on a separate disk system from the data. This is for two reasons: performance and protection. On a dedicated disk, access to the transaction log is faster because it doesn't have to contend with database reads/writes. Placing the transaction log contents on a dedicated disk also enhances the data protection plan. Always try to use a SAN drive for the data and the log if possible.

Split tempdb

Increase the number of `tempdb` data files to be at least equal to the number of processors assigned for SQL Server, in order to reduce `tempdb` contention. In addition, create files of equal size.

Databases

Separate production databases and development (test) databases. Production and nonproduction databases should not reside on the same physical server. This not only separates the two functions, production and test, but also prevents anyone from consuming server resources that are needed for production.

Security and Roles

Include security needs during design. Consider encrypting sensitive pieces of data such as credit card numbers and social security numbers.

Use the fixed server roles and create custom database roles if needed. Avoid assigning individual users special permissions. Create custom database roles that suit your particular situation, and assign users to the appropriate roles.

Auto Create and Auto Update

At the database level, keep Auto Create Statistics on and Auto Update Statistics on. The SQL Server Query Optimizer has the ability to use statistics on columns that are not indexed in order to create more optimal execution plans. Sometimes it is more efficient to use column statistics instead of an index to optimize query performance. If you notice performance problems with updating a specific index with the `STATISTICS_NORECOMPUTE` option, then turn off Auto Update at the index level, not at the database level.

Size

Properly size the database and log files. Pre-size the data file, transaction log file, and the `tempdb` database to avoid or minimize file expansions during operations. Properly size the `mdf` and `ldf` default setting in the `model` database, as every time SQL Server is restarted, the old `tempdb` database is deleted and a new one is created based on the configuration setting in the `model` database. Certain options, such as database growth, should be automatic. Again, in exceptional cases you do not want to turn on auto growth. It is not applicable for Very Large Databases (VLDB).

Auto Shrink and Auto Close

Keep the `Auto_Shrink` and `Auto_Close` options off. These are two options you will never want to enable on a production database.

When `Auto_Close` is set to on, the database is shut down automatically when no one connects to it, and its resources are freed. When a user tries to use the database again, the database regains resources and reopens. Frequent closing and reopening of the database causes delays for users. The overhead of closing and reopening the database can be significant, even affecting performance.

When `Auto_Shrink` is set to on, SQL Server will automatically shrink a database file when more than 25 percent of the space in the database file is unused. Database shrinking hogs CPU. If the size of the file is big, shrinking could take minutes or even hours. Users will notice a sudden performance hit while the shrinking is in progress.

In Chapter 20, we will show you an exemplary policy, `Database Auto Options Disabled`, to enforce this standard.

Design and Performance

While designing your database, design it keeping performance in mind. You cannot really tune performance when your database is in production, as it involves rebuilding tables/indexes, rewriting queries, and so on. The time to tune is during design and development. Use the graphical execution plan in Query Analyzer or the `SHOWPLAN_TEXT` or `SHOWPLAN_ALL` commands to analyze queries.

Ensure that queries do "index seek" instead of "index scan" or "table scan." Avoid "hash join" and "bookmark lookup," as they are expensive operations. The hash join will be used if there are no adequate indexes on the joined columns. Building the hash tables can be very expensive. Bookmark lookups are a mechanism to navigate from a non-clustered index row to the actual data row in the base table (clustered index) in order to fetch all the required columns. Make sure appropriate indexes are created to run queries efficiently.

Store Unstructured Data

In SQL Server 2000, files and images should not be stored as BLOBs in database tables. Storing unstructured data, such as PDFs, Word documents, Project Plan MPPs, Power Point PPTs, and image files, as `TEXT` or `IMAGE` data types in a SQL Server table risks performance problems and should be avoided. An alternative is to use the table to store the locations or links to the physical files, return this information to the application, and then have the application retrieve the file. Storing XML documents as BLOBs (i.e., `TEXT` or `NTEXT`) may be acceptable, but requires review and approval by the data architect. It may be acceptable to store an XML document if the purpose is to use the XML capabilities of SQL Server.

Starting from SQL Server 2005, use the `varbinary(max)` data type to store unstructured data. In SQL Server 2008, if the average of the BLOB data is more than 1MB, enable the `FILESTREAM` option and stream access the data with Win32 APIs.

More Performance Guidelines

The following guidelines are important to adhere to as well:

❑   SQL Server should be installed on its own database server to avoid contention with applications.

❑   Run DBCC commands during off-peak hours.

❑   Keep transactions as short as possible.

❑   Touch as little data as possible during a transaction.

❑   Never wait for user input in the middle of a transaction. This eliminates the possibility of "enlisting" in an ADO or COM+ transaction.

❑ Never run a transaction in SQL server directly. Run everything from application unless you are a DBA. Use transactions only for administrative work in SQL Server directly.

❑ Access tables in the same order in stored procedures, triggers, and development code consistently to avoid deadlocks.

Data Protection Standards and Best Practices

The following guidelines outline best practices for data protection standards:

❑ Create a separate maintenance plan for backing up the system databases. Do not mix user database backups with system database backups.

❑ It is not necessary to backup the `tempdb` because it is rebuilt each time SQL Server starts.

❑ Keep a script of the functional database schema in a secure location on the network. This comes in handy if you need to know the structure of the database in production or you need to recover a database that does not have any backup left (although you should not allow yourself to be in such a situation).

❑ Use Windows Authentication, rather than SQL Server Authentication.

❑ Windows Authentication provides additional security and is recommended.

❑ Because of the security risk, do not use the SQL Server extended stored procedure `xp_cmdshell`.

Backup Policy

Typically, a full database backup should be scheduled for every database at 11:00 PM, and transactional log backup should be scheduled for every 15 minutes. For companies that are not active on weekends, for a VLDB, full backup should be scheduled every Saturday at 11:00 PM, and a differential backup should be scheduled for every night at 11:00 PM except on Saturday and Sunday. Transactional log backup should be scheduled for every 15 minutes.

Tape backup of all the local backups should also be scheduled. Though this is not a DBA's job, you should keep track of the tape backups and ensure that database backups are going to the tapes.

SQL Server Production Standards

Follow your company's change management process. Do not implement a code onto the production server just because you have permission. Remember Murphy's law: "*If anything can go wrong, it will.*"

High Availability and Disaster Recovery

In the production environment, wherever possible, try to have a cluster server. If that's not possible, at least attach the SAN drive for data files like .mdf and .ndf, and log files like .ldf.

If you do not have a SAN replication infrastructure, try to have a DR environment with log shipping or database mirroring, or third-party replication, etc.

The Administration Database

Every SQL Server instance should have an *admin* database. The admin database holds objects, procedures, and functions related to SQL Server administration. For example, this could be a stored procedure to get the databases that have not been backed up for 24 hours, a stored procedure to audit scheduled jobs, a table to consolidate backup or job history, or a table to hold server performance data. You will see the use of the admin database in Chapters 17 and 19.

The Scratch Database

Every SQL server instance should also have a *scratch* database, which is predominantly used for temporary administrative purposes, such as storing a table before implementing a major change on a table; copying the existing copy of a stored procedure before implementing changes to a production database; or restoring a database from a historical tape backup to compare data with a current production database, and so on.

Centralized Inventory Server

At least one *centralized inventory server* for SQL Server inventory tracking is necessary to store the information about all the SQL Server hosts and servers in your environment. Information regarding administration and monitoring from all the SQL Servers is also stored in this database. The inventory server should be reside on a cluster and be replicated across regions to ensure the highest availability. Chapter 15 discusses how to build an inventory database over an existing or new environment. Following Chapter 15, we will design monitoring solutions based on the inventory.

Database File Location and RAID

Depending on your budget, your drives should have a RAID configuration such as RAID 1 + 0 or RAID 1 for the data file drive, RAID 1 + 0 or RAID 5 for the log file drive, and RAID 1 + 0 or RAID 5 for the tempdb drive.

When creating a database, make sure data files such as .mdf, .ndf, the log file .ldf, and tempdb are created on separate drives.

Segregation

Try to keep different features of SQL Server on different host machines. Do not put both the OLTP environment (Database Engine) and the OLAP environment (SSAS) on the same host. Similarly, do not put both the OLTP environment and the DSS environment (SSRS) on the same host.

Features

Do not install features that are not going to be used on the production boxes. For example, if you are not going to use Integration Services on a particular production box, do not install it.

PowerShell Coding Standard

Windows PowerShell is extremely versatile. When you have something more flexible, it calls for standard. You don't want DBAs or system engineers writing duplicate code and using different styles of writing, which leads to a lack of uniformity and more confusion, resulting in wasted resources. Use the following guidelines to create standards:

❑ **Version**: Decide which Windows PowerShell version your company is going to support. Avoid using CTP versions in production.

❑ **Install**: Include Windows PowerShell either as a part of your Windows build or include it as a post-Windows install task.

❑ **PowerShell title**: Try to stick with one title in the PowerShell window. Use something standard such as the following:

```
$host.ui.RawUI.WindowTitle = "Windows PowerShell"
```

❑ **PowerShell prompt**: Decide on a prompt for Windows PowerShell in your environment — something that is distinguishable, such as `PowerPC PS C:\>`.

❑ **Script naming convention**: Use the same verb-noun format used by the Windows PowerShell cmdlets, such as `Backup-DataBase.ps1` or `Ping-Host.ps1`.

Default Parameters

Make sure every script has the minimum following three parameters:

❑ `-Debug`: Runs the script in debug mode

❑ `-Help`: Shows the help file

❑ `-Mail`: E-mails the results of the script to the appropriate contacts, such as the DBA group or the business units

Log File

Any log files created by the PowerShell script should have a naming convention, such as `HostName_ServerName_ScriptName_yyyymmdd_hhmmss.log`.

Log Format

Inside the log file, the format of the log should be as follows:

```
YYYY-MM-DD HH:MM:SS Error/Information/Warning Message
```

The log file should be written only in Unicode. Do not write a log file in ASCII format. Keep in mind that you may have servers worldwide.

Comments

Be generous when writing comments. Make sure you have a standard comment heading, such as the following:

```
# ==============================================================
#
# NAME: MonitorDeadlocks.ps1
#
# AUTHOR: Yan and MAK
# DATE   : 5/1/2008
#
# COMMENT: This script collects the information about threads and resources involved
    in deadlocks.
# ==============================================================
```

Display

When you display a message, make sure you follow a proper format. The following is an example:

```
YYYY-MM-DD HH:MM:SS error/Information/Warning Message
```

Variable Naming Convention

Variable names should be plain English and something related to your program's functionality. Do not, for example, name a variable $a, $marilynmonroe. Use proper casing for variable names, and declare explicitly the data type for each variable — for example, [string] $MyHost. If necessary, suffix variables with comments, as shown in the following example:

```
[string] $Squotes = "'" # -- Set variable for embedded Single Quote.
[string] $Dquotes = '"' # -- Set variable for embedded Double Quote.
```

Try to define and use more functions rather than call a script from another script if the code is reusable.

Exception Handling

Try to set the following variable globally on the top of the script and handle all the exceptions within the script after major cmdlets:

```
$erroractionpreference="SilentlyContinue"
```

There are three ways you could handle exceptions. Based on the requirements, you could use one of the following methods:

Method 1:

```
Using Errvariable named parameter and ErrorAction named parameter. Example

$AFSwmi=get-wmiobject -class Win32_service -computername $hostname -Errorvariable
    ERR -ErrorAction Silentlycontinue
```

```
if ($ERR)
{
Write-Msg -errnumber 2 -message "Can't connect to the remote computer $hostname"
Write-Msg -errnumber 2 -message $ERROR[0]
}
else
.....
```

Method 2:

Using Test-Path cmdlet before executing external commands , executables and batch files etc.

Example

```
$Result=Test-Path -Path "C:\mybatch.bat"
if($Result)
{
$asl= C:\mybatch.bat param1 param2
$asl
}
else
{
Write-Msg -ErrNumber 2 -Message "MyBatch.bat not found in C:\"
}
```

Method 3:

Using Trap command.

```
trap [Exception] {
write-Msg -ErrNumber 2 -Message $_.Exception.GetType().FullName;
write-Msg -ErrNumber 2 -Message $_.Exception.Message;
$ERR=1
continue;
}
$domain = "MyDomain"
$computer = [ADSI]("WinNT://" + $Hostname + ",computer")
if (-not $ERR)
{ ..
```

Summary

As mentioned at the beginning of this chapter, defining standards and specifying the standards in a document is very important for any organization. It helps avoid rework and structures the efforts of both the developer and the database administrator. Feel free to use this chapter as the baseline for your standards and to improve upon it.

This chapter illustrated various SQL Server standards for various aspects of SQL Server and Power-Shell: development; database design, including best practices; data protection; production; and Windows PowerShell coding.

15

Building SQL Server Inventory

In a complex enterprise environment, it can be a daunting task to track and manage hundreds or even thousands of SQL Server hosts and instances. Business units inside the company constantly ask for new instances to be built for new projects, or for migration of existing projects. SQL Server instances reside on different hosts with different operating systems and hardware. It is critical to have an inventory that includes every instance in the environment, and use it to keep up with changes on every instance. This inventory can also be used for auditing, capacity planning, and budget planning.

This chapter presents an inventory tracking solution tailored for SQL Server. The topics discussed include the following:

- ❑ SQL Server inventory

- ❑ Hosts

- ❑ Clusters

- ❑ ClusterNodes table

- ❑ Servers

- ❑ Databases

- ❑ Supplementary tables

SQL Server Inventory

The inventory is stored in a centralized SQL Server database. The database should be set up preferably on a failover cluster instance with at least two nodes. If the company has servers in different regions — say, North America (NA), Europe (EU), and Asia (AS), then each region should have a replicated copy of the centralized database to reduce network bandwidth for reads across continents, and increase redundancy. Peer-to-peer replication introduced in SQL Server 2005 is very suitable in this scenario.

Because we are just demonstrating how to set up an inventory, in our simplified example the inventory database resides on the default instance on a standalone host POWERPC. We store the data and log file under D:\Microsoft SQL Server\MSSQL10.MSSQLSERVER\MSSQL\DATA. We'll first create the inventory database and call it SQL_Inventory. Here is the script, CreateSQL_Inventory.sql:

```
CREATE DATABASE [SQL_Inventory] ON
(NAME = N'SQL_Inventory',
FILENAME = N'D:\Microsoft SQL
Server\MSSQL10.MSSQLSERVER\MSSQL\DATA\SQL_Inventory.mdf',
SIZE = 1024MB , MAXSIZE = UNLIMITED, FILEGROWTH = 1024MB )
LOG ON
(NAME = N'SQL_Inventory_log',
FILENAME = N'D:\Microsoft SQL
Server\MSSQL10.MSSQLSERVER\MSSQL\DATA\SQL_Inventory_log.LDF',
SIZE = 512MB , MAXSIZE = UNLIMITED, FILEGROWTH = 10%)
GO
```

When you create your own inventory database, please make sure you change the path to work for your environment.

We also define two variables, $inventoryServer and $inventoryDatabase, which store the inventory database information in the library file dbaLib.ps1 under C:\DBAScripts. We can just refer to the two variables later when connecting with the inventory database.

```
####################################################
# Define inventory server and database
####################################################
[String] $inventoryServer="POWERPC,1433"
[String] $inventoryDatabase="SQL_Inventory"
```

In our example environment, we have five machines on which SQL Server instances have been installed:

1. POWERPC: Hosts a default instance MSSQLSERVER and INSTANCE1

2. POWERSERVER3: Hosts a default instance MSSQLSERVER

3. DEMOPC: Hosts a default instance MSSQLSERVER and named instance CH0DE1

4. NODE1: One of the two nodes of the Windows Cluster PowerCluster. The Windows cluster hosts a default failover cluster instance SQL2008CLUSTER.

5. NODE2: One of the two nodes of the Windows Cluster PowerCluster. The Windows cluster hosts a default failover cluster instance SQL2008CLUSTER.

Considering the complexity of the enterprise environment, the scripts shown in this chapter can be run in an environment with different Windows operating systems, including Windows 2000 Server, Windows

Server 2003, Windows Vista and Windows Server 2008, and different SQL Server products, including SQL Server 2000, 2005, and 2008.

In the next chapter, we will show you how we installed the named instance INSTANCE1 on POWERPC and the failover cluster default instance SQLCLUSTER2008, and how we used the scripts in this chapter to record the host and server information before and after the installations.

The inventory database contains the following primary tables:

- ❑ **Hosts**: Stores information about SQL Server hosts
- ❑ **Clusters**: Stores information about SQL Server clusters
- ❑ **ClusterNodes**: Stores information about nodes in each SQL Server cluster
- ❑ **Servers**: Stores information about SQL Server instances
- ❑ **ServerDatabases**: Stores information about each database on each SQL Server

Hosts

The Hosts table contains information about all the SQL server hosts. The schema of the Hosts table is described in Table 15-1.

Table 15-1: Hosts Table Schema

Column	DataType	Description
hostID	int identity(1000,1)	ID of the host; and the primary key
hostName	varchar(128)	Name of the SQL Server host
region	char(2)	Region in which the SQL Server host is located (e.g., NA, EU, and AS)
location	char(2)	Code of the city in which the SQL host is located (e.g., NY for New York, CH for Chicago)
description	varchar(500)	Description of purposes of the SQL Server host
primaryBU	varchar(128)	Primary business unit that owns the host
timeZone	varchar(128)	Standard time zone of the host
enableDaylightSavingsTime	bit	Indicates if daylight saving time (DST) is enabled on the host
domain	varchar(128)	Domain of the host

Continued

Table 15-1: Hosts Table Schema *(continued)*

Column	DataType	Description
manufacturer	varchar(128)	Name of the host's computer manufacturer (e.g. Dell, HP)
model	varchar(128)	Product name that the manufacturer gives to the host
systemType	varchar(128)	System running on the Windows-based computer (e.g., X86-based PC, 64-bit Intel PC)
systemStartupOptions	varchar(128)	List of the options for starting up the computer system running Windows
numberOfProcessors	tinyint	Number of logical processors available on the computer
numberOfLogicalProcessors	tinyint	Number of physical processors available on the computer
totalPhysicalMemory	bigint	Total size of physical memory
countryCode	varchar(128)	Country code that the host uses
lastBootUpTime	smalldatetime	Date and time the host was last restarted
locale	varchar(128)	Language identifier used by the host
OS	varchar(128)	Operating system used by the host
version	varchar(128)	Version number of the operating system
servicePackMajorVersion	varchar(10)	Major version number of the service pack of the OS installed on the host
servicePackMinorVersion	varchar(10)	Minor version number of the service pack of the OS installed on the host
buildNumber	varchar(20)	Build number of an operating system
installDate	smalldatetime	When the host was first built or rebuilt
totalVisibleMemorySize	bigint	Number, in kilobytes, of physical memory available to the operating system. This value does not necessarily indicate the true amount of physical memory, but what is reported to the operating system as available to it.

Continued

Table 15-1: Hosts Table Schema *(continued)*

Column	DataType	Description
totalVirtualMemorySize	bigint	Number, in kilobytes, of virtual memory
pagingFileSize	bigint	Total number of kilobytes that can be stored in the operating system paging files — 0 (zero) indicates that there are no paging files.
IP1	varchar(128)	IP Address 1 used by the host
IP2	varchar(128)	IP Address 2 used by the host
IP3	varchar(128)	IP Address 3 used by the host
IP4	varchar(128)	IP Address 4 used by the host
IP5	varchar(128)	IP Address 5 used by the host
IP6	varchar(128)	IP Address 6 used by the host
createDate	smalldatetime	Date and time the host record was created
updateDate	smalldatetime	Date and time the host record was last updated

Here is a SQL script, CreateHosts.sql, to create the Hosts table:

```
USE [SQL_Inventory]
GO
IF EXISTS (SELECT * FROM sys.objects WHERE object_id = OBJECT_ID(N'[dbo].[Hosts]')
AND type in (N'U'))
DROP TABLE [dbo].[Hosts]
GO
CREATE TABLE [dbo].[Hosts](
[hostID] [int] IDENTITY(1000,1) NOT NULL CONSTRAINT PK_hostID PRIMARY KEY CLUSTERED,
[hostName] [varchar](128) NOT NULL CONSTRAINT IX_hostName UNIQUE,
[region] [char](2) NOT NULL,
[location] [char](2) NOT NULL,
[description] [varchar](500) NULL,
[primaryBU] [varchar](128) NOT NULL,
[timeZone] [varchar](128) NULL,
[enableDaylightSavingsTime] [bit] NULL,
[domain] [varchar](128) NULL,
[manufacturer] [varchar](128) NULL,
[model] [varchar](128) NULL,
[systemType] [varchar](128) NULL,
[systemStartupOptions] [varchar](128) NULL,
[numberOfProcessors] [tinyint] NULL,
[numberOfLogicalProcessors] [tinyint] NULL,
[totalPhysicalMemory] [bigint] NULL,
```

```
[countryCode] [varchar](128) NULL,
[lastBootUpTime] [smalldatetime] NULL,
[locale] [varchar](128) NULL,
[OS] [varchar](128) NULL,
[version] [varchar](128) NULL,
[servicePackMajorVersion] [varchar](10) NULL,
[servicePackMinorVersion] [varchar](10) NULL,
[buildNumber] [varchar](20) NULL,
[installDate] [datetime] NULL,
[totalVisibleMemorySize] [bigint] NULL,
[totalVirtualMemorySize] [bigint] NULL,
[pagingFileSize] [bigint] NULL,
[IP1] [varchar](128) NULL,
[IP2] [varchar](128) NULL,
[IP3] [varchar](128) NULL,
[IP4] [varchar](128) NULL,
[IP5] [varchar](128) NULL,
[IP6] [varchar](128) NULL,
[createDate] [smalldatetime] NOT NULL,
[updateDate] [smalldatetime] NOT NULL,
) ON [PRIMARY]
GO
```

We also need a stored procedure, uspUpsertHosts, to insert a host record when the host does not exist in the inventory, or update a host record when the host already exists. This stored procedure will be called later in the Upsert-Host.ps1 script to manage the Hosts table. The following script, uspUpsertHosts.sql, is used to create the stored procedure uspUpsertHosts:

```
SET ANSI_NULLS ON
GO
SET QUOTED_IDENTIFIER ON
GO
USE [SQL_Inventory]
GO
IF EXISTS (SELECT * FROM sys.objects WHERE object_id =
OBJECT_ID(N'[dbo].[uspUpsertHosts]') AND type in (N'P', N'PC'))
DROP PROCEDURE [DBO].[uspUpsertHosts]
GO
CREATE PROCEDURE [dbo].[uspUpsertHosts]
                @hostName    [varchar] (128),
                @region    [char] (2),
                @location    [char] (2),
                @description    [varchar] (500),
                @primaryBU    [varchar] (128),
                @timeZone    [varchar] (128),
                @enableDaylightSavingsTime    [bit],
                @domain    [varchar] (128),
                @manufacturer    [varchar] (128),
                @model    [varchar] (128),
                @systemType    [varchar] (128),
                @systemStartupOptions    [varchar] (128),
                @numberOfProcessors    [tinyint],
                @numberOfLogicalProcessors    [tinyint],
                @totalPhysicalMemory    [bigint],
                @countryCode    [varchar] (128),
```

```
                        @lastBootUpTime    [smalldatetime],
                        @locale   [varchar] (128),
                        @OS    [varchar] (128),
                        @version    [varchar] (128),
                        @servicePackMajorVersion    [varchar] (10),
                        @servicePackMinorVersion    [varchar] (10),
                        @buildNumber    [varchar] (20),
                        @installDate    [smalldatetime],
                        @totalVisibleMemorySize    [bigint],
                        @totalVirtualMemorySize    [bigint],
                        @pagingFileSize    [bigint],
                        @IP1    [varchar] (128),
                        @IP2    [varchar] (128),
                        @IP3    [varchar] (128),
                        @IP4    [varchar] (128),
                        @IP5    [varchar] (128),
                        @IP6    [varchar] (128)
AS
DECLARE @ERRORCODE [int], @ERRMSG [varchar] (128)

-- If the host doesn't exist in the Hosts table, then perform an insertion.
IF NOT EXISTS (SELECT hostID FROM dbo.Hosts WHERE hostName=@hostName)
    INSERT [dbo].[Hosts]
        ( hostName
        , region
        , location
        , description
        , primaryBU
        , timeZone
        , enableDaylightSavingsTime
        , domain
        , manufacturer
        , model
        , systemType
        , systemStartupOptions
        , numberOfProcessors
        , numberOfLogicalProcessors
        , totalPhysicalMemory
        , countryCode
        , lastBootUpTime
        , locale
        , OS
        , version
        , servicePackMajorVersion
        , servicePackMinorVersion
        , buildNumber
        , installDate
        , totalVisibleMemorySize
        , totalVirtualMemorySize
        , pagingFileSize
        , IP1
        , IP2
        , IP3
        , IP4
        , IP5
        , IP6
```

```
            , createDate
            , updateDate
            )
        VALUES(
          @hostName
            , @region
            , @location
            , @description
            , @primaryBU
            , @timeZone
            , @enableDaylightSavingsTime
            , @domain
            , @manufacturer
            , @model
            , @systemType
            , @systemStartupOptions
            , @numberOfProcessors
            , @numberOfLogicalProcessors
            , @totalPhysicalMemory
            , @countryCode
            , @lastBootUpTime
            , @locale
            , @OS
            , @version
            , @servicePackMajorVersion
            , @servicePackMinorVersion
            , @buildNumber
            , @installDate
            , @totalVisibleMemorySize
            , @totalVirtualMemorySize
            , @pagingFileSize
            , @IP1
            , @IP2
            , @IP3
            , @IP4
            , @IP5
            , @IP6
            , GETDATE()
            , GETDATE()
            )
-- If the host already exists in the Hosts table, then perform an update.
ELSE
UPDATE [dbo].[Hosts]
    SET [region] = @region
        ,[location] = @location
        ,[description] = @description
        ,[primaryBU] = @primaryBU
        ,[timeZone] = @timeZone
        ,[enableDaylightSavingsTime] = @enableDaylightSavingsTime
        ,[domain] = @domain
        ,[manufacturer] = @manufacturer
        ,[model] = @model
        ,[systemType] = @systemType
        ,[systemStartupOptions] = @systemStartupOptions
        ,[numberOfProcessors] = @numberOfProcessors
        ,[numberOfLogicalProcessors] = @numberOfLogicalProcessors
```

```
              ,[totalPhysicalMemory] = @totalPhysicalMemory
              ,[countryCode] = @countryCode
              ,[lastBootUpTime] = @lastBootUpTime
              ,[locale] = @locale
              ,[OS] = @OS
              ,[version] = @version
              ,[servicePackMajorVersion] = @servicePackMajorVersion
              ,[servicePackMinorVersion] = @servicePackMinorVersion
              ,[buildNumber] = @buildNumber
              ,[installDate] = @installDate
              ,[totalVisibleMemorySize] = @totalVisibleMemorySize
              ,[totalVirtualMemorySize] = @totalVirtualMemorySize
              ,[pagingFileSize] = @pagingFileSize
              ,[IP1] = @IP1
              ,[IP2] = @IP2
              ,[IP3] = @IP3
              ,[IP4] = @IP4
              ,[IP5] = @IP5
              ,[IP6] = @IP6
              ,[updateDate] = GETDATE()
    WHERE hostName=@hostName


    SET @ERRORCODE = @@ERROR
        IF @ERRORCODE <> 0
            BEGIN
                SET @ERRMSG = 'Insert failed - ' + OBJECT_NAME(@@PROCID)
                SET @ERRMSG = @ERRMSG + ' Error Code: ' + RTRIM(CONVERT(CHAR, @ERRORCODE))
                RAISERROR (@ERRMSG, 16, 1)
                 RETURN (-1)
            END
        ELSE
    RETURN (0)
    GO
```

After the `Hosts` table has been defined and the associated stored procedure has been created, we need a script, `Upsert-Host.ps1`, to insert a SQL Server host record into the inventory when we are about to install an SQL Server instance on it. This host can be a standalone host or a node in a SQL Server cluster. After the installation, if you run the script against the same host for the second time, the script will update the information for the existing host record. The usage of this script is as follows:

```
Upsert-Host -hostName <string[]> -region <string[]> -location <string[]> -primaryBU
<string[]> [-description <string[]>]
```

The complete script, which is available for download from the Wrox website for this book at www.wrox.com, is as follows:

```
# ================================================================
#
# NAME: Upsert-Host.ps1
#
# AUTHOR: Yan and MAK
# DATE  : 6/8/2008
#
# COMMENT: This script inserts a SQL Server host record into inventory.
```

```
#        If the host already exists, then this script updates the existing host record.
# Example: Upsert-Host.ps1 -hostName POWERPC -region NA -location CH -primaryBU STP -
description 'For STP application testing'
# =================================================================

#################################################################
# Initialize parameters
#################################################################
param (
        [switch]$help,
        [string]$hostName = {},  # Name of the host to add into inventory.
        [string]$region = {},  # Region of the SQL Server host. For example, NA, EU and
AS.
        [string]$location = {},  # Code of the city in which the SQL host locates. For
example, NY for New York, CH for Chicago.
        [string]$primaryBU = {},  # Primary BU that owns this host
        [string]$description = {}  # Brief description of the host. For example, which
application/project the host supports.
    )

function ConvertBoolToBit([Boolean] $expr)
{
        if ($expr) { return "1" }
        else { return "0" }
}


function ConvertOSTime([String] $osTime)
{
        return $osTime.SUBSTRING(0, 4) + "-" + $osTime.SUBSTRING(4, 2) + '-' +
$osTime.SUBSTRING(6, 2) + ' ' + '
                $osTime.SUBSTRING(8, 2) + ':' + $osTime.SUBSTRING(10, 2)
}


#################################################################
# Main Program
#################################################################
[String] $strUpsertSql=""

if ( $help ) {
        "Usage: UpSert-Host -hostName <string[]> -region <string[]> -location
<string[]> -primaryBU <string[]> [-description <string[]>]"
        exit 0
}

if ( $hostName.Length -eq 0 ) {
        "Please enter a host name."
        exit 1
}

if ( $region -notmatch '^NA|EU|AS$' ) {
        "The region is invalid. Please enter NA, EU or AS."
        exit 1
}
```

```
if ( $location -notmatch '^\w{2}$' ) {
        "The location is invalid. Please enter a 2-character city code."
        exit 1
}

if ( $primaryBU.Length -eq 0 ) {
        "Please enter a primary BU."
        exit 1
}

# Construct the insert statement
$strUpsertSql = $strUpsertSql + "exec uspUpsertHosts '$hostName', '$region',
'$location', '$description', '$primaryBU', "

# Get the time zone
$reg = [WMIClass]"\\$hostName\root\default.stdRegProv"
$HKEY_LOCAL_MACHINE = 2147483650
$strKeyPath = "SYSTEM\CurrentControlSet\Control\TimeZoneInformation"

if ($reg.GetStringValue($HKEY_LOCAL_MACHINE,$strKeyPath,"TimeZoneKeyName").svalue) {
        $strUpsertSql = $strUpsertSql + "'" + $reg.GetStringValue($HKEY_LOCAL_MACHINE,
            $strKeyPath,"TimeZoneKeyName").svalue  + "', "
}
else
{
        $strUpsertSql = $strUpsertSql + "'" + $reg.GetStringValue($HKEY_LOCAL_MACHINE,
            $strKeyPath,"StandardName").svalue  + "', "
}

$cs = Get-WMIObject -computerName $hostName -class Win32_ComputerSystem

# Get the setting of the daylight savings time
# This property is only available for Windows XP or later
if ($cs.EnableDaylightSavingsTime) {
        $enableDST=(ConvertBoolToBit $cs.EnableDaylightSavingsTime)
}
else
{
        $strKeyPath = "SYSTEM\CurrentControlSet\Control\TimeZoneInformation"
        switch ($reg.GetDWORDValue($HKEY_LOCAL_MACHINE,$strKeyPath,"
            DisableAutoDaylightTimeSet").uValue) {
        1          {$enableDST="0"}
        default         {$enableDST="1"}
        }
}

# Get the number of logical processors
# This property is only available for Windows XP or later
if ($cs.NumberOfLogicalProcessors) {
        $numLogicalProcessors=$cs.NumberOfLogicalProcessors
}
else
{
        $numLogicalProcessors=$cs.NumberOfProcessors
}
```

```
$strUpsertSql = $strUpsertSql + $enableDST + ", '" + $cs.Domain + "', '" '
+ $cs.Manufacturer.Trim() + "', '" + $cs.Model.Trim() + "', '" +
$cs.SystemType + "', '"'
+ $cs.SystemStartupOptions + "', " + $cs.NumberOfProcessors + "," '
+ $numLogicalProcessors + ", " + $cs.TotalPhysicalMemory + ", "

# Get the Operating System information, such as country code, last bootup time, etc.
$os = Get-WMIObject -computerName $hostName -class Win32_OperatingSystem

$strUpsertSql = $strUpsertSql + "'" + $os.CountryCode + "', '" + (ConvertOSTime
$os.LastBootUpTime) + "', '" + $os.Locale + "', '" '
+ $os.Name + "', '" + $os.Version + "', '" + $os.ServicePackMajorVersion + "', '" '
+ $os.ServicePackMinorVersion + "', '" + $os.BuildNumber + "', '" + (ConvertOSTime
$os.InstallDate) + "', " '
+ $os.TotalVisibleMemorySize + ", " '
+ $os.TotalVirtualMemorySize + ", " + $os.SizeStoredInPagingFiles

# Get the IP address information.
$IPArr= ( get-wmiobject -computername $hostname -class
"Win32_NetworkAdapterConfiguration" | where {$_.IpEnabled -match "True" } )

if ($IPArr.Length) {
        for ($i=0; $i -lt 6; $i++) {

                if ($i -lt $IPArr.Length) {
                        $strUpsertSql = $strUpsertSql + ", '" + $IPArr[$i].IPAddress[0]
+ "'"
                }
                else {
                        $strUpsertSql = $strUpsertSql + ", ''"
                }
        }
}
else {
        $strUpsertSql = $strUpsertSql + ", '" + $IPArr.IPAddress[0] + "', '', '',
'', '', ''"
}

$strUpsertSql=$strUpsertSql + ";"
$strUpsertSql

Invoke-Sqlcmd -Query $strUpsertSql -ServerInstance $inventoryServer -Database
$inventoryDatabase
```

We pass the host name, region, location, and primary BU (business unit) to the script. The description is optional. The script connects with the host to retrieve machine-specific information from the `Win32_ComputerSystem` and `Win32_OperatingSystem` classes, and stores the information in the `Hosts` table.

Figure 15-1 shows the result from running the following commands:

```
. C:\DBAScripts\dbaLib.ps1
# Add a DBA inventory host.
```

```
C:\DBAScripts\Upsert-Host.ps1 -hostName POWERPC -region NA -location CH -primaryBU
DBA -description 'DBA Inventory Server'

# Add a database host for testing Straight Through Processing (STP) application.
C:\DBAScripts\Upsert-Host.ps1 -hostName POWERSERVER3 -region NA -location NY
-primaryBU STP -description 'STP application test server'

# Add a database host for Global Wealth Management (GWM) unit.
C:\DBAScripts\Upsert-Host.ps1 -hostName DEMOPC -region NA -location CH -primaryBU
GWM -description 'Database Server for GWM'

# Add node 1 of a cluster for Investment Banking Division (IBD).
C:\DBAScripts\Upsert-Host.ps1 -hostName NODE1 -region NA -location CH -primaryBU
IBD -description 'IBD database cluster node 1'

# Add node 2 of a cluster for Investment Banking Division (IBD).
C:\DBAScripts\Upsert-Host.ps1 -hostName NODE2 -region NA -location CH -primaryBU
IBD -description 'IBD database cluster node 2'
```

Figure 15-1

After the insertions, the `Hosts` table appears as shown in Figure 15-2.

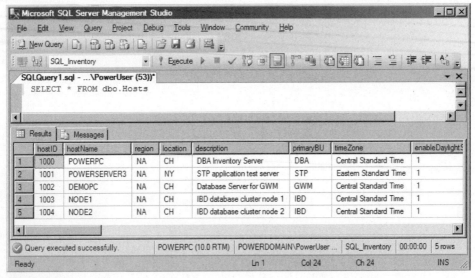

Figure 15-2

Clusters

The `Clusters` table contains information on all the SQL Server clusters. The schema of the `Clusters` table is shown in Table 15-2.

Table 15-2: Clusters Table Schema

Column	DataType	Description
ClusterID	int identity(1000,1)	ID of the SQL Server cluster
SQLClusterName	varchar(128)	Name of the SQL Server cluster
WindowsClusterName	varchar(128)	Name of the Windows cluster on which this SQL Server cluster runs
numberOfNodes	tinyint	Number of the nodes in the SQL Server cluster
clusteringMethod	varchar(128)	Method used for clustering, such as Veritas or MSCS
createDate	smalldatetime	Date and time the cluster record was created
updateDate	smalldatetime	Date and time the cluster record was last updated

Here is a script, `CreateClusters.sql`, to create the `Clusters` table:

```
USE [SQL_Inventory]
GO
IF EXISTS (SELECT * FROM sys.objects WHERE object_id = OBJECT_ID(N'[dbo].[Clusters]')
AND type in (N'U'))
DROP TABLE [dbo].[Clusters]
GO
CREATE TABLE [dbo].[Clusters](
clusterID Int identity(1000,1) NOT NULL CONSTRAINT PK_clusterID PRIMARY KEY
CLUSTERED,
SQLClusterName [varchar](128) NOT NULL,
WindowsClusterName Varchar(128) NOT NULL,
numberOfNodes Tinyint,
clusteringMethod Varchar(128),
createDate Smalldatetime NOT NULL,
updateDate Smalldatetime NOT NULL
)
GO
```

We also need a stored procedure, `uspUpsertClusters`, to insert a cluster record when the cluster does not exist in the inventory, or to update a cluster record when the cluster already exists. This stored procedure will be called later in the `Upsert-Cluster.ps1` script to manage the `Clusters` table. The following script, `uspUpsertClusters.sql`, is used to create the stored procedure `uspUpsertClusters`:

```
USE [SQL_Inventory]
GO
IF   EXISTS (SELECT * FROM sys.objects WHERE object_id =
OBJECT_ID(N'[dbo].[uspUpsertClusters]') AND type in (N'P', N'PC'))
DROP PROCEDURE [dbo].[uspUpsertClusters]
GO
CREATE PROCEDURE [DBO].[uspUpsertClusters]
                    @SQLClusterName    [varchar] (128),
                    @WindowsClusterName    [varchar] (128),
                    @numberOfNodes    [tinyint] ,
                    @clusteringMethod    [varchar] (128)
AS
DECLARE @ERRORCODE [int], @ERRMSG [varchar] (128)

-- If the cluster doesn't exist in the Clusters table, then perform an insertion.
IF EXISTS (SELECT ClusterID FROM [dbo].[Clusters] WHERE SQLClusterName=
@SQLClusterName)
BEGIN
        UPDATE [dbo].[Clusters]
        SET        [WindowsClusterName]=@WindowsClusterName,
              [numberOfNodes]=@numberOfNodes,
              [clusteringMethod]=@clusteringMethod,
              [updateDate]=getDate()
        WHERE SQLClusterName=@SQLClusterName
END
-- If the cluster already exists in the Clusters table, then perform an update.
ELSE
```

```
BEGIN
            INSERT [dbo].[Clusters]
        ( SQLClusterName
        , WindowsClusterName
        , numberOfNodes
        , clusteringMethod
        , createDate
        , updateDate
        )
    VALUES(
            @SQLClusterName
                , @WindowsClusterName
                , @numberOfNodes
                , @clusteringMethod
                , GETDATE()
                , GETDATE()
                )
END

SET @ERRORCODE = @@ERROR
IF @ERRORCODE <> 0
        BEGIN
            SET @ERRMSG = 'Upsert failed - ' + OBJECT_NAME(@@PROCID)
            SET @ERRMSG = @ERRMSG + ' Error Code: ' + RTRIM(CONVERT(CHAR, @ERRORCODE))
            RAISERROR (@ERRMSG, 16, 1)
            RETURN (-1)
        END
    GO
```

After the Clusters table has been defined and the associated stored procedure has been created, we need a script, Upsert-Cluster.ps1, to insert a SQL Server cluster name, its Windows cluster name, the number of nodes it has, and the clustering method it uses. If MSCS (Microsoft Clustering Service) is used, then the SQL Server cluster name is the name of a Network Name resource, and it is different from the Windows cluster name. If VCS (Veritas Cluster Server) is used, then the SQL Server cluster name is the name of an IPService resource, and it can be the same as the Windows cluster name. The Upsert-Cluster.ps1 script inserts a cluster record if the cluster doesn't exist, or updates the information for the existing cluster record if the cluster already exists in the Clusters table. The usage of this script is as follows:

```
Upsert-Cluster.ps1 -SQLClusterName <string[]> -WindowsClusterName <string[]> -
numberOfNodes <int16> -clusteringMethod <string[]>
```

The following complete script is available for download from the Wrox website for this book:

```
#================================================================
#
# NAME: Upsert-Cluster.ps1
#
# AUTHOR: Yan and MAK
# DATE  : 6/8/2008
#
# COMMENT: This script inserts a SQL Server cluster record into inventory.
```

```
# If the cluster already exists, then this script updates the existing cluster record.
# Example: Upsert-Cluster.ps1 -SQLClusterName SQL2008CLUSTER -WindowsClusterName
PowerCluster -numberOfNodes 2 -clusteringMethod MSCS
#=============================================================

##############################################################################
# Initialize parameters
##############################################################################
param (
        [switch]$help,
        [string]$SQLClusterName = {},   # IP Name of the SQL Server failover cluster.
        [string]$WindowsClusterName = {},   # IP Name of the Windows server cluster.
        [Int16]$numberOfNodes = {},   # Number of nodes in the SQL Server failover
cluster.
        [string]$clusteringMethod = {}  # Clustering method used to cluster the Windows
Servers.
    )


##############################################################################
# Main Program
##############################################################################
[String] $strUpsertSql=""

if ( $help ) {
        "Usage: Upsert-Cluster.ps1 -SQLClusterName <string[]> -WindowsClusterName
<string[]> -numberOfNodes <Int16> -clusteringMethod <string[]>"
exit 0
}

if ( $SQLClusterName.Length -eq 0 ) {
        "Please enter a SQL Server failover cluster."
        exit 1
}

if ( $WindowsClusterName.Length -eq 0 ) {
        "Please enter a Windows server cluster name."
        exit 1
}


if ( $numberOfNodes -le 0 ) {
        "The number of nodes must be greater than zero."
        exit 1
}

if ( $clusteringMethod.Length -eq 0 ) {
        "Please enter a clustering method."
        exit 1
}

# Construct the insert statement.
$strUpsertSql = $strUpsertSql + "exec uspUpsertClusters '$SQLClusterName',
'$WindowsClusterName', $numberOfNodes, '$clusteringMethod';"
$strUpsertSql
```

```
Invoke-Sqlcmd -Query $strUpsertSql -ServerInstance $inventoryServer -Database
$inventoryDatabase
```

For example, let's insert the SQL Server cluster SQL2008CLUSTER on the Windows cluster PowerCluster into the inventory (see Figure 15-3):

```
. C:\DBAScripts\dbaLib.ps1
C:\DBAScripts\Upsert-Cluster.ps1 -SQLClusterName SQL2008CLUSTER -WindowsClusterName
PowerCluster -numberOfNodes 2 -clusteringMethod MSCS
```

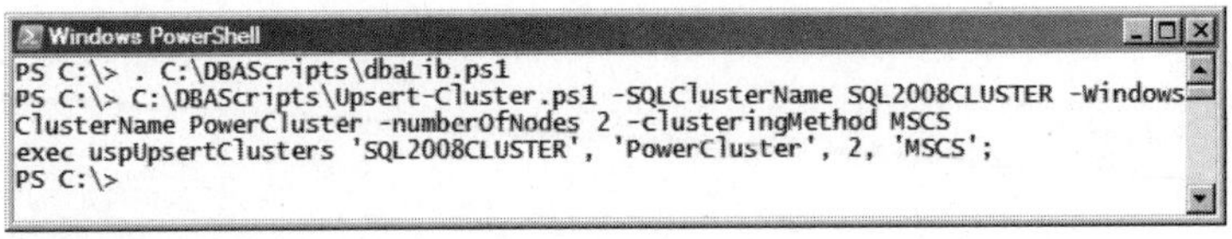

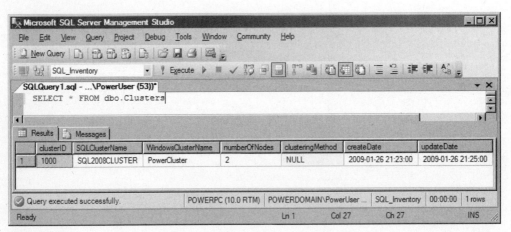

Figure 15-3

After the insertion, the Clusters table appears as shown in Figure 15-4.

Figure 15-4

ClusterNodes

The ClusterNodes table associates SQL Server clusters with their individual nodes. The schema of the ClusterNodes table is shown in Table 15-3.

Here is the script to create the ClusterNodes table:

```
USE [SQL_Inventory]
GO
IF EXISTS (SELECT * FROM sys.objects WHERE object_id = OBJECT_ID(N'[dbo]
```

```
.[ClusterNodes]') AND type in (N'U'))
DROP TABLE [dbo].[ClusterNodes]
GO
CREATE TABLE [dbo].[ClusterNodes](
clusterID int,
nodeID int,
createDate smalldatetime NOT NULL,
updateDate smalldatetime NOT NULL
)
GO
```

Table 15-3: ClusterNodes Table Schema

Column	DataType	Description
clusterID	int	ID of the SQL Server cluster. This ID comes from the Clusters table.
nodeID	int	Host ID of a node in the cluster. This ID comes from the Hosts table.
createDate	smalldatetime	Date and time the cluster node record was created.
updateDate	smalldatetime	Date and time the cluster node record was last updated.

We also need a stored procedure, uspUpsertClusterNodes, to associate the host ID of a new cluster node with the ID of its cluster. This stored procedure will be called later in the Upsert-ClusterNode.ps1 script to manage the ClusterNodes table. The script uspUpsertClusterNodes.sql, shown here, is used to create the stored procedure uspUpsertClusterNodes:

```
USE [SQL_Inventory]
GO
IF  EXISTS (SELECT * FROM sys.objects WHERE object_id =
 OBJECT_ID(N'[dbo].[uspUpsertClusterNodes]') AND type in (N'P', N'PC'))
DROP PROCEDURE [dbo].[uspUpsertClusterNodes]
GO
CREATE PROCEDURE [DBO].[uspUpsertClusterNodes]
                @SQLClusterName    [varchar] (128),
                @nodeName    [varchar] (128)
AS
DECLARE @ERRORCODE [int], @ERRMSG [varchar] (128)
DECLARE @clusterID [int], @nodeID [int]

-- Get cluster ID
IF EXISTS ( SELECT clusterID FROM [dbo].[Clusters] WHERE SQLClusterName=
@SQLClusterName)
        SELECT @clusterID=clusterID FROM [dbo].[Clusters] WHERE
SQLClusterName=@SQLClusterName
ELSE
        SELECT @clusterID=0

-- Get host ID of the node
```

```
IF EXISTS ( SELECT hostID FROM [dbo].[Hosts] WHERE hostName=@nodeName)
        SELECT @nodeID=hostID FROM [dbo].[Hosts] WHERE hostName=@nodeName
ELSE
        SELECT @nodeID=0

-- If the cluster does not exist in the Clusters table, raise an error and then quit.
IF (@clusterID = 0)
BEGIN
        SET @ERRMSG = 'Upsert failed - ' + OBJECT_NAME(@@PROCID)
        SET @ERRMSG = @ERRMSG + 'SQL Server Cluster ' + @SQLClusterName + ' does not
exist in the inventory.'
        RAISERROR (@ERRMSG, 16, 1)
        RETURN (-1)
END

-- If the node does not exist in the Hosts table, raise an error and then quit.
IF (@nodeID = 0)
BEGIN
        SET @ERRMSG = 'Upsert failed - ' + OBJECT_NAME(@@PROCID)
        SET @ERRMSG = @ERRMSG + 'Host ' + @nodeName + ' does not exist in the
inventory.'
        RAISERROR (@ERRMSG, 16, 1)
        RETURN (-1)
END

-- If the cluster node record already exists in the inventory, then perform an update.
IF EXISTS (SELECT * FROM [dbo].[ClusterNodes] WHERE clusterID=@clusterID and
nodeID=@nodeID)
BEGIN
        UPDATE [dbo].[ClusterNodes]
        SET        [updateDate]=getDate()
        WHERE clusterID=@clusterID and nodeID=@nodeID
END
-- If the cluster node record does not exist in the inventory, then perform an
insertion.
ELSE
BEGIN
 INSERT [dbo].[ClusterNodes]
        ( clusterID
        , nodeID
        , createDate
        , updateDate
        )
 VALUES(
        @clusterID
        , @nodeID
        , GETDATE()
        , GETDATE()
        )
END

SET @ERRORCODE = @@ERROR
IF @ERRORCODE <> 0
      BEGIN
        SET @ERRMSG = 'Upsert failed - ' + OBJECT_NAME(@@PROCID)
```

```
            SET @ERRMSG = @ERRMSG + ' Error Code: ' + RTRIM(CONVERT(CHAR, @ERRORCODE))
            RAISERROR (@ERRMSG, 16, 1)
            RETURN (-1)
        END
GO
```

The `Upsert-ClusterNode.ps1` script invokes the `uspUpsertClusterNodes` stored procedure and adds new cluster node information to the `ClusterNodes` table. The usage of this script is as follows:

```
Upsert-ClusterNode.ps1 -SQLClusterName <string[]> -nodeName <string[]>
```

The complete script, also available for download from the Wrox website, is as follows:

```
#=================================================================
#
# NAME: Upsert-ClusterNode.ps1
#
# AUTHOR: Yan and MAK
# DATE  : 6/8/2008
#
# COMMENT: This script inserts a SQL Server ClusterNode record into inventory.
# If the ClusterNode already exists, then this script updates the existing
ClusterNode record.
# Example: Upsert-ClusterNode.ps1 -SQLClusterName SQL2008CLUSTER -nodeName NODE1
#=================================================================

###############################################################################
# Initialize parameters
###############################################################################
param (
        [switch]$help,
        [string]$SQLClusterName = {}, # IP Name of the SQL Server failover cluster.
        [string]$nodeName = {} # Host name of the node being added.
    )


###############################################################################
# Main Program
###############################################################################
[String] $strUpsertSql=""

if ( $help ) {
    "Usage: Upsert-ClusterNode.ps1 -SQLClusterName <string[]> -nodeName <string[]>"
    exit 0
}

if ( $SQLClusterName.Length -eq 0 ) {
    "Please enter a SQL Server failover cluster name."
    exit 1
}

if ( $nodeName.Length -eq 0 ) {
    "Please enter a node name."
    exit 1
```

```
}

$strUpsertSql = $strUpsertSql + "exec uspUpsertClusterNodes '$SQLClusterName',
'$nodeName';"
$strUpsertSql

Invoke-Sqlcmd -Query $strUpsertSql -ServerInstance $inventoryServer -Database
$inventoryDatabase
```

The following inserts the two nodes of the SQL Server cluster SQL2008CLUSTER, NODE1 and NODE2 (see Figure 15-5):

```
. C:\DBAScripts\dbaLib.ps1
C:\DBAScripts\Upsert-ClusterNode.ps1 -SQLClusterName SQL2008CLUSTER -nodeName NODE1

C:\DBAScripts\Upsert-ClusterNode.ps1 -SQLClusterName SQL2008CLUSTER -nodeName NODE2
```

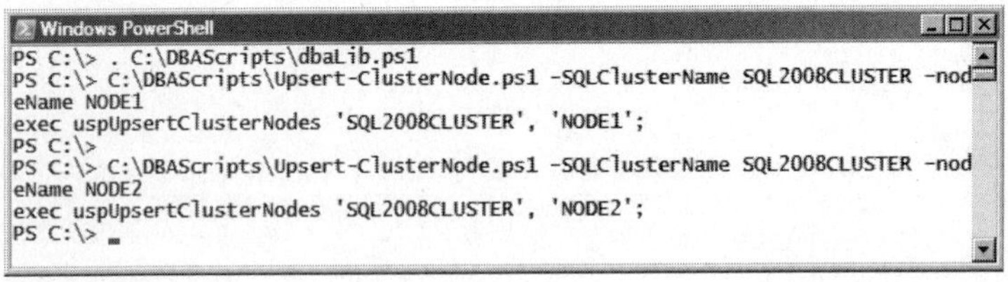

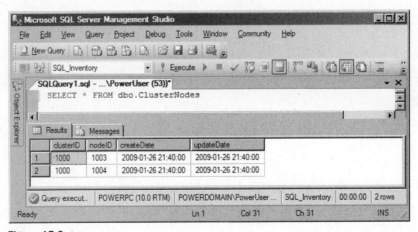

Figure 15-5

Figure 15-6 shows the `ClusterNodes` table after the script was executed.

Figure 15-6

Servers

The `Servers` table contains information about all the SQL Server instances. The schema of the `Servers` table is shown in Table 15-4.

Table 15-4: Servers Table Schema

Column	DataType	Description
serverID	int identity(1000,1)	ID of the SQL Server
instanceName	varchar(128)	MSSQLSERVER for the default instance. For a named instance, instanceName = serverName.
hosted	int	Contains the ID of the standalone host of the SQL Server. Null if the server is on a cluster.
clustered	int	Contains the ID of the cluster hosting this server. Null if the server is on a standalone host.
Status	char(1)	Status of this server. Possible values include D (Development), Q (Quality Assurance), P (Production), U (User Acceptance Testing), and R (Disaster Recovery).
tcpPort	varchar(10)	TCP port on which the SQL Server is listening
serverNetwork Protocols	varchar(128)	Network protocols used by the SQL server
Type	varchar(10)	2008, 2005, or 2000
Edition	varchar(128)	Enterprise, Standard, or Developer
Version	varchar(20)	10.0.1300
servicePack	varchar(10)	Service pack installed on the SQL Server
startupParameters	varchar(512)	Parameters used at SQL Server startup
systemDbDevice	varchar(512)	Path to the directory that contains system databases
errorLogLocation	varchar(512)	Path to the SQL Server `ErrorLog`
Collation	varchar(128)	Collation of the SQL Server
minMemory	bigint	Minimum memory configured for the SQL Server

Continued

Table 15-4: Servers Table Schema *(continued)*

Column	DataType	Description
maxMemory	bigint	Maximum memory configured for the SQL Server
AWEEnabled	bit	Indicates whether Address Windowing Extensions (AWE) is enabled
maxUser Connections	int	Maximum number of user connections that are allowed to connect with the SQL Server at the same time
createDate	smalldatetime	Date and time the server record was created
updateDate	smalldatetime	Date and time the server record was last updated

Here is a SQL script, `Create-Servers.ps1`, to create the `Servers` table:

```
USE [SQL_Inventory]
GO
IF EXISTS (SELECT * FROM sys.objects WHERE object_id = OBJECT_ID(N'[dbo].[Servers]')
AND type in (N'U'))
DROP TABLE [dbo].[Servers]
GO
CREATE TABLE [dbo].[Servers](
[serverID] [int] IDENTITY(1000,1) NOT NULL CONSTRAINT PK_serverID PRIMARY
KEY CLUSTERED,
[instanceName] [varchar](128) NOT NULL,
[hostID] [int] NULL,
[clusterID] [int] NULL,
[status] [char](1) NOT NULL,
[tcpPort] [smallint] NULL,
[serverNetworkProtocols] [varchar](128) NULL,
[type] [varchar](10) NULL,
[edition] [varchar](128) NULL,
[version] [varchar](20) NULL,
[servicePack] [varchar](10) NULL,
[startupParameters] [varchar](512) NULL,
[systemDbDevice] [varchar](512) NULL,
[errorLogLocation] [varchar](512) NULL,
[collation] [varchar](128) NULL,
[minMemory] [bigint] NULL,
[maxMemory] [bigint] NULL,
[AWEEnabled] [bit] NULL,
[maxUserConnections] [int] NULL,
[createDate] [smalldatetime] NULL,
[updateDate] [smalldatetime] NULL,
)
```

We need a stored procedure, `uspUpsertServers`, to insert a server record when the server does not exist in the inventory, or to update a server record when the server already exists. This stored procedure will be called later in the `Upsert-Server.ps1` script to manage the `Servers` table. In this stored procedure, we test the parameters of the host name and the cluster name, and only one name should be valid. If a server exists on a standalone host, then the `clusterID` column for the server record must be null, and the `hostID` column must be valid. If a server exists on a cluster, then the `hostID` column must be null, and the `clusterID` column must be valid. Here is the script used to create the stored procedure `uspUpsertServers`:

```
USE [SQL_Inventory]
GO
IF EXISTS (SELECT * FROM sys.objects WHERE object_id =
OBJECT_ID(N'[dbo].[uspUpsertServers]') AND type in (N'P', N'PC'))
      DROP PROCEDURE [dbo].[uspUpsertServers]
GO
CREATE PROCEDURE [dbo].[uspUpsertServers]
                  @instanceName    [varchar] (128),
                  @status    [char] (1),
                  @hostName    [varchar] (128),
                  @clusterName [varchar] (128),
                  @tcpPort    [varchar] (10),
                  @serverNetworkProtocols    [varchar] (128),
                  @type    [varchar] (10),
                  @edition    [varchar] (128),
                  @version    [varchar] (128),
                  @servicePack    [varchar] (128),
                  @startupParameters    [varchar] (512),
                  @systemDbDevice    [varchar] (512),
                  @errorLogLocation    [varchar] (512),
                  @collation    [varchar] (128),
                  @minMemory    [bigint],
                  @maxMemory    [bigint],
                  @AWEEnabled    [bit],
                  @maxUserConnections    [int]
AS
DECLARE @ERRORCODE [int], @ERRMSG [varchar] (128)
DECLARE @hostID [int], @clusterID [int]

-- If the server resides on a standalone host
IF (@hostName is NOT Null)
BEGIN
      -- Verify the host name
      SELECT @hostID = hostID FROM [dbo].[HOSTS] WHERE hostName=@hostName

      IF (@hostID > 0)
            BEGIN
            -- If the server does not exist in the inventory, perform an insertion.
            IF NOT Exists ( SELECT serverID FROM dbo.Servers
                        WHERE instanceName = @instanceName and hostID = @hostID)
                  INSERT INTO [dbo].[Servers]
                  ( instanceName
                  , hostID
                  , clusterID
                  , status
                  , tcpPort
                  , serverNetworkProtocols
```

```
        , type
        , edition
        , version
        , servicePack
        , startupParameters
        , systemDbDevice
        , errorLogLocation
        , collation
        , minMemory
        , maxMemory
        , AWEEnabled
        , maxUserConnections
        , createDate
        , updateDate
        )
    VALUES(
            @instanceName
        , @hostID
        , NULL
        , @status
        , @tcpPort
        , @serverNetworkProtocols
        , @type
        , @edition
        , @version
        , @servicePack
        , @startupParameters
        , @systemDbDevice
        , @errorLogLocation
        , @collation
        , @minMemory
        , @maxMemory
        , @AWEEnabled
        , @maxUserConnections
        , GETDATE()
        , GETDATE()
        )
-- If the server already exists in the inventory, perform an update.
ELSE
        UPDATE [SQL_Inventory].[dbo].[Servers]
        SET [status] = @status
        ,[tcpPort] = @tcpPort
        ,[serverNetworkProtocols] = @serverNetworkProtocols
        ,[type] = @type
        ,[edition] = @edition
        ,[version] = @version
        ,[servicePack] = @servicePack
        ,[startupParameters] = @startupParameters
        ,[systemDbDevice] = @systemDbDevice
        ,[errorLogLocation] = @errorLogLocation
        ,[collation] = @collation
        ,[minMemory] = @minMemory
        ,[maxMemory] = @maxMemory
        ,[AWEEnabled] = @AWEEnabled
        ,[maxUserConnections] = @maxUserConnections
        ,[updateDate] = GETDATE()
```

```
                        WHERE instanceName = @instanceName and hostID = @hostID
              END
-- If the host name is invalid, raise an error and exit.
        ELSE
              BEGIN
                    SET @ERRMSG = 'Upsert failed - ' + OBJECT_NAME(@@PROCID)
                    SET @ERRMSG = @ERRMSG + ' Host ' + @hostName + ' does not exist.
Please add the host first.'
                    RAISERROR (@ERRMSG, 16, 1)
                    RETURN (-1)
          END
END
-- If the server resides on a cluster
ELSE
BEGIN
      -- Verify the cluster name
      SELECT @clusterID = clusterID FROM [dbo].[Clusters] WHERE
SQLClusterName=@clusterName
      IF (@clusterID > 0)
            BEGIN
            -- If the server does not exist in the inventory, perform an insertion.
            IF NOT Exists ( SELECT serverID FROM dbo.Servers WHERE instanceName =
@instanceName and clusterID = @clusterID)
                    INSERT INTO [dbo].[Servers]
                    ( instanceName
                    , hostID
                    , clusterID
                    , status
                    , tcpPort
                    , serverNetworkProtocols
                    , type
                    , edition
                    , version
                    , servicePack
                    , startupParameters
                    , systemDbDevice
                    , errorLogLocation
                    , collation
                    , minMemory
                    , maxMemory
                    , AWEEnabled
                    , maxUserConnections
                    , createDate
                    , updateDate
                    )
                    VALUES(
                        @instanceName
                        , NULL
                        , @clusterID
                        , @status
                        , @tcpPort
                        , @serverNetworkProtocols
                        , @type
                        , @edition
                        , @version
                        , @servicePack
```

```
                        , @startupParameters
                        , @systemDbDevice
                        , @errorLogLocation
                        , @collation
                        , @minMemory
                        , @maxMemory
                        , @AWEEnabled
                        , @maxUserConnections
                        , GETDATE()
                        , GETDATE()
                    )
            -- If the server already exists in the inventory, perform an update.
            ELSE
                    UPDATE [SQL_Inventory].[dbo].[Servers]
                    SET [instanceName] = @instanceName
                     ,[hostID] = NULL
                     ,[clusterID] = @clusterID
                     ,[status] = @status
                     ,[tcpPort] = @tcpPort
                     ,[serverNetworkProtocols] = @serverNetworkProtocols
                     ,[type] = @type
                     ,[edition] = @edition
                     ,[version] = @version
                     ,[servicePack] = @servicePack
                     ,[startupParameters] = @startupParameters
                     ,[systemDbDevice] = @systemDbDevice
                     ,[errorLogLocation] = @errorLogLocation
                     ,[collation] = @collation
                     ,[minMemory] = @minMemory
                     ,[maxMemory] = @maxMemory
                     ,[AWEEnabled] = @AWEEnabled
                     ,[maxUserConnections] = @maxUserConnections
                     ,[updateDate] = GETDATE()
                    WHERE instanceName = @instanceName and clusterID = @clusterID
            END
        -- If the cluster name is invalid, raise an error and exit.
        ELSE
                BEGIN
                    SET @ERRMSG = 'Upsert failed - ' + OBJECT_NAME(@@PROCID)
                    SET @ERRMSG = @ERRMSG + ' Cluster ' + @clusterName + '
does not exist. Please add the cluster first.'
                    RAISERROR (@ERRMSG, 16, 1)
                    RETURN (-1)
                END
END

SET @ERRORCODE = @@ERROR
IF @ERRORCODE <> 0
    BEGIN
        SET @ERRMSG = 'Upsert failed - ' + OBJECT_NAME(@@PROCID)
        SET @ERRMSG = @ERRMSG + ' Error Code: ' + RTRIM(CONVERT(CHAR, @ERRORCODE))
        RAISERROR (@ERRMSG, 16, 1)
        RETURN (-1)
    END
GO
```

After installing a SQL Server instance, we need a script, `Upsert-Server.ps1`, to insert the SQL server record into the inventory. This script calls the `uspUpsertServers` stored procedure. For a SQL Server instance on a standalone host, we pass a host name. For a SQL Server instance on a cluster, we pass a cluster name. This script connects to the HKLM registry hive of the SQL Server host/cluster and retrieves the TCP/IP port number on which the instance is listening. Then it connects with the SQL Server instance with the port number, and retrieves the other information such as version, edition, and server configurations. If we run the script against the same server for the second time, the script will update the information for the existing server record. The usage of this script is as follows:

```
Upsert-Server -instanceName <string[]> <<-hostName <string[]>|-clusterName
<string[]>> -status <string[]>
```

The complete script, which is available for download from the Wrox website for this book, is as follows:

```
#==============================================================
#
# NAME: Upsert-Server.ps1
#
# AUTHOR: Yan and MAK
# DATE   : 6/8/2008
#
# COMMENT: This script adds a server record into inventory.
#          If the server already exists, then this script updates the existing server
record.
# Example: Upsert-Server -instanceName MSSQLSERVER -hostName POWERPC -status U
#==============================================================


#########################################################################
# Initialize parameters
#########################################################################
param (
        [switch]$help,
        [string]$instanceName = {},   # Name of the SQL Server instance to add into
inventory. For a default instance, it is MSSQLSERVER.
        [string]$hostName = {},   # Name of the SQL Server host.
        [string]$clusterName = {},   # Name of the SQL Server cluster.
        [string]$status = {}  # Status of the SQL Server instance. Possible values
include D, Q, P, U and R.
    )

# This function connects with a SQL Server instance [$pHostName\$pInstanceName,
$pTcpPort] to execute a SQL query $pSql.
function execSQL([String] $pHostName, [String] $pInstanceName, [String]
$pSql, [String] $pTcpPort)
{
        if ( $pInstanceName -eq 'MSSQLSERVER' ) {
                (Invoke-Sqlcmd -Query "$pSql" -ServerInstance "$pHostName,$pTcpPort" -
Database master).Column1
        }
        else {
                (Invoke-Sqlcmd -Query "$pSql" -ServerInstance
"$pHostName\$pInstanceName,$pTcpPort" -Database master).Column1
        }
}
```

```
# This function returns the statements that can be used to get a server configuration
in a column called Column1.
function getConfigSql([String] $option)
{
        $strSql = "CREATE TABLE #temp (name nvarchar(35), minimum int, maximum int,
config_value int, run_value int)'n"
        $strSql = $strSql + "INSERT INTO #temp EXEC (''exec sp_configure
''''$option''''''')'n"
        $strSql = $strSql + "SELECT run_value as Column1 from #temp'n"
        $strSql = $strSql + "DROP TABLE #temp'n"

        return $strSql
}

# This function connects to the HKLM registry hive of the SQL Server host $pHostName
# and retrieve the TCP/IP port number that the instance $pInstanceName is
listening on.
function getTcpPort([String] $pHostName, [String] $pInstanceName)
{
        $strTcpPort=""

        $reg = [WMIClass]"\\$pHostName\root\default:stdRegProv"
        $HKEY_LOCAL_MACHINE = 2147483650

        # Default instance
        if ($pInstanceName -eq 'MSSQLSERVER') {
                #SQL Server 2000 or SQL Server 2005/2008 resides on the same server
as SQL Server 2000
                $strKeyPath =
"SOFTWARE\Microsoft\MSSQLServer\MSSQLServer\SuperSocketNetLib\Tcp"
$strTcpPort=$reg.GetStringValue($HKEY_LOCAL_MACHINE,$strKeyPath,
"TcpPort").svalue
                if ($strTcpPort) {
                        Set-Variable -Name instanceRegPath -Value
"SOFTWARE\Microsoft\MSSQLServer\MSSQLServer" -Scope 1
                        return $strTcpPort
                }

        }
        else {
                #SQL Server 2000 or SQL Server 2005/2008 resides on the same server as
SQL Server 2000
                $strKeyPath = "SOFTWARE\Microsoft\Microsoft SQL
Server\$pInstanceName\MSSQLServer\SuperSocketNetLib\Tcp"
$strTcpPort=$reg.GetStringValue($HKEY_LOCAL_MACHINE,
$strKeyPath,"TcpPort").svalue
                if ($strTcpPort) {
                        Set-Variable -Name instanceRegPath -Value "SOFTWARE\Microsoft
\Microsoft SQL Server\$pInstanceName\MSSQLServer" -Scope 1
                        return $strTcpPort
                }
        }

        #SQL Server 2005
        for ($i=1; $i -le 50; $i++) {
```

```
                $strKeyPath = "SOFTWARE\Microsoft\Microsoft SQL Server\MSSQL.$i"
                $strInstanceName=$reg.GetStringValue($HKEY_LOCAL_MACHINE,
$strKeyPath,"").svalue

                if ($strInstanceName -eq $pInstanceName) {
                        $strKeyPath = "SOFTWARE\Microsoft\Microsoft SQL Server\MSSQL.$i
\MSSQLServer\SuperSocketNetLib\tcp\IPAll"
$strTcpPort=$reg.GetStringValue($HKEY_LOCAL_MACHINE,
$strKeyPath,"TcpPort").svalue

                        Set-Variable -Name instanceRegPath -Value
"SOFTWARE\Microsoft\Microsoft SQL Server\MSSQL.$i\MSSQLServer" -Scope 1
                        return $strTcpPort
                }
        }

        #SQL Server 2008
        $strKeyPath = "SOFTWARE\Microsoft\Microsoft SQL
Server\MSSQL10.$pInstanceName\MSSQLServer\SuperSocketNetLib\Tcp\IPAll"
$strTcpPort=$reg.GetStringValue($HKEY_LOCAL_MACHINE,
$strKeyPath,"TcpPort").svalue
        if ($strTcpPort) {
                Set-Variable -Name instanceRegPath -Value "SOFTWARE\Microsoft\Microsoft
SQL Server\MSSQL10.$pInstanceName\MSSQLServer" -Scope 1
                return $strTcpPort
        }

        return ""
}

# This function connects to the HKLM registry hive of the SQL Server host $pHostName
# and retrieve the network protocols used by the instance $pInstanceName.
function getServerNetWorkProtocols([String] $pHostName, [String] $pInstanceName)
{
        $strProtocols=""

        $reg = [WMIClass]"\\$pHostName\root\default:stdRegProv"
        $HKEY_LOCAL_MACHINE = 2147483650

        $strKeyPath = "$instanceRegPath\SuperSocketNetLib"
        #SQL Server 2000
        $arrValues=$reg.GetMultiStringValue($HKEY_LOCAL_MACHINE,
$strKeyPath,"ProtocolList").sValue
        if ($arrValues) {
                $arrValues | foreach -process { $strProtocols=$strProtocols + $_ + ',' }
                return $strProtocols.Substring(0, $strProtocols.Length-1)
        }
        #SQL Server 2005 or 2008
        else {
                $strKeyPath = "$instanceRegPath\SuperSocketNetLib\Tcp"
                $intEnabled=$reg.GetDWORDValue($HKEY_LOCAL_MACHINE,
$strKeyPath,"Enabled").uvalue
                if ($intEnabled) {
                        if ($intEnabled -eq 1) { $strProtocols='tcp,' }
```

```
                                    $strKeyPath — "SOFTWARE\Microsoft\Microsoft SQL
Server\MSSQL.$instanceNo\MSSQLServer\SuperSocketNetLib\Np"
$intEnabled=$reg.GetDWORDValue($HKEY_LOCAL_MACHINE,
$strKeyPath,"Enabled").uvalue
                        if ($intEnabled -eq 1) { $strProtocols=$strProtocols + 'np,' }


                        $strKeyPath = "SOFTWARE\Microsoft\Microsoft SQL
Server\MSSQL.$instanceNo\MSSQLServer\SuperSocketNetLib\Sm"
$intEnabled=$reg.GetDWORDValue($HKEY_LOCAL_MACHINE,
$strKeyPath,"Enabled").uvalue
                        if ($intEnabled -eq 1) { $strProtocols=$strProtocols + 'sm,' }


                        $strKeyPath = "SOFTWARE\Microsoft\Microsoft SQL
Server\MSSQL.$instanceNo\MSSQLServer\SuperSocketNetLib\Via"
$intEnabled=$reg.GetDWORDValue($HKEY_LOCAL_MACHINE,
$strKeyPath,"Enabled").uvalue
                        if ($intEnabled -eq 1) { $strProtocols=$strProtocols + 'via,' }


                        return $strProtocols.Substring(0, $strProtocols.Length-1)
                }
        }
}


# This function connects to the HKLM registry hive of the SQL Server host $pHostName
# and retrieve the startup parameters used by the instance $pInstanceName.
function getStartupParameters([String] $pHostName, [String] $pInstanceName)
{
        $reg = [WMIClass]"\\$pHostName\root\default:stdRegProv"
        $HKEY_LOCAL_MACHINE = 2147483650

        $strKeyPath = "$instanceRegPath\Parameters"
        $arrValues=$reg.EnumValues($HKEY_LOCAL_MACHINE,$strKeyPath).sNames

        #SQL Server 2000
        if ($arrValues) {
                for ($i=0; $i -lt $arrValues.Length; $i++) {
                        $strParameters=$strParameters +
$reg.GetStringValue($HKEY_LOCAL_MACHINE,$strKeyPath,$arrValues[$i]).svalue + ";"
                }
                return $strParameters
        }

        #SQL Server 2005
        for ($i=1; $i -le 50; $i++) {
                $strKeyPath = "SOFTWARE\Microsoft\Microsoft SQL Server\MSSQL.$i"
$strInstanceName=$reg.GetStringValue($HKEY_LOCAL_MACHINE,
$strKeyPath,"").svalue

                if ($strInstanceName -eq $pInstanceName) {
                        $strKeyPath = "SOFTWARE\Microsoft\Microsoft SQL
Server\MSSQL.$i\MSSQLServer\Parameters"
$arrValues=$reg.EnumValues($HKEY_LOCAL_MACHINE,
$strKeyPath).sNames
```

```
                         if ($arrValues) {
                                for ($i=0; $i -lt $arrValues.Length; $i++) {
                                       $strParameters=$strParameters +
$reg.GetStringValue($HKEY_LOCAL_MACHINE,$strKeyPath,$arrValues[$i]).svalue + ";"
                                }
                                return $strParameters
                         }
                 }
        }

        #SQL Server 2008
        $strKeyPath = "SOFTWARE\Microsoft\Microsoft SQL
Server\MSSQL10.$pInstanceName\MSSQLServer\Parameters"
        $arrValues=$reg.EnumValues($HKEY_LOCAL_MACHINE,$strKeyPath).sNames

        if ($arrValues) {
                for ($i=0; $i -lt $arrValues.Length; $i++) {
                       $strParameters=$strParameters +
$reg.GetStringValue($HKEY_LOCAL_MACHINE,$strKeyPath,$arrValues[$i]).svalue + ";"
                }
                return $strParameters
        }
}

#############################################################################
# Main Program
#############################################################################
[String] $strUpsertSql=""

[String] $instanceRegPath = '' # Registry path for the instance

if ( $help ) {
        "Usage: Upsert-Server -serverName <string[]> <<-hostName <string[]>|
-clusterName <string[]>> -status <string[]>"
        exit 0
}

if ( $instanceName.Length -eq 0 ) {
        "Please enter an instance name."

        if ($instanceName -ieq 'mssqlserver') {
                $instanceName='MSSQLSERVER'
        }
        exit 1
}

if (( $hostName.Length -eq 0)  -and ($clusterName.Length -eq 0)) {
        "Please enter a host name or a cluster name."
        exit 1
}

if (( $hostName.Length -gt 0) -and ($clusterName.Length -gt 0)) {
        "You only need to enter either a host name or a cluster name."
        exit 1
}
```

```
if ( $status -notmatch '^D|Q|P|U|R$' ) {
        "The status is invalid. Please enter D, Q, P, U or R."
        exit 1
}

[String] $sqlNetworkName="" # For standalone host, it is the same as $hostName. For
cluster, it is the same as $clusterName
[String] $windowsNetworkName="" # For standalone host, it is the same as $hostName.
For cluster, it is the WindowsClusterName from the Clusters table.

if ($hostName.Length -gt 0) {
        $sqlNetworkName=$hostName
        $windowsNetworkName=$hostName
}
else {
        $sqlNetworkName=$clusterName

        # Find the Windows Cluster Name
        $strQuerySql="SELECT WindowsClusterName FROM Clusters WHERE
SQLClusterName='$clusterName'"
        $sqlCluster=Invoke-Sqlcmd -Query $strQuerySql -ServerInstance $inventoryServer
-Database $inventoryDatabase

        $windowsNetworkName=$sqlCluster.WindowsClusterName
}

$tcpPort=(getTcpPort $windowsNetworkName $instanceName)
# If tcpPort is not available, the server or the host doesn't exist.
if ($tcpPort -eq "") {
        "Tcp port is not found. Please check the server name and the host/cluster name."

        exit 2
}

if ($hostName.Length -gt 0) {
        $strUpsertSql = $strUpsertSql + "exec uspUpsertServers '$instanceName',
'$status', '$hostName', Null, '$tcpPort', "
}
else {
        $strUpsertSql = $strUpsertSql + "exec uspUpsertServers '$instanceName',
'$status', Null, '$clusterName', '$tcpPort', "
}

$strUpsertSql = $strUpsertSql + "'" + (getServerNetWorkProtocols $windowsNetworkName
$instanceName) + "', "

$strQuerySql = "SELECT CASE SUBSTRING(CONVERT(nvarchar, ServerProperty
('ProductVersion')), 1, CHARINDEX('.', convert(nvarchar,
ServerProperty('ProductVersion')))-1 ) WHEN '10' THEN '2008' WHEN '9' THEN '2005' WHEN
'8' THEN '2000' END"
$strUpsertSql = $strUpsertSql + "'" + (execSQL $sqlNetworkName $instanceName
$strQuerySql $tcpPort) + "', "

$strQuerySql = "Select ServerProperty('Edition')"
$strUpsertSql = $strUpsertSql + "'" + (execSQL $sqlNetworkName $instanceName
```

```
$strQuerySql $tcpPort) + "', "

$strQuerySql = "Select ServerProperty('ProductVersion')"
$strUpsertSql = $strUpsertSql + "'" + (execSQL $sqlNetworkName $instanceName
$strQuerySql $tcpPort) + "', "

$strQuerySql = "Select ServerProperty('ProductLevel')"
$strUpsertSql = $strUpsertSql + "'" + (execSQL $sqlNetworkName $instanceName
$strQuerySql $tcpPort) + "', "

$strParameters =(getStartupParameters $windowsNetworkName $instanceName)
$strUpsertSql = $strUpsertSql + "'" + $strParameters + "', "

$strQuerySql = "select top 1 filename as Column1 from dbo.sysfiles"
$strUpsertSql = $strUpsertSql + "'" + (execSQL $sqlNetworkName $instanceName
$strQuerySql $tcpPort | Split-Path -parent) + "', "

$strErrorLog=( $strParameters.Split(";") | where {$_.StartsWith("-e")} )
$strUpsertSql = $strUpsertSql + "'" + $strErrorLog.Substring(2, $strErrorLog
.Length-2) + "', "

$strQuerySql = "Select ServerProperty('Collation')"
$strUpsertSql = $strUpsertSql + "'" + (execSQL $sqlNetworkName $instanceName
$strQuerySql $tcpPort) + "', "

$strQuerySql = ( getConfigSql "min server memory" )
$strUpsertSql = $strUpsertSql + ( execSQL $sqlNetworkName $instanceName
$strQuerySql $tcpPort) + ", "

$strQuerySql = ( getConfigSql "max server memory" )
$strUpsertSql = $strUpsertSql + ( execSQL $sqlNetworkName $instanceName
$strQuerySql $tcpPort) + ", "

$strQuerySql = ( getConfigSql "awe enabled" )
$strUpsertSql = $strUpsertSql + ( execSQL $sqlNetworkName $instanceName
$strQuerySql $tcpPort) + ", "

$strQuerySql = ( getConfigSql "user connections" )
$strUpsertSql = $strUpsertSql + ( execSQL $sqlNetworkName $instanceName
$strQuerySql $tcpPort) + " "

$strUpsertSql = $strUpsertSql + ";"

$strUpsertSql

Invoke-Sqlcmd -Query $strUpsertSql -ServerInstance $inventoryServer -Database
$inventoryDatabase
```

Before running the script, ensure that you can connect to all the servers remotely with the TCP/IP protocol and confirm that the advanced options setting is enabled:

1. Advanced options are enabled on the servers:

    ```
    exec sp_configure 'show advanced options', 1
    reconfigure
    ```

2. The TCP/IP protocol should be enabled for every server, and TCP/IP ports on which SQL servers listen should not be blocked by Windows Firewall. Verify the connectivity remotely.

3. The IPAll option should be enabled for the TCP/IP protocol. This is usually the case in production environments.

Now add the SQL Server instances in our environment:

```
. C:\DBAScripts\dbaLib.ps1
C:\DBAScripts\Upsert-Server -instanceName MSSQLSERVER -hostName POWERPC -status P

C:\DBAScripts\Upsert-Server -instanceName INSTANCE1 -hostName POWERPC -status P

C:\DBAScripts\Upsert-Server -instanceName MSSQLSERVER -hostName DEMOPC -status D

C:\DBAScripts\Upsert-Server -instanceName CHODE1 -hostName DEMOPC -status D

C:\DBAScripts\Upsert-Server -instanceName MSSQLSERVER -clusterName SQL2008CLUSTER
-status P

C:\DBAScripts\Upsert-Server -instanceName MSSQLSERVER -hostName POWERSERVER3
-status P
```

Figure 15-7 shows the output from running the script.

As shown in Figure 15-8, all six SQL Server instances have been added to the `Servers` table and all the columns related to the server information have been populated.

Databases

The `Databases` table contains information about all user databases on all SQL Server instances. The schema of the `Databases` table is shown in Table 15-5.

Here is a `CreateDatabases.ps1` script to create the `Databases` table:

```
USE [SQL_Inventory]
GO
IF  EXISTS (SELECT * FROM sys.objects WHERE object_id = OBJECT_ID(N'[dbo]
.[Databases]') AND type in (N'U'))
DROP TABLE [dbo].[Databases]
GO
CREATE TABLE [dbo].[Databases](
[databaseID] int IDENTITY(1000,1) CONSTRAINT PK_databaseID PRIMARY KEY CLUSTERED,
[serverID] int NOT NULL,
[databaseName] [varchar](128) NOT NULL,
[createDate] [smalldatetime] NOT NULL,
[updateDate] [smalldatetime] NOT NULL
)
```

Figure 15-7

We also need a stored procedure, `uspUpsertDatabases`, to insert a database record when the database does not exist in the inventory, or to update a record when the database already exists. This stored procedure will be called later in the `Upsert-Database.ps1` script to manage the `Databases` table. The script `uspUpsertDatabases.sql` shown here is used to create the stored procedure `uspUpsertDatabases`:

```
USE [SQL_Inventory]
GO
IF  EXISTS (SELECT * FROM sys.objects WHERE object_id =
OBJECT_ID(N'[dbo].[uspUpsertDatabases]') AND type in (N'P', N'PC'))
      DROP PROCEDURE [dbo].[uspUpsertDatabases]
GO
CREATE PROCEDURE [DBO].[uspUpsertDatabases]
                  @serverID     [int] ,
                  @databaseName    [varchar] (128)
```

```
AS
DECLARE @ERRORCODE [int], @ERRMSG [varchar] (128)

-- If the database already exists in the inventory, then perform an update.
IF EXISTS (SELECT databaseID FROM [dbo].[Databases] WHERE serverID=@serverID and
databaseName=@databaseName)
BEGIN
      UPDATE [dbo].[Databases]
      SET     [updateDate]=getDate()
      WHERE serverID=@serverID and databaseName=@databaseName
END
-- If the database does not exist in the inventory, then perform an insertion.
ELSE
BEGIN
          INSERT [dbo].[Databases]
          ( serverID
          , databaseName
          , createDate
          , updateDate
          )
   VALUES(
          @serverID
           , @databaseName
           , GETDATE()
           , GETDATE()
           )
END

SET @ERRORCODE = @@ERROR
IF @ERRORCODE <> 0
      BEGIN
          SET @ERRMSG = 'Upsert failed - ' + OBJECT_NAME(@@PROCID)
          SET @ERRMSG = @ERRMSG + ' Error Code: ' +
   RTRIM(CONVERT(CHAR, @ERRORCODE))
          RAISERROR (@ERRMSG, 16, 1)
          RETURN (-1)
      END
GO
```

We now need a script, Upsert-Database.ps1, to collect a list of databases on all our database servers. This script connects to every server in our inventory, gets the list of user databases, and inserts them into the inventory. The script is available for download from the Wrox website for this book:

```
#==========================================================
#
# NAME: Upsert-Database.ps1
#
# AUTHOR: Yan and MAK
# DATE   : 6/8/2008
#
# COMMENT: This script collects all the user databases on all the servers and saves
them into inventory.
#==========================================================
```

```
##############################################################################
# Initialize parameters
##############################################################################
param (
        [switch]$help
    )



##############################################################################
# Main Program
##############################################################################
[String] $strUpsertSql=""
[String] $strQuerySql=""

if ( $help ) {
        "Usage: Upsert-Database.ps1"
        exit 0
}

# Get all the servers in our inventory
$strQuerySql="SELECT h.hostName as SQLNetworkName, s.serverID, s.tcpPort
FROM dbo.Servers s
JOIN dbo.Hosts h on h.hostID=s.hostID
UNION
SELECT c.SQLClusterName as SQLNetworkName, s.serverID, s.tcpPort
FROM dbo.Servers s
JOIN dbo.Clusters c on c.clusterID=s.clusterID"

$sqlServers=Invoke-Sqlcmd -Query $strQuerySql -ServerInstance $inventoryServer
-Database $inventoryDatabase

# Loop through all the servers and get the user databases on each of them.
Foreach ($sqlServer in $sqlServers) {

        $strUpsertSql=""

        $sqlNetworkName=$sqlServer.SQLNetworkName
        $sqlServerID=$sqlServer.serverID
        $sqlTcpPort=$sqlServer.tcpPort

        # On SQL Server 2005 and 2008, query the system view sys.databases.
        # SQL Server 2000 does not have the system view sys.databases, so the
sysdatabases table needs to be used instead.
        $strQuerySql="DECLARE @objid int
        SELECT @objid = OBJECT_ID(N'sys.databases')

        IF @objid IS NOT NULL
                SELECT [name] FROM sys.databases WHERE [name] NOT IN ('master', 'model',
'msdb', 'tempdb')
        ELSE
                SELECT [name] FROM dbo.sysdatabases WHERE [name] NOT IN ('master',
'model', 'msdb','tempdb');"

        $sqlDatabases=Invoke-Sqlcmd -Query $strQuerySql -ServerInstance
"$sqlNetworkName,$sqlTcpPort" -Database master
```

```
            if ($sqlDatabases) {
                    Foreach ($sqlDatabase in $sqlDatabases) {
                            $strUpsertSql=$strUpsertSql + "exec uspUpsertDatabases " +
$sqlServerID + ", '" + $sqlDatabase.name + "';'n"
                    }
            }

            # Insert the user databases into the inventory.
            if ($strUpsertSql.Length -gt 0) {
                    $strUpsertSql
                    Invoke-Sqlcmd -Query $strUpsertSql -ServerInstance $inventoryServer
-Database $inventoryDatabase
            }
}
```

Run the script as follows:

```
. C:\DBAScripts\dbaLib.ps1
C:\DBAScripts\Upsert-Database.ps1
```

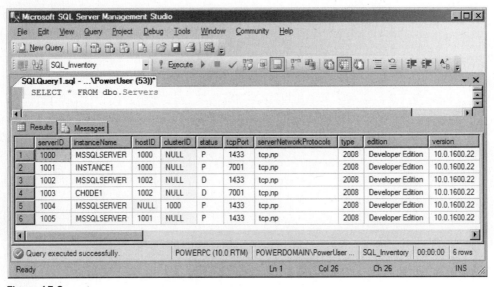

Figure 15-8

Figure 15-9 shows the output.

All the user databases are picked up by the script. Figure 15-10 shows the databases that have been inserted after running the script.

To facilitate the creation of the tables and stored procedures, all the SQL scripts have been consolidated into a script called SQL_Inventory.sql.

Table 15-5: Databases Table Schema

Column	DataType	Description
databaseID	int identity(1000,1)	ID of the database
serverID	int	ID of the server that hosts the database
databaseName	varchar(128)	Name of the database
createDate	smalldatetime	Date and time the database record was created
updateDate	smalldatetime	Date and time the database record was last updated

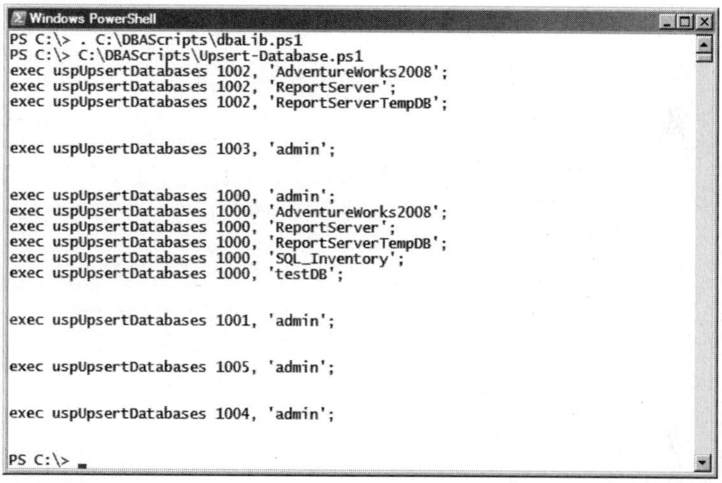

```
Windows PowerShell
PS C:\> . C:\DBAScripts\dbaLib.ps1
PS C:\> C:\DBAScripts\Upsert-Database.ps1
exec uspUpsertDatabases 1002, 'AdventureWorks2008';
exec uspUpsertDatabases 1002, 'ReportServer';
exec uspUpsertDatabases 1002, 'ReportServerTempDB';


exec uspUpsertDatabases 1003, 'admin';


exec uspUpsertDatabases 1000, 'admin';
exec uspUpsertDatabases 1000, 'AdventureWorks2008';
exec uspUpsertDatabases 1000, 'ReportServer';
exec uspUpsertDatabases 1000, 'ReportServerTempDB';
exec uspUpsertDatabases 1000, 'SQL_Inventory';
exec uspUpsertDatabases 1000, 'testDB';


exec uspUpsertDatabases 1001, 'admin';


exec uspUpsertDatabases 1005, 'admin';


exec uspUpsertDatabases 1004, 'admin';

PS C:\>
```

Figure 15-9

Supplementary Tables

We also need supplementary tables to store support personnel information for the following reasons:

❏   The global DBA group can operate on the "follow the sun" support model. It is important to clarify the support shift for each region. When the monitoring system discovers a server issue, it automatically sends out e-mail notifications based on the support shift. However, we also need to take holidays into consideration. When a region observes a holiday, the system should send e-mail to all the other regions instead.

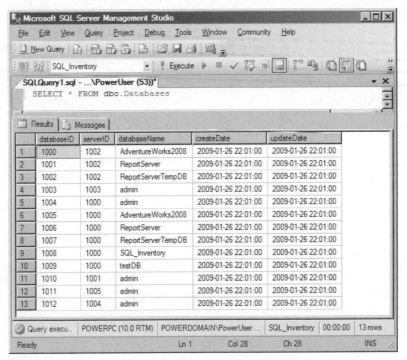

Figure 15-10

❑   Application servers use SQL Servers as a backend. In case of a database outage, the BU own-
ers/users need to be contacted and updated with the status of the SQL Server instance. Therefore, we also need to store BU contacts for each server. If several BUs share databases on a server,
then the BU contacts should be associated with both database and server.

Here is a list of supplementary tables:

❑   `ServerBUContacts`: This table stores business unit contacts for each server. See Table 15-6.

❑   `Regions`: This table defines all the regions in the company, such as NA (North America), EU
(Europe), and AS (Asia). See Table 15-7.

❑   `RegionSupportShifts`: This table defines the time each region starts or stops support for the
globe based on the "follow the sun" model. All the times are GMT. Each region has a dedicated
e-mail group. See Table 15-8.

❑   `RegionHolidays`: Because we also need to consider that each region has different holidays, this
table stores holidays for each region. See Table 15-9.

For two reasons, we present only the table schema. One, the support model for each company can be
different. For a nonglobal company, there is no need to define regions. We only provide an example
on how to set up the support model. Two, none of the following tables store information from physical
systems, so we do not need to connect to the physical hosts or SQL server instances using Windows
PowerShell. It should be very easy to write stored procedures and scripts to insert data into these tables.

Table 15-6: ServerBUContacts (all user defined)

Column	DataType	Description
serverID	int	ID of the associated SQL Server
databaseID	int	If databaseID is null, then the BU contact is for the entire server. Otherwise, the BU contact is associated with this database only.
BUContactEmail	varchar(256)	E-mail address of the BU user. This can be an individual's e-mail or an e-mail group.
BUContactPage	varchar(256)	Page address of the BU user
BUContactPhone	varchar(20)	Phone number of the BU user
preferredContactMethod	varchar(1)	Preferred method of contact by BU (e.g., M for e-mail, P for page, N for phone number)
createDate	smalldatetime	Date and time the BU contact record was created
updateDate	smalldatetime	Date and time the BU contact record was last updated

Table 15-7: Regions

Column	DataType	Description
regionID	char(2)	Regions that DBAs support (e.g., EU, NA, AS)
regionDescription	varchar(256)	Description of the region (e.g., Europe, North America, Asia)

Table 15-8: RegionSupportShifts

Column	DataType	Description
regionID	char(2)	ID of the region
dbaContactEmailGroup	varchar(256)	Contact e-mail group of each region (e.g., lndba, nydba, asdba)
startTime	Time (new data type introduced in SQL Server 2008)	Starting time of the support shift, based on GMT
endTime	Time	Ending time of the support shift, based on GMT

Table 15-9: RegionHolidays

Column	DataType	Description
regionID	char(2)	ID of the region
startDate	smalldatetime	Starting date and time of the holiday, based on GMT
endDate	smalldatetime	Ending date and time of the holiday, based on GMT
createDate	smalldatetime	Date and time the holiday record was created

Summary

This chapter demonstrated how to set up a SQL Server inventory database, and add SQL Server standalone hosts, clusters, servers, and databases in an existing or new environment into the inventory. This approach will help DBAs in an enterprise environment to track and manage hundreds or even thousands of SQL Server hosts and instances effectively and efficiently. Subsequent chapters will build administrative and monitoring solutions on top of this inventory to improve the manageability and scalability of your SQL Server plant.

16

SQL Server Installation

In Chapter 15, we built an inventory consisting of SQL Server instances and their hosts. What should you do to ensure that every server in our inventory is available to users and applications that use it? How do you maintain a stable and high-performance database environment? How do you ensure that in cases of hardware or software failures, you will be able to recover the databases in a timely fashion to meet the SLA? These are all responsibilities of the database administrator (DBA).

In this chapter, we focus on the first DBA responsibility in the life cycle of a SQL Server instance: SQL Server installation. Our approach simplifies the massive installation of tens or hundreds of servers. It will help alleviate the workload in a great deal in enterprise environments, where one or more servers are built every week.

This chapter covers the following topics:

- ❑ Installation procedure and template
- ❑ Standalone installation example
- ❑ Cluster installation example

Installation Procedure and Template

If you are installing one or more SQL servers per week, it would be worthwhile to consider automating the process. Automation makes the life of a DBA much easier. It simplifies the installation process and minimizes human error. If your organization has standards for SQL Server installation, you can enforce them in the installation scripts.

Installation binaries of SQL Server have evolved drastically. The command-line-based installation has evolved from `SetupSQL.exe` with an `iss` file in SQL Server 2000 to `Setup.exe` with either parameters or an `ini` configuration file in SQL Server 2005 and 2008. Though the `ini` configuration files belong to the traditional way of performing a command-line installation, it is very useful and simple to install.

This chapter details the process of a command-line installation of SQL Server 2008 using a customized SQL Server template file and Windows PowerShell. Please note that the setup parameters defined for SQL Server 2005 are different. If you are using SQL Server 2005, you will need to change the template file. The installation process of SQL Server 2000 varies even more, and it involves the creation of `iss` files, thus more changes are needed. The solution presented in this chapter is tailored for SQL Server 2008.

SQL Server 2008 comes in many flavors:

- ❏ Enterprise
- ❏ Standard
- ❏ Developer
- ❏ Workgroup
- ❏ Web
- ❏ Compact
- ❏ Express

SQL Server features vary according to edition. We focus on the first three editions only because the Workgroup, Web, and Express editions are meant for limited use, and the Compact edition is for mobile devices.

SQL Server includes many components that implement features other than RDBMS functionality. These components can be categorized as server components or client tools. The `server` components include the following:

- ❏ Database Engine Services
- ❏ Analysis Services
- ❏ Reporting Services
- ❏ Integration Services

The client tools include the following:

- ❏ SQL Server Management Studio
- ❏ SQL Server Configuration Manager
- ❏ SQL Server Profiler
- ❏ Database Engine Tuning Advisor
- ❏ Business Intelligence Development Studio
- ❏ Connectivity Components

If you are trying to install only the client tools of SQL Server, there is no need for a template file because the installation is straightforward and just needs a setup parameter. The command-line installation in this chapter deals with installation of Database Engine–related components and client tools. You can choose to install two features with the Database Engine:

❑ Replication

❑ Full-Text Search

To give you a visual of the components, Figure 16-1 shows the list of features included if you install SQL Server 2008 with the Installation Wizard.

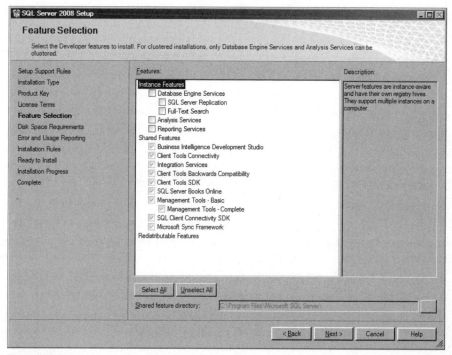

Figure 16-1

Before starting the installation, you need to put the installation binaries on a file server. Assume that the SQL Server installation binaries are copied to a shared folder SQL2008Install on a file server DEMOPC, and name the SQL Server installation binary directories as follows:

```
\\DEMOPC\SQL2008Install\ENT\
\\DEMOPC\SQL2008Install\STD\
\\DEMOPC\SQL2008Install\DEV\
```

DEV stands for developer edition; STD stands for Standard edition; and ENT stands for Enterprise edition.

Because you need to keep track of SQL Server instances in your environment, before installing SQL Server on a host or a Windows cluster, it is also assumed that the host or cluster nodes have been added to your inventory, as demonstrated in Chapter 15.

For example, before installing a new instance on a standalone host POWERPC, you need to run the Upsert-Host.ps1 script as follows:

```
. C:\DBAScripts\dbaLib.ps1
# Add a DBA inventory host.
C:\DBAScripts\Upsert-Host.ps1 -hostName POWERPC -region NA -location CH
-primaryBU DBA -description 'DBA Inventory Server'
```

The output is shown in Figure 16-2.

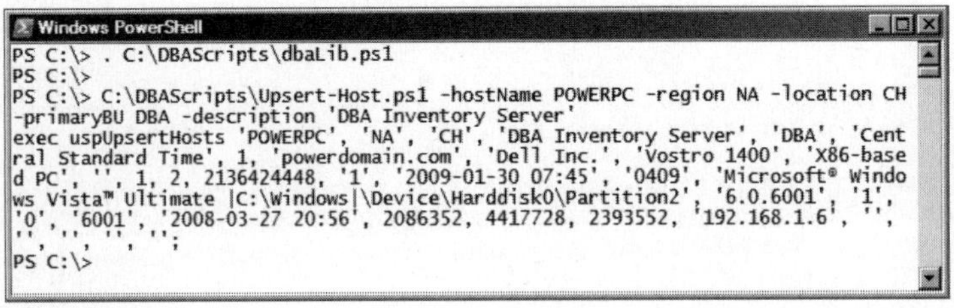

Figure 16-2

Before installing a new failover cluster instance, SQL2008CLUSTER, on a two-node Windows MSCS cluster PowerCluster, you need to run the Upsert-Host.ps1 script to insert the individual nodes, NODE1 and NODE2; the Upsert-Cluster.ps1 script to insert the cluster; and the Upsert-ClusterNode.ps1 script to associate the nodes with the cluster:

```
. C:\DBAScripts\dbaLib.ps1
# Add node 1 of a cluster for Investment Banking Division (IBD).
C:\DBAScripts\Upsert-Host.ps1 -hostName NODE1 -region NA -location CH
-primaryBU IBD -description 'IBD database cluster node 1'

# Add node 2 of a cluster for Investment Banking Division (IBD).
C:\DBAScripts\Upsert-Host.ps1 -hostName NODE2 -region NA -location CH
-primaryBU IBD -description 'IBD database cluster node 2'

C:\DBAScripts\Upsert-Cluster.ps1 -SQLClusterName SQL2008CLUSTER
-WindowsClusterName PowerCluster -numberOfNodes 2 -clusteringMethod MSCS

C:\DBAScripts\Upsert-ClusterNode.ps1 -SQLClusterName SQL2008CLUSTER -nodeName NODE1

C:\DBAScripts\Upsert-ClusterNode.ps1 -SQLClusterName SQL2008CLUSTER -nodeName NODE2
```

The output is shown in Figure 16-3.

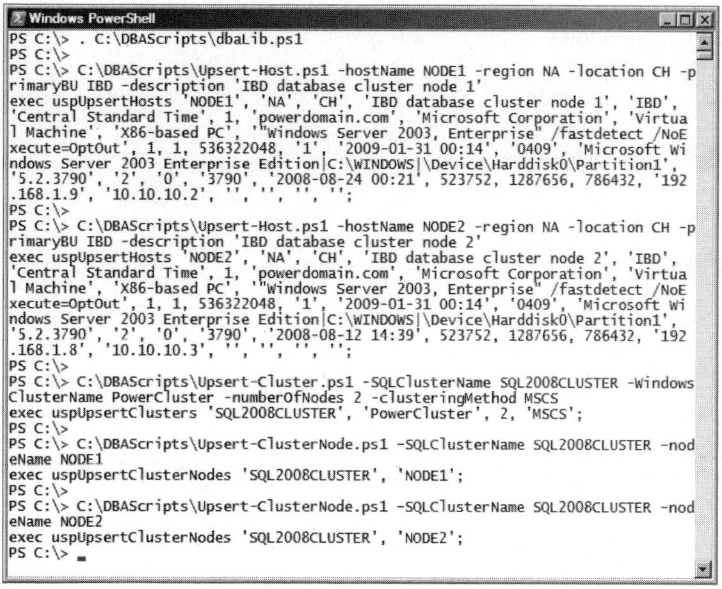

Figure 16-3

SQL Server Installation Template

It would be quite tedious and error-prone to put together all the setup parameters, so we have created a template file. The bare form of the template file is shown here:

```
# SQL Server installation type - STANDALONE or CLUSTER
SQLINSTALLTYPE=

# Name of the new SQL Server instance. MSSQLSERVER for default instance.
INSTANCENAME=
# Status of the SQL Server instance.
# Possible values include D for Development, Q for QA, P for Production,
U for UAT and R for Distaster Recovery.
STATUS=

# Location of SQL Server installation binaries
SQLDISTSVR=

# SQL Server edition ENT, STD, DEV
SQLEDITION=

# SQL SERVER Version - 2008, 2005 or 2000. Our script only supports 2008.
SQLVERSION=

# SQL Server Service pack - blank (for RTM), SP1, SP2. Our script only supports RTM.
SQLSERVICEPACK=

# SQL Server Features - SQL, SQLEngine, Replication, FullText, AS, RS,
IS, TOOLS, BIDS, BOL
FEATURES=
```

```
# SQL Server Security Mode. SQL for Mixed Mode. Blank for Windows Authentication Mode.
SECURITYMODE=

# User or group that will be provisioned with the sysadmin permissions.
# Make sure to include the account with which you will be running
Perform-PostSetupTasks.ps1
# so the post-setup tasks can be performed successfully.
SQLSYSADMINACCOUNTS=

# SQL Server service account
SQLSVCACCOUNT=

# SQL Server Agent Account
AGTSVCACCOUNT=

# Integrated Services Account
ISSVCACCOUNT=

# SQL Server binary directory
INSTANCEDIR=

# SQL Server shared component directory
INSTALLSHAREDDIR=

# SQL Server database files root directory
INSTALLSQLDATADIR=

# User database data directory
SQLUSERDBDIR=

# User database log directory
SQLUSERDBLOGDIR=

# tempdb data directory
SQLTEMPDBDIR=

# tempdb log directory
SQLTEMPDBLOGDIR=

# Backup directory
SQLBACKUPDIR=

# SQL Collation
SQLCOLLATION=

# Static TCP port number to be used
TCPPORT=

# Specify 0 to disable or 1 to enable the error reporting
ERRORREPORTING=

######################################################################
#                     STANDALONE PARAMETERS                          #
######################################################################
```

```
# Name of the standalone host on which the instance is being installed.
# For cluster, this should be blank.
HOSTNAME=

# Specify 0 to disable or 1 to enable the Named Pipes protocol
NPENABLED=


############################################################################
#                        CLUSTER PARAMETERS                                #
############################################################################
# Specify the domain group that contains the SQL Server service account
# and will be used to control access to SQL Server objects, and other
   cluster resources.
SQLDOMAINGROUP=

# Specify the domain group that contains the SQL Server Agent service account.
AGTDOMAINGROUP=

# Specifies the network name for the SQL Server cluster.
FAILOVERCLUSTERNETWORKNAME=

# Specify the cluster group that will contain the SQL Server resources.
FAILOVERCLUSTERGROUP=

# Names of the shared disk resources that will be used to store SQL Server data.
FAILOVERCLUSTERDISKS=

# Network IP address for the new failover instance in the format of
# "IP Protocl;IP Address;Public Network Name;Subnet Mask"
FAILOVERCLUSTERIPADDRESSES=
```

You'll need an installation script that reads the template file and parses the parameters to generate a Setup.exe command. Then the script invokes the command to install a new instance. The complete script, Install-Instance.ps1, follows here, and is available for download from the Wrox website for this book at www.wrox.com:

```
#===============================================================
#
# NAME: Install-Instance.ps1
# DATE  : 10/13/2008
# AUTHOR: Yan & MAK
# COMMENT: This script reads the template file, parses the parameters to generate
a Setup.exe command,
#          and then invokes the command to install a new instance.
#          Run this script on the standalone host or the active node of the cluster
#          that you want to install the new SQL Server instance on.
#
#          In the cluster case, this script installs a single-node cluster
#          and outputs the Setup.exe command you can run on each node you want to
add to the cluster.
#
# Example:
# Install-Instance.ps1 -filename C:\sqltemplate.txt -sapwd
xxxxxxxx -sqlsvcpwd xxxxxxxx -agtsvcpwd xxxxxxxx
#===============================================================
```

```
#########################################################################
# Initialize parameters
#########################################################################
param
(
        [switch] $help,
        [String] $filename={},
        [String] $sapwd={}, # sa password
        [String] $sqlsvcpwd={}, # SQL Server service account password
        [String] $agtsvcpwd={} # SQL Server Agent service account password
)


#########################################################################
# Function to install standalone instance
#########################################################################
Function InstallStandalone()
{
        [String] $installString=""

        # Construct the Setup.exe command from the parameters in the template file.
        $installString=$template.SQLDISTSVR + $template.SQLEDITION
+ "\Setup.exe /q /ACTION=Install "
        $installString=$installString + " /FEATURES=" +$template.FEATURES
        $installString=$installString + " /INSTANCENAME=" + $instanceName

        # Set the sa password only when SECURITYMODE is "SQL"
        if (( $template.SECURITYMODE.Length -gt 0 ) -and ( $sapwd.Length -gt 0 )) {
                $installString=$installString + " /SECURITYMODE=" +
$template.SECURITYMODE
                $installString=$installString + " /SAPWD=" + $sapwd
        }

        $installString=$installString + " /SQLSYSADMINACCOUNTS=" +
$template.SQLSYSADMINACCOUNTS

        $installString=$installString + " /SQLSVCACCOUNT=" +
$template.SQLSVCACCOUNT
        # Set the SQL Server service account password only when
SQLSVCPASSWORD is not blank.
        # For built-in accounts, such as LOCALSYSTEM, no password is needed.
        if ( $sqlsvcpwd.Length -gt 0 ) {
                $installString=$installString + " /SQLSVCPASSWORD=" + $sqlsvcpwd
        }

        $installString=$installString + " /AGTSVCACCOUNT=" +
$template.AGTSVCACCOUNT
        # Set the SQL Server Agent service account password only when
AGTSVCPASSWORD is not blank.
        # For built-in accounts, such as LOCALSYSTEM, no password is needed.
        if ( $agtsvcpwd.Length -gt 0 ) {
                $installString=$installString + " /AGTSVCPASSWORD=" + $agtsvcpwd
        }

        # Set the account for Integration Services.
        if ( $template.ISSVCACCOUNT.Length -gt 0 ) {
```

```
                    $installString=$installString + " /ISSVCACCOUNT=" +
$template.ISSVCACCOUNT
        }

        # Set the directories for SQL Server binary, shared components, database
files and backups
        $installString=$installString + " /INSTANCEDIR=" + $template.INSTANCEDIR
        $installString=$installString + " /INSTALLSHAREDDIR=" +
$template.INSTALLSHAREDDIR
        $installString=$installString + " /INSTALLSQLDATADIR=" +
$template.INSTALLSQLDATADIR

        if ( $template.SQLUSERDBDIR.Length -gt 0 ) {
                $installString=$installString + " /SQLUSERDBDIR=" +
$template.SQLUSERDBDIR
        }

        if ( $template.SQLUSERDBLOGDIR.Length -gt 0 ) {
                $installString=$installString + " /SQLUSERDBLOGDIR=" +
$template.SQLUSERDBLOGDIR
        }

        if ( $template.SQLTEMPDBDIR.Length -gt 0 ) {
                $installString=$installString + " /SQLTEMPDBDIR=" +
$template.SQLTEMPDBDIR
        }

        if ( $template.SQLTEMPDBLOGDIR.Length -gt 0 ) {
                $installString=$installString + " /SQLTEMPDBLOGDIR=" +
$template.SQLTEMPDBLOGDIR
        }

        if ( $template.SQLBACKUPDIR.Length -gt 0 ) {
                $installString=$installString + " /SQLBACKUPDIR=" +
$template.SQLBACKUPDIR
        }

        $installString=$installString + " /SQLCOLLATION=" + $template.SQLCOLLATION
        $installString=$installString + " /ERRORREPORTING=" +
$template.ERRORREPORTING

        # Enable TCP/IP protocol by default
        $installString=$installString + " /TCPENABLED=1"

        # Standalone specific parameter
        $installString=$installString + " /NPENABLED=" + $template.NPENABLED

        "Installing SQL Server instance " + $instanceName + " ..."
        $installString + "`n"

        # Invoke the Setup.exe command on the local computer
        Invoke-Expression $installString

}
```

```
###########################################################################
# Function to install failover cluster instance
###########################################################################
Function InstallCluster()
{
        [String] $installString=""

        # Construct the Setup.exe command from the parameters in the template file.
        $installString=$template.SQLDISTSVR + $template.SQLEDITION  +
"\Setup.exe /q /ACTION=InstallFailoverCluster "
        $installString=$installString + " /FEATURES=" +$template.FEATURES
        $installString=$installString + " /INSTANCENAME=" + $instanceName

        # Set the sa password only when SECURITYMODE is "SQL"
        if (( $template.SECURITYMODE.Length -gt 0 ) -and ( $sapwd.Length -gt 0 )) {
                $installString=$installString + " /SECURITYMODE=" +
$template.SECURITYMODE
                $installString=$installString + " /SAPWD=" + $sapwd
        }

        $installString=$installString + " /SQLSYSADMINACCOUNTS=" +
$template.SQLSYSADMINACCOUNTS

        $installString=$installString + " /SQLSVCACCOUNT=" +
$template.SQLSVCACCOUNT
        # Set the SQL Server service account password only when SQLSVCPASSWORD
is not blank.
        # For built-in accounts, such as LOCALSYSTEM, no password is needed.
        if ( $sqlsvcpwd.Length -gt 0 ) {
                $installString=$installString + " /SQLSVCPASSWORD=" + $sqlsvcpwd
        }

        $installString=$installString + " /AGTSVCACCOUNT=" +
$template.AGTSVCACCOUNT
        # Set the SQL Server Agent service account password only when AGTSVCPASSWORD
is not blank.
        # For built-in accounts, such as LOCALSYSTEM, no password is needed.
        if ( $agtsvcpwd.Length -gt 0 ) {
                $installString=$installString + " /AGTSVCPASSWORD=" + $agtsvcpwd
        }

        # Set the account for Integration Services.
        if ( $template.ISSVCACCOUNT.Length -gt 0 ) {
                $installString=$installString + " /ISSVCACCOUNT=" +
$template.ISSVCACCOUNT
        }

        # Set the directories for SQL Server binary, shared components, database
files and backups
        $installString=$installString + " /INSTANCEDIR=" + $template.INSTANCEDIR
        $installString=$installString + " /INSTALLSHAREDDIR=" +
$template.INSTALLSHAREDDIR
        $installString=$installString + " /INSTALLSQLDATADIR=" +
$template.INSTALLSQLDATADIR
```

```
        if ( $template.SQLUSERDBDIR.Length -gt 0 ) {
                $installString=$installString + " /SQLUSERDBDIR=" +
$template.SQLUSERDBDIR
        }

        if ( $template.SQLUSERDBLOGDIR.Length -gt 0 ) {
                $installString=$installString + " /SQLUSERDBLOGDIR=" +
$template.SQLUSERDBLOGDIR
        }

        if ( $template.SQLTEMPDBDIR.Length -gt 0 ) {
                $installString=$installString + " /SQLTEMPDBDIR=" +
$template.SQLTEMPDBDIR
        }

        if ( $template.SQLTEMPDBLOGDIR.Length -gt 0 ) {
                $installString=$installString + " /SQLTEMPDBLOGDIR=" +
$template.SQLTEMPDBLOGDIR
        }

        if ( $template.SQLBACKUPDIR.Length -gt 0 ) {
                $installString=$installString + " /SQLBACKUPDIR=" +
$template.SQLBACKUPDIR
        }

        $installString=$installString + " /SQLCOLLATION=" + $template.SQLCOLLATION
        $installString=$installString + " /ERRORREPORTING=" +
$template.ERRORREPORTING

        # Cluster specific parameters
        $installString=$installString + " /SQLDOMAINGROUP=" +
$template.SQLDOMAINGROUP
        $installString=$installString + " /AGTDOMAINGROUP=" +
$template.AGTDOMAINGROUP
        $installString=$installString + " /FAILOVERCLUSTERNETWORKNAME=" +
$template.FAILOVERCLUSTERNETWORKNAME
        $installString=$installString + " /FAILOVERCLUSTERGROUP=" +
$template.FAILOVERCLUSTERGROUP
        $installString=$installString + " /FAILOVERCLUSTERDISKS=" +
$template.FAILOVERCLUSTERDISKS
        $installString=$installString + " /FAILOVERCLUSTERIPADDRESSES=" +
$template.FAILOVERCLUSTERIPADDRESSES

        "Installing a single-node SQL Server failover cluster instance " +
$instanceName
        "The SQL Server cluster group is " + $template.FAILOVERCLUSTERNETWORKNAME
+ " ..."

        $installString + "`n"

        # Invoke the Setup.exe command on the local computer
        Invoke-Expression $installString

        # Create the Setup.exe command you can run on each node you want to
add to the cluster.
```

```
        "After confirm that the single-node cluster was installed successfully,
please run the following Setup command on each node you want to add to the cluster.`n"

        $installString=""
        $installString=$template.SQLDISTSVR + $template.SQLEDITION +
"\Setup.exe /q /ACTION=AddNode "
        $installString=$installString + " /INSTANCENAME=" + $instanceName

        $installString=$installString + " /SQLSVCACCOUNT=" +
$template.SQLSVCACCOUNT
        if ( $sqlsvcpwd.Length -gt 0 ) {
                $installString=$installString + " /SQLSVCPASSWORD=" + $sqlsvcpwd
        }

        $installString=$installString + " /AGTSVCACCOUNT=" +
$template.AGTSVCACCOUNT
        if ( $agtsvcpwd.Length -gt 0 ) {
                $installString=$installString + " /AGTSVCPASSWORD=" + $agtsvcpwd
        }

        $installString + "`n"
}

##########################################################################
# Main Program
##########################################################################

if ( $help ) {
        "Usage: Install-Instance.ps1 -filename <string[]> -sapwd [<string[]>]
-sqlsvcpwd [<string[]>] -agtsvcpwd [<string[]>]"
        exit 0
}

if ( $filename.Length -eq 0 ) {
        "Please enter a template file name."
        exit 1
}

# Read the template file and parse the parameters
$file=Get-Content $filename
$file | Foreach-Object {$template = @{}}
{$template[$_.split('=')[0]] = $_.split('=')[1]}

[String] $instanceName=$template.INSTANCENAME

if ($template.SQLINSTALLTYPE -eq "STANDALONE")
{
        # Invoke the function to install a standalone instance
        InstallStandalone
}
elseif ($template.SQLINSTALLTYPE -eq "CLUSTER")
{
        # Invoke the function to install a failover cluster instance
        InstallCluster
```

```
}
else {
        "Invalid installation type!"
        exit 2
}
}
```

Standalone Installation Example

In this example, we install a named instance, INSTANCE1, on POWERPC using the template file and the installation script. We take the bare-form template file and fill in the parameter values for the new standalone SQL Server instance and save it under the C:\DBAScripts directory. The template file, StandaloneTemplate.txt, is shown here:

```
# SQL Server installation type - STANDALONE or CLUSTER
SQLINSTALLTYPE=STANDALONE

# Name of the new SQL Server instance. MSSQLSERVER for default instance.
INSTANCENAME=INSTANCE1

# Status of the SQL Server instance.
# Possible values include D for Development, Q for QA, P for Production, U for
UAT and R for Distaster Recovery.
STATUS=P

# Location of SQL Server installation binaries
SQLDISTSVR=\\DEMOPC\SQL2008Install\

# SQL Server edition ENT, STD, DEV
SQLEDITION=DEV

# SQL SERVER Version - 2008, 2005 or 2000. Our script only supports 2008.
SQLVERSION=2008

# SQL Server Service pack - blank (for RTM), SP1, SP2. Our script only supports RTM.
SQLSERVICEPACK=

# SQL Server Features - SQL, SQLEngine, Replication, FullText, AS, RS, IS,
TOOLS, BIDS, BOL
FEATURES=SQL,IS,Tools,BOL,BIDS

# SQL Server Security Mode. SQL for Mixed Mode. Blank for Windows Authentication Mode.
SECURITYMODE=SQL

# User or group that will be provisioned with the sysadmin permissions.
# Make sure to include the account with which you will be running
Perform-PostSetupTasks.ps1
# so the post-setup tasks can be performed successfully.
SQLSYSADMINACCOUNTS="PowerDomain\SqlService" "PowerDomain\PowerUser"

# SQL Server service account
SQLSVCACCOUNT="PowerDomain\SqlService"
```

```
# SQL Server Agent Account
AGTSVCACCOUNT="PowerDomain\SqlService"

# Integrated Services Account
ISSVCACCOUNT="NT Authority\Network Service"

# SQL Server binary directory
INSTANCEDIR="C:\Program Files\Microsoft SQL Server"

# SQL Server shared component directory
INSTALLSHAREDDIR="C:\Program Files\Microsoft SQL Server"

# SQL Server database files root directory
INSTALLSQLDATADIR="D:\SQLServer"

# User database data directory
SQLUSERDBDIR=

# User database log directory
SQLUSERDBLOGDIR=

# tempdb data directory
SQLTEMPDBDIR=

# tempdb log directory
SQLTEMPDBLOGDIR=

# Backup directory
SQLBACKUPDIR=

# SQL Collation
SQLCOLLATION=SQL_Latin1_General_CP1_CI_AS

# Static TCP port number to be used
TCPPORT=7001

# Specify 0 to disable or 1 to enable the error reporting
ERRORREPORTING=1

#######################################################################
#    STANDALONE PARAMETERS                                            #
#######################################################################
# Name of the standalone host on which the instance is being installed.
# For cluster, this should be blank.
HOSTNAME=POWERPC

# Specify 0 to disable or 1 to enable the Named Pipes protocol
NPENABLED=1

#######################################################################
#    CLUSTER PARAMETERS                                               #
#######################################################################
# Specify the domain group that contains the SQL Server service account
# and will be used to control access to SQL Server objects, and other
cluster resources.
```

```
SQLDOMAINGROUP=

# Specify the domain group that contains the SQL Server Agent service account.
AGTDOMAINGROUP=

# Specifies the network name for the SQL Server cluster.
FAILOVERCLUSTERNETWORKNAME=

# Specify the cluster group that will contain the SQL Server resources.
FAILOVERCLUSTERGROUP=

# Names of the shared disk resources that will be used to store SQL Server data.
FAILOVERCLUSTERDISKS=

# Network IP address for the new failover instance in the format of
# "IP Protocl;IP Address;Public Network Name;Subnet Mask"
FAILOVERCLUSTERIPADDRESSES=
```

After going through the template file and filling in the values, you can run the `Install-Instance.ps1` script as follows. Please run the script under a local administrator account. The `sa` password is passed to the script and will be set to `Pa$$w0rd`. The password for the service account `PowerDomain\SqlService`, which will be used for SQL Server and SQL Server Agent, is `P@ssw0rd`:

```
C:\DBAScripts\Install-Instance.ps1 C:\DBAScripts\StandaloneTemplate.txt -sapwd
'Pa$$w0rd' -sqlsvcpwd 'P@ssw0rd' -agtsvcpwd 'P@ssw0rd'
```

As shown in Figure 16-4, the installation script generates the setup command based on the template file, and installs the new instance, INSTANCE1, on the computer POWERPC.

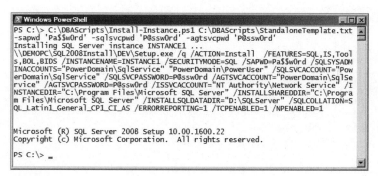

Figure 16-4

You can check the logs under `C:\Program Files\Microsoft SQL Server\100\Setup Bootstrap\Log` to ensure that the instance has been installed successfully.

After confirming the success of the installation, you can continue to perform the post-setup tasks:

1. Change the TCP port to a static port as specified in the template file.
2. Add the server into the inventory.

The `Perform-PostSetupTasks.ps1` script, which follows, is available for download from the Wrox website for this book:

```
# ============================================================
#
# NAME: Perform-PostSetupTasks.ps1
# DATE  : 10/13/2008
# AUTHOR : Yan & MAK
#
# COMMENT: This script performs post-setup tasks, which includes
#          1. Change the TCP port to a static port as specified in the template file
#          2. Add the server into the inventory.
#
#          Run this script on the SQL Server standalone host or the active node
# of the SQL Server cluster.
#
# Example:
# Perform-PostSetupTasks.ps1 -filename <string[]>
# ============================================================

##########################################################################
# Initialize parameters
##########################################################################
param
(
        [switch] $help,
        [String] $filename={} # Template file name
)


##########################################################################
# Post-setup tasks
##########################################################################

if ( $help ) {
        "Usage: Perform-PostSetupTasks.ps1 -filename <string[]>"
        exit 0
}

if ( $filename.Length -eq 0 ) {
        "Please enter a template file name."
        exit 1
}


# Read the template file and parse the parameters.
$file=Get-Content $filename
$file | Foreach-Object {$template = @{}} {$template[$_.split('=')[0]] =
$_.split('=')[1]}

[String] $instanceName=$template.INSTANCENAME
[String] $sqlNetworkName=""
[String] $tcpport=$template.TCPPORT

# Check whether the SQL Server 2008 instance has been installed successfully.
```

```
$sqlservice=Get-WmiObject -namespace root\Microsoft\SqlServer\ComputerManagement10
-class SqlService -filter "DisplayName='SQL Server ($instanceName)'"

# If the SQL Server instance has been installed successfully
if ($sqlservice)
{
        # Standalone instance
        if ($template.SQLINSTALLTYPE -eq "STANDALONE") {

                # Get rid of unnecessary double quotes
                $sqlNetworkName=$template.HOSTNAME.Replace("`"", "")

                # Set TCP port as specified in the template file
                "Setting TCP port to " + $tcpport + " ..."
                # Disable dynamic ports
                $dynamicPorts=Get-WmiObject -namespace root\Microsoft\SqlServer\
ComputerManagement10 -class ServerNetworkProtocolProperty `
                -filter "PropertyName='TcpDynamicPorts' and IPAddressName='IPAll'
and InstanceName='$instanceName'"
                $dynamicPorts.SetStringValue("") | Out-Null
                # Set static port
                $staticPort=Get-WmiObject -namespace root\Microsoft\SqlServer\
ComputerManagement10 -class ServerNetworkProtocolProperty `
                -filter "PropertyName='TcpPort' and
IPAddressName='IPAll' and InstanceName='$instanceName'"
                $staticPort.SetStringValue($tcpport) | Out-Null

                # Restart server for the new port number to take effect ...
                $sqlservice.StopService() | Out-Null
                $sqlservice.StartService() | Out-Null

                "Waiting for the SQL Server service to be completely recovered ..."
                Start-Sleep 60

                # Execute Upsert-Server to insert the new instance into the inventory
                "Adding new instance to the inventory ..."
                Invoke-Sqlcmd -Query "exec sp_configure 'show advanced options', 1;
RECONFIGURE" `
                -ServerInstance "$sqlNetworkName,$tcpport" -Database master

                [String] $upsertString="C:\DBAScripts\Upsert-Server -instanceName "
+ $instanceName `
                + " -hostName " + $sqlNetworkName + " -status " + $template.STATUS

                $upsertString + "`n"

                Invoke-Expression $upsertString
        }

        #Failover cluster instance
        elseif ($template.SQLINSTALLTYPE -eq "CLUSTER") {

                # Get rid of unnecessary double quotes
                $sqlNetworkName=$template.FAILOVERCLUSTERNETWORKNAME
.Replace("`"", "")
```

```
                # Set TCP port as specified in the template file
                "Setting TCP port to " + $tcpport + " ..."
                # Disable dynamic ports
                $dynamicPorts=Get-WmiObject -namespace root\Microsoft\SqlServer\
ComputerManagement10 -class ServerNetworkProtocolProperty `
                    -filter "PropertyName='TcpDynamicPorts' and IPAddressName='IPAll' and
InstanceName='$instanceName'"
                $dynamicPorts.SetStringValue("") | Out-Null
                # Set static port
                $staticPort=Get-WmiObject -namespace root\Microsoft\SqlServer\
ComputerManagement10 -class ServerNetworkProtocolProperty `
                    -filter "PropertyName='TcpPort' and IPAddressName='IPAll' and
InstanceName='$instanceName'"
                $staticPort.SetStringValue($tcpport) | Out-Null

                # Restart server for the new port number to take effect ...
                $sqlservice.StopService() | Out-Null
                $sqlservice.StartService() | Out-Null

                "Waiting for the SQL Server cluster group to be completely
recovered ..."

                Start-Sleep 300

                # Execute Upsert-Server to insert the new instance into the
inventory
                "Adding new instance to the inventory ..."
                Invoke-Sqlcmd -Query "exec sp_configure 'show advanced options', 1;
RECONFIGURE" `
                    -ServerInstance "$sqlNetworkName,$tcpport" -Database master

                [String] $upsertString="C:\DBAScripts\Upsert-Server
-instanceName " + $instanceName `
                    + " -clusterName " + $sqlNetworkName + " -status " +
$template.STATUS

                $upsertString + "`n"

                Invoke-Expression $upsertString
        }
        else {
                "Invalid installation type!"
                exit 2
        }
}
# If the SQL Server instance does NOT exist
else {
        "Cannot detect the SQL Server instance $instanceName. Please make sure
the instance is running."
        exit 3
}}
```

Run the `Perform-PostSetupTasks.ps1` script to configure the newly created instance, INSTANCE1, on PowerPC, and insert it into the inventory. Before running the script, make sure the instance is running. Please run the script under an account that is a local administrator and a member of the `sysadmin` server role in the new instance:

```
. C:\DBAScripts\dbaLib.ps1
C:\DBAScripts\Perform-PostSetupTasks.ps1 C:\DBAScripts\StandaloneTemplate.txt
```

As shown in Figure 16-5, the script sets the TCP port to the static port 7001 as specified in the template file.

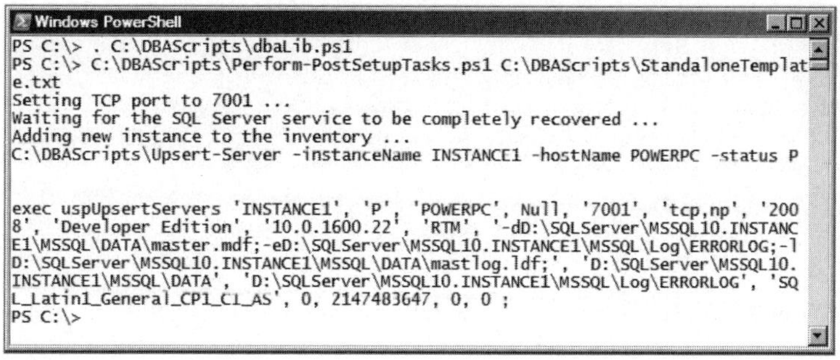

Figure 16-5

Next, it restarts the SQL Server instance INSTANCE1 in order for the new port number to take effect. Then it adds the new server into the inventory.

Cluster Installation Example

You can follow the same procedure to create a SQL Server failover cluster instance. This example installs a default failover cluster instance on a SQL Server cluster group SQL2008CLUSTER on the Windows cluster PowerCluster. To begin, fill in the parameter values in the template file ClusterTemplate.txt and save it under the C:\DBAScripts directory:

```
# SQL Server installation type - STANDALONE or CLUSTER
SQLINSTALLTYPE=CLUSTER

# Name of the new SQL Server instance. MSSQLSERVER for default instance.
INSTANCENAME=MSSQLSERVER

# Status of the SQL Server instance.
# Possible values include D for Development, Q for QA, P for Production, U
for UAT and R for Distaster Recovery.
STATUS=P

# Location of SQL Server installation binaries
SQLDISTSVR=\\DEMOPC\SQL2008Install\

# SQL Server edition ENT, STD, DEV
SQLEDITION=DEV

# SQL SERVER Version - 2008, 2005 or 2000. Our script only supports 2008.
SQLVERSION=2008

# SQL Server Service pack - blank (for RTM), SP1, SP2. Our script only supports RTM.
SQLSERVICEPACK=
```

395

```
# SQL Server Features - SQL, SQLEngine, Replication, FullText, AS,
RS, IS, TOOLS, BIDS, BOL
FEATURES=SQL,Tools,BOL

# SQL Server Security Mode. SQL for Mixed Mode. Blank for Windows Authentication Mode.
SECURITYMODE=

# User or group that will be provisioned with the sysadmin permissions.
# Make sure to include the account with which you will be running
Perform-PostSetupTasks.ps1
# so the post-setup tasks can be performed successfully.
SQLSYSADMINACCOUNTS="PowerDomain\SqlService" "PowerDomain\PowerUser"

# SQL Server service account
SQLSVCACCOUNT="PowerDomain\SqlService"

# SQL Server Agent Account
AGTSVCACCOUNT="PowerDomain\SqlService"

# Integrated Services Account
ISSVCACCOUNT=

# SQL Server binary directory
INSTANCEDIR="C:\Program Files\Microsoft SQL Server"

# SQL Server shared component directory
INSTALLSHAREDDIR="C:\Program Files\Microsoft SQL Server"

# SQL Server database files root directory
INSTALLSQLDATADIR="D:\SQLServer"

# User database data directory
SQLUSERDBDIR=

# User database log directory
SQLUSERDBLOGDIR="L:\SQLServer\MSSQL10.MSSQLSERVER\MSSQL\Log"

# tempdb data directory
SQLTEMPDBDIR=

# tempdb log directory
SQLTEMPDBLOGDIR="L:\SQLServer\MSSQL10.MSSQLSERVER\MSSQL\Log"

# Backup directory
SQLBACKUPDIR=

# SQL Collation
SQLCOLLATION=SQL_Latin1_General_CP1_CI_AS

# Static TCP port number to be used
TCPPORT=7001
```

```
# Specify 0 to disable or 1 to enable the error reporting
ERRORREPORTING=1

#####################################################################
#                     STANDALONE PARAMETERS                         #
#####################################################################
# Name of the standalone host on which the instance is being installed.
# For cluster, this should be blank.
HOSTNAME=

# Specify 0 to disable or 1 to enable the Named Pipes protocol
NPENABLED=

#####################################################################
#                      CLUSTER PARAMETERS                           #
#####################################################################
# Specify the domain group that contains the SQL Server service account
# and will be used to control access to SQL Server objects, and other
cluster resources.
SQLDOMAINGROUP="PowerDomain\SQLAdmins"

# Specify the domain group that contains the SQL Server Agent service account.
AGTDOMAINGROUP="PowerDomain\SQLAdmins"

# Specifies the network name for the SQL Server cluster.
FAILOVERCLUSTERNETWORKNAME="SQL2008CLUSTER"

# Specify the cluster group that will contain the SQL Server resources.
FAILOVERCLUSTERGROUP="SQL Server 2008 Group"

# Names of the shared disk resources that will be used to store SQL Server data.
FAILOVERCLUSTERDISKS="SQL Data" "SQL Log"

# Network IP address for the new failover instance in the format of
# "IP Protocl;IP Address;Public Network Name;Subnet Mask"
FAILOVERCLUSTERIPADDRESSES="IPv4;192.168.1.12;Public;255.255.255.0"
```

On the active node of the Windows cluster PowerCluster, run the Install-Instance.ps1script to install a single-node failover cluster instance MSSQLSERVER on a SQL Server cluster group SQL2008CLUSTER. Please run the script under a local administrator account. The password for the service account, PowerDomain\SqlService, that will be used for SQL Server and SQL Server Agent, is P@ssw0rd. Because you are configuring the new instance to use Windows Authentication mode in the template file, no sa password is passed:

```
C:\DBAScripts\Install-Instance.ps1 C:\DBAScripts\ClusterTemplate.txt -sqlsvcpwd
'P@ssw0rd' -agtsvcpwd 'P@ssw0rd'
```

As shown in Figure 16-6, the script generates the Setup.exe command to install a single-node failover cluster instance MSSQLSERVER on a SQL Server cluster group SQL2008CLUSTER.

Figure 16-6

You can check the logs under `C:\Program Files\Microsoft SQL Server\100\Setup Bootstrap\Log` to ensure that the instance has been installed successfully. The script also prints out the `Setup.exe` command, which can be used to add additional nodes to the cluster SQL2008CLUSTER. After confirming the success of the installation, you can run the command as a local administrator on other nodes of the Windows cluster PowerCluster, as shown in Figure 16-7. Please note that no failovers are necessary.

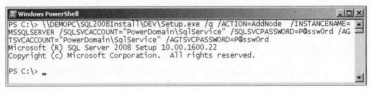

Figure 16-7

After confirming that the failover cluster instance has been installed and configured successfully on all the nodes, you can continue to perform the post-setup tasks on the active node. Before running the script, please ensure that the failover cluster instance is running. Run the script under an account that is a local administrator and a member of the `sysadmin` server role in the new instance:

```
. C:\DBAScripts\dbaLib.ps1
C:\DBAScripts\Perform-PostSetupTasks.ps1 C:\DBAScripts\ClusterTemplate.txt
```

As shown in Figure 16-8, the script sets the TCP port to the static port 7001 as specified in the template file. Next, it restarts the SQL Server failover cluster instance in order for the new port number to take effect. Please note that the service is restarted before an automatic failover happens. Then the script adds the new instance into the inventory.

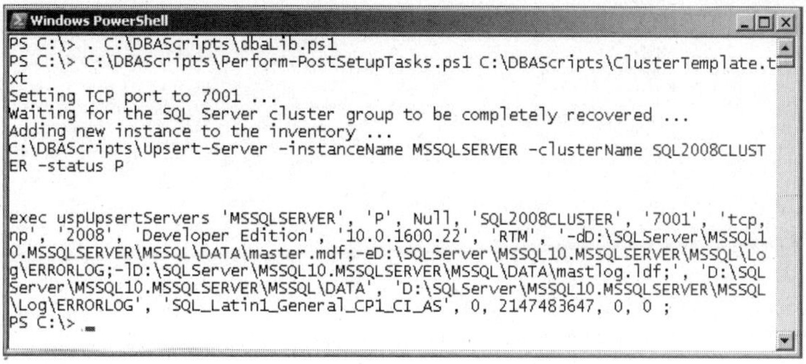

```
Windows PowerShell                                                    _ □ x
PS C:\> . C:\DBAScripts\dbaLib.ps1
PS C:\> C:\DBAScripts\Perform-PostSetupTasks.ps1 C:\DBAScripts\ClusterTemplate.t
xt
Setting TCP port to 7001 ...
Waiting for the SQL Server cluster group to be completely recovered ...
Adding new instance to the inventory ...
C:\DBAScripts\Upsert-Server -instanceName MSSQLSERVER -clusterName SQL2008CLUST
ER -status P

exec uspUpsertServers 'MSSQLSERVER', 'P', Null, 'SQL2008CLUSTER', '7001', 'tcp,
np', '2008', 'Developer Edition', '10.0.1600.22', 'RTM', '-dD:\SQLServer\MSSQL1
0.MSSQLSERVER\MSSQL\DATA\master.mdf;-eD:\SQLServer\MSSQL10.MSSQLSERVER\MSSQL\Lo
g\ERRORLOG;-lD:\SQLServer\MSSQL10.MSSQLSERVER\MSSQL\DATA\mastlog.ldf;', 'D:\SQL
Server\MSSQL10.MSSQLSERVER\MSSQL\DATA', 'D:\SQLServer\MSSQL10.MSSQLSERVER\MSSQL
\Log\ERRORLOG', 'SQL_Latin1_General_CP1_CI_AS', 0, 2147483647, 0, 0 ;
PS C:\> _
```

Figure 16-8

Summary

This chapter presented a solution for a bulk SQL Server installation with a template file and two installation scripts. By simply adding values in the template file, you can run the installation scripts to install and configure standalone or cluster failover SQL Server instances. Subsequent chapters will continue to focus on automation. You will see that the combination of Windows PowerShell and SQL Server 2008 can take you a long way.

17

Collecting SQL Server Performance and Host Performance Data

The previous two chapters covered PowerShell and T-SQL procedures related to SQL Server inventory and database administration and installation. In this chapter you are going to see the various methods used to collect performance-related data from SQL Server. Performance bottlenecks can arise on three different resources: disk, memory, and CPU. Collecting performance-related data from SQL Server is very important for any troubleshooting. This chapter illustrates how to collect such data related to these resources.

SQL Server 2008 comes with the new feature Performance Data Collection. This chapter covers some functionality of the Data Collector by using Windows PowerShell. This chapter will also help you understand how to execute SQL Server stored procedures on a remote machine and bring the output data from one server to another.

There are two types of performance-related data activities. One is collecting performance-related data from the host; the other is collecting performance-related data related to the SQL Server instance. Both are equally important for troubleshooting any performance-related issues. Performance-related data collection can be scheduled on-host or off-host depending on the company and resource utilization.

SQL Server Performance Data Collection

First we'll collect information related to SQL Server. Data collection based on SQL Server–related performance is usually an on-host job because it involves large amounts of data and you don't want to fill up the network bandwidth. As discussed in the previous chapter, there will always be an administration database on the SQL Server instance that you install. Any method you use to collect data requires two components: a place to store the data, which would be a database, and the scripts that get the performance data from the host or the SQL Server.

If you haven't created such a database, then create the following admin database now:

```
create database admin
go
use admin
go
```

Now create the following tables that store the SQL Server–related performance data. You can execute the following T-SQL commands on every server or make it a part of the SQL Server installation. Here we are creating five tables in the admin database:

❑   AWEAllocated

❑   LogFileUsage

❑   TopQueries

❑   TaskCount

❑   TopMemConsumption

The table AWEAllocated stores data related to the amount of memory allocated by the memory clerks used by Address Windowing Extensions (AWE). SQL Server supports AWE, which enables the use of physical memory over 4 gigabytes (GB) on 32-bit versions of Microsoft Windows operating systems. The table LogFileUsage stores data related to log file usage in every database on the server. The table TopQueries will store data related to the top ten queries being executed based on CPU usage. The table TaskCount will store data related to SQL Scheduler on the server. The table TopMemConsumption stores data related to all the memory clerks that are currently active in the server. Here is the code to create the tables:

```
SET ANSI_NULLS ON
GO
SET QUOTED_IDENTIFIER ON
GO

USE [admin]
GO

/****** Object:  Table [dbo].[AWEAllocated]   Script Date: 08/21/2008 11:47:19 ******/
IF  EXISTS (SELECT * FROM sys.objects WHERE object_id = OBJECT_ID(N'[dbo].
   [AWEAllocated]') AND type in (N'U'))
DROP TABLE [dbo].[AWEAllocated]
GO

CREATE TABLE [dbo].[AWEAllocated](
 [AWE allocated, Mb] [bigint] NULL,
 [servername] [sysname] NULL,
 [datestamp] [datetime] NULL
) ON [PRIMARY]

GO

/****** Object:  Table [dbo].[LogFileUsage]   Script Date: 08/21/2008 11:47:49 ******/
IF  EXISTS (SELECT * FROM sys.objects WHERE object_id = OBJECT_ID(N'[dbo].
   [LogFileUsage]') AND type in (N'U'))
```

```
DROP TABLE [dbo].[LogFileUsage]
GO

CREATE TABLE [dbo].[LogFileUsage](
 [servername] [nvarchar](128) NULL,
 [instance_name] [nchar](128) NULL,
 [Log File(s) Used Size (KB)] [bigint] NOT NULL,
 [datestamp] [datetime] NOT NULL
) ON [PRIMARY]

GO

/****** Object:  Table [dbo].[TopQueries]    Script Date: 08/21/2008 12:24:27 ******/
IF  EXISTS (SELECT * FROM sys.objects WHERE object_id = OBJECT_ID(N'[dbo].
   [TopQueries]') AND type in (N'U'))
DROP TABLE [dbo].[TopQueries]
GO

CREATE TABLE [dbo].[TopQueries](
 [Servername] [nvarchar](128) NULL,
 [creation_time] [datetime] NOT NULL,
 [last_execution_time] [datetime] NOT NULL,
 [row_no] [bigint] NULL,
 [l1] [bigint] NULL,
 [total_worker_time] [numeric](26, 6) NULL,
 [AvgCPUTime] [numeric](38, 18) NULL,
 [LogicalReads] [bigint] NOT NULL,
 [LogicalWrites] [bigint] NOT NULL,
 [execution_count] [bigint] NOT NULL,
[AggIO] [bigint] NULL,
 [AvgIO] [numeric](38, 18) NULL,
[query_text] [nvarchar](max) NULL,
 [db_name] [nvarchar](128) NULL,
 [object_id] [int] NULL,
 [datestamp] [datetime] NOT NULL
) ON [PRIMARY]

GO

/****** Object:  Table [dbo].[TaskCount]    Script Date: 08/21/2008 11:48:02 ******/
IF  EXISTS (SELECT * FROM sys.objects WHERE object_id = OBJECT_ID(N'[dbo].
   [TaskCount]') AND type in (N'U'))
DROP TABLE [dbo].[TaskCount]
GO

CREATE TABLE [dbo].[TaskCount](
 [scheduler_id] [int] NOT NULL,
 [current_tasks_count] [int] NOT NULL,
 [runnable_tasks_count] [int] NOT NULL,
 [servername] [sysname] NULL,
 [datestamp] [datetime] NULL
) ON [PRIMARY]
GO

/****** Object:  Table [dbo].[TopMemConsumption]    Script Date: 08/21/2008
   11:48:15 ******/
```

```
IF  EXISTS (SELECT * FROM sys.objects WHERE object_id = OBJECT_ID(N'[dbo].
   [TopMemConsumption]') AND type in (N'U'))
DROP TABLE [dbo].[TopMemConsumption]
GO

CREATE TABLE [dbo].[TopMemConsumption](
 [servername] [nvarchar](128) NULL,
 [type] [nvarchar](60) NOT NULL,
 [SPA Mem, Kb] [bigint] NULL,
 [datestamp] [datetime] NOT NULL
) ON [PRIMARY]

GO
```

Now create the following procedure that retrieves the data from various dynamic management views (DMVs) and stores the SQL server–related performance data into the tables you just created. The DMVs used in this procedure are as follows:

❑ `sys.dm_os_schedulers`

❑ `sys.dm_os_memory_clerks`

❑ `sys.dm_exec_query_stats`

❑ `sys.dm_exec_sql_text`

❑ `sys.dm_os_performance_counters`

Microsoft introduced dynamic management views and functions to get server state information that can be used to monitor the health of a server instance, diagnose problems, and tune performance. We use the preceding DMVs to get specific information:

❑ Log file usage from `sys.dm_os_performance_counters`

❑ AWE memory from `sys.dm_os_memory_clerks`

❑ Top ten queries from `sys.dm_exec_query_stats` and `sys.dm_exec_sql_text`

❑ SQL Server Scheduler task counts from `sys.dm_os_schedulers`

❑ Top memory consumption by type of memory clerk from `sys.dm_os_memory_clerks`

```
USE [admin]
GO

/****** Object:  StoredProcedure [dbo].[uspCollectPerfData]    Script Date: 08/21/2008
   11:53:23 ******/
IF  EXISTS (SELECT * FROM sys.objects WHERE object_id = OBJECT_ID(N'[dbo].
   [uspCollectPerfData]') AND type in (N'P', N'PC'))
DROP PROCEDURE [dbo].[uspCollectPerfData]
GO

CREATE PROCEDURE  uspCollectPerfData as
set nocount on

INSERT INTO TaskCount (servername,scheduler_id,current_tasks_count,
   runnable_tasks_count,datestamp )
```

```
SELECT @@SERVERNAME,
scheduler_id,current_tasks_count,runnable_tasks_count, GETDATE()
FROM sys.dm_os_schedulers
WHERE scheduler_id < 255

INSERT INTO AWEAllocated (servername, [AWE allocated, Mb],datestamp )
SELECT @@SERVERNAME,
SUM(awe_allocated_kb) / 1024 as [AWE allocated, Mb], GETDATE()
FROM sys.dm_os_memory_clerks

INSERT INTO LogFileUsage (servername,instance_name,[Log File(s) Used Size
    (KB)],datestamp)
SELECT @@SERVERNAME,
instance_name,cntr_value 'Log File(s) Used Size (KB)', GETDATE()
FROM sys.dm_os_performance_counters
WHERE counter_name = 'Log File(s) Used Size (KB)'
order by instance_name desc

INSERT INTO TopMemConsumption (servername, type,[SPA Mem, Kb] ,datestamp)
SELECT TOP 10 @@SERVERNAME,
type, SUM(single_pages_kb) as [SPA Mem, Kb], GETDATE()
FROM sys.dm_os_memory_clerks
GROUP BY type
ORDER BY SUM(single_pages_kb) DESC


INSERT INTO TopQueries (
Servername,creation_time,
last_execution_time,
row_no,
l1,
total_worker_time,
AvgCPUTime,
LogicalReads,
LogicalWrites,
execution_count,
AggIO,
AvgIO,
query_text,
db_name ,
object_id ,
datestamp)
select Top 10 @@SERVERNAME,
       creation_time
,       last_execution_time
,rank() over(order by (total_worker_time+0.0)/
 execution_count desc,
 sql_handle,statement_start_offset ) as row_no
,       (rank() over(order by (total_worker_time+0.0)/
 execution_count desc,
 sql_handle,statement_start_offset ))%2 as l1
,       (total_worker_time+0.0)/1000 as total_worker_time
,       (total_worker_time+0.0)/(execution_count*1000)
 as [AvgCPUTime]
,       total_logical_reads as [LogicalReads]
```

```
,          total_logical_writes as [LogicalWrites]
,          execution_count
,          total_logical_reads+total_logical_writes as [AggIO]
,          (total_logical_reads+total_logical_writes)/
 (execution_count+0.0) as [AvgIO]
,          case when sql_handle IS NULL
               then ' '
               else ( substring(st.text,(qs.statement_start_offset+2)/2,
     (case when qs.statement_end_offset = -1
     then len(convert(nvarchar(MAX),st.text))*2
     else qs.statement_end_offset
     end - qs.statement_start_offset) /2  ) )
          end as query_text
,          db_name(st.dbid) as db_name
,          st.objectid as object_id,
GETDATE()
from sys.dm_exec_query_stats  qs
cross apply sys.dm_exec_sql_text(sql_handle) st
where total_worker_time  > 0
order by (total_worker_time+0.0)/(execution_count*1000)

GO
```

You can create the preceding tables and procedures using the SQLPerfmonDDL.sql file available for download from the Wrox website for this book. Once you have executed the preceding script, you have created the tables where you can store all the performance-related data and the stored procedure to collect the performance data.

The next step is to create the script that actually gets the performance-related data from the servers.

Now create the PowerShell script C:\DBASripts\Collect-SQLPerfmonData.ps1, as shown in the following code. This script accepts a server name as parameter and then executes the uspCollectPerfData stored procedure created earlier on that server:

```
#==============================================================
#
# NAME: Collect-SQLPerfmonData.ps1
#
# AUTHOR: Yan and MAK
# DATE  : 5/1/2008
#
# COMMENT: This script collects SQL Server performance data from a SQL Server
    instance
#==============================================================

param (
  [string] $serverName
)

. C:\DBAScripts\dbaLib.ps1

if ( $serverName.Length -eq 0 ) {
"Please enter a server name."
     exit 1
}
```

```
Invoke-Sqlcmd -Query "exec dbo.[uspCollectPerfData]" -ServerInstance $serverName
    -Database "admin"
```

Now execute the script to collect the performance data for the default instance on the host PowerServer3, as shown here:

```
C:\DBAScripts\Collect-SQLPerfmonData.ps1 "PowerServer3"
```

This will execute the procedure uspCollectPerfData on the SQL Server instance PowerServer3 and store the SQL Server performance-related data in the following listed tables:

❑   AWEAllocated

❑   LogFileUsage

❑   TopQueries

❑   TaskCount

❑   TopMemConsumption

Next, query all the tables that hold performance data related to storage, memory, and tasks, as shown here:

```
Use admin
go
select * from dbo.AWEAllocated
select * from dbo.LogFileUsage
select * from dbo.TaskCount
select * from dbo.TopMemConsumption
select ServerName, Query_text, * from dbo.TopQueries
```

Figure 17-1 illustrates the data collected in the table AWEAllocated for the server PowerServer3.

Figure 17-1

Figure 17-2 illustrates the data collected in the table LogFileUsage for all the databases from the server PowerServer3. You can see the Log File Used size in kilobytes.

	servername	instance_name	Log File(s) Used Size (KB)	datestamp
1	POWERSERVER3	TestDatabase	238	2009-02-08 14:15:08.200
2	POWERSERVER3	tempdb	425	2009-02-08 14:15:08.200
3	POWERSERVER3	SQL_Inventory	376	2009-02-08 14:15:08.200
4	POWERSERVER3	mssqlsystemresource	308	2009-02-08 14:15:08.200
5	POWERSERVER3	msdb	360	2009-02-08 14:15:08.200
6	POWERSERVER3	model	420	2009-02-08 14:15:08.200
7	POWERSERVER3	master	380	2009-02-08 14:15:08.200
8	POWERSERVER3	AdventureWorks2008	388	2009-02-08 14:15:08.200
9	POWERSERVER3	admin	485	2009-02-08 14:15:08.200
10	POWERSERVER3	_Total	3380	2009-02-08 14:15:08.200

Figure 17-2

Figure 17-3 illustrates the total task count and runnable task count for each scheduler in the table `TaskCount`.

	scheduler_id	current_tasks_count	runnable_tasks_count	servername	datestamp
1	0	12	0	POWERSERVER3	2009-02-08 14:15:08.200
2	1	15	0	POWERSERVER3	2009-02-08 14:15:08.200

Figure 17-3

Figure 17-4 illustrates the memory consumption by each memory clerk type in the table `TopMemConsumption` from the server PowerServer3.

	servername	type	SPA Mem, Kb	datestamp
1	POWERSERVER3	CACHESTORE_SQLCP	6856	2009-02-08 14:15:08.200
2	POWERSERVER3	CACHESTORE_PHDR	5072	2009-02-08 14:15:08.200
3	POWERSERVER3	MEMORYCLERK_SOSNODE	3296	2009-02-08 14:15:08.200
4	POWERSERVER3	USERSTORE_DBMETADATA	2328	2009-02-08 14:15:08.200
5	POWERSERVER3	USERSTORE_SCHEMAMGR	2008	2009-02-08 14:15:08.200
6	POWERSERVER3	MEMORYCLERK_SQLGENERAL	1064	2009-02-08 14:15:08.200
7	POWERSERVER3	MEMORYCLERK_SQLSTORENG	880	2009-02-08 14:15:08.200
8	POWERSERVER3	CACHESTORE_SYSTEMROWSET	800	2009-02-08 14:15:08.200
9	POWERSERVER3	MEMORYCLERK_SQLCLR	488	2009-02-08 14:15:08.200
10	POWERSERVER3	OBJECTSTORE_SERVICE_BROKER	400	2009-02-08 14:15:08.200

Figure 17-4

Figure 17-5 illustrates the top queries based on total CPU time collected in the table `TopQueries` from the server PowerServer3. You can see the actual T-SQL statements in the column `Query_text`.

	ServerName	Query_text	Servername	creation_time
1	POWERSERVER3	SELECT dtb.collation_name AS [Collation], dtb.name AS [D...	POWERSERVER3	2009-02-08 07:24:41.827
2	POWERSERVER3	SELECT dtb.name AS [Name], dtb.database_id AS [ID], C...	POWERSERVER3	2009-02-08 07:53:49.153
3	POWERSERVER3	IF EXISTS (SELECT * FROM sys.objects WHERE object_i...	POWERSERVER3	2009-02-08 07:53:37.437
4	POWERSERVER3	SELECT dtb.name AS [Database_Name], 'Server[@Name...	POWERSERVER3	2009-02-08 07:24:35.483
5	POWERSERVER3	SELECT SCHEMA_NAME(obj.schema_id) AS [Schema], o...	POWERSERVER3	2009-02-08 13:27:47.217
6	POWERSERVER3	SELECT SCHEMA_NAME(xproc.schema_id) AS [Schema],...	POWERSERVER3	2009-02-08 13:27:47.593
7	POWERSERVER3	SELECT param.parameter_id AS [ID], param.name AS [Na...	POWERSERVER3	2009-02-08 13:30:39.373
8	POWERSERVER3	SELECT SCHEMA_NAME(tt.schema_id) AS [Schema], tt.n...	POWERSERVER3	2009-02-08 13:27:46.890
9	POWERSERVER3	select * from dbo.TopQueries	POWERSERVER3	2009-02-08 14:15:04.687
10	POWERSERVER3	SELECT SCHEMA_NAME(tbl.schema_id) AS [Schema], tbl...	POWERSERVER3	2009-02-08 13:27:46.903

Figure 17-5

This SQL Server performance-related data-collection PowerShell script can be scheduled to run on-host as a SQL Server Agent job with a PowerShell job step or a scheduled task.

SQL Server Host Performance Data Collection

Though host-related performance data is more important for Windows operations, it is necessary for SQL Server DBAs to collect such data for any analysis related to performance troubleshooting.

Host-related performance data can be obtained using the WMI object and stored in a centralized database. That centralized database could be created in the inventory server.

You may be wondering why you are going to use the inventory server to collect host-related performance data, and the `admin` database for SQL Server–related performance data. A SQL Server host many have more than one SQL Server instance. However, each instance will have its own `admin` database, creating a dilemma regarding which instance you should use to collect host-related performance data.

Another reason to choose a centralized database is to distribute the load. All host-related performance is collected in a centralized database and all SQL Server instances related to performance data are collected on each instance.

The next script creates the database `PerfMon_DB` on the inventory server:

```
USE [master]
GO

/****** Object:  Database [PerfMon_DB]    Script Date: 08/23/2008 03:09:13 ******/
IF  EXISTS (SELECT name FROM sys.databases WHERE name = N'PerfMon_DB')
DROP DATABASE [PerfMon_DB]
GO

CREATE DATABASE PerfMon_DB
Go
```

Now create the tables where all the host-related performance data will be stored:

- ❑ `PerfDisk_PhysicalDisk`: Stores data related to physical disk information
- ❑ `PerfRawData_PerfOS_Memory`: Stores information related to memory usage
- ❑ `PerfRawData_PerfOS_Processor`: Stores information about the processor
- ❑ `PerfRawData_PerfProc_Process`: Stores information about processes
- ❑ `PerfRawData_Tcpip_NetworkInterface`: Stores information about the network

Performance bottlenecks could occur on any of these resources. Here is the code:

```
USE [PerfMon_DB]
GO

/****** Object:  Table [dbo].[PerfDisk_PhysicalDisk]    Script Date: 08/23/2008
   03:29:25 ******/
IF  EXISTS (SELECT * FROM sys.objects WHERE object_id = OBJECT_ID(N'[dbo].
   [PerfDisk_PhysicalDisk]') AND type in (N'U'))
DROP TABLE [dbo].[PerfDisk_PhysicalDisk]
GO

CREATE TABLE PerfDisk_PhysicalDisk(
Hostname varchar(100) NULL ,
___GENUS int NULL ,
___CLASS varchar(100) NULL ,
___SUPERCLASS varchar(100) NULL ,
___DYNASTY varchar(100) NULL ,
___RELPATH varchar(100) NULL ,
___PROPERTY_COUNT int NULL ,
___DERIVATION varchar(100) NULL ,
```

```
___SERVER varchar(100) NULL ,
___NAMESPACE varchar(100) NULL ,
___PATH varchar(100) NULL ,
AvgDiskBytesPerRead bigint NULL ,
AvgDiskBytesPerRead_Base bigint NULL ,
AvgDiskBytesPerTransfer bigint NULL ,
AvgDiskBytesPerTransfer_Base bigint NULL ,
AvgDiskBytesPerWrite bigint NULL ,
AvgDiskBytesPerWrite_Base bigint NULL ,
AvgDiskQueueLength bigint NULL ,
AvgDiskReadQueueLength bigint NULL ,
AvgDisksecPerRead bigint NULL ,
AvgDisksecPerRead_Base bigint NULL ,
AvgDisksecPerTransfer bigint NULL ,
AvgDisksecPerTransfer_Base bigint NULL ,
AvgDisksecPerWrite bigint NULL ,
AvgDisksecPerWrite_Base bigint NULL ,
AvgDiskWriteQueueLength bigint NULL ,
Caption varchar(100) NULL ,
CurrentDiskQueueLength bigint NULL ,
Description varchar(100) NULL ,
DiskBytesPersec bigint NULL ,
DiskReadBytesPersec bigint NULL ,
DiskReadsPersec bigint NULL ,
DiskTransfersPersec bigint NULL ,
DiskWriteBytesPersec bigint NULL ,
DiskWritesPersec bigint NULL ,
Frequency_Object bigint NULL ,
Frequency_PerfTime bigint NULL ,
Frequency_Sys100NS bigint NULL ,
Name varchar(100) NULL ,
PercentDiskReadTime bigint NULL ,
PercentDiskTime bigint NULL ,
PercentDiskWriteTime bigint NULL ,
PercentIdleTime bigint NULL ,
SplitIOPerSec bigint NULL ,
Timestamp_Object bigint NULL ,
Timestamp_PerfTime bigint NULL ,
Timestamp_Sys100NS bigint NULL ,
datestamp datetime default getdate())
/****** Object:  Table [dbo].[PerfRawData_PerfOS_Memory]    Script Date: 08/23/2008
   03:29:25 ******/
IF  EXISTS (SELECT * FROM sys.objects WHERE object_id = OBJECT_ID(N'[dbo].
   [PerfRawData_PerfOS_Memory]') AND type in (N'U'))
DROP TABLE [dbo].PerfRawData_PerfOS_Memory
GO

CREATE TABLE PerfRawData_PerfOS_Memory(
Hostname varchar(100) NULL ,
___GENUS bigint NULL ,
___CLASS varchar(100) NULL ,
___SUPERCLASS varchar(100) NULL ,
___DYNASTY varchar(100) NULL ,
___RELPATH varchar(100) NULL ,
___PROPERTY_COUNT bigint NULL ,
```

```
    ___DERIVATION varchar(100) NULL ,
    ___SERVER varchar(100) NULL ,
    ___NAMESPACE varchar(100) NULL ,
    ___PATH varchar(100) NULL ,
    AvailableBytes bigint NULL ,
    AvailableKBytes bigint NULL ,
    AvailableMBytes bigint NULL ,
    CacheBytes bigint NULL ,
    CacheBytesPeak bigint NULL ,
    CacheFaultsPersec bigint NULL ,
    Caption varchar(100) NULL ,
    CommitLimit bigint NULL ,
    CommittedBytes bigint NULL ,
    DemandZeroFaultsPersec bigint NULL ,
    Description varchar(100) NULL ,
    FreeAndZeroPageListBytes bigint NULL ,
    FreeSystemPageTableEntries bigint NULL ,
    Frequency_Object bigint NULL ,
    Frequency_PerfTime bigint NULL ,
    Frequency_Sys100NS bigint NULL ,
    ModifiedPageListBytes bigint NULL ,
    Name varchar(100) NULL ,
    PageFaultsPersec bigint NULL ,
    PageReadsPersec bigint NULL ,
    PagesInputPersec bigint NULL ,
    PagesOutputPersec bigint NULL ,
    PagesPersec bigint NULL ,
    PageWritesPersec bigint NULL ,
    PercentCommittedBytesInUse bigint NULL ,
    PercentCommittedBytesInUse_Base bigint NULL ,
    PoolNonpagedAllocs bigint NULL ,
    PoolNonpagedBytes bigint NULL ,
    PoolPagedAllocs bigint NULL ,
    PoolPagedBytes bigint NULL ,
    PoolPagedResidentBytes bigint NULL ,
    StandbyCacheCoreBytes bigint NULL ,
    StandbyCacheNormalPriorityBytes bigint NULL ,
    StandbyCacheReserveBytes bigint NULL ,
    SystemCacheResidentBytes bigint NULL ,
    SystemCodeResidentBytes bigint NULL ,
    SystemCodeTotalBytes bigint NULL ,
    SystemDriverResidentBytes bigint NULL ,
    SystemDriverTotalBytes bigint NULL ,
    Timestamp_Object bigint NULL ,
    Timestamp_PerfTime bigint NULL ,
    Timestamp_Sys100NS bigint NULL ,
    TransitionFaultsPersec bigint NULL ,
    TransitionPagesRePurposedPersec bigint NULL ,
    WriteCopiesPersec bigint NULL ,
    datestamp datetime default getdate())

/****** Object:  Table [dbo].[PerfRawData_PerfOS_Processor]    Script Date: 08/23/2008
    03:29:25 ******/
IF  EXISTS (SELECT * FROM sys.objects WHERE object_id = OBJECT_ID(N'[dbo].
    [PerfRawData_PerfOS_Processor]') AND type in (N'U'))
```

```
DROP TABLE [dbo].PerfRawData_PerfOS_Processor
GO
CREATE TABLE PerfRawData_PerfOS_Processor(
Hostname varchar(100) NULL ,
___GENUS bigint NULL ,
___CLASS varchar(100) NULL ,
___SUPERCLASS varchar(100) NULL ,
___DYNASTY varchar(100) NULL ,
___RELPATH varchar(100) NULL ,
___PROPERTY_COUNT bigint NULL ,
___DERIVATION varchar(100) NULL ,
___SERVER varchar(100) NULL ,
___NAMESPACE varchar(100) NULL ,
___PATH varchar(100) NULL ,
C1TransitionsPersec bigint NULL ,
C2TransitionsPersec bigint NULL ,
C3TransitionsPersec bigint NULL ,
Caption varchar(100) NULL ,
Description varchar(100) NULL ,
DPCRate bigint NULL ,
DPCsQueuedPersec bigint NULL ,
Frequency_Object bigint NULL ,
Frequency_PerfTime bigint NULL ,
Frequency_Sys100NS bigint NULL ,
InterruptsPersec bigint NULL ,
Name varchar(100) NULL ,
PercentC1Time bigint NULL ,
PercentC2Time bigint NULL ,
PercentC3Time bigint NULL ,
PercentDPCTime bigint NULL ,
PercentIdleTime bigint NULL ,
PercentInterruptTime bigint NULL ,
PercentPrivilegedTime bigint NULL ,
PercentProcessorTime bigint NULL ,
PercentUserTime bigint NULL ,
Timestamp_Object bigint NULL ,
Timestamp_PerfTime bigint NULL ,
Timestamp_Sys100NS bigint NULL ,
datestamp datetime default getdate())

/****** Object:  Table [dbo].[PerfRawData_PerfProc_Process]    Script Date: 08/23/2008
   03:29:25 ******/
IF  EXISTS (SELECT * FROM sys.objects WHERE object_id = OBJECT_ID(N'[dbo].
   [PerfRawData_PerfProc_Process]') AND type in (N'U'))
DROP TABLE [dbo].PerfRawData_PerfProc_Process
GO
CREATE TABLE PerfRawData_PerfProc_Process(
Hostname varchar(100) NULL ,
___GENUS bigint NULL ,
___CLASS varchar(100) NULL ,
___SUPERCLASS varchar(100) NULL ,
___DYNASTY varchar(100) NULL ,
___RELPATH varchar(100) NULL ,
___PROPERTY_COUNT bigint NULL ,
___DERIVATION varchar(100) NULL ,
```

```
___SERVER varchar(100) NULL ,
___NAMESPACE varchar(100) NULL ,
___PATH varchar(100) NULL ,
Caption varchar(100) NULL ,
CreatingProcessID bigint NULL ,
Description varchar(100) NULL ,
ElapsedTime bigint NULL ,
Frequency_Object bigint NULL ,
Frequency_PerfTime bigint NULL ,
Frequency_Sys100NS bigint NULL ,
HandleCount bigint NULL ,
IDProcess bigint NULL ,
IODataBytesPersec bigint NULL ,
IODataOperationsPersec bigint NULL ,
IOOtherBytesPersec bigint NULL ,
IOOtherOperationsPersec bigint NULL ,
IOReadBytesPersec bigint NULL ,
IOReadOperationsPersec bigint NULL ,
IOWriteBytesPersec bigint NULL ,
IOWriteOperationsPersec bigint NULL ,
Name varchar(100) NULL ,
PageFaultsPersec bigint NULL ,
PageFileBytes bigint NULL ,
PageFileBytesPeak bigint NULL ,
PercentPrivilegedTime bigint NULL ,
PercentProcessorTime bigint NULL ,
PercentUserTime bigint NULL ,
PoolNonpagedBytes bigint NULL ,
PoolPagedBytes bigint NULL ,
PriorityBase bigint NULL ,
PrivateBytes bigint NULL ,
ThreadCount bigint NULL ,
Timestamp_Object bigint NULL ,
Timestamp_PerfTime bigint NULL ,
Timestamp_Sys100NS bigint NULL ,
VirtualBytes bigint NULL ,
VirtualBytesPeak bigint NULL ,
WorkingSet bigint NULL ,
WorkingSetPeak bigint NULL ,
WorkingSetPrivate bigint NULL ,
datestamp datetime default getdate())

/****** Object:  Table [dbo].[PerfRawData_Tcpip_NetworkInterface]
   Script Date: 08/23/2008 03:29:25 ******/
IF  EXISTS (SELECT * FROM sys.objects WHERE object_id = OBJECT_ID(N'[dbo].
   [PerfRawData_Tcpip_NetworkInterface]') AND type in (N'U'))
DROP TABLE [dbo].PerfRawData_Tcpip_NetworkInterface
GO
CREATE TABLE PerfRawData_Tcpip_NetworkInterface(
Hostname varchar(100) NULL ,
___GENUS bigint NULL ,
___CLASS varchar(100) NULL ,
___SUPERCLASS varchar(100) NULL ,
___DYNASTY varchar(100) NULL ,
___RELPATH varchar(300) NULL ,
```

```
___PROPERTY_COUNT bigint NULL ,
___DERIVATION varchar(100) NULL ,
___SERVER varchar(100) NULL ,
___NAMESPACE varchar(100) NULL ,
___PATH varchar(300) NULL ,
BytesReceivedPersec bigint NULL ,
BytesSentPersec bigint NULL ,
BytesTotalPersec bigint NULL ,
Caption varchar(100) NULL ,
CurrentBandwidth bigint NULL ,
Description varchar(100) NULL ,
Frequency_Object bigint NULL ,
Frequency_PerfTime bigint NULL ,
Frequency_Sys100NS bigint NULL ,
Name varchar(100) NULL ,
OutputQueueLength bigint NULL ,
PacketsOutboundDiscarded bigint NULL ,
PacketsOutboundErrors bigint NULL ,
PacketsPersec bigint NULL ,
PacketsReceivedDiscarded bigint NULL ,
PacketsReceivedErrors bigint NULL ,
PacketsReceivedNonUnicastPersec bigint NULL ,
PacketsReceivedPersec bigint NULL ,
PacketsReceivedUnicastPersec bigint NULL ,
PacketsReceivedUnknown bigint NULL ,
PacketsSentNonUnicastPersec bigint NULL ,
PacketsSentPersec bigint NULL ,
PacketsSentUnicastPersec bigint NULL ,
Timestamp_Object bigint NULL ,
Timestamp_PerfTime bigint NULL ,
Timestamp_Sys100NS bigint NULL ,
datestamp datetime default getdate())
```

You can create the preceding tables and procedures using the `HostPerfmonDLL.sql` file.

Next, create the `C:\DBAScripts\Collect-HostPerfmon.ps1` script. This Windows PowerShell script is going to get various performance-related information using `Get-WMIObject`. `Get-WMIObject` retrieves the information from the following WMI classes from the remote machine:

- `Win32_PerfRawData_PerfDisk_PhysicalDisk`

- `Win32_PerfRawData_PerfOS_Memory`

- `Win32_PerfRawData_PerfOS_Processor`

- `Win32_PerfRawData_PerfProc_Process`

- `Win32_PerfRawData_Tcpip_NetworkInterface`

The script also generates insert statements on-the-fly and stores them in a file `perfmondata.sql`. Then it executes the file, which basically stores the data in the following tables, respectively, in the `PerfMon_DB` database on the inventory server:

- `PerfDisk_PhysicalDisk`

- `PerfRawData_PerfOS_Memory`

❑   PerfRawData_PerfOS_Processor

❑   PerfRawData_PerfProc_Process

❑   PerfRawData_Tcpip_NetworkInterface

The complete Collect-HostPerfmon.ps1 script is available for download on the Wrox website for this book. A portion of the script is shown here to get you started:

```
#===============================================================
#
# NAME: Collect-HostPerfmondata.ps1
#
# AUTHOR: Yan and MAK
# DATE  : 5/1/2008
#
# COMMENT: This script collects performance data from a SQL Server host.
#===============================================================

param ([String] $hostname)

. C:\DBAScripts\dbaLib.ps1


if ( $hostname.Length -eq 0 ) {
"Please enter a host name."
        exit 1
}

$filename = "c:\DBAScripts\perfmondata.sql"

out-file -inputobject "use PerfMon_DB" -filepath $filename -encoding "Default"
out-file -inputobject "GO" -filepath $filename -encoding "Default" -append
out-file -inputobject "set nocount on" -filepath $filename -encoding "Default" -append

out-file -inputobject "GO" -filepath $filename -encoding "Default" -append
out-file -inputobject "set quoted_identifier off" -filepath $filename -encoding
    "Default" -append
out-file -inputobject "GO" -filepath $filename -encoding "Default" -append

# Get physical disk information from the Win32_PerfRawData_PerfDisk_PhysicalDisk
    WMI class
# and insert into the PerfDisk_PhysicalDisk table.


$PerfDisk_PhysicalDisk=get-wmiobject -class Win32_PerfRawData_PerfDisk_PhysicalDisk
    -computername $hostname
$tsql=""

foreach ($perfdata1 in $PerfDisk_PhysicalDisk) {
$tsql="insert into dbo.PerfDisk_PhysicalDisk
(Hostname,___GENUS,___CLASS,___SUPERCLASS,___DYNASTY,___RELPATH,___PROPERTY_COUNT,
    ___DERIVATION,___SERVER,___NAMESPACE,___PATH,
AvgDiskBytesPerRead,AvgDiskBytesPerRead_Base,AvgDiskBytesPerTransfer,
    AvgDiskBytesPerTransfer_Base,AvgDiskBytesPerWrite,
AvgDiskBytesPerWrite_Base,AvgDiskQueueLength,AvgDiskReadQueueLength,
```

```
      AvgDisksecPerRead,AvgDisksecPerRead_Base,
  AvgDisksecPerTransfer,AvgDisksecPerTransfer_Base,AvgDisksecPerWrite,
      AvgDisksecPerWrite_Base,AvgDiskWriteQueueLength,
  Caption,CurrentDiskQueueLength,Description,DiskBytesPersec,DiskReadBytesPersec,
      DiskReadsPersec,DiskTransfersPersec,
```

Now execute the script `c:\DBAScripts\Collect_HostPerfmonData.ps1`:

```
  C:\DBAScripts\Collect-HostPerfmonData.ps1 PowerServer3
```

Note that PowerServer3 is the host name from where we are getting all the performance data. `$InventoryServer` is the inventory server where the `PerfMon_DB` database is created.

When executed, this script creates the SQL script file `C:\DBAScripts\perfmondata.sql` on-the-fly and executes the file using the `Invoke-Sqlcmd` cmdlet.

After running the preceding script, you can see the data populating the database `PerfMon_DB` on the inventory server, as shown in Figure 17-6. Execute the following Transact SQL command to see the results:

```
  use PerfMon_DB
  go

  select * from dbo.PerfDisk_PhysicalDisk
  select * from dbo.PerfRawData_PerfOS_Memory
  select * from dbo.PerfRawData_PerfOS_Processor
  select * from dbo.PerfRawData_PerfProc_Process
  select * from dbo.PerfRawData_Tcpip_NetworkInterface
```

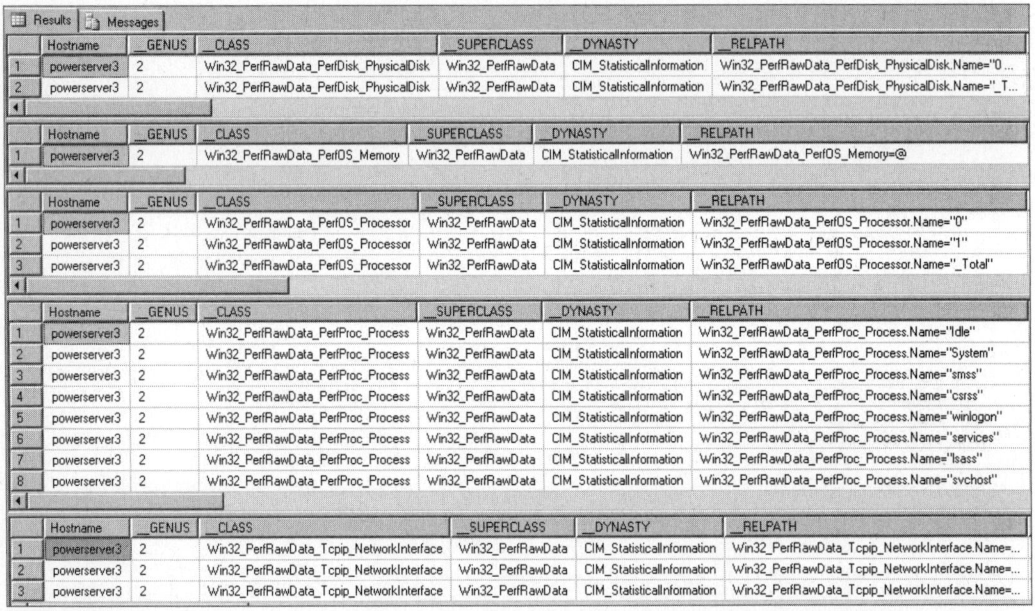

Figure 17-6

This script can be scheduled to run regularly — say, every fifteen minutes — from the inventory server to collect the performance data of a SQL Server host or a group of SQL Server hosts by running multiple `Collect-HostPerfmonData.ps1` commands.

Summary

This chapter illustrated how to collect SQL Server–related performance data on different SQL Server instances, and host-related performance data from the host, and import them into the inventory server database. This chapter should have given you a general idea of how to use dynamic management views, Windows PowerShell, and stored procedures to get performance-related data. It is hoped that the information provided here enables you to develop your own code or modify these codes to fit your needs.

18

Monitoring SQL Server

Proactive monitoring is essential to ensure the stability of your SQL Server environment. Proactive monitoring means finding problems and potential service outages before they occur. As a DBA, you need to ensure that every SQL server instance in your environment is running and healthy, and that no users experience connection problems. You also need to keep track of the reboot schedule of each SQL Server host because regular reboots help improve server performance, and capture any OS or SQL Server errors before they evolve into critical issues.

Oftentimes, an improperly designed application causes blockings and deadlocks. When processes are blocked, users think something is wrong with the database server (and that you are not doing your job). To save everyone a lot of grief, you should capture the blockings or deadlocks as they occur, and notify users that their processes need to be examined before they call you on your hotline.

In this chapter and Chapter 19, we will implement these critical monitoring tasks. This chapter covers the following topics.

- ❑ Pinging SQL Server hosts

- ❑ Checking SQL Server–related services on SQL Server hosts

- ❑ Checking uptime of SQL Server hosts

- ❑ Monitoring Windows event logs

- ❑ Monitoring SQL Server error log

- ❑ Monitoring blockings

- ❑ Monitoring deadlocks

Pinging SQL Server Hosts

Even before monitoring the various components of SQL Server, the most important thing to monitor is whether the host machine is reachable. You can use the `Ping-Host` function to perform this task. The `Ping-Host` function is used to ping one host. If the host can be pinged, then a green message is printed out. Otherwise, a red message is printed out to alert the administrator. The function is shown here:

```
Function Ping-Host  ([string] $hostname )
{
        [String] $alertSubject=""
        [String] $alertMessage=""

        $status=Get-WmiObject Win32_PingStatus -Filter "Address='$hostname'" |
Select-Object statuscode
        if($status.statuscode -eq 0)
        {
                Write-Host "$hostname is reachable." -background "GREEN" -foreground
"BLACK"
        }
        else
        {
                Write-Host "$hostname is NOT reachable." -background "RED" -
foreground "BLACK"
        }
}
```

Save this function in your library file so that it can be easily sourced into other scripts later. For the example in this book, this function will be put into our library file `C:\DBAScripts\dbaLib.ps1`. However, this function only prints out messages in the console. When a host is down or not reachable, the DBA group usually needs to be notified so that proper timely actions can be taken such as escalating the problem to the system administrator. In this book, we will notify the DBA through e-mail. However, in an enterprise environment, it is not plausible to expect the DBA group to read through hundreds or even thousands of alert e-mails every day and not miss anything. In this kind of environment, an alert management system, such as Netcool, is usually in place to consolidate all the alerts and display them on a user's console.

If your company has an alert management system in place, you can easily incorporate the scripts in this book by simply changing the scripts to send a SNMP trap message or whatever message the alert management system requires instead of an e-mail. For the purposes of this book, we need a function called `Send-Email` to send e-mails. Because this function is going to be used often to send notifications, it will also be placed in the library file `C:\DBAScripts\dbaLib.ps1`. Oftentimes, a particular SMTP server is used to send e-mails. This SMTP server can be defined as the default server in the library file. If your SMTP server needs identification, then you will need to specify the SMTP user name and password. You can also define the sending and receiving e-mail addresses used by the DBA group as default in the library file for easy reference. The common variables and `Send-Email` function are shown here:

```
#######################################################
# Define the default SMTP server and e-mail group used by DBA
# Please change the SMTP server, the sending and receiving e-mail addresses before you
```

```
start running this script!
###################################################
$smtpServer="smtp.powerdomain.com"
$fromAddress="yanpan@powerdomain.com"
$toAddress="yanpan@powerdomain.com"
$smtpUserName=""
$smtpPassword=""

################################################### Add function to send e-mail
###################################################
Function Send-Email([String] $smtpServer, [String] $from, [String] $to, [String]
$subject, [String] $body, [String] $userName, [String] $password)
{
        if ($userName.Length > 0 ) {
                $credential=New-Object System.Net.NetworkCredential -argumentList
$userName, $password
                Send-MailMessage -From $from -To $to -Subject $subject -Body $body -
SmtpServer $smtpServer -Credential $credential
        }
        else {
                Send-MailMessage -From $from -To $to -Subject $subject -Body $body -
SmtpServer $smtpServer
        }
}
```

Please change the values for the SMTP server, sending and receiving e-mail addresses in the dbaLib.ps1
file before you start running the scripts in this chapter and next chapter in your environment!

Now we can just call the `Send-Email` function in the `Ping-Host` function to send a notification e-mail
when a host is not reachable. The complete `Ping-Host` function is shown here:

```
Function Ping-host  ([string] $hostname )
{
        [String] $alertSubject=""
        [String] $alertMessage=""

        $status=Get-WmiObject Win32_PingStatus -Filter "Address='$hostname'" |
Select-Object statuscode
        if($status.statuscode -eq 0)
        {
            Write-Host "$hostname is reachable." -background "GREEN" -foreground
"BLACK"
        }
        else
        {
                Write-Host "$hostname is NOT reachable." -background "RED" -
foreground "BLACK"

                # An alert e-mail is sent if the host cannot be pinged.
                Write-Host "Sending an e-mail regarding $hostname ..."
                $alertSubject="Ping Status"
                $alertMessage="$hostName is not reachable. Please check."
```

```
                    Send-Email $smtpServer $fromAddress $toAddress $alertSubject
$alertMessage $smtpUserName $smtpPassword
       }
}
```

In Chapter 15, we set up an inventory database named `SQL_Inventory`. Now we need a script to go through the SQL Server hosts in the inventory and ping each host using the `Ping-Host` function. The complete `Ping-Hosts.ps1` script is shown here:

```
####################################################
# Source in our library file
####################################################
. C:\DBAScripts\dbaLib.ps1

[String] $strQuerySql=""
[String] $sqlHostName=""

$strQuerySql="SELECT hostName FROM dbo.Hosts"

# Gets the list of SQL Server hosts from the inventory database
$sqlHosts=Invoke-Sqlcmd -Query $strQuerySql -ServerInstance $inventoryServer -
Database $inventoryDatabase

# Ping every SQL Server host
Foreach ($sqlHost in $sqlHosts) {
        $sqlHostName=$sqlHost.hostName
        Ping-host $sqlHostName
}
```

As you can see, the `Ping-Hosts.ps1` script and the library file `C:\DBAScripts\dbaLib.ps1` are sourced in the beginning so the script can call the `Ping-Host` function later. Let's run the script to check the status of the hosts:

```
C:\DBAScripts\Ping-Hosts.ps1
```

Figure 18-1 shows two cluster nodes, NODE1 and NODE2, that cannot be pinged.

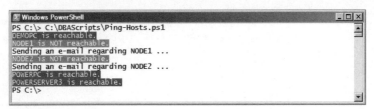

Figure 18-1

Two e-mails are sent, one for each node. A sample alert message is shown in Figure 18-2.

Now you can query all the hosts from the SQL_Inventory database by executing continued `Ping-Hosts.ps1` and sending notifications if any host cannot be pinged. This script can be scheduled to run every half hour or fifteen minutes depending on the service level agreement.

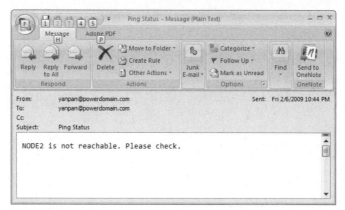

Figure 18-2

Checking SQL Server–related Services on SQL Server Hosts

Pinging hosts is just the first step in monitoring SQL Server. Once you know that you can ping a host and it is reachable, you should check whether SQL Server–related services are healthy. If a service that is set to start automatically is not running for some reason, then you need to capture that. If a service's status is not OK, indicating something such as an error or hanging when stopping, then you need to capture that as well.

The following example creates a function, Check-Services, that would capture these exceptions from the SQL Server–related services on a host:

```
Function Check-Services([String] $hostName)
{
        [String] $alertSubject=""
        [String] $alertMessage=""

        # Get SQL Server related services on the host
        $services=Get-WmiObject -class Win32_Service -computername $hostName
| Where-Object {$_.name -like '*SQL*'}

        foreach ( $service in $services)
        {
                # If a service that is set to start automatically is not running,
then write a red error message and send an alert e-mail.
                if ($service.State -ne "Running" -and $service.StartMode -eq "Auto")
                {
                        $alertSubject="Service Exception"
                        $alertMessage="On " + $hostName + ", the service " +
$service.Name + " is set to AutoStart, but it is " + $Service.State + ".
Please check."
                        Write-Host $alertMessage -background "RED" -foreground
"BLACK"
```

```
                              Write-Host "Sending an e-mail regarding" $service.Name "on"
$hostName "..."
                                   Send-Email $smtpServer $fromAddress $toAddress
$alertSubject $alertMessage $smtpUserName $smtpPassword
                        }
                        # If the status of a service is not OK, then write a red error
message and send an alert e-mail.
                        elseif ($service.Status -ne "OK") {
                                $alertSubject="Service Exception"
                                $alertMessage="On " + $hostName + ", the status of the
service " + $service.Name + " is " + $Service.State + ". Please check."
                                Write-Host $alertMessage -background "RED" -foreground
"BLACK"

                                Write-Host "Sending an e-mail regarding" $service.Name "on"
$hostName "..."
                                   Send-Email $smtpServer $fromAddress $toAddress
$alertSubject $alertMessage $smtpUserName $smtpPassword
                        }
                }
        }
}
```

This function is added to the `C:\DBAScripts\dbaLib.ps1` file. We still need a script to go through the SQL Server hosts in the inventory and check each host using the `Check-Services` function. However, unlike the `Ping-Hosts.ps1` script, which checks every node of a cluster, we only check the active node of the cluster using the Windows cluster name, as SQL Server services only run on the active node. The script, shown here, is called `Check-Services.ps1`:

```
####################################################
# Source in our library file
####################################################
. C:\DBAScripts\dbaLib.ps1

[String] $strQuerySql=""
[String] $sqlHostName=""

$strQuerySql="SELECT hostName
FROM dbo.Hosts h LEFT JOIN dbo.ClusterNodes cn ON h.hostID=cn.nodeID
WHERE cn.clusterID IS NULL
UNION
SELECT WindowsClusterName as hostName
FROM dbo.Clusters"

# Gets the list of SQL Server hosts from the inventory database
$sqlHosts=Invoke-Sqlcmd -Query $strQuerySql -ServerInstance $inventoryServer -
Database $inventoryDatabase

# Check SQL Server related services on every SQL Server host
Foreach ($sqlHost in $sqlHosts) {
        $sqlHostName=$sqlHost.hostName
        Check-Services $sqlHostName
}
```

Now execute the `Check-Services.ps1` script:

```
C:\DBAScripts\Check-Services
```

When the preceding PowerShell script is executed, the results shown in Figure 18-3 are returned.

Figure 18-3

Three services on DEMOPC are set to `AutoStart`, but they are stopped. Three individual e-mails are sent regarding the three services. A sample alert message is shown in Figure 18-4.

Figure 18-4

As shown in Chapter 9, you can also query the `SqlService` class provided by the WMI Provider for Configuration Management to check the SQL Server–related services.

The next example adds another function called `Check-SqlServices` to `dbaLib.ps1` to check the SQL Server 2008–related services:

```
Function Check-SqlServices ([string] $hostName )
{
        [String] $alertSubject=""
        [String] $alertMessage=""

        # Get SQL Server related services on the host
```

```
        $services=Get-WmiObject -namespace
root\Microsoft\SqlServer\ComputerManagement10 -class SqlService -computername
$hostName

        foreach ( $service in $services)
        {
                # If a service that is set to start automatically is not running,
then write a red error message and send an alert e-mail.
                if ($service.State -ne 4 -and $service.StartMode -eq 2)
                {
                        $alertSubject="Service Exception"
                        $alertMessage="On " + $hostName + ", the service " +
$service.ServiceName + " is set to AutoStart, but its state is " + $Service.State +
".Please check."
                        Write-Host $alertMessage -background "RED" -foreground
"BLACK"

                        Write-Host "Sending an e-mail regarding"
$service.ServiceName "on" $hostName "..."
                        Send-Email $smtpServer $fromAddress $toAddress
$alertSubject $alertMessage $smtpUserName $smtpPassword
                }
                # You can add more exceptions here by adding more elseif cases.
        }
}
```

This function is also added to the `C:\DBAScripts\dbaLib.ps1` file. Now we create another script to go through the SQL Server hosts in the inventory, checking each host using the `Check-SqlServices` function. The `Check-SqlServices.ps1` script is shown here:

```
################################################### Source in our library file
###################################################
. C:\DBAScripts\dbaLib.ps1

[String] $strQuerySql=""
[String] $sqlHostName=""

$strQuerySql="SELECT hostName
FROM dbo.Hosts h LEFT JOIN dbo.ClusterNodes cn ON h.hostID=cn.nodeID
WHERE cn.clusterID IS NULL
UNION
SELECT WindowsClusterName as hostName
FROM dbo.Clusters"

# Gets the list of SQL Server hosts from the inventory database
$sqlHosts=Invoke-Sqlcmd -Query $strQuerySql -ServerInstance $inventoryServer -
Database $inventoryDatabase

# Check SQL Server related services on every SQL Server host
Foreach ($sqlHost in $sqlHosts) {
        $sqlHostName=$sqlHost.hostName
        Check-SqlServices $sqlHostName
}
```

Execute the `Check-SqlServices.ps1` script. As shown in Figure 18-5, its output is similar to the `Check-Services.ps1` script. However, notice that one more service, the Service for Integration Services, `MsDtsServer100`, on PowerServer3 is returned, which was missed by the `Check-Services.ps1` script. This is because the `Check-Services` function filters all the Windows services and returns only the ones that have "SQL" in their name. Obviously, "MsDtsServer100" doesn't contain a substring "SQL." The Service for Reporting Services ReportServer also doesn't contain "SQL" in its name. Therefore, the `Check-SqlServices` script, which uses the `SqlService` class provided by the WMI Provider for Configuration Management, is more suitable for checking SQL Server–related services.

```
C:\DBAScripts\Check-SqlServices.ps1
```

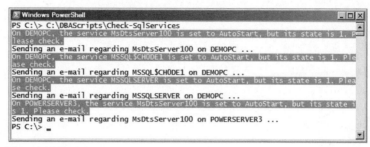

Figure 18-5

A sample alert message is shown in Figure 18-6.

Figure 18-6

Checking Uptime of SQL Server Hosts

A Windows system needs to reboot regularly in order to run as efficiently as possible. Windows systems that do not reboot regularly can be susceptible to memory leaks, fragmentation, and performance issues, and the root cause of any subsequent problems or instability becomes difficult to ascertain. Besides that,

Microsoft releases patches on a monthly basis and many require reboots. Therefore, it is always useful to know when a SQL Server host was last rebooted — that is, its uptime. Uptime helps us decide when to schedule a reboot.

As you learned in Chapter 15, the `Upsert-Host.ps1` script queries the `Win32_OperatingSystem` WMI class on each host, and updates the OS information in the `Hosts` table. One of the columns, `lastBootUpTime`, contains the last time each host was rebooted.

Let's create a script to call `Upsert-Host.ps1` on all the SQL Server hosts in our inventory. The `Update-SQLServerHosts.ps1` script is shown here:

```
####################################################
# Source in our library file
####################################################
. C:\DBAScripts\dbaLib.ps1

[String] $strQuerySql=""
[String] $strCommand=""

# Construct Upsert-Host.ps1 commands for every host in the inventory
$strQuerySql="SELECT 'C:\DBAScripts\Upsert-Host.ps1 -hostName ' + hostName
+ ' -region ' + region + ' -location ' + location
+ ' -primaryBU '" + primaryBU
+ '" -description '" + description + ''" as Command
FROM dbo.Hosts"

$commands=Invoke-Sqlcmd -Query $strQuerySql -ServerInstance $inventoryServer -
Database $inventoryDatabase

# Execute the Upsert-Host.ps1 commands
Foreach ($command in $commands) {
        $strCommand=$command.Command
        Invoke-Expression $strCommand
}
```

Execute the `Update-SQLServerHosts.ps1` script to update host information (see Figure 18-7):

```
C:\DBAScripts\Update-SQLServerHosts.ps1
```

As long as the host information is up-to-date, simply run the following query against the `Hosts` table and you will get how many days, hours, and minutes the hosts have been up:

```
USE SQL_Inventory

SELECT Convert(char(20), GETDATE(), 20) AS [Now]

SELECT hostName, lastBootUpTime,
DATEDIFF(MINUTE, lastBootUpTime, GETDATE())/24/60 as 'Days',
DATEDIFF(MINUTE, lastBootUpTime, GETDATE())/60
- (DATEDIFF(MINUTE, lastBootUpTime, GETDATE())/24/60)*24 as 'Hours',
DATEDIFF(MINUTE, lastBootUpTime, GETDATE())
```

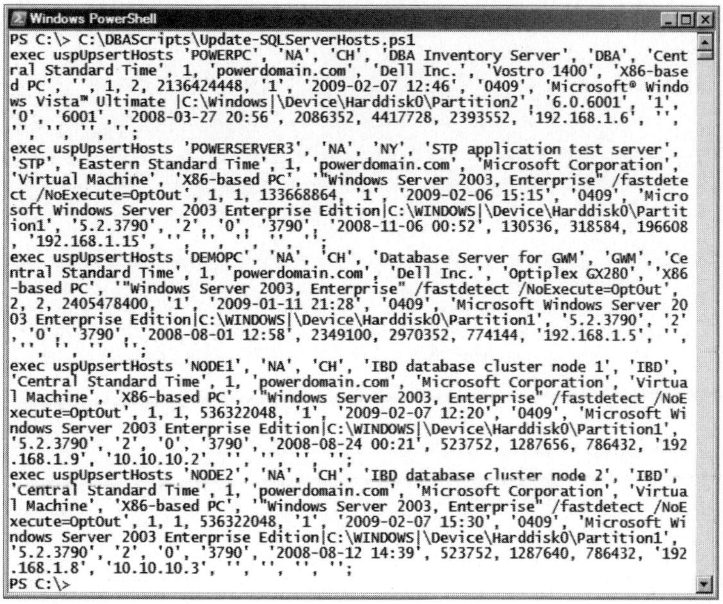

Figure 18-7

```
    - (DATEDIFF(MINUTE, lastBootUpTime, GETDATE())/60)*60 as 'Minutes'
FROM dbo.Hosts
```

Figure 18-8 shows the uptime of all the SQL Server hosts.

Monitoring Windows Event Logs

SQL Server runs on top of the Windows operating system. Its performance depends heavily on the health of that underlying operating system, and it needs the system to provide it with enough resources to handle its workload. For example, if the I/O system degrades because one disk in a RAID group fails, then the I/O performance of the SQL Server will also suffer. Sessions connecting to SQL Server will wait longer for I/O operations to complete, or even get stuck.

Similarly, if the speed and duplex settings of the network card on the SQL Server host do not match the settings on the connecting network switch port, the sending and receiving of network packages by SQL Server can slow down significantly. Sessions will hang waiting for network resources, and end-users will start seeing Web pages time out. Therefore, it is very important to monitor the overall operating system.

System events are stored in Windows event logs. The System log and Application log are the most useful. In the rest of this chapter, we will talk about the on-host monitoring of Windows event logs and the SQL Server error log. We actually already have the tools to tackle a single host. We described how to monitor Windows event logs using the `Get-EventLog` cmdlet in Chapter 6, and how to monitor SQL Server error log using the WMI Provider for Server Events in Chapter 10. Let's put these tools to use.

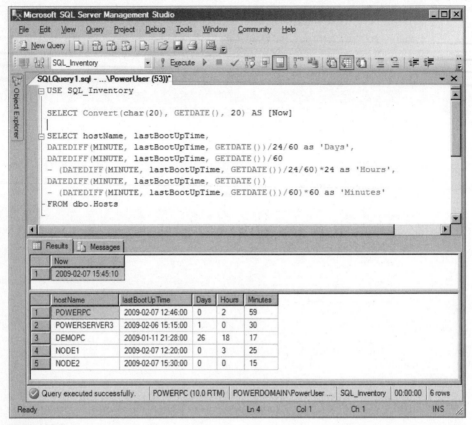

Figure 18-8

Chapter 6 showed you how to filter the Application log in a date range and sort the results:

```
Get-EventLog -LogName "Application" | Where-Object {$_.EntryType -eq "Error"} |
Where-Object {($_.TimeGenerated -gt "2009/01/27") -and ($_.TimeGenerated -lt
"2009/01/28")} | Sort-Object TimeGenerated -descending | Format-Table -auto
```

You should monitor the System and Application logs by querying them regularly. Every query should return the errors that occurred in the last interval. The preceding command just needs to be customized to filter the events that occurred since the last time the log was queried. Suppose that we defined the query interval in a variable called $sleepseconds. By default, the value of this variable is set to 60, which means one minute. We save the last query time in a variable called $startTime, and the current time in a variable called $cutoffTime. Each time, we query the events between $startTime and $cutoffTime. If any error has been found, we send an alert e-mail. Between each query, we wait for the query interval, $sleepseconds, and then query the event logs again. Here is the Monitor-WindowsEventLogs.ps1 script:

```
####################################################
# Initialize parameters
####################################################
```

```
param (
        [Int32]$sleepseconds=60 # Default query interval is 60 seconds (1 minute)
    )

#################################################### Source in our library file
###################################################
. C:\DBAScripts\dbaLib.ps1

# Initialize alert messages
[String] $sysAlertMessage = ""
[String] $appAlertMessage = ""

# Start querying the event log entries $sleepseconds ago
[DateTime] $startTime = (Get-Date).AddSeconds(-$sleepseconds)
[DateTime] $cutoffTime = Get-Date


while ($true) {
        # Look for errors in the System Log that occur between now and $sleepseconds
ago
        # and send an e-mail if any error has been found.
        $sysAlertMessage = (Get-EventLog -logname "System" | Where-Object
{$_.EntryType -eq "Error"} '
                    | Where-Object {($_.TimeGenerated -gt $startTime) -and
($_.TimeGenerated -le $cutoffTime)} '
                    | Select-Object MachineName, Message, Source, TimeGenerated |
Format-List | Out-String)

        if ($sysAlertMessage) {
                Send-Email $smtpServer $fromAddress $toAddress "System Error"
$sysAlertMessage $smtpUserName $smtpPassword
        }

        # Look for errors in the Application Log that occur between now and
$sleepseconds ago
        # and send an e-mail if any error has been found.
        $appAlertMessage = $alertMessage + (Get-EventLog -logname "Application" |
Where-Object {$_.EntryType -eq "Error"} '
                    | Where-Object {($_.TimeGenerated -gt $startTime) -and
($_.TimeGenerated -le $cutoffTime)} '
                    | Select-Object MachineName, Message, Source, TimeGenerated |
Format-List | Out-String)

        if ($appAlertMessage) {
                Send-Email $smtpServer $fromAddress $toAddress "Application Error"
$appAlertMessage $smtpUserName $smtpPassword
        }

        Start-Sleep -s $sleepseconds # Wait for $sleepseconds to query again

        # Set the new starting and ending times
        $startTime = $cutoffTime
        $cutoffTime = Get-Date
}
```

Note that the query interval can be changed by passing a different value to the $sleepseconds parameter.

Now we are ready to create our installation script Install-MonitorWindowsEventLogs.ps1 to copy the Monitor-WindowsErrorLogs.ps1 script from the local host to the C:\DBAScripts directory on every remote host and create a scheduled task to kick off the script at system startup on every host. The following script creates a scheduled task like this on a host named POWERPC:

```
SCHTASKS /Create /S $sqlHostName /RU $sqlUserName /RP $sqlPassword /SC ONSTART /F /TN
"Monitor_WindowsEventLogs_POWERPC" /TR "powershell.exe C:\DBAScripts\Monitor-
WindowsEventLogs.ps1 60"
```

The installation script Install-MonitorWindowsEventLogs.ps1 is shown next. As you can see, this script first gets the list of SQL Server hosts from the inventory. Then it copies the Monitor-WindowsEventLogs.ps1 script, installs the scheduled task Monitor_WindowsEventLogs, and starts the task on each host.

```
####################################################
# Initialize parameters
####################################################
param (
        [Int32]$sleepseconds=60 # Default interval is 60 seconds (1 minute)
    )


####################################################
# Source in our library file
####################################################
. C:\DBAScripts\dbaLib.ps1

[String] $strQuerySql=""
[String] $sqlHostName=""
[String] $sqlUserName="POWERDOMAIN\SqlService"
[String] $sqlPassword="P@ssw0rd" # Password for POWERDOMAIN\SqlService
[String] $localHostName=(Get-ChildItem Env:\ComputerName).Value

$strQuerySql="SELECT hostName FROM dbo.Hosts"

# Get all SQL Server hosts
$sqlHosts=Invoke-Sqlcmd -Query $strQuerySql -ServerInstance $inventoryServer -
Database $inventoryDatabase

Foreach ($sqlHost in $sqlHosts) {
        $sqlHostName=$sqlHost.hostName

        # Copy the Monitor-WindowsEventLogs.ps1 script from the local host to all the
remote hosts.
        If ($sqlHostName -ne $localHostName) {
                If (-not (Test-Path \\$sqlHostName\C$\DBAScripts -pathType
container)) {
                        New-Item \\$sqlHostName\C$\DBAScripts -type directory |
Out-Null
                }

                # Copy both the Monitor-WindowsEventLogs.ps1 script and the library
```

```
file dbaLib.ps1.
                    Copy-Item C:\DBAScripts\Monitor-WindowsEventLogs.ps1
\\$sqlHostName\C$\DBAScripts -force
                    Copy-Item C:\DBAScripts\dbaLib.ps1 \\$sqlHostName\C$\DBAScripts -
force
        }

        "Creating schedule task on $sqlHostName ..."
        SCHTASKS /Create /S $sqlHostName /RU $sqlUserName /RP $sqlPassword /SC
ONSTART '
        /F /TN "Monitor_WindowsEventLogs_$sqlHostName" '
        /TR "powershell.exe C:\DBAScripts\Monitor-WindowsEventLogs.ps1
$sleepseconds"

        # Start the scheduled task immediately
        SCHTASKS /RUN /S $sqlHostName /TN "Monitor_WindowsEventLogs_$sqlHostName"
}
```

To install it on every host, run the following command:

```
C:\DBAScripts\Install-MonitorWindowsEventLogs.ps1
```

As shown in Figure 18-9, the script creates a schedule task `Monitor_WindowsEventLogs` on all the hosts in our environment.

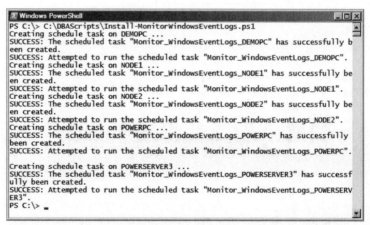

Figure 18-9

A sample alert e-mail sent by the scheduled task is shown in Figure 18-10. The detailed information about the error is contained in the e-mail.

Monitoring SQL Server Error Log

SQL Server error log provides critical information about any current or potential problems detected by the SQL Server Database Engine. Problems are logged as errors with different error numbers followed by detailed error descriptions. For example, if SQL Server is running out of locks, then an error with error number 1204 is reported and the following description is recorded into the SQL Server error log:

```
Error: 1204, Severity: 19, State: 1
The SQL Server cannot obtain a LOCK resource at this time. Rerun your statement when
there are fewer active users or ask the system administrator to check the SQL Server
lock and memory configuration
```

Figure 18-10

This error stops the processing of the current statement and causes a rollback of the active transaction, which needs to be brought to the DBA's attention. The DBA can then change the "Locks" server configuration option, or reexamine the server memory settings. Therefore, as a part of his or her administrative responsibilities, the DBA needs to ensure that every server is being monitored and that critical SQL Server errors are picked up in a timely fashion.

In Chapter 10, we created a function called Get-WMIEvent. The function creates an event subscription called sqlevents. The event subscription registers to events specified by an event query and watches for server events in an infinite loop until the Esc key is pressed manually. The manual stopping mechanism is not useful for automatic and continuous multi-host monitoring. We will create a similar function called Notify-WMIEvent without the stopping mechanism. This function also sends out an alert e-mail to the DBA when an error occurs:

```
function Notify-WMIEvent([string] $eventQuery, [string] $namespace, [string[]]
$properties)
{

# Initialize alert message variables
[String] $alertSubject="SQL Server Error at " + (Get-Date).ToString
('yyyy-MM-dd hh:mm')
[String] $alertMessage=""

# If an event subscription called "sqlevents" already exists, unregister it first.
```

```
if (Get-EventSubscriber 'sqlevents' -ErrorAction SilentlyContinue) {
        Unregister-Event "sqlevents"
}

# Create an event subscription called "sqlevents" that registers to the events
specified by the $eventQuery under the $namespace.
Register-WmiEvent -Namespace $namespace -Query $eventQuery -SourceIdentifier
"sqlevents"

while ($true) {
        # Get new events
        $objEvents=Get-Event -SourceIdentifier "sqlevents" -ErrorAction
SilentlyContinue

        # If new events arrive, then retrieve the event information.
        if ($objEvents) {
                # Loop through the collection of new events
                for ($i=0; $i -lt $objEvents.Count; $i++) {
                        # Construct the alert message from the error event information.
                        $alertMessage = $objEvents[$i].SourceEventArgs.NewEvent |
Format-List $properties | Out-String

                        # Send an alert e-mail.
                        Send-Email $smtpServer $fromAddress $toAddress $alertSubject
$alertMessage $smtpUserName $smtpPassword

                        # Remove the event after its information has been processed.
                        Remove-Event -EventIdentifier $objEvents[$i].EventIdentifier -
ErrorAction SilentlyContinue
                }
        }
}
}
```

This function is added into the library file, dbaLib.ps1. We will now create another script to call this Notify-WMIEvent function. The Monitor-SQLServerErrorLog.ps1 script will run continuously as a scheduled task in the background, which starts every time the SQL Server host starts, and stops when the host shuts down. The script will be saved under the directory C:\DBAScripts.

The Notify-WMIEvent function takes a WQL query, a namespace, and a list of selected properties of events as parameters. We are interested only in errors with a severity level of 17 and higher, which indicate software or hardware errors, and error messages from policy check (Severity 16). We can just take the WQL query from the MonitorErrorLog.ps1 script in Chapter 10:

```
$query = "SELECT * FROM ERRORLOG WHERE Severity >= 16"
```

As shown in Chapter 10, the namespace is in the format root\Microsoft\SqlServer\ServerEvents\instance _name. For a default instance, the namespace is root\Microsoft\SqlServer\ServerEvents\MSSQLSERVER. For a named instance CH0DE1, the namespace is root\Microsoft\SqlServer\ServerEvents\CH0DE1. The instance name is available in the instanceName column in the Servers table from the inventory database. We will pass the instance name as a parameter to the Monitor-SQLServerErrorLog.ps1 script so we can easily monitor multiple instances on the same host using the same script:

```
C:\DBAScripts\Monitor-SQLServerErrorLog.ps1 MSSQLSERVER
```

What properties do we want to monitor? We certainly want to know the error number, severity, and the text description that comes with the error. To identify the source of the error, we would also like to know the computer name and instance name. We include all these properties of the ERRORLOG class in the $selections variable and pass them to the Notify-WMIEvent function:

```
$selections= "ComputerName","SQLInstance","Error","Severity","TextData"
```

We also need to consider cluster cases. In a cluster, the monitoring script should run only on the active node, as the SQL Server instance runs only on the active node. Therefore, we need to check whether the SQL Server Database Engine service runs on the local host. Only when the service is running does the monitoring begin. Let's put the Monitor-SQLServerErrorLog.ps1 script together:

```
###################################################
# Initialize parameters
###################################################
param (
        [string]$instanceName
    )

###################################################
# Source in our library file
###################################################
. C:\DBAScripts\dbaLib.ps1

[String] $sqlServiceName=""

# Get the Database Engine service name of the SQL Server instance $instanceName
if ($instanceName -eq 'MSSQLSERVER') {
        $sqlServiceName='MSSQLSERVER'
}
else {
        $sqlServiceName='MSSQL$' + $instanceName
}

# Only if the SQL Server instance is running, the monitoring starts.
if ((Get-Service $sqlServiceName).Status -eq 'Running') {
        $query= "SELECT * FROM ERRORLOG WHERE Severity >= 16"
        $sqlNamespace= "root\Microsoft\SqlServer\ServerEvents\$instanceName"
        $selections= "ComputerName","SQLInstance", "Error","Severity","TextData"

        Notify-WMIEvent $query $sqlNamespace $selections
}
```

To install this script as a scheduled task on the SQL Server hosts in our inventory, we create another script to copy the Monitor-SQLServerErrorLog.ps1 script from the local host to every remote host, and create a scheduled task to kick off the script at system startup on every host. The script to create a scheduled task for a default instance looks like this, where P@ssw0rd is the password for PowerDomain\SqlService:

```
SCHTASKS /Create /S PowerPC /RU PowerDomain\SqlService /RP P@ssw0rd /SC ONSTART /TN
Monitor_SQLErrorLogs_MSSQLSERVER /TR "powershell.exe C:\DBASCRIPTS\Monitor-
SQLServerErrorLog.ps1 MSSQLSERVER"
```

In the case of a named instance, we just need to replace MSSQLSERVER in the preceding script with the name of a named instance.

The following code example shows the installation script Install-MonitorErrorLogsTask.ps1. As you can see, this script first gets the list of standalone hosts and cluster nodes, along with the SQL Server instances on them. Then it copies the Monitor-SQLServerErrorLog.ps1 script, installs the scheduled task Monitor_SQLErrorLogs, and starts the task on each host:

```
################################################# Source in our library file
#################################################
. C:\DBAScripts\dbaLib.ps1

[String] $strQuerySql=""
[String] $sqlHostName=""
[String] $sqlInstanceName=""
[String] $sqlUserName="POWERDOMAIN\SqlService"
[String] $sqlPassword="P@ssw0rd" # Password for POWERDOMAIN\SqlService
[String] $localHostName=(Get-ChildItem Env:\ComputerName).Value

# Get all the standalone hosts and cluster nodes with their instances in the
inventory.
$strQuerySql="SELECT h.hostName, s.instanceName
FROM dbo.Servers s
JOIN dbo.Hosts h on h.hostID=s.hostID
UNION
SELECT h.hostName, s.instanceName
FROM dbo.Servers s
JOIN dbo.Clusters c ON s.clusterID=c.clusterID
JOIN dbo.ClusterNodes cn ON c.clusterID = cn.clusterID
JOIN dbo.Hosts h ON cn.nodeID = h.hostID"

$sqlServers=Invoke-Sqlcmd -Query $strQuerySql -ServerInstance $inventoryServer -
Database $inventoryDatabase

Foreach ($sqlServer in $sqlServers) {
        $sqlHostName=$sqlServer.hostName
        $sqlInstanceName=$sqlServer.instanceName

        # Copy the Monitor-SQLServerErrorLog.ps1 script from the local host to
all the remote hosts.
        If ($sqlHostName -ne $localHostName) {
                # If the C:\DBAScripts directory does not exist on the destination
host, create it.
                If (-not (Test-Path \\$sqlHostName\C$\DBAScripts -pathType
container)) {
                        New-Item \\$sqlHostName\C$\DBAScripts -type directory |
Out-Null
                }

                # Copy both the Monitor-SQLServerErrorLog.ps1 script and the library
file dbaLib.ps1.
                Copy-Item C:\DBAScripts\Monitor-SQLServerErrorLog.ps1
```

```
\\$sqlHostName\C$\DBAScripts -force
                Copy-Item C:\DBAScripts\dbaLib.ps1 \\$sqlHostName\C$\DBAScripts -
force
        }

        "Creating schedule task on $sqlHostName ..."
        SCHTASKS /Create /S $sqlHostName /RU $sqlUserName /RP $sqlPassword /SC
ONSTART '
        /F /TN "Monitor_SQLErrorLogs_$sqlInstanceName" '
        /TR "powershell.exe C:\DBAScripts\Monitor-SQLServerErrorLog.ps1
$sqlInstanceName"

        # Start the scheduled task immediately
        SCHTASKS /RUN /S $sqlHostName /TN "Monitor_SQLErrorLogs_$sqlInstanceName"
}
```

Before running the script, make sure you have the latest copy of Monitor-SQLServerErrorLog.ps1 under C:\DBAScripts on the host from which you are running Install-MonitorErrorLogsTask.ps1. In addition, the execution policy of Windows PowerShell on every SQL Server host needs to be Unrestricted (please see the section "Script Commands" in Chapter 2).

Execute the scripts to install the scheduled tasks:

```
C:\DBAScripts\Install-MonitorErrorLogsTask.ps1
```

Figure 18-11 shows that the script creates a scheduled task Monitor_WindowsEventLogs on all the hosts in our environment.

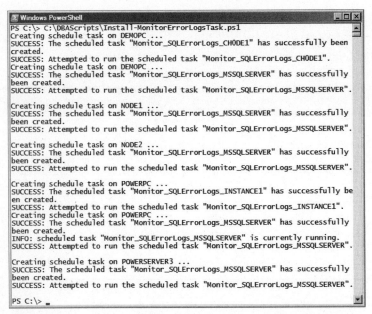

Figure 18-11

Let's test the scheduled tasks by creating an error with severity 18 by raising an error on the default instance on PowerPC:

```
raiserror ('this is a test', 16, 1) with log
```

As shown in Figure 18-12, the error picked up the scheduled task and an e-mail is sent to yanpan@powerdomain.com with detailed information about the error.

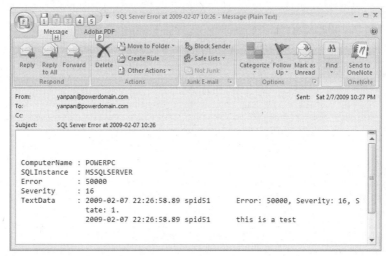

Figure 18-12

Monitoring Blockings

If you are a DBA at your company, then it is very likely that you have been involved in troubleshooting blocking and deadlock issues. I can't count how many times I have received calls from BU users complaining that their processes were running for an unusually long time. When I checked the processes running on their server, I often saw that their processes were being blocked by other processes, waiting for resources to be released.

DBAs should be proactive, rather than reactive, in dealing with blockings. We should not wait for the blocking or deadlock problems to become noticeable to the end-users. We should monitor blockings and deadlocks as they occur and take appropriate actions.

In this chapter, we created the Notify-WMIEvent function to monitor the SQL Server error log, which takes a WQL query, a namespace, and a list of selected properties of events as parameters. Following what we did to monitor the SQL Server error log, we will also create a monitoring script similar to the Monitor-SQLServerErrorLog.ps1 script, and an installation script to install the script as a scheduled task on each SQL Server host. In the new blocking monitoring script, we only need to change the parameter values of the Notify-WMIEvent function to monitor blockings.

As you saw in Chapter 10, the trace event class BLOCKED_PROCESS_REPORT reports blocked processes. By default, this class is disabled. To enable this class, we need to run sp_configure to configure the blocked process threshold option. This option specifies the threshold, in seconds, at which blocked process reports are generated. For example, to define the threshold as five minutes, set the value of the option to 300:

```
exec sp_configure 'show advanced options', 1
GO
RECONFIGURE
GO
exec sp_configure 'blocked process threshold', 300
GO
RECONFIGURE
GO
```

This setting change becomes effective immediately without a server restart. We will run this query to configure all the servers in our inventory.

Now we need to set up the parameters of the Notify-WMIEvent function. We can take the WQL query from Chapter 10:

```
$query = "SELECT * FROM BLOCKED_PROCESS_REPORT"
```

As the Monitor-SQLServerErrorLog.ps1 script, our new blocking monitoring script will accept the SQL Server instance name as a parameter, and use the instance name to determine the namespace, root\Microsoft\SqlServer\ServerEvents\instance_name. The new Monitor-Blocking.ps1 script can be used to monitor multiple instances on the same host using the same script:

```
C:\DBAScripts\Monitor-Blocking.ps1 $instanceName
```

Out of all the properties of the BLOCKED_PROCESS_REPORT event class, the computer name, SQL Server instance name, database ID, and event post time provide when and where the event occurs. The Duration property indicates how long (in milliseconds) the process was blocked. The TextData property is also useful. It provides details about each process that participated in the blocking:

```
$selections= "ComputerName", "SQLInstance", "DatabaseID", "PostTime", "Duration",
"TextData"
```

Here is the Monitor-Blocking.ps1 script that will be copied to each SQL Server host and run on the host. Note that this script is very similar to the Monitor-SQLServerErrorLog.ps1 script. The only differences lie in the values of the parameters of the Notify-WMIEvent function, $query and $selections. You can see how easy it is to reuse the scripts we created earlier and make minor changes to monitor different event classes of interest:

```
###################################################
# Initialize parameters
###################################################
param (
          [string]$instanceName
     )

##########################################################################
# Source in our library file
##########################################################################
. C:\DBAScripts\dbaLib.ps1
```

```
[String] $sqlServiceName=""

# Get the Database Engine service name of the SQL Server instance $instanceName
if ($instanceName -eq 'MSSQLSERVER') {
        $sqlServiceName='MSSQLSERVER'
}
else {
        $sqlServiceName='MSSQL$' + $instanceName
}

# Only if the SQL Server instance is running, the monitoring starts.
if ((Get-Service $sqlServiceName).Status -eq 'Running') {
        $query = "SELECT * FROM BLOCKED_PROCESS_REPORT"
        $sqlNamespace= "root\Microsoft\SqlServer\ServerEvents\$instanceName"
        $selections= "ComputerName", "SQLInstance", "DatabaseID", "PostTime",
"Duration", "TextData"
        Notify-WMIEvent $query $sqlNamespace $selections
}
```

As shown earlier in the section on monitoring the SQL Server error log, we need another script, Install-MonitorBlocking.ps1, to copy the Monitor-Blocking.ps1 script to every host in our inventory and install a scheduled task to kick off the script at system startup. The command to create a scheduled task looks like this:

```
SCHTASKS /Create /S PowerPC /RU PowerDomain\SqlService /RP P@ssw0rd /SC ONSTART /TN
Monitor_Blocking_$instanceName /TR "powershell.exe D:\DBAScripts\Monitor-
Blocking.ps1 $instanceName"
```

Now we are ready to create our installation script, Install-MonitorBlocking.ps1. It is very similar to the Install-MonitorErrorLogsTask.ps1 script. However, in addition to copying the monitoring script and creating a scheduled task, Install-MonitorBlocking.ps1 also needs to configure the "blocked process threshold" option. Therefore, the script must get the TCP/IP port number from the inventory:

```
####################################################
# Source in our library file
####################################################
. C:\DBAScripts\dbaLib.ps1

[String] $strQuerySql=""
[String] $sqlHostName=""
[String] $sqlInstanceName=""
[String] $tcpPort=""
[String] $sqlClusterName=""
[String] $sqlUserName="POWERDOMAIN\SqlService"
[String] $sqlPassword="P@ssw0rd"
[String] $localHostName=(Get-ChildItem Env:\ComputerName).Value

$strQuerySql="SELECT h.hostName, s.instanceName, '' as clusterName, tcpPort
FROM dbo.Servers s
JOIN dbo.Hosts h on h.hostID=s.hostID
UNION
SELECT h.hostName, s.instanceName, c.SQLClusterName as clusterName, tcpPort
FROM dbo.Servers s
```

```
JOIN dbo.Clusters c ON s.clusterID=c.clusterID
JOIN dbo.ClusterNodes cn ON c.clusterID = cn.clusterID
JOIN dbo.Hosts h ON cn.nodeID = h.hostID"

$sqlServers=Invoke-Sqlcmd -Query $strQuerySql -ServerInstance
$inventoryServer -Database $inventoryDatabase

# Here is the query to enable the "blocked process threshold" option
$strQuerySql="exec sp_configure 'show advanced options', 1
GO
RECONFIGURE
GO
exec sp_configure 'blocked process threshold', 300
GO
RECONFIGURE
GO"

Foreach ($sqlServer in $sqlServers) {
        $sqlHostName=$sqlServer.hostName
        $sqlInstanceName=$sqlServer.instanceName
        $tcpPort=$sqlServer.tcpPort
        $sqlClusterName=$sqlServer.clusterName

        if ($sqlClusterName.Length -eq 0) {
                "Changing the threshold on $sqlHostName,$tcpPort"
                Invoke-Sqlcmd -Query $strQuerySql -ServerInstance
"$sqlHostName,$tcpPort" -Database master
        }
        else {
                "Changing the threshold on $sqlClusterName,$tcpPort"
                Invoke-Sqlcmd -Query $strQuerySql -ServerInstance
"$sqlClusterName,$tcpPort" -Database master
        }

        # Install the Monitor-Blocking.ps1 script on all the hosts excluding the
current host that we are copying the script from.
        If ($sqlHostName -ne $localHostName) {
                # If the C:\DBAScripts directory does not exist on the destination
host, create it.
                If (-not (Test-Path \\$sqlHostName\C$\DBAScripts -pathType
container)) {
                        New-Item \\$sqlHostName\C$\DBAScripts -type directory
                }

                # Copy both the Monitor-Blocking.ps1 script and the library file
dbaLib.ps1.
                Copy-Item C:\DBAScripts\Monitor-Blocking.ps1
\\$sqlHostName\C$\DBAScripts -force
                Copy-Item C:\DBAScripts\dbaLib.ps1 \\$sqlHostName\C$\DBAScripts -
force
        }

        "Creating schedule task on $sqlHostName ..."
        SCHTASKS /Create /S $sqlHostName /RU $sqlUserName /RP $sqlPassword /SC
ONSTART '
```

```
        /F /TN "Monitor_Blocking_$sqlInstanceName" '
        /TR "powershell.exe C:\DBAScripts\Monitor-Blocking.ps1 $sqlInstanceName"

    # Start the scheduled task immediately
    SCHTASKS /RUN /S $sqlHostName /TN "Monitor_Blocking_$sqlInstanceName"
}
```

Before running the script, make sure you have the latest copy of `Monitor-Blocking.ps1` under `C:\DBAScripts` on the host from which you are running `Install-MonitorBlocking.ps1`. In addition, the execution policy of Windows PowerShell on every SQL Server host needs to be unrestricted (for more information, see the `Set-ExecutionPolicy` cmdlet in the section "Script Commands" in Chapter 2).

Execute the scripts to install scheduled tasks:

```
C:\DBAScripts\Install-MonitorBlocking.ps1
```

As shown in Figure 18-13, the script configures the "blocked process threshold" option, and creates and starts scheduled tasks on all the hosts in our environment.

Figure 18-13

In Chapter 10, you saw how to create a blocking using SQL queries. Let's run the same queries to create a blocking on the default instance on PowerPC and test the scheduled tasks. Open a query window in SSMS and run the following query:

```
USE AdventureWorks2008

IF  EXISTS (SELECT * FROM sys.objects WHERE object_id = OBJECT_ID(N'[dbo].[Test]')
```

```
AND type in (N'U'))
DROP TABLE [dbo].[Test]
GO

CREATE TABLE Test (i int)

INSERT Test SELECT 1
GO
BEGIN TRAN
UPDATE Test SET i = 1
WAITFOR DELAY '00:10:00'
COMMIT
```

This session holds exclusive locks for 10 minutes on the Test table.

In another query window in SSMS, run this query:

```
USE AdventureWorks2008
UPDATE Test SET i = 1
```

As shown in Figure 18-14, the blocking is picked up by Monitor-Blocking.ps1 and an alert e-mail is sent to yanpan@powerdomain.com with detailed information about the blocking.

Monitoring Deadlocks

To monitor deadlocks, we just follow the preceding approach and create a new monitoring script, Monitor-Deadlock.ps1, and an installation script to install the script as a scheduled task on each SQL Server host. In the new blocking monitoring script, we only need to change the parameter values of the Notify-WMIEvent function to monitor blockings. The DEADLOCK_GRAPH event class contains the deadlock events; therefore, the event query parameter is as follows:

```
$query = "SELECT * FROM DEADLOCK_GRAPH"
```

Like the previous monitoring scripts, our new deadlock monitoring script, Monitor-Deadlock.ps1, will accept the SQL Server instance name as a parameter, and use the instance name to determine the namespace, root\Microsoft\SqlServer\ServerEvents\instance_name. The Monitor-Deadlock.ps1 script can be used to monitor multiple instances on the same host:

```
C:\DBAScripts\Monitor-Deadlock.ps1 $instanceName
```

Out of all the properties of the DEADLOCK_GRAPH event class, the computer name, SQL Server instance name, and start time provide when and where the event occurs. The TextData property provides details about each process that participated in the deadlock:

```
$selections= "ComputerName", "SQLInstance", "StartTime", "TextData"
```

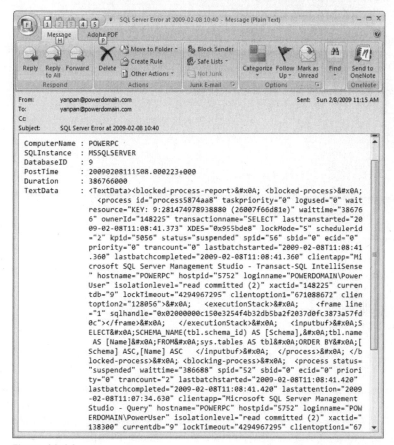

Figure 18-14

Here is the `Monitor-Deadlock.ps1` script that will be copied to each SQL Server host and run on the host. Note that this script is very similar to the `Monitor-SQLServerErrorLog.ps1` and `Monitor-Blocking.ps1` scripts. The only differences lie in the values of the parameters of the `Notify-WMIEvent` function, `$query` and `$selections`:

```
####################################################
# Initialize parameters
####################################################
param (
        [string]$instanceName
    )


####################################################
# Source in our library file
####################################################
```

```
. C:\DBAScripts\dbaLib.ps1

[String] $sqlServiceName=""

# Get the Database Engine service name of the SQL Server instance $instanceName
if ($instanceName -eq 'MSSQLSERVER') {
        $sqlServiceName='MSSQLSERVER'
}
else {
        $sqlServiceName='MSSQL$' + $instanceName
}

# Only if the SQL Server instance is running, the monitoring starts.
if ((Get-Service $sqlServiceName).Status -eq 'Running') {
        $query = "SELECT * FROM DEADLOCK_GRAPH"
        $sqlNamespace = "root\Microsoft\SqlServer\ServerEvents\$instanceName"
        $selections= "ComputerName", "SQLInstance", "StartTime", "TextData"

        Notify-WMIEvent $query $sqlNamespace $selections
}
```

We still need an installation script, Install-MonitorDeadlock.ps1, to copy the Monitor-Deadlock.ps1 script to every host in our inventory and install a scheduled task to kick off the script at system startup. The command to create a scheduled task looks like this:

```
SCHTASKS /Create /S PowerPC /RU PowerDomain\SqlService /RP P@ssw0rd /SC ONSTART /TN
Monitor_Deadlock_$instanceName /TR "powershell.exe D:\DBAScripts\Monitor-
Deadlock.ps1 $instanceName"
```

Now we are ready to create our installation script Install-MonitorDeadlock.ps1. It is very similar to the Install-MonitorErrorLogsTask.psi script. The only differences lie in the copied script name, Monitor-Deadlock.ps1, and the scheduled task name Monitor_Deadlock. The installation script, Install-MonitorDeadlock.ps1, is shown here:

```
####################################################
# Source in our library file
####################################################
. C:\DBAScripts\dbaLib.ps1

[String] $strQuerySql=""
[String] $sqlHostName=""
[String] $sqlInstanceName=""
[String] $sqlUserName="POWERDOMAIN\SqlService"
[String] $sqlPassword="P@ssw0rd" # Password for POWERDOMAIN\SqlService
[String] $localHostName=(Get-ChildItem Env:\ComputerName).Value

# Get all the standalone hosts and cluster nodes with their instances in the
inventory.
$strQuerySql="SELECT h.hostName, s.instanceName
FROM dbo.Servers s
JOIN dbo.Hosts h on h.hostID=s.hostID
UNION
SELECT h.hostName, s.instanceName
FROM dbo.Servers s
```

```
JOIN dbo.Clusters c ON s.clusterID=c.clusterID
JOIN dbo.ClusterNodes cn ON c.clusterID = cn.clusterID
JOIN dbo.Hosts h ON cn.nodeID = h.hostID"

$sqlServers=Invoke-Sqlcmd -Query $strQuerySql -ServerInstance $inventoryServer -
Database $inventoryDatabase

Foreach ($sqlServer in $sqlServers) {
        $sqlHostName=$sqlServer.hostName
        $sqlInstanceName=$sqlServer.instanceName

        # Copy the Monitor-Deadlock.ps1 script from the local host to all the
remote hosts.
        If ($sqlHostName -ne $localHostName) {
                # If the C:\DBAScripts directory does not exist on the destination
host, create it.
                If (-not (Test-Path \\$sqlHostName\C$\DBAScripts -pathType
container)) {
                        New-Item \\$sqlHostName\C$\DBAScripts -type directory |
Out-Null
                }

                # Copy both the Monitor-Deadlock.ps1 script and the library file
dbaLib.ps1.
                Copy-Item C:\DBAScripts\Monitor-Deadlock.ps1
\\$sqlHostName\C$\DBAScripts -force
                Copy-Item C:\DBAScripts\dbaLib.ps1 \\$sqlHostName\C$\DBAScripts -
force
        }

        "Creating schedule task on $sqlHostName ..."
        SCHTASKS /Create /S $sqlHostName /RU $sqlUserName /RP $sqlPassword /SC
ONSTART '
        /F /TN "Monitor_Deadlock_$sqlInstanceName" '
        /TR "powershell.exe C:\DBAScripts\Monitor-Deadlock.ps1 $sqlInstanceName"

        # Start the scheduled task immediately
        SCHTASKS /RUN /S $sqlHostName /TN "Monitor_Deadlock_$sqlInstanceName"
}
```

Execute the script to install scheduled tasks:

```
C:\DBAScripts\Install-MonitorDeadlock.ps1
```

As shown in Figure 18-15, the script creates and starts scheduled tasks on all the hosts in our environment.

Let's test the scheduled tasks by creating a deadlock on the default instance on PowerPC, as in Chapter 10. Open a query window in SSMS and run this query:

```
USE AdventureWorks2008
GO

CREATE TABLE Test (i int)
```

```
INSERT Test SELECT 1
GO
BEGIN TRAN
UPDATE Test SET i = 1
WAITFOR DELAY '00:00:30'
UPDATE Test2 SET i = 1
WAITFOR DELAY '00:02:00'
COMMIT

DROP TABLE Test
```

```
Windows PowerShell
PS C:\> C:\DBAScripts\Install-MonitorDeadlock.ps1
Creating schedule task on DEMOPC ...
SUCCESS: The scheduled task "Monitor_Deadlock_CHODE1" has successfully been crea
ted.
SUCCESS: Attempted to run the scheduled task "Monitor_Deadlock_CHODE1".
Creating schedule task on DEMOPC ...
SUCCESS: The scheduled task "Monitor_Deadlock_MSSQLSERVER" has successfully been
 created.
SUCCESS: Attempted to run the scheduled task "Monitor_Deadlock_MSSQLSERVER".
Creating schedule task on NODE1 ...
SUCCESS: The scheduled task "Monitor_Deadlock_MSSQLSERVER" has successfully been
 created.
SUCCESS: Attempted to run the scheduled task "Monitor_Deadlock_MSSQLSERVER".
Creating schedule task on NODE2 ...
SUCCESS: The scheduled task "Monitor_Deadlock_MSSQLSERVER" has successfully been
 created.
SUCCESS: Attempted to run the scheduled task "Monitor_Deadlock_MSSQLSERVER".
Creating schedule task on POWERPC ...
SUCCESS: The scheduled task "Monitor_Deadlock_INSTANCE1" has successfully been c
reated.
INFO: scheduled task "Monitor_Deadlock_INSTANCE1" is currently running.
SUCCESS: Attempted to run the scheduled task "Monitor_Deadlock_INSTANCE1".
Creating schedule task on POWERPC ...
SUCCESS: The scheduled task "Monitor_Deadlock_MSSQLSERVER" has successfully been
 created.
INFO: scheduled task "Monitor_Deadlock_MSSQLSERVER" is currently running.
SUCCESS: Attempted to run the scheduled task "Monitor_Deadlock_MSSQLSERVER".
Creating schedule task on POWERSERVER3 ...
SUCCESS: The scheduled task "Monitor_Deadlock_MSSQLSERVER" has successfully been
 created.
SUCCESS: Attempted to run the scheduled task "Monitor_Deadlock_MSSQLSERVER".
PS C:\>
```

Figure 18-15

This session holds exclusive locks on the Test table, and tries to update the Test2 table.

Within 30 seconds, in another SSMS query window, run this query:

```
USE AdventureWorks2008
GO

CREATE TABLE Test2 (i int)

INSERT Test2 SELECT 1
GO
BEGIN TRAN
UPDATE Test2 SET i = 1
WAITFOR DELAY '00:00:30'
UPDATE Test SET i = 1
WAITFOR DELAY '00:02:00'
COMMIT

DROP TABLE Test2
```

This session holds exclusive locks on the Test2 table, and tries to update the Test table. We have a deadlock situation here because these two sessions are blocking each other and trying to update the table the other process is holding.

As shown in Figure 18-16, the deadlock is picked up by the scheduled task Monitor_Deadlock_MSSQLSERVER and an e-mail is sent to yanpan@powerdomain.com with detailed information about the deadlock.

Figure 18-16

Please note that if you run both Monitor_Deadlock and Monitor_Blocking jobs at the same time, depending on the blocked process threshold, Monitor_Blocking might pick up the deadlock before Monitor_Deadlock is able to pick up the deadlock. Therefore, you might not see deadlock notification e-mails. Therefore, please adjust the threshold accordingly.

Summary

An important part of a DBA's job is monitoring not only the health of SQL Server instances, but also the health of their hosts. Proactive monitoring ensures the smooth operation of your SQL Server environment, and reduces frustration and confusion for your end-users.

In this chapter, we have demonstrated some powerful monitoring scripts that implemented off-host monitoring tasks, such as pinging hosts and checking SQL Server–related services; and on-host monitoring tasks, such as monitoring Windows event logs, the SQL Server error log, and blockings and deadlocks. The `Notify-WMIEvent` function created in this chapter utilizes the WMI provider for Server Events and the new Eventing feature in Windows PowerShell 2.0 to capture SQL Server events. By simply changing the event query and the properties passed to this function, we built monitoring scripts for different event classes.

We also demonstrated how to install the monitoring scripts as scheduled tasks on SQL Server hosts. The scripts created in this chapter can serve as templates for building your own DBA toolbox, and you can easily customize them to monitor events you are interested in. In short, this chapter provides a simple and feasible solution for enterprise monitoring.

The next chapter continues our exploration of monitoring as it relates to disk space usage, database files, and backups.

19

Monitoring Disk Space Usage, Database Files, and Backups

In an enterprise environment, an unavoidable task is monitoring the free disk space on SQL server hosts to ensure that no system or database drives are running low on space. In addition, the growth of the database files needs to be monitored to ensure there is sufficient space on disks to accommodate future storage needs. It is better to plan ahead, rather than panic when you run out of disk space. In this chapter, we will create extra tables in the inventory databases to hold space information. This chapter also presents sample Windows PowerShell scripts that can be executed against the list of servers stored in the inventory database to collect the space information.

Backup and recovery is one of the most important aspects of database administration. Important information saved in a database needs to be protected against hardware, software, or human errors. Therefore, you need to develop a backup and recovery plan, and monitor the database backups to ensure conformance to the plan.

This chapter covers the following topics:

- ❑ Monitoring disk space usage

- ❑ Monitoring database file growth

- ❑ Monitoring backups

Monitoring Disk Space Usage

In Chapter 15, an inventory database named SQL_Inventory was set up to hold information about hosts, servers, and databases. We can add a DiskSpace table to the SQL_Inventory database to hold the information regarding disk space usage. SQL Server database files can reside on the local drive only. Therefore, we will only store the space information of the local drives on every host in our inventory in the DiskSpace table. The DiskSpace table includes the drive letter, total size of the drive, and free space on the drive. In order to determine the composition of the space, it also includes the size of the space used by each type of database file: data, log, FILESTREAM, and full text. The schema of the table is shown in Table 19-1.

Table 19-1: Schema of the DiskSpace Table

Column	DataType	Description
hostID	int	ID of the host or active cluster node
drive	Char(1)	Drive letter, such as C, D, etc.
totalSize(KB)	Bigint	Total size of the drive
freeSpace(KB)	Bigint	Free space on the drive
total_datafile_size(KB)	Bigint	Total size of the data files on the drive
total_logfile_size(KB)	Bigint	Total size of the log files on the drive
total_filestream_size(KB)	Bigint	Total size of the FILESTREAM files on the drive
total_fulltext_size(KB)	Bigint	Total size of the full-text catalogs on the drive
createDate	smalldatetime	Date and time this disk space record was created
updateDate	Smalldatetime	Date and time this disk space record was last updated

The SQL script CreateDiskSpace.sql creates the DiskSpace table:

```
USE [SQL_Inventory]
GO
IF  EXISTS (SELECT * FROM sys.objects WHERE object_id =
OBJECT_ID(N'[dbo].[DiskSpace]') AND type in (N'U'))
DROP TABLE [dbo].[DiskSpace]
GO
CREATE TABLE [dbo].[DiskSpace](
[hostID] [int],
[drive] [char](1) NOT NULL,
[totalSize(KB)] [bigint],
[freeSpace(KB)] [bigint],
[total_datafile_size(KB)] bigint,
[total_logfile_size(KB)] bigint,
[total_filestream_size(KB)] bigint,
[total_fulltext_size(KB)] bigint,
[createDate] [smalldatetime] NOT NULL default getDate(),
[updateDate] [smalldatetime] NOT NULL default getDate()
)
GO
```

To populate this table, we first query the `Win32_LogicalDisk` WMI class for a drive type of 3, which means local drives. An example of this was already shown in Chapter 5 when we discussed the file system. Run the following command against all the hosts in our inventory to get all the instances of the `Win32_LogicalDisk` class:

```
Get-WmiObject -Class Win32_LogicalDisk -filter "DriveType=3" |
Select-Object DeviceID, FreeSpace | Format-Table -auto
```

Here is the script `uspUpsertDiskspace.sql` to create a stored procedure `uspUpsertDiskSpace`. This stored procedure inserts a new drive record if the drive doesn't exist in the table, or updates a drive record if the drive already exists. Notice that only the first four columns of the `DiskSpace` table, which reflect hostID, drive letter, total drive size, and free drive space, are populated:

```
USE [SQL_Inventory]
GO
IF  EXISTS (SELECT * FROM sys.objects WHERE object_id =
OBJECT_ID(N'[dbo].[uspUpsertDiskSpace]') AND type in (N'P', N'PC'))
DROP PROCEDURE [dbo].[uspUpsertDiskSpace]
GO
CREATE PROCEDURE [DBO].[uspUpsertDiskSpace]
                @hostID    int,
                @drive char(1),
                @totalSize bigint,
                @freeSpace bigint
AS
DECLARE @ERRORCODE [int], @ERRMSG varchar(128)

-- If the drive already exists in the DiskSpace table, then perform an update.
IF exists (SELECT hostID FROM DiskSpace WHERE hostID=@hostID and drive=@drive)
    UPDATE [dbo].[DiskSpace]
    SET [totalSize(KB)]=@totalSize,
        [freeSpace(KB)]=@freespace,
        [updateDate] = GETDATE()
    WHERE hostID=@hostID and drive=@drive
-- If the drive does not exist in the DiskSpace table, then perform an insertion.
ELSE
    INSERT [dbo].[DiskSpace]
          ( hostID
          , drive
          , [totalSize(KB)]
          , [freeSpace(KB)]
          , createDate
          , updateDate
          )
    VALUES(
          @hostID
          , @drive
          , @totalSize
          , @freeSpace
          , GETDATE()
    , GETDATE()
          )

    SET @ERRORCODE = @@ERROR
```

```
IF @ERRORCODE <> 0
    BEGIN
        SET @ERRMSG = 'Upsert failed - ' + OBJECT_NAME(@@PROCID)
        SET @ERRMSG = @ERRMSG + ' Error Code: ' + RTRIM(CONVERT(CHAR, @ERRORCODE))
        RAISERROR (@ERRMSG, 16, 1)
        RETURN (-1)
    END
ELSE
    RETURN (0)

GO
```

To update the next four columns of the DiskSpace table, we need to know how much space on each drive is used for data files, log files, FILESTREAM, data and full-text catalogs. Because a host can contain more than one SQL Server instance, we need to query every SQL Server instance on a host and add up the space. For example, the following SQL query returns the space usage of each drive for an instance:

```
USE master

SELECT drive, isNull([0],0) as [total_datafile_size], isNull([1],0) as
[total_logfile_size],
isNull([2],0) as [total_filestream_size], isNull([4],0) as [total_fulltext_size]
FROM
    (SELECT LEFT(physical_name, 1) as drive, type, SUM(size * 8) as total_size
    FROM sys.master_files
    GROUP BY left(physical_name,1), type) AS SourceTable
    PIVOT
    (
    SUM(total_size)
FOR type IN ([0], [1], [2], [4])
) AS PivotTable
```

The subquery selects from the sys.master_files, which contains all the database files, groups the files by drive and file type, and adds up the sizes of the database files. The available types are listed here:

```
0 -Data files
1- Log files
2- FILESTREAM data
4- Fulltext catalogs
```

Next, the intermediate table is pivoted on the type column. The four type values become four column headings, and we have four columns that contain total file size for each type by an instance.

We store disk space usage of SQL Server instances in a utility table DiskUsageByServer. After we go through all the instances on all the hosts and save the drive usage of each instance, we can add up the disk space of all the instances on a particular host to get the total usage for each drive on that host.

Table 19-2 shows the schema of the utility table, DiskUsageByServer.

Table 19-2: Schema of the DiskUsageBy Server Table

Column	DataType	Description
hostID	int	ID of the host
drive	Char(1)	Drive letter, such as C, D, etc.
dataSize	Bigint	Total size of the data files on the drive
logSize	Bigint	Total size of the log files on the drive
filestreamSize	Bigint	Total size of the FILESTREAM files on the drive
fulltextSize	Bigint	Total size of the full-text catalogs on the drive

The following script, CreateDiskUsageByServer.sql, creates the DiskUsageByServer table:

```
USE [SQL_Inventory]
GO
IF  EXISTS (SELECT * FROM sys.objects WHERE object_id =
OBJECT_ID(N'[dbo].[DiskUsageByServer]') AND type in (N'U'))
DROP TABLE [dbo].[DiskUsageByServer]
GO
CREATE TABLE [dbo].[DiskUsageByServer](
[hostID] [int],
[drive] [char](1) NOT NULL,
[dataSize] bigint,
[logSize] bigint,
[filestreamSize] bigint,
[fulltextSize] bigint)
GO
```

We also need a stored procedure to insert a drive record. Here is the uspInsertDiskUsageByServer.sql script to create the stored procedure:

```
USE [SQL_Inventory]
GO
IF  OBJECTPROPERTY(OBJECT_ID(N'[DBO].[uspInsertDiskUsageByServer]'),  N'IsProcedure')
= 1
    DROP PROCEDURE [DBO].[uspInsertDiskUsageByServer]
GO
CREATE PROCEDURE [DBO].[uspInsertDiskUsageByServer]
                @hostID   int,
                @drive char(1),
                @dataSize bigint,
                @logSize bigint,
                @filestreamSize bigint,
                @fulltextSize  bigint
AS
DECLARE @ERRORCODE [int], @ERRMSG varchar(128)
```

```
INSERT [dbo].[DiskUsageByServer]
(    hostID
   , drive
   , [dataSize]
   , [logSize]
   , [filestreamSize]
   , [fulltextSize]
)
VALUES(
     @hostID
   , @drive
   , @dataSize
   , @logSize
   , @filestreamSize
   , @fulltextSize
)

SET @ERRORCODE = @@ERROR
IF @ERRORCODE <> 0
BEGIN
    SET @ERRMSG = 'Insert failed - ' + OBJECT_NAME(@@PROCID)
    SET @ERRMSG = @ERRMSG + ' Error Code: ' + RTRIM(CONVERT(CHAR, @ERRORCODE))
    RAISERROR (@ERRMSG, 16, 1)
    RETURN (-1)
END
ELSE
    RETURN (0)
GO
```

After we collect the disk space used by all the instances on all the hosts and populate the utility table, we can group the data by host and drive, and add up the total size used for each database file type on each drive of every host. Then we can update the DiskSpace table using this query:

```
UPDATE ds
SET [total_datafile_size(KB)]=du.dataSize, [total_logfile_size(KB)]=du.logSize,
[total_filestream_size(KB)]=du.streamSize, [total_fulltext_size(KB)]=du.fulltextSize

FROM DiskSpace ds
JOIN (SELECT hostID, drive, sum(dataSize) as dataSize, sum(logSize) as logSize,
    sum(filestreamSize) as streamSize, sum(fulltextSize) as fulltextSize
    FROM DiskUsageByServer
    GROUP BY hostID, drive) du
ON ds.hostID=du.hostID and ds.drive=du.drive
```

For a cluster, the space used by SQL Server database files should be counted only on the active node, not on the passive node. Therefore, we need to query the the NetBIOS name on which a SQL Server instance is currently running, by running the following query:

```
SELECT SERVERPROPERTY('ComputerNamePhysicalNetBIOS')
```

In a cluster scenario, this query returns the computer name of the active node.

Putting the pieces together, here is the complete script for Update-DiskSpace.ps1. You can download this script from the Wrox site for this book at www.wrox.com:

```
####################################################
# Source in our library file
####################################################
. C:\DBAScripts\dbaLib.ps1

[String] $strQuerySql=""
[String] $strInsertSql=""
[String] $strUpsertSql=""
[String] $strUpdateSql=""

# Empty the utility table DiskUsageByServer.
[String] $sqlQuerySql="TRUNCATE TABLE [dbo].[DiskUsageByServer];"

Invoke-Sqlcmd -Query $sqlQuerySql -ServerInstance $inventoryServer -Database
$inventoryDatabase


# Gets all the SQL Server hosts.
$strQuerySql="SELECT hostID, hostName FROM Hosts"

$sqlhosts=Invoke-Sqlcmd -Query $strQuerySql -ServerInstance $inventoryServer
-Database $inventoryDatabase

# Loop through the list of hosts.
Foreach ($sqlhost in $sqlhosts) {
        $strUpsertSql=""

        $sqlHostID=$sqlhost.hostID
        $sqlHostName=$sqlhost.hostName

        ###############################################################
        # First step, for every host, gets all the local drives.
        # Insert into or Update the DiskSpace table with the total size and free space
of each drive on the host.

        $devices=Get-WmiObject -computerName $sqlHostName -Class Win32_LogicalDisk -
filter "DriveType=3"

        Foreach ($device in $devices) {
                $strUpsertSql = $strUpsertSql + "exec uspUpsertDiskSpace " + $sqlHostID
+ ", '" '
                + $device.DeviceID.SubString(0,1) + "', " + $device.Size/1024 + ", " +
$device.FreeSpace/1024 + ";`n"

        }

        $strUpsertSql
        Invoke-Sqlcmd -Query $strUpsertSql -ServerInstance $inventoryServer -Database
$inventoryDatabase


        ###############################################################
        # Second step, query every instance on the host.
        # Insert into the DiskUsageByServer table with the space used for data files,
log files, FILESTREAM and full text catalogs on every instance.
```

```
$strInsertSql=""

# Get the instances on a host.
# The first SELECT gets standalone instances for a standalone host,
# and the second SELECT gets clustered instances for a cluster node.
$strQuerySql="SELECT h.hostName as SQLNetworkName, s.tcpPort
FROM dbo.Servers s
JOIN dbo.Hosts h ON s.hostID= h.hostID
WHERE h.hostID=$sqlHostID
UNION
SELECT c.SQLClusterName as SQLNetworkName, s.tcpPort
FROM dbo.Servers s
JOIN dbo.Clusters c ON s.clusterID=c.clusterID
JOIN dbo.ClusterNodes cn ON c.clusterID = cn.clusterID
WHERE cn.nodeID = $sqlHostID"


$sqlServers=Invoke-Sqlcmd -Query $strQuerySql -ServerInstance $inventoryServer
-Database $inventoryDatabase

# Loop through the list of instances on the host.
Foreach ($sqlServer in $SqlServers) {
        if (!$sqlServer) { break }

        $sqlNetworkName=$sqlServer.SQLNetworkName
        $tcpPort=$sqlServer.tcpPort

        # Get the NetBIOS name on which the instance of SQL Server is currently
running.
        # In a cluster, it returns the host name of the active node.
        $strQuerySql="SELECT SERVERPROPERTY('ComputerNamePhysicalNetBIOS') AS
hostName"

        $physicalHost=Invoke-Sqlcmd -Query $strQuerySql -ServerInstance
"$sqlNetworkName,$tcpPort" -Database master

        # If the host is a standalone host or the active node of a cluster, then
add a record
        # to the DiskUsageByServer table that associates the space used by the
instance with the host.
        if ($physicalHost.hostName -ieq $sqlHostName) {

                # Get the information of how much space on all the drives is used
for data files, log files,
                # FILESTREAM and full text catalogs by the instance.
                $strQuerySql="SELECT drive, isNull([0],0) as
[total_datafile_size], isNull([1],0) as [total_logfile_size],
                isNull([2],0) as [total_filestream_size], isNull([4],0) as
[total_fulltext_size]
                FROM
                (SELECT LEFT(physical_name, 1) as drive, type, SUM(size * 8) as
total_size
                FROM sys.master_files
                GROUP BY left(physical_name,1), type) AS SourceTable
                PIVOT
```

```
                                    (
                                    SUM(total_size)
                                    FOR type IN ([0], [1], [2], [4])
                                    ) AS PivotTable;"

                                    $results=Invoke-Sqlcmd -Query $strQuerySql -ServerInstance
   "$sqlNetworkName,$tcpPort" -Database master

                                    # Loop through the list of drives, and insert into the
   DiskUsageByServer table.
                                    foreach ($result in $results) {
                                       $strInsertSql=$strInsertSql + "exec uspInsertDiskUsageByServer "
   + $sqlHostID + ", '" + $result.drive + "', " '
                                       + $result.total_datafile_size + ", " + $result.total_
   logfile_size + ", " '
                                       + $result.total_filestream_size + ", " +
   $result.total_fulltext_size + ";`n"
                                    }
                                  }
                               }

                        if ($strInsertSql -ne "") {
                               $strInsertSql
                               Invoke-Sqlcmd -Query $strInsertSql -ServerInstance $inventoryServer -
   Database $inventoryDatabase
                        }

                  }

   # Use the information in the DiskUsageByServer table to update the DiskSpace table.
   $strUpdateSql="UPDATE ds
   SET [total_datafile_size(KB)]=du.dataSize, [total_logfile_size(KB)]=du.logSize,
   [total_filestream_size(KB)]=du.streamSize, [total_fulltext_size(KB)]=du.fulltextSize

   FROM DiskSpace ds
   JOIN (SELECT hostID, drive, sum(dataSize) as dataSize, sum(logSize) as logSize,
          sum(filestreamSize) as streamSize, sum(fulltextSize) as fulltextSize
          FROM DiskUsageByServer
          GROUP BY hostID, drive) du
   ON ds.hostID=du.hostID and ds.drive=du.drive"

   Invoke-Sqlcmd -Query $strUpdateSql -ServerInstance $inventoryServer -Database
   $inventoryDatabase
```

Run the script in our environment. Figure 19-1 shows the output.

```
   C:\DBAScripts\Update-DiskSpace.ps1
```

Run this query in the SQL_Inventory database:

```
   SELECT h.hostName, ds.*
   FROM dbo.DiskSpace ds JOIN dbo.Hosts h
   ON ds.hostID=h.hostID
```

```
Windows PowerShell                                                    _ □ X
PS C:\> C:\DBAScripts\Update-DiskSpace.ps1
exec uspUpsertDiskSpace 1002, 'C', 32764532, 1586412;
exec uspUpsertDiskSpace 1002, 'D', 45351492, 15365724;


exec uspInsertDiskUsageByServer 1002, 'D', 209280, 12416, 280, 0;
exec uspInsertDiskUsageByServer 1002, 'C', 26688, 3576, 0, 0;


exec uspUpsertDiskSpace 1003, 'C', 10474348, 4177476;
exec uspUpsertDiskSpace 1003, 'D', 5237156, 5094988;
exec uspUpsertDiskSpace 1003, 'L', 5229124, 5195996;
exec uspUpsertDiskSpace 1003, 'M', 2088418, 2071204;
exec uspUpsertDiskSpace 1003, 'Q', 506015.5, 496545;


exec uspInsertDiskUsageByServer 1003, 'D', 24320, 2304, 0, 0;
exec uspInsertDiskUsageByServer 1003, 'L', 0, 512, 0, 0;


exec uspUpsertDiskSpace 1004, 'C', 10474348, 5686024;
exec uspUpsertDiskSpace 1004, 'D', 0, 0;
exec uspUpsertDiskSpace 1004, 'L', 0, 0;
exec uspUpsertDiskSpace 1004, 'M', 0, 0;
exec uspUpsertDiskSpace 1004, 'Q', 0, 0;


exec uspUpsertDiskSpace 1000, 'C', 81919996, 22333492;
exec uspUpsertDiskSpace 1000, 'D', 74288120, 49651884;


exec uspInsertDiskUsageByServer 1000, 'D', 1338176, 554176, 0, 0;
exec uspInsertDiskUsageByServer 1000, 'D', 24320, 2560, 0, 0;


exec uspUpsertDiskSpace 1001, 'C', 10474348, 4489384;
exec uspUpsertDiskSpace 1001, 'D', 5237156, 5176756;


exec uspInsertDiskUsageByServer 1001, 'D', 25600, 3064, 0, 0;


PS C:\>
```

Figure 19-1

Figure 19-2 shows that the disk usage for each host has been populated.

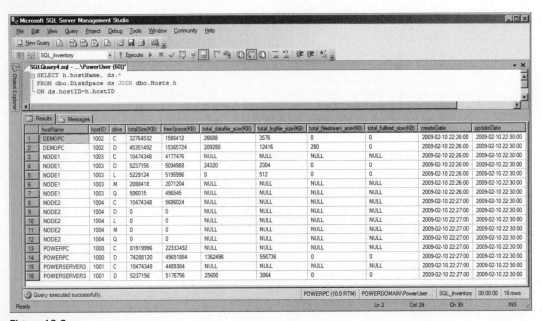

	hostName	hostID	drive	totalSize(KB)	freeSpace(KB)	total_datafile_size(KB)	total_logfile_size(KB)	total_filestream_size(KB)	total_fulltext_size(KB)	createDate	updateDate
1	DEMOPC	1002	C	32764532	1586412	26688	3576	0	0	2009-02-10 22:26:00	2009-02-10 22:30:00
2	DEMOPC	1002	D	45351492	15365724	209280	12416	280	0	2009-02-10 22:26:00	2009-02-10 22:30:00
3	NODE1	1003	C	10474348	4177476	NULL	NULL	NULL	NULL	2009-02-10 22:26:00	2009-02-10 22:30:00
4	NODE1	1003	D	5237156	5094988	24320	2304	0	0	2009-02-10 22:26:00	2009-02-10 22:30:00
5	NODE1	1003	L	5229124	5195996	0	512	0	0	2009-02-10 22:26:00	2009-02-10 22:30:00
6	NODE1	1003	M	2088418	2071204	NULL	NULL	NULL	NULL	2009-02-10 22:26:00	2009-02-10 22:30:00
7	NODE1	1003	Q	506015	496545	NULL	NULL	NULL	NULL	2009-02-10 22:26:00	2009-02-10 22:30:00
8	NODE2	1004	C	10474348	5686024	NULL	NULL	NULL	NULL	2009-02-10 22:27:00	2009-02-10 22:30:00
9	NODE2	1004	D	0	0	NULL	NULL	NULL	NULL	2009-02-10 22:27:00	2009-02-10 22:30:00
10	NODE2	1004	L	0	0	NULL	NULL	NULL	NULL	2009-02-10 22:27:00	2009-02-10 22:30:00
11	NODE2	1004	M	0	0	NULL	NULL	NULL	NULL	2009-02-10 22:27:00	2009-02-10 22:30:00
12	NODE2	1004	Q	0	0	NULL	NULL	NULL	NULL	2009-02-10 22:27:00	2009-02-10 22:30:00
13	POWERPC	1000	C	81919996	22333492	NULL	NULL	NULL	NULL	2009-02-10 22:27:00	2009-02-10 22:30:00
14	POWERPC	1000	D	74288120	49651884	1362496	556736	0	0	2009-02-10 22:27:00	2009-02-10 22:30:00
15	POWERSERVER3	1001	C	10474348	4489384	NULL	NULL	NULL	NULL	2009-02-10 22:27:00	2009-02-10 22:30:00
16	POWERSERVER3	1001	D	5237156	5176756	25600	3064	0	0	2009-02-10 22:27:00	2009-02-10 22:30:00

Figure 19-2

Monitoring Database Files

As stated in the beginning of this chapter, it is important to monitor the size and growth of database files to ensure that they have enough space to grow. To hold the database file space usage, we add a DatabaseSpace table to the SQL_Inventory database. The schema of the table is shown in Table 19-3.

Table 19-3: Schema of the DatabaseSpace Table

Column	DataType	Description
databaseID	int	ID of the database
dataSize(KB)	Bigint	Total size of the data files of the database
unallocatedData(KB)	Bigint	Unallocated space in the data files
maxDataSize(KB)	Varchar(15)	Maximum size of the data files
dataAutogrow	Bit	0 – File is fixed size and will not grow 1 – File will grow automatically
logSize(KB)	Bigint	Total size of the log files of the database
unallocatedLog(KB)	Bigint	Unallocated space in the log files
maxLogSize(KB)	Varchar(15)	Maximum size of the log files
logAutogrow	Bit	0 – File is fixed size and will not grow 1 – File will grow automatically
createDate	smalldatetime	Date and time this database space record was created

As you can see, the DatabaseSpace table indicates the total size of the data and log files, their maximum size, whether they are allowed to grow, and their unallocated space. Here is the CreateDatabaseSpace.sql script to create the DatabaseSpace table:

```
USE [SQL_Inventory]
GO
IF  EXISTS (SELECT * FROM sys.objects WHERE object_id = OBJECT_ID(N'[dbo]
.[DatabaseSpace]') AND type in (N'U'))
DROP TABLE [dbo].[DatabaseSpace]
go
CREATE TABLE [dbo].[DatabaseSpace](
[databaseID] [int],
[dataSize(KB)] bigint,
[unallocatedData(KB)] bigint,
[maxDataSize(KB)] varchar(15),
dataAutogrow bit,
[logSize(KB)] bigint,
[unallocatedLog(KB)] bigint,
```

```
[maxLogSize(KB)] varchar(15),
logAutogrow bit,
[createDate] [smalldatetime] NOT NULL default getDate()
)
GO
```

This table stores the space usage of each database. The unallocated space in the data files is calculated from allocation units. It is not always possible to know which database file an allocation unit resides in because an allocation unit belongs to a data space (a filegroup or a partition on a filegroup), not a file. If a filegroup has two files, then you don't know what allocation unit is from which file in the filegroup. You can certainly go down to the filegroup level if you want to know whether a huge table or a partition will run out of space, but in most cases you only need to monitor on the database level. Therefore, we consider all the data files to belong to a database in an entirety, and log files in an entirety.

Now we create a stored procedure, uspInsertDatabaseSpace, to insert into this table. The complete script, uspInsertDatabaseSpace.sql, to create the stored procedure is shown here:

```
USE [SQL_Inventory]
GO
IF  EXISTS (SELECT * FROM sys.objects WHERE object_id =
OBJECT_ID(N'[dbo].[uspInsertDatabaseSpace]') AND type in (N'P', N'PC'))
DROP PROCEDURE [dbo].[uspInsertDatabaseSpace]
GO
CREATE PROCEDURE [DBO].[uspInsertDatabaseSpace]
@databaseID int,
@dataSize bigint,
@unallocatedData bigint,
@maxDataSize varchar(15),
@dataAutogrow bit,
@logSize bigint,
@unallocatedLog bigint,
@maxLogSize varchar(15),
@logAutogrow bit
AS
DECLARE @ERRORCODE [int], @ERRMSG varchar(128)

INSERT [dbo].[DatabaseSpace]
(    databaseID
  , [dataSize(KB)]
  , [unallocatedData(KB)]
  , [maxDataSize(KB)]
  , [dataAutogrow]
  , [logSize(KB)]
  , [unallocatedLog(KB)]
  , [maxLogSize(KB)]
  , [logAutogrow]
  , createDate
        )
VALUES(
    @databaseID
  , @dataSize
  , @unallocatedData
```

```
            , @maxDataSize
            , @dataAutogrow
            , @logSize
            , @unallocatedLog
            , @maxLogSize
            , @logAutogrow
            , GETDATE()
                )

SET @ERRORCODE = @@ERROR
IF @ERRORCODE <> 0
        BEGIN
            SET @ERRMSG = 'Insert failed - ' + OBJECT_NAME(@@PROCID)
            SET @ERRMSG = @ERRMSG + ' Error Code: ' + RTRIM(CONVERT(CHAR,
@ERRORCODE))
            RAISERROR (@ERRMSG, 16, 1)
            RETURN (-1)
        END
ELSE
        RETURN (0)

GO
```

For a database, the following script calculates the space allocated to data and log files, their maximum size, and the autogrowth mode:

```
SET NOCOUNT ON

DECLARE @dataSize bigint, @reservedSize bigint, @maxDataSize varchar(15),
@dataAutogrow bit
DECLARE @logSize bigint, @logused decimal(3,1), @maxLogSize varchar(15),
@logAutogrow bit

-- Get the total space reserved for data pages.
SELECT @reservedSize=sum(a. total_pages)*8
FROM sys.allocation_units a
WHERE type in (1, 2, 3)

-- Get the total space used by data files.
-- Unallocated Space in the data files = Total size of data files - Total space
reserved for data pages
SELECT @dataSize=sum(convert(bigint, size))*8 FROM sys.database_files WHERE type=0

-- Since all the data files are considered in an entirety, if the max size of any of
the data files is set to Unlimited,
-- then the max size of data files is Unlimited. Otherwise, add up the max size of all
the data files.
IF (SELECT count(name) FROM sys.database_files WHERE (type = 0) and (max_size =
-1) ) > 0
        SELECT @maxDataSize = 'Unlimited'
ELSE
        SELECT @maxDataSize = convert(varchar(15), sum(convert(bigint, max_size))* 8)
        FROM sys.database_files
```

```
         WHERE (type = 0)

-- Since all the data files are considered in an entirety, if any of
the data files is set to autogrow,
-- then the data files are considered to be able to autogrow.
IF ((SELECT count(name) FROM sys.database_files WHERE (type = 0)
and (growth > 0)) ) > 0
        SELECT @dataAutogrow =1
ELSE
        SELECT @dataAutogrow =0

-- Get the total space used by log files.
SELECT @logSize=sum(size)*8 FROM sys.database_files WHERE type=1

-- Since all the log files are considered in an entirety, if the max size of any of the
log files is set to Unlimited,
-- then the max size of log files is Unlimited. Otherwise, add up the max size of
all the log files.
IF (SELECT count(name) FROM sys.database_files WHERE (type = 1) and (max_size =
-1) ) > 0
        SELECT @maxLogSize = 'Unlimited'
ELSE
        SELECT @maxLogSize = convert(varchar(15), sum(convert(bigint, max_size))* 8)
        FROM sys.database_files
        WHERE (type = 1)

-- Since all the log files are considered in an entirety, if any of the log files is
set to autogrow,
-- then the log files are considered to be able to autogrow.
IF ((SELECT count(name) FROM sys.database_files WHERE (type = 1) and
(growth > 0)) ) > 0
        SELECT @logAutogrow =1
ELSE
        SELECT @logAutogrow =0

CREATE TABLE #logspace
([Database Name] varchar(100),
[Log Size] decimal(15,2),
[Log Space Used (%)] decimal(3,1),
Status bit
)

-- Get the current size of the transaction log and the percentage of log space used
for the database
INSERT INTO #logspace EXEC('DBCC SQLPERF(LOGSPACE) WITH NO_INFOMSGS ')
SELECT @logused=[Log Space Used (%)] FROM #logspace WHERE [Database Name] = db_name()
DROP TABLE #logspace

-- Consolidate the information of the database
SELECT @dataSize as dataSize, (@dataSize- @reservedSize) as unallocatedData,
@maxDataSize as maxDataSize, @dataAutogrow as dataAutogrow,
@logSize as logSize, convert(bigint, @logSize * (100-@logused)/100) as
unallocatedLog, @maxLogSize as maxLogSize, @logAutogrow as logAutogrow
```

Save the script into a SQL script file, dbspace.sql, under C:\DBAScripts. We will run this SQL script against all the databases in our inventory in another script, Insert-DatabaseSpace.ps1, which you can download from the Wrox website for this book:

```
#####################################################
Source in our library file
#####################################################
. C:\DBAScripts\dbaLib.ps1

[String] $strUpsertSql=""
[String] $strQuerySql=""
[String] $strScriptFile="C:\DBAScripts\dbspace.sql"

$strQuerySql="SELECT h.hostName as SQLNetworkName, s.tcpPort, db.databaseName,
db.databaseID
FROM dbo.Databases db JOIN dbo.Servers s on db.serverID=s.serverID
JOIN dbo.Hosts h on h.hostID=s.hostID
UNION
SELECT c.SQLClusterName as SQLNetworkName, s.tcpPort, db.databaseName, db.databaseID
FROM dbo.Databases db JOIN dbo.Servers s on db.serverID=s.serverID
JOIN dbo.Clusters c on c.clusterID=s.clusterID"

$sqlDatabases=Invoke-Sqlcmd -Query $strQuerySql -ServerInstance $inventoryServer -
Database $inventoryDatabase

Foreach ($sqlDatabase in $sqlDatabases) {
        $strUpsertSql=""

        $sqlNetworkName=$sqlDatabase.SQLNetworkName
        $tcpPort=$sqlDatabase.tcpPort
        $sqlDatabaseName=$sqlDatabase.databaseName
        $sqlDatabaseID=$sqlDatabase.databaseID

        #Gets the information of how much space on each drive is used for data files,
log files, file stream and full text catalogs.
        $result=Invoke-Sqlcmd -InputFile $strScriptFile -ServerInstance
"$sqlNetworkName,$tcpPort" -Database $sqlDatabaseName

        $strUpsertSql="exec p_Upsert_DatabaseSpace " + $sqlDatabaseID + ", " '
        + $result.dataSize + ", " + $result.unallocatedData + ", '" +
$result.maxDataSize + "', " + $result.dataAutogrow + ", " '
        + $result.logSize + ", " + $result.unallocatedLog + ", '" +
$result.maxLogSize + "', " + $result.logAutogrow + ";"

        $strUpsertSql
        Invoke-Sqlcmd -Query $strUpsertSql -ServerInstance $inventoryServer -Database
$inventoryDatabase

}
```

Run the script in our environment. Figure 19-3 shows the output.

```
C:\DBAScripts\Insert-DatabaseSpace.ps1
```

Now run the following query in the `SQL_Inventory` database:

```
SELECT h.hostName, s.instanceName, db.databaseName, ds.*
FROM dbo.DatabaseSpace ds JOIN Databases db ON ds.databaseID = db.databaseID
JOIN dbo.Servers s ON db.serverID=s.serverID
JOIN dbo.Hosts h ON s.hostID=h.hostID
```

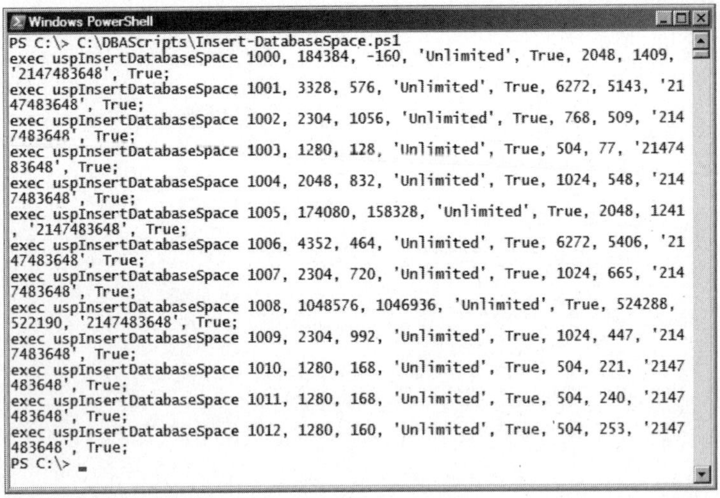

Figure 19-3

As shown in Figure 19-4, the space usage of each database has been collected.

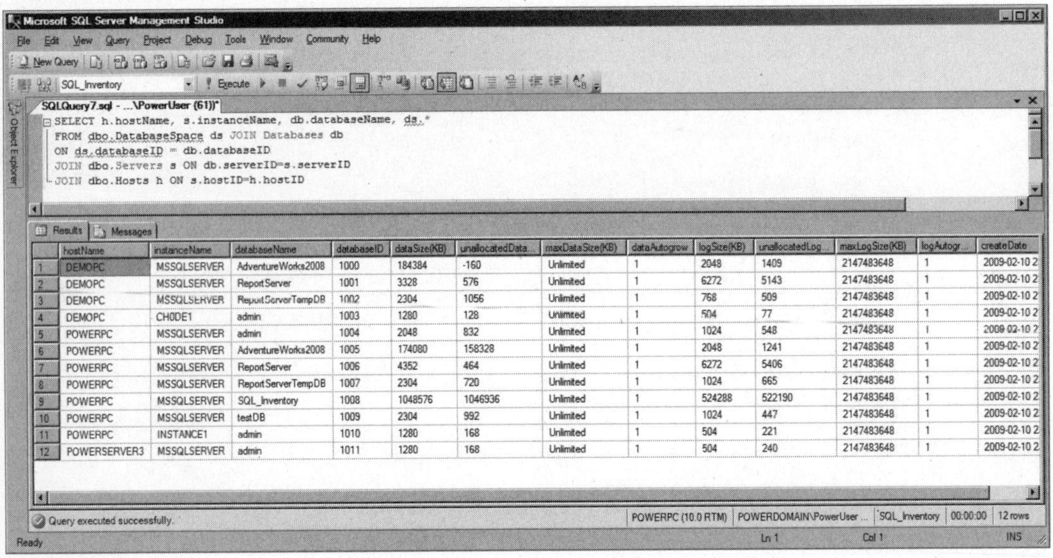

	hostName	instanceName	databaseName	databaseID	dataSize(KB)	unallocatedData...	maxDataSize(KB)	dataAutogrow	logSize(KB)	unallocatedLog...	maxLogSize(KB)	logAutogr...	createDate
1	DEMOPC	MSSQLSERVER	AdventureWorks2008	1000	184384	-160	Unlimited	1	2048	1409	2147483648	1	2009-02-10 2
2	DEMOPC	MSSQLSERVER	ReportServer	1001	3328	576	Unlimited	1	6272	5143	2147483648	1	2009-02-10 2
3	DEMOPC	MSSQLSERVER	ReportServerTempDB	1002	2304	1056	Unlimited	1	768	509	2147483648	1	2009-02-10 2
4	DEMOPC	CH0DE1	admin	1003	1280	128	Unlimited	1	504	77	2147483648	1	2009-02-10 2
5	POWERPC	MSSQLSERVER	admin	1004	2048	832	Unlimited	1	1024	548	2147483648	1	2009-02-10 2
6	POWERPC	MSSQLSERVER	AdventureWorks2008	1005	174080	158328	Unlimited	1	2048	1241	2147483648	1	2009-02-10 2
7	POWERPC	MSSQLSERVER	ReportServer	1006	4352	464	Unlimited	1	6272	5406	2147483648	1	2009-02-10 2
8	POWERPC	MSSQLSERVER	ReportServerTempDB	1007	2304	720	Unlimited	1	1024	665	2147483648	1	2009-02-10 2
9	POWERPC	MSSQLSERVER	SQL_Inventory	1008	1048576	1046936	Unlimited	1	524288	522190	2147483648	1	2009-02-10 2
10	POWERPC	MSSQLSERVER	testDB	1009	2304	992	Unlimited	1	1024	447	2147483648	1	2009-02-10 2
11	POWERPC	INSTANCE1	admin	1010	1280	168	Unlimited	1	504	221	2147483648	1	2009-02-10 2
12	POWERSERVER3	MSSQLSERVER	admin	1011	1280	168	Unlimited	1	504	240	2147483648	1	2009-02-10 2

Figure 19-4

Based on the information in these two tables, there are many ways to utilize the `DiskSpace` and `DatabaseSpace` tables, including the following:

❑   Generate an exception report that either lists the drives and databases whose free space is under a pre-defined threshold or raises an alert when the threshold is reached. If our threshold is 80%, the corresponding SQL statements are as follows:

❑   When a drive has less than 20% free space for future growth of data, log, FILESTREAM, and full-text data combined.

```
USE SQL_Inventory
GO
SELECT h.hostName, ds.drive
FROM dbo.DiskSpace ds
JOIN dbo.Hosts h ON ds.hostID = h.hostID
WHERE  ([total_datafile_size(KB)] + [total_filestream_size(KB)] +
[total_fulltext_size(KB)] + [total_logfile_size(KB)]) * 0.2 > [freeSpace(KB)]
```

❑   When a database has less than 20% unallocated space for either data or log, and the data or log cannot grow automatically.

```
USE SQL_Inventory
GO

SELECT h.hostName, s.instanceName, db.databaseName
FROM dbo.DatabaseSpace ds
JOIN dbo.Databases db ON ds.databaseID = db.databaseID
JOIN dbo.Servers s ON s.serverID = db.serverID
JOIN dbo.Hosts h ON h.hostID = s.hostID
WHERE (convert(dec(15,1),ds.[unallocatedData(KB)]) * 100.0 /
convert(dec(15,1),ds.[dataSize(KB)]) < 20) and (ds.dataAutogrow=0)
UNION
SELECT h.hostName, s.instanceName, db.databaseName
FROM dbo.DatabaseSpace ds
JOIN dbo.Databases db ON ds.databaseID = db.databaseID
JOIN dbo.Servers s ON s.serverID = db.serverID
JOIN dbo.Hosts h ON h.hostID = s.hostID
WHERE (convert(dec(15,1),ds.[unallocatedLog(KB)]) * 100.0 /
convert(dec(15,1),ds.[logSize(KB)]) < 20) and (ds.logAutogrow=0)
```

❑   When the maximum size of the data or log of a database allows less than 20% growth from the current size, and the data or log cannot grow automatically.

```
USE SQL_Inventory
GO

SELECT h.hostName, s.instanceName, db.databaseName
FROM dbo.DatabaseSpace ds
JOIN dbo.Databases db ON ds.databaseID = db.databaseID
JOIN dbo.Servers s ON s.serverID = db.serverID
JOIN dbo.Hosts h ON h.hostID = s.hostID
WHERE (convert(dec(15,1),ds.[dataSize(KB)]) * 100.0 /
```

```
convert(dec(15,1),ds.[maxDataSize(KB)]) > 0.8) and (ds.dataAutogrow=0)
UNION
SELECT h.hostName, s.instanceName, db.databaseName
FROM dbo.DatabaseSpace ds
JOIN dbo.Databases db ON ds.databaseID = db.databaseID
JOIN dbo.Servers s ON s.serverID = db.serverID
JOIN dbo.Hosts h ON h.hostID = s.hostID
WHERE (convert(dec(15,1),ds.[logSize(KB)]) * 100.0 /
convert(dec(15,1),ds.[maxLogSize(KB)]) > 0.8) and (ds.logAutogrow=0)
```

❑ Collect the database space usage regularly and save it in the `DatabaseSpace` table. Based on the historical data, you can calculate the rate at which the databases grow. Furthermore, by calculating how much the databases will grow in one year based on the current growth rate, you can do capacity planning for each host.

Monitoring Backups

We all know that database backups are the bread-and-butter tasks of the database administrator job. We cannot have any database running without backups. Without proper and prompt backups it is not possible to recover a database in the event of data corruption or failures. Therefore, it is critical to monitor the backups continuously.

As discussed in Chapter 14, every SQL Server instance should have an `admin` database. The `admin` database holds objects, procedures, and functions that are related to SQL Server administration. We are going to create in the `admin` database a stored procedure to find any databases that have not been backed up in a certain number of minutes. Shown in the following example is the stored procedure `uspMonitorBackups`, which queries the `msdb.dbo.backupset` table for the last backup date:

```
USE [admin]
GO

IF  EXISTS (SELECT * FROM sys.objects WHERE object_id =
OBJECT_ID(N'[dbo].[uspMonitorBackups]') AND type in (N'P', N'PC'))
DROP PROCEDURE [dbo].[uspMonitorBackups]
GO

CREATE PROCEDURE uspMonitorBackups @backuptype char(1), @numOfMinutes int
as
--D = Database
--I = Differential database
--L = Log
--F = File or filegroup
--G = Differential file
--P = Partial
--Q = Differential Partial
--Example: Exec admin.dbo.uspMonitorBackups 'D',24

declare @dbname varchar(2000)
select name as Databasename
from master.dbo.sysdatabases
where name not in ('tempdb')
and name not in
```

```
(select distinct database_name
from msdb.dbo.backupset
group by database_name
having datediff(minute, max(backup_start_date),getdate()) < @numOfMinutes
)
```

This stored procedure accepts two parameters. The first parameter is the type of database backup you want to monitor, and the second parameter is the number of hours.

The different backup types are as follows:

```
D = Database
I = Database Differential
L = Log
F = File or Filegroup
G = File Differential
P = Partial
Q = Partial Differential
```

Save the stored procedure in a SQL script file `uspMonitorBackups.sql` under `C:\DBAScripts`. You can incorporate the creation of this stored procedure as one of the post-setup tasks in the SQL Server installation script or write a PowerShell script to install the stored procedure on every SQL Server in your environment.

After this stored procedure has been created in the `admin` database on every SQL Server instance, you can schedule a job to run regularly from the inventory server to execute the stored procedure on every server, consolidate the results from every server in an exception report, and then send the exception report to the DBA group. If a server has specific backup requirements, then you can schedule separate SQL Server agent jobs on that server to check the specific requirements regularly. For either case, you can create a PowerShell function called `Check-Backups` to accept the parameters for the stored procedure and execute the stored procedure. Save the function in the library file `C:\DBAScripts\dbaLib.ps1`.

```powershell
Function Check-Backups ([String] $instanceName, [String] $backuptype, [Int32]
$minutes)
{
[String] $strResult=""

$results=Invoke-Sqlcmd -Query "Exec dbo.uspMonitorBackups '$backuptype', $minutes"
-ServerInstance $instanceName -Database "admin"

if ($results) {
        for ($i=0; $i -lt $results.Count; $i++) {
                if ($results[$i].Databasename) {
                        $strResult = $strResult + $results[$i].Databasename + "`n"
                }
        }

        $strResult="The following databases on $instanceName have not been backed up in
$minutes minutes:`n" + $strResult
        Write-Output $strResult
}

}
```

Notice we use `Write-Output`, not `Write-Host`, in the script so that the resultant string objects can be further processed and consolidated into an exception report. `Write-Host` actually sends objects directly to `Out-Host` behind the scenes, and no objects are left in the pipeline after `Write-Host` executes.

For example, if your company's policy requires that at least one full database backup should be taken every day, then you can schedule a PowerShell script to run every, say, twelve hours on the inventory server to call the `Check-Backups` function and execute the `uspMonitorBackups` stored procedure against every server, and create an exception report. The `C:\DBAScripts\Monitor-Backups.ps1` script is shown here:

```
######################################################
# Initialize parameters
######################################################
param (
        [String] $backupType = 'D', # The backup type to check. Defaults to Full
Database backups.
        [Int32] $minutes = 1440, # The number of minutes in which backups have not been
taken. Defaults to 1440 minutes, 1 day.
        [switch] $help
    )


##########################################################################
# Source in our library file
##########################################################################
. C:\DBAScripts\dbaLib.ps1

if ( $help ) {
        "Usage: Monitor-Backups.ps1 [-backupType <string[]>] [-minutes <Int32>]"
        exit 0
}

# Get all the standalone and failover cluster instances
[String] $strQuerySql="SELECT h.hostName as SQLNetworkName, s.instanceName, s.tcpPort
FROM dbo.Servers s
JOIN dbo.Hosts h ON s.hostID= h.hostID
UNION
SELECT c.SQLClusterName as SQLNetworkName, s.instanceName, s.tcpPort
FROM dbo.Servers s
JOIN dbo.Clusters c ON s.clusterID=c.clusterID
JOIN dbo.ClusterNodes cn ON c.clusterID = cn.clusterID"

[String] $subject="Backup Exception Report"
[String] $exceptions=""
[String] $strResult=""

$sqlServers=Invoke-Sqlcmd -Query $strQuerySql -ServerInstance $inventoryServer -
Database $inventoryDatabase

# Loop through the list of SQL Server instances and run the Check-Backups function
# against each instance to get the backup exceptions.
Foreach ($sqlServer in $sqlServers) {
        $sqlNetworkName=$sqlServer.SQLNetworkName
```

```
        $sqlInstanceName=$sqlServer.instanceName
        $tcpPort=$sqlServer.tcpPort

        $strResult=""

        if ($sqlInstanceName -ieq 'MSSQLSERVER') {
                $strResult=(Check-Backups "$sqlNetworkName,$tcpPort" $backupType
$minutes)
                if ($strResult -ne "") {
                        $exceptions=$exceptions + $strResult + "`n"
                }
        }
        else {
                $strResult=(Check-Backups "$sqlNetworkName\$sqlInstanceName,$tcpPort"
$backupType $minutes)
                if ($strResult -ne "") {
                        $exceptions=$exceptions + $strResult + "`n"
                }
        }
}

# Send the exceptions to the DBA group
if ($exceptions -ne "") {
        "Exceptions found. Sending the exception report ..."
        Send-Email $smtpServer $fromAddress $toAddress $subject $exceptions
$smtpUserName $smtpPassword
}
else {
        "No exceptions found."
}
```

Now execute the script C:\DBAScripts\Monitor-Backups.ps1, as shown in Figure 19-5:

```
C:\DBAScripts\Monitor-Backups.ps1 D 1440
```

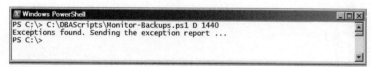

Figure 19-5

When the script is executed, it retrieves a list of databases that do not have a full database backup in the past 1,440 minutes, i.e., 24 hours, and sends an e-mail, as shown in Figure 19-6.

If one business unit decides that the transaction logs on their server need to be backed up every 30 minutes to minimize data loss, you can schedule a SQL Server Agent job on that particular server to meet that need. The job has one PowerShell step that runs the following command:

```
C:\DBAScripts\Monitor-Backups.ps1 L 30
```

Figure 19-7 shows the job and its step.

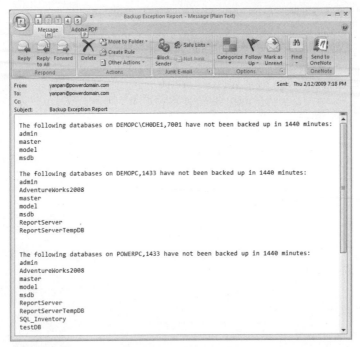

Figure 19-6

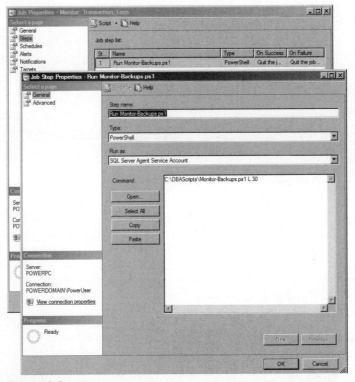

Figure 19-7

Summary

As a DBA, you never want your SQL Server to run out of space. When that happens, the server freezes and user processes stop. In no time, your phone rings and frustrated users are on the other end of the line. Therefore, it is important to monitor free space on local drives. We have discussed how to monitor disk space usage. When a database does not have enough free space and cannot grow for any reason, user processes that insert data into the database stop as well. You have seen in this chapter how to monitor space at the database level.

Backups are the lifeline of a database. If a database becomes corrupted, most of the time you can only rely on backups to recover the database. This chapter described how to monitor backups of all types.

In the next chapter we will define SQL Server policies to enforce SQL Server standards automatically, which makes the DBA's life easier.

## 20

Defining Policies

Policy-Based Management is a new feature in SQL Server 2008 that helps with SQL Server administration. It enables database administrators to manage SQL Server instances by intent through clearly defined policies, thereby reducing the potential for administrative errors. Policies can be applied against a group of servers, thus improving the scalability of monitoring and administration.

In this chapter, we will use the same class to create two exemplary policies and install them on the SQL Servers in our environment. These two policies actually implement the standard that was defined in Chapter 14. One of the policies we will discuss enforces a stored procedure naming convention. The other policy ensures that both the Auto_Shrink and the Auto_Close options are set to off. This chapter goes on to discuss the value of both of these policies.

Stored Procedure Naming Convention Policy

Chapter 12 explained how to define policies using the SMO class `Microsoft.SqlServer .Management.Dmf`. We created a condition called "No server access" and then we defined a policy called `Domain guest cannot access server`, whereby we applied the condition to prevent the domain guest login POWERDOMAIN\Guest from accessing SQL Server. We are going to use the same class to define policies and conditions in this chapter.

In Chapter 14, one of the SQL Server standards that we defined involves the stored procedure naming conventions. Remember that stored procedure names should describe the work they do and be prefixed with "usp." Use a verb abbreviation to describe the work, such as Insert, Delete, Update, Select, Upsert, or Get.

This convention doesn't apply to system databases because the system stored procedures clearly have more free-form names. However, it clearly separates stored procedures from other types of database objects, and ensures that stored procedure names are easy to follow. We would like to apply this naming convention to the admin database and ensure that all the stored procedures created for database administration purposes conform to the naming convention.

To do that, we need to create a condition `Stored Procedure Name` to specify the stored procedure naming convention. The expression in the condition should look like this:

```
(@Name LIKE 'usp%' )
```

We also need to create another condition called `admin database` to restrict the policy to apply to only the admin database. We will apply this condition to the object set of the new policy.

The function to create the policy is shown in the following example. The first parameter, `$pNetworkName`, is either the host name of a standalone SQL Server instance or the SQL Server cluster name of a failover cluster instance. The second parameter is the instance name. The third parameter is the TCP/IP port on which the instance is listening.

```
Function CreateStoredProcNamingConventionPolicy([String] $pNetworkName, [String]
$pInstanceName, [String] $pTcpPort)
{
$sqlConnection=New-Object System.Data.SqlClient.SqlConnection
$sqlConnection.ConnectionString="Server=$pNetworkName,$pTcpPort;Database=master;
Integrated Security=True"
$storeConnection=New-Object
Microsoft.SqlServer.Management.Sdk.Sfc.SqlStoreConnection($sqlConnection)
$store=New-Object Microsoft.SqlServer.Management.Dmf.PolicyStore ($storeConnection)

if (Get-ChildItem -path SQLSERVER:\SQLPolicy\$pNetworkName\$pInstanceName\Policies |
Where-Object {$_.Name -eq 'Stored Procedure Naming Convention'}) {
        "Dropping the existing 'Stored Procedure Naming Convention' policy from the
instance $pInstanceName on $pNetworkName ..."
        (Get-ChildItem -path SQLSERVER:\SQLPolicy\$pNetworkName\$pInstanceName\
Policies | Where-Object {$_.Name -eq 'Stored Procedure Naming Convention'}).Drop()
}
if (Get-ChildItem -path SQLSERVER:\SQLPolicy\$pNetworkName\$pInstanceName\Conditions
| Where-Object {$_.Name -eq 'Stored Procedure Name'}) {
        "Dropping the existing 'Stored Procedure Name' condition from the
instance $pInstanceName on $pNetworkName ...."
        (Get-ChildItem -path SQLSERVER:\SQLPolicy\$pNetworkName\$pInstanceName\
Conditions | Where-Object {$_.Name -eq 'Stored Procedure Name'}).Drop()
}
if (Get-ChildItem -path SQLSERVER:\SQLPolicy\$pNetworkName\$pInstanceName\ObjectSets
| Where-Object {$_.Name -eq 'Stored Procedure Naming Convention_ObjectSet'}) {
        "Dropping the existing object set 'Stored Procedure Naming
Convention_ObjectSet' from the instance $pInstanceName on $pNetworkName ..."
        (Get-ChildItem -path SQLSERVER:\SQLPolicy\$pNetworkName\$pInstanceName
\ObjectSets | Where-Object {$_.Name -eq 'Stored Procedure Naming
Convention_ObjectSet'}).Drop()
}
if (Get-ChildItem -path SQLSERVER:\SQLPolicy\$pNetworkName\$pInstanceName
\Conditions | Where-Object {$_.Name -eq "admin database"}) {
        "Dropping the existing 'admin database' condition from the instance
$pInstanceName on $pNetworkName ..."
        (Get-ChildItem -path SQLSERVER:\SQLPolicy\$pNetworkName\$pInstanceName
\Conditions | Where-Object {$_.Name -eq "admin database"}).Drop()
}
```

```
#Create "Stored Procedure Name" condition
"Creating the 'Stored Procedure Name' condition on the instance $pInstanceName on
$pNetworkName ..."
$condition=New-Object Microsoft.SqlServer.Management.Dmf.Condition ($store,
'Stored Procedure Name')
$operator=New-Object Microsoft.SqlServer.Management.Dmf.ExpressionNodeOperator
("LIKE", "@Name", "'usp%'")
$condition.ExpressionNode=$operator
$condition.Facet='StoredProcedure'
$condition.Create() | Out-Null

#Create "admin database" condition
"Creating the 'admin database' condition on the instance $pInstanceName on
$pNetworkName ..."
$condition2=New-Object Microsoft.SqlServer.Management.Dmf.Condition ($store,
"admin database")
$operator=New-Object Microsoft.SqlServer.Management.Dmf.ExpressionNodeOperator
("EQ", "@Name", "'admin'")
$condition2.ExpressionNode=$operator
$condition2.Facet='Database'
$condition2.Create() | Out-Null

# Create an object set object that includes every stored procedure in the admin
database
"Creating the object set 'Stored Procedure Naming Convention_ObjectSet' on the
instance $pInstanceName on $pNetworkName ..."
$objectSet=New-Object Microsoft.SqlServer.Management.Dmf.ObjectSet($store,
'Stored Procedure Naming Convention_ObjectSet')
$objectSet.Facet="StoredProcedure"
$targetSet=$objectSet.TargetSets["Server/Database/StoredProcedure"]
$targetSet.SetLevelCondition($targetSet.GetLevel("Server/Database"),
"admin database") | Out-Null
$targetSet.Enabled=1
$objectSet.Create() | Out-Null

# Create "Stored Procedure Naming Convention" policy. The execution mode of this
policy is set to "On Change - Prevent".
"Creating the 'Stored Procedure Naming Convention' policy on the instance
$pInstanceName on $pNetworkName ..."
$policy=New-Object Microsoft.SqlServer.Management.Dmf.Policy ($store,
'Stored Procedure Naming Convention')
$policy.Condition=$condition.Name
$policy.ObjectSet=$objectSet.Name
$policy.AutomatedPolicyEvaluationMode="Enforce"
$policy.Enabled=1
$policy.Create() | Out-Null

# Confirm the policy has been created correctly.
if (Get-ChildItem -path SQLSERVER:\SQLPolicy\$pNetworkName\$pInstanceName\Policies |
Where-Object {$_.Name -eq 'Stored Procedure Naming Convention'}) {
        Get-ChildItem -path SQLSERVER:\SQLPolicy\$pNetworkName\$pInstanceName
\Policies | Where-Object {$_.Name -eq 'Stored Procedure Naming Convention'} `
        | Select AutomatedPolicyEvaluationMode, Condition, Enabled, ID, IdentityKey,
```

```
Name, ObjectSet, Parent, CreatedBy, CreateDate
}
else {
        "Failed to create 'Stored Procedure Naming Convention' policy on the instance
$pInstanceName on $pNetworkName."
}


}
```

Now we just need another piece of code to retrieve all the servers from the inventory, and then connect to every server and install the "Stored Procedure Naming Convention" policy using the preceding function. Here is the code:

```
####################### MAIN BODY #################################
[String] $sqlNetworkName=""
[String] $sqlInstanceName=""
[String] $tcpPort=""

$strQuerySql="SELECT h.hostName as SQLNetworkName, s.instanceName, s.tcpPort
        FROM dbo.Servers s
        JOIN dbo.Hosts h ON s.hostID= h.hostID
        UNION
        SELECT c.SQLClusterName as SQLNetworkName, s.instanceName, s.tcpPort
        FROM dbo.Servers s
        JOIN dbo.Clusters c ON s.clusterID=c.clusterID
        JOIN dbo.ClusterNodes cn ON c.clusterID = cn.clusterID"

# Get all the SQL Server instances from the inventory
$sqlServers=Invoke-Sqlcmd -Query $strQuerySql -ServerInstance $inventoryServer
-Database $inventoryDatabase

# Loop through the list of SQL Server instances and create the "Stored Procedure
Naming Convention" policy on each instance.
if ($sqlServers) {
        Foreach ($sqlServer in $sqlServers) {
                $sqlNetworkName=$sqlServer.SQLNetworkName
                if ($sqlServer.instanceName -ieq 'MSSQLSERVER') {
                        $sqlInstanceName="default"
                }
                else {
                        $sqlInstanceName=$sqlServer.instanceName
                }
                $tcpPort=$sqlServer.tcpPort

                #Create the "Stored Procedure Naming Convention" policy
                CreateStoredProcNamingConventionPolicy $sqlNetworkName
$sqlInstanceName $tcpPort
        }
}
```

The complete script is `Install-StoredProcNamingConventionPolicy.ps1`. You can download the script from the website for this book at www.wrox.com. Execute this script to install the policy on every SQL Server in the inventory.

```
C:\DBAScripts\Install-StoredProcNamingConventionPolicy.ps1
```

Figure 20-1 shows the output from running the script in our environment.

```
Windows PowerShell
PS C:\> C:\DBAScripts\Install-StoredProcNamingConventionPolicy.ps1
Creating the 'Stored Procedure Name' condition on the instance CH0DE1 on DEMOPC
...
Creating the 'admin database' condition on the instance CH0DE1 on DEMOPC ...
Creating the object set 'Stored Procedure Naming Convention_ObjectSet' on the i
nstance CH0DE1 on DEMOPC ...
Creating the 'Stored Procedure Naming Convention' policy on the instance CH0DE1
 on DEMOPC ...


AutomatedPolicyEvaluationMode : Enforce
Condition                     : Stored Procedure Name
Enabled                       : True
ID                            : 58
IdentityKey                   : Policy[@Name='Stored Procedure Naming Conventio
                                n']
Name                          : Stored Procedure Naming Convention
ObjectSet                     : Stored Procedure Naming Convention_ObjectSet
Parent                        : PolicyStore (Smo.Server='DEMOPC\CH0DE1')
CreatedBy                     : POWERDOMAIN\PowerUser
CreateDate                    : 2/12/2009 10:50:13 PM

Creating the 'Stored Procedure Name' condition on the instance default on DEMOP
C ...
Creating the 'admin database' condition on the instance default on DEMOPC ...
Creating the object set 'Stored Procedure Naming Convention_ObjectSet' on the i
nstance default on DEMOPC ...
Creating the 'Stored Procedure Naming Convention' policy on the instance defaul
t on DEMOPC ...
AutomatedPolicyEvaluationMode : Enforce
Condition                     : Stored Procedure Name
Enabled                       : True
ID                            : 9
IdentityKey                   : Policy[@Name='Stored Procedure Naming Conventio
                                n']
Name                          : Stored Procedure Naming Convention
ObjectSet                     : Stored Procedure Naming Convention_ObjectSet
Parent                        : PolicyStore (Smo.Server='DEMOPC')
CreatedBy                     : POWERDOMAIN\PowerUser
CreateDate                    : 2/12/2009 10:50:16 PM

Creating the 'Stored Procedure Name' condition on the instance INSTANCE1 on POW
ERPC ...
Creating the 'admin database' condition on the instance INSTANCE1 on POWERPC ..
.
```

Figure 20-1

Note that you need to ensure that the SQL Server Browser service is running on the remote computer if you get the following warning message:

```
WARNING: 'CH0DE1' not available: Failed to connect to server . --> A network-related
or instance-specific error occurred while establishing a connection to SQL Server.
The server was not found or was not accessible. Verify that the instance name is
correct and that SQL Server is configured to allow remote connections. (provider:
SQL Network Interfaces, error: 26 - Error Locating Server/Instance Specified)
```

To see this policy in action, let's try to create a stored procedure called dba_MonitorBackups in the admin database on the default instance, POWERPC. The policy will prevent the stored procedure from being created:

```
USE admin
GO
CREATE PROCEDURE dba_MonitorBackups @backuptype char(1), @numOfMinutes int
as

declare @dbname varchar(2000)
select name as Databasename
from master.dbo.sysdatabases
where name not in ('tempdb')
```

```
and name not in
(select distinct database_name
from msdb.dbo.backupset
group by database_name
having datediff(minute, max(backup_start_date),getdate()) < @numOfMinutes
)
```

As shown in Figure 20-2, the execution failed with the following error message:

```
Policy 'Stored Procedure Naming Convention' has been violated by
'SQLSERVER:\SQL\POWERPC\DEFAULT\Databases\admin\StoredProcedures
\dbo.dba_MonitorBackups'.
This transaction will be rolled back.
Policy condition: '@Name LIKE 'usp%''
Policy description: ''
Additional help: '' : ''
Statement: 'CREATE PROCEDURE dba_MonitorBackups @backuptype char(1), @numOfMinutes
int
as

declare @dbname varchar(2000)
select name as Databasename
from...'.
Msg 3609, Level 16, State 1, Procedure sp_syspolicy_dispatch_event, Line 65
The transaction ended in the trigger. The batch has been aborted.
```

Therefore, the Stored Procedure Naming Convention policy prevents the stored procedure dba_MonitorBackups from being created because its name does not comply with the policy.

Auto_Close and Auto_Shrink Off Policy

Auto_Close and Auto_Shrink are two options you never want to enable on a production database.

When Auto_Close is set to On, the database is shut down automatically when no one connects to it and its resources are freed. When a user tries to use the database again, the database regains resources and reopens. On a production database, which is regularly accessed by users, frequent closing and reopening of the database causes delays for the users. The overhead of closing and reopening the database can be significant, even affecting performance. When Auto_Close is set to On, you can see messages like the one below repeat in the SQL Server error logs, indicating reopenings of the database :

```
2008-07-20 08:24:31.25 spid51    Starting up database 'MNHOST'.
```

When Auto_Shrink is set to On, SQL Server automatically shrinks a database file when more than 25 percent of the space in the database file is unused. Database shrinking hogs CPU. In addition, if the file size is large, it can take minutes or even hours to shrink the file. Users will notice slowed performance while the shrinking is in progress. Even in a development server, enabling these two options rarely provides benefits. Therefore, it is important for the DBA to ensure that both options are set to Off on all databases.

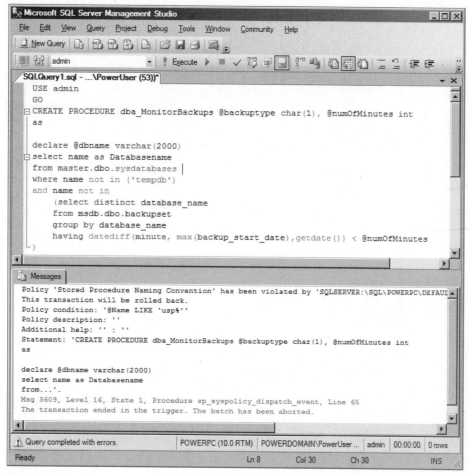

```
Microsoft SQL Server Management Studio                                    _ □ ×
File   Edit   View   Query   Project   Debug   Tools   Window   Community   Help
New Query
admin                              Execute
SQLQuery1.sql - ...\PowerUser (53))*                                        × 
    USE admin
    GO
    CREATE PROCEDURE dba_MonitorBackups @backuptype char(1), @numOfMinutes int
    as

    declare @dbname varchar(2000)
    select name as Databasename
    from master.dbo.sysdatabases |
    where name not in ('tempdb')
    and name not in
        (select distinct database_name
         from msdb.dbo.backupset
         group by database_name
         having datediff(minute, max(backup_start_date),getdate()) < @numOfMinutes
    )

Messages
    Policy 'Stored Procedure Naming Convention' has been violated by 'SQLSERVER:\SQL\POWERPC\DEFAUL
    This transaction will be rolled back.
    Policy condition: '@Name LIKE 'usp%''
    Policy description: ''
    Additional help: '' : ''
    Statement: 'CREATE PROCEDURE dba_MonitorBackups @backuptype char(1), @numOfMinutes int
    as

    declare @dbname varchar(2000)
    select name as Databasename
    from...'.
    Msg 3609, Level 16, State 1, Procedure sp_syspolicy_dispatch_event, Line 65
    The transaction ended in the trigger. The batch has been aborted.

Query completed with errors.    POWERPC (10.0 RTM)   POWERDOMAIN\PowerUser ...   admin   00:00:00   0 rows
Ready                                          Ln 8         Col 30        Ch 30              INS
```

Figure 20-2

The following function creates a policy called "Database Auto Options Disabled" to force every database on a server to disable both options. Similar to the CreateStoredProcNamingConventionPolicy function shown earlier, the first parameter, $pNetworkName, is either the host name of a standalone SQL Server instance or the SQL Server cluster name of a failover cluster instance. The second parameter is the instance name. The third parameter is the TCP/IP port on which the instance is listening:

```
Function CreateAutoOptionsOffPolicy([String] $pNetworkName, [String] $pInstanceName,
[String] $pTcpPort)
{

$sqlConnection=New-Object System.Data.SqlClient.SqlConnection
$sqlConnection.ConnectionString="Server=$pNetworkName,$pTcpPort;Database=master;
Integrated Security=True"
$storeConnection=New-Object Microsoft.SqlServer.Management.Sdk.Sfc
```

```
.SqlStoreConnection($sqlConnection)
$store=New-Object Microsoft.SqlServer.Management.Dmf.PolicyStore ($storeConnection)

if (Get-ChildItem -path SQLSERVER:\SQLPolicy\$pNetworkName\$pInstanceName\Policies |
Where-Object {$_.Name -eq 'Database Auto Options Disabled'}) {
        "Dropping the existing 'Database Auto Options Disabled' policy from the
instance $pInstanceName on $pNetworkName ..."
        (Get-ChildItem -path SQLSERVER:\SQLPolicy\$pNetworkName\$pInstanceName
\Policies | Where-Object {$_.Name -eq 'Database Auto Options Disabled'}).Drop()
}
if (Get-ChildItem -path SQLSERVER:\SQLPolicy\$pNetworkName\$pInstanceName\Conditions
| Where-Object {$_.Name -eq 'Auto Options Disabled'}) {
        "Dropping the the existing Auto Options Disabled condition from the instance
$pInstanceName on $pNetworkName ..."
        (Get-ChildItem -path SQLSERVER:\SQLPolicy\$pNetworkName\$pInstanceName
\Conditions | Where-Object {$_.Name -eq 'Auto Options Disabled'}).Drop()
}
if (Get-ChildItem -path SQLSERVER:\SQLPolicy\$pNetworkName\$pInstanceName\ObjectSets
| Where-Object {$_.Name -eq 'Database Auto Options Disabled_ObjectSet'}) {
        "Dropping the existing 'Database Auto Options Disabled_ObjectSet' object set
from the instance $pInstanceName on $pNetworkName ..."
        (Get-ChildItem -path SQLSERVER:\SQLPolicy\$pNetworkName\$pInstanceName
\ObjectSets | Where-Object {$_.Name -eq 'Database Auto Options
Disabled_ObjectSet'}).Drop()
}

#Create "Auto Options Disabled" condition
"Creating 'Auto Options Disabled' condition on the instance $pInstanceName on
$pNetworkName ..."
$condition=New-Object Microsoft.SqlServer.Management.Dmf.Condition ($store,
'Auto Options Disabled')
$operator=New-Object Microsoft.SqlServer.Management.Dmf.ExpressionNodeOperator
("AND", "@AutoClose = False()", "@AutoShrink = False()")
$condition.ExpressionNode=$operator
$condition.Facet='IDatabaseOptions'
$condition.Create() | Out-Null

# Create an object set object that includes every database.
"Creating object set on the instance $pInstanceName on $pNetworkName ..."
$objectSet=New-Object Microsoft.SqlServer.Management.Dmf.ObjectSet($store, 'Database
Auto Options Disabled_ObjectSet')
$objectSet.Facet="IDatabaseOptions"
$targetSet=$objectSet.TargetSets["Server/Database"]
$targetSet.Enabled=1
$objectSet.Create() | Out-Null

# Create "Database Auto Options Disabled" policy. The execution mode of this policy is
set to "On Change - Log Only".
"Creating 'Database Auto Options Disabled' policy on the instance $pInstanceName on
$pNetworkName ..."
$policy=New-Object Microsoft.SqlServer.Management.Dmf.Policy ($store, 'Database Auto
Options Disabled')
$policy.Condition=$condition.Name
$policy.ObjectSet=$objectSet.Name
```

```
$policy.AutomatedPolicyEvaluationMode="CheckOnChanges"
$policy.Enabled=1
$policy.Create() | Out-Null


# Confirm the policy has been created correctly.
if (Get-ChildItem -path SQLSERVER:\SQLPolicy\$pNetworkName\$pInstanceName\Policies |
Where-Object {$_.Name -eq 'Database Auto Options Disabled'}) {
        Get-ChildItem -path SQLSERVER:\SQLPolicy\$pNetworkName\$pInstanceName
\Policies | Where-Object {$_.Name -eq 'Database Auto Options Disabled'} `
        | Select AutomatedPolicyEvaluationMode, Condition, Enabled, ID, IdentityKey,
Name, ObjectSet, Parent, CreatedBy, CreateDate
}
else {
        "Failed to create 'Database Auto Options Disabled' policy on the instance
$pInstanceName on $pNetworkName."
}


}
```

Needed now is another piece of code to retrieve all the servers from the inventory and then connect to every server and install the "Database Auto Options Disabled" policy using the preceding function:

```
######################## MAIN BODY ##################################
[String] $sqlNetworkName=""
[String] $sqlInstanceName=""
[String] $tcpPort=""

$strQuerySql="SELECT h.hostName as SQLNetworkName, s.instanceName, s.tcpPort
        FROM dbo.Servers s
        JOIN dbo.Hosts h ON s.hostID= h.hostID
        UNION
        SELECT c.SQLClusterName as SQLNetworkName, s.instanceName, s.tcpPort
        FROM dbo.Servers s
        JOIN dbo.Clusters c ON s.clusterID=c.clusterID
        JOIN dbo.ClusterNodes cn ON c.clusterID = cn.clusterID"

# Get all the SQL Server instances from the inventory
$sqlServers=Invoke-Sqlcmd -Query $strQuerySql -ServerInstance $inventoryServer
-Database $inventoryDatabase

# Loop through the list of SQL Server instances and create the "Database Auto Options
Disabled" policy on each instance.
if ($sqlServers) {
        Foreach ($sqlServer in $sqlServers) {
                $sqlNetworkName=$sqlServer.SQLNetworkName
                if ($sqlServer.instanceName -ieq 'MSSQLSERVER') {
                        $sqlInstanceName="default"
                }
                else {
                        $sqlInstanceName=$sqlServer.instanceName
                }
                $tcpPort=$sqlServer.tcpPort
```

```
                      #Create the "Database Auto Options Disabled" policy
                      CreateAutoOptionsOffPolicy $sqlNetworkName $sqlInstanceName $tcpPort
          }
     }
```

The complete script is in `Install-AutoOptionsOff.ps1`. Execute this script to install the policy on every SQL Server in the inventory:

```
C:\DBAScripts\Install-AutoOptionsOff.ps1
```

Figure 20-3 shows the output from running the script in our environment.

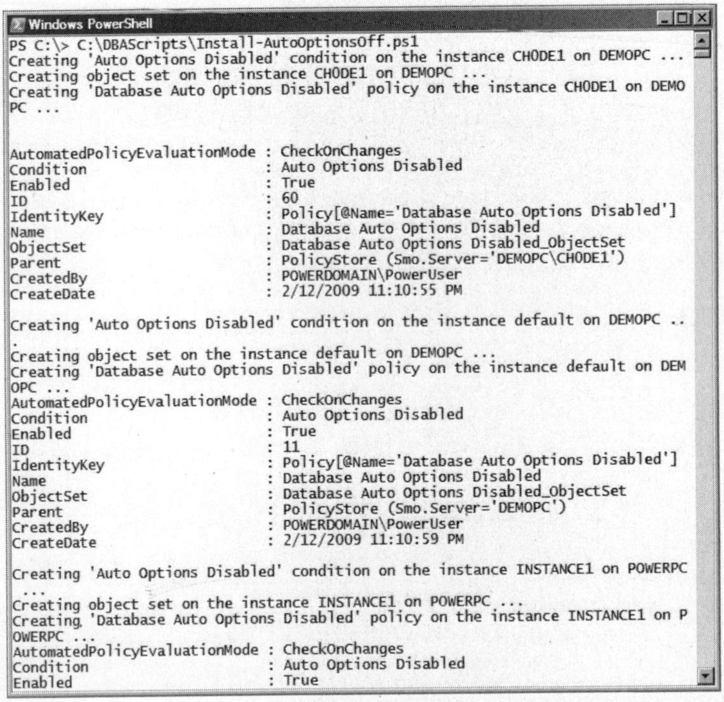

Figure 20-3

If any database violates the policy, an error message with an error number of 34053 will be logged to the SQL Server Error log and the Application log. For example, if you try to enable the `AutoClose` option on the `admin` database, then you will get the following message in the SQL Server Error log:

```
2009-02-12 23:14:52.23 spid33s     Error: 34053, Severity: 16, State: 1.
2009-02-12 23:14:52.23 spid33s     Policy 'Database Auto Options Disabled' has been
violated by target 'SQLSERVER:\SQL\POWERPC\DEFAULT\Databases\admin'.
```

If you allow SQL Server to write to the Application log, then you'll receive the following error message in the Application log:

```
Policy 'Database Auto Options Disabled' has been violated by target 'SQLSERVER:\SQL
\POWERPC\DEFAULT\Databases\admin'.
```

Errors logged into the SQL Server Error log and the Application log will be picked up by the monitoring mechanism discussed in Chapter 18 (see "Monitoring SQL Server Error Logs" and "Monitoring Windows Event Logs").

Summary

Policy-Based Management enables you to transform policies and standards defined on paper to SQL Server policies at the server and database level. In this chapter, you learned how to use two policies to automatically enforce two standards that were defined in Chapter 14 (one for the stored procedure naming convention and the other for disabling the `Auto_Close` and `Auto_Shrink` options). You also learned how to use PowerShell scripts to mass deploy policies on all the servers in the inventory. You can customize the scripts shown in this chapter to create your own company policies, and thus reduce the need for manual auditing and enforcement. The next chapter covers another DBA responsibility: generating DDL scripts for database objects.

21

Generating Database Scripts

Generating Data Definition Language (DDL) scripts for a database and its objects is also a SQL Server database administration task. Generating such scripts is very useful for comparing changes in the DDLs between two different dates. It also helps in copying the schema and objects from one server to another. This chapter covers generating DDL scripts for the following:

❑ Databases

❑ Schemas

❑ User-defined data types

❑ Tables

❑ User views

❑ Stored procedures

❑ Functions

❑ XML schemas

❑ Users

Scripting Databases

Throughout this chapter you will use the .NET-based object library SMO. You learned how to write SMO programs in Windows PowerShell in Chapter 13, and now you will use two major SMO classes in this chapter:

❑ `Microsoft.SqlServer.Management.Smo.Scripter`

❑ `Microsoft.SqlServer.Management.Smo.Server`

Chapter 21: Generating Database Scripts

For some tasks, such as scripting stored procedures, you will also be using the SMO class `Microsoft.SqlServer.Management.Smo.StoredProcedure`.

This chapter describes how to use SQL Server Management Objects (SMO) to script databases and its objects. All the scripts in this chapter store the SQL script files generated to a directory named `C:\scdata`. Let's first create this directory:

```
New-Item -Path C:\ -Name scdata -Type directory
```

Create the following `C:\DBAScripts\Script-Db.ps1` script. This script generates a DDL statement that takes three parameters: a server name, a database, and a file path. The server name indicates where the database resides. The file path points to the file where we are going to store the generated DDL for the database.

The following example first loads the SMO assembly file. It then creates a SMO Server object, `$srv`, and a Scripter object, `$MyScripter`. Then it connects to the database and uses the Script method to generate a script, storing that to a variable `$scrContent`. Then it adds the `"Go"` statement to every string that was generated by the script method and stores it to the variable `$scrContent2`. Finally it generates the filename based on the current timestamp, using the `Get-Date` cmdlet to get a `System.DateTime` object and querying the object's properties, such as year, month, and day, and exporting the content of the variable `$scrContent` to the file.

```
#==============================================================
#
# NAME: Script-Db.ps1
#
# AUTHOR: Yan and MAK
# DATE   : 5/1/2008
#
# COMMENT: This script generates DDL statement for the given database
#==============================================================

param
(
[string] $SQLServername,
[string] $Databasename,
[string] $filepath

)
[reflection.assembly]::LoadWithPartialName("Microsoft.SqlServer.Smo") | Out-Null
$MyScripter=New-Object ("Microsoft.SqlServer.Management.Smo.Scripter")
$srv=New-Object "Microsoft.SqlServer.Management.Smo.Server" $SQLServername
$MyScripter.Server=$srv

$scrcontent=$MyScripter.Script($srv.databases["$Databasename"])

$date=Get-Date
$suffix="_"+$date.year.tostring()+"_"+$date.month.tostring()+"_"
+$date.day.tostring()
$filepath=$filepath+$databasename+"_db_"+$suffix+".sql"
$scrcontent2="use [master]"+"`r`n"+"Go"+"`r`n"

foreach ($str in $scrcontent)
```

```
    {
               $scrcontent2=$scrcontent2+ $str+"`r`n"+"Go"+"`r`n"

    }
    Out-File -inputobject $scrcontent2 -filepath $filepath -encoding "Default"
```

Before executing the script, use the Set-Location cmdlet to change the location of the script folder to C:\DBAScripts if you are not on that folder:

```
    Set-Location C:\DBAScripts
```

Now execute C:\DBAScripts\Script-Db.ps1 as shown here:

```
    .\Script-Db.ps1 PowerServer3 Adventureworks2008 C:\scdata\
```

When the preceding C:\DBAScripts\Script-DB.ps1 is executed, it generates the DDL commands for creating the database Adventureworks2008 and stores the generated commands on to the file C:\scdata\Adventureworks2008_db_2009_2_15.sql. The file name is generated on the fly. The prefix of the filename is generated based on the database name that is passed as the parameter plus the word "_db_". The suffix of the filename is generated based on the current timestamp when the script was executed (see Figure 21-1).

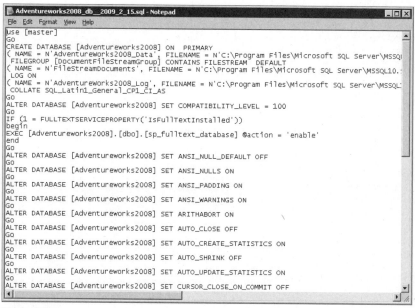

Figure 21-1

Scripting Schemas

You know that the schema is separated from the database user beginning with SQL Server 2005; that separation continues in SQL Server 2008. Generating DDL for a schema is just as important as generating DDL for databases.

Now create the following script, `C:\DBAScripts\Script-Schema.ps1`. This generates DDL statements for all schemas in a database when executed. It is similar to `Script-DB.ps1`. This script uses the `foreach` loop to iterate through all the schemas, and generates the scripts for each schema using the `script` method.

```
#===============================================================
#
# NAME: Script-Schema.ps1
#
# AUTHOR: Yan and MAK
# DATE  : 5/1/2008
#
# COMMENT: This script generates DDL statement for all schemas from the given database
#===============================================================

param
(
  [string] $ServerName,
  [string] $DatabaseName,
  [string] $filepath
)

[reflection.assembly]::LoadWithPartialName("Microsoft.SqlServer.Smo") | Out-Null

$MyScripter=New-Object("Microsoft.SqlServer.Management.Smo.Scripter")

$srv=New-Object "Microsoft.SqlServer.Management.Smo.Server" "$ServerName"

$db = $srv.Databases["$DatabaseName"]

$MyScripter.Server=$srv

$date=Get-Date

$suffix="_"+$date.year.tostring()+"_"+$date.month.tostring()+"_"
+$date.day.tostring()

$filepath=$filepath+$databasename+"_schema_"+$suffix+".sql"

$scrcontent="use [$databasename]"+"`r`n"+"Go"+"`r`n"


foreach ($sch in $db.Schemas)
{
        $scrcontent=$scrcontent+ $sch.script()+"`r`n"+"Go"+"`r`n"
}

Out-File -inputobject $scrcontent -filepath $filepath -encoding "Default"
```

Now execute the script as shown here:

```
.\Script-Schema.ps1 PowerServer3 Adventureworks2008 C:\scdata\
```

When the preceding `C:\DBAScripts\Script-Schema.ps1` is executed, it generates the DDL commands for creating all the Schemas in the database Adventureworks2008 and stores the generated commands on to the file `C:\scdata\Adventureworks2008_schema_2009_2_15.sql`. The file name is generated on the fly. The prefix of the filename is generated based on the database name that is passed as the parameter plus the word "_schema_". The suffix of the filename is generated based on the current timestamp when the script was executed (see Figure 21-2).

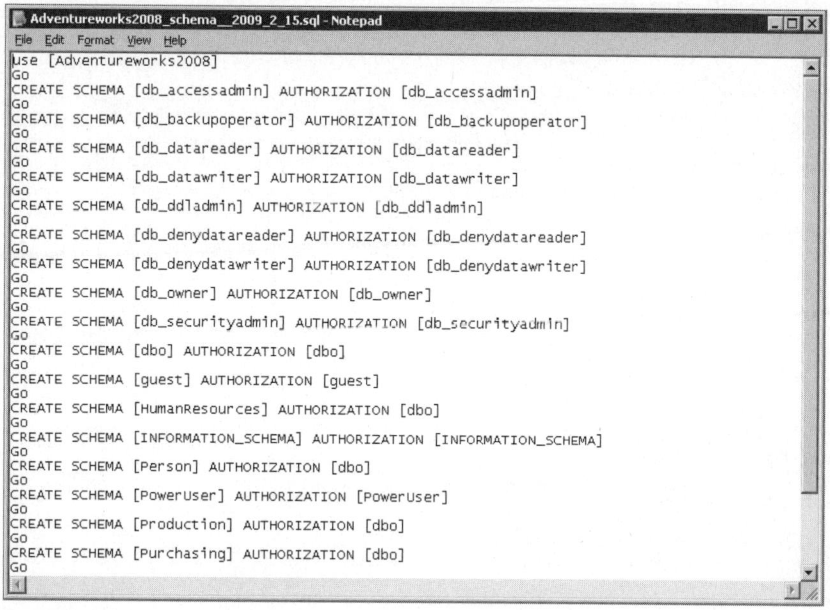

Figure 21-2

Scripting User-Defined Data Types

This section illustrates the method to generate all the user-defined data types on a given database. The script created in this section is also similar to `Script-DB.ps1`. It uses the `foreach` loop to iterate through all the user-defined data types available on the database and generates the scripts for each one using the `script` method. Create the following script, named `C:\DBAScripts\Script-UDDtype.ps1`:

```
# ================================================================
#
# NAME: Script-UDDtype.ps1
#
# AUTHOR: Yan and MAK
# DATE   : 5/1/2008
#
# COMMENT: This script generates DDL statement for User Defined Data Type
# ================================================================

param
(
  [string] $ServerName,
  [string] $DatabaseName,
  [string] $filepath
)
```

```
[reflection.assembly]::LoadWithPartialName("Microsoft.SqlServer.Smo") | Out-Null
$MyScripter=New-Object("Microsoft.SqlServer.Management.Smo.Scripter")
$srv=New-Object "Microsoft.SqlServer.Management.Smo.Server" "$ServerName"
$db=$srv.Databases["$DatabaseName"]

$MyScripter.Server=$srv
$date=Get-Date
$suffix="_"+$date.year.tostring()+"_"+$date.month.tostring()+"_"+
$date.day.tostring()
$filepath=$filepath+$databasename+"_uddtype_"+$suffix+".sql"

$scrcontent="use [$databasename]"+"`r`n"+"Go"+"`r`n"
Out-File -inputobject $scrcontent -filepath $filepath -encoding "Default"

foreach ( $type in $db.UserDefineddataTypes )
{
        $spcontent=$type.script()

        Out-File -inputobject $spcontent -filepath $filepath -encoding "Default"
-append
        $suffix2="`r`n"+"Go"+"`r`n"
        Out-File -inputobject $suffix2 -filepath $filepath -encoding "Default"
-append
}
```

Now execute the script as shown here:

```
.\Script-UDDtype.ps1 PowerServer3 Adventureworks2008 C:\scdata\
```

When the preceding `C:\DBAScripts\Script-UDDtype.ps1` is executed, it generates the DDL commands for creating all the User Defined Data Types in the database Adventureworks2008 and stores the generated commands on to the file `C:\scdata\Adventureworks2008_uddtype_2009_2_15.sql`. The file name is generated on the fly. The prefix of the filename is generated based on the database name that is passed as the parameter plus the word "_uddtype_". The suffix of the filename is generated based on the current timestamp when the script was executed (see Figure 21-3).

The following script, `C:\DBAScripts\Script-UDtype.ps1`, generates all user-defined types that are based on .NET data types in the database. This script is also similar to `Script-DB.ps1`. It uses the `foreach` loop to iterate through all the user-defined data types available on the database and generates the scripts for each one using the `script` method:

```
# ==============================================================
#
# NAME: Script-UDtype.ps1
#
# AUTHOR: Yan and MAK
# DATE  : 5/1/2008
#
# COMMENT: This script generates DDL statement User Defined Type.
# ==============================================================

param
(
```

```
    [string] $ServerName,
    [string] $DatabaseName,
    [string] $filepath
)

[reflection.assembly]::LoadWithPartialName("Microsoft.SqlServer.Smo") | Out-Null
$MyScripter=New-Object("Microsoft.SqlServer.Management.Smo.Scripter")
$srv=New-Object "Microsoft.SqlServer.Management.Smo.Server" "$ServerName"
$db = $srv.Databases["$DatabaseName"]

$MyScripter.Server=$srv
$date=Get-Date
$suffix="_"+$date.year.tostring()+"_"+$date.month.tostring()+"_"
+$date.day.tostring()
$filepath=$filepath+$databasename+"_udtype_"+$suffix+".sql"

$scrcontent="use [$databasename]"+"`r`n"+"Go"+"`r`n"
Out-File -inputobject $scrcontent -filepath $filepath -encoding "Default"

$spcontent =""
foreach ( $udtype in $db.UserDefinedTypes )
{
$udtype.script()
$spcontent=$udtype.script()
$spcontent

Out-File -inputobject $spcontent -filepath $filepath -encoding "Default" -append
$suffix2="`r`n"+"Go"+"`r`n"
Out-File -inputobject  $suffix2 -filepath $filepath -encoding "Default" -append
}
```

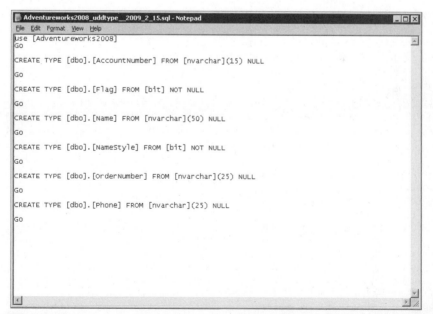

Figure 21-3

Execute the script as shown here:

```
.\Script-UDtype.ps1 PowerServer3 Adventureworks2008 C:\scdata\
```

If you do not have user-defined types, then the generated file, such as `Adventureworks2008_udtype`
`_2009_2_15.sql`, will be empty.

> *The prefix of the filename is generated based on the database name that is passed as the parameter plus
> the word "_udtype_". The suffix of the filename is generated based on the current timestamp when the
> script was executed.*

Scripting Tables

Tables are the most important objects in the database because that is where most of the data is stored.
However, tables have other dependent objects such as indexes, constraints, keys, and so on. When you
are trying to generate a DDL script for a table, it is important to generate DDL statements for all the
related dependent objects as well.

The following script, `C:\DBAScripts\Script-Table.ps1`, generates all the tables, constraints, indexes,
and keys in the database. This script is similar to `Script-DB.ps1`. It uses the `foreach` loop to iterate
through all the tables, indexes, default constraints, check constraints, primary key constraints, foreign
key constraints, and triggers available on the database, and generates the scripts for each of them using
the `script` method.

```
# =============================================================
#
# NAME: Script-Table.ps1
#
# AUTHOR: Yan and MAK
# DATE  : 5/1/2008
#
# COMMENT: This script generates DDL statement for all tables
#
# =============================================================

param
(
   [string] $ServerName,
   [string] $DatabaseName,
   [string] $filepath
)

[reflection.assembly]::LoadWithPartialName("Microsoft.SqlServer.Smo") | Out-Null
$Scripter=New-Object("Microsoft.SqlServer.Management.Smo.Scripter")
$srv=New-Object "Microsoft.SqlServer.Management.Smo.Server" "$ServerName"
$db = $srv.Databases["$DatabaseName"]
$Scripter.Server=$srv
$date=get-date
$suffix="_"+$date.year.tostring()+"_"+$date.month.tostring()+"_"
+$date.day.tostring()
```

```
$filepath=$filepath+$databasename+"_table_"+$suffix+".sql"

$scrcontent="use [$databasename]"+"`r`n"+"Go"+"`r`n"

foreach ( $Table in $db.Tables )
{
        $scrcontent =$scrcontent +$table.script()

        $Scripter.Options.DriPrimaryKey = $true

        foreach ( $Index in $Table.Indexes )
        {
                if( $Index.IndexKeyType -eq [Microsoft.SqlServer.Management.Smo
.IndexKeyType]::DriPrimaryKey )
                {
                        $scrcontent =$scrcontent +$Index.script()+"`r`n"+"Go"+"`r`n"
                }
                else
                {
                        $scrcontent =$scrcontent +$Index.script()+"`r`n"+"Go"+"`r`n"
                }
        }

        $Scripter.Options.DriPrimaryKey = $false

        foreach ( $Check in $Table.Checks )
        {
                $Scripter.Options.DriChecks = $true
                $scrcontent =$scrcontent +$check.script()+"`r`n"+"Go"+"`r`n"
                $Scripter.Options.DriChecks = $false
        }

        foreach ( $DmlTrigger in $Table.Triggers )
        {
                $scrcontent =$scrcontent  +$dmltrigger.script()+"`r`n"+"Go"+"`r`n"
        }

        foreach ( $Column in $Table.Columns )
        {
                if ( $Column.DefaultConstraint -ne $null )
                {
                        $scrcontent =$scrcontent+$Column.DefaultConstraint.script()
+"`r`n"+"Go"+"`r`n"
                }
        }

}

foreach ( $Table in $db.Tables )
{
        $Scripter.Options.DriForeignKeys = $true

        foreach ( $ForeignKey in $Table.ForeignKeys )
```

```
        {
                $scrcontent =$scrcontent +$ForeignKey.script()+"`r`n"+"Go"+"`r`n"
        }

        $Scripter.Options.DriForeignKeys = $false

}

Out-File -inputobject $scrcontent -filepath $filepath -encoding "Default"
```

Now execute the script as shown here:

```
.\Script-Table.ps1 PowerServer3 Adventureworks2008 C:\scdata\
```

When the preceding C:\DBAScripts\Script-Table.ps1 is executed, it generates the DDL commands for creating all the tables in the database Adventureworks2008 and stores the generated commands on to the file C:\scdata\Adventureworks2008_table_2009_2_15.sql. The file name is generated on the fly. The prefix of the filename is generated based on the database name that is passed as the parameter plus the word "_table_". The suffix of the filename is generated based on the current timestamp when the script was executed (see Figure 21-4).

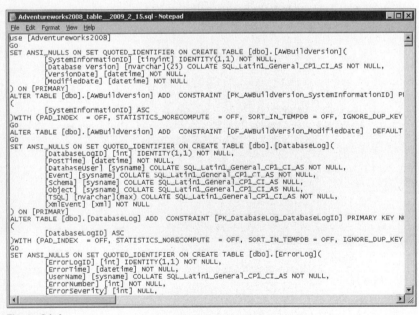

Figure 21-4

Scripting User Views

Next, create the following script, C:\DBAScripts\Script-View.ps1, that generates all the user views in the database. This script is similar to the Script-DB.ps1 script. It uses the foreach loop to iterate through all the views available on the database and generates the scripts for each view using the script method.

```
# ================================================================
#
# NAME: Script-View.ps1
#
# AUTHOR: Yan and MAK
# DATE  : 5/1/2008
#
# COMMENT: This script generates DDL statement for views
#
# ================================================================

param
(
   [string] $ServerName,
   [string] $DatabaseName,
   [string] $filepath
)

[reflection.assembly]::LoadWithPartialName("Microsoft.SqlServer.Smo") | Out-Null
$MyScripter=New-Object("Microsoft.SqlServer.Management.Smo.Scripter")
$srv=New-Object "Microsoft.SqlServer.Management.Smo.Server" "$ServerName"
$db = $srv.Databases["$DatabaseName"]

$MyScripter.Server=$srv
$date=Get-Date
$suffix="_"+$date.year.tostring()+"_"+$date.month.tostring()+"_"
+$date.day.tostring()
$filepath=$filepath+$databasename+"_view_"+$suffix+".sql"

$scrcontent="use [$databasename]"+"`r`n"+"Go"+"`r`n"
Out-File -inputobject $scrcontent -filepath $filepath -encoding "Default"

foreach ( $view in $db.views )
{
        if ( $view.IsSystemObject -eq $false )
        {
                $spcontent=$view.script()

                Out-File -inputobject $spcontent -filepath $filepath -encoding "
Default" -append
                $suffix2="`r`n"+"Go"+"`r`n"
                Out-File -inputobject $suffix2 -filepath $filepath -encoding "
Default" -append
        }
}
```

Execute the script as shown here:

```
.\Script-View.ps1 PowerServer3 Adventureworks2008 C:\scdata\
```

When the preceding C:\DBAScripts\Script-View.ps1 is executed, it generates the DDL commands for creating all the views in the database Adventureworks2008 and stores the generated commands on to the file C:\scdata\Adventureworks2008_view_2009_2_15.sql. The file name is generated on the fly. The prefix of the filename is generated based on the database name that is passed as the parameter plus the word "_view_". The suffix of the filename is generated based on the current timestamp when the script was executed (see Figure 21-5).

```
Adventureworks2008_view__2009_2_15.sql - Notepad                          _ □ X
File  Edit  Format  View  Help
use [Adventureworks2008]
GO

SET ANSI_NULLS ON
SET QUOTED_IDENTIFIER ON

CREATE VIEW [HumanResources].[vEmployee]
AS
SELECT
      e.[BusinessEntityID]
     ,p.[Title]
     ,p.[FirstName]
     ,p.[MiddleName]
     ,p.[LastName]
     ,p.[Suffix]
     ,e.[JobTitle]
     ,pp.[PhoneNumber]
     ,pnt.[Name] AS [PhoneNumberType]
     ,ea.[EmailAddress]
     ,p.[EmailPromotion]
     ,a.[AddressLine1]
     ,a.[AddressLine2]
     ,a.[City]
     ,sp.[Name] AS [StateProvinceName]
     ,a.[PostalCode]
     ,cr.[Name] AS [CountryRegionName]
     ,p.[AdditionalContactInfo]
FROM [HumanResources].[Employee] e
     INNER JOIN [Person].[Person] p
       ON p.[BusinessEntityID] = e.[BusinessEntityID]
     INNER JOIN [Person].[BusinessEntityAddress] bea
     ON bea.[BusinessEntityID] = e.[BusinessEntityID]
     INNER JOIN [Person].[Address] a
     ON a.[AddressID] = bea.[AddressID]
     INNER JOIN [Person].[StateProvince] sp
     ON sp.[StateProvinceID] = a.[StateProvinceID]
```

Figure 21-5

Scripting Stored Procedures

The next script, C:\DBAScripts\Script-SP.ps1, generates all the stored procedures in the database. This script is similar to the Script-DB.ps1 script. It uses the foreach loop to iterate through all the stored procedures available on the database and generates the scripts for each one using the script method. Here, we also use the PreFetchObject method. The PreFetchObject method enables collections to be fully populated with objects with one network trip to the instance of Microsoft SQL Server. Prefetching is an optimization used when the whole collection of objects is required.

```
# ==============================================================
#
# NAME: Script-SP.ps1
#
# AUTHOR: Yan and MAK
# DATE   : 5/1/2008
#
# COMMENT: This script generates DDL statement for all stored procedures
#
# ==============================================================
```

```
param
(
  [string] $ServerName,
  [string] $DatabaseName,
  [string] $filepath
)

[reflection.assembly]::LoadWithPartialName("Microsoft.SqlServer.Smo") | Out-Null
$MyScripter=New-Object("Microsoft.SqlServer.Management.Smo.Scripter")
$srv=New-Object "Microsoft.SqlServer.Management.Smo.Server" "$ServerName"
$db = $srv.Databases["$DatabaseName"]

$db.PrefetchObjects([Microsoft.SqlServer.Management.Smo.StoredProcedure])

$MyScripter.Server=$srv
$date=Get-Date
$suffix="_"+$date.year.tostring()+"_"+$date.month.tostring()+"_"
+$date.day.tostring()
$filepath=$filepath+$databasename+"_storedprocedure_"+$suffix+".sql"

$scrcontent="use [$databasename]"+"`r`n"+"Go"+"`r`n"
Out-File -inputobject $scrcontent -filepath $filepath -encoding "Default"

foreach ( $sp in $db.StoredProcedures )
{
        if ( $sp.IsSystemObject -eq $false )
        {
                $spcontent=$sp.script()

                Out-File -inputobject $spcontent -filepath $filepath -encoding "Default"
-append
                $suffix2=""`r`n"+"Go"+"`r`n"
                Out-File -inputobject  $suffix2 -filepath $filepath -encoding "Default"
-append
        }
}
```

Now execute the script as shown here:

```
.\Script-SP.ps1 PowerServer3 Adventureworks2008 C:\scdata\
```

When the preceding `C:\DBAScripts\Script-SP.ps1` is executed, it generates the DDL commands for creating all the Stored Procedures in the database Adventureworks2008 and stores the generated commands on to the file `C:\scdata\Adventureworks2008_storedprocedure_2009_2_15.sql`. The file name is generated on the fly. The prefix of the filename is generated based on the database name that is passed as the parameter plus the word "_storedprocedure_". The suffix of the filename is generated based on the current timestamp when the script was executed (see Figure 21-6).

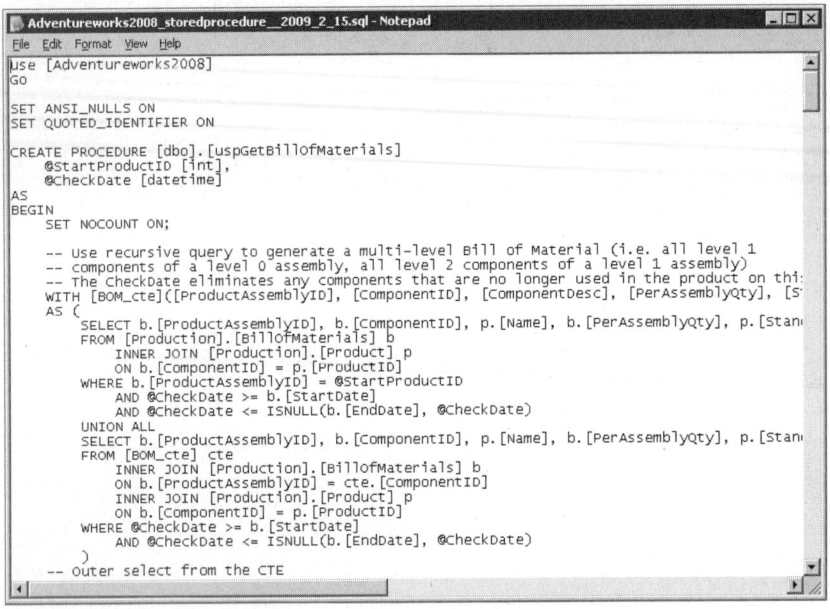

Adventureworks2008_storedprocedure__2009_2_15.sql - Notepad

File Edit Format View Help

```
use [Adventureworks2008]
Go

SET ANSI_NULLS ON
SET QUOTED_IDENTIFIER ON

CREATE PROCEDURE [dbo].[uspGetBillofMaterials]
    @StartProductID [int],
    @CheckDate [datetime]
AS
BEGIN
    SET NOCOUNT ON;

    -- Use recursive query to generate a multi-level Bill of Material (i.e. all level 1
    -- components of a level 0 assembly, all level 2 components of a level 1 assembly)
    -- The CheckDate eliminates any components that are no longer used in the product on thi
    WITH [BOM_cte]([ProductAssemblyID], [ComponentID], [ComponentDesc], [PerAssemblyQty], [S
    AS (
        SELECT b.[ProductAssemblyID], b.[ComponentID], p.[Name], b.[PerAssemblyQty], p.[Stan
        FROM [Production].[BillOfMaterials] b
            INNER JOIN [Production].[Product] p
            ON b.[ComponentID] = p.[ProductID]
        WHERE b.[ProductAssemblyID] = @StartProductID
            AND @CheckDate >= b.[StartDate]
            AND @CheckDate <= ISNULL(b.[EndDate], @CheckDate)
        UNION ALL
        SELECT b.[ProductAssemblyID], b.[ComponentID], p.[Name], b.[PerAssemblyQty], p.[Stan
        FROM [BOM_cte] cte
            INNER JOIN [Production].[BillOfMaterials] b
            ON b.[ProductAssemblyID] = cte.[ComponentID]
            INNER JOIN [Production].[Product] p
            ON b.[ComponentID] = p.[ProductID]
        WHERE @CheckDate >= b.[StartDate]
            AND @CheckDate <= ISNULL(b.[EndDate], @CheckDate)
        )
    -- Outer select from the CTE
```

Figure 21-6

Scripting Functions

The next script shows all the functions in the database. This script, named `Script-Function.psi`, is similar to `Script-DB.ps1`. It uses the `foreach` loop to iterate through all the functions available on the database and generates the scripts for each function using the `script` method.

```
# ================================================================
#
# NAME: Script-Function.ps1
#
# AUTHOR: Yan and MAK
# DATE  : 5/1/2008
#
# COMMENT: This script generates DDL statement for all functions
#
# ================================================================

param
(
  [string] $ServerName,
  [string] $DatabaseName,
  [string] $filepath
)

[reflection.assembly]::LoadWithPartialName("Microsoft.SqlServer.Smo") | Out-Null
$MyScripter=New-Object("Microsoft.SqlServer.Management.Smo.Scripter")
$srv=New-Object "Microsoft.SqlServer.Management.Smo.Server" "$ServerName"
$db = $srv.Databases["$DatabaseName"]

$MyScripter.Server=$srv
$date=Get-Date
```

```
$suffix="_"+$date.year.tostring()+"_"+$date.month.tostring()+"_"
+$date.day.tostring()
$filepath=$filepath+$databasename+"_function_"+$suffix+".sql"

$scrcontent="use [$databasename]"+"`r`n"+"Go"+"`r`n"
Out-File -inputobject $scrcontent -filepath $filepath -encoding "Default"

foreach ( $function in $db.UserDefinedFunctions )
{
        if ( $function.IsSystemObject -eq $false )
        {
                $spcontent=$function.script()

                Out-File -inputobject $spcontent -filepath $filepath -encoding "
Default" -append
                $suffix2="`r`n"+"Go"+"`r`n"
                Out-File -inputobject  $suffix2 -filepath $filepath -encoding "
Default" -append
        }
}
```

Execute the script as shown here:

```
.\Script-Function.ps1 PowerServer3 Adventureworks2008 C:\scdata\
```

When the preceding `C:\DBAScripts\Script-Function.ps1` is executed, it generates the DDL commands for creating all the user defined functions in the database Adventureworks2008 and stores the generated commands on to the file `C:\scdata\Adventureworks2008_function_2009_2_15.sql`. The file name is generated on the fly. The prefix of the filename is generated based on the database name that is passed as the parameter plus the word "_function_". The suffix of the filename is generated based on the current timestamp when the script was executed (see Figure 21-7).

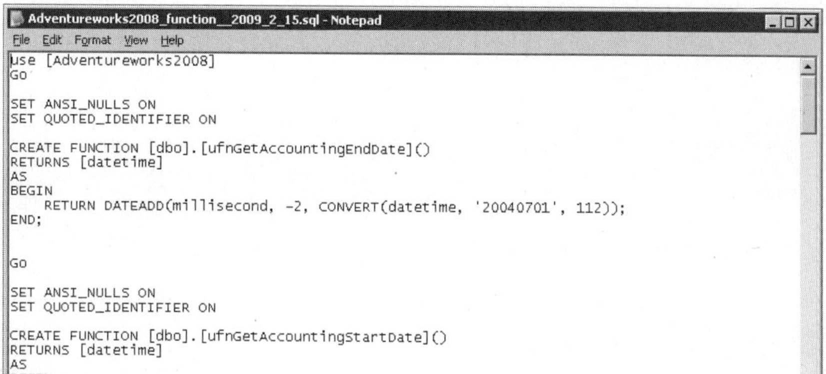

Figure 21-7

501

Scripting XML Schemas

Now create the following script, C:\DBAScripts\Script-XMLSchema.ps1, that generates all the XML schemas in the database. This script is similar to the Script-DB.ps1 script. It uses the foreach loop to iterate through all the XML schemas available on the database and generates the scripts for each one using the script method.

```
# ================================================================
#
# NAME: Script-XMLSchema.ps1
#
# AUTHOR: Yan and MAK
# DATE   : 5/1/2008
#
# COMMENT: This script generates DDL statement for all XML Schema
#
# ================================================================
param
(
   [string] $ServerName,
   [string] $DatabaseName,
   [string] $filepath
)

[reflection.assembly]::LoadWithPartialName("Microsoft.SqlServer.Smo") | Out-Null
$MyScripter=New-Object("Microsoft.SqlServer.Management.Smo.Scripter")
$srv=New-Object "Microsoft.SqlServer.Management.Smo.Server" "$ServerName"
$db = $srv.Databases["$DatabaseName"]

$MyScripter.Server=$srv
$date=Get-Date
$suffix="_"+$date.year.tostring()+"_"+$date.month.tostring()+"_"
+$date.day.tostring()
$filepath=$filepath+$databasename+"_xml_"+$suffix+".sql"

$scrcontent="use [$databasename]"+"`r`n"+"Go"+"`r`n"
Out-File -inputobject $scrcontent -filepath $filepath -encoding "Default"

foreach ( $xml in $db.XmlSchemaCollections)
{
        $spcontent=$xml.script()

        Out-File -inputobject $spcontent -filepath $filepath -encoding "Default"
-append
        $suffix2="`r`n"+"Go"+"`r`n"
        Out-File -inputobject  $suffix2 -filepath $filepath -encoding "Default"
-append
}
```

Execute the script as shown here:

```
.\Script-XMLSchema.ps1 PowerServer3 Adventureworks2008 C:\scdata\
```

When the preceding `C:\DBAScripts\Script-XMLSchema.ps1` is executed, it generates the DDL commands for creating all the XML Schema in the database Adventureworks2008 and stores the generated commands on to the file `C:\scdata\Adventureworks2008_xml_2009_2_15.sql`. The file name is generated on the fly. The prefix of the filename is generated based on the database name that is passed as the parameter plus the word "_xml_". The suffix of the filename is generated based on the current timestamp when the script was executed (see Figure 21-8).

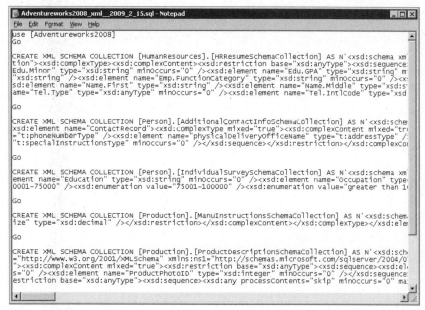

Figure 21-8

Scripting Users

You may want to create the following script, `C:\DBAScripts\Script-User.ps1`, which will generate all the users in the database. This script is similar to the `Script-DB.ps1` script. It uses the `foreach` loop to iterate through all the users available on the database and generates the scripts for each user using the `script` method.

```
# =================================================================
#
# NAME: Script-User.ps1
#
# AUTHOR: Yan and MAK
# DATE   : 5/1/2008
#
# COMMENT: This script generates DDL statement for all users
#
# =================================================================
```

```
param
(
    [string] $ServerName,
    [string] $DatabaseName,
    [string] $filepath
)

[reflection.assembly]::LoadWithPartialName("Microsoft.SqlServer.Smo") | Out-Null
$MyScripter=New-Object("Microsoft.SqlServer.Management.Smo.Scripter")
$srv=New-Object "Microsoft.SqlServer.Management.Smo.Server" "$ServerName"
$db = $srv.Databases["$DatabaseName"]

$MyScripter.Server=$srv
$date=Get-Date
$suffix="_"+$date.year.tostring()+"_"+$date.month.tostring()+"_"
+$date.day.tostring()
$filepath=$filepath+$databasename+"_user_"+$suffix+".sql"

$scrcontent="use [$databasename]"+"`r`n"+"Go"+"`r`n"
Out-File -inputobject $scrcontent -filepath $filepath -encoding "Default"

foreach ( $user in $db.Users )
{
        if ( $user.IsSystemObject -eq $false )
        {
                $spcontent=$user.script()

            Out-File -inputobject $spcontent -filepath $filepath -encoding "Default"
-append
                $suffix2="`r`n"+"Go"+"`r`n"
                Out-File -inputobject  $suffix2 -filepath $filepath -encoding "Default"
-append
        }
}
```

Now execute the script as shown here:

```
.\Script-User.ps1 PowerServer3 Adventureworks2008 C:\scdata\
```

When the preceding C:\DBAScripts\Script-User.ps1 is executed, it generates the DDL commands for creating all the users in the database Adventureworks2008 and stores the generated commands on to the file C:\scdata\Adventureworks2008_user_2009_2_15.sql. The file name is generated on the fly. The prefix of the filename is generated based on the database name that is passed as the parameter plus the word "_user_". The suffix of the filename is generated based on the current timestamp when the script was executed (see Figure 21-9).

From all the Windows PowerShell scripts related to database object scripting (see Figure 21-10), you can see that each one generated corresponding SQL files accordingly (see Figure 21-11).

If you want to generate all the objects, constraints, stored procedures, functions, users, data types, and views from one single script, you could either merge all the preceding scripts into one or use the

`SMO.Transfer` method. The `Transfer` object is a tool object that provides programmatic control over copying schemas and data to other instances of SQL Server. We do not illustrate that method here, but we encourage you to explore that option yourself.

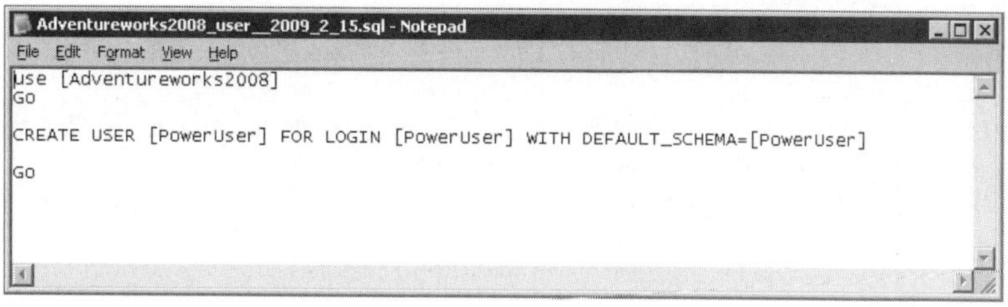

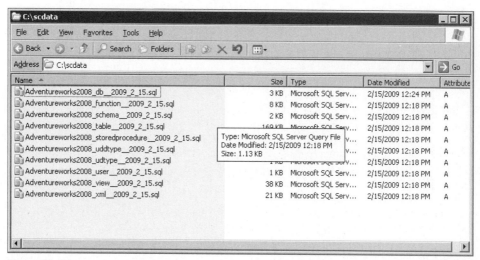

Figure 21-9

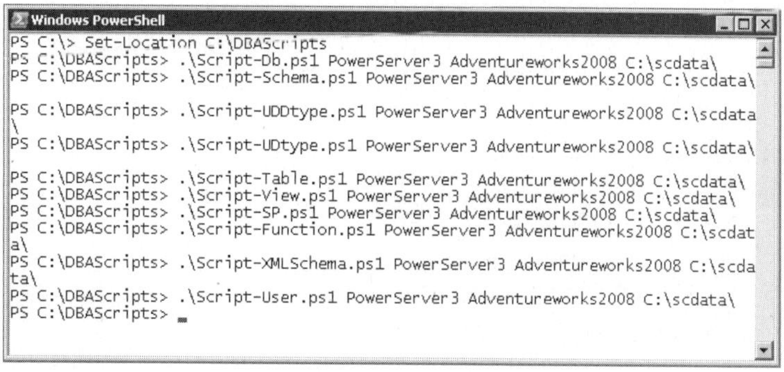

Figure 21-10

Figure 21-11

You could schedule all the preceding Windows PowerShell scripts to run on a nightly basis. You could then compare the generated file from one script on a particular day with the generated file from the same script from another day and see if anything changed.

Summary

This chapter illustrated various ways to create DDL scripts for databases, schemas, tables, functions, stored procedures, users, user-defined data types, and so on. Windows PowerShell enables you to use .NET-based object library SQL Server Management Objects (SMO) to script the database objects.

This book has provided all the necessary information you need about Windows PowerShell with respect to SQL Server database administration. You have seen plenty of examples demonstrating how valuable Windows PowerShell scripts can be for improving the manageability of a SQL Server plant. We hope you enjoyed reading this book and that you learned both sides of system and database administration with Windows PowerShell. We also hope that the solutions presented in this book help you manage your own environment and make your life easier.

cmdlets

If you need detailed information on any of the cmdlets listed in this Appendix, please execute the cmdlet `Get-Help` with the name of the cmdlet you are interested in as a parameter, as shown below:

```
Get-Help Get-WMIObject -Full
```

For more information about `Get-Help`, refer to Chapter 2.

If you need detailed information on some of the cmdlets' related programming, snapins, please execute cmdlet `Get-Help` as shown below:

```
Get-Help About_PSSnapins
```

To get the list of available help related to `About*`, execute the cmdlet `Get-Help` as shown below:

```
Get-Help About*
```

cmdlets Related to Core Snap-ins

Add-History cmdlet: Adds entries to the end of the session history — that is, the list of commands entered during the current session. You can use the `Get-History` cmdlet to get the commands and pass them to `Add-History`, or export the commands to a CSV or XML file and then import the commands, and pass the imported file to `Add-History`. You can use this cmdlet to add specific commands to the history or to create a single history file that includes commands from more than one session.

Add-PSSnapIn cmdlet: Adds one or more registered Windows PowerShell snap-ins to the current session. After the snap-ins are added, you can use the cmdlets and providers that the snap-in supports in the current session. To add the snap-in to all future Windows PowerShell sessions, add an `Add-PSSnapin` command to your Windows PowerShell profile. For more information about profiles, refer to Chapter 4.

Clear-History cmdlet: Deletes commands from the command history — that is, the list of commands entered during the current session. Without parameters, `Clear-History` deletes all commands from the session history, but you can use the parameters of `Clear-History` to delete selected commands.

Enter-PSSession cmdlet: Starts an interactive session with a single remote computer. During the session, the commands that you type run on the remote computer, just as though you were typing directly on the remote computer. You can have only one interactive session at a time. Typically, you use the `ComputerName` parameter to specify the name of the remote computer, but you can also use a session that you create by using `New-PSSession` for the interactive session. To end the interactive session and disconnect from the remote computer, use the `Exit-PSSession` cmdlet or type **Exit**.

Exit-PSSession cmdlet: Ends interactive sessions that you started by using `Enter-PSSession`. You can also use the `EXIT` keyword to end an interactive session. The effect is the same as using `Exit-PSSession`.

Export-Console cmdlet: Exports the names of the Windows PowerShell snap-ins (PSSnapins) in the current session to a Windows PowerShell console file (`.psc1`). You can use this cmdlet to save the snap-ins for use in future sessions. To add the snap-ins in the `.psc1` console file to a session, start Windows PowerShell (`powershell.exe`) at the command line, such as by using `Cmd.exe` or another Windows PowerShell session, and use the `PSConsoleFile` parameter of `PowerShell.exe` to specify the console file.

ForEach-Object cmdlet: Performs an operation on each of a set of input objects. The input objects can be piped to the cmdlet or specified by using the `InputObject` parameter. The operation to perform is described within a script block, which is provided to the cmdlet as the value of the `Process` parameter. The script block can contain any Windows PowerShell script. Within the script block, the current input object is represented by the `$_` variable. In addition to the script block that describes the operations to be carried out on each input object, you can provide two additional script blocks: one is specified as the value of the `Begin` parameter, and runs before the first input object is processed; the other is specified as the value of the `End` parameter, and runs after the last input object is processed. The evaluation results of all the script blocks, including the ones specified with `Begin` and `End`, are passed down the pipeline.

Get-Command cmdlet: Gets basic information about cmdlets and other elements of Windows PowerShell commands in the session, such as aliases, functions, filters, scripts, and applications. `Get-Command` gets its data directly from the code of a cmdlet, function, script, or alias, unlike `Get-Help`, which gets its information from help topic files. Without parameters, `Get-Command` gets all of the cmdlets and functions in the current session. `Get-Command *` gets all Windows PowerShell elements and all of the non–Windows-PowerShell files in the Path environment variable (`$env:path`). It groups the files in the Application command type. You can use the `Module` parameter of `Get-Command` to find commands that were added to the session by adding a Windows PowerShell snap-in or importing a module.

Get-Help cmdlet: Displays information about Windows PowerShell cmdlets and concepts. To get a list of all cmdlet help topic titles, type **get-help ***. If you type **get-help** followed by the exact name of a help topic or a word unique to a help topic, `Get-Help` displays the topic contents. If you enter a word or word pattern that appears in several help topic titles, `Get-Help` displays a list of the matching titles. If you enter a word that does not appear in any help topic titles, then Get-Help displays a list of topics that include that word in their contents. In addition to **get-help**, you can also type **help** or **man**, which displays one screen of text at a time, or **<cmdlet-name> -?**, which is identical to Get-Help, but works only for cmdlets. You can display the entire cmdlet help file or selected parts of the file, such as the syntax, parameters, or examples. You can also use the Online parameter to display an online version of a cmdlet help file in your Internet browser. Conceptual help topics in Windows PowerShell begin with "about_," such as "about_comparison_operators." To see all "about_" topics, type **get-help about_***. To see a particular topic, type **get-help about_<topic-name>**, such as **get-help about_comparison operators**.

Get-History cmdlet: Gets the session history, or the list of commands entered during the current session. Windows PowerShell automatically maintains a history of each session. You can save the session history in XML or CSV format. By default, history files are saved in the home directory, but you can save the file in any location.

Get-Job cmdlet: Gets objects that represent the background jobs that were started in the current session. You can use Get-Job to get jobs that were started by using Start-Job, or by using the AsJob parameter of any cmdlet. Without parameters, a Get-Job command gets all jobs in the current session. You can use the parameters of Get-Job to get particular jobs. The job object that Get-Job returns contains useful information about the job, but it does not contain the job results. To get the results, use the Receive-Job cmdlet. A Windows PowerShell background job is a command that runs "in the background" without interacting with the current session. Typically, you use a background job to run a complex command that takes a long time to complete. For more information about background jobs in Windows PowerShell, type **get-help about_jobs**.

Get-PSSession cmdlet: Gets the Windows PowerShell sessions (PSSessions) that were created in the current session. Without parameters, Get-PSSession gets all of the PSSessions created in the current session. You can use the parameters of Get-PSSession to get the sessions that are connected to particular computers or to identify sessions by their name, ID, or instance ID. For more information about Windows PowerShell sessions, type **get-help about_PSSessions**.

Get-PSSnapIn cmdlet: Gets objects representing each Windows PowerShell snap-in added to the current session or registered on the system. The snap-ins are listed in the order in which they are detected. Get-PSSnapin gets only registered snap-ins. To register a Windows PowerShell snap-in, use the InstallUtil tool included the Microsoft .NET Framework 2.0. For instructions, see "How to Register Cmdlets, Providers, and Host Applications" in the *Windows PowerShell Programmer's Guide* on MSDN.

Invoke-Command cmdlet: Runs commands on a local or remote computer and returns all output from the commands, including errors. With a single Invoke-Command command, you can run commands on multiple computers. To run a single command on a remote computer, use the ComputerName parameter. To run a series of related commands that share data, create a PSSession (a persistent connection) on the remote computer, and then use the Session parameter of Invoke-Command to run the command in the PSSession. You can also use Invoke-Command on a local computer to evaluate or run a string in a script block as a command. Windows PowerShell converts the script block to a command and runs the command immediately in the current scope, instead of just echoing the string at the command line. Before using Invoke-Command to run commands on a remote computer, read about_remote. To see important notes about the use of this cmdlet, type **get-help invoke-command -full**.

Invoke-History cmdlet: Runs commands from the session history. You can pass objects representing the commands from Get-History to Invoke-History, or identify commands in the current history by using their ID number. To find the identification number of a command, use Get-History.

New-PSSession cmdlet: Creates a Windows PowerShell session (PSSession) on a local or remote computer. When you create a PSSession, Windows PowerShell establishes a persistent connection to the remote computer. Use a PSSession to run multiple commands that share data, such as a function or the value of a variable. To run commands in a PSSession, use the Invoke-Command cmdlet. To use the PSSession to interact directly with a remote computer, use the Enter-PSSession cmdlet. For more information, see about_PSSessions. You can run commands on a remote computer without creating a PSSession by using the ComputerName parameter of Enter-PSSession or Invoke-Command. When you use the ComputerName parameter, Windows PowerShell creates a temporary connection that is used for the interactive session or for a single command and is then closed.

Receive-Job cmdlet: Gets the results (output and/or errors) of Windows PowerShell background jobs. Use Receive-Job to get the results of jobs started by using Start-Job or the AsJob parameter of any cmdlet. You can get the results of all jobs or identify jobs by name, ID, instance ID, computer name, location, or session, or by submitting a job object. When you start a Windows PowerShell background job, the job starts, but the results do not appear immediately. Instead, the command returns an object that represents the background job. The job object contains useful information about the job, but it does not contain the results. This method enables you to continue working in the session while the job runs. For more information about background jobs in Windows Power-Shell, type **get-help about_jobs**. To get the results of the command, use the Receive-Job cmdlet. Receive-Job gets the results (output and errors) that have been generated by the time that the Receive-Job command is submitted. If the results are not yet complete, you can run additional Receive-Job commands to get the remaining results. By default, job results are deleted from the system when you receive them, but you can use the Keep parameter to save the results so that you can receive them again. To delete the job results, receive them again (without the Keep parameter), close the session, or use the Remove-Job cmdlet to delete the job from the session.

Remove-Job cmdlet: Deletes Windows PowerShell background jobs that were started by using Start-Job or the AsJob parameter of any cmdlet. You can use this cmdlet to delete all jobs or delete selected jobs based on name, ID, instance ID, command, or state, or by passing a job object to Remove-Job. Without parameters or parameter values, Remove-Job has no effect. Before deleting a running job, use the Stop-Job cmdlet to stop the job. If you try to delete a running job, the command fails. You can use the Force parameter of Remove-Job to delete a running job. If you do not delete a background job, the job remains in the global job cache until you close the session in which the job was created.

Remove-PSSession cmdlet: Closes the Windows PowerShell sessions (PSSessions) in the current session. It stops any commands that are running in the PSSessions, ends the PSSession, and releases the resources that the PSSession was using. If the PSSession is connected to a remote computer, Remove-PSSession also closes the connection between the local and remote computers. If you have saved the PSSession in a variable, the session object remains in the variable, but the state of the PSSession is Closed.

Remove-PSSnapIn cmdlet: Removes a Windows PowerShell snap-in from the current session. You can use it to remove snap-ins that you have added to Windows PowerShell, but you cannot use it to remove the snap-ins that are installed with Windows PowerShell. After a snap-in is removed from the current session, it is still loaded, but the cmdlets and providers in the snap-in are no longer available in the session.

Set-PsDebug cmdlet: Turns script debugging features on and off, sets the trace level, and toggles strict mode. When the `Trace` parameter is set to 1, each line of the script is traced as it is executed. When the parameter is set to 2, variable assignments, functions, and script calls are also traced. If the `Step` parameter is specified, you are prompted before each line of the script is executed.

Set-StrictMode cmdlet: Configures `strict` mode for the current scope (and all child scopes) and turns it on and off. When `strict` mode is on, Windows PowerShell generates a terminating error when the content of an expression, script, or script block violates basic best-practice coding rules. Use the `Version` parameter to determine which coding rules are enforced. Unlike the `Set-PSDebug` cmdlet, `Set-StrictMode` affects only the current scope and its child scopes, so you can use it in a script or function without affecting the global scope. When `Set-StrictMode` is off, uninitialized variables (Version 1) are assumed to have a value of 0 or $null, depending on type. References to non-existent properties return $null. and the results of invalid function syntax vary with the error. Unnamed variables are not permitted.

Start-Job cmdlet: Starts a Windows PowerShell background job on the local computer. A Windows PowerShell background job runs a command "in the background" without interacting with the current session. When you start a background job, a job object is returned immediately, even if the job takes an extended time to complete. You can continue to work in the session without interruption while the job runs. The job object contains useful information about the job, but it does not contain the job results. When the job completes, use the `Receive-Job` cmdlet to get the results of the job. For more information about background jobs, type **get-help about_jobs**. To run a background job on a remote computer, use the `AsJob` parameter, which is available on many cmdlets, or use the `Invoke-Command` cmdlet to run a `Start-Job` command on the remote computer. For more information, see `about_remote_jobs`.

Stop-Job cmdlet: Stops Windows PowerShell background jobs that are in progress. You can use this cmdlet to stop all jobs or stop selected jobs based on their name, ID, instance ID, or state, or by passing a job object to `Stop-Job`. You can use `Stop-Job` to stop jobs that were started by using `Start-Job` or the `AsJob` parameter of `Invoke-Command`. When you stop a background job, Windows PowerShell completes all tasks that are pending in that job queue and then ends the job. No new tasks are added to the queue after this command is submitted. This cmdlet does not delete background jobs. To delete a job, use `Remove-Job`.

Wait-Job cmdlet: Waits for Windows PowerShell background jobs to complete before it displays the command prompt. You can wait until any background job is complete or until all background jobs are complete, and set a maximum wait time for the job. You can use `Wait-Job` to get background jobs that were started by using `Start-Job` or the `AsJob` parameter of `Invoke-Command`. When the commands in the job are complete, `Wait-Job` displays the command prompt and returns a job object so you can pipe it to another command.

Where-Object cmdlet: Creates a filter that controls which objects will be passed along a command pipeline. It filters objects passed to it as pipelined input or objects provided as the value of the `InputObject` parameter. It determines which objects to pass along the pipeline by evaluating a script block, which may include a reference to an object being filtered. If the result of the evaluation is `True`, the object being processed is passed along the pipeline; otherwise, the object is discarded.

cmdlets Related to the PowerShell Management Snap-in

Add-Computer cmdlet: Adds computers to a domain or workgroup. It also creates a domain account for any computer added to the domain without an account. You can use the parameters of this cmdlet to specify an OU and domain controller, to perform an unsecure join, and to restart the computer automatically. To get the results of the command, use the Verbose and Passthru parameters.

Add-Content cmdlet: Appends content to a specified item or file. You can specify the content by typing it in the command or by specifying an object that contains the content.

Checkpoint-Computer cmdlet: Creates a system restore point on the local computer. This cmdlet runs only on Windows Vista and Windows XP.

Clear-Content cmdlet: Deletes the contents of an item, such as deleting the text from a file, but does not delete the item. As a result, the item exists, but is empty. Clear-Content is similar to Clear-Item, but works on files, rather than aliases and variables.

Clear-EventLog cmdlet: Deletes all of the entries from the specified Event logs on the local computer or remote computers. To use Clear-EventLog, you must be a member of the Administrators group on the affected computer. The EventLog cmdlet works only on classic Event logs. To get events from logs that use the Windows Eventing technology in Windows Vista and later versions of Windows, use Get-Event.

Clear-Item cmdlet: Deletes the value of an item but does not delete the item. For example, Clear-Item can delete the value of a variable, but it does not delete the variable. Each Windows PowerShell provider defines the value that is used to represent a cleared item. Clear-Item is similar to Clear-Content, but works on aliases and variables, rather than files.

Clear-ItemProperty cmdlet: Deletes the value of a property but does not delete the property. You can use this cmdlet to delete the data from a registry value.

Complete-Transaction cmdlet: Commits an active transaction. When you commit a transaction, the commands in the transaction are finalized and the data affected by the commands is changed. If the transaction includes multiple subscribers, then in order to commit the transaction, you must enter one Complete-Transaction command for every Start-Transaction command. The Complete-Transaction cmdlet is one of a set of cmdlets that support the transactions feature in Windows PowerShell. For more information, see about_transactions.

Convert-Path cmdlet: Converts a path from a Windows PowerShell path to a Windows PowerShell provider path.

Copy-Item cmdlet: Copies an item from one location to another in a namespace. Copy-Item does not delete the items being copied. The particular items that the cmdlet can copy depend on the Windows PowerShell providers available. For example, when used with the FileSystem provider, it can copy files and directories; when used with the Registry provider, it can copy registry keys and entries.

Copy-ItemProperty cmdlet: Copies a property and value from a specified location to another location. For example, you can use Copy-ItemProperty to copy one or more registry entries from one registry key to another registry key.

Debug-Process cmdlet: Attaches a debugger to one or more running processes on a local computer. You can specify the processes by their process name or process ID (PID), or you can pipe process objects to Debug-Process. Debug-Process attaches the debugger currently registered for the process. Before using this cmdlet, verify that a debugger is downloaded and correctly configured.

Disable-ComputerRestore cmdlet: Turns off the System Restore feature on one or more file system drives. As a result, it attempts to restore the computer but does not affect the specified drive. To disable System Restore on any drive, it must be disabled on the system drive, either first or concurrently. To re-enable System Restore, use the Enable-ComputerRestore cmdlet. To find the state of System Restore for each drive, use Rstrui.exe.

Enable-ComputerRestore cmdlet: Turns on the System Restore feature on one or more file system drives. As a result, you can use tools, such as the Restore-Computer cmdlet, to restore the computer to a previous state. By default, System Restore is enabled on all eligible drives, but you can disable it, such as by using the Disable-ComputerRestore cmdlet. To enable (or re-enable) System Restore on any drive, it must be enabled on the system drive, either first or concurrently. To find the state of System Restore for each drive, use Rstrui.exe.

Get-ChildItem cmdlet: Gets the items in one or more specified locations. If the item is a container, it gets the items inside the container, known as *child items*. You can use the Recurse parameter to get items in all child containers. A location can be a file system location, such as a directory, or a location exposed by another provider, such as a registry hive or a certificate store.

Get-ComputerRestorePoint cmdlet: Gets the restore points on the local computer. This cmdlet can also display the status of the most recent attempt to restore the computer. You can use the information returned by Get-ComputerRestorePoint to select a restore point, and you can use the sequence number to identify a restore point for the Restore-Computer cmdlet.

Get-Content cmdlet: Gets the content of the item at the location specified by the path, such as the text in a file. It reads the content one line at a time and returns an object for each line.

Get-EventLog cmdlet: Gets events and Event logs on the local and remote computers. Use the parameters of Get-EventLog to search for events by using their property values. Get-EventLog gets only the events that match all of the specified property values. The EventLog cmdlet works only on classic Event logs. To get events from logs that use the Windows Eventing technology in Windows Vista and later versions of Windows, use Get-Event.

Get-Hotfix cmdlet: Gets the quick-fix engineering (QFE) updates that have been applied to the local computer or to remote computers by Component-Based Servicing.

Get-Item cmdlet: Gets the item at the specified location. It does not get contents of the item at the location unless you use a wildcard character (*) to request all contents of the item. The Get-Item cmdlet is used by Windows PowerShell providers to enable you to navigate through different types of data stores.

Get-ItemProperty cmdlet: Gets the properties of the specified items. For example, you can use Get-ItemProperty to get the value of the LastAccessTime property of a file object. You can also use Get-ItemProperty to view registry entries and their values.

Get-Location cmdlet: Gets an object that represents the current directory, much like the pwd (print working directory) command. When you move between Windows PowerShell drives (PsDrives), Windows

PowerShell retains your location in each drive. You can use `Get-Location` to find your location in each drive. You can also use `Get-Location` to get the current directory at run time, and use it in functions and scripts, such as in a function that displays the current directory in the Windows PowerShell prompt. If you use the `Push-Location` cmdlet to add locations to a path stack, you can use the `Stack` parameter of `Get-Location` to display the current stack.

`Get-Process` cmdlet: Gets the processes on a local or remote computer. Without parameters, `Get-Process` gets all of the processes on the local computer. You can also specify a particular process by process name or process ID (PID) or pass a process object through the pipeline to `Get-Process`. By default, `Get-Process` returns a process object that has detailed information about the process and supports methods that enable you to start and stop the process. You can also use the parameters of `Get-Process` to get file version information for the program that runs in the process, and get the modules that the process loaded.

`Get-PSDrive` cmdlet: Gets the Windows PowerShell drives in the current console. You can get a particular drive or all drives in the console. `Get-PSDrive` gets the following drives: Windows logical drives on the computer, including drives mapped to network shares; drives exposed by Windows PowerShell providers, such as the Certificate, Function, and Alias drives and the HKLM and HKCU drives exposed by the Windows PowerShell Registry provider; and drives that you create by using `New-PSDrive`.

`Get-PSProvider` cmdlet: Gets the Windows PowerShell providers in the current session. You can get a particular drive or all drives in the session. Windows PowerShell providers enable you to access a variety of data stores as though they were file system drives. For information about Windows PowerShell providers, type **get-help about_Providers**.

`Get-Service` cmdlet: Gets objects representing the services on a local computer or a remote computer, including running and stopped services. You can direct `Get-Service` to get only particular services by specifying the service name or display name of the services, or you can pipe service objects to `Get-Service`.

`Get-Transaction` cmdlet: Gets an object that represents the current transaction in the session. This cmdlet never returns more than one object because only one transaction is active at a time. If you start one or more independent transactions (by using the `Independent` parameter of `Start-Transaction`), the most recently started transaction is active, which is the transaction returned by `Get-Transaction`. When all active transactions have either been rolled back or committed, `Get-Transaction` shows the transaction that was most recently active in the session. The `Get-Transaction` cmdlet is one of a set of cmdlets that support the transactions feature in Windows PowerShell. For more information, see `about_transactions`.

`Get-WmiObject` cmdlet: Gets instances of `WMI` classes or information about available classes. The `ComputerName` parameter can always be used to target a remote computer. If the `List` parameter is specified, the cmdlet gets information about the `WMI` classes available in a specified namespace. If the `Query` parameter is specified, the cmdlet runs a `WMI` query language (WQL) statement. *Note*: `Get-WmiObject` does not use the Windows PowerShell remoting infrastructure to perform remote operations. You can use the `ComputerName` parameter of `Get-WmiObject` even if your computer does not fulfill the requirements for Windows PowerShell remoting and is not configured for remoting in Windows PowerShell.

`Invoke-Item` cmdlet: Performs the default action on the specified item. For example, it runs an executable file or opens a document file in the application associated with the document file type. The default action depends on the type of item and is determined by the Windows PowerShell provider that provides access to the data.

Join-Path cmdlet: Combines a path and child-path into a single path. The provider supplies the path delimiters.

Limit-EventLog cmdlet: Sets the maximum size of a classic Event log, how long each event must be retained, and what happens when the log reaches its maximum size. You can use it to limit the Event logs on local or remote computers. The EventLog cmdlets work only on classic Event logs. To get events from logs that use the Windows Eventing technology in Windows Vista and later versions of Windows, use Get-Event.

Move-Item cmdlet: Moves an item, including its properties, contents, and child items, from one location to another. The same provider must support the locations. For example, it can move a file or subdirectory from one directory to another or move a registry subkey from one key to another. When you move an item, it is added to the new location and deleted from its original location.

Move-ItemProperty cmdlet: Moves a property of an item from one item to another. For example, it can move a registry entry from one registry key to another registry key. When you move an item property, it is added to the new location and deleted from its original location.

New-Item cmdlet: Creates a new item and sets its value. The type of items that can be created depends upon the location of the item. For example, in the file system, New-Item is used to create files and folders. In the registry, New-Item creates registry keys and entries. New-Item can also set the value of the items that it creates. For example, when creating a new file, New-Item can add initial content to the file.

New-PSDrive cmdlet: Creates a Windows PowerShell drive (PsDrive) that is "mapped" to or associated with a location in a data store, such as a network drive, a directory on the local computer, or a registry key. You can use the PsDrives that you create to access data in the associated data store, just like you would do with any mapped drive. You can change locations into the drive (set-location, cd, or chdir) and access the contents of the drive (get-item, get-childitem, dir). However, the PsDrives are known only to Windows PowerShell. You cannot access them by using Windows Explorer, WMI, COM, or .NET, or by using tools such as Net Use. PsDrives exist only in the current Windows PowerShell console. To make the drive persistent, you can export the console to which you have added the drive or save a New-PSDrive command in your Windows PowerShell profile. To delete a drive that was created by New-PSDrive, use Remove-PSDrive.

New-Service cmdlet: Creates a new entry for a Windows service in the registry and in the service database. A new service requires an executable file that executes during the service. The parameters of this cmdlet enable you to set the display name, description, startup type, and dependencies of the service.

New-WebServiceProxy cmdlet: Enables you to use a Web service in Windows PowerShell. The cmdlet connects to a Web service and creates a Web service proxy object in Windows PowerShell. You can use the proxy object to manage the Web service. A Web service is an XML-based program that exchanges data over a network, particularly over the Internet. The Microsoft .NET Framework provides Web service proxy objects that represent the Web service as a .NET object.

Pop-Location cmdlet: Changes to the location most recently pushed onto the stack by using Push-Location. You can pop a location from the default stack or from a stack that you create by using Push-Location.

Push-Location cmdlet: Adds ("pushes") the current location to the top of a list of locations, called a *stack*. You can push the current location onto a default stack or onto a stack that you create. If you specify a path, Push-Location pushes the current location onto the stack, and then changes to the location specified by the path. You cannot push a location onto the stack unless it is the current location.

Remove-Computer cmdlet: Removes local and remote computers from their current workgroup or domain. When you remove a computer from a domain, Remove-Computer also disables the computer's domain account. When the computer is in a domain, you must provide credentials, even when they are the credentials of the current user, and you must restart the computer to make the change effective. To get the results of the command, use the Verbose and PassThru parameters.

Remove-EventLog cmdlet: Deletes an Event log file from a local or remote computer and unregisters all of its event sources for the log. You can also use this cmdlet to unregister event sources without deleting any Event logs. The EventLog cmdlets work only on classic Event logs. To get events from logs that use the Windows Eventing technology in Windows Vista and later versions of Windows, use Get-Event.

Remove-Item cmdlet: Deletes one or more items. Because it is supported by many providers, it can delete many different types of items, including files, directories, registry keys, variables, aliases, and functions.

Remove-ItemProperty cmdlet: Deletes a property and its value from an item. You can use it to delete registry values and the data that they store.

Remove-PSDrive cmdlet: Deletes Windows PowerShell drives that you created by using New-PSDrive. Remove-PSDrive cannot delete Windows drives or mapped network drives created by using other methods. Also, you cannot delete the current working drive. Deletes WMI classes and instances.

Rename-Computer cmdlet: Renames computers in workgroups and domains. When you rename a computer in a domain, Rename-Computer also changes the name in the computer's domain account. You cannot use Rename-Computer to rename domain controllers. When renaming a remote computer in a domain, you must provide credentials, even when they are the current user's credentials. When renaming any computer in a domain, you must restart the computer to effect the name change.

Rename-Item cmdlet: Changes the name of a specified item. This cmdlet does not affect the contents of the item being renamed. You cannot use Rename-Item to move an item, such as by specifying a path along with the new name. To move and rename an item, use the Move-Item cmdlet.

Rename-ItemProperty cmdlet: Changes the name of a specified item property. The value of the property is not changed. For example, you can use Rename-ItemProperty to change the name of a registry entry.

Reset-ComputerMachinePassword cmdlet: Changes the machine account password that the computers use to authenticate to the domain controllers in the domain. You can use it to reset the passwords of local and remote computers.

Resolve-Path cmdlet: Interprets the wildcard characters in a path and displays the items and containers at the location specified by the path, such as the files and folders or registry keys and subkeys. The names appear just as they are represented in the drive, including capitalization.

Restart-Computer cmdlet: Restarts the operating system on the local and remote computers. You can use the parameters of Restart-Computer to run the restart operations as a background job, to specify the authentication levels and alternate credentials, to limit the operations that run concurrently, and to force an immediate restart. This cmdlet does not require Windows PowerShell remoting unless you use the `AsJob` parameter.

Restart-Service cmdlet: Sends a stop message and then a start message to the Windows Service Controller for a specified service. If a service was already stopped, then it is started without notifying you of an error. You can specify the services by their service names or display names, or you can use the `InputObject` parameter to pass an object that represents each service you want to restart.

Restore-Computer cmdlet: Restores the local computer to the specified system restore point. A `Restore-Computer` command restarts the computer. The restore is completed during the restart operation.

Resume-Service cmdlet: Sends a resume message to the Windows Service Controller for each of the specified services. If they have been suspended, then they resume service. If they are currently running, then the message is ignored. You can specify the services by service name or display name, or you can use the `InputObject` parameter to pass a service object that represents the services you want to resume.

Set-Content cmdlet: A string-processing cmdlet that writes or replaces the content in the specified item, such as a file. Whereas the `Add-Content` cmdlet appends content to a file, `Set-Content` replaces the existing content. You can type the content in the command or send content through the pipeline to `Set-Content`.

Set-Item cmdlet: Changes the value of an item, such as a variable or registry key, to the value specified in the command.

Set-ItemProperty cmdlet: Changes the value of the property of the specified item. You can use the cmdlet to establish or change the properties of items. For example, you can use `Set-ItemProperty` to set the value of the `IsReadOnly` property of a file object to true. You also use `Set-ItemProperty` to create and change registry values and data. For example, you can add a new registry entry to a key and establish or change its value.

Set-Location cmdlet: Sets the working location to a specified location. That location could be a directory, a subdirectory, a registry location, or another location stack.

Set-Service cmdlet: Changes the properties of a local or remote service, including status, description, display name, and start mode. You can use this cmdlet to start, stop, or suspend (pause) a service. To identify the service, enter its service name or submit a service object, or pipe a service name or service object to `Set-Service`.

Show-EventLog cmdlet: Opens Event Viewer on the local computer and displays in it all of the classic `Event` logs on the local computer or a remote computer. To open Event Viewer on Windows Vista and later versions of Windows, the current user must be a member of the Administrators group on the local computer. The `EventLog` cmdlets work only on classic `Event` logs. To get events from logs that use the Windows Eventing technology in Windows Vista and later versions of Windows, use `Get-Event`.

Split-Path cmdlet: Returns only the specified part of a path, such as the parent directory, a child directory, or a file name. It also can display the items that are referenced by the split path and indicate whether the path is relative or absolute. You can use this cmdlet to display or submit only a selected part of a path.

Start-Process cmdlet: Starts one or more processes on the local computer. To specify the program that runs in the process, enter an executable file or script file, or a file that can be opened by using a program on the computer. If you specify a non-executable file, `Start-Process` starts the program that is associated with the file, much like the `Invoke-Item` cmdlet. You can use the parameters of `Start-Process` to specify options, such as loading a user profile, starting the process in a new window, or using alternate credentials.

Start-Service cmdlet: Sends a start message to the Windows Service Controller for each of the specified services. If a service is already running, then the message is ignored without error. You can specify the services by their service name or display name, or you can use the `InputObject` parameter to supply a service object representing the services that you want to start.

Start-Transaction cmdlet: Starts a transaction, which is a series of commands that are managed as a unit. A transaction can be completed ("committed") or it can be completely undone ("rolled back"), restoring any data changed by the transaction to its original state. Because the commands in a transaction are managed as a unit, either all commands are committed or all commands are rolled back. By default, transactions are rolled back automatically if any command in the transaction generates an error, but you can use the `RollbackPreference` parameter to change this behavior. The cmdlets used in a transaction must be designed to support transactions. Cmdlets that support transactions have a `UseTransaction` parameter. To perform transactions in a provider, the provider must support transactions. The Windows PowerShell Registry provider in Windows Vista and later versions of Windows supports transactions. You can also use the `System.Management.Automation.TransactedString` class to include expressions in transactions on any version of Windows that supports Windows PowerShell. Other Windows Power-Shell providers can also support transactions. Only one transaction can be active at a time. If you start a new, independent transaction while a transaction is in progress (neither completed nor undone), the new transaction becomes the active transaction, and you must commit or roll back the new transaction before making any changes to the original transaction. The `Start-Transaction` cmdlet is one of a set of cmdlets that support the transactions feature in Windows PowerShell. For more information, see `about_transactions`.

Stop-Computer cmdlet: Shuts down computers remotely. It can also shut down the local computer. You can use the parameters of `Stop-Computer` to run the shutdown operations as a background job, to specify the authentication levels and alternate credentials, to limit the concurrent connections that are created to run the command, and to force an immediate shutdown. This cmdlet does not require Windows PowerShell remoting unless you use the `AsJob` parameter.

Stop-Process cmdlet: Stops one or more running processes. You can specify a process by process name or process ID (PID), or pass a process object to `Stop-Process`. `Stop-Process` works only on processes running on the local computer. On Windows Vista and later versions, to stop a process that is not owned by the current user, you must open Windows PowerShell with the "Run as administrator" option. In addition, you are prompted for confirmation unless you use the `Force` parameter.

Stop-Service cmdlet: Sends a stop message to the Windows Service Controller for each of the specified services. You can specify the services by their service name or display name, or you can use the `InputObject` parameter to pass a service object representing the services that you want to stop.

Suspend-Service cmdlet: Sends a suspend message to the Windows Service Controller for each of the specified services. While suspended, the service is still running but its action is halted until resumed, such as by using `Resume-Service`. You can specify the services by service name or display name, or you can use the `InputObject` parameter to pass a service object representing the services that you want to suspend.

Test-Connection cmdlet: Sends Internet Control Message Protocol (ICMP) echo request packets ("pings") to one or more remote computers and returns the echo response replies. You can use this cmdlet to determine whether a particular computer can be contacted across an IP network. Use the parameters of Test-Connection to specify both the sending and the receiving computers, to run the command as a background job, to set a timeout and number of pings, and to configure the connection and authentication. Unlike the traditional "ping" command, Test-Connection returns a Win32_PingStatus object that you can investigate in Windows PowerShell.

Test-Path cmdlet: Determines whether all elements of the path exist. It returns TRUE ($true) if all elements exist and FALSE ($false) if any are missing. It can also tell whether the path syntax is valid and whether the path leads to a container or a terminal (leaf) element.

Undo-Transaction cmdlet: Rolls back the active transaction. When you roll back a transaction, the changes made by the commands in the transaction are discarded and the data is restored to its original form. If the transaction includes multiple subscribers, an Undo-Transaction command rolls back the entire transaction for all subscribers. By default, transactions are rolled back automatically if any command in the transaction generates an error. However, transactions can be started with a different rollback preference and you can use this cmdlet to roll back the active transaction at any time. The Undo-Transaction cmdlet is one of a set of cmdlets that support the transactions feature in Windows PowerShell. For more information, see about_transactions.

Use-Transaction cmdlet: Adds a script block to an active transaction. This enables you to do transacted scripting using transaction-enabled .NET objects. The script block can contain only transaction-enabled .NET objects, such as instances of the System.Management.Automation.TransactedString class. The UseTransaction parameter, which is optional for most cmdlets, is required when using this cmdlet. The Use-Transaction cmdlet is one of a set of cmdlets that support the transactions feature in Windows PowerShell. For more information, see about_transactions.

Wait-Process cmdlet: Waits for one or more running processes to be stopped before accepting input. In the Windows PowerShell console, this cmdlet suppresses the command prompt until the processes are stopped. You can specify a process by process name or process ID (PID), or pipe a process object to Wait-Process. Wait-Process works only on processes running on the local computer.

Write-EventLog cmdlet: Writes an event to an Event log. To write an event to an Event log, the Event log must exist on the computer and the source must be registered for the Event log. The EventLog cmdlets work only on classic event logs. To get events from logs that use the Windows Eventing technology in Windows Vista and later versions, use Get-Event.

cmdlets Related to the Security Snap-in

ConvertFrom-SecureString cmdlet: Converts a secure string (System.Security.SecureString) into an encrypted standard string (System.String). Unlike a secure string, the encrypted standard string can be saved in a file for later use. The encrypted standard string can be converted back to its secure string format by using the ConvertTo-SecureString cmdlet. If an encryption key is explicitly specified by using the Key or SecureKey parameters, the Rijndael encryption algorithm is used. The key specified must have a length of 128, 192, or 256 bits because those are the key lengths supported by the Rijndael encryption algorithm. If no key is specified, then the Windows Data Protection API (DPAPI) is used to encrypt the standard string representation.

ConvertTo-SecureString cmdlet: Converts encrypted standard strings into secure strings. It can also convert plain text to secure strings. It is used with `ConvertFrom-SecureString` and `Read-Host`. The secure string created by the cmdlet can be used with cmdlets or functions that require a parameter of type `SecureString`. The secure string can be converted back to an encrypted, standard string using the `ConvertFrom-SecureString` cmdlet. This enables it to be stored in a file for later use. If the standard string being converted was encrypted with `ConvertFrom-SecureString` using a specified key, that same key must be provided as the value of the `Key` or `SecureKey` parameter of the `ConvertTo-SecureString` cmdlet.

Get-Acl cmdlet: Gets objects that represent the security descriptor of a file or resource. The security descriptor contains the access control lists (ACLs) of the resource. The ACL specifies the permissions that users and user groups must have in order to access the resource.

Get-AuthenticodeSignature cmdlet: Gets information about the `Authenticode` signature in a file. If the file is not signed, the information is retrieved but the fields are blank.

Get-Credential cmdlet: Creates a credential object for a specified user name and password. You can use the credential object in security operations. The cmdlet prompts the user for a password or user name and password. Users are prompted through a dialog box or at the command line, depending on the system registry setting.

Get-ExecutionPolicy cmdlet: Gets the execution policy that is effective in the shell. The execution policy is determined by the user preference that you set by using `Set-ExecutionPolicy` and the `Group` Policy settings for the Windows PowerShell execution policy. The default is `Restricted`.

Get-PfxCertificate cmdlet: Gets an object representing each specified `.pfx` certificate file. A `.pfx` file includes both the certificate and a private key.

Set-Acl cmdlet: Changes the security descriptor of a specified resource, such as a file or a registry key, to match the values in a security descriptor that you supply. To use `Set-Acl`, use the `Path` parameter to identify the resource whose security descriptor you want to change, and use the `AclObject` parameter to supply a security descriptor that has the values you want to apply. `Set-Acl` uses the value of the `AclObject` parameter as a model and changes the values in the resource's security descriptor to match the values in the `AclObject` parameter.

Set-AuthenticodeSignature cmdlet: Adds an Authenticode signature to any file that supports Subject Interface Package (SIP). In a Windows PowerShell script file, the signature takes the form of a block of text that indicates the end of the instructions executed in the script. If there is a signature in the file when this cmdlet runs, that signature is removed.

Set-ExecutionPolicy cmdlet: Changes the user preference for the execution policy of the shell. To run this command on Windows Vista, you must use the Run As Administrator option when starting Windows PowerShell, even if you are a member of the Administrators group on the computer. The execution policy is part of the security strategy of Windows PowerShell. It specifies whether you can load configuration files (including your Windows PowerShell profile) and run scripts, and which scripts, if any, must be digitally signed before they will run.

cmdlets Related to the Utility Snap-in

Add-Member cmdlet: Adds a user-defined custom member to an instance of a Windows PowerShell object. Enables you to add the following types of members: `AliasProperty`, `CodeProperty`, `NoteProperty`,

ScriptProperty, PropertySet, CodeMethod, MemberSet, and ScriptMethod. You set the initial value of the member by using the Value parameter. In the case of AliasProperty, ScriptProperty, CodeProperty, and CodeMethod, you can supply additional information by using the SecondValue parameter. The additional members are added to the particular instance of the object that you pipe to Add-Member or specify using the InputObject parameter. The additional member is only available while that instance exists. You can use the Export-Clixml cmdlet to save the instance, including the additional members, to a file. The information stored in that file can be used by the Import-Clixml cmdlet to recreate the instance of the object.

Add-Type cmdlet: Enables you to define a .NET class in your Windows PowerShell session. You can then instantiate objects (by using the New-Object cmdlet) and use the objects, just as you would use any .NET object. If you add an Add-Type command to your Windows PowerShell profile, the class will be available in all Windows PowerShell sessions. You can specify the type by indicating an existing assembly or source code files, or you can specify source code in line or saved in a variable. You can even specify only a method and Add-Type will define and generate the class. You can use this feature to make Platform Invoke (P/Invoke) calls to unmanaged functions in Windows PowerShell. If you specify source code, Add-Type compiles the specified source code and generates an in-memory assembly containing the new .NET types. You can use the parameters of Add-Type to specify an alternative language and compiler (CSharp is the default), compiler options, assembly dependencies, the class namespace, and the names of the type and the resulting assembly.

Clear-Variable cmdlet: Deletes the data stored in a variable, but it does not delete the variable. As a result, the value of the variable is NULL (empty). If the variable has a specified data or object type, Clear-Variable preserves the type of the object stored in the variable.

Compare-Object cmdlet: Compares two sets of objects. One set of objects is the Reference set and the other is the Difference set. The result of the comparison indicates whether a property value appeared only in the object from the Reference set (indicated by the <= symbol), only in the object from the Difference set (indicated by the => symbol) or, if the IncludeEqual parameter is specified, in both objects (indicated by the == symbol).

ConvertFrom-Csv cmdlet: Creates objects from comma-separated, variable-length (CSV) strings that are generated by the ConvertTo-Csv cmdlet. You can use the parameters of the ConvertFrom-Csv cmdlet to specify the column header row, which determines the property names of the resulting objects, to specify the item delimiter, or to direct ConvertFrom-Csv to use the list separator for the current culture as the delimiter. The objects that ConvertFrom-CSV creates are CSV versions of the original objects. The property values of the CSV objects are string versions of the property values of the original objects. The CSV versions of the objects do not have any methods. You can also use the Export-Csv and Import-Csv cmdlets to convert objects to CSV strings in a file (and back). These cmdlets are the same as the ConvertTo-Csv and ConvertFrom-Csv cmdlets, except that they save the CSV strings in a file.

ConvertFrom-StringData cmdlet: Converts a string that contains one or more "name=value" pairs into a hash table. Because each "name=value" pair must be on a separate line, here-strings are often used as the input format. The ConvertFrom-StringData cmdlet is considered to be a safe cmdlet that can be used in the DATA section of a script or function. When used in a DATA section, the contents of the string must conform to the rules for a DATA section. For details, see about_data_sections.

ConvertTo-Csv cmdlet: Returns a series of comma-separated, variable-length (CSV) strings representing the objects that you submit. You can then use the ConvertFrom-Csv cmdlet to recreate objects from the CSV strings. The resulting objects are CSV versions of the original objects that consist of string representations of the property values, and no methods. You can also use the Export-Csv and Import-Csv cmdlets to convert .NET objects to CSV strings (and back). `Export-Csv` is the same as `ConvertTo-Csv` except that it saves the CSV strings in a file. You can use the parameters of the `ConvertTo-Csv` cmdlet to specify a delimiter other than a comma or to direct `ConvertTo-Csv` to use the default delimiter for the current culture. For more information, type **get-help export-csv-full** and see the Notes section.

ConvertTo-Html cmdlet: Converts .NET objects into HTML that can be displayed in a Web browser. You can use this cmdlet to display the output of a command in a Web page. You can use the parameters of `ConvertTo-Html` to select object properties, to specify a table or list format, to specify the HTML page title, to add text before and after the object, and to return only the table or list fragment, instead of a strict DTD page. When you submit multiple objects to `ConvertTo-Html`, Windows PowerShell creates the table (or list) based on the properties of the first object that you submit. If the remaining objects do not have one of the specified properties, then the property value of that object is an empty cell. If the remaining objects have additional properties, those property values are not included in the file.

ConvertTo-Xml cmdlet: Creates an XML-based representation of one or more .NET objects. To use this cmdlet, pipe one or more objects to the cmdlet or use the `InputObject` parameter to specify the object. When you pipe multiple objects to `ConvertTo-XML` or use the `InputObject` parameter to submit multiple objects, `ConvertTo-XML` returns a single XML document that includes representations of all the objects. This cmdlet is similar to `Export-Clixml` except that `Export-Clixml` stores the resulting XML in a file. `ConvertTo-XML` returns the XML, so you can continue to process it in Windows PowerShell.

Disable-PSBreakpoint cmdlet: Disables breakpoints, points in a script where execution stops temporarily so that you can examine the instructions, which ensures that they are not hit when the script runs. You can use it to disable all breakpoints, or specify breakpoints by submitting breakpoint objects or breakpoint IDs. Technically, this cmdlet changes the value of the `Enabled` property of a breakpoint object to False. To re-enable a breakpoint, use the `Enable-PSBreakpoint` cmdlet. Breakpoints are enabled by default when you create them by using the `Set-PSBreakpoint` cmdlet. `Disable-PSBreakpoint` is one of several cmdlets designed for debugging Windows PowerShell scripts. For more information about the Windows PowerShell debugger, type **get-help about_debuggers**.

Enable-PSBreakpoint cmdlet: Re-enables disabled breakpoints, points in a script where execution stops temporarily so that you can examine the instructions. You can use it to enable all breakpoints, or specify breakpoints by submitting breakpoint objects or breakpoint IDs. Newly created breakpoints are automatically enabled, but you can disable them by using the `Disable-PSBreakpoint` cmdlet. Technically, this cmdlet changes the value of the `Enabled` property of a breakpoint object to `True`. `Enable-PSBreakpoint` is one of several cmdlets designed for debugging Windows PowerShell scripts. For more information about the Windows PowerShell debugger, type **get-help about_debuggers**.

Export-Alias cmdlet: Exports the aliases in the current session to a file. If the output file specified does not exist, the cmdlet will create it. `Export-Alias` can export the aliases in a particular scope or all scopes, and it can generate the data in CSV format or as a series of `Set-Alias` commands that you can add to a session or to a Windows PowerShell profile.

Export-Clixml cmdlet: Creates an XML-based representation of an object or objects and stores it in a file. You can then use the `Import-Clixml` cmdlet to recreate the saved object based on the contents of that file. This cmdlet is similar to `ConvertTo-XML` except that `Export-Clixml` stores the resulting XML in a file. `ConvertTo-XML` returns the XML, so you can continue to process it in Windows PowerShell.

Export-Csv cmdlet: Creates a comma-separated, variable-length (CSV) file representing the objects you submit. You can then use the `Import-Csv` cmdlet to recreate objects from the CSV strings in the files. The resulting objects are CSV versions of the original objects that consist of string representations of the property values, and no methods. You can also use the `ConvertTo-Csv` and `ConvertFrom-Csv` cmdlets to convert .NET objects to CSV strings (and back). `Export-Csv` is the same as `ConvertTo-Csv` except that it saves the CSV strings in a file. You can use the parameters of the `Export-Csv` cmdlet to specify a delimiter other than a comma or to direct `Export-Csv` to use the default delimiter for the current culture. When you submit multiple objects to `Export-Csv`, it organizes the file based on the properties of the first object you submit. If the remaining objects do not have one of the specified properties, the property value of the object is null, as represented by two consecutive commas. If the remaining objects have additional properties, those property values are not included in the file. For more information, type **get-help export-csv -full** and see the Notes section.

Export-PSSession cmdlet: Gets cmdlets, functions, aliases, and other command types from another session on a local or remote computer and saves them in a Windows PowerShell script module file (`.psm1`). To add the commands from the script module file to a session, use the `Add-Module` cmdlet. Unlike `Import-PSSession`, which imports commands from another session into the current session, `Export-PSSession` immediately saves the commands in a script module file. The commands are not imported into the current session. To export commands, first use the `New-PSSession` cmdlet to connect to the session that has the commands you want to export. Then use the `Export-PSSession` cmdlet to export the commands. By default, `Export-PSSession` exports all commands, except for commands that already exist in the session, but you can use the `PSSnapin`, `CommandName`, and `CommandType` parameters to specify the commands to export.

Format-Custom cmdlet: Formats the output of a command as defined in an alternate view. `Format-Custom` is designed to display views that are not just tables or lists. You can use the views defined in the `*format.PS1XML` files in the Windows PowerShell directory or you can create your own views in new `PS1XML` files and use the `Update-FormatData` cmdlet to add them to Windows PowerShell.

Format-List cmdlet: Formats the output of a command as a list of properties in which each property is displayed on a separate line. You can use `Format-List` to format and display all or selected properties of an object as a list (`format-list *`). Because more space is available for each item in a list than in a table, Windows PowerShell displays more properties of the object in the list, and the property values are less likely to be truncated.

Format-Table cmdlet: Formats the output of a command as a table, with selected properties of the object in each column. The object type determines the default layout and properties displayed in each column, but you can use the `Property` parameter to select the properties that you want to see. You can also use a hash table to add calculated properties to an object before displaying it and to specify the column headings in the table. To add a calculated property, use the `Property` parameter and type a hash table for the parameter value. Create an `Expression` key in the hash table and assign to the key an expression that calculates a value. The hash table can also have `Label`, `Format`, and `Alignment` keys.

Format-Wide cmdlet: Formats objects as a wide table that displays only one property of each object. You can use the `Property` parameter to determine which property is displayed.

Get-Alias cmdlet: Gets the aliases (alternative names for commands and executable files) in the current session. This includes built-in aliases, aliases that you have set or imported, and aliases that you have added to your Windows PowerShell profile. By default, `Get-Alias` takes an alias and returns the command name. When you use the `Definition` parameter, `Get-Alias` takes a command name and returns its aliases.

Get-Culture cmdlet: Gets information about the current culture settings. This includes information about the current language settings on the system, such as the keyboard layout, and the display format of items such as numbers, currency, and dates. You can also use the `Get-UICulture` cmdlet, which gets the current user interface culture on the system. The UI culture determines which text strings are used for user interface elements, such as menus and messages.

Get-Date cmdlet: Gets a `DateTime` object that represents the current date or a date that you specify. It can format the date and time in several Windows and UNIX formats. You can use `Get-Date` to generate a date or time character string, and then send the string to other cmdlets or programs.

Get-Host cmdlet: Gets an object that represents the program hosting Windows PowerShell. The default display includes the Windows PowerShell version number and the current region and language settings that the host is using, but the host object contains a wealth of information, including detailed information about the version of Windows PowerShell currently running, the current culture, and the UI culture of Windows PowerShell. You can also use this cmdlet to customize features of the host program user interface, such as text and background colors.

Get-Member cmdlet: Gets the "members" (properties and methods) of objects. To specify the object, use the `InputObject` parameter or pipe an object to `Get-Member`. To retrieve information about static members (members of the class, not of the instance), use the `Static` parameter. To get only certain types of members, such as `NoteProperties`, use the `MemberType` parameter.

Get-PSBreakPoint cmdlet: Gets all of the breakpoints, points in a script where execution stops temporarily so that you can examine the instructions, that are set in the current console. You can also get only a selected breakpoint by specifying the breakpoint ID. `Get-PSBreakpoint` is one of several cmdlets designed for debugging Windows PowerShell scripts. For more information about the Windows Power-Shell debugger, type **get-help about_debuggers**.

Get-PSCallStack cmdlet: Displays the current call stack. Although it is designed to be used with the Windows PowerShell debugger, you can use this cmdlet to display the call stack in a script or function outside of the debugger. To run a `Get-PSCallStack` command while in the debugger, type **k** or **get-pscallstack**.

Get-Random cmdlet: Gets a randomly selected number. If you submit a collection of objects to `Get-Random`, it gets one or more randomly selected objects from the collection. Without parameters or input, `Get-Random` returns a randomly selected 32-bit unsigned integer between 0 and `Int32.MaxValue` (0x7FFFFFFF, or 2,147,483,647). You can use the parameters of `Get-Random` to specify a seed number, minimum and maximum values, and the number of objects returned from a submitted collection.

Get-TraceSource cmdlet: Gets the trace sources for Windows PowerShell components currently in use. You can use the data to determine which Windows PowerShell components you can trace. When tracing, the component generates detailed messages about each step in its internal processing. Developers use the trace data to monitor data flow, program execution, and errors. The tracing cmdlets were designed for Windows PowerShell developers, but they are available to all users.

Get-UICulture cmdlet: Gets information about the current user interface (UI) culture settings for Windows. The UI culture determines which text strings are used for user interface elements, such as menus and messages. You can also use the `Get-Culture` cmdlet, which gets the current culture on the system. The culture determines the display format of items such as numbers, currency, and dates.

Get-Unique cmdlet: Compares each item in a sorted list to the next item, eliminates duplicates, and returns only one instance of each item. The list must be sorted in order for the cmdlet to work properly.

Get-Variable cmdlet: Gets the Windows PowerShell variables in the current console. You can retrieve just the values of the variables by specifying the ValueOnly parameter and you can filter the variables returned by name.

Group-Object cmdlet: Displays objects in groups based on the value of a specified property. Group-Object returns a table with one row for each property value and a column that displays the number of items with that value. If you specify more than one property, Group-Object first groups by the values of the first property, and then, within each property group, it groups by the value of the next property.

Import-Alias cmdlet: Imports an alias list from a file.

Import-Clixml cmdlet: Imports a CLIXML file with data that represents .NET objects and creates the objects in Windows PowerShell.

Import-Csv cmdlet: Creates objects from comma-separated, variable-length (CSV) files that are generated by the Export-Csv cmdlet. You can use the parameters of the Import-Csv cmdlet to specify the column header row, which determines the property names of the resulting objects, to specify the item delimiter, or to direct Import-Csv to use the list separator for the current culture as the item delimiter. The objects that Import-CSV creates are CSV versions of the original objects. The property values of the CSV objects are string versions of the property values of the original objects. The CSV versions of the objects do not have any methods. You can also use the ConvertTo-Csv and ConvertFrom-Csv cmdlets to convert objects to CSV strings (and back). These cmdlets are the same as the Export-Csv and Import-Csv cmdlets except that they do not save the CSV strings in a file.

Import-LocalizedData cmdlet: Designed to enable scripts to display user messages in the UI language selected by the current user. Import-LocalizedData imports data from .psd1 files in language-specific subdirectories of the script directory into a local variable specified in the command. The cmdlet selects the subdirectory and file based on the value of the $PsUICulture automatic variable. When you use the local variable in the script to display a user message, the message appears in the user's UI language. You can use the parameters of Import-LocalizedData to specify an alternate UI culture, path, and filename, and to suppress the error message that appears if the .psd1 files are not found. The Import-LocalizedData cmdlet supports script internationalization in Windows PowerShell 2.0. This initiative aims to better serve users worldwide by making it easy for scripts to display user messages in the UI language of the current user. For more information, including the format of the .psd1 files, type **get-help about_script_internationalization**.

Import-PSSession cmdlet: Imports cmdlets, functions, aliases, and other command types from a session on a local or remote computer into the current session. You can import any command that Get-Command can find in the other session. Use an Import-PSSession command to import commands from a customized shell, such as an Exchange shell, or from a session that includes Windows PowerShell modules and snap-ins, or other elements that are not in the current session. To import commands, first use the New-PSSession cmdlet to connect to the session from which you will import. Then use the Import-PSSession cmdlet to import the commands. By default, Import-PSSession imports all commands, except for commands that exist in the current session. To overwrite a command, use the CommandName parameter. You can use imported commands just as you would use any command in the session. When you use an imported command, the imported part of the command actually runs in the session from which it was imported, but the remote operations are handled entirely by Windows PowerShell. You need not even be aware of them, except that you must keep the connection to the other session (PSSession) open. If you close it, the imported commands are no longer available. Because imported commands might take longer to run than local commands, `Import-PSSession` adds an `AsJob` parameter to every imported command. This parameter enables you to run the command as a Windows PowerShell background job. For more information, see `about_jobs`. When you use `Import-PSSession`, Windows PowerShell adds the imported commands to a temporary module that exists only in your session, and returns an object that represents the module. To make the imported commands available in other sessions, use the `Export-PSSession` cmdlet.

Invoke-Expression cmdlet: Evaluates or runs a specified string as a command, and returns the results of the expression or command. Without `Invoke-Expression`, a string submitted at the command line would be returned (echoed) unchanged.

Measure-Command cmdlet: Runs a script block or cmdlet internally, times the execution of the operation, and returns the execution time.

Measure-Object cmdlet: Calculates the property values of certain types of objects. `Measure-Object` performs three types of measurements, depending on the parameters in the command. The `Measure-Object` cmdlet performs calculations on the property values of objects. It can count objects and calculate the minimum, maximum, sum, and average of the numeric values. For text objects, it can count and calculate the number of lines, words, and characters.

New-Alias cmdlet: Creates a new alias in the current Windows PowerShell session. Aliases created by using `New-Alias` are not saved after you exit the session or close Windows PowerShell. You can use the `Export-Alias` cmdlet to save your alias information to a file; and you can later use `Import-Alias` to retrieve that saved alias information.

New-Object cmdlet: Creates an instance of a .NET or COM object. You can specify either the type of a .NET class or a Programmatic Identifier (ProgID) of a COM object. By default, you type the fully qualified name of a .NET class, and the cmdlet returns a reference to an instance of that class. To create an instance of a COM object, use the `ComObject` parameter and specify the ProgID of the object as its value.

New-TimeSpan cmdlet: Creates a `TimeSpan` object that represents a specified period of time. You can use a `TimeSpan` object to add or subtract time from `DateTime` objects.

New-Variable cmdlet: Creates a new variable in Windows PowerShell. You can assign a value to the variable while creating it, or assign or change the value after it is created. Use the parameters of `New-Variable` to set the properties of the variable, such as those that create read-only or constant variables, to set the scope of a variable, and to determine whether variables are public or private. Typically, you create a new variable by typing the variable name and its value, such as **"$var = 3,"** but you can use the `New-Variable` cmdlet to use its parameters.

Out-Default cmdlet: Sends the output to the default formatter and the default output cmdlet. This cmdlet has no effect on the formatting or output. It is a placeholder that enables you to write your own `Out-Default` function or cmdlet.

Out-File cmdlet: Sends output to a file. You can use this cmdlet instead of the redirection operator (>) when you need to use its parameters.

Out-GridView cmdlet: Sends the output from a command to a grid view window where the output is displayed in an interactive table. This feature requires Microsoft .NET Framework 3.5 with Service Pack 1. You can use the following features of the table to examine your data:

❏ **Search** — Use the Search in Results box at the top of the window to search the text in the table. You can search for text in a particular column, search for literals, and search for multiple words.

❏ **Sort** — To sort the data, click a column header. Click again to toggle from ascending to descending order.

❏ **Group** — You can arrange the data in groups with the same property value. To turn on grouping, right-click anywhere in the column heading row and select Show in Groups. Then, click a column heading to group the data by the values in that column. To turn off grouping, right-click the column header row and select Show in Groups again.

❏ **Filter** — Use the Out-GridView filter pane to create rules to filter the data. This is very useful for very large data sets, such as Event logs.

❏ **Copy and paste** — To copy rows of data from Out-GridView, use Ctrl+C (copy). You can paste the data into any text or spreadsheet program. The command output that you send cannot be preformatted, such as by using the Format-Table or Format-Wide cmdlets. For more information, see the Notes and Examples.

Out-Host cmdlet: Sends output to the Windows PowerShell host for display. The host displays the output at the command line. Because Out-Host is the default, you do not need to specify it unless you want to use its parameters to change the display.

Out-Null cmdlet: Sends output to NULL, in effect deleting it.

Out-Printer cmdlet: Sends output to the default printer or to an alternate printer, if one is specified.

Out-String cmdlet: Converts the objects that Windows PowerShell manages into an array of strings. By default, Out-String accumulates the strings and returns them as a single string, but you can use the stream parameter to direct Out-String to return one string at a time. This cmdlet enables you to search and manipulate string output as you would in traditional shells when object manipulation is less convenient.

Read-Host cmdlet: Reads a line of input from the console. You can use it to prompt a user for input. Because you can save the input as a secure string, you can use this cmdlet to prompt users for secure data, such as passwords, as well as shared data.

Remove-PSBreakpoint cmdlet: Deletes a breakpoint. Enter a breakpoint object or a breakpoint ID. When you remove a breakpoint, the breakpoint object is no longer available or functional. If you have saved a breakpoint object in a variable, the reference still exists but the breakpoint does not function. Remove-PSBreakpoint is one of several cmdlets designed for debugging Windows PowerShell scripts. For more information about the Windows PowerShell debugger, type **get-help about_debuggers**.

Remove-Variable cmdlet: Deletes a variable and its value from the scope in which it is defined, such as the current session. You cannot use this cmdlet to delete variables that are set as constants or those that are owned by the system.

Appendix A: cmdlets

Select-Object cmdlet: Gets only the specified properties of an object or set of objects. It can also select unique objects from an array of objects or it can select a specified number of objects from the beginning or end of an array of objects. If you use `Select-Object` to select specified properties, it copies the values of those properties from the input objects and creates new objects that have the specified properties and copied values. Use the `Property` parameter to specify the properties you want to select. Alternately, use the `First, Last, Unique, Skip,` and `Index` parameters to select particular objects from an array of input objects. For more specific object filtering, use the `Where-Object` cmdlet. You can also use `Select-Object` to add calculated properties to an object. To add a calculated property, use the `Property` parameter and type a hash table for the parameter value. Create an `Expression` key in the hash table and assign to the key an expression that calculates a value. The hash table can also have a `Name` key.

Select-String cmdlet: Searches for text and text patterns in input strings and files. You can use it like Grep in UNIX, and Findstr in Windows. `Select-String` is based on lines of text. By default, `Select-String` finds the first match in each line and, for each match, it displays the filename, line number, and all text in the line containing the match. However, you can direct it to detect multiple matches per line, display text before and after the match, or display only a Boolean (true or false) that indicates whether a match is found. `Select-String` uses regular expression matching, but it can also perform a simple match that searches the input for the text that you specify. `Select-String` can display all of the text matches or stop after the first match in each input file. It can also display all text that does not match the specified pattern, You can also specify that `Select-String` expect a particular character encoding, such as when searching files of Unicode text.

Send-MailMessage cmdlet: Sends an e-mail message from within Windows PowerShell.

Set-Alias cmdlet: Creates or changes an alias (alternate name) for a cmdlet or for a command element, such as a function, a script, a file, or other executable. You can also use `Set-Alias` to reassign a current alias to a new command, or to change any of the properties of an alias, such as its description. Unless you add the alias to the Windows PowerShell profile, changes to an alias are lost when you exit the session or close Windows PowerShell.

Set-Date cmdlet: Changes the system date and time on the computer to a date and time that you specify. You can specify a new date and/or time by typing a string or by passing a `DateTime` or `TimeSpan` object to `Set-Date`. To specify a new date or time, use the `Date` parameter. To specify a change interval, use the `Adjust` parameter.

Set-PSBreakpoint cmdlet: Sets a breakpoint in a script or in any command run in the current session. You can use `Set-PSBreakpoint` to set a breakpoint before executing a script or running a command, or during debugging, when stopped at another breakpoint. *Note:* `Set-PSBreakpoint` cannot set a breakpoint on a remote computer. To debug a script on a remote computer, copy the script to the local computer and then debug it locally. Each `Set-PSBreakpoint` command creates one of the following three types of breakpoints:

- **Line breakpoint** — Sets breakpoints at particular line and column coordinates
- **Command breakpoint** — Sets breakpoints on commands and functions
- **Variable breakpoint** — Sets breakpoints on variables

You can set a breakpoint on multiple lines, commands, or variables in a single `Set-PSBreakpoint` command, but each `Set-PSBreakpoint` command sets only one type of breakpoint. At a breakpoint, Windows PowerShell temporarily stops executing and gives control to the debugger. The command prompt changes to "<DBG>" and a set of debugger commands become available for use. However, you can use the `Action` parameter to specify an alternative response, such as conditions for the breakpoint or instructions to perform additional tasks (e.g., logging or diagnostics). The `Set-PSBreakpoint` cmdlet is one of several cmdlets designed for debugging Windows PowerShell scripts. For more information about the Windows PowerShell debugger, type **help about_debuggers**.

Set-TraceSource cmdlet: Configures, starts, and stops a trace of a Windows PowerShell component. You can use it to specify which components will be traced and where the tracing output is sent.

Set-Variable cmdlet: Assigns a value to a specified variable or changes the current value. If the variable does not exist, the cmdlet creates it.

Sort-Object cmdlet: Sorts objects in ascending or descending order based on the values of the object's properties. You can specify a single property or multiple properties (for a multi-key sort), and select a case-sensitive or case-insensitive sort. You can also direct `Sort-Object` to display only the objects with a unique value for a particular property.

Start-Sleep cmdlet: Suspends the activity in a script or session for the specified period of time. You can use it for many tasks, such as waiting for an operation to complete, or pausing before repeating an operation.

Tee-Object cmdlet: Sends the output of a command in two directions (like the letter T). It stores the output in a file or variable, and sends it down the pipeline. If `Tee-Object` is the last command in the pipeline, the command output is displayed in the console.

Trace-Command cmdlet: Configures and starts a trace of the specified expression or command. It works like `Set-TraceSource` except that it applies only to the specified command.

Update-FormatData cmdlet: Updates and adds `format.ps1xml` files to the current console. You can use it to reload currently loaded files, to add new `format.ps1xmls` files to the console, or to reorder the precedence of the files. The Windows PowerShell formatting files are XML files with a `.ps1xml` filename extension. The XML tags in the formatting files define the default display views for each .NET object that Windows PowerShell displays. You can create your own format `.ps1xml` files to change an existing object view or to create views for a new object. You do not need to restart the shell to update the format data. When used without parameters, `Update-FormatData` reloads all currently loaded formatting files, including files added to the current console with a previous `Update-FormatData` command. Use this command to reload changed files.

Update-List cmdlet: Adds and removes items from a property value of an object, and then returns the updated object. This cmdlet is designed for properties that contain collections of objects. The `Add` and `Remove` parameters add and remove individual items from the collection, respectively. The `Replace` parameter replaces the entire collection. If you don't specify a property in the command, `Update-List` returns an object that describes the update, instead of updating the object. You can submit the update object to cmdlets that change objects, such as `Set-*` cmdlets. This cmdlet works only when the property that is being updated supports the IList interface that `Update-List` uses. Also, any `Set-*` cmdlets that accept an update must support the IList interface. The core cmdlets installed with Windows PowerShell do not support this interface. To determine whether a cmdlet supports `Update-List`, see the cmdlet help topic.

Update-TypeData cmdlet: Updates the current extended type configuration by reloading the `*.types.ps1xml` files into memory. Extended type information is normally loaded when Windows

PowerShell requires the type information it contains. The `Update-TypeData` cmdlet can be used to preload all type information. It is particularly useful when you are developing types and want to load those new types for testing purposes.

Write-Debug cmdlet: Writes debug messages to the console from a script or command. By default, debug messages are not displayed in the console, but you can display them by using the `Debug` parameter or the `$DebugPreference` variable.

Write-Error cmdlet: Writes an error to the console. Use the `Message` parameter to specify the text of the error message. Use the other parameters to provide details about the error, and to explain how and why it occurred, and how the user should respond. You can also use the `ErrorRecord` or `Exception` parameters to describe the error, instead of an error message.

Write-Host cmdlet: Customizes output. You can specify the color of text by using the `ForegroundColor` parameter, and you can specify the background color by using the `BackgroundColor` parameter. Use the `Separator` parameter to specify a string to use to separate displayed objects. The particular result depends on the program that is hosting Windows PowerShell.

Write-Output cmdlet: Sends the specified object down the pipeline to the next command. If the command is the last in the pipeline, then the object is displayed in the console. `Write-Output` sends objects down the primary pipeline, also known as the *output stream* or the *success pipeline*. To send error objects down the error pipeline, use `Write-Error`. This cmdlet is typically used in scripts to display strings and other objects on the console. However, because the default behavior is to display the objects at the end of a pipeline, it is generally not necessary to use the cmdlet. For example, `"get-process | write-output"` is equivalent to `"get-process."`

Write-Progress cmdlet: Displays a progress bar in a Windows PowerShell command window that depicts the status of a running command or script. You can select the indicators that the bar reflects and the text that appears above and below the progress bar.

Write-Verbose cmdlet: Writes text to the verbose message stream in Windows PowerShell. Typically, the verbose message stream is used to deliver information about command processing that is used for debugging a command. When you use the `Write-Verbose` cmdlet for your detailed information, users can decide whether they want to display or hide the information by setting the value of the `$VerbosePreference` variable.

Write-Warning cmdlet: Writes a warning message to the Windows PowerShell host. The response to the warning depends on the value of the user's `$WarningPreference` variable and the use of the `WarningAction` common parameter.

Index

SYMBOLS

A

B

SQL Server (continued)